CN 940.431
AN 72337

PASSCHENDAELE IN PERSPECTIVE:
The Third Battle of Ypres

Northern College
Library

NC09078

THE N   E

D0988371

NSLEY

PASSCHENDAELE IN PERSPECTIVE

The Third Battle of Ypres

LEO COOPER
LONDON

First published in Great Britain in 1997
by
LEO COOPER
190 Shaftesbury Avenue, London WC2H 8JL
an imprint of
Pen & Sword Books Ltd,
47 Church Street,
Barnsley, South Yorkshire S70 2AS

© Peter Liddle, 1997

A CIP record for this book is available from the British Library

ISBN
0 85052 552 7 Hardback edition
0 85052 588 8 Paperback edition

The right of Peter Liddle to be identified as author of this
Work has been asserted by them in accordance with the
Copyright, Designs and Patents Act, 1988

All rights reserved. No part of this publication may be
reproduced, in any form or by any means, without permission from the
publishers.

Typeset by Phoenix Typesetting, Ilkley, West Yorkshire.

Printed in Great Britain by Redwood Books Ltd,
Trowbridge, Wilts

This book is dedicated to the memory of all the men who served in the Salient during the Third Battle of Ypres, to their families anxious for them at the time and to their descendants respectful of their forbears in Flanders fields.

Contents

Part III   MILITARY EFFECTIVENESS, IDENTITY AND EXPERIENCE

Part IV   THE BRITISH HOME FRONT

Part V   PASSCHENDAELE: THE INSPIRATION, FASCINATION AND DISCORDANCE OF AN ENDURING LEGACY

IX

List of Illustrations

22 An important aspect of the work of the RFC over the Salient was photo reconnaissance; this oblique aerial photograph shows Belgian Wood in the German sector near Hollebeke, August 1917. The wing of the aircraft is visible, somewhat out of focus, on the right hand side. (L.Beaumont-Tansley, Liddle Collection) Chapter 11

23 Perhaps the best known British single-seat fighter of the First World War was the Sopwith Camel. No 45 Squadron was much involved in the fighting during 1917 around Ypres, and this photograph is said to record "A" Flight's last operation before the Squadron was transferred to Italy. (J.Bruce/G.S.Leslie Collection) Chapter 11

24 One of the most successful fighters on the Allied side was the SE5A; B4863 was first allocated to the RFC in France on 23 August 1917 and was first flown by Captain J.T.B.McCudden of No 56 Squadron on 6 September 1917. It was in this aircraft that he took part in the combat of 23 September 1917, which ended in the death of Werner Voss. (J.Bruce/ G.S.Leslie Collection) Chapter 11

25 The DH4 was widely used as a day bomber, and was most effective when powered by a Rolls Royce Eagle engine. This example, A7583, was an aircraft of No 57 Squadron and is here seen in German hands after being forced down in combat over Roulers on 2 October 1917. Its pilot, 2nd Lieutenant C.G.Crane, was made a prisoner of war, but his observer, 2nd Lieutenant W.L.Inglis, was killed in the combat. (J.Bruce/G.S.Leslie Collection) Chapter 11

26 The wreckage of a German aeroplane in Houthulst forest, Autumn 1917. (L.H.Matthews, Liddle Collection) Chapter 11

27 German prisoners of war acting as stretcher bearers at an advanced dressing station on the Menin Road, September 1917. (R.S.Goodman, Liddle Collection) Chapter 12

28 A narrow-gauge railway being used to convey wounded to the rear. (A.Medcalf, Liddle Collection) Chapter 12

29 The extreme northern end of the trench system on the Western Front: sand dunes around Nieuport. German positions viewed from the Belgian lines. (Liddle Collection) Chapter 13

30 Barbed wire entanglements among the dunes at Nieuport - the sea visible in the distance. (Liddle Collection) Chapter 13

31 Men of the 11th Battalion South Wales Borderers, 38th Welsh Division, behind the lines in the Ypres Salient, late summer 1917.

The 38th Division were popularly known as "Lloyd George's Welsh army". (E.S.Nevell, Liddle Collection) Chapter 14

Between pages 290 and 291

On the following day, Cripps was on artillery co-operation duties, assisting in the direction of fire of 8" howitzers but he also had to drop propaganda pamphlets over the German lines. While engaged on a patrol to assist in the neutralization of the fire (N.F.) of enemy batteries on 12 September, his sporting instincts – some might say unsporting- led him to attempt to machine-gun ducks on the Yser marshes. *(B.U.S.Cripps, Liddle Collection)* page 168

List of Maps

Chronology

1917	WESTERN FRONT	OTHER FRONTS & NAVAL WAR	HOME FRONTS & WORLD EVENTS
JAN		5th: Balkans – Austro-German forces continue to advance in Rumania, capturing Braila.	5th: Rome Conference.
	8th: MacMullen ordered to draw up new plan for Flanders offensive.	8th: Balkans – Austro-German forces capture Focsani in Rumania 8th: Conference at Pless – German political and military leaders approve unrestricted submarine warfare.	
	15th: British and French Governments approve Nivelle's plan.		23rd: Japan secures special rights in Manchuria.
	30th: Plumer's plan for Flanders.	(British merchant ship losses – Jan total: 49 ships; 153,899 tons)	
		31st: Germany resumes unrestricted submarine warfare.	
FEB			3rd: United States Government severs relations with Germany.
	9th: Rawlinson Plan		
	14th: MacMullen Plan presented.		
	23rd: Germans effect a preliminary withdrawal between Arras & Soissons.	25th: Mesopotamia – British recapture Kut el Amara.	17th: Australia – Hughes forms National War Government.
		(British merchant ship losses – Feb total: 105 ships; 310,868 tons)	26th: Calais Conference. 26th: Russia – general mutiny of troops in St Petersburg

1917	WESTERN FRONT	OTHER FRONTS & NAVAL WAR	HOME FRONTS & WORLD EVENTS
MAR			1st: German attempts at anti-American alliance with Mexico publicised in the US press.
	4th: Main German withdrawal leading by 5.4.17 to withdrawal from Bapaume, Peronne, Roye, Noyon, Chauny.	11th: Mesopotamia – Baghdad occupied by the British. 11th: Balkans – Second Battle of Monastir & Battle of Lake Presba (until 19.3.17).	10th: Russia – strikes break out, soldiers join workers. 12th: Russia – Provisional Government formed. Formation of Petrograd Soviet. 13th: London Conference. 14th: Russia Petrograd Soviet issues` Army Order No. 1'. 15th: Russia – Tsar Nicholas II abdicates. 17th: France – resignation of Briand's government. Ribot the new French Prime Minister. 17th: Germany – Reichstag galvanised by Russian Revolution, establishes committee to consider constitutional reform.
	18th: Plumer's plan for Messines.	(British merchant ship losses – March total: 127 ships; 352,344 tons).	20th: Britain – first meeting of the Imperial War Cabinet.
APR	3rd: Haig agrees to Messines plan. 6th: Compiègne Conference.		6th: United States declares war on Germany. 7th: Germany – Kaiser promises franchise reform 7th: Cuba declares war on Germany.
	9th: Battles of Arras begin (end 24.5.17)		11th: All-Russian Conference of Soviets votes to continue the War. 13th: Bolivia severs relations with Germany
	13th: Nivelle requests that Haig agrees to a delay in the French offensive – agreed.		15th: Germany – cutting of the bread ration – growing unrest.

1917	WESTERN FRONT	OTHER FRONTS & NAVAL WAR	HOME FRONTS & WORLD EVENTS
APRIL	16th. Second Battle of the Aisne (`Nivelle Offensive') – until 20.4.17.		16th. Germany – outbreak of mass demonstrations and strikes.
		17th: Palestine – Second Battle of Gaza (until 19.4.17)	16: Russia – Lenin arrives in Petrograd.
		24th: Mesopotamia: British take Samarra.	
		24th: Balkans – Battle of Doiran (until 25.4.17)	
	29th: French Army – beginning of indiscipline, leading to mutinies.	30th: Sir L C Money's analysis of shipping lossess presented to the British Govt.	29th: Pétain becomes CGS of the French Army.
		(British merchant ship losses – April total: 169 ships; 526,447 tons).	
MAY	3rd: Bullecourt		3rd: Russia – Bolshevik inspired demonstrations in Petrograd.
	4th: Aisne offensive.		4th: Paris Conference.
	7th: Haig briefs Army Commanders on summer plans.		
		10th: British navy implements convoy system.	10th: Britain – beginning of May strikes.
		12th: Italy – Tenth Battle of Isonzo (until 8.6.17).	
	15th: General Pétain succeeds Nivelle as French Commander-in-Chief.		16th: Russia – Kerensky becomes Minister of War.
	20th: Aisne offensive ends. 20th: British troops begin to move north.		
		(British merchant ship losses – May total: 122 ships; 345,293 tons).	23rd: Hungary – Government of Count Tisza resigns, succeeded by Count Esterhazy (15.6.17).
JUN	5th: Letter from Pétain to Haig announcing that the French First Army, under General Anthoine, is to take part in the Flanders campaign.		
	7th: Battle of Messines begins (until 14.6.17)		

1917	WESTERN FRONT	OTHER FRONTS & NAVAL WAR	HOME FRONTS & WORLD EVENTS
JUN	10th: New German troops arrive in the Ypres sector.		
			11th: Britain: first meeting of the War Policy Committee.
			12th: Greece – abdication of King Constantine, in favour of Alexander.
	14th: von Lossberg arrives to begin additional Flanders defences. 14th: RFC squadrons withdrawn from Flanders to UK.		13th: Britain – worst German air raids of the War (162 killed; 432 injured). 18th: Austria – Government of Count Claus Martinitz resigned, succeeded by government under Count von Seidler.
	26th: First U.S. troops arrive in France.		26th: Greece – Venizelos becomes Prime Minister. 27th: Greece enters the War on Allied side.
		28th: Palestine – Gen. Sir E Allenby assumes command.	
		29th: Russia – Kerensky offensive begins (until 7.7.17). (British merchant ship losses – June total: 122 ships; 398,773 tons).	
JUL			6th: Germany – Matthias Erzberger, leading Centre Party figure, calls for a peace policy.
	10th: Germans launch attack at Nieuport.	11th: Mesopotamia – attack on Ramadi.	12th: Germany – Bethmann-Hollweg resigns as Chancellor.
			14th: Germany – Dr Michaelis the new Chancellor.
	15th: Third Ypres – preliminary bombardment starts. [for anticipated 'z' day of 25 July]		16th: Russia – Bolshevik attempt to seize power ends in failure (18.6.17).
		18th: Russia – German counter- offensive begins.	18th: Russia – Lenin flees to Finland.

1917	WESTERN FRONT	OTHER FRONTS & NAVAL WAR	HOME FRONTS & WORLD EVENTS
JUL			19th: Germany – Reichstag passes peace resolution.
			21st: Russia – Kerensky becomes Prime Minister.
	25th: Gough and Anthoine want delay.	22nd: Balkans – Battle of Maraseti (first phase, until 1.8.17)	
	BATTLES OF THIRD YPRES		
	31st: Battle of Pilckem Ridge (until 2.8.17).	(British merchant ship losses – July total: 99 ships; 359,539 tons)	(German aeroplane attacks on Britain – July losses: 87 killed and 249 injured).
AUG		1st: Russia – Gen. Brusilov succeeded by Gen. Kornilov.	
		6th: Balkans – Battle of Maraseti (second phase, until 3.9.17).	4th: Liberia declares war on Germany.
			9th: Hungary – Esterhazy's ministry resigns; succeeded by Count Wekerle (21.8.17).
			11th: Britain – Arthur Henderson resigns from War Cabinet over the proposed Stockholm Conference.
			14th: China declares war on Germany.
	15th: Battle of Hill 70 (Lens) – until 25.8.17.		
	16th: Battle of Langemarck.	17th: Italy – Eleventh Battle of Isonzo (until 12.9.17).	16th: Germany – Gen. Groener removed from War Office.[1]
	20th: Second Battle of Verdun (until 15.12.17).	(British merchant ship losses – August total: 91 ships; 331,370 tons).	(German aeroplane attacks on Britain – Aug losses: 44 killed and 71 injured).
SEPT		1st: Battle of Riga (until 5.9.17).	2nd: Germany – OHL creates Fatherland Party.
			8th: Russia – Kornilov coup defeated.
			12th: France – Painlevé becomes Prime Minister.

1917	WESTERN FRONT	OTHER FRONTS & NAVAL WAR	HOME FRONTS & WORLD EVENTS
SEPT	20th: Battle of Menin Road Ridge (until 25.9.17). Involvement of Anzac and South African troops.		
	25th: Inter-Allied Conference at Boulogne.		
	26th: Battle of Polygon Wood (until 3.10.17).	28th: Mesopotamia – British capture Ramadi.	26th: Canada – compulsory military service introduced.
		(British merchant ship losses – September total: 78 ships; 186,647 tons)	(German aeroplane attacks on Britain – Sept losses: 210 killed and 391 injured).
OCT	4th: Battle of Broodseinde.		5th: Peru severs relations with Germany.
	9th: Battle of Poelcappelle. 12th: First Battle of Passchendaele.	11th: Baltic Islands – German attack on, leading to capture 20.10.17.	9th: Egypt – Sultan Ahmed Fuad succeeds Sultan Hussein Kamil.
	23rd: Battle of Malmaison (until 1.11.17).	24th: Italy; Twelfth Battle of Isonzo (Caporetto) – until 26.12.17. [26.10.17: French and British divisions ordered to Italy].	25th: Russia – Bolsheviks form Military Revolutionary Committee.
	26th: Second Battle of Passchendaele.	27th: Palestine – Third Battle of Gaza (until 7.11.17)	26th: Brazil declares war on Germany. 29th: Italy – Orlando becomes Prime Minister (following resignation of Bozelli, 25.10.17).
		(British merchant ship losses – October total: 86 ships; 261,873 tons)	(German aeroplane attacks on Britain: Oct losses: 21 killed and 63 injured).
NOV			1st: Germany – Dr Michaelis resigns as Chancellor; succeeded by Count von Hertling. 2nd: Balfour Declaration.
	6th: Canadian Corps capture Passchendaele.	5th: Mesopotamia – Battle of Tikrit.	5th: Rapallo Conference – idea of Supreme War Council.

1917	WESTERN FRONT	OTHER FRONTS & NAVAL WAR	HOME FRONTS & WORLD EVENTS
NOV		7th: Italy – Gen. Cadorna replaced by Gen. Diaz as Commander-in-Chief of Italian forces.	7th: Russia – Bolsheviks seize power in Petrograd.
	10th: End of Battles of Third Ypres.	10th: Italy – Italian troops in position on Piave.	16th: France – Clemenceau becomes Prime Minister.
	20th: Battle of Cambrai (until 3.12.17)	(British merchant ship losses – November total: 64 ships; 175,194 tons).	
DEC		5th: Russia – Armistice between Russia and the Central Powers.	
		6th: Balkans – Truce of Focsani: hostilities cease between Rumania and the Central Powers.	6th: Finland proclaims independence.
	7th: BEF Conference on defensive measures in 1918.		7th: U.S. declares war on Austria-Hungary.
		9th: Palestine – Allenby takes Jerusalem.	7th: Ecuador severs relations with Germany.
			17th: Canadian elections: victory for ruling coalition.
		22nd: Russia – negotiations for a peace treaty begin at Brest-Litovsk.	22nd: Britain – Lord Rhondda's rationing scheme comes into force.
			24th: Britain – dismissal of Jellicoe.
		(British merchant ship losses – Dec total: 85 ships; 257,807 tons).	(German aeroplane attacks on Britain – Dec total: 22 killed and 113 injured).

Political and Military Command in 1917

GREAT BRITAIN

H.M. King George V

WAR CABINET
Prime Minister: David Lloyd George
Lord President: Lord Curzon
Chancellor of the Exchequer: Andrew Bonar Law
Minister without portfolio: Arthur Henderson (resigned August 1917)
Minister without portfolio: Lord Milner
Minister without portfolio: Lieutenant-General Jan Smuts
(from June 1917)
Minister without portfolio: Sir Edward Carson (from July 1917)
Minister without portfolio: George Barnes (from August 1917)
Cabinet Secretary: Sir Maurice Hankey

GOVERNMENT MINISTERS
Lord Chancellor: Lord Finlay
Lord Privy Seal: Lord Crawford
Secretary of State for Foreign Affairs: Arthur Balfour
Secretary of State for Home Affairs: Sir George Cave
Secretary of State for War: Lord Derby
Secretary of State for India: Austen Chamberlain
(until July, succeeded by E S Montagu)
Secretary of State for the Colonies: Walter Long
First Lord of the Admiralty: Sir Eric Geddes
(succeeded Sir Edward Carson in July 1917)
Minister of Labour: J Hodge (until August, succeeded by G H Roberts)
Minister of Blockade: Lord Robert Cecil
Minister for Reconstruction: Dr Christopher Addison
(Minister for Munitions until July 1917)
Minister for Munitions: Winston Churchill (from July 1917)

Director General of National Service: Neville Chamberlain (succeeded by Sir Auckland Geddes August 1917)
President of the Air Board: Lord Cowdray (until November, succeeded by Lord Rothermere)
President of the Board of Trade: Sir A Stanley
President of the Board of Agriculture: Rowland Prothero
Shipping Controller: Sir Joseph Maclay
Food Controller: Lord Devonport (succeeded by Lord Rhondda, May 1917)
President of the Local Government Board: Lord Rhondda (until June, succeeded by W Hayes Fisher)
Chancellor of the Duchy of Lancaster: Sir F Cawley
Chief Secretary for Ireland: H E Duke
Secretary for Scotland: Rt Hon R Munro
President of the Board of Education: H A L Fisher
Attorney-General: Sir F E Smith
Postmaster-General: A Illingworth
Solicitor-General: Sir Gordon Hewart

WAR POLICY COMMITTEE
David Lloyd George
Lord Curzon
Lord Milner
Lieutenant-General Jan Smuts
Secretary: Sir Maurice Hankey

ADMIRALTY
First Lord of the Admiralty: Sir Eric Geddes (succeeded Sir Edward Carson in July 1917)
First Sea Lord: Admiral Sir John Jellicoe (until December 1917)
Deputy First Sea Lord: Vice-Admiral Sir Roslyn Wemyss
Commander-in-Chief of the Grand Fleet: Admiral Sir David Beatty

WAR OFFICE
Secretary of State for War: Lord Derby
Chief of the Imperial General Staff: General Sir William Robertson
Director of Military Operations: Major-General F Maurice
Under Secretary of State for War: J I MacPherson

GHQ
Commander In Chief: Field Marshal Sir Douglas Haig
Chief Of Staff: Lieutenant-General Sir Launcelot Kiggell
Deputy Chief of Staff: Major-General Richard Butler
Artillery Adviser: Major-General Noel Birch
Director Of Intelligence: Brigadier-General John Charteris
Director Of Military Operations: Major-General John Davidson

Meteorological Adviser: Lieutenant-Colonel Ernest Gold
Press Censor: Major Neville Lytton
Quartermaster-General: Lieutenant-General Sir R.C. Maxwell
Director General of Transportation: Major-General Philip Nash (from
June, succeeded Major-General Sir E Geddes)
Engineer-in Chief: Major-General Robert Rice (until October 1917)
Director General of Medical Services: Lieutenant-General Sir Arthur
Sloggett

ARMY COMMANDERS
GOC Second Army: General Sir Herbert Plumer
GOC Fourth Army: General Sir Henry Rawlinson
GOC Fifth Army: General Sir Hubert Gough

CORPS COMMANDERS
[during Third Ypres]
GOC I Corps: Lieutenant-General Sir Arthur Holland
GOC II Corps: Lieutenant-General Sir Claud Jacob
GOC V Corps: Lieutenant-General Sir Edward Fanshawe
GOC IX Corps: Lieutenant-General Sir Alexander Hamilton-Gordon
GOC X Corps: Lieutenant-General Sir Thomas Morland
GOC XIII Corps: Lieutenant-General Sir William McCracken
GOC XIV Corps: Lieutenant-General F.R. the Earl of Cavan
GOC XV Corps: Lieutenant-General Sir John DuCane
GOC XVIII Corps: Lieutenant-General Sir Ivor Maxse
GOC XIX Corps: Lieutenant-General Sir H E Watts

BRITISH DOMINIONS

PRIME MINISTERS
Prime Minister of Australia: William Hughes
Prime Minister of Canada: Sir Robert Borden
Prime Minister of Newfoundland: Sir E P Morris
Prime Minister of New Zealand: W F Massey
Prime Minister of South Africa: General Louis Botha

MILITARY COMMAND
GOC Canadian Corps: Lieutenant-General Sir Arthur Currie
GOC I Anzac Corps: Lieutenant-General Sir William Birdwood
GOC II Anzac Corps: Lieutenant General Sir Alexander Godley
Commander South African Brigade: Brigadier-General F S Dawson

FRANCE

President: Raymond Poincaré

PRIME MINISTERS

Aristide Briand (until 17 March 1917)
Alexandre Ribot (until 12 September 1917)
Paul Painlevé (until 16 November 1917)
Georges Clemençeau

WAR MINISTRY
War Ministers:
Général L H Lyautey (until 17 March 1917)
Paul Painlevé (combined with premiership from 12 September 1917)
Georges Clemençeau (from 16 November 1917, combined with premiership)

Chief of the General Staff: Général F Foch (Pétain from 29.4.17 until 15.5.17)

MILITARY COMMAND
Commander-in-Chief: Général H P Pétain (from 17.5.17)
Pétain's Chief of Staff: Général Debeney
Commander of the First Army: Général Anthoine (from 15.6.17)
Chief of Staff, First Army: Colonel Peschart d'Ambly
Commander 1st Army Corps: Général Lacapelle
Commander 36th Army Corps: Général Nollet

GERMANY

Kaiser Wilhelm II

CHANCELLORS
Theobald von Bethmann Hollweg (until 13 July 1917)
Dr Georg Michaelis (until 1 November 1917)
Count von Hertling

MILITARY COMMAND
Chief of the General Staff: Field Marshal P von Hindenburg
Chief Quartermaster General: General Erich Ludendorff
Army Group Commander: Crown Prince Rupprecht of Bavaria
Crown Prince Rupprecht's Chief of Staff: General von Kuhl
Commander of the Fourth Army: General Sixt von Armin
Chief of the General Staff of the Fourth Army: General von Lossberg

FRANCE

Presidents: Raymond Poincaré

PRIME MINISTERS
Aristide Briand (until 20 March 1917)
Alexandre Ribot (until 12 September 1917)
Paul Painlevé (until 16 November 1917)
Georges Clemenceau

WAR MINISTERS

General H. Lyautey (until 20 March 1917)
Paul Painlevé (combined with Premiership from November 1917)
Georges Clemenceau (from 16 November 1917, combined with Premiership)

Chief of the General Staff: General Ferdinand Foch (from April 1917)

MILITARY COMMAND

Commander-in-Chief: General Robert Nivelle (until 15 May 1917, then General Philippe Pétain)
Commander of the Reserve Army Group: General Humbert, then
General Fayolle; First Army: General Debeney; Fourth
Army: General Gouraud; Sixth Army: General Mazel, etc.
Commander-in-Chief, Armies of the East: General Sarrail

GERMANY

Kaiser: Wilhelm II

CHANCELLORS

Theobald von Bethmann-Hollweg (until 14 July 1917)
Dr Georg Michaelis (until 1 November 1917)
Count von Hertling

MILITARY COMMAND

Chief of the General Staff: Field Marshal Paul von Hindenburg
Deputy Chief of the General Staff: Erich Ludendorff
Army Group Commanders: Crown Prince Rupprecht of Bavaria,
German Crown Prince, Chief of Staff General von der Schulenburg;
Commander of Armies in the East: General Max Hoffmann
Chief, Navy High Command: Admiral Henning von Holtzendorff

xxxiv

Acknowledgements

In a collaborative work of this nature, the editor's first acknowledgement must be to his fellow contributors. Without exception it has been a pleasure to work with them and gratefully I acknowledge the privilege of having their time commitment, scholarly examination of their sources and the end-product in the form of their chapters in the book. Behind the labours, fitted in between other pressing duties, there seem to have been well-springs of enthusiasm in contributing to this book. To four people in particular, three of them contributors, I owe a great deal. Ian Whitehead readily accepted the responsibility of assistant editorial work, compiled the bibliography, devised and produced the chronology and command annexes, even more significantly the index and regularly visited Leeds for discussions on the book as it developed. Matthew Richardson has read and commented usefully upon my writing, as well as supporting every aspect of scholarly activity within the Liddle Collection with exemplary efficiency constantly leavened with keenness. Peter Chasseaud has somehow found time within his own teaching and writing, vastly to enhance the book with the professional skills of a cartographer inspired by a very special understanding of the Western Front and, once again, after all that he has done to help with books, T.V. and CD Rom productions from the Collection, Alasdair Cheyne, with help from Matthew, has ensured that appropriate photographs and facsimile documents add distinction to the book.

I am deeply indebted to Bob Carrington and Albert Smith who used the Liddle Collection cataloguing cross-reference system to provide me with a range of personal experience material for my own chapter. This cross-referencing system has had countless hours of selfless service by archive volunteers over the last twenty or so years. It makes research in the Collection easy but someone still had, in the case of the 3rd Ypres, to locate the document from the catalogue and photocopy that which was relevant - a time-taking task cheerfully undertaken by these good friends.

Of course while the writing or editorial work was being undertaken, the burden increased on staff in the Liddle collection. Matthew Richardson again helped here as did Kate Peters and the regular volunteers in the Liddle Collection. Carolyn Mumford transcribing tape-recordings, Terry

Mumford putting these transcripts in place and compiling cross-references, Jacqueline Wynne Jones, Braham Myers, Albert Smith, John Wooley, Michael Regan, Bob Pykett, Keith and Brenda Clifton have all given freely their now experienced labour in the Collection. My blessings were multiplied: my good friend, Hugh Cecil, assisted me with proof reading in time, I am sure, he could ill afford from his own work.

Claire Harder, Secretary in the Collection, Secretary to the Friends of the Collection and Girl Friday towards the production of the book, has brought to bear on the book her experience of assisting with *Facing Armageddon*. Not least important, she has kept calm and invariably pleasant whilst juggling with her various responsibilities which have included her own post-graduate studies.

In view of the excellence of Pen & Sword's service in the production of several of the editor's books, notably *Facing Armageddon* [with Hugh Cecil], I had no hesitation in putting this Passchendaele book with Pen & Sword Books and from Barnsley, Barbara Bramall has ensured that the firm's reputation has been maintained.

I would like to thank all copyright holders for their generous readiness to allow material under their control, illustrations, maps or textual, to appear in the book, most notably the Controller of H.M.S.O. and, concerning photographs, Major-General S.N. Gower, the Director of the Australian War Memorial and the authorities at the Canadian National Archives, the New Zealand Army Memorial Museum and the South African National Museum of Military History. Every effort has been made by contributors to locate current holders of copyright in text and illustrations but the editor apologizes for any omissions which may have occurred in this respect and would welcome information so that amendments can be made in future editions.

There may be further acknowledgements I should have made for help or encouragement and I hope I may be excused for any accidental omissions but in conclusion I do thank my very dear wife, Louise and our children, Felicity, Alexander and Duncan, for their forbearance. A house move, as writing and general editorial duties drew together was as welcome as rain in the Salient in August 1917 and I am conscious that our successful emergence from this experience without damage or casualties is as a result of their enthusiasm for life and its challenges. My thanks to them as ever.

Peter Liddle
University of Leeds,
June 1997.

Introduction

The Third Battle of Ypres ranks with other features of the First World War as a subject of unending debate with compelling, tragic, and, as is charged, culpable associations. The massacre of Armenians, the Dardanelles/ Gallipoli campaign, the Somme, the fateful Russian revolutions, the drowning of merchant seamen and the starvation of civilians by blockade, may not all offer an identifiable link to Passchendaele but they have a similar resonance.

In the light of what was known at the time, was the proposal for a major offensive on the Western Front launched from the Ypres Salient in the second half of 1917, a sound concept? Then, were the methods employed to realize the great design, well-judged? Given the evidence available to British High Command, political and military, was it at some stage clear that the overall plan had failed, that re-thinking was required – indeed, should all offensive operations have been cancelled long before the attempts to advance were operationally abandoned? Like the fall of adjacent dominoes toppling over in turn, the sequence of questions is not readily stopped.

If the evidence were clearly to point towards cancellation, why was such evidence ignored? What weight may properly be placed on any external factors, maritime or French, which at the time supported the argument for maintaining the offensive. Eighty years on, these are still the questions which face anyone interested in the First World War in general and the Western Front in particular. They are questions with which the editor of this work has long wrestled, none of the books dedicated to the subject seeming to provide satisfactory answers. The provision of some satisfactory answers for general readership is the purpose of *Passchendaele in Perspective*.

The book is designed to have even-handedness as a principle consistently upheld. It strives to avoid special pleading as rigorously as it eschews the peddling of prejudice. It has a further characteristic in its general approach to the subject. In all those chapters looking back to 1917, the source material which tells the story or supports the interpretation, in the main, dates from the period in question.

Furthermore, a serious attempt has been made to produce a more comprehensive as well as a more balanced book than has previously been published on Third Ypres. The means chosen to achieve this, begin with a serious consideration of German response to the British offensive and continue with a concern separately to look at French and Commonwealth involvement, but, additionally, there are new approaches, new topics for examination and new insights which substantiate the claim that the book is innovatively all-embracing.

In 1995/6, Hugh Cecil and the editor of this Passchendaele book worked to prepare for publication *Facing Armageddon: the First World War Experienced*, a book with an avowedly international character. A great deal was learned from this successful exercise. It convinced the editors of what could be gained by drawing together in one volume the knowledge of scholars who have examined, and evaluated, relevant documentation in non-English language archives and of course in Commonwealth and other archives. The Armageddon exercise also encouraged the provision of an opportunity here, in this new book, for younger historians with their fresh outlook to co-operate with established scholars in the field of First World War studies. If the seasoned historian were to have gained a reputation free from any charge of having offered layer upon layer of first-held views repeated, then the application together of emerging and proven talent towards a subject so compelling as Passchendaele was surely an exciting prospect.

There remains another distinctive approach which gives a special character to this book. From the start the design has been to ensure that understanding of the battle was illuminated by specialists whose knowledge was not usually aired in the same company as that of the more traditional military, political and social presentations. Several of the chapters in this book appear here as a direct result of this thinking and the nature of others bears witness to it. Surveying and mapping the Salient, weather factors, the weapons and equipment of the B.E.F., the Salient as an inspiration of artistic and literary expression, surviving memorabilia of the battle and the vestiges on the ground today of the 1917 battlefield, these have not been subjects extensively examined before in books which evaluated High Command or sought to record personal battle experience. Thereby, much was absent in books which claimed comprehensive treatment of the battle and in *Passchendaele in Perspective*, the intention is that this should be remedied.

The book is divided into five parts of which the first is entitled, *The Setting and Those who Set the Scene*. In Chapter One, *The World War Context*, John Bourne argues persuasively that it was the overall context of the war which in fact required the Flanders Offensive and in this lay its contemporary significance with its distinctive Russian, French, Maritime and even Imperial aspects. There is no difficulty in selecting American entry into the war, the French mutinies and the Russian Revolutions as the events which dominate the year – for Russians, French and Americans,

Passchendaele scarcely concentrated their thinking in the Summer of 1917 but Bourne makes the telling point that, after Verdun and the Somme, Britain had to face the "reality of the Great War", British statesmen being "compelled to fight a war which allowed no freedom for alternative methods of waging war". He acknowledges that this reality was "still unacceptable to some". His target here is Lloyd George but his comment might well have been addressed to many who have written about the war.

The Home Front context within which Passchendaele was set had a wider framework than one structured simply between Whitehall and Westminster. The morale of the nation's work force, and of potential or actual soldiers in the U.K. and the state of public opinion responding to information on the progress of the battle, were factors which had to be carefully watched by departments of Government. In Chapter Two, *Lloyd George, the War Cabinet, and High Politics*, it is the political heart of this scene which is considered by John Turner, and most particularly the war within the war, the war between Lloyd George and the Generals.

The 'high command' on both sides is outlined, the alliances, the tactics, manoeuvres and engagements. We can enjoy the paradox of Asquith, the spurned Liberal leader, yoked to Haig, the epitome of the conservative establishment in uniform, but, if Passchendaele itself were a distasteful subject, certainly a sad subject for study, then the scene laid out by Turner matches it. One almost has to remind oneself that in addition to the advance of personal ambition, the practice of disloyalty, the struggle for ascendancy between old and new establishments, there was also real concern about the way most effectively to wage the war.

Evidence is put before the reader of these anxieties catalysed by the Lansdowne letter. We are even given an example from the B.E.F., a letter from a politically well-connected officer documenting the drained confidence of some senior military figures with whom he was associated. Turner makes no excuse for Lloyd George's conduct, nor indeed for Haig and Robertson in the struggle for supreme authority in the military direction of the war, but he chooses to stress the limitations upon the Prime Minister's freedom of action, his dependence upon the support of the Conservative Party and on the Russian, Italian and French factors. This is notably at variance with the conclusions reached by Trevor Wilson and Robin Prior who, in *Passchendaele, the Untold Story*, categorically affirm Lloyd George's responsibility for allowing the continuance of a battle he had the authority to halt.

Haig was left with his command of the B.E.F. and with his Flanders battle and Lloyd George with but one tactical achievement, the sacking of Robertson as C.I.G.S. This particular war was in no sense over and, in Robertson's replacement, the slippery Sir Henry Wilson, the Prime Minister now had a General on his side, at least for this moment of their mutual need.

In Chapter Three, *Field Marshal Sir Douglas Haig and Passchendaele*, Frank Vandiver looks first at the Nivelle / Lloyd George accord as the manifestation of the distrust between the British Prime Minister and the Commander-in-Chief B.E.F. from which so much ill-consequence followed. Haig's intended Flanders offensive was first circumvented by Lloyd George's agreement to the French plans for the Chemin des Dames offensive and then, when the Flanders endeavour was sanctioned, French incapacity to deliver their promised help was one of the reasons for the delayed start of the battle.

In his examination of Haig's strategic objectives and exercise of command, Vandiver recognizes that Haig's choice of Gough to lead the Northern half of the Flanders operation was less than shrewd and he also accepts, as Haig himself did, that if Charteris were guilty of an over-optimistic assessment of the nearness to breaking of the German morale, then Haig too must be culpable in this respect.

On the charge that there was a lack of clarity in Haig's mind as to what might realistically be achieved as the battle developed and what he judged must be sought, a breakthrough, Vandiver again recognizes a degree of confusion. It might be added that this confusion encapsulates the Franco-British dilemma throughout the central years of the war: with the loss of strategic initiative to the Germans, the forces of the entente were condemned to attack against all tactical advantage and to strive both to break the strength and will of the entrenched enemy and for the possibility of actually breaking through his lines decisively.

This American historian believes that Haig honourably took up the gauntlet in 1917 as the only possible alternative to a potentially disastrous British inactivity on the Western Front. In so doing, and more particularly in what was to follow, the undeniable 1918 achievement, his reputation, Vandiver considers, has been unfairly sullied.

In Chapter Four, *The German High Command*, Heinz Hagenlücke makes the German perspective clear as a British attack from the Salient was awaited. A militarily defensive stance had been decreed while victory was won by the U-boat. This stance reflected not just a reasonable strategic and tactical appraisal but a recognition of political factors with regard to German war aims. "A huge part of German society itself deemed the annexation of the country [Belgium] very valuable" is one of several noteworthy asides made by Hagenlücke in his chapter.

From mid-April, the German High Command had detected the likelihood of a British offensive in Flanders, recognising the U-boat bases on the Belgian coast as a key strategic objective. It is instructive to read this German historian's account of the desperately undertaken changes in methods of defence as the battle developed and that even these changes failed to avert losses so serious that "irreparable damage" was endured by the German forces engaged. It seems in fact that the achievement of avoiding defeat at Third Ypres was ruinously costly to the Germans, and Hagenlücke's point needs to be borne in mind by all involved in the endless debate over attrition, its grim virtues or its senseless waste.

In the Second Part of the book, *Problems, Plans and Performance and*

British Operational Command, Paddy Griffith, in Chapter Five, looks at *The Tactical Problem: Infantry, Artillery and the Salient*. With the significant distinction that Griffith actually sees Passchendaele as a British victory, the complementary nature of his conclusions and those put forward by Heinz Hagenlücke is remarkable. For Griffith, the Third Battle of Ypres, despite the appalling difficulties which, for periods of weeks, made ground unconquerable, shows the B.E.F. practising lessons learned from earlier attempts to assault strongly held positions. The means by which to achieve a really useful degree of surprise was not yet within the grasp of the B.E.F. but artillery planning was striving for more sophistication. The creeping barrage, as employed earlier in the year, was offering infantry a new, far more effective, protection of an advance towards initial objectives despite difficulties of co-ordination and the limitations of such a barrage once front line positions had been won.

In Griffith's view, Third Ypres was fought and won "by virtue of the dominance of [British] artillery and the endurance of their infantry". He adds the sad tailpiece that no such thinking as the B.E.F. had directed to the tactics of attack, the gradual coming together of an integrated weapons system [including the aeroplane], had been focused on the problems of defence. There would be a price to pay for this in the Spring of the following year.

That ejecting the enemy from the Belgian coast and preventing him from exercising a maritime threat to the United Kingdom, was conceptually a consideration from the very loss of that coast in October 1914, is made clear in Chapter Six on *Passchendaele: the Maritime Dimension*. Geoffrey Till, looks initially at pre-war consideration of Britain's geo-political position and it is as well to be reminded that in just over six months of the outbreak of war, the Dardanelles/Gallipoli venture, first, drew all strategic thought of a diversionary nature away from the North Sea and towards the Eastern Mediterranean and then later discredited to a considerable extent the idea of combined operations. Ironically the idea was kept afloat by the U-boat threat to Channel communications and supply of the B.E.F. There was also, for the military, the harsh reality that trench warfare left but one flank unturned, the North Sea coast, and for advantage to be taken of that, twin-service collaboration would again have to be essayed.

It seems undeniable that the debate over Grand Strategy; national needs; maritime insecurity; Royal Navy deployment; military requirements and opportunities; the dominance and competence of leading personnel; were all interwoven with the launching and maintenance of the Ypres Offensive in 1917. Geoffrey Till establishes that the maritime dimension was central as a strategic factor in Passchendaele planning and remained as an intended means of its realization until military failure, away from the coast, decreed otherwise.

The less well-known role of the French at Third Ypres, is the subject of Chapter Seven, *Third Ypres and the Restoration of Confidence in the ranks of the French Army*. Allain Bernède explains the context within which the new French Commander-in-Chief, General Pétain, attempted to achieve his twofold aim, first of restoring confidence within the ranks of the French Army after the failure and dire consequence of the Chemin des Dames Offensive, and second of regaining British respect for French military capacity. A limited task with infantry protected to the maximum by an adequacy of artillery: by these means the French earned success in their sector. Anglo-French collaboration was planned in detail and in many senses carried out well. There were, as might be expected, areas of disagreement and in the end Sir Douglas Haig deeply resented the early closing down of the French effort. Bernède relates this and seems to accept Haig's stricture as a reasonable perception. However, he points out that the French commitment to Third Ypres, following upon the events of April/May, was the most significant they made to the offensive in that year and, the French historian tartly reminds us, it was observed by the French that the economy of their methods of attack was noticed but not practised by British High Command.

Ian Beckett in Chapter Eight, *Operational Command: The Plans and the Conduct of Battle,* examines *Command* within its operational parameters. He considers that the structure of command at the time of Third Ypres needed reform and notes ironically a beneficial consequence of the battle, in that reform was precipitated, involving the removal of two of the most senior at G.H.Q., men whose influence hampered the effectiveness of the B.E.F. The author tackles first the pre-war conceptual origin of a Flanders offensive and then traces further consideration of the Belgian coast as a military objective in each of the first three years of war. Sir Douglas Haig, in particular, was keen to bring the enemy to decisive battle in Flanders but it has been charged that Haig later hid his sustained but unrealistic belief in a major breakthrough behind the dubious defence that, quite apart from the U-boat bases and the need to shield the weakened French, the battle was maintained to grind down the capacity of the German Army to continue the war. Beckett is in sympathy with this charge and draws into further discussion the geographical divergence of the objectives of Haig's breakthrough – the coast and the rail and communications centre inland at Roulers. It might be mentioned here that to reach a point where the railway junctions came under fire was an explicitly marked step threatening from inland German retention of the coast.

It is clear that the Haig/Gough command relationship was unsatisfactory in ways which to some extent parallel the problems between Ian Hamilton and his senior subordinate commanders at Helles and Suvla on the Gallipoli Peninsula in April and August 1915 respectively but with reference to the work of staffs in operational command and the "unremitting burden" evidently felt by one Staff Officer, Neill Malcolm, Gough's Chief of Staff, Beckett might well have drawn attention to that burden endured by the Commander-in-Chief himself and Plumer's Chief of Staff, Harington, who did not fail under stress.

Not everyone will agree with Beckett's generally unsympathetic review of G.H.Q. in operation, indeed not everyone contributing to this book. Some would aver that insufficient allowance is made by critics of command in operation for the pressure of unfolding and new circumstance on decision makers in the eye of the storm. Sometimes the input of the enemy into the equation of battle seems diminished or neglected by those exposing every perceived flaw in the direction of British military endeavour. It would be a shame if Clausewitz and the friction factor in war were not still judged to be worth our close attention.

A concluding point here might be made. In examining the success of British arms in 1918 after the stemming of the German offensives, it is increasingly being put forward that the improvement in operational methods as they emerged came by initiatives from the lower echelons of command. If this were to be proved the case, then at least it can be countered that these initiatives were not stifled from above.

It is likely that much of the information on Cartography and Artillery Survey in Chapter Nine, *Field Survey in the Salient: Cartography and Artillery Survey in the Flanders Operations in 1917*, will be new to most readers and indeed to many contributors in this book [as it was to the editor]. It is hard to imagine the practice and further development of a science, in this case that of artillery survey, taking place under more adverse conditions than those obtaining in the Salient at the time of Third Ypres. Peter Chasseaud writes authoritatively on the massive contribution of the technological weapon of engineer and artillery survey in what was in a dominant sense a battle of guns and howitzers. Chasseaud ensures that a landscape which, in the imagination, is familiar, is given new detail widening one's vision of the military problems being tackled: "Topographers had to struggle forward to field battery positions with weighty plane-tables and tripods strapped to their backs, and Trig observers had to get up to the heavies carrying theodolites and tripods . . . Pushing the trig skeleton forward was vitally important for fixing battery positions and targets, as well as O.P.'s and microphone bases, but was seriously hampered by weather conditions unsuitable for observation, the state of the ground, by continual heavy shelling and by road congestion which prevented survey parties from moving forward".

In Chapter Ten, *The Flanders Battleground and the Weather in 1917*, John Hussey systematically demolishes the case against Haig that, in the face of clear meteorological evidence, he launched an offensive which was bound to founder in mud because August would have its "usual" heavy rain and that disaster was being invited by the over-optimistic, stubborn Haig who only listened to advice which was in conformity with his intention.

We are reminded first that there was every reason to attack in Flanders, that there was little freedom and no good argument for attacking elsewhere. Second, it is made clear that the military campaigner [unless of course he were suddenly to shatter peace with the sword and initiate military operations at a place and time of his own choosing] can seldom select ideal conditions of terrain, season and weather. Instead he has, in the main, to make do with what circumstances decree. On occasion, gambles have to be taken and the weather gamble for Third Ypres was scarcely on the same scale of fatefulness as that which launched the D-Day assault of June 1944. Historically, modern warfare simply has to cope with prevailing ground and weather conditions, and sometimes those conditions are severe. There are many examples: Marlborough in the Netherlands, the flooding at Walcheren in 1944. In the First World War, the freezing flat-lands on either side of the flooded Tigris or, this time on elevated ground, the drenching, icy rain and slippery rock tracks of the hills outside of Jerusalem, demonstrate that there is scant reason for seeing the soldiering misery of the Salient as without parallel.

Hussey then moves from such comparative matters, subjective as they are, to something beyond contention – properly presented statistical evidence, dating from the period and shrewdly analysed by Philip Griffiths of the University of Birmingham, and backed by Hussey's own study of the daily weather diaries. The evidence is conclusive: the August weather was **exceptionally** bad [and October too was worse than might have been expected]. There was indeed statistically based evidence and the meteo-rologists were abreast of the science of their time but it could not allow for such totally abnormal weather. Such data as existed was carefully studied as provided by Haig's meteorological adviser, so the Commander in Chief can scarcely be accused of ignoring advice.

After relying so heavily on verifiable data, and winning his battle hands down, it is perhaps understandable that John Hussey ventures onto the more dangerous ground of hypothesis: if only the Nivelle Offensive were to have been called off earlier, what might then have been achieved by a consequentially earlier start to an offensive from the Salient? Not everyone may agree with him here, but the daily weather statistics of the high summer should provoke further thought.

In several senses, Jack Bruce and Kevin Kelly's Chapter Eleven on *The Royal Flying Corps and the Struggle for Supremacy in the Air over the Salient*, widens the vision of those whose eye on the battle remains at ground level. Set out before us is the impressive strength and the location of British aerial resources committed to the battle and the range of its tasks is explained. The numerical and technical strength of the German air arm is considered and a vignette given of the celebrated Werner Voss.

It may not be generally appreciated that a Belgian air contribution and, in some strength, French pilots and observers, were in support at the battle but Bruce and Kelly establish this and remind the reader of Guynemer and Fonck, both of whom were in combat over the Salient.

The focus is sharply on the multi-role air support of the soldiers on the ground and there is some irony in the fact that concentration upon this essential work was affected by external political pressures, a not unfamiliar circumstance for British command on the Western Front. German aero-plane air raids on London and the South East of England temporarily drew away from the Salient two key fighter units and then resulted in the re-deployment of British bombers away from the battle for reprisal raids on German territory. It might be added here that Trenchard, in command of the R.F.C. in France, had submitted to the War Cabinet in June that the best security for London against bombing was the capture of the Belgian coast and the forced withdrawal Eastwards of the German bomber airfields near Ghent. To Haig and Jellicoe may be added Trenchard in giving this strategic objective the highest priority.

It is clear that Third Ypres marked no critical change in the waging of the war in the air but, to balance the loss of machines, if not of men, the struggle provided an invaluable proving of the merits or otherwise of British aircraft and equipment. The wise decisions made in Britain over the selection of aircraft frames and engines for mass production to meet what-ever the New Year would hold, were founded at least in part, on what had been proven in the skies over the Salient in the second half of 1917.

In the eyes of most people, battle and medical services conjure up solely the image of finding and bringing wounded or receiving wounded initially at the Regimental Aid Post. At the Regimental Aid Post, cases would receive their first treatment and they would be evacuated first by stretcher and then, at a later stage, by horse-drawn or motor ambulance conveying them to dressing stations. Thereafter they would be taken to Base hospi-tals by train, ambulance or barge. Awareness that men, before and during battle, have to be kept fit and free from illness by, not least, efficient sani-tary arrangements, slips out of consideration. Similarly, while there will be sympathetic identification with wounded in pain, not much thought may be given to the problem for medical personnel dealing with various types of wound by their gravity or location in the body still less to the classifi-cation of those rendered mentally or emotionally ineffective as soldiers.

Ian Whitehead, in Chapter Twelve, *Third Ypres – Casualties and British Medical Services: an Evaluation*, establishes immediately that the rôle of the Royal Army Medical Corps certainly did embrace the issues of hygiene and sanitation. He goes as far as stating that, "disease prevention was undoubtedly the most important challenge facing the RAMC" and explains both the organization and the measures by which the problem was tackled.

The second R.A.M.C. responsibility, that of the initial evacuation and treatment of wounded, was one from which lessons from the Somme were well-learned and again Whitehead demonstrates that despite the foul ground conditions for transportation of wounded, the organisation set in place and its personnel stood up well to the challenge of the series of battles which make up Third Ypres.

There was careful planning within the overall organization of hospitals for receiving and treating head injuries, chest injuries, fractured limbs at different casualty clearing stations, even specialist treatment centres for easily cured diseases like scabies. The reader is introduced to some of the measures employed to clean wounds preventing the onset of gangrene and also the developing work in blood transfusion.

Not everything was managed with smooth efficiency and it seems that the work of the R.A.M.C. suffered to some extent by the exercise of control from the Adjutant-General's branch. Practical problems were also consequent upon a desire to operate on cases as soon as possible and therefore placing casualty clearing stations well forward within proximity of targets for enemy shelling.

It was in the area of responsibility for making a soldier, as quickly as possible, fit for return to duty and assessing and treating mentally or emotionally disturbed men that particular difficulties arose. That the categorization of such cases had a relationship to the award of war pensions is one of many insights Whitehead offers his readers. He makes it plain that "there was a reluctance to recognize emotional shell shock as an illness, since many military and medical officers continued to believe that its supposed sufferers were either malingerers or men of poor calibre", but at least a new system was in place for dealing with such cases before the Third Battle of Ypres commenced and we learn what this entailed and, as a further indication of learning from experience, what was done for those suffering from the new German weapon, mustard gas. In a section of this book dealing with problems, Whitehead charts a record of considerable success achieved by the medical services.

Geoffrey Till, in his chapter on the Maritime Dimension, has set the scene for Andrew Wiest's *The Planned Amphibious Assault* in Chapter Thirteen. The one seriously considered combined operation to outflank the opponent on the Western Front has been less fully covered in scholarship, one may presume, because it never took place. However, the strategic potential and the fascination revealed here of the evidence of the long-sustained reality of the concept in top-level planning, deserves our close attention, attention which many will find compulsive as Wiest describes the practical detail worked out to carry through the amphibious landing successfully.

We learn of the design, construction and testing of an unprecedented, 200 yard long vessel for transportation, lashed between monitors and conveying tanks, guns and men for a shore landing. To the surprise which this may engender in the reader, might be added the assault training of the men themselves in a high security coastal camp given some additional immunity by report of the men carrying some infection. From the camp, tanks are driven up and over a newly-constructed sea wall built to simulate the obstruction which would be faced.

With the readiness of the force in practical matters and in high morale, one can sense the tension, then the frustration as the probability of launching the attack diminished into possibility and then into cancellation. Andrew Wiest leaves us to ponder whether an extra degree of boldness in High Command might have paid dividends. Haig held to the imaginative concept for long. Nevertheless he had the evidence of the uniformly swift

German reaction to attack and the poor record of ships against shore batteries. Might he have gambled, sanctioning the assault without waiting for what always had seemed to him the essential pre-cursor, evidence of a breakout from the Salient? Is Haig thereby displaying his limitation or his wise acceptance of reality? With these questions arises another: do we really know enough about the strength of German forces on the coast or within immediate reach of the coast?

In Part Three, *Military Effectiveness, Identity and Experience*, John Lee in Chapter Fourteen, *The British Divisions at Third Ypres* is partisan in a way which can properly be defended. Lee sees it as entirely unwarranted that the burden borne by British troops in relation to that carried by their Commonwealth comrades, should be inadequately recognized. He goes further than this and, by exemplification, demonstrates that for the British divisions there is not just a record of endurance but one of successful soldiering at stages during the campaign.

On the first day of the battle, British divisions in the centre and on the left did particularly well, taking 6,000 prisoners and numerous objectives as the letter which concludes this introduction documents. Then, in appalling conditions offering every disadvantage to the attacker saddled with unrealistic objectives, the cost of failure led to bitterly expressed resentment among those who survived. However, weather, tactics and the setting of objectives were to change for the better and again British divisions earned success before insuperable circumstances returned.

Accustomed as most readers will be, to think in terms of regimental or battalion pride, and, as some will consider just as significant with regard to fighting efficiency, down to units still smaller, companies, platoons, sections or the undesignated tiny groups of 'mates', Lee shows that men could under certain circumstances identify closely with something much larger, a division of troops, in number perhaps approaching eighteen thousand. Lee shows that it was not just Welsh, Scottish, Irish or Ulstermen who could feel pride in belonging to so large a collection of their uniformed countrymen but that, within England, there were divisions with regional associations or with successful battle experience or with commanders who fostered pride in divisional identity. Some such divisions, from throughout the United Kingdom, developed around these factors a fine fighting reputation and when an explanation is sought for this, the division's cohesion as a unit and the 'divisional' thinking of regimental officers and men have to come into the equation.

Though there *is* reference to the question of the Australians bearing a disproportionate burden during the battle, Ashley Ekins, in Chapter Fifteen, *The Australians at Passchendaele*, has chosen to examine Australian morale, before and during the battle. His continuing research into Australian soldier discipline and the incidence of Courts-Martial, gives him a valuable statistical index to assist in this. There is a second theme to the chapter and again statistics are used, casualties and yards of ground won, and they are used to endorse his judgement of the unprofitability of the offensive. The relationship between his two themes is self-evident.

Fromelles, Pozières and Mouquet Farm in 1916, Bullecourt in both April and May of the following year and then Messines, had been stern tests for the Australians. Ekins quotes from the celebrated C.E.W. Bean that there had been: "too much hard fighting to welcome the prospect of more", a statement which no doubt would have been endorsed by United Kingdom, Canadian, New Zealand and South African troops. Nevertheless, benefitting from drier weather and adequate artillery support, Australian soldiers earned striking success in late September at the Battle of Menin Road and at Polygon Wood. However, these successes were dearly bought and Ekins shows that tensions arose over what they were being required to tackle and those strains were evident even between battalion commanders and the officers and men subject to their authority.

The next success, Broodseinde, was more costly still, and when weather and ground conditions turned decisively against them, failure attended all endeavour to make progress towards Poelcappelle and Passchendaele. With casualties and frustration mounting, so did weariness, resentment and indiscipline. Ekins records the Australian divisions as exhausted, demoralised and "at their lowest ebb in the war". He marshals statistics to prove his points, though it is intriguing to note the disparity between Australian and Canadian Court-Martial numbers in the same period. Thanks not least to Ashley Ekins work in this area, comparative statistics are available and no doubt some challenging implications will, in due course, be drawn.

As for the recovery of the Australians from their lowest ebb and towards the level which first assisted in avoiding defeat in 1918 and then shared in the achievement of victory, Ekins offers as explanation the creation of a unified Australian Corps, nearly four months on a quiet sector and, at the same time, common throughout the B.E.F. "the beginnings of a growing technological and tactical proficiency".

That Canadians uniquely won achievement from the Third Battle of Ypres is a frequently expressed case with which several chapter authors in this book would take issue. What is incontestable is that in the changed nature of the battle from its original concept, it was the Canadians who captured the final, [far more limited] objective, Passchendaele itself. In Chapter Sixteen, *The Canadians at Passchendaele*, Dean Oliver explains the means by which the Corps won its victory in the Salient and makes a striking observation on a longer-term significance of this achievement.

The reluctance with which the Canadians, already of course experienced in the Salient, returned to it in 1917, is made abundantly clear, but, made just as evident, is their state of professional competence on entry into the Salient for the later stages of the battle. It was this competence at every level which had distinguished their success at Vimy. "Good officers, sound planning, technical expertise and innovative tactics" were, according to Oliver, the "real keys to Canadian success".

It is to be noted that Oliver will not have the significance of the Canadian victory over-blown while acknowledging that a realistic appraisal would, in Canada, take time to limit the airy myths which grew in the wake of the accomplishment – the Empire, the Allies, saved by Canadian arms. As to the futility of the battle, a perspective from which Canadians were some-what insulated by reason of their capture of Passchendaele, Oliver informs the reader that the best book on the battle as a Canadian experience, that by Daniel G Dancocks [*Legacy of Valour*, 1988] affirms that such a judge-ment is quite simply "wrong".

What the Canadians proved throughout the war, was that they were great learners and with appropriate tactical innovations to their credit. Oliver documents this but adds that "hard fighting, bravery and collective determination" needed to be present in full measure too. Concerning the one lesson wrongly learned or misapplied, we are informed by this Canadian that Passchendaele proved to post-war Governments in the Dominion that a part-time army – of course so much cheaper too – could answer Canada's defence commitments and in this manner the develop-ment of a viable Regular Army was forestalled. In view of the professionalism necessarily developed to win their victories in France, such a conclusion was indeed an ironic legacy of Passchendaele.

With the exception of a mounted rifle brigade in Palestine, it was New Zealand's national army on war service, which gave a special character to *The New Zealand Division at Passchendaele*, Chapter Seventeen, the subject of Chris Pugsley's contribution to this book. As the 'sole focus of national attention and political concern', the New Zealand division's performance was watched as closely from the other side of the world as it was by G.H.Q. in France.

As with all troops, what they would face in an offensive, would be condi-tioned, among other things, by the thoroughness of their training, the realism of the objectives set, the effectiveness of their artillery support, the strength of the opposition, the nature of the ground and events as they developed to left and right of them on the day. For the New Zealanders, there was a further factor which, on a good day could be overcome, but on a bad day had the most grim consequence. Pugsley paints a stark contrast between the efficiency of the staff work and divisional command of Major-General Sir Andrew Russell and that of his Corps Commander, Lieutenant-General Sir Alexander Godley, officer in command, II Anzac Corps.

The case for Russell is certainly established beyond doubt and is greatly to his credit and to the credit of his staff and the men of the division. Training, preparations, plans, meticulously thorough checking and rehearsal, brought outstanding success at Messines and, where New Zealand losses had been incurred unnecessarily there, it had been as a result of Russell's requirements being overruled. Thereafter, when new tactical procedures were recommended, Russell required the closest attention to following such methods in practice exercises.

On 4 October, in the Third Battle of Ypres, the division went into action to seize Gravenstafel Ridge and achieved its objectives though rain drowned the prospect of developing this success. It was the attempt required by Godley and against the doubts expressed by Russell, to renew the drive forward from 9 and 10 October, into a morass, which led to high losses, no gain and great bitterness.

It has to be accepted that the conditions were atrocious but, from Corps level, nothing had been done to improve the route up into the battle zone. Field Artillery had either failed to get up into position to support the infantry assault or had not found sufficiently stable positions accurately to carry out their fire programme. In due course, Passchendaele was to fall, but not to New Zealand troops. Well might Russell write in his diary for 12 October of "New Zealand's blackest day". It was a cruel reward for soldiers of a provenly good division.

In Chapter Eighteen on *South Africans in Flanders: Le Zulu Blanc,* Bill Nasson vividly evokes the distinctive background of troops with Boer, South African, English and a Scottish heritage. Their separateness was bound together into unity by distant and recent history, a far off, spacious, dry homeland and current confinement in wet, war-torn Flanders, their military traditions and, we are told with a literary raising of an eyebrow, their perceived entitlement and certainly claim to the black South African tradition of martial prowess. Nasson also nicely observes Flemish misconception that African soldiers would surely not be white, something which, for these particular troops, may have been, at best, a reflection of local ignorance. South African soldiers, in common with all who endured the Salient, were harrowed by their experience and yet they too wrought out limited achievement from limitless disadvantage.

The editor, in Chapter Nineteen, *Passchendaele Experienced: Soldiering in the Salient during the Third Battle of Ypres,* has attempted to broaden the picture of soldiering in the Salient to include more than the front line infantryman or the Gunner at his battery. The essential work in the rear areas and then along the lines of communication is shown to be subject to the same climate, to similar ground condition problems and at least to a degree of the shelling which would be expected near the forward positions.

It is also important to appreciate that in those more advanced positions, the ground was not invariably an impassable morass and thus attacking successes were, on occasion, achieved. As in earlier periods of the war, indeed it might be said as universally in war, soldiers showed adaptability, resourcefulness, ingenuity, as well as endurance. Their spirits drained by days of awfulness could be wonderfully uplifted by the smell of sizzling bacon and, when nearly all those positive influences in sustaining morale had been peeled away by sheer weariness, sodden misery, the loss of too many friends, sights and shocks too shattering, then for almost all men, there remained their self-respect before their fellows, their regard for their comrades, the family pride of their unit. It was usually just enough to keep them going.

German Werth leaves the reader in no doubt, in Chapter Twenty, *Flanders 1917 and the German Soldier*, that British shelling and infantry assault, the climate and ground conditions and the sheer length of the war, reduced German soldiers to an hitherto unprecedented pitch. They held to their task; Charteris in his over-optimistic assessment of their collapsed morale was proved wrong. To be wrong is sufficient in itself, but, reading Werth, one wonders by how much!

No one reading Chapter Twenty-One, *The Weapons and Equipment of the British Soldier at Passchendaele*, will be left without an enhanced understanding of the practicalities of soldiering in the Salient. From what the individual wore and worked with, to that of the co-operation in teams of machine-gunners, field gunners or tanks, Matthew Richardson has described analytically the relationship between inanimate objects and their function. By the use of both contemporary technical manuals and personal experience material, he has documented something which complements the work of Paddy Griffith in establishing that the British soldier's equipment and weaponry had "reached a zenith of efficiency" in aiding him to carry out his work even under the most adverse circumstances.

What constituted Army Law, what happened to those soldiers who defaulted in any respect, what held men to their tasks; these are the subjects Peter Scott tackles in Chapter Twenty-Two, *Law and Orders: Discipline and Morale in the British Armies in France, 1917*.

We may guess at the need, in a hugely expanded Army establishment, for junior officers to educate themselves in matters relating to Courts-Martial and for the Army, as it did, to bring additional legal expertise in at various levels of Army advocacy. Peter Scott provides chapter and verse in this and on other issues like the constituent elements which sustained morale, the work of Provost Marshals and of the Regimental Police.

Not everyone will agree with his dismissal of the deterrence factor in the capital punishment debate – indeed how can one know for sure in this – but there can be little doubt of the appropriateness of Scott's borrowing a phrase in a contemporary Government report on the Home Front labour force: after all that had been endured in the Salient during the battle, the B.E.F. remained "loyal and temperamentally conservative".

In Part Four, *The British Home Front*, the first of the two subjects examined is that of the presentation of 'news' information about the battle by Press and film agencies. The central points which emerge from Stephen Badsey and Philip Taylor's Chapter Twenty-Three, *Images of Battle: The Press, Propaganda and Passchendaele*, are that the "weak and disorganised nature of the British propaganda organizations at the time of Third Ypres prevented them from pursuing any coherent Home Front policy [of propaganda] other than in very general terms". The authors make clear that there were Flanders factors too which inhibited the dissemination of news, not really military censorship but the dangers and difficulties, indeed near impossibility, of getting the drama of action pictures from the exposed flat battlefield. We are told that the cine-cameramen in fact did better in this than was achieved by still camera photographs!

Changes in the organisation of propaganda and changes in its focus (from persuading elites to concentrating upon the masses) were happening during the very months of Passchendaele. However, these changes in themselves are full of interest, not least, the growth of Lord Beaverbrook's empire. What is not discussed but is perhaps worth consideration, is whether graphically detailed newspaper coverage of the cost of the fighting would have weakened the sinews of Home Front factory or household. If it would, then the absence of such reportage was fundamentally beneficial to a nation in the peril of war.

The interdependence of the armed services, agriculture and industry in the national war effort is readily understood but the tensions created by the manpower demands of each is the subject of Chapter Twenty-Four, *The 'Recruiting Margin' in Britain: Debates on Manpower during the Third Battle of Ypres*. Here, Keith Grieves paints a picture of the priority of War Office claims upon available manpower now being seriously challenged by both agriculture and industry at the very time that Government confidence in Military use of its manpower was at a lower ebb than ever before. This of course lent strength to the civilian side in the argument.

Grieves illustrates the issues being fought in case after case at the local level, the tribunals, where appeals against military service were held. Needs, in terms of the local, never mind the national economy, frequently prevailed over military argument against exemption from the provisions of the Military Service acts. It has to be said that agriculture and industry, denuded of their pre-war accustomed manpower surplus and each expanding to meet the crises of the war, had a powerful case, whereas the claims of the War Office were under challenge. There are reasons for believing that the Government may have got the balance wrong in weighing the merits of opposing cases: certainly this was Winston Churchill's judgement in his 8 December 1917 appeal to the War Cabinet.

The final section of the book, Part Five, is entitled: *Passchendaele: the Inspiration, Fascination and Discordance of an Enduring Legacy*. Paul Gough's, Chapter Twenty-Five, *'An Epic of Mud': Artistic Interpretations of Third Ypres*, provides a particularly good example of how a specialist can bring his reader from familiar into unfamiliar terrain in such a way that there is a ready understanding of new concepts as they are explained and, in this particular case, of practical problems for the painter as individual artists answer challenges to them in their different ways.

In the context of this book, it may be reasonable to observe that the battlefield was not invariably an 'epic of mud' but there is no doubt that as Gough helpfully deals with the artist's handling of space, shape, colour, light, texture, detail, the presence and use of the human figure, methods of actually applying paint, one among many powerful images remains and is little invalidated by the artist's licence in weapon identification – the depiction of the landscape as a strange marine world: "the liquified battlefield as a swelling turbulent mass liberally dotted with wreckage and detritus, where exploding mines [sic] crash like gigantic breakers on the sandbagged breaker of a trench".

Old Comrades Association commemoration of Western Front experience has always served, just as with National 1914-18 war remembrance, to focus on the Somme and Third Ypres experience. Playing its part in keeping alive an awareness of Passchendaele in the national psyche, before radio and television became the dominant agent for such mental associations, were the poems and novels of those who had been there in 1917. These men, inspired by a range of emotional reaction to their experience and choosing some form of literary expression suited either to their talent or need, provide us with the literary legacy of Passchendaele. In Chapter Twenty-Six, *Passchendaele – A Selection of British and German War Veteran Literature*, Hugh Cecil will almost certainly surprise the reader as he explains that, this arguably most ghastly battle of all, nowhere near matches in volume or excellence of literary production, its predecessor in prolonged awfulness, the Somme. Cecil shows there are some simple reasons for this. Many of the writers who had, by August 1917, established a literary reputation were now dead and of those who survived or who were emerging with their talents, some did not serve in the Salient during the Third Battle of Ypres. Edmund Blunden, Herbert Read and the sad figure of Ivor Gurney were to serve there and write from their experience in poetic form.

For those who wrote as novelists, the number is of course larger and the quality more varied than the high standards achieved by the three poets. Cecil draws our attention to the strikingly divergent message behind the work of Robert Briffault, Ernest Raymond and Patrick Miller. Henry Williamson also drew lessons from the war but the irony here was that these lessons played their part in formulating his own political convictions, convictions which discredited him as a man and unfairly shadowed his literary reputation.

Some British and German writers of memoirs of their war experience, held views, different from but no less fixed, than those of Williamson. Guy Chapman is a prime example, Cecil informing us that Chapman, who wrote so affectionately of the men in his battalion, believed that they were "needlessly wasted by a prodigal military system serving a cynical civilian leadership".

Concerning Third Ypres, the literary honours seem to belong to Edmund Blunden's *Undertones of War*, though the works of Ernst Jünger and Rudolf Binding in their different ways offer rival German claims. Cecil concludes his chapter with attention to the expression in literature of what was, in khaki, almost a man's moral life jacket – sardonic humour. Quite evidently a novel or memoir which sought to convey the essence of soldiering in the Salient had in truth, to demonstrate that an earthy or morbid sense of humour helped to keep one's days within the realms of redemption.

The Flemish tapestry woven by Mark Derez in Chapter Twenty-Seven, *A Belgian Salient for Reconstruction: People and Patrie, Landscape and Memory*, has a design which recognises the centuries-old link between the United Kingdom and Flanders and demonstrates that the setting which, pre-1914, had drawn the architectural pilgrim from across the Channel, would, from 1919, draw from the same source, pilgrims inspired by a far more poignant goal and to a setting transformed by the ravage of war.

Derez, however, does not allow this theme excessively to dominate his chapter. Because of what had been done to Flanders fields, villages and towns, the problems of post-war reconstruction drew together Flemish, Belgian and international agencies to work together, sometimes in uneasy harness. The photographs in this book convey something of the scale of the task, but the debates reconstruction engendered and the tensions which arose, provide for Derez a focus for many perceptive observations. For example, and with nice irony, he draws attention to the contrasting consequences of the benevolence of two Americans directed towards the plight of the country and its people. An American engineer named Knox devoted his entire fortune and three years of life in endeavouring to develop a machine to deal with land drainage and levelling. In every sense he was to be unrewarded. On the other hand, Henry Ford gave ten tractors for work on the farms being re-established. This resulted in the purchase by Belgium of another hundred and twenty of his machines. Seed corn indeed.

From Derez we learn about the continuing harvest of steel from fields within the former salient, about the restoration of farming activity and, delightfully detailed, about the two types of wooden shacks provided uniformly to house the returning families each of course with varying numbers of persons and each 'householder' having different needs.

The debate over architectural reconstruction and of memorializing the dead was as subject to dispute as every other move towards a new, post-conflict, normality. Delegates at wartime conferences, held beyond Belgium's unoccupied boundaries, heard proposals where modernists and conservatives offered their contrasting ways forward. The attraction in 1919 of an opportunity for reconstruction on an hitherto unimaginable scale, let flood predictably conflicting ideas on townscape development. Aesthetes advocated preservation of ruins appropriately to symbolize the affliction from which the towns had suffered. There were however others who wanted meticulously detailed rebuilding of what had been destroyed.

Even when such matters had been resolved, there was room for contention over the newly-erected local memorials to those who had died. If the British were to have won respect for the way they commemorated every single fallen soldier, their cemeteries used up a phenomenally large amount of land, land which quite reasonably was viewed as lost by the Flemish farmer.

In his conclusion, Derez informs us on Flemish "thinking" about the Great War and clearly he shows that it has been influenced by the second great conflict which, in the area of the former salient, left more scars upon the soul than upon the landscape. Ypres today, he concludes, is associated with a new popular pacifism, its landscape more at risk from unrestrained development than from any other threat.

It is the contention of the Editor and Matthew Richardson in Chapter Twenty-Eight, *Passchendaele and Material Culture: the Relics of Battle*, that those artefacts which have survived their presence in the Salient in 1917, have, in common with all such vestiges of conflict, a significance which changes as time increasingly distances them from the event. For the soldier who originally souvenired some relic, it is likely that in his older years it came to symbolize his irrecoverable youth, the days when great things were done, dangers were faced and he was in the midst of tests which proved his manhood. For later generations, the associations and symbolism change; the object is no longer a talisman of youth but a fragile link to a past now variously interpreted according to new values, values which, in time, are themselves subject to change.

However, battle artefacts have a less chameleon appeal too: through them, it is possible to picture and understand the function of an object so preserved, presenting a more scientific, or at least, practical, awareness of events in the past. Each item, with other such artefacts, can play a small part in reaching an understanding of the nature and course of a particular battle, and, at the same time, it allows us what may well be an uncomfortable empathy with the soldier at war. Liddle and Richardson choose items from Passchendaele which vividly illustrate their argument.

From Armistice Day onwards in 1918, the geographical proximity of Ypres to Channel ports took on a different significance from that which it had held in 1917. For the first individual and group pilgrimages to the Salient in 1919 and the coach loads visiting the Flanders battleground today, the relative cheapness and easiness of the journey from the United Kingdom, have added attraction to each visitor's interest in going, even the need to go. What there is to see, how people react to their experience, are but two of the questions addressed by Paul Reed in Chapter Twenty-Nine, *Vestiges of War: Passchendaele Revisited*.

For all such visits, the city is the starting and concluding point, Passchendaele, the St James of Compostella, the furthermost and sacred goal of the journey. The whole landscape and, ironically, Passendale [as we must call it] above all, is so mercifully transformed from its 1917 appearance that the solidly unchanged features, of course the pill boxes, and the more fragile vestiges, the evocatively described Bremen Redoubt, are all the more precious in aiding any attempt to feel the frightful vibrations of the past in their historic setting.

Unchanged too are the cemeteries with all around them changing. The genesis of these places of tranquillity, memorializing the violence of the past, is explained and generically classified by Reed. The museums, the great deeds, especially poignant details, and above all the endless march of names, shadowy flickering figures in khaki crossing our minds as on an early cine-screen, they are all catalogued here.

We learn of the tours and the guide books, ancient and modern, charting a ground for long, and perhaps again, considered hallowed, sanctified by endeavour and its cost. One gets the feeling that today's visitor, peering through curtains drawn over his past, would be infinitely well-resourced if he were to consider the points made by Reed, not least his reminding us of that poignant reflection by Field Marshal Plumer, on those with no known graves, when he dedicated the Menin Gate: "They are not missing – they are here".

Where does the balance of judgement fall in this study of the Third Battle of Ypres prepared eighty years after it was fought, yet still within living memory of a handful of men? Sensible scholarship accepts that the nature of the war exerted severe constraint over High Command strategic initiative and that the tactical problems for infantry assault were chilling. Readers of this book will have no doubt that the Belgian coast and Roulers were eminently justifiable objectives but thereafter, there are developments which encourage argument. Within this book, some differing opinions are expressed but, in the final chapter, *Passchendaele: Verdicts Past and Present*, Brian Bond magisterially surveys what has been written, deals with some of the controversial issues which have been examined and re-examined in the past and puts forward what he judges can reasonably be accepted today. He recognizes, as of course we all do, that we have but reached a stage in a debate which will go on.

Here, this introduction is to be concluded, not by an historian but by the words of a man who had just experienced the first days of the battle and was still in a state of emotional turmoil. His reaction provides a subtext of personal experience for the considerations of historians privileged in studying the battle and in not having been there at the time.

B.E.F. August 8 / 1917
My dear father,
I fear very much that you will have been worrying about me during the past 10 days. Well perhaps there was ample reason for doing so though I have delayed telling you directly that such was the case until we are as we are now – miles from the line in peace and quietness.

In a speech to us this morning the Divisional General told us practically that we could write home and tell all our folks all about it – without of course mentioning names. So I hasten to avail myself of this rather unusual privilege – though time seems scarcer than ever.

Our three weeks away back from the line was not rest – it was hard detailed training for the coming battle. I entered into it very thoroughly and enjoyed it much. I quite felt fit for my allotted task when the time for the fight arrived.

I am proud to say that this Brigade attained every objective exactly to the tick of each allotted time, that it gained more ground and took more prisoners than any other Brigade in the whole push. Moreover it never yielded a yard of ground despite withdrawals on right and left. I think we are justly proud of ourselves and for a host of reasons I would not have missed it for anything. I am glad to have had a share in it – it was a great experience.

That puts the brighter side – the details are of heartbreaking fatigue, of stern physical hardships – of mud toil pain and death. But one is proud to think of the stoutheartedness and the grit and endurance shown.

I shall never forget zero hour on July 31st. The Barrage was positively stupendous and I stood on the parapet of our assembly trench just awestruck. Five minutes later it was my turn to go over and we got our men sorted out into some sort of artillery formation. Then we advanced after the infantry to the third Bosche line where we quickly got into action and put up a long range barrage of fire. Two hours later we went forward again and in the afternoon put up two more barrages – our fire being directed well into the bosche lines of course. Then my section became a reserve section.

By the end of the first day all objectives were taken and the hanging on process began. Unfortunately the rain began also and the next three days were a perfect nightmare. I went forward again on the 1st day to take charge of the guns in the line of resistance. Can you imagine anything more hopeless than having to hang on indefinitely to a water-logged trench, without dugouts, without overcoats and without hot food of any description and with the Bosche shelling and the rain pouring at its worst? I think it was the worst experience I have had – in 48 hours everybody was about deadbeat, shivering all the time with the trenches ankle to waist deep in water. On my second personal reporting to the CO at HQ he kept me there for 12 hours – had it not been for that I am sure I should have been ill. He put a man on to massaging my feet – gave me a dry shirt and socks and made me sleep in his little Hun dugout and woke me up every 2 hours – to dose me up with Rum! If I never found any value in rum before I certainly did last week. I returned to my job much fitter and finding my chaps still in the same muddy watery conditions felt almost sorry I'd had such special treatment. The remaining three days were a vast improvement for we got cover and shelter in a huge Bosche stronghold and by the time we came out and our clothes were approximately dry – and our spirits equally approximately high. It was a good strafe – a real taste of hard war and though I certainly did nothing to boast about at all, I think I did my job quite respectably. We lost Playfair (my sub) Donovan (the violinist) and Sutherland (o/c 4 section) wounded, and Head (o/c 2 section) killed. I took 36 men in and had 20 killed and wounded including my sergeant and corporal. So you can see we had a pretty thin time and now that we are away from it we are feeling pretty done up – the natural reaction I guess. Our o/c was jolly good and did everything possible for us. It is horrid losing so many good fellows. I had six killed and I suppose it will be my painful duty to write to their relatives in a day or two.

By the way I had my kit blown up – I had made a little pile of it and for ease in getting about was working without it. The chief losses are my Thermos – the glass shattered into little pieces – and my razor and all toilet things. I can buy all these out here though. By the way my waterproof watch wasn't waterproof although it was too much to expect it to keep going when you couldn't see it on my wrist for a great patch of mud!

My legacy from last week is one very sore foot and a very tired feeling all over. But both will be put right after 48 hours here. This is a jolly little place – I am in a tent in a meadow with pleasant wooded hills in sight.

I must stop now – we are crammed out with the work of re-organisation.

Much love as always and every good wish for your improvement in health.

Your affectionate son

Douglas

You'll have to show this letter to the others – I've no time to write any more.

Douglas A. Crockatt, Lt. Machine Gun Corps
[O.C. No. 3 Section, 117 M.G. Coy, 39 Division,
XVIII Corps, Fifth Army]

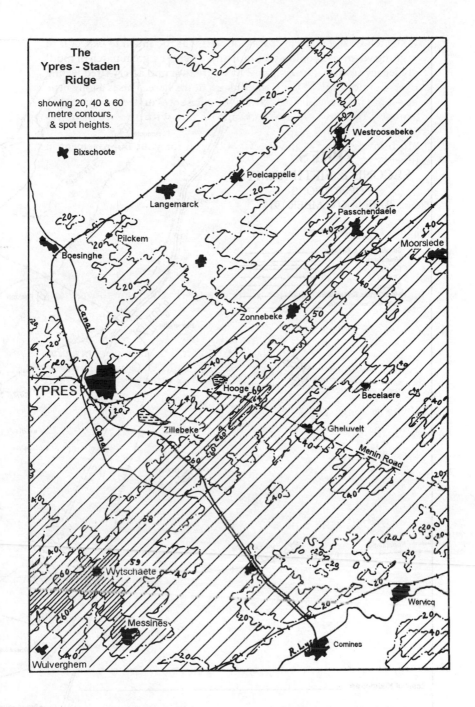

The Ypres - Staden Ridge

showing 20, 40 & 60 metre contours, & spot heights.

Bixschoote

Westroosebeke

Poelcappelle

Langemarck

Passchendaele

Pilckem

Moorslede

Boesinghe

Zonnebeke

YPRES

Hooge

Becelaere

Zillebeke

Gheluvelt

Menin Road

Wytschaete

Messines

Wervicq

Wulverghem

R. Lys

Comines

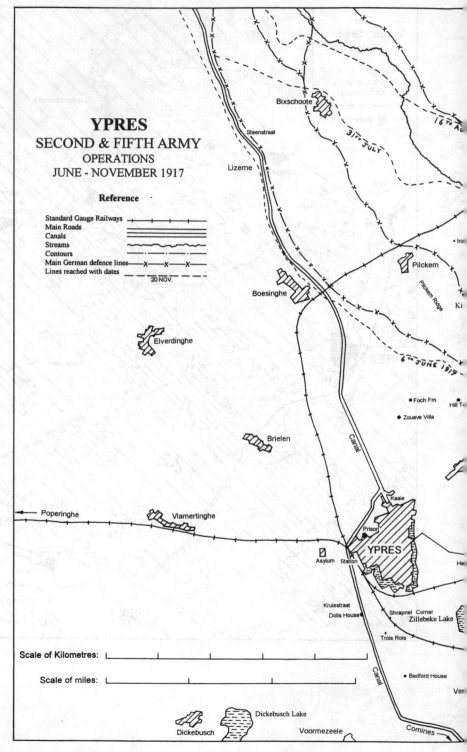

YPRES

SECOND & FIFTH ARMY
OPERATIONS
JUNE - NOVEMBER 1917

Reference

Standard Gauge Railways	
Main Roads	
Canals	
Streams	
Contours	
Main German defence lines	—x—x—x—
Lines reached with dates	

20 NOV.

Bixschoote

Steenstraat

31st JULY

16 TH A

Lizeme

Pilckem

Pilckem Ridge

Ki

Boesinghe

Elverdinghe

6 TH JUNE 1917

Iro

Foch Fm

Hill T

Zouave Villa

Brielen

Canal

Kaaie

Poperinghe

Vlamertinghe

Prison

YPRES

Asylum   Station

He

Kruisstraat

Dolis House

Shrapnel Corner

Zillebeke Lake

Trois Rois

Scale of Kilometres:

Scale of miles:

Canal

Bedford House

Ver

Dickebusch Lake

Dickebusch

Voormezeele

Comines

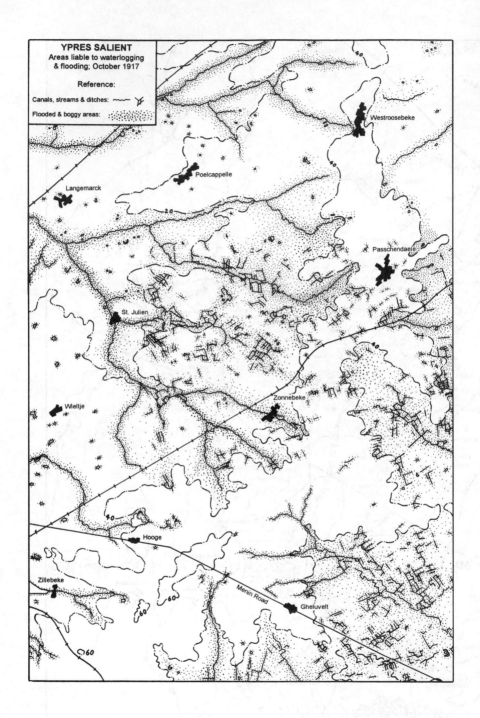

YPRES SALIENT
Areas liable to waterlogging
& flooding; October 1917

Reference:

Canals, streams & ditches:

Flooded & boggy areas:

Westroosebeke

Poelcappelle

Langemarck

Passchendaele

St. Julien

Wieltje

Zonnebeke

Hooge

Zillebeke

Menin Road

Gheluvelt

Part I

The Setting and Those Who set the Scene

Chapter 1

The World War Context

John Bourne

'... I keep thinking how big it is, the *war*, and how impossible it is to write about, and how useless it is to get angry, that's such a trivial reaction, it doesn't, it doesn't do any sort of justice to the to the to the tragedy, you know you spend your entire life out there obsessed with this tiny little sector of the Front, I mean *thirty yards* of sandbags, that's the war, you've no conception of anything else, and now I think I can see all of it, vast armies, flares going up, *millions* of people, *millions, millions*.'

Pat Barker, The Eye in the Door (Harmondsworth: Penguin, 1994), p. 220.

There are some who dispute the status of the Great War as a 'true' World War.[1] This is perverse. The conflict *was* global. Major wars were fought not only in western, eastern and southern Europe, but also in the middle east and the Caucasus. A lesser – guerrilla – war tied down more than 100,000 British Empire troops in East Africa. Surface fleets and submarines contested naval supremacy on and under the oceans of the world. But this was far from all. The insatiable demands of war extended far beyond the battlefields, not least because two of the major belligerents, Great Britain and France, were imperial powers with access to global resources of manpower, raw materials and food. The 'British' Army eventually recruited 1.6M Indians, 630,000 Canadians, 412,000 Australians, 136,000 South Africans, 130,000 New Zealanders and approximately 50,000 Africans as well as several hundred thousand Chinese 'coolies'. The 'French' Army recruited 600,000 North and West Africans as combat troops and a further 200,000 as labourers. The ability of the Entente to command the manpower and natural resources of Africa, Asia, Australasia and north and south America made a major contribution to victory. The political and economic impact of this global mobilization was also immense.[2]

It is sometimes difficult to appreciate the global nature of the war in British writing and British remembrance. These have been, and generally remain, thoroughly Anglo-centric and Western Front in their focus. British perceptions of the war also often appear curiously disproportionate, not least in relation to 1917. For the Russians, 1917 was the year of Revolution, the end of one tyranny and the beginning of another. For the French, it was *'l'année troublé'*, the year of national exhaustion and mutiny. For the Americans, it was the year of national exhilaration. The United States took centre spot on the world stage, inaugurating the 'American century'. For the British, 1917 seems symbolically to have become the year Siegfried Sassoon threw the ribbon of his Military Cross into the river Mersey. This gesture has gradually assumed an inconographic status, not least perhaps because Sassoon's 'Soldier's Declaration' against the continuance of the war was published in *The Times* on 31 July, the same day that Sir Douglas Haig launched his Flanders offensive. This is invariably known by the name of the battle which concluded it, 'Passchendaele'. The very name, suggestive of Christ's suffering, haunts the British national memory. It was the 'campaign of the mud', emblematic, like Sassoon's gesture, of the brutality and futility of Britain's most unpopular and uncomfortable war. Front line soldiers were not alone in being unable to see beyond the sandbagged confines of the trench system. British perceptions of 1917 have often been bogged down there, too. But only by looking beyond them, at the world war context, can Britain's war in 1917 be understood.

Although 1917 has strong claims to be regarded as one of the most important years of the twentieth century, it was not the key year of the First World War. That accolade must go to 1916. Verdun, the Somme and the Brusilov Offensive tore away what remained of the last vestiges of the 'short-war' illusion. The implications of the 'long-war' reality inexorably imposed themselves. They proved largely unpalatable to most governments. Victory was no longer something in the gift of armies alone. It would require the full mobilization of national resources at previously unimaginable levels. This would not be easy or cheap to achieve. There would be a high price to pay: the abandonment of cherished beliefs and ways of doing things; a potentially dangerous political compromise with popular aspirations. There was a general awareness among the elites of the great powers that the continuance of the war beyond 1916 might break the political and social structure of pre-war Europe. They paused to consider the alternative, a compromise peace, only to recoil from its apparent admission of failure and defeat. Instead, a 'win the war' spirit came to the fore among the reconstituted governments of Germany, France and Britain, and even to some extent Russia. In 1917 the gamblers would, once more, return to the gaming tables. There would be another throw of the dice. Victory, not peace, would terminate the suffering. And the victors would decide the future at home as well as abroad.

1916 had proved an exceptionally difficult year for Germany. Germany had more invested in the success of a short war than any other belligerent. The German Army's failure to deliver a quick victory had correspondingly severe implications. Many of these concerned the British. Belief that a quick victory was possible had led pre-war German planners to discount British belligerency. The true costs of this miscalculation became apparent in 1916. The appearance of a British Army of fifty divisions on the Western Front was as surprising to the Germans as it was remarkable to the British themselves. British perceptions of the battle of the Somme have been transfixed by the tragic events of a single day, 1 July. German perceptions were rather different. From the middle of 1916 they were dominated by an uncomfortable realization of the accumulating weight of Allied manpower and material superiority, not least in artillery. This was immediately acknowledged by Hindenburg and Ludendorff when they succeeded Falkenhayn in command of the German armies at the end of August. The offensive at Verdun was scaled down. More than 310,000 males born in 1898 were rushed into the army three months before they were due for conscription. A review of operational procedures was undertaken and, by December, a new defensive doctrine, 'Principles of Command for the Defensive Battle in Position Warfare', had been promulgated and disseminated. Re-equipment and re-training of the Army began in earnest. In the spring of 1917 the German Army in France retreated to a series of linked defensive positions, characterized by an intricate system of mutually supporting strongpoints, dense belts of barbed wire and great depth. The German line was shortened by 25 miles, freeing a reserve of 13 divisions. The German Supreme Command was convinced that the Allies would renew their offensives in the West in 1917. They had no wish to repeat the experience of the Somme. This time they would be ready.

These changes did not imply German acceptance of the inevitable. The German instinct to seek the knock-out blow remained. Verdun seemed, in retrospect, an aberration. 'Attrition' offered only the prospect of eventual submission to Allied manpower and material superiority. The state of German domestic morale was already giving considerable cause for concern. The winter of 1916–17, the 'turnip winter', was exceptionally severe. Germany's ramshackle bureaucracy seemed incapable either of increasing supplies of food or of distributing fairly such supplies as existed. The idea of equality of sacrifice was exposed as a cruel sham. The state of Germany's principal ally, Austria-Hungary, was even more worrying. Austria was close to exhaustion and desperate for peace. The 31-year-old Emperor, Karl, who had succeeded the aged Franz Joseph in November 1916, believed a compromise peace was essential to the survival of his empire. His clumsy feelers to the Allies sounded alarm bells in Berlin. Germany's need to end the war quickly remained as great as ever. This was beyond the power of the army in 1917. German hopes were transferred to the navy. The navy was only too willing to encourage them.

During the winter of 1916 the German Supreme Command convinced itself and the Kaiser that resort to 'unrestricted' submarine warfare, the sinking of merchant ships without warning, could defeat the British by 1 August 1917 and end the war on German terms. The decision was riddled with wishful thinking and proved catastrophic in its consequences.

The chances of the German navy being able to deliver a victory were always improbable. Its capacity to wage submarine warfare was woefully inadequate. When unrestricted submarine warfare was declared on 1 February 1917, the navy had fewer than half the number of U-boats needed to mount an effective blockade of Great Britain and only a third of these was of true ocean-going vessels. At any one time two-thirds of the U-boat fleet were unavailable for action, either en route to the war zones or returning from them. This numerical inadequacy was never repaired. The submarine building programme barely kept up with losses. This was bad enough, but it was not all. The Germans not only overestimated their own strength but also underestimated that of their enemy. Britain was the world's greatest naval power. It was unlikely that she would simply give up in the face of the U-boats. Increased domestic supplies of food were sought. Three million acres of grassland were brought under the plough. Local food rationing was introduced, eventually followed by a national system. Convoying of merchant ships began. More effective use of available shipping was made. An emergency shipbuilding programme was instituted. New anti-submarine technologies and tactics were developed. The U-boat crews paid a high price for their government's over-confidence. Worst of all, the strategy of unrestricted submarine warfare deliberately risked the probability of American intervention. In 1917 Germany repeated the mistake made in 1914 with regard to Britain, again convincing herself that the war would be won before the United States' even more contemptible little army could have any effect. This ignored the instantaneous impact which American belligerency would have on the naval war. This not only immediately increased the resources available for use against the U-boats but also liberated British strategy from the restraints imposed by American neutrality. The Royal Navy was free to pursue the blockade of Germany with even greater ruthlessness. The willingness to risk the addition of American manpower and economic resources to the Allied cause in a continuing war was even more reckless and ultimately condemned Germany to defeat.

For France, too, 1916 had been a year of trial. The French war-effort during the Great War was an epic of national resistance. It has rarely received just treatment in British historiography. France had borne the brunt of the war in the West from the beginning. The French Army's attacks dwarfed in scale and casualties those of the British. That the French were able to endure, let alone compete against, the military and industrial might of Germany required an extraordinary degree of military and economic mobilization, made even more remarkable by the loss to the Germans in 1914 of so many economic and industrial resources. And, on top of all this came the purgatory of Verdun. By the end of 1916, France was approaching exhaustion. French soldiers of high idealism and selfless commitment had been repeatedly flung against the German lines by commanders of iron resolution. But their efforts were barren of strategic achievement. The German Army still occupied a tenth of the soil of France.

'Les Boches sont à Noyon,' Clemenceau's *Le Chien Enchainé* daily reminded its readers. There was an almost universal desire for the war to end. But in France, as in Germany, victory not peace emerged as the instrument of deliverance.

France's national dilemma was reflected in that of her prime minister, Aristide Briand. Briand was in a difficult position. His coalition government, which had been in office since October 1915, was never able to impose itself on French policy and strategy. His was a complicated balancing act between a strong parliamentary Radical block, upon which his majority depended and which sought subordination of the military, and the power of the French High Command. By the end of 1916 popular unrest and pacifist agitation added to his difficulties. Something had to be done. There seemed no prospect of peace on terms which would be politically or morally acceptable. Germany remained too strong and too intransigent for that. Briand, like France, needed a victory. He moved swiftly to achieve one. The parliamentary Radicals were placated by Joffre's removal from the High Command, effected through a skilful piece of political manoeuvring. He was replaced by Robert Nivelle. Briand, and France, looked to Nivelle to end the nation's suffering.

France in the winter of 1916–17 displayed many of the characteristics of a patient with a terminal illness. Conventional medical opinion had been tried and found wanting. It could offer only more of the same ineffective treatment. But then along came Nivelle, the plausible, self-confident quack with a miracle cure. He told the patient what he most wanted to hear. 'Follow my instructions and all will be well. Not only can I cure you, but the cure will not hurt.' France's destiny would rest on Nivelle's ability to repeat on the grand scale what he had achieved on the small scale at Verdun. A massive artillery barrage would rupture the German line. French troops would pour through the gap, roll up the Germans and end the war. All in forty-eight hours. In the unlikely event of failure, the offensive would be stopped. There would be 'no more Verduns'. Even recounting these events in tranquillity eighty years later takes one's breath away. The plan's reckless arrogance was a measure of French despair. Not everyone was convinced. Mounting criticism in the French Army and government led to the resignation of the war minister, General Lyautey, and the fall of the Briand coalition. Briand's successors failed to stop the Nivelle Offensive, which approached its apotheosis amid mounting political polarization and volatility.

The chances of the Nivelle Offensive succeeding were never great. The German anticipation of an attack by the 'retreat to the Hindenburg Line' effectively eliminated what chances there were. Despite this, the attack went ahead along the Aisne on 16 April. It achieved negligible gains at great cost. The true costs, however, could not be counted simply in casualties. The failure of the Nivelle Offensive struck a damaging blow to French national morale. Political demoralization and polarization followed. So did mutiny. About half the French Army was affected. Serious disturbances

7

continued from the end of April to the middle of June. The worst fears of France's allies had come perilously close to fulfilment. The French Army was, temporarily at least, out of the war as an offensive force.

This was a dispiriting state of affairs for the recently-formed British government to contemplate. They found no comfort in the condition of Britain's other major ally, Russia, which by the end of 1916 was in an even worse state than France.

Treatment of Russia's contribution to the war in British writing has fared even worse than that of France. Perceptions have been completely overshadowed by the October Revolution of 1917 and by Bolshevik 'revolutionary defeatism' which acquiesced in a Carthaginian peace and took Russia out of the war. Subsequent Soviet-dominated Russian historiography has done nothing to correct these perceptions. The historical significance of the Bolshevik Revolution, however, should not be allowed to obscure the major contribution which the Russian Army made to the Allied war effort. The Russians displayed an unhesitating willingness to co-operate with the Anglo-French alliance. It is doubtful whether, without the Russian contribution, Germany could have been defeated by Britain and France alone. The prospect of a Russian withdrawal from the war was therefore a chilling one.

This prospect became all too real in March 1917. On 8 March a strike in Petrograd developed into an uprising. Two days later the troops sent to suppress it killed their officers and joined the revolution. The Tsar abdicated on 15 March. A liberal Provisional Government was formed. Its grip on power was always weak. Events were out of control. Food shortages, inflation, administrative disintegration and socialist propaganda carried chaos beyond the towns into the army and the countryside. Peasants seized the land. Peasant soldiers refused to fire on them, instead deserting in large numbers to ensure that they did not miss their share. But the government's fatal weakness was to preach peace and continue the war. The Kerensky Offensive in July 1917 led to mass Bolshevik-inspired protests. Its failure finally shattered the Army's resolve. Soldiers 'voted with their feet'. The 'failure' of the Provisional Government to end the war is usually regarded as important because of the opportunity which it offered to the Bolsheviks to seize power. But it was important for a different reason. It kept Russia in the war for another year. A wounded, weakened Russia perhaps, but one which the German Army could not ignore and one which it was compelled to attack again at Riga in September. This was the final act of sacrifice made by the Russian Army to keep faith with its western Allies. Its consequences were, arguably, profound.

To set against these distressing developments there was only the entry of the United States into the war. The United States' declaration of war on Germany, on 6 April 1917, was historic, for America and for the world. The United States saw itself as an arbitrator. President Wilson had tried to broker a negotiated peace before. His failure led to the realization that the USA could not dictate a peace if it did not enter the war. The incompetence of German policy allowed Wilson to convince American political and public opinion that it was right to do so. He was however careful to maintain his distance. The United States became an Associated Power, not an Ally. If the New World was coming in to redress the balance of the Old it would do so on its own terms and for its own (self-proclaimed noble) ends.

Militarily, however, American belligerency did little to compensate for the weakening of the Russian and French armies. The United States was a feeble military power. Its active service army had fewer than 130,000 men, largely destitute of artillery; its air force was tiny and obsolete; its 'sea-lift' capacity 'less than that of Norway'.[3] Nivelle's successor, Pétain, declared his policy to be that of 'waiting for the Americans and the tanks'. His wait was likely to be a long one. There was no prospect of a significant American military contribution on the Western Front for at least a year. The consequences of this were not lost on the British government.

The generation of British statesmen who conducted the Great War had one thing in common. They were all Imperialists. They could not contemplate an acceptable future for their country in which it ceased to be a great Imperial power. British involvement in the war was occasioned primarily by the desire to secure and maintain this status. Britain's political leaders needed no encouragement to pay attention to the 'world war context'. For a country like Great Britain, with global responsibilities, global ambitions and global dilemmas, it was always a 'world war'. British strategy took full account of this from the outset.

The dominant influence on British strategy for the first two years of the war was that of Lord Kitchener. Kitchener was a man of penetrating insight and careful calculation, not at all the 'Oriental mystic' of Lloyd George's caricature. He shared the view that Britain's principal war aim was to ensure the long-term security and survival of the Empire. On this, Britain's future prosperity and political stability would depend. The Empire's long-term security was threatened not only by Germany, but potentially also by France, Russia and Japan, Britain's allies, and by the neutral United States. In order to achieve the aim, it was essential that Britain not only win the war but also dictate the peace. Such an outcome was more likely if Britain finished the war as the strongest member of the victorious coalition. Kitchener took a pessimistic view of the military capabilities of Britain's principal allies, France and Russia, and had a deep respect for the power of Germany. He could not envisage an outcome to the war satisfactory to British interests which acquiesced in a French or Russian defeat. In order to avert these possibilities it would be necessary to raise a mass British Army and keep it in the field for 'three years'. The purpose of this army was not only to keep the French and Russians in the war but also eventually to deliver the knock-out blow against Germany. Kitchener expected this to be in 1917 when the combined effect of French and Russian blows had rendered the German Army ripe for defeat.[4]

The problems which this strategy faced were fundamental to British conduct of the war. They were posed by the power of the German Army

9

and the unwillingness of the French to conform to Kitchener's view of their role. The French wanted the 'Boches' out of their country. They were unwilling to wait for the British to remove the Germans at some distant time convenient to themselves. The French wanted to deliver the knock-out blow and as soon as possible. No other strategy was politically or morally acceptable to France. And there was nothing the British could do to prevent its prosecution. But the price the French paid for their attempt to deliver a victory of annihilation in 1915 rendered them, not the Germans, ripe for defeat by the spring of 1916. Kitchener's armies found themselves thrown into battle a year before they were ready, not to finish off the Germans but to prevent the Germans finishing off the French. During the Somme campaign it became horribly apparent that the British Army had neither the skill nor the means to knock the German Army out of the war. Their role would be much more unpleasant, that of partici-pating fully and bloodily in the preparation of the German Army for defeat. The reality of the Great War, still unacceptable to some, was that British statesmen were compelled to fight a war which allowed no freedom for alternative methods of waging war. This reality formed the principal part of David Lloyd George's grim inheritance when he replaced Asquith as prime minister in December 1916. It was one which he was reluctant to accept.

Lloyd George's rise to power resulted from considerable 'insider' dissat-isfaction with Asquith's conduct of the war. This owed as much to Asquith's manner as to his policies. 'Tell me, Mr Asquith,' Lady Maud Tree is famously supposed to have asked, 'do you take an interest in the war?' No one would ever ask the question of Lloyd George. He was the person-ification of energy and determination. His job was simple: to win the war. The fall of the Asquith Coalition cleared the political decks to enable him to do this. Among his first public utterances, he expressed his preference for a 'knock-out blow' and a 'war to the finish'. These declarations were in marked contrast to his carefully constructed post-war image as the man of prudence struggling heroically but ineffectually to restrain the grandiose ambitions of a politically powerful, but boneheaded, military *junta* buttressed by Royal and press influence. Lloyd George's dilemma, like Briand's, encapsulated that of the nation. He was compelled to fight the war he had to, not the war he wanted to. Unlike Briand, however, he later succeeded in shifting the blame to others.

Contemplation of the 'world war context' did not make Lloyd George's first Christmas in 10 Downing Street a comfortable one. And the New Year brought no relief. During the first four months of Lloyd George's premier-ship the carefully constructed foundations of Kitchener's strategy disintegrated.[5] German U-boats threatened the Royal Navy's command of the sea and raised the spectre of starvation. The US Federal Reserve Board's advice to Americans, on 28 November 1916, not to lend any more money to the belligerents devastated British credit and compromised Britain's capacity to act as banker to the Entente. The Russian Revolution, the failure of the Nivelle Offensive and the mutiny of the French Army brought into question the ability of the Entente to resist, much less to defeat, the military power of Germany. The political situation in both Russia and France was volatile and unpredictable. The possibility of Britain's allies seeking a separate peace was as real as it was alarming. British national morale also gave cause for concern. A wave of strikes in the engineering industry in May undermined the government's self confidence in the level of sacrifice the British people would be willing to accept. The spectre not only of defeat but also of revolution danced before the War Cabinet's eyes. Lloyd George, like Briand and Ludendorff, needed a victory, preferably soon, striking and cheap. Like them, he failed to achieve one.

Lloyd George was appalled by the Somme. He had no wish to see a repetition, but a repetition was what he got. The 'world war context' made this difficult to avoid. The Russians and French appeared incapable of further major offensive effort. The Americans were not ready. Italy, too, was suffering a crisis of morale. Food shortages were severe, political alienation, defeatism and pacifism rife. The Italian government was unenthusiastic at the prospect of 'hosting' a 'Lloyd George offensive' on its territory. The French were also adamantly opposed to the transfer of any British troops from the Western Front, where they were the most reliable bulwark against a German attack. There was always the Middle East, but Lloyd George's attempts to re-direct British military resources to Palestine or Mesopotamia brought him into renewed conflict with his Chief of the Imperial General Staff, General Sir William Robertson.

Robertson had, perhaps, the clearest and bleakest understanding of Britain's strategic position. The weakness of the French and Russian armies meant that the British Army must play a full part in defeating the Germans. This could only be done on the Western Front where the bulk of the German Army was deployed on the territory of Britain's closest ally whose defeat or withdrawal from the war could not be contemplated. Robertson was no blinkered 'Westerner'. He was fully aware of the importance of the Empire, but he was dubious about the advantages of ruthlessly prosecuting the war against Turkey. Defeat by the Turks would be disastrous. Britain should maintain a minimum level of military force in Egypt and Mesopotamia to ensure against that. But victory over the Turks might be disastrous, too because of the extended obligations and the challenges which would ensue. Robertson favoured detaching Turkey from the Central Powers by diplomacy. He did everything in his power – even beyond his authority – in 1917 to minimize the prospect of Britain inflicting a humiliating defeat on Turkey.[6] He contemplated the prospect of the Ottoman Empire's dismemberment with alarm.

Robertson's views were more prudent than those of his prime minister. Lloyd George's desire to bring about the defeat of the Ottoman Empire had embroiled him, by the end of 1917, in a policy which embraced acts of naked imperialism (together with the French), sponsorship of Arab nationalism by support for the Arab Revolt and encouragement of Zionist aspirations through the Balfour Declaration. It was truly a war of illusions. It is also doubtful whether a victory in Palestine would serve Lloyd George's purpose of boosting Allied morale. The evidence of the first clear-cut British victory of the war, General Maude's capture of Baghdad in March 1917, was not encouraging. Its impact on British national morale was negligible. That on Britain's allies was nil.

The War Cabinet faced hard choices in the spring of 1917. The hardest choice of all was, perhaps, no choice. If the government wanted to keep the French and Russians in the war, if it wanted to maintain military pressure on the German armies, if it wanted a morale-boosting victory to steady Allied popular morale, the British Army would have to attack. Lloyd George could persuade neither his professional military advisers nor his Cabinet colleagues nor parliament nor his Allies that an attack other than on the Western Front would be prudent or effective. The Commander-in-Chief of the British Expeditionary Force, Field-Marshal Sir Douglas Haig, favoured an attack in Flanders. Here, unlike on the Somme – a battle-ground of French choosing, the German Army would not be able to retreat without compromising its entire position on the Western Front. They would therefore have to stand and if they stood they would be broken. Sir William Robertson was less sanguine. He doubted whether the British Army could knock the Germans out of the war single-handedly in 1917, but he was sure that a Flanders offensive would contribute significantly to the wearing down of the German Army and undermine Germany's willingness and ability to continue the war. How, otherwise, was Germany to be defeated? The Royal Navy was also enthusiastic. An offensive in Flanders would protect the Channel ports, threaten Germany's ability to wage submarine warfare from bases at Ostend and Zeebrugge and, most importantly of all, remove the nightmare of Germany retaining post-war control of the Channel coast in any negotiated settlement. The Flanders campaign was not the personal whim of Sir Douglas Haig. The 'world war' context demanded an offensive. Allied political opinion demanded an offensive on the Western Front. British political and military opinion supported it. The War Cabinet approved it. Their approval was contingent on the offensive's continuing 'success', but in the event they proved neither able nor willing to call it off. The option of not playing was unavailable to the British government. And Flanders was the only game in town. It was, perhaps, not the ideal way to make war, but it was the way wars are generally made. Lloyd George's subsequent attempts to claim otherwise were not only 'disingenuous', but mendacious and misleading.

Notes

1 See, for example, John Keegan, ed., *Who's Who in World War II* (London: Routledge, 1995), Introduction.
2 See Bernard Waites, 'Peoples of the Underdeveloped World', in Hugh Cecil and Peter H. Liddle, eds., *Facing Armageddon. The First World War Experienced* (London; Leo Cooper, 1996), pp. 596–614.

3   Holger H. Herwig, *The First World War. Germany and Austria-Hungary 1914–1918* (London: Arnold, 1996), p. 320.
4   For an account of the evolution of Kitchener's strategy, see David French, *British Strategy and War Aims, 1914–1916* (London: Allen & Unwin, 1986).
5   For an account of the disintegration of Kitchener's strategy, see David French, *The Strategy of the Lloyd George Coalition, 1916–1918* (Oxford: Clarendon Press, 1995), pp. 40–66.
6   Robertson ordered General Allenby, GOC-in-C Egypt from June 1917, to inflate the number of troops he would need to launch a successful offensive in Palestine in the belief that no such reinforcements would be forthcoming and no such offensive would take place. He erred. Lloyd George ordered Allenby to attack anyway. He captured Jerusalem on 9 December 1917. Subsequent revelation of Robertson's subterfuge weakened his position and contributed to his dismissal in February 1918.

Chapter 2

Lloyd George, the War Cabinet and High Politics

John Turner

From the view point of Westminster and Whitehall, the Passchendaele campaign began to emerge as an idea late in 1916. At first it was little more than a conditional clause in an agreement between British and French commanders. In May 1917, it became the preferred strategic option for the Western Front, because the 'Nivelle' offensive, on which so many hopes had rested, failed ignominiously and an offensive in Flanders to take the Channel ports was Haig's favoured plan. Lloyd George and the War Cabinet had little enthusiasm either for the idea or for the military commanders who were putting it into action, but had little option but to allow it to continue while they tried to find a way to control Haig and outflank Robertson. Until November, political anxieties about the campaign were focused not on the merits of the plan or the progress of the battle, but on the politics of civil-military relations and the strategic control of British forces in France. The weary and inconclusive end of the fighting season brought a new political reality, as the pressure for a negotiated peace grew in Westminster, in the labour movement, and in the trenches. The government was forced to launch a political offensive against 'defeatism' which culminated in the destruction of the historic Liberal Party, the consequent reconstruction of the party-political system and the consolidation of the Conservative forces which dominated British politics for the next two decades. 'Passchendaele' thus had causes and consequences which were rooted in the crisis of the British state which accompanied the First World War.

THE NEW COALITION AND GENERAL NIVELLE

The Lloyd George Coalition came into being in December 1916. Leading Conservatives in the coalition ministry which had governed under HH Asquith since May 1915 decided that they could no longer bear to serve under Asquith or alongside his principal Liberal lieutenants, Walter Runciman and Reginald McKenna. Somewhat paradoxically and very late in a complicated Palace revolution, the same Conservatives decided that they would be prepared to serve under David Lloyd George, even though he had for nearly two decades been the Liberal whom Conservatives most liked to hate. His main qualification was the strong position he had taken in favour of 'a more vigorous prosecution of the war' and against the prevailing philosophy of the Asquith régime, which had been to exercise great caution in taking control either of the civilian economy or of the strategic direction of the war, which it had tended to leave to the generals. Lloyd George had been one of the few Liberals to support compulsory military service and to criticize the reluctance of McKenna, the Chancellor of the Exchequer, to jeopardize the financial stability of the country by throwing every resource into the war. He was publicly identified in the autumn of 1916 with a demand for a 'knockout blow', a new great effort which would defeat the German army in a short time.

Lloyd George's new government was dominated by Conservatives. Andrew Bonar Law, the leader of the party, became Chancellor and a member of the small War Cabinet which replaced Asquith's larger and more diffuse War Committee. Other Conservatives in the War Cabinet were Lord Curzon, a former Viceroy of India who had taken a leading part in Conservative politics in the Lords, and Lord Milner, a former High Commissioner in South Africa, who was closely associated with an extreme imperialist position and, to a greater extent even than Curzon, was a confirmed opponent of democracy (which he dismissed as 'flapdoodle'). With the rather ineffective counterweight of the Labour leader, Arthur Henderson, and the regular presence of Arthur Balfour, a former Conservative prime minister who had become Foreign Secretary in the new régime, these figures constituted the supreme executive body of the British war effort. In their hands, ostensibly, lay control of British strategy and the chance of an Entente victory in the great struggle.

The central paradox of War Cabinet government was that these men were profoundly divided amongst themselves about the principal strategic questions of the war. Lloyd George had been a supporter of all out war since the spring of 1915, and an ally of the generals in their call for military conscription, which had finally been achieved in two stages in January and June 1916. On the other hand, he had also been a consistent critic of the strategy of concentrating military effort on the Western Front, and had supported various proposals for peripheral attacks on Germany's allies with the intention of inducing them to make separate peace agreements; his favourites were the support of Italian forces against the Austrians in North East Italy, and the Salonika campaign which sought to cut the supply line between Germany and Turkey by an expedition mounted from the Northern Aegean port. Under the Asquith Coalition he had been Minister of Munitions, responsible for supplying the materials of war in huge quantities to the Western Front, and often trying to supply more than the commanders admitted to needing. He was, however, a stern critic of Lord Kitchener's conduct of the War Office.[1]

When Kitchener was drowned on his way to Russia on 5 June 1916, Asquith persuaded Lloyd George to take on the War Office. He began his new job on 6 July, five days after the beginning of the first Somme offensive which had by then won three square miles of ground at the cost of over 60,000 casualties. Relations between the new Secretary of State and the military hierarchy deteriorated rapidly. In September, he told Marshal Foch, the French commander at the Somme, that 'he gave Haig all the guns and ammunition and men he could use and nothing happened'.[2] The comment was leaked by Foch to the British High Command and by Haig's staff to the *Morning Post,* which launched a savage attack on Lloyd George for undermining the generals. The campaign of press attrition continued, with damaging leaks from both sides. Lloyd George chafed under the convention that Sir William Robertson, the Chief of the Imperial General Staff, gave military advice direct to the Cabinet without the intervention of the Secretary of State for War. Eventually, on 3 November 1916, the Secretary of State presented the War Committee with a comprehensive indictment of the conception and execution of Britain's strategic policy.

The strategic outcome of the developing debate was seen at an Inter-Allied conference at Chantilly on 15 November, where the generals from both sides agreed to repeat in 1917 the offensive strategy which had failed in 1916. This was orchestrated by Robertson and presented as a *fait accompli* to the political leaders of France and Britain, who met separately in Paris on the same day. Politically, Asquith's apparent spinelessness in dealing with military advice goaded Lloyd George into mounting his final devastating attack on the Coalition government, in which he was first supported by Bonar Law and Edward Carson, the Ulster Unionist leader, and finally joined by Curzon and other Conservative grandees including Balfour, Austen Chamberlain, Robert Cecil, and Walter Long. Because Carson was regarded, for many reasons, as a difficult colleague, Milner came into the War Cabinet at the last minute in his place.

Curzon, Chamberlain, Cecil and Long were among the Conservative leaders who most loathed and distrusted Lloyd George. Until 7 December, the day after Asquith resigned, they were widely believed to prefer Asquith to Lloyd George. Their eventual adherence to the new Coalition was to some extent secured by Lloyd George's solemn promise that he would not interfere with the strategic judgement of Robertson and Haig. The creation of a political coalition strong enough to take control of strategy had been achieved by undertaking to retain military control over strategic matters. Lloyd George almost certainly hoped to be able to finesse these troublesome colleagues for whose intellect and political cunning he had little respect. Arthur Balfour, who had been sceptical of land offensives for much longer than Lloyd George, was nevertheless more diffident about denying the wishes of his Conservative colleagues, as was Bonar Law; and Milner, who shared Lloyd George's intellectual contempt for the military hierarchy, had no power-base in the Conservative party in Parliament.

The new government had to decide within a few days how to proceed with the offensive already agreed. The French cabinet had also fallen and representatives of the new ministries met on 26 and 27 December to decide the next step. By this time, Robertson had nearly blocked any alternative strategies emerging from the new War Cabinet. The only current alternative proposal to a new attack on the Western Front was a diversionary manoeuvre in the Balkans supplied through Salonika. Colonel Maurice Hankey, the new War Cabinet secretary observed that 'the new War Cabinet is really up against it, as they don't believe in Robertson's "Western Front" policy, but they will never find a soldier to carry out their "Salonika" policy'.[3] Instead, the new government tried to persuade the French to support an offensive on the Italian front. Unsuccessful in this, the government eventually gave in to military advice in mid-January when shown a plan by General Robert Nivelle, a French artillerist who had previously won distinction at Verdun. The Nivelle plan called for a diversionary attack by the British Army, a main attack by the French and so to a breakthrough by both armies. Haig wanted, as a side effect, to relieve the Channel ports, and wrote into what was in effect to be the start of the 1917 campaign planning, a promise that, in the summer, British divisions would be transferred from southern positions supporting the French flank to carry out an offensive in Flanders.

Haig and Nivelle soon fell out. Haig noticed that the plan exposed the British army to the risk of 'heavy losses with the possibility of no showy successes',[4] and began to drag his feet, blaming the inadequacy of the French railway system for his inability to mount an attack. Nivelle's complaints led the War Cabinet to call a meeting with the French government at Calais on 26–27 February. Lloyd George had manufactured an opportunity and used it well. At the conference it was decided that 'as between Haig and Nivelle, Ll.G. should support the latter',[5] and as a result Haig was formally subordinated to Nivelle for the period of the offensive. Though the circumstances behind this conference have been variously interpreted, there is no doubt whatsoever of the serious political and military consequences which ensued. Haig fought back, winding up the Press and second rank Conservative ministers such as Austen Chamberlain and Walter Long, and appealing, as he had sometimes done before, directly to the royal household.

This highly personalised and politicised approach to the conduct of civil-military relations, which was characteristic of Haig, so unnerved Nivelle that he made an informal request to Lloyd George that Haig should be removed from his command.[6] This provoked a remarkable but very secret upheaval in War Cabinet thinking, which conclusively, and in many ways paradoxically, prepared the way for the Flanders offensive. Lloyd George asked Colonel Hankey to prepare a memorandum to show whether the time had come to sack Haig, and risk the political opprobrium that such a step might bring. Hankey, who was not the simple, upstanding, apolitical Royal Marine officer that he sometimes pretended to be, took the precaution of taking soundings in the War Cabinet and found that none but

Bonar Law was prepared to give political support for sacking Haig. Convinced that it was impossible to get rid of Haig, Hankey advised that if Haig were to be left in place the best strategic option was to allow him to withdraw his troops from the southern commitment which was implied by Nivelle's plans, and concentrate instead on the northern flank:

> ... we strike into relatively new country, where the enemy must either fight or surrender important objectives ... Moreover the expulsion of the enemy from the Belgian coast is not only a primary British interest, but the War Cabinet have repeatedly insisted that from the point of view of the allies as a whole, viz. that of combating submarine warfare, it is of almost vital importance.[7]

Lloyd George was convinced. Between the War Cabinet of 6 March, when he was highly critical of Haig, and that of 8 March when the situation was reviewed again, his attitude, carefully reported by Robertson, was transformed.[8] On 14 March, the War Cabinet formally permitted Haig to prepare for a Flanders attack if the Nivelle offensive failed.[9] Haig and Robertson had won the first political battle on the road to Passchendaele.

'ALL THE WAR CABINET BELIEVE WE CANNOT BEAT THE BOSH' [SIC][10]

Haig's contribution to the Nivelle campaign began on 9 April with a diversionary attack towards Arras. The French assault was delayed by bad weather, and began only on 16 April. Within two days it had manifestly failed, and the French government, a new ministry under Ribot which had replaced the previous Briand government, prepared to sack Nivelle. Neither Lloyd George nor Haig believed French assurances that the attack would continue, and Haig prepared to 'take up the "alternative plan" in earnest'.[11] This implied a renewed offensive, but an offensive on Haig's own terms.

The War Cabinet was now in a cleft stick. The strategic position was clearly bad, in fact worse than they knew. Although Nivelle had been favoured by Lloyd George precisely because his tactical methods promised to reduce casualties by intensive use of artillery, the battering taken by French troops on the Chemin des Dames front had been so severe that front-line morale had begun to collapse. Units began to mutiny in late April, and the deterioration continued and spread across the French front during May and June. Haig realized the effect on French troops' fighting condition as early as the end of April, but concealed the later details of mutinies from his political masters.[12] As a result, the majority of the War Cabinet, with Lloyd George expressing some reservations, decided to press the French for a renewal of the offensive at an inter-Allied conference in Paris on 4 May. The outcome was a decision to continue attacks with limited objectives. The leading candidate was Haig's Flanders plan, which was launched with an assault on Messines Ridge on 7 June. Significantly, Pétain, the new French Commander-in-Chief, was unable to commit troops in support. On the same day as the attack was launched, a new War Cabinet committee, the War Policy Committee, was set up to decide between an extension of the Messines Ridge offensive into a full-scale campaign and alternatives. These alternatives included proposals to wait out the summer and divert resources to the Italian front where there was supposedly a hope of inflicting grave damage on the Austrians.

Milner, who had worked hard to get the committee set up, was profoundly worried about the effect of high casualty rates on Britain's ability to continue the war. Though hardly squeamish about loss of life, he was concerned about the labour supply and anxious that the tactical promises of Nivelle's assault had not been fulfilled. By 17 June, he had come to the conclusion that 'we were not justified in throwing away so many men on the Western Front'.[13] This was a difficult conclusion to follow through. On the one hand, Hankey, who was close to the civilian leaders, was arguing that the best approach was to 'conserve our strength in the main theatre until next year, when with America's co-operation, and with Russia reorganized, we may hope for better results'. Yet he acknowledged that some action had to be taken and 'This can best be done by fighting a great battle with the object of recovering the Flanders coast, which would be the most effective way of reducing our shipping losses'.[14] On the other hand, Haig was convinced that 'victory on the Western Front means victory everywhere and a lasting peace. And I have no further doubt that the British Army in France is capable of doing it, given adequate drafts and guns'.[15] Some doubts in the minds of Robertson and of Derby, the Secretary of State for War who was generally regarded as the 'soldier's pet' rather than a serious decision-maker, were overborne by Haig's optimism, an optimism which ultimately was justified. In response to Haig it proved impossible for Milner or anyone else to make a politically strong case for any alternative strategic concept.

Haig presented his plan to the Committee on 19 June, to be met by Lloyd George with a warning, which he had made often enough before, that there was not enough manpower to press home the sort of attack that Haig wanted. Lloyd George's position by now was a poignant reminder of Reginald McKenna's position a year before, which Lloyd George had so strenuously resisted. A war of attrition on the Western Front, requiring a continuous supply of drafts to replace casualties, drained the male labour force and threatened the supply of munitions, home-grown food, and ships (and thus of food imports). McKenna had feared the economic and financial consequences. To some extent he had been vindicated by the country's near-bankruptcy in December 1916, when the United States Federal Reserve Board, on the President's instruction, had nearly got to the point of stopping British credit, a move which would have paralysed not only the war effort but the whole of the British economy. On top of all this, Lloyd George in 1917 feared industrial unrest and even civil disorder in imitation of the revolution which had just overthrown the Tsarist government in Russia. He also looked forward in alarm to a Peace Conference at

19

which Britain was militarily and economically exhausted while 'America was still overwhelmingly strong, and Russia had perhaps revived her strength'.[16]

These short and long term concerns for Britain's survival led Lloyd George to argue for a postponement of the Western offensive until 1918, and a diversion of resources to Italy. None of this had any effect on Robertson and Haig, who recognized that since the alternative plans were unworkable, the only possible solution was a Flanders attack. No matter how much Lloyd George observed that 'similar reasons to those given now had always been adduced as to why we should do better than last time', the soldiers held the day. The only way to prevent Haig from carrying out his Flanders offensive was to sack him – and to replace him with whom, it might be asked? The events of March had made it clear that Lloyd George and his colleagues were unable to carry out any such plan. The inconclusive discussions of late June determined the outcome of the War Policy Committee's deliberations, for although the final approval of Haig's proposal was delayed until 20 July, the intervening period was not occupied by debate or new strategic thinking, and, in the absence of anything new, the Flanders offensive seemed bound to happen.

CONTROLLING THE SOLDIERS

The War Cabinet's subsequent concern with the Passchendaele campaign was strangely detached from the military problems of the battlefield itself. The armies of Russia, which had girded themselves for and launched, as agreed with the British and French Governments, an offensive after the fall of Tsarism, collapsed in mid-July with consequences which were ultimately fatal for the new Provisional Government and immediately very awkward for the Western allies. As usual, both sides in the strategic debate used the new situation as an argument for their preferred options. Robertson argued for reinforcement to the Western Front to keep German troops away from the East; Lloyd George demanded reinforcements to strengthen Italy against the Austrians. Lloyd George had a further hope, undisclosed to the military advisers, that Austria was about to sue for a separate peace. These geopolitical concerns were inextricably bound up with Lloyd George's determination to re-establish civilian control over strategy by imposing an Allied General Staff which would control the war from the Channel to the Adriatic. This in turn created a political storm, which preoccupied Parliament until November. The Third Battle of Ypres itself, traumatic for the armies in France and fateful in its consequences for the future course of the war, was largely ignored until its failure acquired political meaning at the very end of the year.

An Allied General Staff was proposed by General Foch, the French Chief of the General Staff, whose main concern was the co-ordination of action on the Western Front between Haig and the French armies. The French were anxious because Haig's plans required supporting action which would put intolerable strains on French military morale. They were therefore sympathetic, for the moment, to Lloyd George's plans to support the Italian campaign on the Isonzo, and believed that they were unlikely to get what they wanted without a strategic authority controlled by civilians.

In mid-August, the Flanders campaign was brought nearly to a halt by the summer rains. Early in September, Foch pressed for the transfer of troops and guns to the Isonzo, to the immense annoyance of Robertson who commented that:

> ... Lloyd George being keen on the Italian project for the time being and knowing that I am against it and that the French are for it, and as the French keep rubbing in that it is necessary to have a Central Staff at Paris, I can see Lloyd George in the future wanting to agree to some such organisation so as to put the matter in French hands and to take it out of mine.[17]

General Henry Wilson, formerly the British representative at the French headquarters, lobbied the War Cabinet to support the Inter-Allied staff.[18] The Italian government asked for heavy guns, and Foch in early September, visited London to press the matter, thereby precipitating a political crisis in the War Cabinet. Lloyd George seized on Foch's proposal. Haig objected, and won the support of Carson and Smuts, and the disagreement provoked Robert Cecil, Balfour's cousin and deputy at the Foreign Office, to threaten resignation. The malcontents leaked the dispute to the Conservative press, which under the leadership of the *Morning Post*, challenged the government to stop meddling in strategy.[19]

The question of guns for Italy was soon resolved, by Haig's agreement to loan 100 guns on the understanding that they would be sent back when he needed them again in Flanders. The political crisis, on the other hand, gathered momentum. Lloyd George, Milner and Bonar Law had by now become convinced that there would be no progress on the Western Front, and differed among themselves only in the extent to which they were prepared to attack the soldiers in public.[20] News of apparent German proposals for a compromise peace rather confused the issue, because Lloyd George was willing to make large concessions at Russia's expense in order to get German withdrawal in the West while Milner and Bonar Law favoured continuing the war. This dispute was also taken to the public, with Asquith making a well-reported speech denouncing any peace agreement which would not include German withdrawal from Russia. The military commanders insisted that Germany could be defeated on the Western Front even if Russia were forced to withdraw from the struggle, and with this opinion apparently leaked to the press, it was politically impossible to make progress towards a compromise peace.[21]

Lloyd George's solution was to raise the political stakes by pressing for another peripheral attack, this time in Palestine against the Turks, which was reasonably thwarted by Robertson. By now the War Cabinet as a whole was so frustrated by its military advisers that it was open to Lloyd George's suggestion that Henry Wilson and Lord French, Haig's hitherto discredited predecessor as commander in France, should be invited to give strategic advice, 'the which intreague [sic], if unsavoury, is very skilful'[22] as Hankey observed. In fact it was rather less skilful than intended, since resignations were soon threatened from Curzon, Balfour, Cecil (again), Carson and Derby. Resignations were stayed until the reports, both denouncing the offensive on the Western Front, were debated in the War Cabinet on 29 October. This launched a major political debate over the 'unity of command' issue. On 2 November, the War Cabinet approved the constitution for the Supreme War Council, making it clear that it would review and if necessary change the strategic plans suggested by the separate general staffs.[23] Henry Wilson was chosen as British representative, in a deliberate snub to Robertson, and when the new body met for the first time at Rapallo, its first act was to oversee the transfer of more than 200,000 British and French troops to the Italian front, to shore up an ally which had just suffered a rout at the battle of Caporetto. The decision was taken on an eventful day, 7 November, during which the Bolsheviks took the Winter Palace, Allenby broke through in Palestine, and Haig launched the final attack in the Ypres campaign.

While the British army struggled in the swamps of Passchendaele, British politicians struggled in the swamps of Westminster. Lloyd George made a fiery speech in Paris on 12 November denouncing 'patchwork planning' and the tactical methods which had caused so many casualties in past campaigns. He was greeted by a storm of condemnation from the right-wing press both in Britain and in the United States, and the Conservative Party began to boil. Austen Chamberlain, temporarily a back-bencher, was close to the military hierarchy; he spent the second week in November at the front and returned to London to work up the Conservative party in parliament.[24] From the other side, Asquith intervened in the House in support of the generals, alerting Liberals on both sides of the House to the possibility that civil-military relations might be the rock on which the historic Liberal Party would founder.[25] Some sort of a break had been expected by some of Lloyd George's supporters since May, and, during October, preparations were being made for a decisive breach which would lead to a wholesale reconstruction of political parties. The possible programme of a new party, incorporating moderate Conservatives, pro-war Liberals, and 'patriotic' labour representatives, was discussed between Lloyd George, Milner and some others on 15 October.[26] The intensity of intra-party animosity after Lloyd George's Paris speech in November, led Christopher Addison, Lloyd George's chief Liberal henchman, to observe that 'there is no doubt that the General Staff and the Asquithites have made a very strong effort to discredit'[27] the government. These efforts redoubled, but in a far more convoluted way, when Lord Lansdowne transformed the terms of debate by proposing a negotiated peace and Haig launched, but failed to profit from, the battle of Cambrai.

THE POLITICAL AFTERMATH OF THIRD YPRES: FROM THE LANSDOWNE LETTER TO THE RESIGNATION OF ROBERTSON

Third Ypres had indeed produced disappointing results, to say the least, and it was set in a context of wider war weariness and unrest, disastrous in Russia and a matter of growing concern on the Home Front. On 29 November, the Marquess of Lansdowne published a letter in the *Daily Telegraph* calling for a revision of Britain's stated war aims which would make it easier to achieve a negotiated peace with Germany. Lansdowne was a former Conservative Foreign Secretary – he had negotiated the colonial agreements with France which had set up the Entente Cordiale – and an influential figure amongst Conservatives in the House of Lords. Explicit in his letter was a profound fear that the changes which the war had already caused were threatening the very society which Britain was, in his view, fighting to defend. He did not directly criticize the loss of life on the Western Front, but he questioned whether the transformation of industrial society, the strengthening of the labour movement, and the burden of taxation would fatally undermine Britain's political stability.

The Lansdowne letter, coming at the end of an inconclusive and expensive campaigning season, with the party-political system in turmoil and the parliamentary supporters of the governing coalition at odds with one another, and with the possibility of a negotiated peace widely rumoured in the newspapers, terrified the War Cabinet. An immediate and strident campaign of denigration against Lansdowne himself sought to polarize the argument quickly. Proponents of a negotiated peace were unpatriotic and dangerous; unhesitating supporters of the war were the only true patriots. Although Asquith was dextrous enough to denounce the political logic of the Lansdowne letter, many of his Liberal supporters were easily caught in the net and alleged support for Lansdowne's alleged principles became a convenient touchstone which enabled the government to isolate Liberal M.P.s who were not full-hearted supporters of the Coalition. Meshing conveniently with Lloyd George's inclination towards a pro-war centre party, it enabled Lloyd George's allies to prepare the ground for an election campaign which would set pro-war against anti-war parties and result, if all went well, in the return of a strengthened Lloyd George coalition. This scheme took somewhat longer to execute than was intended – the election only took place after the war was over – but it worked extremely well when put into practice and even crippled the Labour Party for a couple of years.[28]

Such a political success should not be allowed to conceal the real dangers which the letter and the associated political crisis revealed. The major difficulty for the War Cabinet was that most of its members fundamentally agreed with Lansdowne's assessment of the socio-political consequences of the war, and furthermore knew that the situation was at least as grave as he implied. On 10 December, the War Cabinet set up a 'Manpower Committee', the principal brief of which was to review the distribution of men between the army and the civilian economy. Though it may seem

23

surprising that no systematic effort had been made before to establish priorities for the use of men, the deliberations of the committee and the evidence placed before it, reveal how convoluted the policy-making processes of British government had become, and how profound was the loss of trust between civilian and military decision-makers.

Hankey, the War Cabinet secretary, dismissed all War Office submissions as 'utterly unreliable'.[29] The War Office asked for 600,000 able-bodied men to be taken from the civilian economy by November 1918, despite evidence that agriculture, shipbuilding and munitions production were nearly at the point of breakdown for lack of labour. An alternative or additional source of conscripts was Ireland, but for the fact that the imposition of conscription there could be expected to cause a political breakdown. Remarkably, the military was now ready to accept that the present manpower situation was so serious that such a risk was justified. Haig admitted that his troops had been exhausted by the campaigns of 1917, and suggested that he would be on the defensive in 1918.[30] Even so, the War Office wanted 'every available man and gun in France' because it expected the Germans to attack before American military strength had built up in the new campaigning season.[31]

Lloyd George and his civilian colleagues thought that this demand was impossible to satisfy. Not only did the army's casualty rate of over 50,000 men a month threaten many crucial sectors of the civilian economy, its demands were also threatening the country's political stability. Eric Geddes, the Minister of National Service, brought to the Manpower Committee a report from his intelligence branch, warning that discharged soldiers were 'in a very disgruntled state . . . the men were thoroughly war-weary . . . they spoke most bitterly of the waste of life during the continued hammerings against the Ypres Ridge this Autumn'.[32] Lloyd George responded that the generals must be made to realize 'how profoundly he was dissatisfied with this expenditure of life, and of the very serious results it was having on the national outlook'.[33]

The War Cabinet was also coming to realize that discontent was not confined to the working classes or the troops. Lansdowne himself, and his overt sympathisers among M.P.s and journalists, were evidence that the civilian élite was not completely reliable.[34] Soon enough it was to become apparent that even senior officers in the army were affected by Lansdowne's views and sympathetic to his reasoning. As an officer in the Guard's Brigade wrote at the end of the year:

> . . . the ordinary Tommy & junior officer has no idea why we are fighting & no ultimate aim or achievement to put before him – He has absolutely nothing to look forward to except Death, if lucky a wound. He knows that if he survives one battle he is due for the next . . . All we want is – A definite statement of our peace terms (not vague terms – i.e. freedom of the seas but facts) . . . people don't seem to realise the extraordinary extent of feeling both among men and officers here, & if they don't soon do something – they must expect them to welcome letters like Lord L's.[35]

The same writer commented that 'officers out here (3 generals I know included) took it up as a kind of gospel-truth and its author as the champion of their cause – i.e. peace on moderate terms'. According to Smuts and Hankey, this was very much the position taken by Haig, who, in January 1918, warned Smuts that the French and Italians were both likely to collapse, that American forces were building up too slowly to be useful, and that an early peace should be arranged by allowing Germany to expand into Russia.[36] However, Haig's diary attributes these views to the War Cabinet, as communicated to him by Smuts.

So profound were the War Cabinet's fears that they responded by making almost exactly the restatement of war aims which Lansdowne had suggested, in the form of a speech made by Lloyd George to a meeting of trade unionists in Caxton Hall on 5 January 1918. They had been careful to undermine Lansdowne's political position beforehand, and the ostensible audience was the people at large, reached through the leaders of labour, rather than the disgruntled middle classes or the war-weary army. But the message was very much the same, and the political intention clear. Although it was necessary to go on fighting the war, the restatement of war aims towards a peace on the basis of national self-determination was an attempt to ensure that the 'working class volcano'[37] did not erupt beneath the government's feet. It was a volcano which might have burst forth either in Britain or among the troops in France.

Simultaneously the War Cabinet struggled to control Haig and Robertson, whose strategic ideas and tactical methods they had come to believe were lethal to the British war effort. The workings of the Supreme War Council offered both an occasion and an excuse. In December, the French government had asked that Haig's armies should take over more of the front line and that a strategic reserve should be set up which could reinforce any part of the line which was threatened by a German attack. These requests were predicated on the assumption that Entente forces would be on the defensive as a result of the exhaustion of the 1917 campaign, and that the French army, in particular, was in need of support. Haig and Robertson resisted, though Robertson supported the idea of a 'reserve' on condition that it was under the control of the Allied Chiefs of Staff rather than his enemy Wilson, the British Military Representative on the Supreme War Council. Lloyd George wanted both to extend the British line, though not by as much as the French wanted, and to create the 'reserve' because it promised to be a body of troops outside the control of Haig. The Supreme War Council, meeting from 30 January to 2 February, accepted most of Lloyd George's points, but neither Robertson nor Haig was prepared to accept this decision. A characteristically vicious political campaign was launched, which involved not only the generals' usual supporters in the right wing press but also the Unionist War Committee, the mouthpiece of Conservative back-benchers least friendly to Lloyd George. The War Cabinet fought back, with Lloyd George and Milner in the lead.

Haig and Robertson were in fact divided on the main issue: Haig was willing to accept the Versailles decision in most respects, and was less aroused by the question of Robertson's authority relative to that of the Permanent Military Representative. This was Lloyd George's opportunity, and Haig was summoned to London to become part of a political manoeuvre.[38] Lloyd George, Milner and Lord Derby, who was himself about to be removed from the War Office, met on the morning of 9 February and drew up a proposal for Henry Wilson to become C.I.G.S. and Robertson to go to Versailles as Permanent Military Representative. There was no doubt that Robertson would refuse this. The same afternoon Haig indicated that he would make no objection, and the Haig-Robertson alliance was broken. Robertson fought back with leaks to favoured journalists, to Conservative M.P.s and even to Asquith, but to no avail. Lloyd George was able to persuade all his Conservative colleagues not to resign, and to persuade the House of Commons that Robertson was, in Haig's words, a 'mulish irreconcilable'.[39] It was a political success. But matters had not progressed as far as Lloyd George had wanted, for reasons expressed with brutal clarity by Milner before the event: 'It is no use having a great rumpus & getting rid of Robertson, if the policy is to be side-tracked for quite different reasons by Haig'.[40] Robertson was the last victim of the Passchendaele campaign. His removal represented the furthest that the War Cabinet was able to get in establishing civilian control of strategy and tactics, for Wilson, his successor, soon proved almost as obstinate in demanding the subordination of civilian and other requirements to the provision of drafts for the Western Front.

PASSCHENDAELE AND BRITISH POLICY-MAKING
Since the establishment of a new Coalition to bring the war under control and move towards victory by methods which would not destroy the British economy, Lloyd George and the War Cabinet had been obliged to watch what had been, in their perception, an offensive which had replicated in methods, cost and futility the failed campaign of the previous summer, to change their war aims in response to civil and military discontent, and still to accept the survival of most of a military élite which believed in all the methods which they distrusted. It was hardly a distinguished record. Even at this remove of time, and with a huge body of evidence on which to draw, explanations of this failure of political intention can only be approximate. Many historians will still accept the verdict of contemporaries that Lloyd George, in particular, was simply too clever by half, and so profoundly incapable of honest dealing that even when he was right he was unable to impose his will. Probably the best explanation is less personal. The evolution of strategic policy in 1917 was conditioned by many contexts, and each must play its part in explaining the War Cabinet's position.

Strategically, as David French has often reminded us,[41] the demands of Britain's allies, and their perennial weaknesses, severely limited British options. The French were genuinely unable to mount a serious offensive after April 1917; the Russians had shot their bolt and fallen back into chaos after August. In the absence of any real support from the Americans, whose entry into the war in April did not presage any troops until the next year, there was only a choice between doing nothing and doing what Haig wanted to do. The peripheral alternatives so much beloved of Lloyd George – the Salonika campaign, the Palestine campaign, the Italian campaign on the Isonzo – were strategically meaningful only if a significant campaign were being fought on the Western Front to occupy German strength while Germany's allies were being picked off or demoralized. Much energy went into argument about whether the peripheral campaigns should be starved of resources, but the true argument was whether German troops could be kept occupied without an Entente offensive in the West, and this was never properly addressed by the civilian members of the War Cabinet.

The second context was straightforwardly political. The Lloyd George Coalition had to survive by retaining the support of the Conservative Party in parliament. There is no doubt that whatever the merits of a strategic case, most Conservative M.P.s were instinctive supporters of the expert authority of military officers and instinctive opponents of Lloyd George. The analysis which led the War Cabinet to want to limit military offensives was actually unpalatable to uninformed back-benchers, because it implied that Britain's military and economic capacity was limited and her global and imperial ambitions were in thrall to financial constraints – which in practice meant the Americans. The argument that the best solution to Britain's predicament was a less 'vigorous prosecution of the war' was simply not understood by a parliamentary party which thought it had accepted Lloyd George as almost the only Liberal with the patriotism and courage to give his and the country's all to the struggle.

Closely related to this difficulty was the strong link between the military hierarchy and the instruments of political propaganda. Senior officers were very closely connected to the right wing press, particularly the *Spectator* and the *Morning Post*. Haig was also close to the Royal Household, which had its own ways of leaking. Well-accustomed to underhand political methods, the generals met Lloyd George's intrigues with intrigues of their own. They were considerably helped by the willingness of Asquith, at least in the months after September 1917, to take up the cause of the generals despite the history of antipathy between the army and the Liberal hierarchy. Soldiers who disliked the strategic preferences of the War Cabinet could rely on newspapers, Conservative M.P.s and disaffected Liberals to back them up in parliament and in public, and thus frustrate the freedom of the War Cabinet to carry out its own plans.

These interlocking contexts go some way to explaining why the development of the Passchendaele campaign from its inception to its inglorious conclusion in November was allowed to proceed, with the support or acquiescence of a political leadership which disliked both the policy and the military men who championed and conducted it. They also explain how the campaign and its results were so important in shaping the politics of the war, creating conditions in which the Lloyd George coalition was forced into the compromises of the Caxton Hall speech, but also into an extreme decision to break up and reform the party system in order to ensure the survival of the régime.

Notes

1   Kitchener had been appointed as a 'non-political' Secretary of State for War because the post was vacant on the outbreak of war and the Liberal government wanted the support of his reputation. He was a bad communicator, and an inflexible strategist, but he had foreseen the need for a mass land army.

2   See John Grigg, *Lloyd George: from peace to war*, London, Methuen, 1985, pp. 380–384.

3   Hankey Diary, 26 December 1916, Churchill College, Hankey Papers 1/1, quoted in Stephen R Roskill, *Hankey: man of secrets*, London, Collins, 1970, p. 348.

4   Haig Diary, 7 February 1917, National Library of Scotland, Haig Papers 110.

5   Hankey Diary, 24 February 1917; War Cabinet Minutes, 24 February 1917, Public Record Office, CAB 23/1.

6   TS note, n.s., 7 March 1917, House of Lords Record Office, Lloyd George Papers F/162/1

7   Holograph note by Hankey, 8 March 1917 (1.30am) CAB 63/19.

8   Robertson to Haig, 6, 8 March 1917, King's College, London, Robertson Papers I/23/11, 12.

9   Haig Diary, 9 March 1917, Haig Papers 111.

10   Rawlinson Diary, 23 July 1917, Rawlinson Papers 1/7. The exception Rawlinson allowed to this generalisation was Jan Smuts, the South African leader, who had joined the War Cabinet.

11   Haig to Robertson, 29 April 1918, Robertson Papers I/23/25.

12   There were many occasions for this but see especially the exchange on 28 April 1917 in Robertson Papers I/23/23 and John Terraine, *Haig: the educated soldier*, pp. 296–305.

13   Diary of Sir Hugh Thornton, 17 June 1917, Bodleian Library, Milner Papers 23/1. Thornton was Milner's private secretary.

14   Memorandum by M.P.A. Hankey, 18 April 1917, CAB 63/20.

15   Haig to Robertson, 28 May 1917, quoted in Robert Blake, *The Private Papers of Douglas Haig*, London, p. 233.

16   7th Meeting of the Cabinet Committee on War Policy, 19 June 1917, CAB 27/6.

17   Robertson to Haig, 9 August 1917, reprinted in Robert Blake, *The Private Papers of Douglas Haig*, p. 251.

18   Wilson Diary, 20–27 August 1917, Imperial War Museum, Henry Wilson Papers. Wilson was notoriously out of sympathy with Robertson and Haig, who both distrusted his ready familiarity with the French.

19   Cecil to Balfour, 4 September, 1917, British Library, Balfour Papers Add. MSS 49738, ff. 150–151; see also Cecil's draft letter of resignation in Robert Cecil Papers, PRO FO 800/196, ff. 240–245. *Morning Post*, 5 September 1917.

20   Milner Diary, 16–20 September 1917, Milner Papers 88; Bonar Law to Lloyd George, 18 September 1917, Lloyd George Papers F/30/2/25.

21   David Woodward, *Lloyd George and the Generals*, pp. 206–207.

22   Hankey Diary, 20 October 1917, Hankey Papers 1/3.

23 War Cabinet Minutes, 2 November 1917, W.C. 262 & 263, CAB 23/3.

24 Chamberlain resigned from the India Office after the publication of the Mesopotamia Report condemned the ineptitude of the Government of India. His activities in November 1917 are recorded in Curzon to Lloyd George, 18 November 1917, Lloyd George Papers F/11/8/18.

25 Cecil Harmsworth to Walter Runciman, November 1917, University of Newcastle, Runciman Papers, WR 161 (2).

26 Addison Diary, 15 October 1917, Bodleian Library, Addison Papers.

27 Addison Diary, 19 November 1917.

28 For an elaboration of this point, see John Turner, *British Politics and the Great War: coalition and conflict, 1915–1918*, London & New Haven: Yale University Press, 1992, pp. 248–333.

29 Hankey Diary, 6 December 1917, Hankey Papers.

30 'Memorandum on the Question of an Extention of the British Front', 15 December 1917, CAB 27/14.

31 General Sir Frederick Maurice (Director of Military Operations) to Lloyd George, 18 December 1917, Lloyd George Papers F/44/3/40.

32 Second Meeting of the Manpower Committee, 11 December 1917, CAB 27/14.

33 Third Meeting of the Manpower Committee, 11 December 1917, ibid.

34 See e.g. Violet Markham to St Loe Strachey (editor of the *Spectator*) on 'the extent of the evil among our own class'. House of Lords Record Office, Strachey Papers S/18/5/1.

35 Victor Cazalet, Household Bn., B.E.F. to Austen Chamberlain, 31 December 1917, Birmingham University Library, Austen Chamberlain Papers, AC 13/3/38.

36 Smuts to Lloyd George, 21 January 1918, Lloyd George Papers F/45/9/9; see also Hankey to Lloyd George, 22 January 1918, Lloyd George Papers F/23/2/11.

37 W. Buckler (a Counsellor at the U.S. Embassy) to Arthur Hugh Frazier, quoted in Frazier to Colonel E.M. House (President Woodrow Wilson's special assistant), 16 January 1918, Yale University Library, House Papers 466/I/58/F282.

38 David Woodward, *Lloyd George and the Generals*, London: Associated University Presses, 1983.

39 Haig Diary, 20 February 1918. Haig Papers 123.

40 Milner to Lloyd George, 8 February 1918, Lloyd George Papers F/38/3/10.

41 David French, *The Strategy of the Lloyd George Coalition*, Oxford: Clarendon Press, 1995.

Chapter Three

Field Marshal Sir Douglas Haig and Passchendaele

Frank E Vandiver

Nineteen seventeen was Field Marshal Sir Douglas Haig's most testing time. His battles that year, especially Passchendaele, were so controversial that they nearly cost him his command and have shadowed his reputation ever since. Wasteful and fruitless, critics charge, stolid examples of martial bankruptcy. Are the critics right? Were the British battles of 1917 unremitting disasters plotted by a cavalryman lost in modern war? Haig's bad year began with a command crisis triggered by Britain's new Prime Minister, David Lloyd George, who sought to subordinate Haig to France's General Robert Georges Nivelle. Although the crisis passed in compromise, the military's confidence in Lloyd George was destroyed beyond repair.[1]

Nivelle convinced the British cabinet that he could win the war on the Western Front if Haig's armies tied down German reserves. As a result Haig agreed to attack near Arras in a limited holding battle. If Nivelle's offensive did not gain the long-sought breakthrough in forty-eight hours it would be stopped and the French would support Haig's cherished offensive in Flanders.[2] Haig, concerned about Admiral Jellicoe's pronouncement that Germany's reinstated policy of unrestricted submarine warfare might starve England into defeat,[3] wanted to break out of the Ypres salient, capture the submarine ports of Ostend and Zeebrugge, turn the enemy right flank at the Dutch frontier and drive on to victory.

That kind of thinking chilled Lloyd George. It sounded too much like German and Allied plans of 1916 which produced Verdun and the Somme. Apparently Western Front generals learned nothing from experience and to Lloyd George, Haig seemed the most egregious Bourbon on the battlefield. A British drive from a bad position toward the bogs of southern Belgium seemed to prove strategic bankruptcy. But when Nivelle's April attack failed in another blood bath along the Chemin-des-Dames (he expected 10,000 casualties, but suffered at least 125,000) and turned into

(i) "One of a set of contemporary postcard caricatures of Field Marshal Sir Douglas Haig. The artist was almost certainly Bert Thomas. *(Peter Scott Collection)*

7ᘔ337

a lingering catastrophe that led to wide-spread French army mutinies, Lloyd George turned to Haig to keep up the war.[4]

What about Haig, now that he shouldered the burden of pressing the enemy? Was he bankrupt of original strategy? Good strategy is not necessarily original, and his ideas were sound, with incontestably valid objectives, the Belgian coast and Roulers. He wanted always to force the war where Germany could not refuse battle, and a look at a Western Front map showed that a British breach beyond Ypres could easily threaten the railway centre at Roulers where German communications in Flanders were hinged. Clearing the Belgian coast would not only ease the submarine crisis but would threaten to outflank a further key centre of German occupied Belgium, Ghent. These two considerations justified a Flanders offensive but Haig held, also, to the unwavering principle of "wearing out" Germany's Army. He believed (erroneously as it happened) that the German Army had been so battered by the Somme, by Nivelle's vainglorious efforts and by British successes at Arras and Vimy Ridge, that a determined British drive – properly aided by the French – might win the war.[5] So firmly did he stick to this belief that he lured some sceptics to reluctant agreement – among them, for a time, Lloyd George.[6]

Nevertheless Haig could take small comfort from being a temporary necessity. Well he knew that the War Cabinet remained split about fighting in France. Bonar Law and Lord Milner resisted Haig's ideas, and when Lloyd George joined them this alliance was opposed by Arthur Balfour, South Africa's General Jan Smuts and Lord Curzon. Although nominally an "Easterner," who sought victory somewhere beyond France, Lord Curzon, in the post-Nivelle crisis, supported the Chief of the Imperial General Staff (CIGS) General Sir William Robertson and Haig.[7] The King supported Haig but he had more influence than power. War Cabinet debate waxed long and tortuous.[8]

Within himself, Haig had confidence. Taciturn, almost inarticulate some said, he rarely showed emotion to his generals, staff or "other ranks," but in a deep and inner keep of his heart held a conviction of the rightness of his thinking, almost a sense of destiny, and this encouraged him to hold firm against compromise in the Flanders venture. Haig's plan rested on confidence in his armies reinforced by estimates of deteriorating enemy conditions provided by his intelligence chief, General John Charteris,[9] and clear grasp of the strategic importance of the areas he planned to attack. Furthermore, it rested on assurances that the French would continue pressure in the Chemin-des-Dames area to prevent detachments of German reserves. It rested, too, on his careful study of Western Front operations – and on a flexibility which made the attack easy to stop. Also, Haig had some hope that a projected Italian offensive would drain German divisions which Russia's collapse might release from the east.[10]

After Arras and Vimy, he believed he had found the way to win: trained troops advancing on defined objectives behind careful and concentrated artillery preparation with reserves ready to consolidate gains. Haig's idea of objectives ran wider and deeper than 'bite and hold' tactics, but it has to be said that he turned to these methods in practice, when his break-through vision receded beyond reach. In explaining his Flanders plan to Army Commanders on 7 May, Haig outlined a two-phased campaign; the Messines-Wytschaete Ridge, which dominated the southern part of the Ypres salient, would be taken by General Sir Herbert Plumer's Second Army to protect the British right flank during the second phase – the drive to capture the Belgian coast "some weeks later." The delay – much against Haig's grain – was forced by the need to continue holding attacks around Arras, as it was impossible to maintain "sufficient resources" on two fronts.[11] Then, too, there would be increased opportunities to change plans if the main drive were broken into two distinct battles. More than that, a distinct break in action might deceive the enemy into thinking the Messines attack a diversion from the Arras front.[12]

Plumer, holding the Ypres sector, had made early preparations to occupy the high ground ahead of his army by tunnelling to set twenty-one mines under Messines Ridge and had scouted approaches to the daunting Gheluvelt plateau.[13] He could advance toward the plateau and follow it toward Roulers. What did Haig want?

In fact, Haig wanted a general advance by British and French forces along the entire Ypres salient and on to the Channel coast, but he wrestled with command problems. Haig had ambivalent feelings about Plumer, but acknowledged the competence of the sixty year old General. There were, however, questions over his record: he had not performed well in the Crater battles of 1916 and his plans for exploiting the capture of Messines Ridge seemed too cautious.[14] So, too, were General Sir Henry Rawlinson's ideas for Ypres activity something of a disappointment. Haig had hoped to have him lead the left flank operations.

On 30 April, 1917, Haig told Fifth Army's commander, General Sir Hubert Gough, that he would command the northern half of the Flanders operation, "including the landing force" in Belgium. There were obvious reasons for Gough's selection. The war put a premium on youth – older commanders usually failed on the Western Front. Gough, forty-seven, was the youngest army commander and Haig liked his energy and drive, despite his over-zealousness at the Somme and poor results at Bullecourt. Quick promotions and Haig's favour, combined with irritating arro-gance, dimmed Gough's popularity. His worst defect, though, was his inattention to staff work. Still, he had dash to him and good Lancer back-ground. To Haig, Gough seemed the best prospect for breaking through the German positions and winning in 1917.[15] Gough moved his staff close to Ypres, began learning his new theatre and preparing a battle plan.

Plumer's Messines battle plan had gone through several changes. The version current in May and June 1917 showed Plumer and his staff increasing masters of the Western Front's siege warfare. Relying on the mines to wreck the German front line and confuse the whole defensive sector, the Second Army would advance under a carefully prepared artillery schedule which would deluge the battlefield as the mines exploded; infantry would follow a barrage toward objectives within their physical strength; reserves of men and guns would move forward to consolidate gains and subdue enemy counter-attacks. Plumer went to corps, divisional and brigade headquarters, discussing details of the upcoming battle, seeking advice and comments, and showing all leaders, down to platoon commanders, a huge model of the Messines-Wytschaete Ridge. They all understood where they were to be located.

Plumer's scheme to capture the ridge with nine divisions after a four day bombardment and destruction of the crest by a million pounds of ammonal looked good, but his proposal then to stop the attack and regroup brought sharp reaction. Haig urged the taking of Messines village and continuation toward a Courtrai-Roulers line, some twenty miles on. Plumer accepted the need to take the whole of the Ridge on the first day, but needed more men for Haig's grand exploitation. His hesitancy troubled the Field Marshal.[16]

Although he stuck to the old Staff College maxim of leaving the battle to officers on the scene, the Commander-in-Chief evolved command techniques as he learned from the war. He had always commented on operational plans, but in 1916 adopted a different management approach.[17] To Plumer and his commanders Haig addressed queries on 20 May which show his careful attention to details:

> Questions for all Corps.
>
> Have you got the enemy's batteries accurately located? Are changes of position occurring, and if so, in what manner? For example, is the enemy occupying alternative positions near vacated ones; is he re-occupying his old ones after a certain lapse of time, or do you see a general tendency to move his batteries back? . . . What information have you about the enemy's system of holding the line? . . .
>
> What is the strength of your mopping-up parties? . . .
>
> Are your infantry trained to deal with low-flying aeroplanes by Lewis Gun and rifle fire? This is most necessary as it is part of the German system now to seek for concentrations of troops at daybreak . . .

Detailed questions were asked of units with specific tasks. What plans did IX Corps have for capturing Wytschaete village? Was X Corps "satisfied with the counter-battery arrangements of the Corps on left? It is vital to your success that these should be most thorough." Haig queried commanders about field tactics and equipment, the use of machine-guns and gas, and the ground they faced.[18]

From the responses he learned where adjustments must be made and where he needed to strengthen the attack. Officers of reasonable initiative responded well to this "Socratic" system, but some eager commanders needed more directions than queries – a lesson Haig learned, painfully. In any case, once the battle was launched, command was, by actual circumstance, devolved from GHQ control and even much further down the chain of authority.

At 3.10 AM, Thursday, 7 June, 1917, Plumer's mines shook the ground like an earthquake and blew the top off Messines Ridge. A terrible kind of beauty caught one German eye as "nineteen gigantic roses with carmine petals, or . . . enormous mushrooms . . . rose up slowly and majestically out of the ground and then split into pieces with a mighty roar." Right after the greatest of man-made explosions, came a torrent of shells as British artillery pounded the front and rear areas and Tommies and Anzacs came up out of their trenches and hunched into the chaos ahead, and into almost no resistance. Swiftly they took the enemy first line and moved on against the crest. Messines village and Wytschaete fell and by 9 AM the ridge was British.[19]

Expecting the usual counter-attacks, the victors began digging-in; confusion confounded German reaction and their few feeble thrusts were beaten back easily. Plumer prepared to move on to his last objective, the so-called Oosttaverne Line. Things got stickier now, since a good many of the German guns extracted from the maelstrom fired on the British infantry as they massed on the ridge crest. When they advanced they came under friendly and hostile fire, as British guns were still laying a protective barrage. The tragedy doubled when attempts to correct the range brought the ridge crest under fire. Here Plumer took his heaviest casualties (24,562)[20] and, by the end of the day he did not quite have all of his objective. However, he had won a great victory. Haig was nearly jubilant when he visited Second Army Headquarters on the afternoon of the 7th, and noted that "the operations today are probably the most successful I have yet undertaken."[21]

Much depended on following up success; the Germans feared further attacks before they re-consolidated.[22] Haig had wanted Plumer to press on to a foothold on the southern end of the Gheluvelt Plateau, the key position from which the Germans could bring enfilading artillery fire on an attack to the North. Secured gains here would anchor Gough's right as he drove on toward Roulers, and plans were made along those lines. Plumer requested three days to get his artillery in place. This seemed too long, and Haig detached two Corps from Second Army to Fifth and asked for a quick programme to get the Plateau. Gough asked for a few days himself and got them – more than Plumer would have needed. Six days later Gough noted heavy enemy defences and said the Gheluvelt attack should be part of his main offensive in six weeks' time.[23]

Problems cropped up quickly. Haig had learned from Pétain something of the shattered condition of the French Army, but was not given the full picture. Indeed, Pétain had promised some support, which he then continually delayed. Then, on 2 June, Pétain announced he could not attack in support of the Flanders drive![24] French failure threatened to undermine Haig's whole programme for 1917; everything he had thought and told the War Cabinet, depended on strong French support.

With tepid support from London, an absence of support from the French, and with reinforced German positions around Ypres, Haig faced daunting uncertainties everywhere. What was Haig to do in these circumstances? Should the offensive be called off, and if so, what would be the likely impact on the course of the War in other sectors? Some hope remained of Pétain pinning down German reserves and he did offer a French Army for co-operation on the British left. With these thin encouragements, Haig determined to go on, if he could get firm approval from London.

Even as Gough's artillery preparation began on 15 July, the War Cabinet had as yet failed to bless the plans.[25] Belatedly, only six days before the infantry went into action, approval came in ambiguous terms from Robertson: "War Cabinet authorizes me to inform you that having approved your plans . . . you may depend on their whole-hearted support and that if and when they decide again to reconsider the situation they will obtain your views before arriving at a decision as to cessation of operations." That sparked Haig's anger, vented in a letter to the Secretary of State for War, Lord Derby, just before battle: "How different to the whole-hearted, almost unthinking support given by our Government to the Frenchman (Nivelle) last January."[26]

Unexpected problems came from the man Haig trusted to carry the offensive through to victory. Gough, after a careful study of ground and objectives, and consultations with Corps commanders, made a "slight" change in Haig's battle order. That understatement hid a major shift in Gough's line of attack. His army would "pivot on the left with the French, while the right flank advanced along the Passchendaele Ridge." Instead of aiming toward Roulers and sweeping up the high ground along Gheluvelt Plateau, Fifth Army would attack northeastward toward the channel ports. Haig apparently agreed to this radical shift that exposed Gough's right, because of confusion about Gough's intentions. The Commander-in-Chief had cautioned Gough on 28 June about the right flank. "I impressed on Gough the vital importance of the ridge . . . , and that the advance north should be limited until our right flank has really been secured on this ridge."[27] The next day Haig visited Gough's Corps commanders, stressing the need to take the Plateau. If heed were not taken of the Commader-in-Chief's warning, Gough would be at the mercy of the German artillery pounding his right flank.

Delays plagued all of July. Gough needed time to replace guns lost in a long artillery battle; the French First Army commander on the left needed time to extend his bombardment which had been slowed by poor weather. These conditions had all kinds of ill portents for Haig. In the lowlands around Ypres, rain brought ground water near the surface. The Tank Corps kept a "swamp map" showing how mud encroached on operating positions – the map spread alarmingly as the month progressed[28] – and weather became a palpable enemy.

At 3.50 AM on 31 July, 2000 guns announced the beginning of the Battle of Pilckem Ridge: fourteen British and two French divisions attacked, covered on the right by five Second Army divisions. On the right and left things went well; in the centre five divisions attacked the Gheluvelt Plateau suffering heavy losses and achieving little gain as counter-attacks engulfed them. As the battle wore on Haig could see that enemy artillery concentrations were higher than reported but he felt satisfied with the day. Casualties ran to about 15,000 with the Germans losing more, including 5,000 prisoners and more than sixty guns. Speed counted in organizing Gough's main attack, scheduled for 3 August, but General Headquarters cautioned careful preparation for the drive's next phase. Clearly Gough had not scored a breakthrough and operational tempo slowed as rains deluged the battlefield and the Germans used mustard gas.[29] Mud slowed everything down. Gough wanted to get on with the battle, but Haig urged patience for better weather and drier ground. This meant, of course, that Haig was beginning to shift back to Plumer's ideas – carefully planned attacks for limited objectives.[30]

Gough tried again for Gheluvelt on 10 August and failed largely because of poor artillery preparation and vigorous counter-attacks. On the 16th, a major drive started toward Langemarck without much success but, on the 19th, a tank attack at St. Julien did surprisingly well. Still, Haig could see a stalemate coming and made a sweeping change of strategy and tactics. By the end of August he had turned the campaign over to Plumer. Pétain had finally helped with attacks at Verdun, 20 August, which netted some 6,000 prisoners and greatly cheered the French, who did not press success. But London loomed again a problem. The Prime Minister made no secret of his sense of vindication concerning his doubts about the wisdom of Haig's plans, and demonstrated his renewed desire to wage war outside of France.[31] An Italian victory in the latest Isonzo offensive beckoned the "Easterners," but Haig would not be deflected, and Lloyd George chose not to exercise his power to over-rule the Field Marshal.

The rest of his offensive fell into the 'bite and hold' pattern as Plumer picked up where Messines left off. The most fearsome concentration of British Artillery ever assembled opened his Battle of the Menin Road. It started on 20 September in acceptable weather, and prospered; the Battle of Polygon Wood followed on 26 September, with good results too, and Haig began again to think of things beyond Ypres' ridges. An interruption of German communications at Roulers now might present a real opportunity for a breakthrough, and much was expected from a renewed drive on 4 October.

Against a back-drop of rains, that made lakes of shell holes, and a War Cabinet toying with having Haig take over more French line, Plumer launched the Battle of Broodseinde. This was initially scheduled for 6 October, but was brought forward to 4 October, to take advantage of the favourable weather conditions. Again careful preparation produced victory. Haig urged a swift follow up but, despite the dry weather in

37

September, conditions under foot remained poor. The constant heavy shelling had churned up the ground, destroying natural water courses and creating a quagmire. Thus, as rain drenched the dreary landscape of the Gheluvelt-Passchendaele plateau, what land there was between the armies became a slimy nightmare of rivulets and half-filled holes where men, animals and equipment slithered, fought, sank and drowned. Plumer drove for Poelcappelle on the 9th with dismal results, but Haig judged that some success had been achieved. Mud, though, won the day. In the pall of that awful battle, Haig saw glimmers of German fatigue. He still hoped to take Passchendaele, but reluctantly began to feel there would be no drive to Roulers, let alone anywhere else in 1917.

Still he clung to a chance – if the weather improved – slim, but a chance to break over the Passchendaele ridge and on to the coast. Gough's tough Anzacs struggled through sticky glue for the ruins of Passchendaele on the 12th and just could not get there. On the 22nd small gains were made, only to be lost; once more on the 26th British troops trudged forward, again on the 28th (Haig noted the 7th division "really engulfed in mud in some places"[32]) and 30th they slithered toward that obliterated village. Canadians finally took it on November 6 and on the 10th Haig let his offensive end on a sodden crest where his armies could survive the winter looking down on enemy lines. Heights did not deceive the Field Marshal; he knew the BEF's new lines were vulnerable.

No army could have given more than Haig's, no men stood so much so long so steadily to such martyrdom. The men had fought beyond all expectation of what might have been endured. They were dazed and worn. Third Ypres had cost about 275,000 British casualties, almost equal to German losses.[33] Morale suffered finally, not in French dimensions, but some spark went from the men who fought so hard for what seemed so little.

What of Douglas Haig in the ruin of his hopes? He was soon preoccupied with a new battle further South – General Sir Julian Byng's tank attack at Cambrai in late November that first proved the value of these behemoths of the battlefield and then faded against counter-attacks. This disappointment, combined with Third Ypres, nearly finished Haig's career. Should Cambrai have been attempted? Did Haig err in deciding to push on after the attack stalled? He accepted responsibility midst a welter of demands for an investigation.

Somehow, in this nadir of his life, he held firm to his growing religious faith, which helped him face a kind of feeding frenzy among old and new critics, who damned his judgment, his aloofness, his strategy, tactics, everything. Lloyd George's criticism broke into the open with attacks on Haig and on the CIGS, Robertson. He implied that had the Cabinet known details of Haig's Third Ypres plans (which, of course, it did), it would have cancelled the campaign. Clearly changes would be made. Particular criticism was reserved for General Charteris and General Sir Launcelot Kiggell. Haig resented the campaign against these two men, seeing it as an oblique attack on himself. He fought, in vain, to retain Charteris and Kiggell – both men went as sacrifices for their leader. Robertson, that tough opponent of Lloyd George's whims, would also go.

The Prime Minister, much as he wanted to, did not remove the Commander-in-Chief. He received strong advice against it and pondered the difficult question of replacement. He wanted no more Sommes and Ypres and had radically changed the high command to prevent this. He would find other ways to trim the Field Marshal to the Cabinet's wind.

One of the most serious questions plaguing Haig's reputation is why he fought Passchendaele at all. What were the alternatives? Nivelle's failure and consequent French mutinies created an emergency, but there were dangers other than French mutinies facing the Allies as the summer of 1917 approached. Russia was all but finished while Austria, showing unexpected recuperative strength, attacked the Italians, the submarines continued to menace and the Americans were still getting organized. The British Army alone could continue putting pressure on the Western Front. Haig took up the burden.

Along with the issue of 'why' is the issue of 'where'. Why did Haig elect to fight in Flanders? To turn the Belgian flank of the German Army might have restored movement to the War, and it might have led to that decisive victory for which Haig searched. This was Haig's clear overall vision and, within it, was that strategically compelling objective, the Belgian coast, the capture of which, it could reasonably be assessed, would considerably reduce the submarine threat.

Tied with 'why' and 'where' is 'when'. Why did Haig launch Third Ypres so late in 1917? That the weather seriously affected the terrain in Flanders was well known by all army staffs. Ideally, Haig should have started his campaign in April or early May, and he did want to attack earlier, but had to defer to Nivelle's April offensive on the Chemin-des-Dames. A vital sub-question: if he wanted to attack earlier, why did Haig accept the delay of almost two months between Messines and the Battle for Pilckem Ridge? Of course, the answer lies in logistics. He had to allow several weeks for re-deployment northward and hoped that the Battle of Messines would screen the movement. Logistics cost some time because road and rail communications had to be established and, men, munitions and supplies shifted. Then, too, local problems dislocated time tables. Gough and the French First Army commander requested extra days for artillery siting and repair, which Haig deplored but allowed. With July almost gone, should Haig have cancelled the offensive? Meteorologists prophesied that there was no reason not to expect good weather in August – time enough for success.[34]

'Why', 'where', 'when', questions lead on to 'who'? Why did Haig pick Gough to lead the heavy end of the attack? This choice ranks, according to most sources, as the worst of Haig's mistakes. Unfamiliar with the field, unfamiliar with his new divisions, but filled with "the cavalry spirit," Gough had almost no credentials for the job. As things worked out, this was proved sound, but Haig liked him, found him easy to work with, approved his gusto and found nothing to condemn in his earlier commands. Haig's own tactical notions had shifted during the protracted slogging around Arras and he came, perhaps unaware of the irony, to think in almost Nivellian terms – breakthrough and mop up on the way to victory.

Unfortunately zest could not make up for confusion – which came to Gough partly because it came to Haig. As planning for the campaign progressed, Gough thought Haig wanted a breakthrough. This, at first, was true, but, as fighting stalled in the mud, Haig turned back to Plumer's slower wearing out fight. All of which indicates some indecision in Haig's mind, as his early plans disintegrated.

In the midst of changed tactics and terrible weather, why did Haig urge Plumer to greater speed and on to Passchendaele itself? Weather and time and position combine in the answer. As shells wrecked the Flanders drainage system and everything turned to bog and slime, Haig grasped a last opportunity to break the German army before winter. Failing that, the Gheluvelt-Passchendaele plateau opened on to good ground for the next campaign. The worried Field Marshal did not panic but became edgy as time raced on and rain swamped him.

With all this, why was Haig so relentlessly determined – seeing success over the next wallow? Most students blame General Charteris. As intelligence chief he briefed Haig on the state of German morale and usually reported it on the verge of collapse. Be it said for Haig that he defended Charteris manfully: "I cannot agree that Charteris should be made 'whipping boy' for the charge of undue optimism brought against myself. His duty is to collect, collate and place before me all evidence obtainable in regard to the enemy ... The responsibility for the judgment formed on the evidence obtained and for the views put forward ... rests on me and not on him ... "[35] There was some shrewd self-assessment in that comment.

A question comes from history: Did Passchendaele accomplish anything? General Erich Ludendorff in *My War Memories, 1914–1918* (1919) acknowledged the exhaustion of Third Ypres and thought German morale never recovered. Field Marshal von Hindenburg in *Out of My Life* (1920) recalled the campaign as wearing beyond belief. Other German commanders felt Passchendaele's dread portents for Germany. Some recent students accept German testimony on the difficulty of defence but reject the idea that Haig's battles were really wearing the enemy out.[36] Can they have it both ways, indeed some economic historians now suggest that the seeds of later German collapse were watered by the demands of the 1917 Flanders campaign.[37]

There is, in all of this, a terrible sadness – not just for the armies but for their commander. Despite retrospective comment to the contrary, there is abundant evidence that Haig 'felt' for his men. He had not accomplished what he believed was possible, but he and his subordinate commanders had learned from an experience that had tested them so seriously and their men to the uttermost. From Arras, Messines, Lens, Third Ypres, and Cambrai, there were clear indications of a different way of war, of an orchestration of machines and men under tighter, shrewder, more scientific direction. Those ideas germinated as the Germans were just held in the Spring of 1918 and then routed in Haig's and his army's splendid "Hundred Days."

Haig emerges from history the dapper, taciturn soldier, untouched, undaunted and aloof. Yet, there is within that picture another man whose devoted post-war work for his demobilized men should not be seen as some sort of expiation of guilt over his failure to nurture them in war. In fact, this 'educated soldier', in John Terraine's admirably appropriate phrase, had, within the constraints of what was possible in 1917, striven for clear strategic objectives, while holding the Germans in battle. In the tragedies of wars and battles there is room for criticism of Haig, as of Ulysses S. Grant and other great captains, but when they lead men to victory it gives one pause for thoughts beyond denigration.

Notes

1   See John Terraine, *Douglas Haig: The Educated Soldier* (London, 1963), pp. 275–276.
2   See Leon Wolff, *In Flanders Fields: The 1917 Campaign* (New York, 1958), pp. 259–260; Victor Bonham-Carter, *The Strategy of Victory, 1914–1918* (New York, 1963), pp. 208–209.
3   At a meeting of the War Cabinet, 20 June 1917, Admiral Jellicoe stated that "there is no good discussing plans for next spring – we cannot go on." Shipping losses to German submarines, he said, would finish England. Haig, who was present, noted in his diary that this comment came as "a most serious and startling" revelation, "a bomb shell for the Cabinet and all present." "No one present shared Jellicoe's view," Haig noted. "and all seemed satisfied that the food reserves in Great Britain are adequate." "To say that this was a 'bomb-shell' was to put it mildly," observes John Terraine in *Haig*, pp. 333–334, and argues that Jellicoe's statement was "the turning-point of the meeting." Lloyd George challenged the Admiral, who stuck to his statement. Discussion of other plans in the meeting Terraine thinks "had now become academic, after Jellicoe's intervention," and various studies have suggested that the Cabinet finally approved plans for Third Ypres because of the sea threat. Robin Prior and Trevor Wilson, in *Passchendaele: The Untold Story* (New Haven and London, 1996), pp. 201–202 n.7, specifically excuse Haig from using this alarmist comment as a prop for his plans, but they wrongly suggest that the whole 'Belgian coast clearance' was an irrelevance.
    But the threat carried some argumentative weight. General Robertson, CIGS, in a "Memorandum *regarding future military* policy," written on 23 June, 1917 in response to Lloyd George's request for more thought about the Western Front versus the Italian Front, observed that "the Admiralty regard it as imperative that we should endeavour to clear the [Belgian] coast," and cites a memorandum, 18 June, from Jellicoe (copy in Haig Papers, H-114, National Library of Scotland). Haig used the argument in discussions with

General Nivelle on 24 April 1917, with French War Minister Paul Painlevé, and Prime Minister Alexandre Ribot on 26 April (Haig Diary). Jellicoe had, in fact, been sounding his alarm for some time. See Robertson to Haig, 26 April 1917, cited in Terraine, *The Road to Passchendaele: The Flanders Offensive of 1917, A Study in Inevitability* (London, 1977), p. 81. Admiral Sir Reginald Bacon, commanding the Dover Patrol, told Haig in January 1916 of the submarine menace and stressed the need to take the Belgian coast (Robert Blake, ed., *The Private Papers of Douglas Haig, 1914–1919* [London, 1952], p. 120).

4   See Alexandre Ribot, *Lettres à un ami, Souvenirs de ma vie politique* (Paris, 1924), pp. 174–177. For Haig's battles at Arras and Vimy Ridge, see Terraine, *Haig*, pp. 284–290, 288–289. See also General Robertson's memo of 23 June 1917: "It is admitted by the War Cabinet that we must continue to be active somewhere on the Western Front . . ." Copy in Haig Papers, H-114.

5   See, for example, Haig's response to Lloyd George's expressed "misgivings" about the military advice he received and his request for rethinking his recommendations for a Flanders drive, addressed to the CIGS, 22 June 1917, in Haig Papers, H-114.

For Nivelle's plans and fate, see Frank E. Vandiver, "Haig, Nivelle, and Third Ypres," *Rice University Studies* (Winter, 1971), pp. 79–80.

6   See Robertson's memorandum of June 23, 1917, cited above, and also Terraine, *The Road to Passchendaele* (London, 1977), p. 75, quoting a letter from Lord Esher to Haig, 21 April 1917, in which Lloyd George's changed opinion is mentioned. "It is almost comic to see how the balance has turned. For the moment I do not think *you* could do wrong."

7   See Terraine, *Haig*, p. 334; Holger H. Herwig and Neil M. Heyman, *Biographical Dictionary of World War I* (Westport, Connecticut and London, 1982).

8   See John Terraine, *Road to Passchendaele*, pp. 93–98.

9   Haig, in a memorandum to Robertson on 22 June 1917 (Haig Papers, H-114), summarized his view of German decline: 1. Shortage of manpower reflected by reduced size of German battalions and breaking up of new divisions to reinforce those in line; 2. Deteriorating economic conditions, reflected in worn field guns and equipment, iron cartridge cases replacing brass, shortages of telephone and telegraph equipment and ammunition, reduction of field rations; 3. "A marked and unmistakable fall in the moral[e] of German troops." These considerations led Haig to the conclusion "that the German Army has already lost much of that *moral* force without which physical power, even in its most terrible form, is but an idle show." He added that "the optimistic views I hold and the advice which I have given are justified by the present condition of our opponent's troops."

10 See OAD 449, 16 May 1917, a letter from Haig to Robertson, in Haig Papers, H-113.

11 OAD 434, 7 May 1917, Haig Papers, H-113.

12 See OAD 449, 16 May 1917, letter from Haig to Robertson, Haig Papers, H-113.

13 Edmonds J, Official History *France and Belgium*, 1917, *Volume II*, pp. 3–4.

14 For Plumer's 'looks' see Terraine, *Haig*, p. 308.

15 See Edmonds J, Official History *France and Belgium*, 1917, vol II pp. 19–20;

Terraine, *Haig*, p. 337; Prior and Wilson, *Passchendaele*, p. 59–51; Herwig and Heyman, *Biographical Dictionary of World War I*, pp. 167–168.

16 Prior and Wilson, *Passchendaele*, pp. 57–58.
17 The term is Terraine's. See his *Haig*, p. 315.
18 Quoted in Terraine, *Haig*, pp. 315–317.
19 The London *Times* covered the Messines fighting with remarkable accuracy. See the issues for 8 & 9 June 1917.
20 See Edmonds J, Official History *France and Belgium, 1917*, Vol II p. 87.
21 Haig Diary, 7 June 1917.
22 See Terraine, *Road to Passchendaele*, p. 121, quoting Hindenburg and Ludendorff.
23 See Edmonds J, Official History *France and Belgium, 1917*, Vol II pp. 89–90; Prior and Wilson, *Passchendaele*, p. 64.
24 See Haig Diary, 2 June 1917.
25 Haig Diary, 20 June 1917. See also Terraine, *Haig*, pp. 335–336.
26 Quoted in Terraine, *Haig*, p. 336.
27 Haig Diary, 28 June 1917.
28 For the swamp maps, see Terraine, *Haig*, p. 342.
29 According to the chief meteorologist at GHQ, "the rainfall directly affecting the first month of the offensive was more than double the average; it was over five times the amount for the same period in 1915 and 1916 (Terraine, *Haig*, p. 348).
30 Haig's concern for conserving manpower is shown by his careful discouragement of small, wasteful attacks.
31 Terraine, *Haig*, p. 354.
32 Quoted in Terraine, *Haig*, p. 370.
33 Casualties are in dispute. Edmonds J, Official History *France and Belgium, 1917*, Vol II pp. 361, puts British losses at 244,897 and estimates German losses at some 400,000. C. R. M. F. Cruttwell in *A History of the Great War, 1914–1918* (Oxford, 1934) says Passchendaele "cost us [the British] about 300,000 as against 400,000. Terraine, *Haig*, pp. 371–372, accepts the British total, but doubts German losses were so high. He returns to the subject in *Road to Passchendaele*, pp., 343–347, examines variant estimates, breaks out numbers for separate operations at Lens and Cambrai, and again accepts Edmonds' British total. After discussing problems inherent in assessing German casualties, Terraine guesses at a total of 260,400. Prior and Wilson, *Passchendaele*, p. 195, give a total of 275,000 British casualties and "just under" 200,000 German, but give no reason for arriving at these figures. Numbers obviously vary with sources. See, for instance, Herwig and Heyman, *Biographical Dictionary of World War I*, p. 178: "the British lost a further 400,000 casualties at Ypres." Leon Wolff, *In Flanders Fields*, p. 259, discusses the confusion of numbers and accepts estimates given in the *Statistics of the Military Effort of the British During the Great War*: British, 448,614; German, 270,710. His numbers triggered a stiff Terraine retort and analysis in *Road to Passchendaele*, pp. 343–344. A. J. P. Taylor, in *The First World War: An Illustrated History* (Harmondsworth reprint, 1987), pp. 192–194, lists 250,000 British casualties to 400,000 German, but adds "no one believes these farcical calculations." Denis Winter, in his controversial *Haig's Command: A Reassessment* (London, 1991), pp. 110–113, concludes that the Germans lost fewer men than the British. Cyril Falls, *The Great War* (Reprint, Norwalk,

Connecticut, 1987), p. 303, suggests 240,000 British casualties and 260,000 German.

34 See Terraine, *Road to Passchendaele*, pp. 205–206.
35 Quoted in Terraine, *Haig*, p. 385.
36 See especially Prior and Wilson, *Passchendaele*, pp. xiv–xv.
37 See Jackson, A, *Germany, the Home Front (2): Blockade, Government and Revolution*, in Cecil, H & Liddle, P H, *Facing Armageddon*, London, Leo Cooper/Pen & Sword, 1996.

Chapter Four

The German High Command

Heinz Hagenlücke

General Falkenhayn's dismissal and the appointment of General Field Marshal Hindenburg and Quarter Master General Ludendorff to the Third *Oberste Heeresleitung* (OHL) on 29 August 1916 meant much more than a mere shift of the personnel in charge.[1] The new High Command fundamentally changed the future conduct of German warfare in many ways. First of all, the OHL gave the order finally to halt the costly fighting around Verdun, to stop Falkenhayn's 'blood mill' once and for all. At the other focal point on the Western Front, the Somme, a tough, unyielding defence was built up, until the B.E.F. had to suspend its offensive there. Next, the operations against Romania were organized, operations which forced that country out of the war in 1916. Finally, the dangerous situation in the Eastern theatre where the Austrians were threatened by the Brusilov offensive, was stabilized. At the end of the year, the very severe crisis of the summer of 1916, when the Central Powers were confronted with a comprehensive offensive of the Entente on all fronts, had been mastered.

The OHL also introduced new fighting tactics and new defensive measures, re-organized and re-structured the army in a way that enabled the Germans to survive the following year on the Western Front and prepared to counter the British effort to break out of the Ypres Salient.

Hindenburg and Ludendorff, who had spent most of their time in the East up to August 1916, and were not familiar with the different circumstances in Belgium and Northern France, took their first journey to the Western Front shortly after their assignment. On 8 September, in order to get acquainted with the situation, a conference of high-ranking officers, divisional commanders and the Chiefs of the two *Heeresgruppen* (Army groups), Crown Prince Rupprecht[2] of Bavaria and the German Crown Prince, took place at Cambrai[3]. During the meeting, the officers illustrated the difficulties the Army had to deal with, the ever increasing shortage of reserves emerging as the main problem. Colonel Bronsart von Schellendorf, Chief of Staff of the Second Army who had fought that year on the Somme, pointed out that the young recruits especially often were not trained

45

enough for the fierce fighting. In consequence, they sustained the greatest casualties of all and this was partly responsible for the shortage in manpower.

During the horrendous *Materialschlachten* of 1916, on the Somme and at Verdun, the German troops indeed had suffered high casualties. In this context, there appeared for the first time the new expression *abgekämpfter* (fought-out) troops. The fighting power of the best divisions too had worsened in a way that severely threatened their efficiency. Colonel Max Hoffmann wrote that 'the feeling of absolute superiority of the German soldiers was lost, and signs of combat fatigue (*Kampfmüdigkeit*) and despondency (*Kleinmut*) were observed in certain quarters.'[4] After two years of constant heavy fighting, the German Army on the Western Front was in a condition which demanded the rehabilitation of its fighting strength by rest and refitting. Ludendorff admitted the bad situation, writing after the war: 'The endeavours of the year 1916 had been too much. The vigour (*Spannkraft*) of the troops had weakened under the enormous fire of the artillery and by own losses. On the Western Front, we were totally exhausted.'[5]

Having heard the complaints, the OHL decided to react. Ludendorff promised to do whatever he could to increase German industrial production and to take care of the manpower problem. The result of that was in a certain way the *Hilfsdienstgesetz* from December 1916, designed to increase industrial and agricultural production, to double or even triple the production of armaments, rifles, machine-guns, guns and *Minenwerfer*.[6]

In view of the bad shape of the troops, the OHL decided to choose a defensive attitude for the next stage of the fighting. Until then, it had been Falkenhayn's requirement that the first trench line should be held however great the human cost.[7] The German troops clung desperately to their positions, becoming easy prey for the enemy artillery. The forward line had to be defended by all means and if lost, recaptured immediately. Such was the British superiority in artillery that, many times, German counter-attacks had to be launched over completely destroyed front-line troops. The deep dug-outs and cellars the soldiers had built to protect themselves from the unrelenting enemy barrage often proved to be man-traps.

Given the experience of the Somme and Verdun, the OHL re-organized their defence, now practising a principle of elasticity and defence-in-depth.[8] The resultant deliberations concerning the defensive system were summed up in the manual *Grundsätze für die Führung in der Abwehrschlacht im Stellungskrieg* (Basic Principles for the conduct of the defence-battle in Position Warfare), issued 1 December 1916.[9] From now on, a retreat from the lines should be ordered, if they were too difficult to hold. If a long lasting shelling were to indicate a large-scale enemy attack, the outposts should leave the first trench and occupy so-called *Trichterstellungen* (shell-hole positions). In those lightly fortified shell-holes, groups consisting of just a few men should gather and continue the fighting. Once the enemy had taken their trenches, specially trained *Eingreifdivisionen* (counter-attack divisions) who were positioned shortly behind the front, were to expel the attackers and recapture it. Behind a lightly-held forward zone, a second line had to be built in a way to preclude a simultaneous artillery attack on both lines. The distance between the two positions should be from 4 to 10 kilometres. Between the first and the second line, dug-outs, heavy concrete pillboxes and other obstacles had to be erected, which could survive an enemy artillery attack. The skeleton of infantry defence was no more the rifle of the single soldier, but the machine-gun. In the first trench only very few machine-guns were posted, most of them were to be found in the second line. The co-operation between artillery and infantry had to be improved and this became a task for the Air Force. Special air force units, *Artillerieflieger-Abteilungen* and *Infanterieflieger-Abteilungen* were formed for aerial reconnaissance purposes. Their job was to observe enemy trenches and batteries and provide the necessary communication between artillery and infantry.

Of course, the Allied forces had held the initiative since the beginning of the Somme operations, so that there was nothing left for the German Army other than to remain on the defensive. Ludendorff, however, not only accepted this premise, but also changed tactics, the main concern being now to avoid any losses, considering the diminishing German manpower stock. The effectiveness of the new system will be discussed later.

During the winter of 1916, the prospects of further fighting were discussed. On 15 January 1917, a briefing at Cambrai took place. A memorandum submitted by General Kuhl, Chief of Staff of the *Heeresgruppe* Crown Prince Rupprecht was discussed by the Staffs of OHL and Prince Rupprecht's Army Group. It was Kuhl's firm belief that the Entente would seek with extreme energy in 1917 for decisive victory. On the Western Front, the French and British would scarcely use the same tactics they had employed in 1916, but would try to break through the German lines at two or three different places. Kuhl did not predict where precisely these attacks would occur but considered an Allied offensive in the Arras area was likely The German Army on the other hand was not in a state to attack, even very limited offensive operations were to be excluded. More than ever, the exhausted troops needed rest, relief and further training: 'It is not the old troops anymore we have to reckon with' he stressed, as many other officers did.[10] The Allied attacks would be so heavy and comprehensive that every *Ersatz,* human and material alike, was needed and could not be wasted in unavailing offensive actions: 'There is nothing left for us but to get ready for the defence against the attacks to be expected and for this purpose to bring the troops to the best possible condition and to renounce all offensive operations . . .'[11]

Ludendorff agreed to all points Kuhl stressed, since this had been his own opinion for a long time. In order to strengthen the front, Ludendorff announced that eight divisions would be transported from Romania to the West and some 13 new divisions prepared. As the culmination of the war was expected on the Western Front, the OHL moved from the former H.Q. Pless in Upper Silesia to the spa town of Bad Kreuznach.

The High Command's strategy for 1917 was simple. Given the Allied superiority in artillery, manpower and every other facility, all operations at the Western Front had to be defensive; the strategic initiative had to be left to the Entente.[12] This did not mean however that Germany would not seek a decisive success elsewhere. The submarines, the new *Wunderwaffe* of the Reich, should provide the victory at sea by starving out England. Thus the Army simply had to hold on at the front until the U-boats had brought England to her knees within six months, as the Admiralty firmly promised. Ludendorff believed in this promise for a considerable time. This meant that the two German submarine bases on the Flemish coast at Zeebrügge and Ostende had to be protected at all costs, although at the time there were a mere 30 boats at the disposal of the officer in command, Admiral von Schröder. These bases were very valuable for the Germans, considering the fact that there were only about 90 submarines operating in the North Sea, so that one third of the U-boat flotilla was stationed on the Belgian coast.[13] These submarines of the smaller B-I and B-II type largely operated in the Channel. A comprehensive retreat from the German lines in the coastal region was out of the question.

At Cambrai, new thoughts were given to a possible withdrawal into the *Siegfried-Stellung*, or Hindenburg-Line (Operation *Alberich*), which had been prepared from September 1916. The operations, starting on 16 March 1917 and accomplished three days later without any enemy intervention, are often considered as a military masterpiece[14]. They shortened the front from 170 to 125 kilometres, set free 13 divisions and 50 heavy batteries, thus providing the OHL with a valuable stock of reserves. Most of all, because of *Alberich* the Allies had to delay their spring-offensive.

After the withdrawal had been completed, the Western Army was then deployed in three major *Heeresgruppen*. The *Heeresgruppe* Crown Prince Rupprecht, consisting of 61 divisions including the Second, Fourth and Sixth Army, defended a zone which stretched from the Flemish coast to La Fère [on the Western Front 151 German divisions then stood against 196 Allied].

Finally, Ludendorff promised that new and better weapons would be handed over to the troops. Beginning in February, each company should receive three, later six, light machine-guns of the new MG 08-15 type and every battalion was to have 18 heavy machine-guns, greatly enhancing the fire power of the troops.

The official *Reichsarchiv* summed up the High Command's strategy for 1917: 'The focus of all thinking was the indubitably impending French and British assault against the German Western Front on the one hand and the hope of a quick result of submarine warfare on the other hand. The conclusion of the war seemed to be just around the corner.'[15]

In the spring of 1917 the German High Command was quite optimistic concerning the further course of the war. Ludendorff even mentioned in

June that the longer the war lasted the better for the Reich since the Entente would have to deal with great difficulties in securing the supply of ammunition.[16] The submarines seemed to fulfil their task in an excellent way, the Admiralty predicted that England would be down on her knees within a few months. Even as late as 20 August 1917, the Chief of the Admiralty, Holtzendorff, assured Crown Prince Rupprecht that by October Britain would be defeated![17]

On the other hand, the ongoing battles had inflicted further damage on the troops. From April to June 1917, the Army had suffered 384,000 casualties on the Western Front, among them 121,000 men killed or missing. From mid-April, bread rations for the troops had to be cut.[18] A crisis of manpower was once again impending, causing the OHL to reduce the *Ersatz* for the Eastern Front drastically. The shortage of ammunition was so critical that the OHL also had to deny quite a few counter-offensive operations which the local commanders in the West had strongly recommended.[19]

The large-scale spring offensive of the Allied forces started on 9 April 1917 – Ludendorff's birthday – when the British attacked at Arras, and captured Vimy Ridge. Following that, on the Aisne and in the Champagne, the Nivelle-Offensive began, but this was disastrous for the French and resulted in widespread mutinies among the French divisions.[20]

The Battle of Messines marked a prelude to the Battle of Flanders.[21] The British preparations for an assault at the Ypres front and near Wytschaete had been detected by the Germans comparatively early, by mid-April.[22] Consequently, defensive measures were stepped-up, especially the rearward position, the so-called *Flandern-Stellung* which was extended, the German positions here thus becoming perhaps the most fortified German front lines of all.[23] It was also noticed by the Germans that the full extent of their line was not a favourable position to defend. On 30 April 1917, General Kuhl recommended a withdrawal from this position, pointing out the negative experiences the German Army had undergone with similar positions during the Battle of Arras.[24] General Sixt von Armin, Commander in Chief of the Fourth Army, and von Lassert, Commander in Chief of the Group Wytschaete, as well as their Staff Officers, however, unanimously voted against his proposal. They argued that a retreat without a fight would have negative repercussions on the morale of the troops. Furthermore, withdrawal did not offer any strategic advantages. As Kuhl noticed quite correctly after the war, the true reason for their refusal was based on a general aversion to give up voluntarily even one inch of ground which had been captured.[25]

In the early hours of 7 June 1917, 19 heavy mines detonated under the German trenches at Messines Ridge, the detonation being 'the largest man-made explosion in recorded history'.[26] Immediately after the blasting, the British artillery opened fire and the infantry moved forward to the first German trench line, which was taken easily, the German troops being shocked and in total disorder.[27] A few hours later, the B.E.F. had captured the Messines Ridge.[28] The assembled *Eingreifdivisionen*, if they reached their objectives through the deadly British barrage at all, were thrown back. When the battle came to an end, seven days after the mines had detonated, the British had taken this valuable position from where the Germans had been able to observe all British movement and direct their artillery fire upon it.

As a consequence of the stubbornness of General Staff Officers, the German casualties at Messines were extremely high: more than 25,000 soldiers had been killed or wounded. With just one mighty punch the Entente had achieved a great success, although the Germans finally prevailed in maintaining at least their positions in the immediate rear. Since the enemy mining seemed to have diminished during the last weeks, nobody at the Fourth Army reckoned with an imminent blasting of the trenches and in this the British had achieved a valuable degree of surprise.

Furthermore, the sudden, unsuspected English attack had a negative effect on the morale of the German troops. Even the official *Reichsarchiv* had to admit that the moral influence of the blasting on the troops was more fatal than the actual casualties caused by it.[29] After the war, General von Kuhl observed: 'The Supreme Command of the Army Group was mistaken in not simply ordering the retreat, in spite of all objections. The German Army could have avoided one of the worst tragedies of the World War.'[30]

If Field Marshal Haig were really to have expected that the Germans would not recognise Messines as the first stage of his great offensive in Flanders, he was wrong.[31] On the contrary, the British main attack at Ypres had long been expected from the German side. Even the public in the Reich anticipated it.[32] In order to do everything that could be done to stand up to the expected Allied onslaught in Flanders and as a consequence of Messines, on 12 June 1917, the most experienced officer in defence matters, Colonel Fritz von Lossberg, was appointed Chief of the General Staff of the Fourth Army.[33] Albrecht von Thaer, Staff Officer at the Group Wytschaete, greeted his arrival at the Army's Headquarters almost enthusiastically: 'I consider it as a true blessing for the matter that Lossberg is in charge. He is a terrifically capable man, a first-class capacity. Everybody trusts him.'[34]

Lossberg's task was to organize and further strengthen the German defence in the elastic way Ludendorff required. Because of the seven-week interval between Messines and the start of the Allied operations on 31 July, Lossberg had more than enough time to do his job. He 'determined to turn the existing defences into the strongest on the Western Front.'[35]

On 16 July, the British started their bombardment of the German lines, indicating that a major offensive was near. Crown Prince Rupprecht noted that the preliminary barrage was even more intense than during the Battle of the Somme. The Germans, however, were prepared for this. The German artillery answered on 13 July with a furious counter-barrage, using the newly developed mustard gas against the British lines. The amount of ammunition that was fired *before* the battle had even started was tremendous. On 28 July, the Fourth Army expended 19 train loads of ammunition![36] All in all, the Army Group was optimistic that the British onslaught could be stopped. Again Crown Prince Rupprecht wrote in his diary on 31 July: 'I am awaiting the attack with great calmness, since on an attacked front we never have been provided with reserves so strong and well trained (*in ihre Rolle so gut einspielte*). . .'.[37]

On the eve of the battle, Crown Prince Rupprecht's *Heeresgruppe* comprised a total of 65.5 divisions: Sixt von Armin's Fourth Army held 10 *Stellungsdivisionen* (plus a cavalry division) at the front and 6 1/3 *Eingreifdivisionen* behind, 1162 guns (550 heavy guns) and roughly 600 aeroplanes. It is interesting to notice that the Germans used the interval Haig granted them between Messines and 31 July hugely to increase their troops, since in mid-June the Fourth Army had only got 12 divisions and 389 guns.[38] Still, apart from aerial resources, the Germans were outnumbered by approximately 1.5 to 1 in manpower[39] and 3 to 1 in artillery. Experience, however, had shown that such disparity did not necessarily guarantee victory for the attacker.

Finally, at 3.50 a.m. on 31 July 1917, the long expected Allied strike commenced, the infantry advancing behind a devastating creeping barrage. General Kuhl described his impression as follows: 'At dawn on 31 July, a hurricane of fire broke out as nobody had ever witnessed before. The whole Flemish ground trembled and seemed to be on fire. This was no simple barrage, it was as if hell had been let loose.'[40]

In the north, the French First Army advanced roughly 2500 yards while in the centre the British made quite an achievement in capturing Pilckem ridge, pushing their line further for about 3000 yards. On the right, however, things did not look so good for the British. The Second Army failed completely to take the key position of Gheluvelt Plateau. Although the Allied barrage had lasted for 14 days and destroyed most of the first lines and wire, many of the rearward German pillboxes, strongholds and machine-gun emplacements were still intact. Furthermore, the greater part of the batteries located in the woods and especially behind the Gheluvelt Plateau where they were hidden from direct British observation could not be suppressed and they concentrated their fire on the attacking British troops. Notwithstanding the Allied counter-battery, the Fourth Army artillery fired 27 train loads of ammunition on the first day of the battle.[41]

The Allied troops took the first German line and the outposts comparatively easily, but the *Eingreifdivisionen*, waiting near the village of Passchendaele, and not hit at all, began their counter-attacks, helping to bring the advance to a halt.[42]

In spite of this all, the Germans suffered considerable losses, too.[43] Albrecht von Thaer noted in his diary, that the first day of the battle witnessed a deadly fight unprecedented in the whole war: 'Whole divisions burn out to slag within few hours and one is crying for more, but they do not come.'[44] From the day of the preliminary British barrage to 31 July, the Fourth Army suffered 30,000 casualties; some batteries, especially heavy ones, were depleted down to 50%. Yet, the Germans had managed to stop the Allied attack, though losing about 2–3,000 yards of their own ground. Given the standards of the Western Front, this was a remarkable success for the Entente. However they had not accomplished their strategic aims, and this was largely because they had been unable to eliminate the German artillery. Some German officers even attributed their success to the alleged superiority of the German infantry.[45]

The breakthrough Field Marshal Haig had hoped for was far out of sight. Correspondingly, the German Army leaders, Crown Prince Rupprecht as well as Ludendorff, were satisfied with the way the battle had developed so far.[46]

The first stage of the battle ended on 31 July; then, heavy rain started, opening a season which provided the worst weather in Belgium for nearly 75 years. The battlefield turned into a gigantic swamp disadvantaging every further attack. The next major attack came on 10 August, when the British took the village of Westhoek but again failed to capture the Gheluvelt Plateau as a whole, and then on the 16th came the Battle of Langemarck.

Up to now, the German elastic defensive system had proved to be successful. Albrecht Thaer observed that the casualties suffered were much lower than at Arras or on the Somme, attributing this to Ludendorff's elastic defence system.[47] While on the Somme the average loss of a division after fourteen days of combat amounted to 4,000 men, at Third Ypres, at least in the beginning, it was only 1,500 to 2,000.[48] This had obvious repercussions on the troops: 'The morale of the troops is much better than last year', Thaer remarked on 23 August.[49]

Meanwhile, after the British disaster at Langemarck, Haig transferred responsibility for seizing the Gheluvelt Plateau from General Gough to General Plumer and the Second Army. Plumer changed the British tactics for the battle into a series of "bite and hold" actions to accomplish the strategic aims. As the frontal attack on the German lines had proved to be impossible, now a strictly limited series of steps, each step winning some 1000 yards, was to be undertaken to secure Allied objectives. Furthermore, the concentration of artillery was increased.[50] It took Plumer several weeks to make the necessary preparations.

The German Staff officers were confused by the fact that during that time, it was comparatively quiet at the front and could not explain the British idleness.[51] Albrecht von Thaer wrote in a letter from 4 September that it got almost boring there[52]; Rupprecht noted on 12 September that the battle seemed to have come to an end and considered relieving some of the divisions.[53]

This time, the Germans were utterly wrong. On 20 September, the third big attack began against Menin Road ridge with an unprecedented 8-hour creeping barrage. Despite furious counter-attacks, the British advanced

1500 yards on average and captured vital posts like Inverness Copse, Glencorse Wood and part of Polygon Wood.

Plumer's new strategy turned out to be extremely successful, causing very heavy casualties among the German troops, Ludendorff describing the British attacks as 'irresistible'[54]. For instance, from eleven counter-attacks the *Eingreifdivisionen* launched at Menin Road ridge, ten failed completely and one pushed back the British only a few hundred yards.[55] Not only had the divisions been held back too far, but they were smashed by Allied artillery and machine-guns before they could even attack.

The OHL was aghast. Against the new British approach to the battle, the Germans could find no remedy; the recapturing of ground once lost was impossible.[56] Albrecht von Thaer wrote on 28 September : "We are going through a really awful experience. I do not know anymore what to do in the face of the British."[57]

The High Command did not know what to do either, but had to react somehow. At the end of September, the OHL decided to modify defensive tactics by returning to the former system practised in 1916.[58] The thinly held forward zone was now again reinforced, concentrating more troops and especially machine-guns there; as little ground as possible was to be conceded.[59] As it had often been proved that the *Eingreifdivisionen* were held back too far, they were brought closer to the front.

The very bloody Battle of Broodseinde – a 'black day'[60] for the Germans – on 4 October – witnessed perhaps the heaviest German casualties of all. The reinforced first German line was virtually smashed by enemy infantry and artillery. The OHL came to the conclusion that the loss of ground was inevitable and turned back to their previously prevailing system. Sixt von Armin ordered on 7 October that the first trench line had to be held very lightly and 500–1,000 yards behind, a main battle zone was to be erected.[61]

This could not stop the British advance either but surprisingly enough, in spite of the bad news from Ypres, Ludendorff was more optimistic than ever. On 6 October, he told Rupprecht by phone that the military situation was 'favourable' and assured him that Germany would eventually win the war by the end of the year, if the Army only would hold its positions in Flanders.[62] The *Heeresgruppe*, however, did not share Ludendorff's assessment. In mid-October, Rupprecht even considered a comprehensive withdrawal into the *Flandern-Stellung* in order to save men and material, which would have included the abandonment of the Navy bases at Zeebrügge and Ostende. This, however, was out of the question, since the submarines were just about to bring final victory to the Reich – at least in Ludendorff's judgement.

At this critical situation, the weather got worse; heavy rain again diminished, in particular, the effect of the artillery, reducing its capacity to destroy all the strongpoints, pillboxes and wire. Bad weather, in general, favoured the defender rather than the attacker; rain became, as Rupprecht noted, 'our most effective ally.'[63]

Still, the battle raged, with heavy fighting at Poelcapelle and around

Passchendaele itself. Ludendorff observed that the British were storming like a 'raging bull' against the German lines.[64] On 6 November, the 2nd Canadian Division finally took Passchendaele, the Germans trying in vain to throw them back. On 10 November, all operations came to a halt, because the weather conditions made any further action futile and the Entente was about to launch an offensive at Cambrai, supported by a great number of tanks.

The British had gained 4½ miles of ground at Ypres since 31 July, but moved themselves into such an unfavourable position, that in spring 1918, when the Germans launched their great offensive, the BEF had to evacuate all those gains within three days.

The OHL's land strategy for the year 1917 was not unreasonable. Hindenburg and Ludendorff clearly recognised that the worn-out troops were simply not in a condition to launch a major offensive against the Allies in the West. Their superiority in manpower, equipment and ammunition could not be matched. Thus, the Army had to remain on the defensive, the first principle being to avoid unnecessary losses. For this reason, the new system of elastic defence was created and the divisions were meticulously trained for it. It is fair to say that the German Army in the West was well prepared for its defensive battles.

Once the British altered their strategy after Plumer had gained control, elastic defence, however, proved not so effective. It seemed as if all tactical innovations, all steps taken to strengthen the defence, could not stop the methodically attacking Allied troops. Indeed, elastic defence 'stopped the bleeding, but did not stop the haemorrhage'.[65] Under the circumstances of overwhelming Allied superiority in artillery, there seemed to be no way to stop their offensive.

If the decision to remain defensive on land were wise, the decision to declare unrestricted submarine warfare was not reasonable at all, since it would, sooner or later, provoke the Americans to enter the war, in the end sealing Germany's fate. But the OHL considered it to be the only way to secure victory for the Reich in 1917.[66]

Since the submarines were to force Britain to peace in 1917, the Navy bases in Flanders had to be protected and as Ypres was the key to the ports, the High Command had little room for a possible retreat. Although the figures differ slightly, one can assume that roughly one third of the German submarines fighting in the North Sea and the Channel was stationed in Flanders. On the other hand, in October 1918, when the war was already lost, Admiral Scheer assured Chancellor Max von Baden that the loss of the Flemish ports had no real influence on the submarine operations.[67]

It should be also noted that the annexation of Belgium was one of the most important Kriegsziele (war aims) the OHL fostered, mainly for military reasons. Moreover, a huge part of German society itself deemed the annexation of the country as very valuable, so that there were also political reasons why Flanders, the symbol of German control of Belgium, could not be given up.

Whatever British records may have revealed later, the OHL attributed Haig's choice of Flanders as the place for the large Allied offensive because of the success of the U-boat campaign starting on 1 February 1917.[68] In July, the U-boats had sunk 811,000 gross tons – according to the German sources.[69] The submarines in the Channel, however, were unable to fulfil their task and could never really disturb the transport of British goods and men to the Western Front.

The German military strategy of 1917 was never discussed outside GHQ with politicians and civilians, the Chancellor, the *Reichstag*, or other institutions. Unlike Britain, where an intensive debate of military operations and objectives took place, no German civilian ruler ever had to give his consent to military operations planned by OHL. This was partly due to the fact that in Germany there was no Imperial Defence Committee, War Policy Committee, War Cabinet or any other institution that co-ordinated civilian policy and military strategy. Given the semi-constitutional structure of the German Empire and the dominance of the military in wartime, no one dared to question the decisions of the High Command. Traditionally, the Chancellor, by appointment bearing responsibility for German policy, did not take an active role in strategic planning; not even Bismarck had done so. Theoretically, Wilhelm II was *Oberster Kriegsherr* (Supreme Warlord) and responsible for the conduct of the war, but he had little influence.[70]

Furthermore, no one in Germany except a few Generals really knew the situation in Flanders. Wilhelm II, for instance, was not informed about the casualties sustained there before 20 August, when the Chief of the *Militärkabinett*, General Lyncker, prompted Sixt von Armin to tell the Kaiser that the fighting had cost the Fourth Army 84,000 losses.[71] On one of the very rare occasions when the *Oberste Heeresleitung* revealed military matters to politicians, no real information was given. When Hindenburg and Ludendorff met with two Reichstag deputies in July 1917 in Berlin during the crisis which led eventually to Chancellor Bethmann Hollweg's dismissal, they talked to them in a general manner, pointing out that the military situation was very favourable.[72] Even while the battle was causing heavy losses amongst the German troops, the OHL was more optimistic than ever that the war would be won soon, Ludendorff even transferred several divisions to the East in late-summer 1917, while the battle in Flanders was still going on.

Third Ypres cost the German Army about 217,000 casualties, with the serious loss of experienced officers: division after division was involved in the battle, roughly half of the German Western Army. Although the British losses were much higher, the Germans could not replenish their manpower reserves in the way the Entente could. From 1918 onwards, American troops would appear on the battleground.

The Passchendaele experience to a certain degree caused Ludendorff to discontinue the defensive attitude of 1917.[73] Just one day after the battle had come to an end, on 11 November 1917 at the Mons Conference, he proposed a major offensive in the year 1918, – the *Michaels-Offensive* – which was designed to secure German victory before the Americans had built up their Army in France. In the event the offensive was to fail and it paved the route to defeat in November 1918.

It has been stated that Third Ypres was the 'worst ordeal of the World war'[74]. Perhaps it was even the most violent *Materialschlacht* of the whole war, as a German officer remarked 10 years after Passchendaele.[75] The outcome of the battle has been considered a huge achievement for the German Army, since in the end the Allies did not break through the German lines. However, the casualties sustained there had inflicted such irreparable damage to the troops, that their fighting power was never fully restored: "The former sharp German sword became blunt".[76]

On 5 December 1917, Crown Prince Rupprecht issued the following order, praising all soldiers who fought during Third Ypres: 'The huge battle in Flanders seems to have come to an end . . . The sons of all German tribes have competed among themselves for heroic bravery and tough tenacity and made the English and French attempt to break through a failure . . . In spite of the unheard of mass-deployment of men and material the enemy has gained nothing. So the Battle of Flanders is a heavy defeat for the foe, for us it is a great victory. Who took part in the battle can be proud of being a *Flandernkämpfer*. Every single combatant can be assured of the gratitude of the Fatherland.'[77]

Notes

1   For the circumstances of Falkenhayn's dismissal see Holger Afflerbach: *Falkenhayn. Politisches Denken und Handeln im Kaiserreich.* München 1994, pp. 437–450 and Karl-Heinz Janßen: "Der Wachsel in der Obersten Heeresleitung 1916", in: *Vierteljahrshefte für Zeitgeschichte* 7 (1959), pp. 337–371.
2   The Army Group was created by Falkenhayn on 25 August 1916.
3   Asprey, pp. 268–69.
4   Hoffmann, vol. II, p. 157.
5   Ludendorff, Erinnerungen, p. 230.
6   Gunther Mai: *Das Ende des Kaiserreiches.* München 1987, pp. 95–105; Asprey, pp. 279–286; Gerald D. Feldman: *Armee, Industrie and Arbeiterschaft in Deutschland 1914 bis 1918.* Berlin/Bonn 1985, pp. 133–206 (Original version: *Army, Industry and Labour in Germany 1914–1918.* Princeton, New Jersey 1966).
7   Rupprecht, vol. III, pp. 110–11.
8   For the German tactical doctrine cf. T. Lupfer.
9   Printed in Ludendorff, Urkunden, pp. 601–640; Reichsarchiv XII, pp. 38–39. Asprey, p. 273, gives a false date of the issue.
10 Reichsarchiv XI, p. 506. This was the shared belief of every staff officer, cf. Kuhl, p. 9. Rupprecht wrote in a letter to the OHL from 27 September 1916: 'It is unmistakable that our infantry is not the same any more.' Rupprecht, vol. II, p. 107.
11 Reichsarchiv XI, p. 508.
12 Kielmansegg, p. 509.
13 Andreas Michelsen: *Der U-Bootskrieg.* Leipzig 1925, pp. 182–185.

14 Groener, p. 420.
15 Reichsarchiv XI, p. 510.
16 Rupprecht, vol. II, p. 226.
17 Rupprecht himself commented: 'The gentlemen of the navy are dangerous optimists.': Vol. II, p. 248.
18 Reichsarchiv XIII, p. 22–23.
19 Reichsarchiv XIII, p. 29.
20 Asprey, pp. 303–310. The mutinies as a result of the violation of the "Live and let live" principle are discussed by Tony Ashworth: *Trench Warfare 1914–1918. The Live and Let Live System*. London 1980, p. 224.
21 For the details see Reichsarchiv XII, pp. 425–476; Beumelburg, p. 24–25.
22 Kuhl, p. 112.
23 Ludendorff, *Erinnerungen*, p. 332.
24 Kuhl, p. 113: Rupprecht, vol. II, p. 155–156.
25 Kuhl, p. 114.
26 Prior/Wilson, p. 61.
27 Rupprecht noted on 10 June that the blasting had caused a panic among the troops. Rupprecht, vol. III, p. 165.
28 Admiral Müller noted on 8 June 1917, the news from Messines had caused quite a depression at GHQ. Müller, p. 292.
29 Reichsarchiv XII, p. 454.
30 Kuhl, p. 114.
31 Prior/Wilson, p. 51.
32 Thaer, p 123 (20 May 1917); Lossberg, p. 294; Beumelburg, p. 28; Rupprecht; v. Einem, p. 318; MacDonald, p. 87. Secretary of War von Stein for instance informed the *Hauptausschuß* of the *Reichstag* on 3 July 1917 that a major Allied offensive was expected in Flanders: *Der Hauptausschuß des Deutschen Reichstags 1915–1918*. Eingeleitet von Reinhard Schiffers. Bearbeitet von Reinhard Schiffers und Manfred Koch in Verbindung mit Hans Boldt. Vol. III, p. 1480.
33 Lossberg, p. 293; Beumelburg, p. 28.
34 'Er ist eben doch ein mordstüchtiger Mann, eine erstklassige Kraft': Thaer, p. 126.
35 Prior/Wilson, p. 71.
36 Rupprecht, vol. II, p. 231.
37 Rupprecht, vol. II, p. 232.
38 Reichsarchiv XIII, p. 54.
39 The strength of a British division at that time was much higher than a German.
40 Kuhl, p. 121.
41 Rupprecht, vol. II, p. 232.
42 Prior/Wilson, pp. 86–96.
43 Kuhl, p. 122.
44 'Ganze Divisionen brennen in wenigen Stunden zu Schlacken aus und man schreit nach neuen, die nicht kommen.' Thaer, p. 130. The phrase "Zu Schlacke verglühen or ausbrennen" emerged during the *Materialschlachten* of 1916, meaning that although a unit had survived a fight physically, it was no more in the condition to continue the combat mentally.
45 So did General v. Einem in a letter from 20 August 1917: Einem, p. 332.
46 Hoffmann, vol. I, p. 174 (Ludendorff being content with the outcome of the battle); Thaer, p. 131 and Rupprecht, vol. II, p. 232.
47 Still, Crownprince Rupprecht's *Heeresgruppe* lost 2020 officers and 83508

Mannschaften (enlisted) between 1 June and 10 August. Rupprecht, vol. II, p. 247.
48 Rupprecht, vol. II, p. 235.
49 Thaer, p. 134.
50 Prior/Wilson, p. 115.
51 Kuhl, p. 123.
52 Thaer, p. 136.
53 Rupprecht, vol. II, p. 260; Ludendorff, *Erinnerungen*, p. 389.
54 Müller, 30 September 1917, p. 323.
55 Prior/Wilson, p. 121.
56 Thaer, p. 138.
57 Thaer, p. 139.
58 Beumelburg, p. 120–121.
59 Rupprecht, vol. II, pp. 269–71.
60 Beumelburg, p. 122.
61 Reichsarchiv XIII, p. 80; Beumelburg, p. 125.
62 Rupprecht, vol. II, p. 268. Ludendorff repeated this on 13 October, Rupprecht wondering what could have led him to believe this.
63 Rupprecht, vol. II, p. 271.
64 Ludendorff, *Erinnerungen*, p. 392.
65 Paul Kennedy: "Military Effectiveness in the First World War", in: Allan R. Millet/Williamson Murray (Eds.): *Military Effectiveness. Volume I: The First World War*. London/Sydney/Wellington 1988, p. 343.
66 Ludendorff, Erinnerungen, p. 245.
67 Conference in Berlin 17 October 1918: Ludendorff, Urkunden, p. 569; Bauer, p. 246.
68 The military communiqué of 1 August 1917 declared that the British wanted to destroy the 'U-boat plague' which was undermining England's naval supremacy from the Flemish coast.
69 Terraine, p. 210, citing Lloyd George, gives the figure of 359,000 gross tons sunk.
70 Cf. Wilhelm Deist: Kaiser Wilhelm II. als Oberster Kriegsherr, in: Wilhelm Deist: *Militär, Staat und Gesellschaft*. München 1991, pp. 1–18.
71 Müller observed that this figure did not seem to have made a great impression on Wilhelm II; Müller, p. 314.
72 Meeting from 14 July 1917: *Die Reichstagsfraktion der deutschen Sozialdemokratie 1898–1918*. Zweiter Teil. Bearbeitet von Erich Matthias und Eberhard Pikart. Düsseldorf 1966, p. 305.
73 Kielmansegg, p. 355.
74 Kuhl, p. 129.
75 Beumelburg, p. 7.
76 Kuhl, p. 131; Ludendorff, *Erinnerungen*, p. 392.
77 Beumelburg, p. 168.

Part II

Problems, Plans and Performance and British Operational Command

Chapter Five

The Tactical Problem: Infantry, Artillery and the Salient[1]

Paddy Griffith

The Great War was the first conflict outside Manchuria to use the full new generation of weapons that had been developed during the 1880s and 1890s. These weapons and related aids included smokeless powders and magazine rifles; Maxim guns; quick-firing artillery with high explosive shells, hydraulic recoil systems and an accurate indirect fire capability; barbed wire, telephones and even radios. To them the Great War itself would add trench mortars, flamethrowers, gas and tanks, as well as a comprehensive bestiary of aircraft designed for every imaginable type of military use. Many of these weapons had been extensively discussed before 1914 by the men who would fill the highest ranks in the armies of the war – but, before the cataclysmic event itself, it had always been very difficult to discern just how each weapon would work on an actual battlefield. In particular it would be impossible to determine the full psychological effect of the new weapons, and their interaction one with another. It was not known, for example, whether the machine gun or the motor cycle would prove to be the more important on the future battlefield, or whether soldiers born in towns would sustain the nervous shock of high explosives better than those born of peasant stock in a tranquil rural environment.

The answers to these questions would not be revealed until a very large number of infantrymen had been fed, more or less as 'guinea pigs', into a grandiose but awesomely clumsy experiment in military technology. That experiment was always foredoomed to be a massive human tragedy, but from the point of view of the technician it did at least have the virtue of defining and fixing the key features of the 'Art of War' for the whole of the remainder of the twentieth century.[2] By the second half of 1917 those features were on the road to being well-known and well understood, and tactical planning was being based on much more sophisticated principles than it had been during the badly-managed first two years of the war.

In essence there were three ways to launch an assault under the new conditions of combat. The most seductive but also the soonest discredited,

61

S E C R E T.

B.M.33/5

12/13 Northd Fus.
1 Lincoln R.
10 York R.
3/4 "The Queens" (RWS) R.
62 M.G.Coy.
62 T.M.Bty.

NOTES ON CONFERENCE HELD AT BRIGADE H.Q. ON 29th & 30th SEPT. 1917.

1. Impress on all ranks the importance of keeping into our barrage. The only means of knowing whether troops are sufficiently close to the barrage is when casualties are inflicted by our own artillery.

2. As soon as strong points are seen, they should be rushed at once. Experience proves that the enemy show little resistance if this is done.

3. If strong points are used as shelters by our troops after capture, it is better to remain on our side of them, rather than inside them.

4. Shovels should be carried by all assaulting troops with the exception of the leading platoons of the attack, who should be as lightly equipped as possible.

5. On October 3rd, machine guns which have been placed at the disposal of battalions should be employed against low flying aeroplanes.

6. Posts must be pushed well forward down forward slopes to cover consolidation, to get a good view and break up counter-attacks.

7. The lines given in Operation Orders should be consolidated

    (i)   By connecting up shell holes into Platoon Posts.

    (ii)   At night form a continuous line.

    (iii) Rear lines must be made as strong as possible.

    (iv) When counter-attack goes forward rear line must be occupied immediately by troops in rear.

8. **Counter-attacks.**

    (i)   Supports and local reserves of battalions will counter-attack immediately on the initiative of local commanders.

    (ii)   Support battalions will counter-attack on the initiative of the Commander.
        After final objective has been taken 3/4 "The Queens" (RWS) Regt. will be Support Battalion and will detail two companies as a support to 12/13th Northd Fus. and two companies as a support to 10th Yorkshire Regt.
        Support Battalion Commanders must keep in close liaison with the local reserves to the sector he is covering and attack immediately if he finds the local supports and reserves have not succeeded in repulsing the enemy. He must, however, be careful not to engage and break up his force prematurely.

(ii) Tactical Considerations. Conclusions drawn from a 62nd Infantry Brigade Conference to prepare operational orders for the Battle of Broodseinde on 4 October. *(K.A.Oswald, Liddle Collection)*

not least by the 'first day' of the Somme, was for the artillery to destroy the enemy first, after which the attacking infantry could occupy his positions without difficulty or danger. The problem with this was that it required an absolutely stupendous and logistically impossible number of heavy shells to destroy all the inhabitants and wire obstacles of even a relatively small section of trench defences. Even then the job could not be done without the creation of major additional obstacles in the form of a morass of shell craters – which at Ypres often became lethally waterlogged. Before the autumn of 1917, furthermore, the British had no certain means of neutralizing the enemy's artillery, which lurked inaccessibly at long ranges, yet provided at least half the effective defence for the enemy's front line trenches. However thoroughly these front line positions might themselves be pulverized by the attacker's artillery therefore, no more than fifty per cent of their dangers could be destroyed unless good counter-battery fire could also be provided.

The second way to launch an attack was for the infantry to do the whole business on its own, in the traditional (or 'colonial') manner, relying mainly on the firepower and cold steel that it could itself carry forward. Losses would clearly be higher if the infantry had to *fight* forward rather than simply occupying empty ground; but to counterbalance this risk there did seem to be some distinct potential advantages in an 'infantry only' attack. In particular it would bypass several higher echelons of command and control, such as the need for constant close liaison with artillery or reliance upon detailed and rigid timetables and master-plans. It allowed local initiative and instant problem-solving by platoon commanders who, under the conditions of the Great War, would encounter delays of many hours if they were to try to pass signals back and forth across the mile or two of ground that separated them from their infantry brigade HQ or artillery regimental HQ.

No one in 1914 had ever believed that unsupported infantry could simply march forward across an empty No Man's Land to fight forward exclusively with its own resources. The power of modern weapons was known to make such a tactic suicidal, and in the event – despite copious subsequent statements to the contrary – the troops were very rarely ordered to do it. [There were doubtless far too many unfortunate occasions on which expected support failed to materialize at the right time and place or when the cover of the terrain proved to be inadequate, thereby producing an impression that the infantry had been asked to do the impossible]. Nevertheless there remained many circumstances in which a covered approach actually could be made with a realistically high expectation of success – whether at night or in fog; down trenches or ditches; through woods or villages, or by short rushes from one shell hole to another. By late 1916 it had unexpectedly been found that a particularly good time for such attacks was in the full daylight of mid-afternoon, when the enemy was likely to be sleeping off the cumulative effects of his night-time fatigue duties, his dawn *Stand To* and his mid-morning breakfast.

SECRET.   B.M.62/107

12/13 Northd Fus.
1 Lincoln R.
10 York R.
3/4 "The Queens" (RWS) R.
62 M.G.Coy.
62 T.M.Bty.

_____

1. All battalions must be ready to interchange positions
    should circumstances compel such a course.

2. The two leading companies of the attacking battalions will
    advance as light as possible, therefore they will not carry
    shovels. The washing kit will be very light. Nothing super-
    fluous will be taken.

3. Greatcoats will be carried forward until Zero day. The
    method of carrying is left to C.Os. They will be dumped
    before Zero hour, in any way, as directed by C.Os.

4. The 1st Lincolnshire Regt. will make arrangements to carry
    out the attack on the 1st objective should circumstances
    compel such a change.

5. While there is a moon bayonets will not be fixed by any
    troops except the usual front line posts and immediate
    supports.

6. The dividing line for the advance of the 62nd and 64th
    Brigades on the final objective will be the visible trees
    on the northern side of JUDGE COPSE.

7. As many officers as possible will take compass bearings on
    their final objectives.

8. Baggage of units will be dumped in Transport Camp.

9. Although the wire is reported light, Battalions will take
    care not to forget wirecutters.

10. The utmost care will be taken over the question of guides.
     The routes must be continuously patrolled before and after
     the attack. They must be marked out by posts, tapes, and
     any other means which C.Os can think of.

11. Owing to enemy bombing at night protecting walls must be
     built for the horses and mules at once. The men may either
     dig down or build walls for themselves.

12. When C.Os move their Battn. H.Q. they must always remember
     to inform Bde. H.Q. the position of their new ones at once.

Capt,
Bde. Major,
62 Infantry Bde.

1-10-17.

(iii) "While there is a moon bayonets will not be fixed . . ." Preliminary Orders
for the 62nd Infantry Brigade before the Battle of Broodseinde. (K.A.Oswald,
Liddle Collection)

There were still many circumstances, in other words, in which it was not suicidal for infantry to try to fight forward on its own. The need for infantry to be trained in this skill therefore remained a high imperative in every army throughout the war, and in fact the techniques themselves by which it might be achieved tended to move forward in leaps and bounds. The initially crude ideas of purely linear mass attacks interspersed by elephantine pauses 'to establish fire supremacy' were quickly superseded by the intense experience of trench raiding by small groups during 1915, with the result that by 1916 there was already an impressive body of 'stormtroop' doctrine available for the infantry of every army on the Western Front. A whole new armoury of light machine-guns, bombs and mortars was created for its use. By its nature however, such warfare had to depend on small scale local initiatives. It could nibble away at the enemy's dominance of No Man's Land and could often capture a few of his front line positions, but it did not make a reliable technique upon which large scale co-ordinated offensives might be planned by Corps, Army or Expeditionary Force HQs.

For the full grand opera of mass assaults at Army level or above, the lessons of the Somme had shown that there was in fact a third way which had not been fully identified during the fumbling first two years of the war, mainly because it must have seemed so complicated and difficult to any peacetime army. Its essence was to combine a dauntingly large number of technically separate elements, each of which took a considerable effort of trial and error to develop. First there was a great game of deception and surprise connected with the assembly of the assault troops opposite the point of attack. This undertaking would achieve its crowning glory only at Cambrai on 20 November 1917 when all the artillery fire could at last be predicted from the map, without the need for pre-registration shoots that would betray both the number and the position of the guns and hence the central fact that a major offensive was being planned in that particular sector. At Messines and Third Ypres this technique had not yet been brought to full maturity, so other associated deception measures were likely to fall short of their required effectiveness. In particular the unexpectedly over-prolonged two week preparatory bombardment before the 'first day' of the Third Ypres battle, 31 July, gave away practically all the surprises that the Allied command would have hoped to spring, and which in fact they often did spring in their offensives from November 1917 onwards.

Second, the increasing range and volume of accurate artillery by the middle of 1917 meant that the preliminary bombardment could act in an interdiction role, as it had already at Messines, in order to cut off the front line enemy soldier from the rear, 'so that he cannot bring up ammunition or replace guns and cannot bring up food or stores without suffering serious loss. To keep him short of food. To reduce his morale.'[3] Even if surprise could not be achieved, in other words, the hope was that the front line enemy soldier could at least be prevented from making any particular use of that fact. Linked with this there was a further sophistication in the minds of British artillery planners, when they made a clear distinction between cratering and non-cratering ammunition. They would hope to use either shrapnel or the new No.106 instant percussion fuse for HE shells to minimize pre-battle cratering on any ground that friendly infantry would eventually have to cross. Many exceptions remained, however, and delayed action / maximum cratering shells would still take up over fifty per cent of most fireplans throughout Third Ypres.

Third, and perhaps most important, the infantry's close artillery support after the Somme was no longer intended to destroy the enemy or his fortifications, but merely to neutralize him for a relatively short period of time. The front line enemy troops would be numbed and forced down to the bottom of their shelters by a comprehensive 'creeping barrage' consisting of as many as eight lines of bursting shells, one behind the other to around 2,000 yards in depth, and along many miles of frontage, all marching

```
S E C R E T.                OPERATION ORDERS NO. 87,      Copy No......//....
                                 by Lieut. Col. A.C. Corfe, D.S.O.,
   Ref: Map ZILLEBEKE         Commanding 11th Bn."THE QUEEN'S OWN"
        6A. 1/10,000.         Royal West Kent Regt.(Lewisham).

                                                     11th September, 1917.

   3. FORMATION &      (a).  The attack will be made in depth, the leap frog
      METHOD OF              method being followed.
      ATTACK.
                       (b).  The Battalion will attack on a 2 Company Front,
                             with 2 platoons of each Company in front line,
                             the remaining platoons, or platoon per Company
                             following behind as support or Company Reserve.
                             The order of attack will be from right to
                             left.-
                                  1st WAVE........."B" Coy.   "C" Coy.
                                  2nd WAVE........."D" Coy.   "A" Coy.

                       (c).  The Battalion will advance in this order behind
                             15th Bn. Hampshire Regiment at sufficient
                             distance not to become involved in their attack,
                             with the 12th East Surrey Regiment on the right.
                                  On capture of BLUE LINE  they will assemble
                             behind it, then close up under the barrage to
                             attack the GREEN LINE which will be captured
                             and consolidated by "B" and "C" Companies.
                             "D" and "A" Companies will consolidate a line 200
                             to 300 yards  in rear of GREEN LINE.
                                  The Supporting or Reserve Platoons  of each
                             Company will in all cases consolidate  150 yards
                             in rear of their respective Companies giving
                             depth to the defence.
```

(iv) Battle Operation Orders for an attack in September 1917 towards Tower Hamlets (see also the associated map shown opposite). The order and the accompanying map are among the papers of D.J.Dean, at the time a platoon commander in the 11th Bn Royal West Kent Regiment. The vertical pencil mark on the map is where Dean has scored over his battalion's start line. *(D.J.Dean VC, Liddle Collection)*

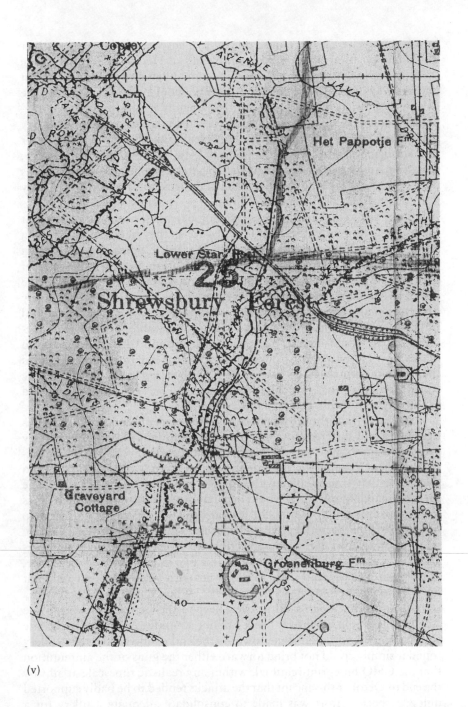

67

forward in step to a pre-arranged timetable. They were designed to smother the enemy positions with judicious mixtures of HE, shrapnel and smoke shells, as well as mortar bombs, machine-gun bullets and anything else that might be available. This numbing barrage would advance through the enemy position at infantry pace, so that friendly troops following immediately behind it could hope to move forward relatively unscathed. They could reach enemy dug-outs before the defenders could rise from the floor to man their weapons. From the point of view of the advancing infantry, therefore, attacking a numbed enemy was found to be almost as good as attacking an enemy who had been totally destroyed – and certainly a very great deal better than attacking without any artillery support at all.

In the Third Ypres battle these creeping barrages, normally planned at Corps level, were often every bit as effective as they had been at Arras in April 1917 and at Messines on 7 June. At Third Ypres they also often included a major 'endgame' phase of consolidation, in which the walls of shells would be maintained in depth for a considerable time, ahead of the positions won by the infantry in their advance. Especially when timely observation and reporting could be sustained, this standing barrage could inflict crippling damage upon the almost inevitable German counter-attacks that would attempt to re-gain lost ground.[4] It did not seem to matter how close to or far from their initial front line the Germans placed their counter-attacking reserves to re-take their front line positions: the Royal Artillery could normally smash them to pieces before they could regain any significant trench that they had lost.[5]

In all these ways the creeping barrage was a very great tactical innovation; but it still suffered from one central limitation. This was that its very success meant that as soon as a particular group of guns had won a particular piece of ground for the infantry, those guns would normally find themselves left behind effective range for any subsequent advance. The forward march of the battle would then have to be delayed until such times as the artillery could be brought forward to support the next great leap forward. In GHQ's initial predictions for the Third Ypres battle, including its plan for 31 July, each such repositioning (or each 'bite and hold' operation) was assumed to need something like two or three days.[6] In practice, however, it was found to require rather nearer a week each time, and not infrequently something nearer two weeks. When Plumer's Second Army took over from Gough's Fifth, even despite the better weather of late August, the whole hand-over needed about a month. And then, in the late October period of liquid slime towards the end of the battle, the artillery found it simply could not bring forward either the guns or the ammunition that the GHQ blueprint required, within any realistic timescale at all.[7] By the end of October this meant that the attacks tended to be badly supported unless a special effort was made to consolidate adequate artillery for a particular push on an ever-narrowing frontage, as General Currie insisted there should be for the Canadian assault on Passchendaele village. Even then, however, the creeping barrages still ran the risk of moving forward faster than the infantry could follow over the treacherous ground. Whereas in dry conditions a 'creeper' and its infantry might comfortably advance 100 yards in about four minutes, by the end of this battle even 100 yards in twelve minutes could be too fast for the infantry to keep up.[8]

The sheer scale of the artillery support required for this type of battle was quite prodigious. The total weekly expenditure of shells for the BEF as a whole during the four months of Third Ypres ran at between two and three million, of which some two thirds must have been fired in the area of the salient, making something like 33,000,000 shells overall in this one battle. The Germans believed that at Ypres they were outnumbered in guns by some three to one (approx.3,500 vs 1,200), later falling to two to one; but in shells it was by a factor of six to one. By October they were complaining of a distinct shortage of ammunition.[9] To this we can add a British estimate that the RFC dropped eight times as many bombs from aircraft as the *Luftwaffe* did.[10]

The raw balance of numbers, of course, provides far from the whole story. The German artillery was notorious for its converging, and therefore concentrated, fire from around the outer circumference of the salient. It also had its observers on the higher ground, whereas the British guns were relatively exposed in the lower ground, and inevitably firing outwards in a much less concentrated way. The Germans also enjoyed a threefold advantage in the use of gas shell: firstly in terms of doctrine, in that they were ahead of the British in understanding the effective counter-battery use of this munition; secondly in technology, in that they already had mustard gas whereas the British did not; and thirdly in tactical posture, in that as defenders they were happy to use persistent gas on the battlefield – ie mustard – since they would not need to send their own soldiers over the contaminated ground whereas the British, as the attackers, would always have to do so. Admittedly the British had the prevailing wind in their favour, and would themselves make great advances in the use of gas shell as this battle unfolded; but that would come too late to ensure a decisive superiority for their artillery in the initial counter-battery duel during the two weeks of bombardment before 31 July. German mustard gas therefore administered a technological surprise on the British during that first phase, and prevented their greatly superior artillery from crushing its German opposite numbers in the way that had been hoped. When the British infantry attack was finally launched on 31 July, it found it was already working in a less than ideal artillery environment, even before the start of the rains.

The Germans hoped to tip the balance still further by deploying only a relatively weak and thinly-spread infantry defence in the forward zone of the battlefield, so that much of the initial British artillery fire would fall either on empty space or on garrison troops whom their commanders considered 'expendable'.[11] This forward screen would still nevertheless be able to inflict some disorganization and damage on the British infantry following behind their creeping barrage, who would then be vulnerable to violent counter-attacks by higher-quality, undamaged German formations coming from the rear. This system of dynamic defence had worked dramatically well against the ill-starred French Nivelle Offensive in April, but at Third Ypres it turned out that the effects of the German counter-attacks were often very much less significant than their planners had hoped, particularly in the face of superior British artillery. Time after time the Germans would find they were sacrificing their 'expendable' first line divisions without being able to cash in, with their counter-attack divisions, on the sort of dramatic scale of pay-back that the sacrifice had been designed to achieve. The limited 'bite and hold' expectations that the British had learned by this time meant that BEF attacks were usually halted and consolidated at the point when they had overrun the German first line system but had not yet over-extended themselves in the way the Germans would have preferred. Moreover, on the rare occasions when the German counter-attacks did manage to make contact with the attacking infantry, as on 31 July itself, they tended to meet quite well-prepared opponents, and so they found themselves involved in scrappy dog-fights rather than in the crushing break-throughs that their planners had envisaged. The peculiar intensity of the fighting at Third Ypres may perhaps be explained as much by this carefully-calculated balance of high aggressive intention from both sides simultaneously, as it may be by any other factor.

'Other factors' were, of course, not difficult to find. The most obvious, clinging and all-pervasive one was the mud. It messed up the first part of the battle in August and the last part of the battle in late October and November, slowing down both sides equally but always working more in favour of the defender making his stand than the attacker trying to move. When the ground was relatively dry, as on 31 July and in the period from late August to early October, the BEF found it could make encouraging advances. At other times it encountered grave difficulties in moving absolutely anything that needed to be moved across the battlefield, regardless of whether that meant hay-boxes or mules; stretcher cases or rum-jars; artillery shells or small arms ammunition – or even the supposedly 'all terrain cross country vehicles' that were the tanks. Some 300 tanks bogged down and sank into the mud during this battle, and such few tactical successes as were gained with them can only be described as 'paltry'. The grim revelation that tanks could not operate off the roads in conditions of heavy rain at Ypres certainly came as something of a body blow to many who had previously believed they could do anything, go anywhere, and had virtually limitless possibilities.

Another contributory factor in the 'friction' facing British attacks was the deep German understanding of concrete. This was of particular importance in the Ypres area, since the water-table was often so high that digging trenches downwards was impracticable. Field fortifications therefore had to be built from the ground upwards, and so concrete pill boxes and shelters became invaluable. The Germans established successive lines of such structures throughout the whole depth of their defences, many of which may still be inspected today. The memoirs of their British attackers – and eventual occupants – are eloquent of the unique strength and shelter that they alone could provide in the lethal but otherwise featureless landscape of this battlefield.[12]

It was perhaps precisely because the pill boxes stood out so obviously as landmarks that on 7 October, following their 'black day' at Broodseinde on the 4th, the Germans switched to a concept of basing their defence more upon scattered machine-gun teams thrown forward of the main line and also, it was hoped, of the main British barrage.[13] The idea was that these microscopically small individual tactical units would escape destruction by artillery, and spring to life on the flanks and rear of the attacking infantry as it swept past. They did admittedly have some successes but in general they amounted to just one more desperate expedient which could not hope to reverse the inevitable trend of the battle.

The British fought and won Third Ypres by virtue of the dominance of their artillery and the endurance of their infantry. Despite the awful conditions and the various tactical surprises that the enemy continued to spring, the 'bite and hold' system kept on moving doggedly forward until it finally ran out of momentum in November. The gains from each 'bite' were not perhaps spectacular, and Haig certainly continued to be impatient for bigger breakthroughs and greater mobility almost up to the end. Nevertheless, by this time the BEF had developed a workable system of offensive tactics against which the Germans ultimately had no answer. It was only unfortunate that the same could not be said of British defensive tactics in March 1918.

Notes

1   This chapter is based upon the author's *Battle Tactics of the Western Front* (Yale University Press, London and New Haven, Conn., 1994); British Official History (OH) 1917 Vol.2; the insights contained in Shelford Bidwell and Dominick Graham, *Firepower: British Army Weapons and Theories of War, 1904–45* (Allen and Unwin, London, 1982), as well as in the works of Robin Prior and Trevor Wilson. PRO documents in the WO 158 series were also very useful, as were the seven essays edited by the author in *British Fighting Methods in the Great War* (Frank Cass, London 1996). In addition to the writers of those essays he would especially like to thank John Hussey, as well as John Bourne, Andrew Grainger, Bill Rogan, Peter Scott, Andy Wiest and everyone in the Western Front Association and other organizations who have been kind enough to discuss these matters with him.

2   A fascinating 1990s 'operational art' perspective is to be found in J B A Bailey, 'The First World War and the birth of modern warfare' in *The Occasional* (SCSI, The Staff College, Camberley), no.22, 1996.

3   PRO WO 158–208, Second Army circular 29 August 1917: 'General Principles on which the artillery plan will be drawn', paragraph ii.

4   Eg Lord Moyne, *Staff Officer: The diaries of Lord Moyne 1914–18* (edited by Brian Bond and Simon Robbins, Leo Cooper, London 1987), pp.168–9.

5   See OH 1917 Vol 2, pp.259, 272–3, 290, 277, 304, 318; G C Wynne, 'The development of the German defensive battle in 1917, and its influence on

British defence tactics' in *Army Quarterly*, 1937 Vol.34: April, pp.15–32 and July, pp.248–266 and Vol.35: October, pp.14–27. See also German Official History, *Der Weltkrieg 1914–18* Band 13 (1942) pp. 77–80 (translated by Colonel R.Macleod as *Great battles fought during the first world war, 1914–18: Flanders 1917.*

6   Brigadier J H Davidson 22 June in PRO 158–20, item 128; and document of 26 June in Appendix XXV to OH 1917 Vol.2 p.436.

7   PRO WO 158–250 and –251, Fifth Army conferences, 31 August to 10 November, make an eloquent testimony to the difficulties Gough and his staff encountered when they tried to 'adapt the shell-pocked sodden ground to our needs'. In essence they discovered that not one class of weapon in their armoury could work effectively when the mud was deep.

8   PRO WO 158–251, item #17, Fifth Army conference 30 October, reporting 58 Division's loss of its barrage.

9   *Abstract of Official Statistics of the Military Effort of the British Empire during the Great War, 1914–20* (HMSO, the War Office, March 1922), p.408 ff.; and *Der Weltkrieg, op cit.*, Vol.13 pp 62–3, 73, 96, 99.

10   PRO WO 158–209: Second Army corps commanders' conference, 24 October.

11   Wynne, *op.cit.*, April 1937, p.22.

12   For example, Charles Carrington, *Soldier From the Wars Returning* (London, Hutchinson 1965), pp.191–7.

13   *Der Weltkrieg, op cit.*, p.80.

Chapter Six

Passchendaele: The Maritime Dimension

Geoffrey Till

Before the war, there had been an unprecedented explosion of theoretical and conceptual interest in the nature and conduct of war. Many of the theorists had taken a particular interest in the British case, either because they too were British or because, like Mahan, they took Britain as a template for other countries. When the war came, British experience seemed to confirm much of what many of them had predicted.

Firstly, there were the bleak assessments of the geographer Sir Halford Mackinder. Most famously in his address before the Royal Geographical Society in 1904 entitled "The Geographic Pivot of History" but in other writings too, Mackinder argued that the maritime British were facing an uncertain future because of the relentless march of new technology.[1] In the shape of railways, for example, this was revitalizing the continental powers against which Britain had historically been pitted, making them more secure against sea-based attack, better able to mobilize their human and material resources and better able to exploit some of the vulnerabilities of maritime Britain. Just after a decade later, in the Spring of 1917, a continental alliance led by Imperial Germany seemed to be on the point of making this all come true. The situation seemed grim indeed, as Lord Beaverbrook later observed:

> The submarine peril was indeed deadly. The year of 1917 opened on a scene of desolation and anxiety. The survival of Britain hung in the balance. On the land, the great forces of German military power massed themselves for an offensive on the Western Front. At sea, the striking power of the U-boat accumulated a terrible intensity. The toll of shipping, with the Channel routes open to constant attack from bases at Zeebrugge, mounted with every month.[2]

Anticipating something of the sort, Mackinder had warned of the necessity for Britain to make the most of its Imperial resources, both material and human, and to consider entering into continental coalitions. A hostile

73

Eurasian land-power, like Russia or Germany, should be confined to a land strategy as much as possible. "A purely oceanic policy is possible even for an insular Power only under temporary conditions which are passing away . . . "[3]

Accordingly, Britain had entered into a continental coalition, fielded a mass continental-style expeditionary army, making extensive use of Imperial manpower, and in the Summer of 1917 launched the second of its major assaults on the German army. And, in part at least, this was motivated by the situation Britain seemed to be facing at sea. "The Army," Admiral Beatty told his wife in April 1917, "are doing all they can to win the war, and we are doing our best to lose it, which is heartbreaking."[4]

The notion that British security could only be founded upon a constructive combination of its sea and land forces working in imaginative conjunction was central to the other great school of British strategists represented by, as they later became, the Navy's Sir Julian Corbett and the Army's Major-General Sir Charles Callwell. Both, in varying degrees, sought to:

> . . . establish the principle that sea-power is generally dependent up to a certain point upon military force, and that it may in certain conditions be reduced to impotence without its aid . . . There is a connection between land-power and sea-power which sailors and soldiers alike are apt to overlook, and which extreme schools of naval thought and of military thought sometimes try to ignore.[5]

Their broad conclusions were two-fold. First, the British should emphasize what would now be called "jointery" in the habits of thought and the style of war that both the Army and the Navy developed. Second, Britain's war-leaders should locate areas for the projection of power where the inherent cost-effectiveness of an expeditionary approach based on the Royal Navy and an Army especially shaped to co-operate with it, could best be deployed. This had been the rationale for the Gallipoli campaign of 1915. Thus Corbett:

> As it was likely that the situation would shortly develop into one of stale-mate, and a successful offensive in the main theatre would be impossible for the Allies until they had greatly increased their supply of men and munitions, it was necessary to consider whether we could not seek decisive results elsewhere.[6]

The Gallipoli campaign, however, had failed not so much through faulty conception as through bad implementation. There was nonetheless a continuing interest in finding theatres of war, or indeed operations of war, in which the principle could be re-applied. At the strategic level during the Passchendaele campaign, this found expression in Lloyd George's continual preference for a switch of resources to Italy, or even for a renewed pressure on Turkey. At the operational level it was illustrated by the sustained interest in the idea of a combined coastal and amphibious assault on the Flanders coast. So how was it that practice came to conform to theory in this perhaps unexpected way?

EMERGENCE OF THE THREAT

The catalyst for the British declaration of war upon Germany in 1914 was the invasion of neutral Belgium. Because it was a "dagger pointed at the heart of England," the British were always particularly sensitive to the menace implied by seizure of that part of the European coastline by any potentially hostile power. The threat soon materialized and Britain's unsuccessful attempt to hold the line at Antwerp was the first response. On 1 January 1915, Churchill pointed out the consequences of failure:

> The battleship *Formidable* was sunk this morning by a submarine in the Channel. Information from all quarters shows that the Germans are steadily developing an important submarine base at Zeebrugge. Unless an operation can be undertaken to clear the coast and particularly to capture this place, it must be recognised that the whole transportation of troops across the Channel will be seriously and increasingly compromised.[7]

In the last Summer before the war, Sir Arthur Conan Doyle, echoing the earlier claims of the French *Jeune Ecole*, had warned the readers of the Strand Magazine that a small Continental power with 16 submarines could destroy British commerce and force the Government to an abject peace. Because the Channel was so narrow, so thick with merchant ships and so close to enemy bases, the threat of U-boat attack was particularly serious there.

The scale of the threat slowly grew until the Summer of 1916 and then began to accelerate through the autumn as the number of U-boats grew and as the larger and more capable UB II boats became part of the Flanders Flotilla. By October 1916, as Jellicoe told the First Sea Lord, "... the menace of the enemy's submarine attack on trade is by far the most pressing question at the present time."[8] Soon after, Jellicoe was himself appointed as First Sea Lord largely to deal with the submarine problem. Through the winter months, the situation worsened. U-boat numbers steadily increased, between 300–350,000 tons of ships were lost a month from October 1916 to January 1917 and, even more ominously in some ways, the ship-tonnage laid up under repair from previous attacks began to clog Britain's ship-yards. In the harsh terms of attritional warfare between industrialized powers, the exchange ratio between U-boats lost and the merchant ships they sank, worsened, day by day. Public confidence in the Admiralty's capacity to cope with this level of damage atrophied.

And then, on 1 February 1917, the Germans took the risk of alienating neutral opinion and renewed their style of submarine warfare which was "unrestricted" in that it did not adhere to the prize rules which had so restricted U-boat effectiveness before. On that day, 23 of the German

Navy's 105 operational U-boats were based in Flanders. The new campaign was immediately successful. Allied losses shot up to 520,000 tons in March 1917 and an appalling 860,000 tons in April. The exchange ratio was 1 U-boat to 53 merchant ships in February, 1:74 in March and a terrible 1:167 in April. This level of loss far exceeded Britain's capacity to recycle previously damaged ships, build new ones or acquire merchant tonnage from other sources. By the end of May, the net annual rate of depletion of British shipping had reached the disastrous level of 25 per cent.[9]

By all the indicators, April 1917 was the month of crisis and, both the level of tonnage lost and the numbers of operational U-boats at sea, settled down subsequently to levels which while not quite catastrophic remained very serious indeed for months to come.

Not surprisingly, the situation was regarded by everyone concerned as extremely serious. Jellicoe himself was amongst the most publicly pessimistic. As early as 19 February, just over a fortnight into the unrestricted submarine campaign, he pointed out:

> It will be seen from a consideration of these figures that the position is exceedingly grave. It is perhaps within the powers of those responsible for the import of food and munitions into this country to state how long we can continue to carry on the war if the losses in merchant ships continue at the present rate.[10]

Jellicoe's comment illustrates what was thought to be the most serious strategic consequence of the U-boats' success – the prospect of an inability to feed the country, supply its war industries and support its expeditions overseas with the declining stock of merchant ships that had so far survived the U-boat campaign. The problem was aggravated by the fact that bad harvests had increased Britain's dependence on Australian grain, which was particularly expensive in shipping terms.[11] Jellicoe's pessimism about both the existing situation, and even more the prospects for the Spring and early Summer of 1917, when weather conditions were likely to increase U-boat effectiveness, led the War Cabinet on 23 March to think the unthinkable, and at least to discuss what Britain might have to do "to secure a reasonable peace."

But, in point of fact, most politicians and most soldiers, while they accepted the fact of the level of loss [a matter of objective fact], did not believe the consequences were as bad, in terms of remaining and projected food-stocks, as Jellicoe seemed sometimes to be making out. And there was indeed, a lack of consistency over time, even a certain imprecision, in Jellicoe's estimates of Britain's future capacity to feed and supply itself.

When on 10 April, Jellicoe showed his new American ally, Rear-Admiral Sims, the real shipping loss figures, he told the startled Sims, 'as quietly as though he were discussing the weather' [at least according to Sims] "It is impossible for us to go with the war if losses like this continue." When Sims asked whether there was a solution, Jellicoe replied: "Absolutely none that we can see now." This was not only a comment about the current effectiveness of the German submarine onslaught, but also, even more worryingly, a bleakly pessimistic view about the Navy's capacity to do very much about it.[12] Such a view, if accurately represented, seemed to confirm all the pre-war prognostications to the effect that new technology would allow Eurasian land-powers to enlist these advances to exploit the critical vulnerabilities of maritime powers.

Thus Haig's reaction to Jellicoe's presentation to the War Policy Committee of 20 June 1917:

> A most serious and startling situation was disclosed today. At today's conference, Admiral Jellicoe, as First Sea Lord, stated that owing to the great shortage of shipping due to German submarines, it would be impossible for Great Britain to continue the war in 1918. This was a bombshell for the cabinet and all present. A full enquiry is to be made as to the real facts on which this opinion of the Naval Authorities is based. No one present shared Jellicoe's view, and all seemed satisfied that the food reserves in Great Britain are adequate. Jellicoe's words were, "There is no good discussing plans for next spring – we cannot go on."[13]

Despite such uncertainties, there was general agreement that the U-boats had brought about a serious situation which, of course, endangered Britain's supplies, but also could undermine its capacity to sustain offensive operations elsewhere. This applied not only to far-flung theatres like Salonika or the vulnerable outer reaches of the Ottoman empire; it could apply even more critically to Britain's capacity to support its army on the Western Front.

This had always been a major concern. The point was that the U-boat was but one aspect of the general naval threat presented by the German Navy. The destroyer and patrol boat flotillas based in Flanders were also a real menace – especially when in conjunction with a renewed U-boat campaign. During the winter of 1916–17, they came out about once a month, attacking transports in the Channel and disrupting the anti-submarine barrage that was intended to stop U-boats breaking out into the Atlantic. Apart from the actual damage they inflicted, they forced the British to maintain their guard in the Channel with forces that might otherwise have been deployed against U-boats elsewhere, or acting in support of the Grand Fleet. Jellicoe was also perfectly aware of the corollary. The more the general U-boat threat sucked the Navy's light forces out of the Channel, the more vulnerable would the Army's supply lines be to local German attack.

There were already between 2 to 3 German destroyer flotillas usually available for such operations in the Channel – a significant force. They could, and did, choose the time and circumstances for a foray; they often caught defending British forces unprepared, struck and were gone before a proper response could be prepared. As Bacon remarked, "It is as easy to stop a raid of express engines with all lights out at night, at Clapham

Junction, as to stop a raid of 33 knot destroyers on a night as black as Erebus in waters as wide as the Channel".[14]

So far, admittedly, such activity had been more of a nuisance than fatal and in fact the celebrated action of the *Swift* and the *Broke* on the night of 20–21 April 1917 caused the Germans to close down their raiding policy for 10 months. But, when he spoke to the War Policy Committee on 20 June 1917, Jellicoe did not know this was the case and expressed his strong concerns about what would happen if the Germans ever realized the extent of the opportunity within their grasp. He was worried,

> that immense difficulties would be caused to the navy if by the winter the Germans were not excluded from the Belgian coast . . . The position would become almost impossible if the Germans realised the use they could make of these ports. The enemy already had three squadrons of destroyers based on Zeebrugge and might increase them to six. If he came out in a concentrated force he could wipe the ships on patrol out of existence. The largest force which he had hitherto sent out at a time was one flotilla, and that was divided. If he came out concentrated he could sweep up the naval forces on patrol, which never exceeded a strength of 7 destroyers and 2 flotilla leaders. He could also attack the French craft, monitors, and the cross-channel coastal traffic.[15]

Haig's reliance on the supplies brought across the Channel made him receptive to all such concerns. As one of his earliest biographers remarked:

> Throughout 1917, the Allied policy, and especially the British policy, was to force a military decision quickly, lest we should be forestalled by the success of the German submarine campaign . . . The successes of the German submarines during 1917 represented a great peril and were, as is well known, the cause of deep and increasing anxiety. They provided a new and most potent argument for the Flanders offensive.[16]

WHAT HAD GONE WRONG?

One commodity, at least, was not in short supply – namely the attribution of blame for what had evidently gone so wrong. Most popular of the explanations by far, both then and since, was the sheer incompetence of the Admiralty particularly under the stewardship of the First Lord, the "Ulster Pirate" Sir Edward Carson[17] and the First Sea Lord, Admiral Jellicoe. The political establishment under Lloyd George was particularly critical. According to Colonel Charles Repington, on 9 February 1917, "Lloyd George said that the Admiralty had been awful, and that the present submarine menace was the result . . . He thought that the apathy and incompetence of the naval authorities were terrible. I asked him why he did not hang somebody."[18]

The criticism could be as severe from within the Navy too, not least from Admiral Beatty, Commander-in-Chief of the Grand Fleet who mourned the fact that, "Unfortunately, the sphere of their activity is outside my domain and I am reduced to hurling insults at them".[19]

While the War Cabinet Secretary Sir Maurice Hankey, could certainly share these views, he also viewed the problem from a much larger and rather more sophisticated perspective. The day before Lloyd George's outburst to Colonel Repington, Hankey wrote in his diary, "My prophecy seems to be coming true, that our military effort would so far exhaust us that we cannot maintain our sea forces and our economic position".[20]

The point had been made by both British schools of strategy before the war. Britain's maritime vulnerabilities had forced her into an uncharacteristically heavy investment in the mass warfare style of the Continent. Arguably, Britain had struck the wrong balance between the maritime/expeditionary and the continental dimensions of its defence policy. Arguably, the costliness and, so far at least, the failure of this approach, had sucked so many resources away from the maritime/expeditionary approach advocated by Corbett, that an indifferent performance at Jutland in 1916, and against the new threat posed by the U-boats a year later, was perhaps the not unexpected result.

It was certainly true, that while Lloyd George took a dim view of Jellicoe's general level of competence, he was unimpressed by Haig, and the style of warfare he thought Haig represented. Lloyd George was constantly looking for some other form of warfare where strategic effectiveness could be bought at a less terrible price in blood and treasure. After the war, progressives like Liddell Hart drew exactly the same conclusion. The real explanation for the dreadful events of 1917 both on land and at sea was to be found not in the alleged professional incompetence of Britain's military leaders [although if true, that would certainly have exacerbated the problem] but in the much wider sphere of grand strategy.

Of course, the many and varied solutions to the crisis of spring 1917 that were proposed, and tried, tended to reflect assumptions about what was the main cause of the problem.

SLOW GLOBAL SOLUTIONS

One of Jellicoe's problems was not only that he could offer no single solution to the U-boat menace but he candidly admitted that one probably did not exist. This was a profoundly unwelcome response to those who hoped for a simple and rapid solution and this made him politically vulnerable. Jellicoe's point, though he rarely expressed it well, was that naval warfare simply could not be reduced to the few simplistic formulae and answers which so many of his critics seemed to expect.

As Balfour had remarked the previous year, "We must for the present be content with palliation . . . [since the submarine menace is] . . . an evil which unfortunately we cannot wholly cure."[21] Instead, the response to the threat that the U-boat posed in the Channel and elsewhere, was in fact a whole package of measures. Some were not the Admiralty's responsibility, including, for example:

- the acquisition and repair of replacement tonnage from as many sources as possible
- rationing of the food and supplies to be carried to and from Britain
- a review of Britain's overseas commitments which required heavy support in shipping [particularly Salonika]
- improving the speed and efficiency with which merchant cargoes were loaded and unloaded at ports, and indeed received from, or despatched to, their inland destinations.

The naval response would also need to be comprehensive and varied, particularly in view of the fact that until the arrival of effective depth charges and ASDIC, it was very difficult to detect and sink submerged submarines. Offensive mine-laying across the various routes that U-boats would have to take to get from their bases in the North Sea and the Channel to the open sea had a role to play. And so, it was thought, did offensive patrolling in areas where merchant shipping was concentrated, particularly in the Western Approaches and the Channel. In a fox-hunting Navy, this response had an instinctive appeal[22] and special hunting detachments of destroyers and patrol boats were maintained at Devonport and Portsmouth for the purpose.

But experience was to show that U-boats, like foxes, often escaped. Newbolt in the Official History tells of one operation in early September 1916 when two or three U-boats managed to sink over thirty British and neutral vessels without suffering any losses in a restricted sea area apparently covered by 49 destroyers and a similar force of patrol boats.[23] Even the Channel, in fact, was quite a big place.

But the real criticism was of the Admiralty's failure to implement the ancient strategy of convoy-and-escort as early as it could have done. This is a huge topic beyond the scope of this chapter, but three points should nevertheless be made. First, it was not self-evident that the ancient strategy of convoy-and-escort was, in fact, applicable in the age of steam and of submarines. The otherwise perceptive Corbett for one thought it was not.[24] Second, the level of escort required was unclear; but what was clear was that the necessary escorts would need to be taken off other apparently essential activities such as protecting the Grand Fleet or mounting hunter patrols. Access to American bases and ports, after the entry of the United States into the war on 6 April 1917, would certainly improve matters.

Third, early experience of convoys in fact was more ambiguous than many of its critics charged. The experimental ones on the Dutch routes [where ambush from the Flanders destroyer and U-boat flotillas was a particular problem] and the French coal trade were carried out in waters which were also heavily patrolled by offensive hunter groups. Secondly, even when convoy-and-escort was introduced, overall losses remained quite high.

And this was the real point. Jellicoe was at least right in arguing that there was no quick and easy solution. While there is certainly substance in the view that he could and should have introduced convoy-and-escort earlier, it was true that the whole combined package of measures was needed to reduce the U-boat threat to more manageable proportions. Moreover, this was a process which inevitably took a good deal of time. The exchange ratio fell back to 1:73 in May, June and July, a level which looked good only in comparison with the catastrophic situation in April. Tonnage losses remained high and even by the very end of 1917, the total level of shipping available was still declining.[25]

So, even in the Spring and early Summer of 1917, and even after the grudging introduction of convoy, the long term situation remained extremely unclear and distinctly worrying. Long term solutions were, in fact, going to be exactly that.

QUICKER LOCAL SOLUTIONS?

Evidently, the Channel was a particular problem, both in its peculiar importance to the British war effort, and in the level of threat the Germans were able to extend against it. It was understandable, then, that many sailors should be interested in dramatic acts against the Flanders ports from which the German submarines and destroyers operated.

This notion fitted in with the long established tenets of orthodox maritime strategy, which held that attacking the bases from which commerce raiders operated [a policy often described in such bucolic metaphors as "stopping the earths" or "stamping out nests"] was much more effective than mounting defensive or offensive patrols on the open oceans. "Those who advocate the small cruisers on patrol," wrote Fred T Jane, "are really no more logical than he who would suggest that instead of destroying the nest, individual hornets should be slain on the wing."[26]

Specifically, two sorts of maritime action were contemplated. The first was bombardment of Zeebrugge and/or Ostende from the sea. This possibility was widely discussed. At the seventh and eighth meetings of the War Council on 8 and 13 January 1915, for instance, the bombardment of Zeebrugge had been suggested. Fisher, then First Sea Lord, had been against it.

Asked whether the bombardment of Zeebrugge would materially lessen the risks to transports and other ships in the English Channel, Lord Fisher replied that he thought not. In his opinion the danger involved in the operation [in loss of ships] would outweigh the results . . . Lord Fisher said that the Navy had not unlimited battleships to lose, and there would probably be losses in any attack on Zeebrugge. He objected to any attack on Zeebrugge without the co-operation of the Army along the coast.[27]

Some sailors were keen to try, however. Zeebrugge was bombarded on November 23 1914 for an hour by the 3rd Battle Squadron in a bid to dissuade the Germans from turning it into a U-boat base. Damage was done but German preparations continued. Vice Admiral Bacon at Dover favoured the bombardment option and was allowed to try his luck against the Bruges canal lock gates at Zeebrugge on 12 May 1917 and Ostende docks on 4 June, but to no lasting significant effect. The trouble was that the lock gates and the port installations were difficult to hit and relatively easy to repair. Moreover, the Germans could always pull their submarines and destroyers back up the canal to Bruges, out of harm's way, should the need arise. To have a lasting effect Zeebrugge and Ostende would need to be *regularly* bombarded.

This would be difficult to organize because the bombarding squadron would have to be defended against German mines and counter-action at sea. Additionally, Ostende and Zeebrugge were in fact arguably one of the most strongly fortified sections of the European coastline and were protected with large coastal guns in an era when majority opinion in the Navy held that modern technology had if anything strengthened the Nelsonic dictum that sailors who attacked forts were fools. As usual, Callwell had made the point before the war, " . . . the opposition of valuable fighting ships to batteries on dry land is not in accordance with sound principles of strategy or of tactics".[28] The Dardanelles experience seemed to have shown him to have been right.

The second option was some kind of blocking operation, in which the Zeebrugge and Ostende exits from what was the real U-boat/destroyer base at Bruges 8 miles inland, could be sealed. Admiral Lewis Bayly had been amongst the first to advocate such an operation in the autumn of 1914, and Admiral Tyrwhitt of the Harwich Force proposed a plan to land a raiding party on the Zeebrugge mole which would then move on to attack the canal lock gates. When this was turned down by Admirals Jellicoe, Bacon and Oliver, he went on to propose an even more ambitious scheme to seize the whole town and use it as an advanced base for an advance on Antwerp.[29] Bacon considered this impractical, preferring the bombardment option. Keyes, however, was more sympathetic to the idea and later developed his own scheme, which turned into the famous St George's Day raid of 23 April 1918.

It was generally thought, and with some justification, that, like the bombardment option, a blocking operation would only effect temporary relief, even if it were successful. Such was the conclusion of Admiral Duff's Anti-submarine Division in February 1917. Jellicoe agreed, telling Beatty in June, "I have got myself much disliked by the Prime Minister and others because I have urged the necessity for this operation and *not* a purely naval bombardment, or rather plus it, and have pointed out that a naval bombardment will never turn the Hun out of Zeebrugge and Ostende".[30]

Only the physical capture and retention of Ostende and Zeebrugge promised what Jellicoe thought he needed. Again this was entirely in line with Callwell's conclusions about, ". . . the same fundamental principle of naval warfare, that the guerre de course can be best checkmated by capturing the bases on which the cruisers of the enemy depend".[31]

And it was here that what was later to be called the "British Way in War" would surely be at its most effective. Its advocates produced a vision of the Army and Navy advancing together, closely co-operating at every step, in a combined operation that would both turn the German flank and capture the Flanders ports. It might even shorten the war and demonstrate the superiority of the British approach to warfare over land-bound continental alternatives. There were two elements to the proposition.

First, the Army would help the Navy command and exploit the seas by capturing the ports from which serious threats emanated. This was what the Navy had wanted from the start. The idea of an overland offensive to clear the Belgian coast and avert the potential maritime threat its ports represented, was much discussed from mid November 1914 to January 1915 when it was overtaken by the much more ambitious Dardanelles operation. Thereafter, the scheme languished and the First Sea Lord rather unfairly complained,

> We are trying to get the Military to advance along the Belgian coast and to try to take Ostende, from which we can bombard Zeebrugge, but they are apathetic ... It is quite extraordinary to me that the Military seem to expect the Navy to be at their beck and call, and do exactly what they want, without any attempt at reciprocation.[32]

As the maritime threat from the Belgian ports worsened, Admiralty interest in such an operation grew, and in November 1916, the War Committee gave the notion top priority: "There is no operation of war to which the War Committee would attach greater importance than the successful occupation, or at least the deprivation to the enemy, of Ostende and especially Zeebrugge".[33]

But the second element of this combined strategy was the corollary of the Admiralty's stress on the Belgian ports, namely the extent to which the Navy could help the Army secure its strategic objectives. This had also been evident from the start. When in the autumn of 1914 after the fall of Antwerp, the German Army had streamed westwards along the Belgian coast, the Navy had been important in helping the Allies hold the line at Nieuport. As Callwell had remarked a few years before, "The importance of naval control in campaigns which have territory bordering on the sea for their scene of action can hardly be exaggerated. It may govern the whole course of the conflict and may decide the issue".[34]

As though to demonstrate the point, in October 1914, Churchill offered Sir John French an inviting prospect of a combined counter-stroke against the German advance:

> If you chose to push your left flank along the sand dunes of the shore to Ostende and Zeebrugge, we could give 100 or 200 heavy guns in absolutely devastating support. For four or five miles inshore we could make you perfectly safe and superior. Here at last you have their flank – if you care to use it: and surely the coast strip held and fed well with troops would clear the whole line out almost to Dixmude and hand it

right back, if it did not clear it altogether. If the attack were quick and sudden, their big guns would all be caught too. We could bring men in at Ostende or Zeebrugge to reinforce you in a hard south-eastern push. There is no limit to what could be done by the extreme left handed push and sea operations along the Dutch frontier.[35]

This was Corbett and Callwell in action. From the start, the outflanking potential of an amphibious assault was seen as an important part of the project. The notion that the flexibility and mobility provided by Britain's command of the sea could allow the British Army to turn the German flank and restore movement to a static theatre in which frontal assaults were terribly costly, made this prospect deeply attractive to the Army. It explains why Robertson advocated it so strongly in the winter of 1914–15 and why Haig took the idea up with such enthusiasm a year later. Nonetheless, as will be discussed later in this volume, Haig's attitude to the coastal advance and the amphibious assault was always tempered with caution. He knew how difficult these actions could be unless the German defenders had already been distressed and distracted by threats from their south-west. Rawlinson made the essential point: " . . . the coastal attack is essentially subsidiary to the Fifth Army attack and will be launched in order to confirm and extend a victory already won".[36]

The strategic interests of the Navy and the Army were so interwoven in the Passchendaele campaign [a point that would have surprised the readers of neither Corbett nor Callwell] that it is difficult to disentangle the extent to which either was responsible for its initiation. Certainly, Jellicoe's concerns about the threat posed by the Belgian ports were a very important factor in the final deliberations of the crucial War Policy committee of 20 June 1917. But the extent to which the *conduct* of the campaign was handed over to the Army and the extent to which Haig made the coastal advance and the amphibious assault secondary to, and conditional upon, the seizure of the Roulers/Staden area is perhaps a better indicator of the real priorities – and, therefore, of the real responsibility for the Passchendaele campaign.

The maritime dimension of the Passchendaele campaign revealed the accuracy of the pre-war predictions of the British strategists Mackinder, Corbett and Callwell in two obvious ways. First, new technology [especially but not exclusively in the shape of the submarine] had indeed shown up Britain's maritime vulnerabilities in the face of a mobilized, industrialized Eurasian land power. Second, the British, in order to compensate for this, had felt impelled to go ashore and engage in the continental style of war – but this had produced problems in the priorities to be followed in the allocation of scarce resources. This dilemma had manifested itself most forcibly in the submarine crisis of spring 1917.

The vulnerabilities that the U-boat campaign demonstrated, played an important, though not necessarily decisive, part in the incremental decision to launch the Passchendaele offensive. But this was not the result of some simplistic notion that once the Flanders ports were captured then all would be well. The Admiralty was perfectly well aware that less than a third of the U-boats facing them in local British waters operated out of Zeebrugge and Ostende; equally, those same U-boats, if forced from Flanders, could be almost as effective if based in Germany. The anti-submarine campaign was an extremely complex one involving a large number of different but inter-connected factors. The seizure of the Flanders coast would help, but it would not be decisive. Yet in the desperate days of spring 1917 when it was obvious that there were no quick and easy answers to the U-boat menace, every possibility had to be exploited.

As worrying in some ways, was the prospect of a surface attack on Britain's cross-Channel communications with its Army and with various vital continental sources of supply. This might well be in association with the use of U-Boats. So far, the German flotilla effort had been capable of little more than irritating guerrilla attacks. Their destroyers and patrol boats were outnumbered, outclassed and could not aspire to commanding the Channel. Indeed, the classic action of 20/21 April 1917 showed that defeating the enemy in battle was still the best way of maintaining that command; after that encounter the Channel was to be quiet for the better part of a year.

But things might not always be so. Britain's age-old nervousness about a hostile power possessing the Channel coast re-surfaced in the shape of a concern about what the Germans might do in the future. Such was certainly Bacon's concern: "Had we been fighting a country with any sea instinct, we might quite possibly have lost the war through deliberately allowing the enemy to establish himself in Belgium and fortify harbours within easy operational distance of our Channel and cross-Channel communications".[37]

U-boats, destroyers, patrol boats, mine-layers – even German aircraft bombing the port facilities of Dunkirk were significant, not so much for the damage they actually inflicted, but as a warning of what might happen if the Germans were ever able to concentrate more resources in that vital area. Britain would lose the war, if it lost the Channel. And if the war against the U-boat elsewhere continued to go as badly as it seemed to be doing in the early Summer of 1917, then there was every prospect, Jellicoe thought, of this happening. For him it was a question of now or never:

> The facts . . . are conclusive in pointing to the absolute necessity of turning the Germans out of northern Belgium at the earliest possible moment. It must be done during the present summer: every day that we wait the difficulties will increase, and every day that we wait the threat from both sea and air becomes greater.
> . . . if we did not clear the Germans out of Zeebrugge before this winter we should have great difficulty in ever getting them out of it.[38]

As things transpired, of course, this was an over-pessimistic view. Britain did retain control of the Channel and it did defeat the U-boat threat, or at least reduce it to manageable proportions, without turning the Germans out of the Flanders ports- just as it was to do again a generation later. But to a beleaguered Admiralty in the Summer of 1917 this would naturally have seemed unlikely; accordingly, everything that might improve the situation just had to be tried.

This was merely the "defensive" aspect of the case, although it is one which has tended to command the attention of those considering the maritime causes of the Passchendaele campaign. However, there were "offensive" maritime possibilities too – in particular the contribution that Britain's sea power could make to a great out-flanking campaign that Haig hoped would transform the war. Such possibilities were at the heart of pre-war strategic discussion.

Jellicoe also made the point that, "The operation cannot be carried out by the navy alone, but it can be carried out as a joint business."[39] In this too, he was echoing the views of Corbett and Callwell. The Passchendaele campaign, as originally intended, had a significant maritime component not merely in terms of why it was launched but also in how it would have been conducted. Paradoxically, the only reason why the essential maritime dimension of Passchendaele was not more clearly revealed through the planned coastal and amphibious assaults, was the failure of Haig's "continental" style assault, away to the south against Roulers. Had that succeeded, the maritime character of the campaign would have been much more obvious.

Notes

1   For a review of Mackinder's ideas, see W.H.Parker, *Mackinder: Geography as an Aid to Statecraft*, [Oxford: Clarendon Press, 1982].

2   Lord Beaverbrook, *Men and Power,1917–1918* [London: Hutchinson,1956]. p. 150.

3   Parker, op cit p 65.

4   Letter of 27 April 1917. B. McL. Ranft [Ed} *The Beatty Papers Vol I* [London: Scolar Press for Naval Records Society, 1989] p. 419.

5   C.E. Callwell, *Military Operations and Maritime Preponderance: Their Relations and Interdependence* [Ed Colin S. Gray] [Annapolis, MD: 1996] pp. 161, 163. the equivalent is Julian S. Corbett, *Some Principles of Maritime Strategy* {Ed Eric Grove] [Annapolis, MD: 1988].

6   Julian S Corbett *Naval Operations* [London: Longmans, Green, 1922] Vol II. p. 66.

7   Quoted in J. Terraine, *The Road to Passchendaele* [London: Leo Cooper, 1984] p. 10.

8   Jellicoe to Beatty, 23 Dec 1916 Quoted in Arthur Marder, *From Dreadnought to Scapa Flow* [London: Oxford University Press, 1969] Vol 4 Year of Crisis, p. 114.

9   Paul G. Halpern, *A Naval History of World War I* [London: UCL Press, 1994] pp 335–380; Ernest C. Fayle, *Seaborne Trade* 3 Vols [London: John Murray, 1920–4] Vol 3. p. 132.

10   Quoted in Andrew A. Wiest, *Passchendaele and the Royal Navy* [London: Greenwood Press, 1995] p. 75.

11   Halpern, op cit, p. 377.

12 It is only fair to say that this is not what Jellicoe said he said to Sims. See A Temple Patterson, *Jellicoe* [London: Macmillans, 1969] p. 170.
13 Quoted Wiest, op cit, p. 108.
14 Quoted H. Newbolt *Naval Operations* op cit Vol IV, p. 64.
15 Quoted Wiest, op cit, p. 107.
16 George A. B. Dewar, *Sir Douglas Haig's Command* [London: Constable, 1922], p. 341.
17 Beaverbrook, op cit p. 17.
18 Quoted Wiest p. 73.
19 Quoted Marder, op cit, p. 112.
20 Quoted Wiest, op cit pp. 73, 77.
21 Quoted Marder, op cit, p. 280.
22 Halpern, op cit p. 343.
23 Newbolt, op cit, p. 377.
24 Corbett, op cit p. 270.
25 Halpern, op cit p. 366.
26 Fred T Jane, *Heresies of Sea Power* [London, Longman, 1906] p. 174.
27 Admiral Lord Fisher, *Memories* [London: Hodder and Stoughton, 1919] p. 79.
28 Callwell, op cit, p. 28.
29 A Temple Patterson, *Tyrwhitt of the Harwich Force* [London: Military Book Society, 1973]. p. 182–3.
30 Wiest op cit, p. 73 and quoted p. 115.
31 Callwell, pp 101, pp. 166–7.
32 Jackson to Jellicoe, 21 Nov 1915, quoted Marder, op cit p. 200.
33 Quoted Wiest, op cit, p. 59.
34 Callwell, op cit, p. 243.
35 Quoted Wiest, op cit, p. 8.
36 Rawlinson to Haig, 20 July 1917. WO 138/239. I am grateful to Dr David Massam for bringing this note to my attention.
37 Admiral Sir Reginald Bacon, *The Dover Patrol* [London: Hutchinson, 1929] Vol II. p. 228.
38 Quoted Wiest, op cit p. 104, 107.

Chapter 7

Third Ypres and the restoration of confidence in the ranks of the French Army

Allain Bernède

Immediately on his appointment as the new Commander in Chief of the French Army after the disaster of the *Chemin des Dames*[1], on 16 and 17 April 1917, General Pétain, was determined as his highest priority to restore confidence in the ranks of his army.

At the time of Paris and Amiens conferences, which took place on 5 and 18 May respectively, the French armies were obviously weakened and the British were insisting once more on the necessity of an offensive in Belgium. This offensive had already been on the agenda in London on 15 January. The mutinies, which had broken out from 29 April[2], revealed more than just a weakening: in fact a very serious crisis, and worst of all, a great loss of confidence among the ranks of the French armies.

Then, quite a strange dialogue was settled between the British and the French. For the British, the major preoccupation was that their communication lines were threatened by the enemy's submarines in the North Sea while, for General Pétain, his main preoccupation was to restore some confidence in his army and *to wait for the Americans*.

THE FRENCH PROBLEM: WHAT SHOULD BE DONE?

General Pétain, Commander-in-Chief from 15 May, believed that two things needed to be done: change the combat method and restore morale. However, these two points together required that no risk be taken. The situation was so tense that the slightest failure would lead to an irreversible defeat for the French Army. Consequently, only two days after he became Commander-in-Chief, Pétain, on 17 May, proposed to the Allies a participation in the operations in Flanders with a Franco-Belgian army under the command of the Belgian King assisted by a French Chief of Staff. Then, on 19 May, he signed his directive number one in which he revealed his resolution to aim at, "weakening the German troops, while preserving his own resources by performing limited attacks, launched by surprise, scattered in time and space, and carried out by major assets, above all artillery in areas where the enemy would be particularly anxious to hold their positions".[3]

Pétain, former infantry teacher at the War College, taught the means by which infantry and artillery could co-operate most effectively; created some *artillery research centres*, reorganised the training[4] of this branch as the infantry was already planning new techniques for "crossing in line"[5] supported by artillery. Moreover, with an affinity to his troops, he set up new rules for the soldier's life with better provision for leave, rest and food. But, at the time when the new Commander-in-Chief took office, the relief of British by French troops in the area of Saint Quentin, shifted the main concentration of British troops towards the River Lys and made necessary a new definition of Anglo-French collaboration.

THE CASSEL CONVENTION, 7 JUNE:

While discussions were in progress over the urgent need to limit German submarine activities in the North Sea, British Staff officers continued their operational planning. General Debeney, co-ordinator of the French armies in the north and north-east,had already received from Field Marshal Haig on 15 May, the operations:

> scheme regarding the action to take the north of La Lys after the taking of the Messines hill . . . The goal of the operations was to take possession of the Belgian coast. The plan was to lead firstly an attack from the Hooge-Steenstraate front to seize the Passchendaele-Staden hill, and the Roulers-Thorout railway lines, thus menacing the rear of German organisations farther northward.[6]

At the end of May, Belgium refused[7] the creation of the Franco-Belgian army. At the same time,the main headquarters[8] operations office negotiated the proper conditions to commit the French army between the British and Belgian ones. "The French forces will have to get a front which will allow the deployment for the attack of two divisions in line, and the following development of their northward manoeuvre".[9]

Finally, a six and a half kilometre front was given to the French, but immediately G.Q.G. noticed that three kilometres were flooded and the rear area was characterized by its bad communications and its scant billeting resources.

During the meeting on 2 June, considering the huge task to be undertaken mainly in terms of "road and railway communication network and water supply",[10] Field Marshal Haig and General Debeney observed that the French will need long delays before launching new offensives.

In the following days, while talks were still going on between both Staff Headquarters, opinions between the British and the French differed to a marked degree. According to Haig, the French units must be under his command whereas Pétain replied that, apart from minor details, the British should "only issue general instructions regarding co-ordination for the attack".[11]

Nevertheless, when Haig, General Ruquoy[12] and General Pétain met in Cassel on 7 June to sign an agreement which would stipulate the exact role of the three armies, Haig obtained the command of operations in Flanders. Since the day before, he had been officially informed that the First French Army, led by General Anthoine[13], had been chosen to be engaged by his side in Flanders.

At that time, French interests demanded such a concession. In the event of failure, the British Army was strong enough to prevent any disintegration from happening. In spite of the major failure in April, the French Army leaders had to show everybody, be it enemies or allies, that their soldiers were still able to achieve success.

THE FIRST FRENCH ARMY IN FLANDERS:

On 9 June, only three days after his appointment, General Anthoine turned up at the St-Omer General Headquarters while his Chief of Staff was already working to solve problems with the British. As soon as the relief of the Belgian troops was achieved, General Anthoine's Staff, of about thirty officers of whom a third dealt with artillery, engineering, road services and railways, settled down in Rexpoede on 16 June. On 22 June, at last, General Anthoine signed his directive number one defining conditions for the employment of his army: "Under the command of Marshal Haig, it will take part in the offensive operation led by the British. It will operate in Hetsas area, at the extreme left, as a pivot for the British Armies. Its goal is to reach Steenbek line between the pond of Blanckaart and the north edge of the Houthulst forest".[14]

General Anthoine had been appointed by Pétain because, on the Champagne front, while leading the Fourth Army, he "obtained an excellent performance of the artillery thanks to a judicious use of the various weapons and services".[15] Thus, he was perfectly in tune with the Commander-in-Chief's conception of artillery use "to break the enemy's morale and will of resistance by crushing them with gun fire".[16] To achieve this technically delicate and politically difficult entreprise, he was given Colonel Peschart d'Ambly[17], as Chief of Staff. He was a man who, from the beginning of the war, had turned out to be what he was in time of peace, "methodical, sensible, calm, energetic and vigorous".[18]

However, the task of the Staff was not to be easy. Although General Lacapelle had led the training of the First Army Corps during its stay at Mailly Camp,[19] the divisions which arrived from 26 June onwards had an uneven quality.

A remarkable effort was made in terms of artillery. Within the First Army Headquarters, for instance, a captain was specifically in charge of dealing with fire-plan. From mid-July on, the First Army front was composed of 60 artillery batteries of 75mm field artillery, i.e. 240 guns. Solidly provided with means of destruction against the enemy's defensive system, this small French Army had 277 pieces of trench artillery with calibres ranging from 58 to 240mm and 164 pieces of heavy artillery with the following calibres: 155mm, 220mm, 8 inches, 270mm and 280mm. The counter-battery provision included 148 long-range pieces of 105mm, 120mm and 155mm, 64 heavy artillery pieces of 305mm, 320mm and 370mm calibre was responsible for the destruction of concrete dugouts.[20] The artillery had for its assistance an aeroplane detachment for the heavy artillery and another for each long-range artillery group. The remaining air strength was comprised of another three squadrons among which was the famous *Cigognes*, two bombing squadrons, one reconnaissance, and one squadron in reserve.

HEADQUARTERS' ACTIVITIES: SUPPLY AND INTELLIGENCE SERVICES:

Beginning work on 21 June, the Staff of the First Army operated virtually as one unit. The 36th Army Corps, located on the coast, did not, for the moment, take part in this work. Immediately, the British insisted on the necessity to accumulate all the supplies ready for launching the offensive on 25 July.

If the operations office were given about a month to establish their plans, the "logistics transport office" had even less time to equip the front, that is to say to reinforce the terrain by upgrading the road, by building railway stations, bringing in the artillery and railway networks then organising resupplying centres, water supply above all, and by allocating and setting up hospitals.

The French had to reduce their demands, for instance in the field of road networks, [only one for the area when two were expected, one for each divisional front], technicians agreed on the fact that the First Army would achieve the necessary works with the help of the British who would provide them with some of the equipment.

In 1917, *the front being nothing but the continuation of the factory*, the problem was to provide the combat zone with railways in order to be able to supply the artillery batteries and ensure the supply of a whole range of necessities, from personnel on leave to rations for 135,000 men, fodder for 40,000 horses and petrol for 3,000 motorized vehicles. When the First Army Corps arrived on 13 July, Rousbrugge station was nothing but a meadow where 424 cars and 288 trucks were unloaded. A hundred and sixty kilometres of roads were restored or widened but only 14 kilometres were built in view of the climate and quality of soil.

The Intelligence Office of General Headquarters informed its counterpart of the First Army that units of the Fourth German Army, led by Von Armin and in the Crown Prince of Bavaria's Army Group, were facing them. However, General Anthoine needed tactical information of another sort "to lead an artillery battle supported by infantry",[21] even if the Belgians confirmed during the relief the numbers of battalions, companies, the numbers of the Landwehr and reserve regiments testifying they really were the troops which had lost Vimy Ridge on the outskirts of Arras in April and May of this year.

As early as 21 June, the first Intelligence note[22] was handed out to confirm the situation report. For successful investigations, the Intelligence Office had three main means, namely, the ground acquisition (SROT) section, a sound acquisition section (SRS) and the air-photograph section (SPA). Thanks to those means, at the end of June, the office identified with certainty 63 artillery positions out of a probable 100 existing.

The study of air-photographs sharpened this information showing that about 50 sites had emplacements and that 25 were made of concrete. Still, nobody could tell how those casemates were armed because most of the time they were only identified when one artillery piece fired. In spite of all, out of the observation synthesis came the following results: the guns seemed to be almost equally divided between the 77mm field guns, cannons and 105mm howitzers, 150mm howitzers and higher calibres. As they did not fit the usual pattern, there had to be a check to see if the observers had not mistaken the 105mm guns for those of 77mm, shooting a new shell the range of which had been increased by the use of new gun carriages.

With regard to aviation, the French counted a total of 17 German units, among which there were 5 fighter squadrons, 7 bombing squadrons, 4 reconnaissance and 1 seaplane flight, but the existence of many more was suspected. A wireless communication jamming-station was detected as well.

As soon as the divisions started the offensive, they knew there was quite a difficult obstacle ahead: the Yser canal, then some more fortified positions before reaching the batteries and billets. The first position aimed at defending the canal banks was made of trenches and blockhouses. Between the canal and the position stood nests of machine-guns and thick belts of barbed-wire.

The divisions were to learn gradually that the second position was of three-lines protected by marshy or flooded areas. Moreover, they realized that further ahead still, there was a third position before the Hindenburg line beyond which was the enemy's resupplying network. Actually, it was only with the publishing of the intelligence note number 44 (3 August), that is to say just after the attack on 31 July, that the divisions would get "reliable intelligence" thanks to the seizure of a German map of the combat area with a scale of 1/20.000.

TWO FRENCH INFANTRY DIVISIONS, ON THE LEFT OF THE BRITISH, FACING THE GERMAN PILLBOXES:

While the Chief of Staff, and the branch heads of the First Army Corps were in Rousbrugge from 21 June onwards, the first 2 divisions which arrived (the 1st and the 51st) relieved battalions of the 4th and 5th Belgian divisions from 26 June. On 10 July, after unloading, the heavy artillery and the162nd and 2nd infantry divisions, the entire 1st Army Corps, started an internal relief which was to end on 19 July.

A note from the "Operations" Office of the First Army[23], dated 17 July, briefed the 1st Infantry Division on its next mission after its return to the front line. Not only was it to have its part of the front, but, most of all, it was to collaborate on its right flank with "the British who commit to this attack a great number of troops and equipment for a series of successive efforts intended to force the Germans into swampy and unprepared areas, to weaken them thoroughly".

From the study of the terrain, the French kept in mind that, in the whole region nestling between the Yser, Bruges and the sea-front, it was not possible to dig an underground shelter, which led the Germans, as well as the Belgians, to build concrete emplacements. That meant that they would not have to face fresh infantry platoons coming out of deep shelters after the shelling. Moreover, the concrete material used, the only one strong enough, required a few months before being able to give entire satisfaction after having dried out. "With a series of efforts",[24] it was hoped that the Franco-British Army would manage to drive the Germans out of what were to be called the *pill-boxes*.

The success of the operation was thus dependent on the destruction of the concrete shelters by the artillery. The High Command, as a result, would only launch the attack after satisfactory results had been obtained.

COMBAT METHOD: COUNTER-BATTERIES

General Anthoine wrote in the orders he gave to the artillery: "Counter-battery fire will be executed without restrictions of projectiles under two conditions, namely: first, the existence of the attacked batteries should be certain; secondly, the shooting should be constantly observed and controlled". Then, he specified that "the enemy's anti-aircraft batteries still have the priority for destruction".[25]

On 15 July at 6am, First Army artillery started its counter-battery fire. Two days later, on 17 July, the weather was getting worse but the attack was still to be launched on 21 July. The French artillerymen, newly arrived at their positions, had no shooting data, the aircraft were stuck on the ground and so preparations for the offensive were delayed, in the end by a full ten days.

The H-hour was finally set at 3.50 a.m. on 31 July. By then, the 1st and 51st infantry divisions had gone up to the front for the second time since 27 July and had started their own reconnaissance missions.

Three phases were scheduled . The first aimed at seizing the first two front lines. The second was to carry on the offensive after a short break to give units enough time for regrouping. At 7.10 a.m., the third phase was to enable the second line battalions to relieve the first line. On 30 July, at 11 a.m., with the attack scheduled for the next day, General Anthoine gave his last orders. Counter-intelligence was high in the list. "No modifications in the firing pace should allow the ears to recognize the various phases of the attack and in order to prevent the enemy aircraft from seeing our troops in their attack position, our planes must keep them away from the French lines".[26]

WAITING FOR 'CAPTAIN JOHN'

In July, the main concern of the Chief of Staff was, along with the equipment responsibilities, to settle details about the co-ordination of artillery. He also wanted to set up communication networks with the British because of the mission allocated to the First Army. From 11 July, by general instruction n°14, the First Army had to be able, at any moment, to cover the left flank of the British Fifth Army. "Captain John will come back"[27] meant there was likely to be a gas attack in the following night ahead of the British front unless Captain John "missed his train".

Facing many difficulties, General Anthoine's Staff, anxious to avoid any risk when the action started, asked for liaison and co-ordinating measures of all kinds. As far as he was able, General Grégoire, in command of the 1st Infantry Division, methodically organized the artillery fire intended to assist crossing the canal. Shrapnel shells were to rake and clear any occupied shell holes ahead of an artillery barrage from about a hundred 75mm guns. The first wave of this barrage would be preceded at 150 metres by an intense shell barrage, that is, a shell every 15 metres and every 30 seconds.

"Whatever the worth of the preparation may be, it would be silly to suppose that not one German or one machine-gun will survive".[28] Officers will have to use what has been studied at Mailly camp as far as machine-gun reductions and mutual unit support were concerned. Units must always be ready to respond to a counter-attack. "The difficult thing is not always to conquer but to keep".[29]

As for General Anthoine, it was all too clear that French credibility was at stake in British eyes.

> We must, he wrote, be entirely confident – and the duty of each officer is to pass on this and [also] that feeling of confidence in his soldiers' hearts, in making them understand the whole importance of a major success for the future in this area so close to Lille and the left of the British army. They have to be told that the 1st Army Corps has been chosen to represent the French in the main battle which will start and that the First Infantry Division will be honoured to fight along with the British Guards Division. I met the generals and officers of the British Guards, they too are proud to have on their left the First Infantry Division whose worth they have clearly witnessed on the Somme battlefields.[30]

TOGETHER INTO THE BATTLE:

In the evening of 31 July, in the chaos of the conquered positions, now being turned into mire, the front line battalions were relieved under extraordinarily difficult conditions. It had been raining since the middle of the afternoon. The offensive got stuck in the mud. Because the British positions on their flank were slightly to the rear, General Anthoine gave the artillery the order to start destroying the new German front line the next day "as would be defined by the reconnaissance mission of the day".[31] Yet it was plain for all to see that, because of the pouring rain, it was not possible to resume the attack. Thus, Anthoine ordered the front divisions to be relieved and strictly following the special order n°31 he ordered his men to wait for the new offensive in order that casualties were minimised. In spite of this instruction to hold rather than to attack, General Anthoine could be satisfied.

As the shelling was maintained, a wireless message from the German batteries was intercepted: "Can't shoot, batteries under fire".[32] That confession was proof that the First Army artillery had fulfilled its counter-battery function. On the evening of 31 July, Sir Douglas Haig sent General Pétain the following telegram:

Operations of First French Army North of Boesinghe, conducted under General Anthoine's command with greatest skill and gallantry, have met with complete success. Assisted by the crossing of the canal skilfully effected on the night of 27th/28th instant, and after a most effective bombardment, the preparatory dispositions for to-day's attack were completed last night without incident. The assault launched this morning in combination with the British armies on their right rapidly gained its whole objectives. Thereafter the French troops pressed on with the greatest ardour beyond their objectives and in spite of the enemy's resistance captured Bixschoote and the powerful German trench systems to south-east and west of the village including Cabaret Kortekeer. By their success the French divisions have most admirably covered and secured the allied flank, and have contributed very largely to today's success. The thanks and congratulations of the British Army are due to all ranks of the First French Army. I am glad to say that while they inflicted very severe casualties on the enemy the losses of the First French Army have been very small indeed.[33]

Brigadier General Seymour commanding the Third Guards Brigade told the Lieutenant Colonel, in command of the 201st Infantry Regiment about both the satisfaction and the honour which the 2nd Scot Guards and Welsh Guards felt when they fought along with them. On 17 August, Haig, in a letter to General Anthoine, wrote about the "French soldiers' consummate skills and hard work".[34]

The Field Marshal was to inspect the French troops on the airfield of Bergues on 19 August and General Anthoine was to be invited to the Guards' parade near Proven on 25 August. However, even though the commanders congratulated one another and although their collaboration was still very good, especially in the field of Intelligence,[35] there were some minor points of conflict.

FRANCO-BRITISH COLLABORATION.

Collaboration had started as early as 24 May when two officers, Colonel Bellaigue de Bughas and Lieutenant Colonel Reynaud, were appointed to General Headquarters BEF, one as the Chief of the French Mission, the other as Director of Services. This was technical co-operation and everything went well. During the conference which took place at British Headquarters on 16 June, the British, French and Belgian representatives agreed on an important effort to improve communications and to set boundaries between the areas where the different armies were deployed, according to the main rail and road junctions.

The lending of equipment, filtration tanks, trucks, locomotive wagons, railway tankers, barges to carry water, river gun-boats, mortars and howitzers (with their ammunition), tents, increased, as well as the exchange of services, ammunition transfer, and the transportation of artillery and labouring units.

On 5 July, the French War Minister ordered the creation of a committee for the "air defence of the territory" and he asked as well for the presence of a British officer. A French artillery officer was appointed by General Anthoine to maintain the technical liaison between the British Fifth Army and the First French Army.

On 15 July, Field Marshal Haig thanked General Anthoine for his "congratulations" which he had expressed on the work achieved by the British troops attached to the First Army. Then, on 17 July, the French set up an Intelligence Staff committee with a view to solving wire and wireless communications within the area of the various armies. The next day, the British, judging that operations must be synchronized, decided that the British forces included in the approaching operation would use Paris time. This was before the 31 July attack. Everybody's interest demanded common action.

On the evening of 31 July, it was clear that the expected result had not really been obtained. According to Captain Renondeau, liaison officer with the British Fifth Army, quoting a report by Lieutenant Colonel Fuller, Chief Staff Officer in the Tank Corps: "it seemed that we had expected more".[36] Besides, with the German artillery being constantly on the move, the Intelligence Branch was disoriented and reported that engaging enemy batteries had proved to be very difficult.

In August, the situation changed completely. The British moved their General Headquarters from St Omer to Blendecques. From that time on, the British and French no longer had the same objectives. Combat methods had to be reviewed to allow the infantry to be able to face counter-attacks. Turning the country into a quagmire with shelling was not proving to be a solution either. To realize and do something about this was to take quite some time, and this would eventually endanger the cohesion of the two armies. As early as 10 August, General Horne wrote to the 1st Army:

I have lately had under consideration the state of affairs in the town of Armentières which was heavily shelled with gas and HE shell on the night 28th/29th July and on succeeding days. Yesterday, I visited the town and found it has been much knocked about, and evacuated by the civilians with the exception of from 1000 to 1200. The majority of these remaining civilians are either very averse to leave their homes, or else are making money out of the troops in the neighbourhood.

If they remain in the town, their presence renders necessary additional police measures to prevent looting houses and cellars, and should a recurrence of the bombardment, especially gas shelling, occur there are no civilian hospital facilities in the town for dealing with casualties.

Their presence would, therefore, be a considerable embarrassment to the troops who would have to control the population and assist in their evacuation, and to our medical organisation which would be obliged to deal with civilian casualties, at a time when they might be fully employed in dealing with battle casualties of our own troops.

I am, therefore, of opinion that the compulsory evacuation of the remaining civilians in Armentières is a tactical necessity, and I hope that steps may be taken as soon as possible to obtain the necessary permission for this measure from the French government.

A considerable amount of voluntary evacuation has already been carried out with the assistance of troops and transport of the XI corps.

The civilian casualties during the bombardments are estimated at about 500 of whom not less than 350 were evacuated by British ambulances.[37]

There was more than one fly in the ointment. Practical difficulties piled up. For instance, the French asked for a second filtration tank from the English on a loan basis through the French Mission but it was refused after a week's procrastination. On 11 September, when the British asked, in anticipation of future operations, for the authorization to set up an aerodrome between Bergues and Hondschoote in the First Army area, they were now to face a refusal. On 28 September, the French High Command would even go as far as to reconsider the authorization for the enlargement of Calais aerodrome which they had initially granted. On 9 October, the British complained to the French Mission about the attitude of the French press:

Cases have recently occured in which local French newspapers have inserted articles with certain details of British operations in contravention of the existing censorship regulations. As an example, "La dépêche de Lille" published valuable information of the effects of the German bombardment of Armentières with gas shells.

I would be glad if steps could be taken to remind the local newspapers that, in the interests of military success, nothing should be inserted in their papers concerning British military operations without censorship by competent military authority. I presume that, wherever possible, the French Mission, to whom the articles would normally be submitted, would obtain the proof from the local British military authorities immediately concerned. Corps Staffs or Army Staffs would, in almost very case, be competent to give the necessary permission.[38]

On 30 October, General Headquarters sent a telegram as a reply: "Please let General Charteris know that the Commander-in-Chief finds it inadvisable to spread false news about sending several divisions to

Salonique by the Allies to win success that could politically counterbalance the Italian retreat".[39]

These were minor divergences, escalating though they were; however, there were to be matters of more fundamental discord.

DIVERGENCES : THE FRENCH GET READY FOR LA MALMAISON.

On 15 September, on the French side, General Nollet replaced General Lacapelle in the fighting area. From that moment on, the Staff of the 36th Army Corps[40] was to replace the staff of the 1st Army Corps in the conduct of operations. However, orders relating to future operations had been modified.

The Commander of the 36th Army Corps "must constantly bear in mind the resumption of the offensive"[41] whereas the Commander of the First Army Corps was to put combat units withdrawn from the fighting, back into action. On the right flank of the French, the 1st Infantry Division re-inforced by every means its liaison with the British left flank formation while at the rear, the 2nd Infantry Division trained its field batteries to fire aerial bursts of shrapnel to deter maintenance work on forward defensive positions so that troops foreseeing an attack, left the front line trenches to settle in shell holes.

Considering that field artillery was no longer particularly useful in Flanders, the French High Command withdrew it to commit it to the area of La Malmaison. However, even though the allocation had been modified and reduced, there still remained 623 pieces of French artillery in Flanders. From then on, in accordance with General Order number 28, dated 18 September, the objective of the next offensive, [still in co-ordination with the British], aimed at encircling the forest of Houthulst. First, in co-ordination with the British on the right flank, the goal was to seize the hill above the southern edge of the forest; second, it was to secure a start line in co-ordination with the Belgians on the French left.

However, relations with the British were deteriorating. The issue of the relief of the French units on the front of the Northern army group poisoned the atmosphere even though Pétain himself came on 6 October to review the 2nd and 162nd divisions, which had recently been withdrawn from the front, in order to show how important Flanders was in his own eyes. General Anthoine could hardly hide his fears concerning the engagements in the offing. He declared: "it is a question of national honour, we have to keep the word we gave to the British . . . "[42]

From 14 September, onwards, fully technical but, in implication, 'politically' serious talks dragged on. How could they lower the flooding which was covering the right bank of the Yser? It would have to be drained by pumps but that could not be done straightaway!

During the attack on 9 October, good booty was obtained with the capture of more than 150 prisoners, 44 machine-guns, 6 bomb-launching devices and quite a significant number of rifles, but the battalions committed to the battle owed their success to the deep and heavy barrage which made up for insufficient prior destruction of the German defences.

The small-scale attack on 22 October aimed at shaping the battlefield for further operations. If the 1st French Infantry Division enabled the 35th British Infantry Division to straighten up its front by protecting its left flank, still there remained an important task, namely the seizure of a bridgehead towards the north-west aimed at securing the Luyghem position.

Altogether, after a ten-kilometre advance, the French front lines reached from the southern to the western edges of the Houthulst forest. Despite casualties and suffering, General Anthoine felt he had succeeded in his mission. The major part of the 'concrete', that is to say the blockhouses area on the French front, was in the hands of the First Army.

On the other hand, Field Marshal Haig claimed that, "we won't win the war if we lounge around".[43] On 19 October, because he had perfectly understood that General Anthoine's army was to be taken away from him, Haig confessed to the French Commander in Chief in the north that the relief of six French divisions by the British forces, would jeopardize the British offensive projects which were planned for the spring of 1918. Haig questioned the French point of view and refused to countenance the B.E.F. being further deployed on defensive fronts rather than being committed to the offensive. Worst of all, during 1917, in Haig's opinion, the British Army had sustained the main effort by itself. The Russian and Italian allies had done nothing while the French had done little.

In a secret report to the French High command, Major Curville, liaison officer at General Headquarters, stated that Field Marshal Haig, the British press and public opinion all seemed convinced that "the French government won't commit its army in expensive operations any longer and wants only one thing, namely to have the British relieve the French as soon as possible. France, by the will of its government, from now on doomed to passivity",[44] would not enjoy any more credibility. This was all the more tragic in that the British were twice to attack Passchendaele – on 6 and 10 November, on the second occasion completing its capture.

To sum up: 1917 had been for France a year full of tensions and dangers. However, with 6 divisions and a total of 135,000 soldiers deployed on a four kilometre front[45], the presence of the First French Army at the side of the British in Flanders represented the highest rate of commitment to an offensive of the French armies in 1917, since the disasters of April and May. Losses were low: 1,625 killed or missing, 6,902 wounded or taken prisoner[46], in spite of the heavy fighting[47]. With a substantial booty of 1,500 prisoners, 43 guns, numerous minenwerfers, hundreds of machine-guns, thousands of rifles, the French soldiers felt that they had dominated the enemy. This had been in line with General Pétain's "limited offensives"[48] policy, aimed at the restoration of his army. In General Anthoine's file, one can read: "this small army, with very limited infantry assets has achieved major success. General Anthoine's economical and rational methods caught the attention of the British command, without modifying its fighting methods which involved high human cost".[49]

Notes

1   The Chemin des Dames draws its name from a road on the narrow ridge between the Aisne river and the Ailette. In the 18th century, the daughters of Louis XV used to go there walking while they were staying in their castle near Laon.

2   These mutinies which took place while seriously disruptive strikes were going on, led to an overall suspicion of treason.

3   General Pétain's directive n°1 of 19 May 1917, in Les Armées françaises dans la Grande Guerre, Paris, Imprimerie nationale 1937, Tome V, annexe numero 235, p. 391.

4   Instruction n°28052 of 29 May, 1917 and directive n°2 of 18 June, 1917.

5   A very complex operation by which the first line of the assault echelon is replaced by a new one without breaking the pace of the action.

6   S.H.A.T. 17 N°339. Fonds de la mission militaire française auprès des armées britanniques, 1917 – secret plan for capitalising upon the capture of Messines Ridge.

7   Since the Belgian constitution did not allow the King to delegate, in one way or another, part of his command authority, the setting up of a Franco-Belgian army with a French Chief of Staff did not materialize; S.H.A.T. 17N°339, as quoted endnote 6: French co-operation with the British and Inter-Allied armies, note of French GQG General Staff, Third Office, 17 May 1917.

8   At Compiègne.

9   S.H.A.T. 17 N°339 G.Q.G. Third Office note of 27 May 1917, matters to be discussed by General Pétain, Marshal Haig and General Ruquoy.

10 S.H.A.T. 17 N°336. Report of French General Headquarters meeting 2 June 1917.

11 S.H.A.T. 19 N°122. Report of 16 June 1917 at advanced G.H.Q.

12 Chief of Staff of the Belgian Army.

13 Ranking first upon graduation at the 'Ecole Polytechnique' and then at the 'Ecole Supérieure de Guerre', General Anthoine was a tall fifty-seven-year old man with a brilliant intelligence, a sharp memory and remarkable willpower.

14 Note n°884/3 S.H.A.T. (Army Historical Department) Reference Number 22 N27.

15 S.H.A.T. Reference Gx/3 644 (New Reference 9 Y D) General Anthoine's private file.

16 Quoted by Captain Delvert in Les operations de la 1'ière armée dans les Flandres, Paris, L. Fournier 1920, p. 72.

17 Fifty-two-year old infantry-man, outstanding graduate from the «Ecole Spéciale Militaire» (ranking 27 out of 394) as well as from the 'Ecole Supérieure de Guerre' (ranking 38 out of 79).

18 S.H.A.T. Reference Gx/4 (New Reference 13 Y D) Colonel D'Ambly's private file.

19 S.H.A.T. Reference Gx/4 298 (New Reference 13 Y D) General Lacapelle's private file.

20 S.H.A.T. 17 N°363 Directive Number 1 of General Anthoine, 22 June 1917.

21 Directive N1 of General Pétain 19 May 1917. In Les Armées françaises dans la Grande Guerre, Paris, Imprimerie nationale, 1937, Tome V, annexe numero 235, p. 391.

22 From 31 June to 30 November 1917, the First Army's Intelligence branch issued 163 Intelligence notes.

23 Note n°884/3 S.H.A.T. (Army Historical Department) Reference N°22N27.

24 ibid.

25 ibid.

26 ibid.

27 S.H.A.T. 27 N27. Note n°389/5. 1st A.C. Third Office 17 July 1917.

28 S.H.A.T. 22 N27 Note number 384/3 1st A.C. 1st I.D. Third Office, 17 July 1917.

29 ibid.

30 ibid.

31 ibid.

32 S.H.A.T. 17 N°363 French Military Mission to the British Armies. Correspondence dated 2 August 1917.

33 S.H.A.T. 17 N°333 Telegram from Field Marshal Sir Douglas Haig to General Pétain, 31 July 1917.

34 Quoted by Captain Delvert in Les operations de la 1'ière armée dans les Flandres, Paris, L. Fournier, 1920, p. 148.

35 Captain Renondeau forwarded information on the enemy's combat methods e.g. leaving few troops in the first lines while strengthening its depth.

36 S.H.A.T. 17 N°364 French Military Mission to the British Armies. Report by Lieutenant-Colonel Fuller, Chief Staff Officer, Tank Corps, dealing with 31 July. Date 3 August 1917 Translation sent by Captain Renondeau, liaison officer to the British Fifth Army, to General Commander in Chief.

37 S.H.A.T. 17 N°333 Note of 10 August 1917 G.H.Q./O/A 288.

38 S.H.A.T. 17 N°333 British Armies in France, French Mission, 9 October 1917.

39 S.H.A.T. 17 N°333 Telegram n°8599/M, 30 October 1917.

40 Its two divisions, 133rd and 29th Infantry Division, had relieved in the line, the divisions of the 1st Army Corps.

41 S.H.A.T. 22 N°2098 Note of 30 September 1917 related to possible manoeuvres carried out by 36th Army corps.

42 S.H.A.T. 17 N°363 Instructions for operations number 52 for the commanding officer of the 36th Army Corps, date 18 October 1917.

43 S.H.A.T. 16 N°1828 Report of Major Cuberville, liaison officer to G.H.Q. dated 16 October 1917.

44 ibid.

45 In 1917, for the battles at la Malmaison and at Verdun, 31,200 and 23,333 soldiers were committed every kilometre, that is 1.2% and 0.09% of the French manpower of that year.

46 On 11 September, Captain Guynemer was reported missing with his plane over Belcapelle.

47 Between 6 and 7 million shells of all calibres were fired by French artillery.

48 Directive N°1 of General Pétain, 19 May 1917. In Les Armées françaises dans la Grande Guerre, Paris, Imprimerie nationale, 1937, Tome V, annexe numero 235, p. 391.

49 S.H.A.T. Reference Gx/3 644 (New Reference 9 Y D) General Anthoine's private file.

Chapter 8

Operational Command: The Plans and the Conduct of Battle

Ian F W Beckett

Before it was seemingly supplanted in the late 1960s and 1970s in the popular imagination by the experience of the Somme, Passchendaele was regarded as the characteristic battle of the Western Front during the Great War, its notoriety aptly summed up by the title of the pamphlet extracted from David Lloyd George's *War Memoirs*, 'The Campaign of the Mud'. To Lloyd George it was variously a 'grisly tragedy', 'one of the greatest disasters of the war' and one of 'the most gigantic, tenacious, grim, futile and bloody fights ever waged in the history of the war'. Of course, as the Official Historian complained, too many confused the fighting for the village of Passchendaele with the campaign as a whole, Third Ypres embracing eight separate battles between 31 July and 10 November 1917, namely Pilckem Ridge (31 July–2 August), Langemarck (16–18 August), Menin Road Ridge (20–25 September), Polygon Wood (26 September–3 October), Broodseinde (4 October), Poelcappelle (9 October), First Passchendaele (12 October) and Second Passchendaele (26 October–10 November). Nevertheless, the climactic struggle for the village of Passchendaele was a convenient shorthand for what Basil Liddell Hart described as 'the gloomiest drama in British military history'[1].

Inevitably, Third Ypres has been taken to reflect upon the command of the British army and the conduct of its operations, the need to excuse 'this senseless campaign', as Lloyd George also subsequently labelled it, producing four entirely different draft versions of the relevant volume of the Official History over a period of nine years before it became with the Cambrai volume the last dealing with the Western Front to be published in 1948.[2] It is recognized, of course, that all armies confronted with trench warfare faced new technical and managerial problems requiring both adjustment and a learning process. Essentially, managerial and technical difficulties were inter-linked and the British Army in particular faced a daunting challenge in expanding from a small pre-war regular army of 247,432 officers and men largely shaped by the demands of colonial warfare into a mass continental-style army with 4.9 million wartime enlistments under both voluntary enlistment and conscription and a peak strength on the Western Front of over 1.5 million men. Of the pre-war officer corps of just 12,738 regulars, only 447 were trained staff officers and, indeed, by 1918 the army required as many officers in staff appointments as it had had in the entire officer corps in 1914.[3]

Unfortunately, however, not only did training in staff duties lack realism but it was also the case that, unlike their German counterparts, British staff officers served commanders and could not issue orders on their own authority. The rigid demarcation between those tasked with operational planning and those tasked with support functions such as supply was also unhelpful. Compounding the difficulties was the absence of any agreed doctrine of command and, of course, few regulars in 1914 had commanded higher formations other than during the annual autumn manoeuvres. Indeed, at the last of the army's annual staff conferences before the war in January 1914, the then Director of Military Training and future CIGS, Sir William Robertson, had concluded that the nature of command was not fully understood within the army.[4]

Assisting the understanding of command, there have been increasing numbers of studies of the operational level in the Great War by historians such as Tim Travers, Dominick Graham, Robin Prior and Trevor Wilson, including the first full scale academic study of Passchendaele by Prior and Wilson. Other aspects of the Passchendaele campaign have also been the subject of recent study including work by David French and William Philpott on the overall strategic background and even on the intended supporting amphibious assault on the Belgian coast by Andrew Wiest and Alf Peacock.[5] Thus, reviewing Passchendaele might provide additional evidence of the nature of the operational level of command within the army at a crucial transitional period between the failures on the Somme in 1916 and the ultimate victory of the army in 1918.

The concept of a British offensive in Flanders was of long standing, its origins lying in pre-war debate concerning what has sometimes been referred to as the 'Belgian option'. Those military decision makers favouring British intervention on the continent in the event of war had been divided between those like Major-General (later Field Marshal) Sir Henry Wilson wishing to afford direct assistance to the French and those like Field Marshal Sir John French desiring an independent military role for the British Expeditionary Force (BEF) in Belgium. Of course, the security of Belgium and the need to deny Germany use of the Channel 'as a hostile base' was the *casus belli* for British entry to the war and it will be recalled that, at the celebrated meetings of the improvised War Council on 4 and 5 August 1914, French pressed strongly for a descent upon Antwerp rather than the planned concentration of the BEF at Mauberge to act in concert with the left flank of the French armies. Subsequently, of course, the BEF transferred from the Aisne to Flanders in October 1914, by which time the Royal Naval Division had been committed to the defence of Antwerp and two additional British divisions formed from regulars brought back from overseas had landed at Zeebrugge. In the event, Antwerp, Zeebrugge and Ostend all fell to the Germans but the salient secured around Ypres at such great cost in the autumn of 1914 continued to hold its strategic significance for the BEF.

Indeed, cross-Channel troop transporting was temporarily suspended and this surface threat remained far more significant than that posed by submarines after the German introduction of unrestricted submarine warfare in February 1917. The First Sea Lord, Admiral Sir John Jellicoe, had frequently expressed anxiety about the impact of U boat depredations on British merchant shipping but the introduction of convoying, delayed though in retrospect it seems, had markedly reduced the submarine threat and so the alarm raised by the First Sea Lord at the War Policy Committee on 20 June was not followed by an immediately shared concern.

Initially, of course, Britain had been the junior military partner to the French and Russians and thus the location of its first major offensive in the summer of 1916 had been dictated by the requirement to co-operate where the British and French lines adjoined astride the Somme. Field Marshal Sir Douglas Haig, who had succeeded French as Commander-in-Chief in December 1915, also subscribed to the concept of an independent British offensive in Flanders. With Britain becoming more dominant within the alliance, this was then given added impetus by the Admiralty's concerns. Thus, after a meeting of the War Committee on 20 November 1916, the prime minister, Asquith, drafted but did not sign a note for the C.I.G.S., General Sir William Robertson, conveying the meeting's conclusion that 'there is no operation of war to which the War Committee would attach greater importance than the successful operation, or at least the deprivation to the enemy, of Ostend and especially Zeebrugge'. In the context of his commitment to the defeat of what he regarded as the principal strength of the German army on the principal war front, Haig's own appreciation of the military situation did not waver through the planning process which ensued, particularly as the collapse of the French Army in the wake of the Nivelle offensive in April 1917, placed yet further responsibility on the British Army. The United States, of course, came into the war in April 1917 but Haig saw little prospect of American forces arriving in time to preserve the alliance and thus only a sustained British effort would hold out any hope of nursing the French through another winter. Haig also shared the prevailing assumption among British policy makers that a victory won and a peace dictated by the Americans would not serve British interests. Believing that he enjoyed a superiority on the chosen front and that German morale was close to collapse, Haig conceived of a Flanders offensive as forcing the Germans to fight for the Channel ports rather than simply withdrawing from the existing front line as they had withdrawn to the new defences of the Hindenburg Line prior to the Nivelle offensive. Indeed, Haig believed it important not to divert forces elsewhere, which might be welcomed by the Germans and lead to possible Allied reverses should the Germans launch their own offensive in the west.[7]

Lloyd George, who had succeeded Asquith as prime minister in December 1916, did not share Haig's optimism with regard to an offensive but, his political courage never matching his strategic convictions, he resorted to subterfuge in order to oppose strategic plans which appalled him. In a sense, his hands were tied by the reaffirmation of the primacy of the Western Front at the Allied conference at Chantilly in November 1916 and by the subsequent failure of Nivelle. Of course, as is well known, he had invested considerable political capital in the latter's success, having attempted to subordinate Haig to Nivelle's authority. While little was known by British politicians of the true state of the French Army in the aftermath of the Nivelle offensive, the War Cabinet was well aware of both the possibility of the French pursuing a separate peace and also the need to retain the military initiative. Having been discredited by the Nivelle episode, Lloyd George was in no position to argue his strategic preferences – now largely based on shifting resources to the Italian front – as superior to those of Haig and Robertson, who had become CIGS in December 1915. Thus, Lloyd George was drawn to accept the conclusions of the military conference at Paris on 4–5 May 1917 that the soldiers should determine the timing and nature of the Allied offensives for the year. Indeed it has to be said that Lloyd George demanded that the French attacks continued, that a knock-out blow was essential but that he himself did not wish to enter into the military arguments. However, such acceptance of plans for an offensive assumed that the objectives would be limited and that the French would fully participate. Moreover, the subsequent discussion of strategic options by the specially convened War Policy Committee brought final agreement for the Flanders offensive only on condition that a step by step approach was adopted and that the offensive should not continue if it proved too costly. In the event, the War Policy Committee did not reconvene until 24 September and the members of the War Cabinet consistently proved unwilling to halt the operations when their fears were fully realised.

Of course, to some extent, Robertson was to conceal the true state of affairs from the politicians in the belief that he must support Haig despite his own misgivings. Certainly, the offensive was presented to the War Policy Committee as a considered step by step campaign and one in which massed use of artillery would minimize British casualties but Haig always intended a significant strategic breakthrough to the Belgian coast.[8] Subsequent post facto justification for sustaining the effort in terms of the state of the French Army and even the wearing down of German morale and strength cannot disguise the original intention. Far from trying to take pressure off the French as he argued, Haig repeatedly urged the French to participate more fully in the campaign. Of course they had promised this and Haig wanted their help, believing that German strength was sufficiently weakened to achieve a decisive victory.[9] Indeed, the intention to achieve a breakthrough was sufficiently explicit in Haig's instructions to Lieutenant-General Sir Hubert Gough of Fifth Army on 28 June 1917 for Gough to continue to plan along such lines, Haig having rejected the concerns of the Director of Military Operations at GHQ, Brigadier-General John Davidson, who favoured consolidation of any breach in the German defences before attempting a rapid exploitation to the rear. If Gough somehow misinterpreted these instructions then the responsibility clearly lay with Haig rather than Gough. As the most recent study of Passchendaele has commented, 'Haig could not have failed to notice that Gough's plan went further in the direction of a breakthrough than that offered by anyone else he had consulted', both General Sir Henry Rawlinson, commanding Fourth Army, and General Sir Herbert Plumer, commanding Second Army, having offered more modest proposals earlier in 1917.[10]

The choice of ground, of course, placed the British at a considerable disadvantage in that, ever since 1914, the Germans had controlled what passed for the high ground across the flat Flanders plain. Not only was it the case that almost any slight rise in the ground provided observation over much of the surrounding countryside, but the British artillery could only be deployed with difficulty to support a major offensive from what remained a relatively narrow salient. Moreover, the German defences were known to be in depth following the transformation in German tactical doctrine over the winter of 1916–17 in response to the lessons learned from the Somme. The doctrine required the construction of three successive trench lines as outpost, battle and rear zones with both artillery and machine-guns fully integrated into a strongpoint-based defence – concrete pillboxes substituted for bunkers in the water-logged soil. This enabled a defensive battle to be fought primarily in a battle zone extending anything from 1,500 to 3,000 yards in depth and with specially designated counter-attack formations poised to intervene as necessary. Following the British success at Messines on 7 June 1917, however, the architect of the new doctrine, Fritz von Lossberg became chief of staff to the German Fourth Army opposite Gough and yet further defensive lines were prepared, extending to five in most sectors and to seven on the key Gheluvelt plateau. On average, the German defences extended to a depth from front to rear of 10–12,000 yards, presenting a formidable barrier to the British. The Germans not only enjoyed excellent observation from the ridge east of Ypres running through Gheluvelt and Passchendaele but could also sight their artillery behind the ridge out of direct British line of vision. Moreover, the central sections of the German lines astride the Menin Road were unsuitable for tanks.[11]

The very geographical nature of the Ypres salient rendered it necessary to undertake preliminary operations to seize the Messines ridge (7–14 June), which otherwise would have enfiladed the British right flank. Messines had figured in the earliest discussions of the forthcoming offensive in November 1916 when the initial planning had been entrusted to Plumer and it had equally featured in the calculations of Rawlinson, brought into the planning process in January 1917 and also Colonel Macmullen of the GHQ Staff, whose unrealistic scheme to overrun the Gheluvelt plateau with tanks while simultaneously seizing both the Pilckem and Messines ridges was only briefly considered. While Plumer had suggested Messines as the first objective in a series of staggered operations, Rawlinson had recommended following up its capture within two or three days. However, as early as 21 March, Haig had warned Nivelle that for logistical reasons, following upon the planned Messines Ridge attack, there would have to be a five to six week gap before the offensive was renewed. As a counter to the logistical argument, it has been suggested by Prior and Wilson that it was primarily to enable Gough and his staff to be brought into the salient since Haig had greater confidence in Gough's more 'thrusting' character.[12] In the event, seven weeks were to elapse between Plumer's assault on Messines and the beginning of the main offensive. It might be noted, moreover, that while the first day of the Messines offensive was spectacularly successful with the assistance of the mines laid under the German lines, Haig insisted on pushing the penetration of the German defences to a depth of 3,000–4,000 yards and ultimately the Battle of Messines resulted in 25,000 casualties for the B.E.F.[13]

Haig believed the prolongation of the Messines operation worthwhile in terms of the attrition of the German defenders and it is certainly true that he conceived of the Passchendaele offensive as a whole as having an attritional impact upon the German Army. Haig told Gough on 30 June that the objective was 'to wear down the enemy, but at the same time, to have an objective' but then suggested both the coast and the ridge as such an objective. Haig's chief of staff, Launcelot Kiggell, also remarked on the attritional objective to Gough on 7 August but it seems that Haig was not able to distinguish between the Belgian coast and the Passchendaele Ridge as the primary objective: in fact, it has been argued that mere possession of the ridge itself became of symbolic importance to Haig. However, as David French has commented, Haig 'never lost sight of the idea that his ultimate objective was to drive the Germans from the coast'.[14]

Certainly, in view of the depth of the German defences, the offensive, as eventually agreed, was highly ambitious. On the first day alone – 31 July – Gough anticipated overrunning the German defence zone to a depth of 5,000 yards: it was a plan with which Plumer apparently concurred although it was heavily criticized by Davidson. The plan then postulated an advance of 12½ miles to the line of the Roulers-Thourout railway by 7/8 August. Beyond that lay the line from Zeebrugge through Bruges to Thielt and then the Dutch frontier. The supporting amphibious operation entrusted to Rawlinson's Fourth Army, for which detailed preparation and special training were undertaken, would have taken the coast around Middelkerke, brought Ostend under fire from British artillery and drawn off German forces opposite Haig.[15] Moreover, the comparative successes at Menin Road Ridge, Polygon Wood and Broodseinde in late September and early October, by which time Plumer's Second Army had taken over responsibility for operations, were still seen by Haig as a prelude to greater success after the frustrations of August. Indeed, as Prior and Wilson have commented, having advanced just three and a half miles in seven weeks, Haig anticipated that the Polygon Wood operation in particular would prove an opportunity to clear the next three and a half miles in just one or two weeks and to reach the coast by 5 November. The theme of Haig's despatches and those accounts penned by his staff officers immediately after the war is that only the deterioration in the weather after 3 October prevented the breakthrough while also stressing the need to continue the operations to assist the French.[16] Again, while Plumer is generally associated with a more limited 'bite and hold' approach to operations, there is no real evidence that he resisted the continuing of the attempt to achieve a breakthrough once the weather deteriorated, considerable doubt having now been thrown on the contention of the Official History that Gough and Plumer urged on Haig the suspension of operations on 7 October.[17]

Nor was it the case that Haig and GHQ were unaware of the deteriorating conditions, the celebrated story of Kiggell's surprise upon going up to the front for the first time on 20 November resting on the dubious source of the Official Historian, Sir James Edmonds, who fed it to Liddell Hart.[18] Haig's diary makes it perfectly clear that liaison officers reported accurately on conditions but the implications were ignored perhaps due to the concern to maintain the schedule of advance to coincide with the amphibious landing, which was only cancelled finally on 15 October following the failure of the first attempt to take Passchendaele village.[19] Even then, Haig declined to halt operations on 26 October and only the final failure to advance further along the Passchendaele ridge on 10 November brought the campaign to an end.

Turning specifically to the nature of command during the campaign, it is now generally known that Haig was well aware of the delicate balance to be struck by a Commander-in-Chief between control of and guidance to subordinates, his Staff College training having inculcated the belief that, while his authority would be impaired by allowing subordinates a free hand, it was still necessary to leave the actual execution of operations to those subordinates once he had laid down the overall strategic parameters. Unfortunately however, in practice, Haig was highly inconsistent in his approach to command, interfering in operational matters on some occasions while failing to assert his authority on others.[20] Thus, the kind of pattern set by Haig in his dealings with Rawlinson at Neuve Chapelle in March 1915 and again in planning the Somme campaign were to be reproduced in his relationship with Gough, whose staff moved after Bullecourt in May to its new headquarters near Poperinghe on 1 June 1917. Gough had known since April that he would play a role in the campaign but had only been informed officially on 13 May. As indicated earlier he certainly assumed that he was intended to break through.[21]

Subsequently, Haig appears to have counselled a more step by step approach but this was never made clear to Gough and, equally, Haig's wish that Gough seize the whole of the dominating Gheluvelt Plateau was another message that was not impressed with sufficient clarity even though it was one repeated by Haig on 28 June, 30 June and 5 July and evidently supported by the commander of Gough's XIV Corps, Lord Cavan. Indeed, Haig not only acquiesced in Gough's refusal to accept the need to embrace the plateau in the initial plan but also Gough's stalling of the original starting date from 15 to 31 July for which, of course, there was good reason – the need to wait for the commander of the French First Army on Gough's left flank, General Anthoine, to complete artillery preparations.[22] Ultimately, Gough himself appears to have realized the error with regard to Gheluvelt. After the war, Sir Charles Broad, who had then been on Fifth Army staff, suggested that Gough had telephoned GHQ on the evening of 31 July and had his request to extend operations to the right rejected but Haig's diary entries for 31 July and 2 August makes this very unlikely. Gough himself claimed that he initiated the decision on 24 August for Plumer's Second Army to take over responsibility for securing the plateau but he also claimed after the war that Plumer resisted the suggestion.[23]

There is some supporting evidence to this effect in the contemporary diary of Gough's chief of staff, Neill Malcolm. Malcolm noted, on 25 August, that 'the flank of our attack is to be extended to include Zandevoorde to be undertaken by 2nd Army' and he went on to comment on the following day that Plumer was not keen on Zandevoorde: 'Unless he undertakes that there is no object in his taking over anything from us'.[24] However, there is no contemporary evidence that Haig over-ruled Gough's supposed recommendation on 16 August that the operations be halted but differences of opinion between Haig and Gough continued to the extent that, as Prior and Wilson have expressed it, Haig's 'bizarre mixture of wild optimism and realistic appraisal' led him both to resolve to replace Gough with Plumer on 24 August for the new operations to gain the Gheluvelt Plateau and yet to leave Gough in effective operational control until 10 September.[25] It has been remarked that, like other army commanders, Gough was afraid of Haig and thus, to quote Tim Travers, the planning of the Passchendaele campaign showed him 'neither brave enough nor perhaps canny enough to either understand or confront an aloof and over-bearing Haig'. Certainly, Gough himself complained after the war that there was insufficient discussion in army commanders' conferences with Haig. Yet, equally, on occasions, as already noted, Haig did not impose himself on Gough. One corps commander, Aylmer Haldane, noted in his diary in September 1917 that it was 'as if the tail were wagging the dog, i.e. Gough and other Army commanders propose operations to which Haig agrees and does not as a rule initiate them'.[26]

If the relationship between Gough and Haig demonstrates a certain inconsistency in command, much the same pertained at army level. Certainly, the contrast in style between Gough and Plumer was marked, Malcolm complaining on one occasion that Plumer's system of command 'merely appears to be to tell the corps to carry on' although this was a view expressed prior to the appointment of Charles 'Tim' Harington as Plumer's Chief of Staff in June 1916. Nonetheless, Plumer's conferences were more of a forum than those of Gough despite the fact that both Gough and Malcolm maintained that they always consulted their own corps commanders regularly during major operations. Of course Malcolm had a case to plead and we must bear this in mind but he specifically rejected the suggestion in one draft of the Official History that there was a bitter difference of opinion between Fifth Army's corps commanders and himself on the objectives to be achieved at Passchendaele.[27] However, neither Gough nor Malcolm made any secret of the fact that, to quote Gough, they were 'very severe towards inefficiency' and both Gough's wartime letters to his sister-in-law and Malcolm's diaries reveal their frequent complaint as Malcolm expressed it in July 1916 of 'this wretched idea of command being interference' on the part of corps. Significantly, there was less dissatisfaction on the part of Gough and Malcolm with Fifth Army's corps commanders in 1917, both being confident in the abilities of Ivor Maxse (XVIII Corps), Cavan (XIV Corps) and Claud Jacob (II Corps) if not in Herbert Watts (XIX Corps). Malcolm was also pleased by the relationship achieved with Anthoine, and with the Royal Flying Corps, which he believed unjustly criticized.[28]

Much has been made of Malcolm's supposed baneful influence on Gough, particularly in the context of the Passchendaele campaign when it has been suggested that the absence of Edward 'Moses' Beddington as Fifth Army's GSO2 – he had been promoted to GSO1 in 8th Division in November 1916 – removed a mitigating voice on behalf of subordinate commanders.[29] It is certainly the case that Haig visited some of Gough's divisional commanders personally on 11 September in the belief that the true situation was being concealed from Gough; that Kiggell reported to Haig on 5 October that Malcolm was primarily responsible for ill feeling between Gough and the Canadian Corps; and that Haig told Gough on 9 December that divisions disliked serving in Fifth Army. Malcolm, of course, was then removed from Fifth Army on 16 December.[30] Similarly, an old friend of Gough, Major-General Llewellyn Pope-Hennessy, testified after the war to an 'atmosphere of terror' within Fifth Army during the campaign. However, while Gough was later persuaded that Malcolm had not been a good chief of staff, this was not his impression at the time and Gough appeared to believe that the main difficulty had been the unwillingness of subordinates to inform Malcolm of their difficulties because Gough invariably accompanied him on visits to units. There is also evidence of the respect in which Malcolm was held within Fifth Army's staff.[31]

Certainly, Malcolm's diaries suggest the unremitting burden on him of preparation for the campaign, not only in terms of the near daily conferences – Malcolm calculated at one point that his office was handling 500,000 words a day over the telegraph wire – but also Malcolm's personal aerial reconnaissances: on 11 July, for example, Malcolm was forced down on one flight by engine failure and, on a second flight, his aircraft broke a strut on landing. Compared with the trenchant views he had expressed on some formations during the Somme, Malcolm's comments during Passchendaele were very restrained, criticism being confined to the 30th Division – 'retainers of the Derby family' – on 4 August, the 42nd and 61st Divisions on 6 September and Lieutenant-General Sir Edward Fanshawe's V Corps, which had replaced XIX Corps in Fifth Army, on 18 September and Fanshawe's BGGS, Brigadier-General R P Benson. For the most part however, Malcolm was well aware of the difficulties facing units, especially once the weather broke. The continuing problems of communication also need to be stressed with army and corps commanders having little opportunity to influence events once men had left the front line trenches. On 1 July 1916, for example, while Rawlinson had had direct telephone contact with corps, corps with divisions, divisions with brigades and brigades with battalions, and he received over 160 messages from corps during the day, he still had no clear idea of the true situation in one corps for eight hours. Similarly, Malcolm remarked of the attack on 16 August 1917, 'More or less the usual experience of battle – very encouraging reports in the morning then getting worse'.[32]

Another measure of Fifth Army's reputation is its relative performance when compared to Second Army. Third Ypres, of course, was a transitional experience in terms of the evolution of operational methods. It did not involve the popular image associated with the Somme of linear formations advancing steadily into German fire. Lessons had been learned and small groups of infantry now utilized looser formations with the man portable fire support of light machine-guns and rifle grenades in order to get forward. Essentially, however, it was an artillery battle and the Royal Artillery had improved immeasurably in terms of the development of more sophisticated methods such as sound-ranging, flash-spotting and survey work, which enabled a new accuracy in indirect and predicted fire and far more refined creeping barrages and counter-battery fire. The difficulty, of course, was that there was still a reluctance to trust entirely to the new methods used at both Arras in April 1917 and at Messines and there was still a preference for longer old-style artillery bombardment which, among other failings, cut up the ground in ways prejudicial to the subsequent movement of artillery forward in support of further advances. Fifth Army's CRA, Herbert Uniacke, one of the best artillerists in the B.E.F., who was not readily consulted by either Gough or Malcolm, later suggested that, while he favoured shorter bombardments, the nature of the Ypres salient itself, rendered it necessary to undertake a longer bombardment in order to cover both the preparations for attack as well as the attack itself.[33]

On 31 July 1917, Fifth Army gained an average of 3,000 yards across a frontage of 13,700 yards after a 15 day preliminary bombardment involving some 3,036 British and French guns: by 2 August, the artillery had fired 4.2 million shells. In theory, this was greater artillery support than that enjoyed by either Third Army at Arras or Plumer at Messines on

7 June but it was still insufficient to accomplish all the tasks set for the artillery, not least counter-battery work when Fifth Army's intelligence greatly underestimated the number of German batteries. The intended depth of advance also lay beyond the range of field artillery support. Subsequent attacks by Fifth Army, such as those in late August, simply did not have sufficient artillery support to succeed.[34] By contrast, the concentration of Plumer's artillery – some 2,195 guns in Second and Fifth Armies firing 3.5 million shells – for the Menin Road operation on 20 September, was three times greater than that on 31 July with the advance restricted to a frontage of 14,500 yards and, more importantly, to a depth of no more than 1,700 yards. Yet even this did not suppress the German batteries. The Polygon Wood operation on 26 September was even more finely tuned to the range of the available artillery with a frontage of just 8,500 yards and a planned advance to a depth of only 1,250 yards.

However the perceived successes of the Menin Road and Polygon Wood were not accomplished cheaply. Moreover, the pace of Plumer's operations thereafter increased, despite the worsening weather and with distinctly less artillery preparation so that, for all intents and purposes, the Poelcappelle and the First Passchendaele operations in October were undertaken without artillery support. As Prior and Wilson have commented, in following a generally north-easterly direction, Plumer's operations were also driving Second Army deeper into a narrow salient, which made it even more difficult to bring artillery to bear and which exposed his infantry to German enfilading fire. Thus, while Fifth Army sustained 86,000 casualties for the gain of three and a half miles in seven weeks, Second Army took 69,000 casualties in September and October (up to the end of First Passchendaele) for an advance of under 4,000 yards. In addition, the Canadian Corps, which effectively took over the conduct of the offensive for the culminating second Passchendaele operation, then suffered some 12,000 casualties for perhaps 700 yards.[35]

In fact, Third Ypres was not as costly as the Somme, amounting to perhaps 275,000 casualties if the preliminary operation at Messines were to be included. The Somme, which had lasted a month longer, had cost perhaps 419,000 casualties. The greater controversy, however, surrounded the estimate of German losses. While Lieutenant-General von Kuhl, chief of staff to the German Northern Army Group, regarded the campaign as the 'greatest martyrdom of the world war', the figure of 400,000 German casualties, given by the British Official History, is unlikely to have been more than 220,000.[36] Haig claimed that he had 'used up' 88 of the 156 German divisions on the Western Front but, over the winter of 1917–18, his own army displayed some signs of despair as measured in terms of the statistical indices of morale that GHQ itself utilized.[37]

Nevertheless, the British Army was extraordinarily resilient and it must be said that the technical means of 'breaking through' defences as opposed to 'breaking into' such defences were not available in 1917 or even 1918. Certainly however, the initial success enjoyed by General Sir Julian Byng's

Third Army at Cambrai on 20 November 1917, was to mark the gathering pace of change within the army. This was so not least in operational methods although, significantly, those changes were increasingly to emanate from the lower echelons of the command structure and neither from GHQ nor army commanders.[38] Indeed, as a result of the campaign, GHQ was substantially restructured, those dismissed including Kiggell and Haig's chief of intelligence, John Charteris. The restructuring was necessary and made at least some contribution to the eventual success of the British Army in the following year.

Notes

1   Ian Beckett, 'Frocks and Brasshats' in Brian Bond (ed.), *The First World War and British Military History* (Clarendon Press, Oxford, 1991), pp. 89–112; David Lloyd George, *War Memoirs* (Ivor Nicolson & Watson, London, 1934), IV, pp. 2110, 2251; Sir James Edmonds, *The Official History of the Great War: Military Operations, France and Belgium, 1917 Volume II* (HMSO, London, 1948), [Hereafter, *OFH*], pp. iii–iv; Basil Liddell Hart, 'The Basic Truths of Passchendaele', *Journal of the Royal United Service Institution* 104, 1959, pp. 433–439.

2   Lloyd George, *War Memoirs*, IV, p. 2240. For the compilation of the Official History's volume on Passchendaele, see Tim Travers, *The Killing Ground: The British Army, the Western Front and the Emergence of Modern Warfare, 1900–1918* (Allen & Unwin, London, 1987), pp. 203–219. For the Official History generally, see also David French, 'Sir James Edmonds and the Official History: France and Belgium' in Bond (ed.), *First World War and British Military History*, pp. 69–86.

3   Ian Beckett, 'Hubert Gough, Neill Malcolm and Command on the Western Front' in Brian Bond and Gary Sheffield (eds.), *The Western Front Revisited: A British Reappraisal on the 80th Anniversary of the Somme* (British Commission for Military History, forthcoming); Peter Scott, 'The Staff of the BEF', *Stand To* 15, 1985, pp. 44–61.

4   Dominick Graham, 'Sans Doctrine: British Army Tactics in the First World War' in Tim Travers and T. Archer (eds.), *Men at War* (Precedent, Chicago, 1982), pp. 69–92; Staff College Library, Reports of the General Staff Conferences, 1906–14, Conference of 12–15 Jan. 1914; Ian Beckett, *Johnnie Gough, VC* (Tom Donovan, London, 1988), pp. 148–149.

5   Travers, *Killing Ground*; Ibid., *How the War Was Won: Command and Technology in the British Army on the Western Front, 1917–18* (Routledge, London, 1992); Shelford Bidwell and Dominick Graham, *Firepower: British Army Weapons and Theories of War, 1904–45* (Allen & Unwin, London, 1982); Robin Prior and Trevor Wilson, *Command on the Western Front* (Blackwell, Oxford, 1992); Ibid., *Passchendaele: The Untold Story* (Yale University Press, New Haven, 1996); David French, *The Strategy of the Lloyd George Coalition, 1916–18* (Clarendon Press, Oxford, 1995); William Philpott, *Anglo-French Relations and Strategy on the Western Front* (Macmillan, London, 1996); Andrew Wiest, *The Royal Navy and Passchendaele* (Greenwood Press, New York, 1995); Alf Peacock, 'The Proposed Landing on the Belgian Coast, 1917', *Gunfire* 11, 1988, pp. 2–50 and 12, 1988, 3–56. On the civil-military disputes surrounding Passchendaele, see also David Woodward, *Lloyd George and the Generals* (University of

Newark Press, 1983) and his edition of *The Military Correspondence of Field Marshal Sir William Robertson, 1915–18* (Bodley Head for Army Records Society, London, 1989).

6   For the evolution of the 'Belgian option', see Philpott, *Anglo-French Relations*, passim; Ibid., 'The Strategic Ideas of Sir John French, *Journal of Strategic Studies* 12, 4, 1989, pp. 458–478; Keith Wilson, 'The War Office, Churchill and the Belgian Option, August to December 1911' in Keith Wilson (ed.), *Empire and Continent* (Mansell, London, 1987), pp. 126–140.

7   P(ublic) R(ecord) O(ffice), Cab 42/24/10, Hankey to Robertson, 22 Nov. 1916; Ibid, Cab 42/24/13, Minutes of War Committee, 20 Nov. 1916. The best expression of Haig's views on the strategy of the Western Front and of the Third Ypres campaign, reflecting what might be termed the case for the defence first elaborated in the 1920s, is to be found in the work of John Terraine. See his *Haig: The Educated Soldier* (Hutchinson, London, 1963) and *The Road to Passchendaele: The Flanders Offensive of 1917 – A Study in Inevitability* (Leo Cooper, London, 1977).

8   French, *Strategy*, pp. 94–123.

9   Tim Travers, 'The Evolution of British Strategy and Tactics on the Western Front in 1918: GHQ, Manpower and Technology', *Journal of Military History* 54, 1990, pp. 173–200; PRO, Cab 45/114, Note by Wynne, 21 Apl. 1945; Ibid., Cab 45/192, Davidson to Edmonds, 10 Aug. 1934; Ibid., WO 158/48, Haig to Petain, 28 Sep. and 19 Oct. 1917; Travers, *How the War Was Won*, pp. 11–19.

10   Travers, *Killing Ground*, pp. 205–206; Prior and Wilson, *Passchendaele*, pp. 75–77; Major-General Sir John Davidson, *Haig: Master of the Field* (London, 1953), pp. 26–32.

11   Prior and Wilson, Passchendaele, pp. 71–73; Bidwell and Graham, *Firepower*, p. 88; Tim Travers, 'A Particular Style of Command: Haig and GHQ, 1916–18', *Journal of Strategic Studies* 10, 3, 1987, pp. 363–376. On German defensive doctrine, see Timothy Lupfer, *The Dynamics of Doctrine* (Combat Studies Institute, Fort Leavenworth, 1981); Martin Samuels, *Command or Control: Command, Training and Tactics in the British and German Armies, 1888–1918* (Frank Cass, London, 1995), pp. 158–197.

12   Prior and Wilson, *Passchendaele*, pp. 45–52.

13   Ibid., pp. 64–66.

14   PRO, WO 158/249, Note by Haig on Fifth Army Order to Corps Commanders, 30 Jun. 1917; *OFH*, p. 131; Davidson, *Haig: Master of the Field*, pp. 26–29; King's College, Liddell Hart Centre for Military Archives (hereafter LHCMA), Kiggell Mss, V/114, Kiggell to Gough, 7 Aug. 1917; French, *Strategy*, p. 127.

15   Andrew Wiest, 'Haig's Abortive Amphibious Assault on Belgium, 1917', *The Historian*, June 1992, pp. 669–682; PRO, Cab 45/114, Note by Wynne on conversation with Davidson, 21 Apl. 1945; Ibid., Cab 45/140, Wynne to Edmonds, 16 Feb. 1944, Gough to Edmonds, 27 May 1945, and note by Wynne on conversation with Gough, 31 May 1945; Davidson, *Haig: Master of the Field*, pp. 26–32. Geoffrey Powell, *Plumer: The Soldier's General* (Leo Cooper, London, 1990) is in error in stating that Gough was the only source for Plumer's support for the first day plan since it was also Davidson's recollection, as stated both in his own book and his conversation with Wynne noted above.

16   Brigadier-General John Charteris, *At GHQ* (Cassell, London, 1931); Ibid.,

Field Marshal Earl Haig (Cassell, London, 1929); Duff Cooper, *Haig* (Faber & Faber, London, 1935–36), 2 vols.; G. A. B. Dewar and J. H. Boraston, *Sir Douglas Haig's Command, 1915–18* (Constable, London, 1922), 2 vols.; David French, 'Sir Douglas Haig's Reputation, 1918–28', *Historical Journal* 28, 4, 1985, pp. 953–60.

17 Prior and Wilson, *Passchendaele*, pp. 160–161.

18 Travers, *Killing Ground*, pp. 108, 120, n. 28; LHCMA, Liddell Hart Mss 11/1927/17, Note of Conversation with Edmonds, 7 Oct. 1927.

19 PRO, WO 158/239, Kiggell to Bacon, 15 Oct. 1917.

20 Travers, *Killing Ground*, pp. 85–126; Gerard de Groot, *Douglas Haig, 1861–1928* (Unwin Hyman, London, 1988), pp. 50–53.

21 General Sir Hubert Gough, *The Fifth Army* (Hodder & Stoughton, London, 1931), pp. 195–198. For Neuve Chapelle and the Somme, see Travers, *Killing Ground*, pp. 127–151.

22 PRO, WO 158/249, Malcolm to Corps Commanders, 30 Jun. and 8 Jul. 1917: Travers, *Killing Ground*, p. 205–214; Prior and Wilson, *Passchendaele*, pp. 73–77, 86–87.

23 LHCMA, Liddell Hart Mss, II/1934/46, Note of Conversation with Broad, 22 Aug. 1934; PRO, Cab 45/140, Gough margin comments on drafts of OFH and Gough to Edmonds, 7 Jun. 1944 and 27 May 1945; Gough, Fifth Army, pp. 206–207.

24 Powell, *Plumer*, p. 210; Malcolm Mss, Diary entries for 25 and 26 Aug. 1917.

25 Anthony Farrar-Hockley, *Goughie* (Hart-Davis, MacGibbon, London, 1973), pp. 224, 229–230; Prior and Wilson, *Passchendaele*, pp. 108–110.

26 Travers, *Killing Ground*, pp. 101–123; PRO, Cab 45/140, Gough to Edmonds, 27 May 1945; Aylmer Haldane Mss, Diary entry for 4 Sep. 1917 quoted by Travers, 'A Particular Style of Command', pp. 363–376.

27 Malcolm Mss, Diary for 10 Jun. 1916; Hubert Gough Mss, Gough to Edmonds, 3 May 1944 and Malcolm to Gough, 24 and 29 Apl. 1944.

28 LHCMA, Edmonds Mss, II/1/43, Gough to Edmonds, 3 May 1923; Beckett, 'Hubert Gough, Neill Malcolm and Command on the Western Front'; Malcolm Mss, Diary entries for 13 Jul. 1916, 18 Jun. and 8 Aug. 1917.

29 Farrar-Hockley, *Goughie*, pp. 228–229.

30 Farrar-Hockley, *Goughie*, pp. 237, 239, Robert Blake (ed.), The Private Papers of Douglas Haig (Eyre & Spottiswoode, London, 1952), pp. 257, 272; Malcolm Mss, Diary entry for 16 Dec. 1917.

31 LHCMA, Liddell Hart Mss, 11/1933/23, Note of conversation with Pope-Hennessy, 14 Oct. 1933; Ibid., 11/1936/31 Note of conversation with Lloyd George and Gough, 27 Jan. 1939; Gough, *Fifth Army*, pp. 134–135; Imperial War Museum, Smith Mss, Smith to mother, 17 Dec. 1917 and 16 May 1918.

32 Malcolm Mss, Diary entries for 11 Jul., 25 Jul., 4 Aug., 16 Aug., 18 Aug., 6 Sep., 18 Sep., 19 Sep., 28 Sep., 30 Sep., 31 Oct. 1917; Prior and Wilson, *Command on the Western Front*, p. 183.

33 Bidwell and Graham, *Firepower*, pp. 89–91; Malcolm Mss, Diary entry for 24 Sep. 1917.

34 *OFH*, p. 138, n.2; Prior and Wilson, *Passchendaele*, pp. 82–84.

35 Prior and Wilson, *Passchendaele*, pp. 115–119, 128, 131, 161–162, 166–167, 199–200.

36 *OFH*, p. xv, 360–363; Prior and Wilson, *Passchendaele*, p. 195.

37 J Brent Wilson, 'The Morale and Discipline of the BEF, 1914–18', Unpub. M.A., New Brunswick, 1978, pp. 67–117, 212–262.

38 Travers, *How The War Was Won*, passim; Prior and Wilson, *Command on the Western Front*, passim.

Quotations from Crown copyright records in the Public Record Office appear by permission of Her Majesty's Controller of Stationery. Grateful acknowledgement is also given for permission to consult and quote from archives in the care of the Trustees of the Imperial War Museum and the Trustees of the Liddell Hart Centre for Military Archives, King's College, London. Particular acknowledgement is given to the assistance of Mrs Denise Boyes (Huber Gough Mss) and Captain Dugald Malcolm (Malcolm Mss) in enabling consultation of archives remaining in private hands.

Chapter 9

Field Survey in the Salient: Cartography and Artillery Survey in the Flanders Operations in 1917

Peter Chasseaud

DEVELOPMENT OF THE SURVEY ORGANISATION.

The contribution of survey to the ultimate British success in 1914–18 has been veiled for too long, deliberately because of the need for secrecy (Haig's despatches only referred obliquely at first to the location work of the field survey companies (FSCs) for this reason), and later, as the war became history, because of lack of comprehension of its achievement. The work of the artillery is frequently invoked, but not the vital contribution made by survey to its effectiveness; in particular to the achievement of surprise through the application of survey data to gunnery ('unregistered' or 'predicted' fire).

Engineer and artillery survey developed rapidly and by 1917 it had evolved into a technological weapon of massive potential; the astounding initial success of the Battle of Cambrai in November was in large part due to the application of survey techniques to gunnery (the Germans had used a similar technique at Riga in September). Enemy batteries had been located by the flash-spotting groups and sound-ranging sections of 3rd FSC, which also surveyed-in the British batteries. Thus all British and enemy batteries and other targets were fixed to the survey grid, the control for which had been built up since 1915 by the sappers. Emphasising the nature of the 'artillery war', Lieutenant-Colonel Harold Winterbotham RE (later a Director General of the Ordnance Survey), one of the principal figures in the British survey organisation, remarked that the vast majority of survey work had been for the artillery[1].

In 1914 it was expected that the war, which would be brief, would be conducted on reproductions of the national maps of France and Belgium, and the BEF had been equipped with 'tactical' maps to the scales of 1:80,000 (France) and 1:100,000 (Belgium). A tiny Topographical Subsection under Major E. M. Jack RE, known as 'Maps GHQ' (another

117

later Director General of the Ordnance Survey), went out with the BEF and was responsible for all survey and mapping matters, including the work of the Printing Company RE; by the end of the war Jack, now Colonel Jack, was responsible for an organization of over 4,000 officers and men who were engaged in the systematic acquisition and application of survey data, and the FSCs were enlarged into field survey battalions. Colonel Jack ('Maps' GHQ) emphasized that their contribution was out of all proportion to their size[2].

The stalemate, starting on the Aisne, immediately demonstrated the need for large-scale (1:40,000 and 1:20,000) maps for artillery work as indirect fire became the rule. When batteries and targets were hidden, and observing oficers could not see both, firing by the map was inevitable. A Ranging Section RE under Captain Winterbotham was rushed to Flanders in November 1914 to help to locate enemy batteries by intersecting a visual signal dropped by an aeroplane over the battery. This section turned to mapping work in early 1915 when it was realized that enlargements of the French 1:80,000 were hopelessly inaccurate for artillery work, and the section also started fixing British heavy batteries before the Neuve Chapelle battle in order to achieve surprise and save expensive ammunition. This enabled range and bearing to the target to be read off the map or calculated trigonometrically and applied to the gun. Batteries were provided with this data in graphic form, and soon with rigid 'artillery boards' on which grid, gun position and targets were plotted. Later, squares of the trench map were pasted onto the grid, thus providing more data for the gunners. All this was the origin of 'predicted' fire, used so successfully at Cambrai, at Hamel, Amiens and later battles in 1918, and at El Alamein and the Rhine crossing in the next war.

During 1915, the survey rapidly expanded. In December 1914, the BEF had been split into two armies, and over the next few months each was given a maps officer and a section of the Printing Company. Between July (when Third Army was formed) and September 1915, these 'maps and printing sections' were enlarged into topographical sections, which became FSCs in February 1916. These sections were responsible for all ground survey and trigonometrical work, map compilation, drawing and printing, panorama photos, and enemy battery location by flash-spotting and sound-ranging. The 1:10,000 scale trench maps haphazardly developed by Intelligence and lithographed at army headquarters or at GHQ, or even printed at Southampton, were replaced in the summer of 1915 by a regular series of 1:10,000 sheets prepared by the topographical sections.

The Belgian national survey was good material, but further south the FSCs had to make a completely new large-scale map to replace the French 1:80,000. They fitted to the old French trig points all available large-scale topographical material such as village (communal), mine, railway and canal plans and then revised these and plotted tactical details such as trenches from air photos. For the area in British hands, the topographers conducted a plane-table survey, again using communal plans as a base.

During 1916, the large-scale trench and artillery map developed into an even more accurate and sophisticated data-plot which also served as a base for overprinting with further intelligence, artillery or other tactical information, especially during the Somme battle. Hostile battery maps evolved, and daily situation maps were printed during operations showing British and German front lines and new trenches. Barrage, target and track maps appeared, and also those recording enemy counter-attacks; these last proved particularly useful for planning dispositions, defensive fire, standing barrages and artillery SOS lines, and were a feature of the operations at Ypres the following year.

Battery survey had developed during the year, a notable advance being the introduction by Capt. B. F. E. Keeling (formerly of the Survey of Egypt), Trig Officer of 4th FSC and from July OC of the new 5th FSC, of the auxiliary trig point later known as a 'bearing picket', near the battery position, to fix and provide line (bearing) for long-range railway guns before 1 July. Keeling was wounded on the Somme, but returned in 1917 to command the new Depot FSC, and later 3rd FSC. In the Autumn of 1916, 3rd FSC made extensive use of such pickets. Towards the end of 1916, it had been found necessary to devolve many survey functions to corps, particularly British battery fixing (field batteries were fixed graphically by plane-tablers, and heavy and siege batteries instrumentally with the theodolite) and the rapid production of tactical maps during operations. Corps topographical sections were therefore formed over the next few months, coming under the FSCs.

Most of the 32 million trench and other maps, used during the war, were printed at the Ordnance Survey at Southampton, though at the end of 1917, an Overseas Branch of the Ordnance Survey was established in France. The number of maps printed at the front by the BEF was tiny at first, but as the FSCs were gradually equipped with more and better printing facilities, the numbers increased dramatically in 1917 and 1918, to that of millions.

ENEMY BATTERY LOCATION; FLASH-SPOTTING & SOUND-RANGING.

When FSCs were formed, they included observation groups for the location of enemy batteries by instrumental flash-spotting (cross-observation, or intersection) from fixed survey posts, sound-ranging sections for locating German guns by recording the arrival of the sound wave at a row of carefully surveyed microphones, and compilation sections for analysing the results from all location sources. By 1917 these were generally allocated to army FSCs on the basis of one observation group and one sound-ranging section per corps. Around Ypres they came under 2nd FSC (Major C. S. Reid RE). In the autumn of 1915, the first British experimental sound-ranging section under the Nobel Prize-winning physicist Lieutenant W. L. Bragg was installed south of Ypres at La Clytte, later moving to Kemmel. Sound-ranging had been mooted before the war in Austria, patented in Germany in 1913, and developed both by the Germans and the French at the end of 1914, the Germans using it in late 1914 in the La Bassée area.

The British used the Bull apparatus, in which signals from microphones were carried to fine filaments suspended in the magnetic field of an Einthoven 'string' galvanometer; these were filmed as the sound wave activated them, thus creating a visual record which was also marked by a time scale. The position of the gun could be calculated from the differences between the times the sound wave arrived at each microphone, but the early microphones responded to all noises except the low frequency gun report. In June 1916, the physicist Lieutenant Tucker, who had joined Bragg's section at Kemmel, invented the hot-wire microphone. This enabled the burst of the enemy's shell, as well as the sound of discharge, to be recorded. By September 1916, all eight British sections (two to each army) were equipped with the new microphone, and the failure of the first year was followed by a sudden transformation of locating. Sound-ranging was the 'Manhattan Project' of the 1914–18 war, employing over 200 British scientists, mathematicians and electrical engineers. Bragg recruited many of Rutherford's research team from Manchester, including Andrade, Nuttal, Marsden, Gray, Darwin, Robinson and Russell[3]. The French and Germans (Max Born was engaged in research), and later the Americans, similarly employed large numbers of scientists in sound-ranging.

During the Somme battle, corps had been evolving a new heavy artillery counter-battery (CB) organisation, based on a CB staff officer (CBSO or 'counter-blaster') who collated location reports from the RFC, artillery forward observation officers (FOOs) and FSC groups and sections. All FSCs had problems ensuring that group observers were watching the same flash. 'Synchronisation' was achieved in June 1916 by the invention of the 'flash and buzzer board' by 3rd FSC's Lieutenant Harold Hemming. This board enabled a controller at group HQ to concentrate observations onto the same enemy battery, thus vastly increasing the number and accuracy of locations. By the end of 1916, each army had a thoroughly efficient and experienced FSC, which not only supplied all the maps and surveyed the British batteries, but also, through its groups and sections, provided accurate locations of hostile batteries to the corps CBSOs. The groups and sections had begun in 1916 to range British guns onto hostile batteries; in bad visibility sound-ranging was the only way of doing this. The flash-spotters also began to 'range on the air burst', a practice delayed in the British army by the shortage of mechanical time-fuzes.

By 1917, there were over twenty British sound-ranging sections, and a corresponding number of observation groups. FSCs had about four of each, giving one per corps and covering the whole front. The success of CB work at Arras and Vimy in April 1917 was largely due to the location of over 90 per cent of German batteries by 1st and 3rd FSCs; flash-spotting and sound-ranging locations being confirmed by air photos. Winterbotham, commanding 3rd FSC, strongly urged the advantage of surprise at Arras, believing that survey had developed sufficiently to neutralize the enemy artillery with a 'hurricane bombardment'; GHQ disagreed, and Allenby was forced to adopt a longer bombardment. Significantly, it was 3rd FSC (under Keeling) which achieved the 'survey surprise' at Cambrai.

The Arras, Vimy and Messines attacks demonstrated the slowness of the sound-ranging sections to move forward and get back into action on new microphone bases. This was largely due to reliance on army or corps signals units for cable-laying, and also to delays in the survey of the microphone positions. 'Maps GHQ' and the FSCs responded by instituting courses in self-sufficiency and mobility; at Cambrai, 'H' Section was in action on its new base in 56 hours, and in 1918 even faster times were achieved. The effectiveness of sound-ranging was enhanced, from August 1917, by the gradual establishment of 'wind sections' in army areas. These monitored changing atmospheric conditions and fed the data to the sections in the line, enabling them to make the appropriate corrections when an enemy battery was located or being ranged on.

SURVEY TRIUMPH AT MESSINES; 2nd FIELD SURVEY COMPANY.

The Messines battle in June 1917 was fought on the same principles as the Arras and Vimy attacks, including the survey of forward positions for batteries which were to advance at zero, and for machine gun barrages. 2nd FSC located over 90 per cent of the hostile batteries, and also prepared special maps, fixed battery positions, made-up artillery boards, and provided survey expertise for mining. It supplied maps printed at Southampton, and at FSC HQ at Cassel, to the assault units. In May, it issued 589,000 maps, most of which were printed by the Ordnance Survey. Corps topographical sections overprinted on brief sheets and distributed these as well. The Maps and Printing Officer, the geologist Ben Lightfoot, organized the drawing, printing and distribution of maps, as well as the taking of panorama photos. At first, like the other FSCs, equipped only with hand-presses, the 2nd received its first power-press, a demy, and photo-mechanical apparatus, in May, enabling it to overprint the barrage maps.

For the first time, an army artillery plan was created, founded on survey data and assisted by gun calibration and meteorological data, and a 1:10,000 barrage map (in several sheets) produced. In previous battles, relatively unco-ordinated barrage maps had been produced by corps and divisions. The creeping barrage relying on the map, first tried at Loos in September 1915, had developed on the Somme and became a crucial element in all big operations. It was a notable feature of the Arras and Vimy attacks.

Heavy batteries were fixed, and artillery boards supplied, by 2nd FSC's Trig Section, under Lieutenant Alexander Simms, who before the war had worked on geodetic survey in Africa. Field batteries were fixed by the corps topographical sections. 2,266 guns and howitzers were concentrated west of the Messines – Wytschaete Ridge, including 756 heavy or medium. At

Arras, 3rd FSC had made a significant innovation by surveying forward positions for the field artillery so that batteries could move up rapidly and pick up their barrage lines immediately from bearing pickets. The same procedure was followed at Messines.

One of the tasks of 2nd FSC was to assist with survey for the tunnelling companies. Positions in the German lines were fixed by intersection and from air photographs, a special series of which was taken for the mine survey:

> The direction of the galleries ... had to be determined very accurately on data obtained from an excellent series of aeroplane photographs taken for the purpose. The best testimony to the precision with which the work was executed, is that all the mines achieved their objectives[4].

Before Messines, GHQ had suggested that corps should form report centres for the rapid reception and transmission of all tactical information (including enemy battery locations) during operations. Tim Harington (Plumer's Chief of Staff) decided to create an Army Report Centre at Locre Château; this began working on 3 June, being linked by buried cables to corps centres at Bailleul, Mont Noir and Reninghelst, and also to corps heavy artillery and divisional headquarters. 2nd FSC played a vital part, because of its well-placed flash-spotting survey posts, and its sound-ranging sections which could give essential information as to enemy artillery activity and areas being shelled.

Enemy batteries had been located by the groups and sections, of 2nd FSC, the RFC and FOOs. 'A' Group had its HQ at Vlamertinghe Château, and covered the Ypres salient; 'B' Group at Kemmel covered the Messines – Wytschaete ridge, and 'C' Group at Armentières covered the Kemmel – Ploegsteert front. For a few months at the beginning of 1917, the artist and writer David Jones served with 'B' Group.

The deployment of 2nd FSC's sound-ranging sections was:

'A' Section	VIII Corps	Northern flank of Ypres salient (N of Bellewaarde Lake)
'N' Section	II Corps	Astride Menin Road
'I' Section	X Corps	Mount Sorrel – St. Eloi
'W' Section	IX Corps	Grand Bois – Wytschaete sector
'M' Section	I ANZAC	Messines – Warneton sector[5]

As the location effort intensified, an increasing number of destructive shoots was carried out, rising from 12 in the week ending 19 April to 120 in the week ending 24 May (109 of which were located by flash). By 31 May the weekly figure was 166, and by 7 June the figure for the last ten days was 438[6]. Barrage rehearsals forced the Germans to disclose hidden batteries, which were picked up by the flash-spotters. A counter-battery map issued three weeks before the attack showed 172 German batteries in the main sector to be attacked[7], while Harington noted that over 200 batteries were systematically dealt with by the British counter-batteries[8]. Of 630 German guns between Mount Sorrel and St. Yves, a quarter of the field pieces and almost half the heavies were destroyed[9].

Major-General Franks, Second Army's GOC, RA, remarked of the survey contribution:

> . . . we had to . . . locate every German gun and get it picketed or knocked out. There were hundreds of German guns in front of us, and between the air photographs, the Field Survey work, flash spotting at night, and sound ranging, we got onto the German guns and knocked them about so badly that they gave us very little trouble indeed during that battle. After the battle . . . We went over all those German battery positions and compared them with the records which had been worked out and mapped, for day by day during the battle fresh counter-battery maps were brought out, showing the positions as they shifted, and we found on comparing results with what we could see on the ground that we had got over 90 per cent of the German guns absolutely accurately located. And what was most wonderful of all was that wherever there was a doubt about the position of a battery, in every case the sound rangers were right: they had beaten everybody in accuracy[10]

A SURVEY DISASTER AT 3rd YPRES; 2nd AND 5th FIELD SURVEY COMPANIES.

TRIG & TOPO.

The relative failure at Ypres was not a failure of survey but rather of strategy and operational planning; the survey organization did its best under impossible conditions. Survey techniques were astonishingly vindicated at Cambrai and in the 1918 battles.

The Ypres battle was fought by Second and Fifth Armies, both 2nd FSC (Major Reid) and 5th FSC (Major F. B. Legh) being involved. Fourth Army, with Major M. N. MacLeod's 4th FSC, was waiting on the coast for the combined operations that never happened. Fifth Army took over Second Army front from Observatory Ridge northwards on 10 June, and on 18 July the strength of 5th FSC was 21 officers and 389 men[11]. From a survey point of view, the change of the main attack frontage from Second to Fifth Army was unwise, as it meant that the incoming 5th FSC had to start from scratch, with no local knowledge, having to learn the ground, identify trig points, and assimilate the existing cartographic material and the unceasing flow of new photographs.

Lieutenant Aldous, 5th FSC's Trig Officer, took over the trig data and mapping of Fifth Army area from 2nd FSC. The primary task was artillery survey, as many new batteries were moving into the salient and their positions, or bearing pickets in each artillery brigade area, had to be fixed. It is significant that when Wyndham Lewis painted 'A Battery Shelled' in this period, he placed the survey instrument (an artillery director) centre stage. Fifth Army took over 203 heavy howitzers and 444 field guns and howitzers from Second Army, but in the next month a further 249 heavy howitzers and 978 field pieces had been transferred from other armies. Other batteries arrived only in the week before the attack[12].

Initially 5th FSC's flash-spotters worked from old 2nd FSC posts, but new microphone positions had to be fixed for the sound-rangers. The shifting of microphone positions and the establishment of new OPs for the observation groups after the battle had started meant that the trig staff were continually surveying in exposed forward areas in some of the worst conditions of the war. Obtaining information about the movements of batteries, and then trying to find them proved exceptionally difficult during this battle. Topographers had to struggle forward to field battery positions with weighty plane-tables and tripods strapped to their backs, and trig observers had to get up to the heavies carrying theodolites and tripods. Fixing trigs and resecting in the swampy wasteland of the Flanders battle-field was an almost impossible task, though right up to the end it was possible for the batteries to see a vital trig point – the ruins of Passchendaele church – a few thousand yards ahead. Pushing the trig skeleton forward was vitally important for fixing battery positions and targets, as well as OPs and microphone bases, but was seriously hampered by weather conditions unsuitable for observation, the state of the ground, by continual heavy shelling and by road congestion which prevented survey parties from moving forward.

MAPS AND PRINTING.

Special sheets could now be produced photo-mechanically and printed on the demy power-presses. The Depot FSC had actually received its first powered press in the autumn of 1916, and now, for the Flanders operations, it set up a printing plant at Haig's Advanced GHQ in a train at Westcappel, 19 miles from Ypres. During the battle it produced the crucial maps on which operational decisions were based:

> German Order of Battle, Situation Maps showing Distribution of the Enemy's Forces, The Enemy's Dispositions, The Enemy's Counter-Attacks against the Fifth and Second Armies, and Hostile Tactical Maps – Enemy's Reserves, Concentrations & Counter Attack Methods East of Ypres[13].

Between June and November, 2nd and 5th FSCs supplemented the regular series by producing series of 1:10,000 demy sheets, covering their respective army fronts. These went into several editions. They were primarily infantry maps, but were also used by field artillery as fighting and barrage maps. Various overprints besides the usual trench plates were added, including layers, secret editions showing British dispositions, occupied shell-holes and posts, barrages, concrete structures, strong points, information from captured German maps, target maps, and wet areas.

They also produced series of 1:20,000 corps front demy sheets, again going into many editions. These were the primary artillery series. They

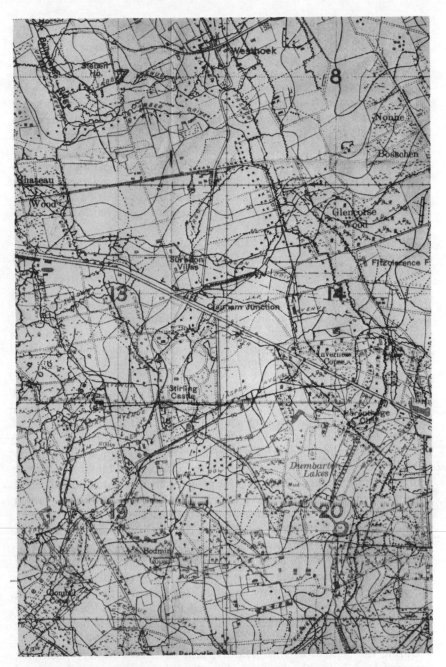

(vi) Trench map (trenches corrected to 30.6.17) of the Gheluvelt Plateau area, showing the Menin Road running past Château Wood (Hooge), Clapham Junction and Inverness Copse. The density of German defences in this crucial area proved an insuperable barrier to the British advance. *(Peter Chasseaud Collection)*

were overprinted with various forms of artillery intelligence, including hostile artillery dispositions, hostile counter-attacks, tracks, routes and artillery targets (harassing fire), enemy reserves and concentrations, red British front line and posts, wet and marshy ground (soil maps), and special CB editions with green woods for the Flying Corps. Some sheets were layered, the better to show ground forms. It became the practice to show concrete works by special signs. The task of compiling hostile battery lists and preparing hostile battery maps was a huge one, and occupied three officers of 5th FSC.

Series of 1:10,000 and 1:20,000 brief sheets and message maps were also produced, often issued down to infantry section commanders, as well as village plans. Some of the brief sheets were overprinted as barrage maps. Altogether, several million maps were issued during the battle.

OPERATIONS.

The bombardment at Ypres posed a special problem for the artillery, and made accurate survey even more vital:

> Facing the entire front of the Fifth Army the German defences, except for a forward observation line, lay on a reverse slope and completely out of sight of ground observers. The success of the preliminary bombardment consequently depended upon direction from aircraft and shooting by the map based on air photographs[14].

On 31 July, the first day of the attack, Second Army on the right did little more than advance its line to obtain better observation and improve its position. Its main task was to act as a flank guard for the major thrust made by Fifth Army and it also lent useful artillery support, aided by 2nd FSC, by attempting to neutralize the important German artillery group hidden behind the Zandvoorde ridge. After 24 August, Haig took a firmer grip on operations because of the poor progress by Fifth Army and decided to give Plumer the crucial task of capturing the Gheluvelt Plateau, which Gough had failed to do. Second Army was ordered to take over Fifth Army front as far north as the Ypres – Roulers railway on 26 August, and this involved the transfer of tasks from 5th to 2nd FSC.

Plumer's step-by-step siege methods were to be essentially those of Messines, an artillery battle relying heavily on survey. Batteries had to be surveyed after each step, enemy batteries and defensive positions located, and new barrage maps prepared. He used 1,295 guns and howitzers, of which 575 were heavy and medium, more than double the allotment to the same frontage for 31 July[15].

During the September fine weather, 2nd FSC fixed battery positions, prepared boards for the heavy and medium batteries, and printed and distributed special maps, particularly for artillery purposes. Sound-ranging sections and observation groups prepared to move forward and establish new bases as soon as possible, to keep enemy batteries neutralized. In the preparatory period from 31 August to 20 September:

Battery positions, pillboxes, machine-gun nests, observation posts, telephone exchanges, were systematically bombarded by the aid of information obtained from air photographs, prisoners' statements, ground observation and other means – counter-battery fire was particularly assisted by the work of the four sound-ranging sections of the 2nd Field Survey Company R.E., using bases east of Ypres ['I' Section], at Zillebeke ['A' Section], on the Wytschaete ridge ['W' Section] and on Hill 63 (Ploegsteert) ['M' Section], covering the whole Second Army area[16].

Second Army Report Centre was still at Locre.

The obliteration of trenches and all other features by the bombardments, and the later revision of German defence tactics on the 'forefield' principle, made it necessary for intelligence officers and cartographers to identify defended crater areas – 'organized shell-holes' were identified by tracks on air photos and indicated on maps by a rash of little red circles. One of the supreme ironies of the Flanders offensive was the creation by the British of their own worst obstacle – the artillery preparation and covering barrages cut up the country so much that tanks ultimately had to be withdrawn from the battle, while guns, men and mules sank beneath the mud. The topography was utterly transformed. Plumer's series of attacks was successful, but was brought to a halt early in October by deteriorating weather. The last few weeks of the battle were fought in such dreadful conditions that the ultimate achievement, the capture by the Canadians of the ruins of Passchendaele, has given its name to the whole of the Third Battle of Ypres in popular memory.

I ANZAC CORPS TOPO SECTION.

The experiences of I ANZAC Corps Topo Section are indicative of the work of such sections. From 1 September, preparatory mapping work was undertaken, and on 5 September, I ANZAC relieved the exhausted II Corps between Hooge and the Ypres – Roulers railway. The Section office opened at Hoograaf, south of Poperinghe, and the drawing staff was kept busy with mapping for the operations of 20 and 26 September. In September, a record number of 30,691 maps was issued including maps printed by 2nd FSC and GHQ, but excluding issues from 2nd FSC direct to divisions. The Section produced 62 different maps during September, big editions being prepared by the Section and printed by the Army Printing & Stationery Services.

During September the Section reseted 54 field batteries, fixed 2 calibration points and supplied 39 artillery boards. A 'Corps model' was built south-east of Busseboom, being kept up to date and corrected from air photographs. It proved of great use to attacking troops.

The Corps was also heavily engaged in October, during the Passchendaele battles. The drawing staff was hard-pressed with mapping for the operations of 4, 9, 12 and 26 October, each requiring 1:10,000 objective maps, barrage maps, up to date corps front maps showing latest enemy work, and 1:5,000 message maps for use in battle.

Work was also done for the Corps 'Q' Branch, Signals, the Chemical Adviser and Intelligence. Staff maps were also kept up to date from air photos and reports. During October, 20,547 maps were issued, 24 field batteries were resected and 40 artillery boards supplied. A plane-table survey of pill-boxes in the Corps area was begun on 22 October; by the end of the month 97 had been fixed. Work on the Corps model had stopped on 5 October after the Broodseinde battle, as the work could not keep pace with the advances. During October, the Section produced 75 different maps.

Between 1 and 14 November, while the Canadian Corps was attacking Passchendaele, I ANZAC was holding the line to its south between Becelaere and the Ypres – Roulers railway. 46 more pill-boxes and 3 field batteries were resected, and 3 map boards supplied. During Third Ypres, three NCOs did all the work of resecting field batteries and other survey work in the Corps area[17].

ENEMY BATTERY LOCATION – 2nd & 5th FSC FLASH-SPOTTING AND SOUND-RANGING.

Following the Messines attack, the groups and sections of 2nd FSC continued with location work on their front from Observatory Ridge to the Lys; their deployment had changed because the northern part of Second Army front had been handed over to Fifth Army. 'A' Group of 2nd FSC, the northernmost group, was initially transferred to 5th FSC. 'B' and 'C' Groups had pushed posts forward onto the Messines – Wytschaete ridge after 7 June.

After Messines, 'N' Section was transferred to 4th FSC on the coast, and soon after to Egypt. 2nd FSC's other sound-ranging sections were deployed as follows: 'A' Section at Zillebeke, 'I' Section south-east of Ypres with a base facing Hollebeke, 'W' Section on the Messines – Wytschaete Ridge, and 'M' Section at Ploegsteert (Hill 63) on the southernmost part of Second Army front. During Third Ypres, 'A' and 'I' Sections were caught in the thick of things, being exposed to heavy shelling for months. The battery area around Zillebeke, Verbrandenmolen and elsewhere east of Ypres, attracted constant German 'area shoots', and these concentrations played havoc with sound-ranging lines. Buried cables were a mixed blessing; while they protected lines from breaks caused by shellfire, if a break did occur it was almost impossible to locate!

The Germans were reinforcing the Ypres front in the full knowledge that the Allies were planning a further attack, and 2nd FSC had the task of locating the new batteries and of supporting Fifth Army to its left with counter-battery fire. A ferocious artillery battle developed, with British batteries in the exposed salient suffering severe losses. By 31 July, the British had still not gained a significant mastery, many German batteries remaining unsubdued. It was a most inauspicious start for Haig's Flanders offensive. Second Army's 'Summaries of Operations' for the weeks ending on the dates given below indicate the intensity of its CB work:

Date	Our Destructive Shoots	Enemy Batteries Neutralized
21st June	87 (with aeroplane or balloon)	734
28th June	111 (101 with aeroplane observation)	360
5th July	45	
12th July	38 observed, & 13 heavy concentrations, & others.	
19th July	n.a.	328
26th July	137	441
16th Aug	140	379
23rd Aug	139	445[18]

The groups and sections had helped to locate these batteries in the first place, and continued to report on their state of activity, which helped to confirm which positions were occupied.

2nd FSC's 'C' Group was heavily embroiled in the Flanders offensive, being lent to 5th FSC from 17 August to 3 September and having to keep lines open over heavily shelled ground to the exposed Westhoek ridge. It later moved to the Broodseinde ridge front. Lines were continually being cut by shellfire (the sound-ranging sections suffering from the same problem), and locations suffered as a result.

5th FSC initially had two sound-ranging sections in the line. 'R' Section had its HQ at Tank Farm, which was shared with a Second Army section, north of Dickebusch Lake. 'Q' Section, covering the northern sector of the Salient, had its HQ in the grounds of Vlamertinghe Château[19]. In June, 'R' Section established for the first time a microphone base on the chord of the Ypres salient, along the line of the Yser and Comines canals, a length of 7,000 yards. The recording apparatus was protected by concrete shelters behind the walls of a barn. The north OP was at La Brique, west of St Jean, inside a small cottage which had been strengthened with concrete. It was thought that short-wave radio might here solve the problem of line-maintenance, but the experiment was not a great success. The trench-set wireless apparatus was linked to a loop aerial consisting of four mercury-vapour light tubes[20], supplied by the drawing office. The south OP at Hellfire Corner suffered from heavy shelling, and this led to a new OP being established near the Section HQ, well behind the microphone line. This proved very successful, particularly in locating high-velocity guns which were used for harassing fire[21].

For the opening of the battle 5th FSC had two groups for flash-spotting. In the north, No. 1 Group (later renumbered 12) had its HQ at Vlamertinghe Château, and OPs at Woesten, Elverdinghe White Mill, Vlamertinghe Château and Goldfish Château. No. 2 Group (later renumbered 13) had its HQ near Brandhoek and posts covering the southern area at Elverdinghe White Mill, Vlamertinghe Château, Château Segard and Wytschaete[22].

The weather broke on 31 July, and August was a dreadful month for observation as well as for fighting, with much rain and wind, and very limited visibility. Following the capture of the Pilckem Ridge on 31 July, No.1 Group was able to move some posts forward between 6 and 12 August. This gave good observation northwards towards the Houthulst Forest and eastwards to Langemarck and Poelcappelle but, in the crucial Gheluvelt Plateau sector in the south, II Corps' attack stalled along the Menin Road, little ground was gained and the Germans retained the best of the observation. The Bellewarde ridge was captured but this only provided observation to the north-east. Useful high ground from Observatory Ridge to Clapham Junction on the Menin Road was also gained, but little work could be done owing to the proximity to the German line, the intensive shelling, the fact that most German artillery was defiladed behind Zandvoorde and the Gheluvelt plateau, the many spurs and re-entrants of the plateau, and poor visibility. No.2 Group was unable to move any posts forward for nearly two weeks after the initial assault. Many men from the groups and sections were gassed or wounded. The intense shelling at the start of the battle cut up the sound-ranging lines so badly that all the personnel of 'R' Section were out in line-repairing parties. On 7 August, an officer was wounded and a photographer killed by a shell while working on the lines[23]. Other, heavy, casualties followed.

The relative failure on the Gheluvelt plateau gave the measure of the strength of the German defences. Though these were broadly known to Fifth Army staff and well mapped, certain features had escaped notice, particularly in the wooded areas. In the first assault, two German maps had been captured showing hidden machine-gun emplacements in the area subsequently to be attacked. Accurate shooting by heavy howitzers would be necessary for their destruction and, luckily, some valuable observation areas had been occupied on 31 July. Unfortunately, it rained for days, the battlefield turned into a swamp and observation was poor. A further attack on 10 August failed, largely because the German artillery concentration about the Gheluvelt plateau could not be located. There were too few periods of good visibility to check from the air the shifting of German batteries to their alternative emplacements – typically they had three or four and, though these were shown on the hostile battery maps produced at frequent intervals by the FSCs, it could not be said with any certainty which were occupied. The German guns had remained unmastered, and British artillery losses were severe. On 16 August, Gough attacked again, but the German batteries remained unsubdued. It proved remarkably difficult for the British artillery to deal even with targets which had been accurately located. To help 5th FSC to locate German batteries more effectively following this failure, 'B' Sound-Ranging Section was formed on 17 August, No. 3 Group being transferred from 2nd to 5th FSC, possibly to provide its nucleus. 'B' Section lost an officer and three men wounded on 7 September[24].

On 24 August, No.2 Group HQ moved from the Canal Bank near Noordhof Farm, north of Ypres, into Ypres itself. Its posts were now between St. Julien and the Menin Road, looking in a generally north-

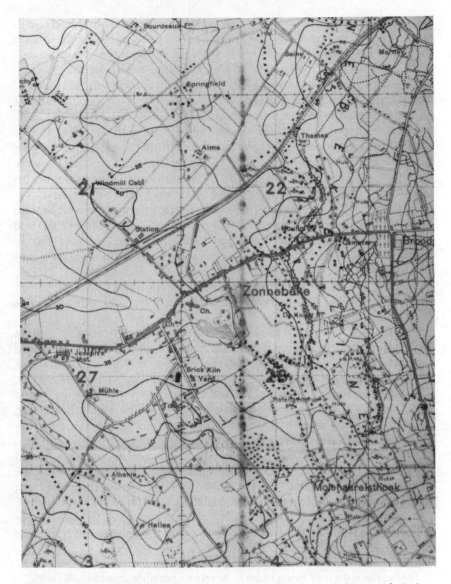

(vii) Trench map (trenches corrected to 8.9.17) of the Zonnebeke-Broodseinde area; concrete works are marked "C". *(Peter Chasseaud Collection)*

eastward direction. The southernmost post of this group had shifted north-wards over 7,000 yards. 5th FSC now had no posts south of the Menin Road. As Fifth Army moved slowly forward through the slough during August, 'R' Section followed up. On 29 August, half of the Section, including its HQ, moved from Tank Farm to a new HQ in the ramparts of Ypres. Its microphone base was now about 5,600 yards long, and ran just behind the old British front, facing towards Zonnebeke and Passchendaele. It was now covering part of the salient rather more to the north-east of its original base, as Second Army took over more front. On 3 September, No.3 Group was transferred back to 2nd FSC, the Gheluvelt plateau frontage having been transferred to Second Army following Gough's failure to advance II Corps onto the high ground traversed by the Menin road.

Preparations for the next series of major attacks, this time with Second Army playing the leading role, began at the end of August; Plumer allowed three weeks to reorganize and make plans. The fine weather during September enabled 5th FSC's observation groups to obtain more locations than during August, and it was also suitable for sound-ranging; 5th FSC having 'B', 'Q' and 'R' Sections in the line. 'B' Section was on V Corps front facing Zonnebeke, Passchendaele and Gravenstafel, the other sections being to its north.

The British, who throughout the war had underestimated German sound-ranging, began to be more concerned about German activity and 'Maps GHQ', on 14 September, issued a document, "Notes on what can be done by our batteries to avoid detection by enemy sound ranging" [25], which outlined the factors making for easy detection by the enemy and listed various precautionary measures which could be taken. Beginning, "Wind is the most potent factor in the problem", it went on to state that "if our Sound Ranging Sections cannot range our batteries owing to an unfavourable wind, the conditions are good for the enemy's Sound Ranging". The advice given, in situations when the wind favoured the enemy, was to fire from several positions simultaneously, to fire salvoes, to use masking fire from neighbouring batteries and, when enemy fire onto a British position was being controlled by sound-ranging, to ask a neigh-bouring howitzer battery of a calibre one down from the enemy's to fire a round or section salvo, preferably at the German battery:

> timing the instant of firing to be as nearly as possible simultaneous with the burst of the enemy shell. The efficacy of this method obviously depends on the confusion of the record by the simultaneous arrival at the German instrument of the sounds of the burst and the howitzer discharge.

It appears that, even at this late date, German sound-ranging was not as good as the British system and could not distinguish between reports when two or more British guns were fired simultaneously, whereas: "This would not confuse the record obtained by the British type of Sound Ranging instrument; on the contrary, it would probably mean more than one location on a single record". Nonetheless, the general noise of battle caused problems for the British sound-rangers.

Plumer's first assault took place on the 20th, but CB and bombardment work had been going on for some weeks. On the day of the attack the observation group officers reported at intervals anything they saw from their survey posts. Information about enemy counter-attacks was particularly sought. On this day an observation group of 5th FSC reported at 5.10pm to V Corps HA (HQ Vlamertinghe Château): "three parties of 20 men coming out of the trench near BELLEVUE and moving down the road towards the front line. 60-pdrs have turned on to search the road" [26]. On 26 September, the OCs groups again reported what they could see, and 'R' Section followed up the advance, moving its HQ to Balls Farm, north-north-west of Pilckem. After the Polygon Wood battle, the boundary between Second and Fifth Armies was shifted northwards, thus giving Second Army the task of capturing the high ground around Passchendaele. 'B' Section was therefore transferred from 5th to 2nd FSC on 30 September, being installed on this front facing Passchendaele. It remained on this front when II ANZAC was relieved by the Canadian Corps on 18 October.

For the 4 October attack, there was no preliminary bombardment, but there was the normal intensive counter-battery work and destruction of strongpoints; the technique to be used at Cambrai seven weeks later was rapidly developing. On this day, 'O' Section arrived from Third Army, remaining with 5th FSC until 2 November. It established its HQ at the White Mill at Elverdinghe. On 6 October, 'O' Section relieved 'R' Section in the line, taking over the latter's base. On 16 October, 'Q' Section moved to west of St. Julien, and on 26 October, 'O' and 'R' Sections changed over, 'O' going out to rest after three weeks in the line![27] This gives some indication of the conditions, as up to October it was usual for sections to remain in place without relief during operations. 2nd FSC's sound-ranging sections were deployed as follows: 'B' Section in the Passchendaele sector, 'I' Section in the Becelaere sector, 'A' Section facing Zandvoorde, 'W' Section on the Wytschaete – Messines ridge, and 'M' Section in the Warneton sector.

The problem of keeping communication through between microphones and the recording apparatus at section HQs became so critical that much time and effort were spent before and during October in attempts to replace the cables with a continuous wave (CW) wireless link. In the end it was decided not to equip the sections with CW sets because of the shortage of skilled operators[28], and, as Colonel Jack noted: "large and cumbersome installations at each microphone and other disadvantages"[29].

In September and October much of the German artillery fire came from behind the Passchendaele – Westroosebeke ridge, and the foul weather in October made location work particularly difficult. During October, the daily "XVIII Corps HA and CB Reports" listed the following "Batteries Reported Active" and "Locations" in total:

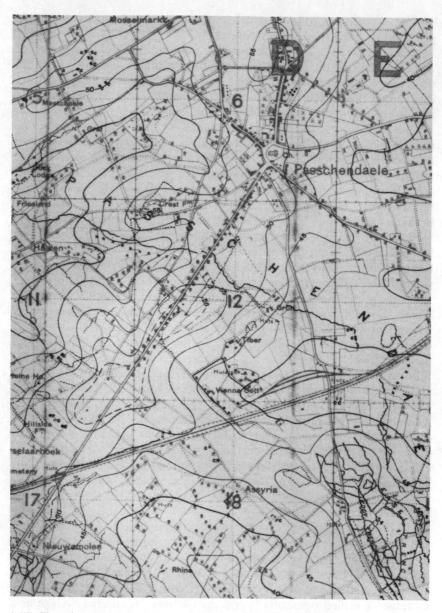

(viii) Trench map (trenches corrected to 8.9.17) of the Passchendaele area;
concrete works are marked "C". *(Peter Chasseaud Collection)*

Batteries Active:	No.	%	Locations:	No.	%
Sound Ranging	3	0.83	Sound Ranging	18	3.85
Observation Section	57	15.7	Observation Section	90	19.27
Kite Balloon	59	16.25	Kite Balloon	25	5.35
RFC	244	67.22	RFC	334	71.52[30]

This is a crucial set of data, as it illustrates the insuperable problems besetting the location units of 2nd and 5th FSCs during the battle. Their lines were continually being cut by shellfire, tanks and traffic, and even had the lines remained through, the bad weather defeated the best efforts of the sound-ranging sections and the observation groups. XVIII Corps Reports for October frequently carried such remarks as: "weather very unfavourable" (19th), "thick ground mist" (20th), "thick ground mist made it quite impossible to locate positions accurately" (22nd), "air observation impossible" (23rd), "no observed shooting possible" (25th), and "low clouds and ground mist" (27th)[31].

The observation groups also suffered from poorly sited OPs, the Germans occupying most of the high ground and siting their batteries in the dead ground behind. Towards the end of the battle, 5th FSC's No. 12 Group had posts west of Kitchener's Wood, 2,000 yards north of Pilckem, east of Pilckem and north-east of St. Julien. No.13 Group's posts were at Hill 29 (NW of Mousetrap Farm), Stray Farm east of Pilckem, south-east of Frezenberg, and west of Kitchener's Wood[32]. 2nd FSC's groups, each with 3 posts in action, were deployed as follows: No. 3 Group (HQ Brandhoek) had posts on the Westhoek Ridge, No. 1 Group (HQ La Clytte) had posts near Hill 60 and Wytschaete, No. 2 Group (HQ Kemmel) had OPs in Wytschaete and Messines, while No. 4 Group (HQ Westhof Farm) had OPs on Hill 63 and in Armentières[33].

The sheer numbers of batteries firing at any one time also reduced the efficacy of these methods of location. Posts were now in captured German pill-boxes, as offering the only cover from shell-fire, and defiladed by the Passchendaele ridge, they looked to the north-east. That closest to the enemy was 5,000 yards from Passchendaele. McLeod of 4th FSC noted on taking over the Ypres front at the end of the battle that:

Facilities for observation were bad on the Northern half of the Army front from POLYGON WOOD northwards and good from this point southwards . . . The situation on the Southern portion of the Army front, as regards groups, was satisfactory. Nos. 1, 2, and 4 Groups were well installed on the high ground between Hill 60 and ARMENTIERES and were getting good results. North of this however the situation was bad, the 3rd. Battle of YPRES had been raging since August and the heavy shelling had completely disorganised the telephone communications of all Groups . . . two O.P.s on the PILCKEM Ridge gave satisfactory observation over the HOUTHULST Forest. The Group H.Q. was however in the Canal Bank N. of YPRES and badly placed, telephonic communication being so bad, that it was necessary to move it further

North. From HOUTHULST southwards however the situation was very bad. No.3 Group, the next Group to the south, had its H.Q. beside the XXII Corps C.B. Office at BRANDHOEK and O.P.s on the WESTHOEK Ridge. Practically no communication existed between H.Q. and the O.P.s, nor could the O.P.s see any flashes but an occasional sky reflection. There was virtually no Field Survey observation between HOUTHULST Forest and HILL 60[34].

This was a damning indictment of the observation arrangements of 5th and 2nd FSCs in the later stages of the Third Battle of Ypres, as inherited by 4th FSC. The reasons, of course, were ground conditions and shelling.

Sound-ranging conditions were bad apart from September; the wind being generally adverse, the prevailing westerlies blowing the sound from the German guns upwards and away from the microphones. Wind sections were also introduced in the autumn to feed data to the sound-ranging sections so that they could adjust their results accordingly. Cables were continually being cut, and casualties among the linesmen were frequent. They began to be responsible for laying as well as maintaining their lines, and this brought them into action more quickly after an advance. Airlines were abandoned in favour of cable laid on the ground, which suffered fewer breaks from shellfire. Frustrated by the lack of locations, the counter-battery staffs insisted that the sections be pushed further forward. Serious disputes arose over this between the CB staffs and the FSCs. Ironically, the sections suffered less from cut wires when they were close up to the line, but between 4,000 to 6,000 yards back they suffered severely from harassing fire. Cut lines and bad weather affected the flash-spotters as well. Intense shellfire destroyed all the trig points, so that survey of microphones and OPs proved particularly difficult.

The Canadian Corps CRA produced a secret "Artillery Report on Passchendaele Operations Oct. 17th to Nov. 18th 1917", which heavily criticized the handling of the groups and sections of 2nd FSC:

Sound Ranging Sections. The base was located too far back and no attempt seems to have been made to establish it further forward. Special silent periods were arranged to facilitate their work. A number of locations were sent in, but they were found to be extremely inaccurate.

Observation Sections. Practically no results of any value were received. The posts were located some thousands of yards in rear of the crest. It was claimed that forward posts could not be established on account of Signal difficulties.

The failure of the Survey Sections illustrates once more the necessity for the transfer of the Flash Spotting and Sound Ranging Sections from Intelligence to Artillery Command.

On October 21st, both [Second] Army R.A. Intelligence and [Second] Army Intelligence were warned of the unsatisfactory state of affairs ... The failure of the above services during an advance of any extent has been apparent throughout the past year and was most noticeable in the last operations. Until such time as the control of these services is placed in the hands of the branch of the service for whose assistance it is primarily intended, it is difficult to see how any improvement is to be effected.[35]

Such criticism may well have been justified. GHQ took the failure of survey observation at Passchendaele seriously enough to take action; MacLeod noted that, in November, GHQ ruled that the tactical employment of groups and sections should be directed by the artillery[36].

Another problem faced by survey, and the CB staff, was the change in German artillery tactics. Alternative positions were used, as well as single and wandering guns to suggest that positions were occupied. Protection was exchanged for concealment, and the days of heavily protected and easily located enemy gun positions were over. Intense concentrations of British fire often fell on empty positions. Closer co-operation between FSCs and artillery was to provide a solution to some of these problems.

On 5 November, 'Q' Section moved its HQ from Vlamertinghe Château, where it had been since the opening of the battle, up to Kitchener's Wood[37]. The microphones had been advanced to the Langemarck area to locate the mass of German artillery in the Houthulst Forest. Otto Dix documented the swamps of this part of the battlefield; for those men trying to maintain the lines, death by suffocation or drowning was added to the more usual hazards of shellfire, gas and machine-guns at long range. In many places the duckboard tracks were the only footing.

On 11 November, five days after the capture of Passchendaele, 5th FSC had two sections in the line, with overlapping bases, 'Q's base, only 3,000 yards from Passchendaele, was a regular 6,500 yards arc with a radius of about 4,400 yards centred on Spriet. Each sub-base (ie the distance between two microphones) was 1,300 yards. 'Q's base extended further to the South than 'R's and lay 2,000 yards to the east at the closest point. 'Q' was linked to II Corps, while 'R' was with XIX Corps. 'R's base was about 5,600 yards long, and irregular but almost straight, facing Poelcappelle, Schaap Balie and Houthulst Forest[38]. A survey officer, conducted by 5th FSC's Maps Officer, Captain T. C. Nicholas, described one of the sound-ranging forward posts:

Nicholas took me past Boesinghe and up in that waste of clay and water to where the shells fall. As soon as the canal is passed and one enters the late Hun territory the outlook is amazing. I had seen Neuve Chapelle and Souchez and Loos but this was beyond them all . . . In this mess of clay and water is mingled wire and shell-cases and bits of men . . . Our objective was an O.P. (sound-ranging) which was situated in a Hun pill box . . . The walls of this one were 8 feet thick to the west and the roof solidly reinforced. A direct hit the day previous to my visit on the roof had done nothing serious. It was a good headquarters for the section. One looked out on that misty day on the sea of holes and clay and water and saw nothing else save two other pill boxes[39].

The efforts of the survey were recognized in Haig's Despatch written at the end of 1917:

Special mention again deserves to be made of the Field Survey Companies, who throughout the year's operations have carried out their important functions with the utmost zeal and efficiency. With the assistance of the Ordnance Survey they have enabled an adequate supply of maps to be maintained in spite of the constant changes of the battle front. Their assistance has also been invaluable to our artillery in locating the enemy's new battery positions during the actual progress of battle[40].

It was recognition of Survey's remarkable endeavour to fulfil essential work under exceptional difficulty.

Notes

1   Winterbotham, H. St.J. L.; *British Survey on the Western Front*, Geographical Journal 1919, p256.
2   Jack, E.M.; *Report on Survey on the Western Front*, War Office, London, 1920, xvi.
3   Chasseaud, Peter, *Topography of Armageddon, A British Trench Map Atlas of the Western Front 1914–1918*, Mapbooks, Lewes, 1991, p10.
4   The History of the Corps of Royal Engineers, Vol V, p476.
5   Author's reconstruction.
6   Second Army's '*Summary of Operations*', PRO WO 158 217.
7   Author's collection.
8   Harington's '*Preliminary Notes on the Messines Operation*', PRO WO 158 302.
9   OH 1917, Vol. 2, p93.
10   Remarks after talk by Winterbotham on 24–2–19, Geographical Journal 1919, p24.
11   5th Field Survey Company War Diary, PRO WO 95 492.
12   OH 1917, Vol. 2, p108.
13   PRO WO 153 1195.
14   Ibid, pp133–4.
15   Ibid, p237.
16   Ibid, p247.
17   I ANZAC Corps Topographical Section War Diary, PRO WO 95 1014.
18   Second Army Operations, PRO WO 158 217.
19   5th FSC War Diary, Op. Cit.
20   Innes, John; *Flash Spotters and Sound Rangers*, George Allen & Unwin, London, 1935, pp 170–1.
21   Ibid, pp171–2.
22   5th FSC War Diary, Op. Cit.
23   Ibid.
24   Ibid.
25   I(c)/6047/123. Author's collection.
26   V Corps Heavy Artillery War Diary, PRO WO 95 756.

27 5th FSC War Diary, Op. Cit.
28 *Supply of Engineer Stores and Equipment; The Work of the Royal Engineers in the European War, 1914–19*, RE Institute, Chatham, c1920, p66.
29 Jack,Op. Cit. p125.
30 XVIII Corps War Diary, PRO WO 95 955.
31 Ibid.
32 5th FSC War Diary, Op. Cit.
33 MacLeod, M.N.; *History of the 4th Field Survey Battalion, 1919*; unpublished typescript in MCE, RE; Map Research & Library Group.
34 Ibid.
35 *'Secret Report . . .'*, p18; in Canadian Corps Heavy Artillery War Diary, PRO WO 95 1959.
36 MacLeod, Op. Cit.
37 5th FSC War Diary, Op. Cit.
38 Ibid.
39 Romer, Carrol; Typescript of diary in private hands. Quoted by kind permission of John Romer.
40 Haig, Sir Douglas; *Sir Douglas Haig's Despatches*, ed Lt. Col. J. H, Boraston, Dent, London & Toronto, 1919, p142.

Chapter 10

The Flanders Battleground and the Weather in 1917

John Hussey

"A change in the weather. Happily, rain – our most effective ally":
Crown Prince Rupprecht of Bavaria, Flanders, 12 October 1917

No one can think of Third Ypres without haunting images of the mud and filth and rain filling his mind; conditions which have made its name of evil memory to this day. A British subaltern vividly described the effects of mud on all movement: "In October the provisional orders for an advance in the direction of Westroosebeke gave my company eight minutes for every 100 yards, but even this pace proved in the course of the month to be far beyond the capacity of men in the prevailing conditions". Nor did conditions spare the other side, for on 21 October 1917 the German Fourth Army reported declining morale among its infantry, upon whom "continuous enemy fire and the effects of the weather in the soaked crater areas fall most heavily, without having the opportunity for rest and relief because enemy attacks follow each other so quickly".[1] It is right and proper to remember these things, but history demands more than remembrance – it calls for understanding – and the peculiar climatic problems of 1917 are still misunderstood even though they are basic to any discussion of the campaign.[2]

The German thrust towards the French Channel ports was the natural sequel to their capture of western Belgium. Had the Allies not held them at Ypres in the autumn of 1914 it is difficult to see how Dunkirk, only 25 miles further west, could have been saved. Ypres was to remain Dunkirk's landward bastion until 1918. Yet even without capturing Dunkirk, a German force holding Ostend and Zeebrugge could dispute command of the Channel, disrupt Thames and East Coast trade and threaten the northern French ports and British communications with France. Hence until after the Zeebrugge raid of April 1918, the British Government and Admiralty were always anxious to destroy or capture German naval bases on the Belgian coast, and this consideration played its part in the British land campaign of 1917. [3]

We should also recognize that Allied policy required that the British should fight not merely on the main battlefront but on that part most convenient logistically: in Picardy, Artois and Flanders; there was never any possibility that the BEF might be deployed between Champagne and Switzerland. We may find the Flemish landscape boring and the climate dull, and we may lament that British soldiers had to fight there, but our political traditions, maritime needs and logistics gave our forebears little choice.

Apart from the Ardennes, which represent the remains of a worn-down mountain chain extending from Germany's Hunsrück and Eifel to re-emerge in the west of England and in Ireland, much of Belgium comprises Tertiary Eocene formations [approximately 65 million years old,] with sands, gravels and marls predominating in Flanders. These are covered in places by later Quaternary silts [about a million years old.] The narrow coastal strip is almost pure sand, but the higher ground starts only a short way inland and, through the industry of generations of Flemish peasants, the countryside in the vale of Ypres and beyond became a flourishing market garden.

Ypres is 22 miles from the sea and stands on the 20 metre (66 feet) contour, though Bixschoote four miles to its north is at only 8.5 metres (30 feet). [4] Eastward from Ypres the country stays at between 20 and 35 metres for several miles, with the Steenbeek stream cutting through at about 15 metres (48 feet) near St Julien. The horizon to the east is bounded by a low and unimpressive ridge running in a generally north-easterly direction from the high ground of Messines and Wytschaete (the latter attaining 80 metres or 264 feet at its highest point) past "Clapham Junction" on the western edge of the Gheluvelt plateau (only 2½ miles from Ypres, and at 65 metres, 213 feet) and Gheluvelt itself somewhat above 50 metres. Thence it continues to the village of Passchendaele (5½ miles from Ypres, at about 50 metres, 165 feet), thereafter sinking into the northern plain. When morning sun lights up the vale, an observer standing on this insignificant ridge has the entire Ypres Salient exposed to clearest view. In places the gradients will be felt by the calf muscles of today's walker, but generally the slopes across the battlefield are slight in the extreme: the British *Official History* puts the gradients as ranging from the imperceptible, to 1 in 60 near Hooge and to 1 in 33 near Zonnebeke. [5]

But "imperceptible" indicates that the water table, inevitably very few feet below the surface, would not easily absorb persistent heavy rain and that damage to the elaborate system of ditches and canals could easily turn the ground into the softest mud. [6] Then there were the numerous streams, which have been described in the *Official History*:

starting in small valleys on the Ypres Ridge, the Steenbeek, Stroombeek, Kortebeek, etc., run at right angles across the [British planned] line of advance; as their lower courses became obstructed by shell-fire, these tended to become sloughs; this was particularly the case near St Julien

141

[on the 15 metre contour], and, a mile farther north, around the Stroombeek. But it must be borne in mind that the ground was divided into wet zones and dry zones. For instance, even late in the battle, on one half-battalion front a trench could be dug, whilst on the other half only a shell-hole position was possible . . . [7]

All this is well known and yet the man in the street tends to think of the country round Ypres as a flat swampy ground with sheets of water everywhere, a sort of non-tropical Zairean basin. Some comparisons with England may therefore be helpful. If we look at Newark and the ten miles to Lincoln, we find country averaging no more than 10 metres in height. York is certainly less than 10 metres above sea level and so is the battlefield of Stamford Bridge seven miles away towards the coast, while Tadcaster (near Towton field) ten miles south-west is at about 10 metres, and the field of Marston Moor seven miles west of York is no more than 20 metres above sea level. One could multiply the examples from other parts of eastern England where Tertiary and Quaternary geology is so evident. In other words, Flanders is a fairly typical North European province, with a typical North European climate: it is *not* some monsoon-like tropical swamp, and the conditions of weather and battle which so afflicted it in 1917 could in certain less happy circumstances of war have obliged our Home Forces to fight an invader in "the swamps" of Stamford Bridge, Towton or Marston Moor – or under "the seasonal rains" of Newark, or the "monsoon climate" of the London basin.[8]

But the soil of Ypres was not good soil for a war in which artillery was the dominant weapon. Underneath it was London clay, mixed with sand and silt. This mixture was unpredictable in balance even for local experts, as the architect of the Menin Gate memorial was to find in 1919. [9] Eighty years of care have doubtless made some changes to surface soils, but the Commonwealth War Graves Commission's modern categorization of three types may serve nonetheless: those close to pure sand, sandy soils, and well-balanced soils.[10] The first group (close to pure sand) is not relevant here, for the names are those of Berlin, Bergen-op-Zoom, and Coxyde (on the Belgian coast); and the third (well-balanced soils) unsurprisingly includes Kemmel, Ploegsteert Wood, and Messines. The sandy soils, however, include Vlamertinghe and Brandhoek (both west of Ypres), Hooge Crater, Poelcappelle and Tyne Cot – as well as Antwerp, Arnhem Oosterbeek and Cologne. Some of their physical properties today can be seen from this table [11]:

Element %	Railway Dug-outs	Hooge Crater	Poel-cappelle	Tyne Cot
clay	10.9	14.1	7.8	12.7
fine silt	8.9	8.5	7.6	8.3
coarse silt	16.8	11.5	13.2	11.6
pure sand	51.4	54.7	56.7	53.4
coarse sand	8.4	7.7	11.3	10.1

This was the ground for the British offensive in the summer and autumn of 1917, ground already familiar from the dry autumn of First Ypres in October and November 1914. [12]

Haig had always known that to take the ridge would "entail very hard fighting lasting perhaps for weeks". Yet weather conditions for much of Third Ypres were so bad that to later generations it has seemed almost incomprehensible that the battle should have continued unchecked until November; indeed it has been asserted that Haig's plans demanded a totally dry season for operations and that GHQ knew perfectly well that the chosen season was invariably one of regular and heavy rain. Lloyd George – who as Prime Minister could have ordered the battle to end at any time – declared that Haig made "a reckless gamble . . . on the chance of a rainless autumn"; Liddell Hart and Leon Wolff emphasized GHQ's foreknowledge of seasonal deluges; and Gerard De Groot insisted that "any rain would have been disastrous . . . Haig's plans required a drought of Ethiopian proportions to ensure success". [13]

It is therefore a duty to truth and commonsense to state that neither Haig nor any British soldier in Flanders expected or suggested that a North European summer and autumn would be without any rain or could be a rainless season. Interestingly, Haig's most violent critic supports my statement, for he quotes a GHQ document of early May 1917 as saying:

> Operations are liable to the danger of interruption by bad weather. *A few hours* of rain brings the brooks into flood which only subsides within periods varying up to *twenty-four* hours. *A few weeks' rain* may make the whole country impracticable for prolonged operations for at least *one week*. |my italics| [14]

Much of the confusion over the forecasts for the summer weather of 1917 is due to an inaccurate claim by Haig's Intelligence chief, Brigadier-General John Charteris, who, having said that "Haig was already [26 July 1917] anxious about the weather conditions that were to be anticipated", added that: "Careful investigation of records of more than eighty years showed that in Flanders the weather broke early each August with the regularity of the Indian monsoon."

It was perhaps the most baffling statement that even Charteris ever made, and coming from a member of GHQ it was seen as the most conclusive evidence of Haig's "guilt". [15] As it confirmed that sufficient meteorological information had been collected, so, by implication, it posited three questions: were those in the BEF's meteorological staff *ignorant*, were they *negligent*, or did Haig *ignore* their advice ?

In the early months of war, the civilian Meteorological Office in London had handled the BEF's weather information, supplying five weather telegrams per day, but the standard observations and the code to transmit them proved inadequate for military needs. In June 1915, therefore, GHQ

St Omer established a three-man Royal Engineers Meteorological Section under a London meteorologist, Ernest Gold [16], who in the years 1907–14 had contributed a score of remarkable scientific papers on his chosen subject. By the end of 1917 his service comprised 16 officers and 82 other ranks at GHQ and in each of the five Armies, plus a specialized Met group from Sound-Ranging of 25 officers and men. It expanded further in 1918 by which time Gold had attained Lieutenant-Colonel's rank. Data was exchanged between centres and disseminated through the "Meteor" four-hourly telegrams, which used standard data but added visibility factors on a geometric progression of distance, the form and amount of low, medium and high cloud, relative humidity, present weather and past weather by two-figure sequences, rainfall (twice daily), and maximum day and minimum night temperatures.[17]

Gold had been among the first to analyse successfully thermal wind effect and the conditions in the troposphere (the air in the first seven miles above the earth) and the stratosphere above it. But though he and his colleagues were aware that surface weather charts told only part of the story, such an essential concept as the weather front (which "revolution-ized" forecasting) was not known until 1919, and it was only after 1939 that sufficient data was available on temperature, wind and humidity in the upper atmosphere to show that it is the higher (rather than lower) level movements which in large measure control surface activity, and that without knowledge of the histories and characteristics of higher level movements, the study of patterns of successive *surface* weather charts could be of only limited help in forecasting future developments. The tech-niques available during the Great War were far in advance of those of, say 1900, but were necessarily over-reliant on analogue forecasts from data on the lower atmosphere. [18] Gold was clearly not *ignorant*, but was he *negli-gent*? The record clears him. Gold records:

The week of fair warm weather and local thunderstorms of the battle of Messines [7–14 June 1917] was forecast before the battle began. The fair weather from the 20th of September to the 3rd of October, 1917, during the advance towards Passchendaele was indicated in the forecasts issued on the 19th of September and following days: the generally unsettled weather after the 4th of October was predicted as to its general character on the 3rd of October, and the details day by day were given with such accuracy as to evoke the special thanks of General Plumer's staff. [19]

A sample of Gold's discussions with Second Army's chief of staff comes from his contemporary notes:

On the morning of the 11th [October 1917] General Harington again rang up and I informed him at 9 a.m. that the indications were for unset-tled weather after a fair interval: that it did not look as if the fair interval would last until noon on the 12th: it might last until 6 a.m. At noon I told General Harington that the chances were just against the fair interval lasting till 6 a.m. though it would probably last until midnight. At 4 p.m. and 5 p.m. I repeated all that I had said before and added that a miracle might save us from rain, but even a miracle could not save us from high winds or gales ... Late on the night of the 11th rain began. At 7 a.m. next morning General Harington rang up to know about fairer intervals. I said there was a chance that we should get one but it was doubtful, and anyhow we were likely to get rain again afterwards. By 9 a.m. the fair interval had come ... The rain began again about midday.[20]

Gold says that he could advise that indications of change from adverse to "favourable" weather for an operation might be:

'in the offing' a considerable time before they can be predicted with confidence – [but] the latter interval is frequently a short one – a day – or a few hours.[21]

But can a postponed or cancelled operation be mounted again without confusion at a day's notice? What happens when a forecast – or worse, several such – prove(s) wide of the mark? The risk of tension between the forecaster and the commanders must have been ever-present, just as the stress upon all of them in such circumstances as those of 11 October might have led to mutual mistrust, self-doubt, cynicism and despair.

Harington and Plumer certainly listened to Gold. But did the Commander-in-Chief? One of Gold's subordinates describes the working day:

The chief task of the day was the preparation of the synoptic chart for the fundamental time of 7 a.m. since the forecast was based on this. This chart, along with the current situations at the various observer stations, was taken to the Colonel as soon as it was prepared. He then made a forecast and the chart, weather particulars from the forward stations and the current forecast were drawn in copying ink on a general weather chart. Copies were then made ... and these were distributed to the various headquarters at GHQ. Early in the forenoon the Colonel visited the Commander in Chief and discussed with him the weather prospects of the day. Reports from local stations arrived throughout the day and at 6 p.m. the data for a new synoptic chart was received and the process repeated except that a general weather chart was not prepared. [22]

Sir Douglas Haig made no complaints over Gold's work, nor did he criticize it through omission from his Despatch on the 1917 battle, for he wrote: "the Meteorological Section has kept me furnished with valuable information concerning the probable course of the weather, in spite of the limited area from which the necessary data are now procurable". The few brief references in his private diary are very quiet and not once during all that ghastly August did he criticize those daily weather briefings or the disappointments they must have brought. As the much delayed offensive drew near there are two references to Gold in the diary: on 30 July: "Rain fell in early morning. At noon glass rising after a slight fall in night . . . The weather specialist assures us that this afternoon will be clear and observation good", while on the 31 July, as battle commenced, he wrote: "Glass steady. Morning dull and coldish. The bright weather reported as coming is slower in its progress than expected by our weather prophet!"[23]

So much, then, for the weather technology of 1917 and the provision of information to the generals. Was the outcome of all those discussions merely what Lloyd George called "a reckless gamble . . . on the chance of a rainless autumn"?[24]

One part of the answer comes from a later war. After a perfect May 1944, the Overlord plan was imperilled early in June by dreadful Channel weather. Group Captain Stagg's meteorological forecast of a brief improvement for 6 June finally decided Eisenhower and his commanders. This greatest gamble in our military history was summed up in Sir Alan Brooke's diary entry of 5 June: "At the worst it may well be the most ghastly disaster of the whole war".[25] *Nothing* in the operations of 1917 approached those stakes. Stagg's remarks in 1971 on the hazards of forecasting (27 years after Overlord and 54 after Third Ypres) are significant here:

The amount and kind of information from that area today [he is speaking of the North Atlantic] is still not enough to allow the normal forecast period to be extended regularly and reliably much beyond 24 hours . . . none of the advances in the last quarter century has disproved the inherent unpredictability of the behaviour of the atmosphere in respect of development, movement and decay of depressions and anticyclones after a day or two, and for small-scale weather features (such as local strengthening of wind or change in cloudiness) after much shorter periods even than that.[26]

As to the other part of the answer to Lloyd George, it so happens that in the last ten years the historical records of Flanders weather have been studied by Philip Griffiths, a young geography student at the University of Birmingham with an interest in weather and trained in modern mathematical climatological techniques. His undergraduate thesis was published in summarized form in 1989 and my debt to his work will be obvious in the following paragraphs.[27]

Before 1914, the principal recording station for Flanders was at Lille, only 16 miles from Ypres (the distance from Dover to Canterbury); there was a small station at Cachtem (two miles east of Roulers and therefore under German control after 1914), a more distant inland one at Brussels (70 miles from Ypres) and another at Cap Gris Nez on the coast (57 miles). Lille's data[28] covers the years 1867–1916 and for statistical purposes here may be analysed by decade and under the quintiles: very dry, dry, normal, wet and very wet. Taking the quarter September, October and November, Griffiths calculated that in the 30 years 1867–96 there were 9 very wet, 6 wet, 8 normal, 3 dry and 4 very dry autumns, but that in the years 1897–1916 the figures were 1 very wet, 4 wet, 2 normal, 7 dry and 6 very dry respectively: that is 13 dry or very dry in 20 years, a noticeable trend towards *dry autumns* . When he took individual months he found that whereas September in Lille was dry or very dry in 11 of the first 30 years, it was dry or very dry in *nine* of the next 20; more interestingly, while October 1867–96 was very wet or wet in 15 years and dry or very dry in 8 years, the comparative 1897–1916 figures showed a very different and encouraging pattern: 3 very wet and 2 wet as against *six* dry and *six* very dry in 20 years.

Griffiths then took these results a stage further by studying them for anti-cyclonic tendencies according to modern analytical formulae. Put very simply, anticyclones are zones of higher barometric pressure than the zones surrounding them, regions of calm air surrounded by light to moderate winds spiralling outwards. An anticyclone suggests quiet and settled weather, sunny and warm in summer, with a stationary or slow moving habit. By classifying each weather type on a five point "C-index" scale ranging from plus 2 for cyclonic to minus 2 for anticyclonic weather and applying this to the daily weather for each September in the 30 years to 1916, Griffiths found that he obtained a Lille total of minus 420, a very high total, showing that 25 of the Septembers were predominantly anticyclonic, and only one (1896) notably cyclonic. For October the result was minus 87, with 17 years more anticyclonic than cyclonic. Griffiths also found that the average rainfall at Lille in October tended to decrease over the 50 years. Any meteorologist studying the records early in 1917 would have noted these trends.

There remains August, about which Charteris had said "the weather broke early each August with the regularity of the Indian monsoon". In 1958 Colonel Gold had publicly contradicted Charteris by stating the meteorological facts and his argument ought to have been conclusive, but there were many – like Liddell Hart and Wolff – who still chose to ignore Gold and cling to Charteris as their sole expert.[29]

When Griffiths took the 30 successive Augusts up to 1916 and subjected them to the C-index test he found that there was a score of minus 14, meaning that there was a slight predominance of anticyclonic patterns, but that there were as many cyclonic Augusts as anticyclonic. What of early August? Griffiths divided Augusts into two 10-day and one 11-day periods: the first period, i.e. 1–10 August (that 'regular early rainy period') was neither strongly cyclonic nor anticyclonic – it had no pattern; the second period was predominantly anticyclonic and the third predominantly cyclonic. And still within these periods there were yet further off-setting factors, and a variance test showed Griffiths that for the period 1887 to 1916 *"there is no reason* to suggest that the weather broke early in the month with any regularity" [p.10, my italics]. He noted also that at Cap Gris Nez 65% of August days were rain-free in 1901–16 and that this was particularly evident in the four years 1913–16 when there were 26, 23, 23 and 21 dry days and when the total monthly rainfall was 17, 28, 22 and 96 mm. respectively (0.7, 1.1, 0.9 and 3.8 inches). Thus Griffiths concluded that "during the summers preceding the [1917] Flanders campaign August days were *more often dry* than wet" [my italics].

This scientific analysis bears repeating. From a meteorologist's standpoint, August might be expected to be reasonably dry, not abnormally wet. It destroys utterly the Charteris statement about Augusts.[30] As for the autumn, we can see the validity of Haig's later comment that "there was no reason to anticipate an abnormally wet October".[31] Based as they were on the best available evidence, Gold's forecasts were not a reckless gamble.

The actual weather record, for the most part terrible, must now be summarized; but the tragedy of Third Ypres' weather does not start with 31 July 1917. In a different sense it starts very early in the year. The British and French Cabinets had insisted on 15–16 January 1917 that Général Nivelle's panacea for instant victory, planned for 1 April "at latest", should take priority over the British Flanders project and Haig was ordered to give full support in Artois until Nivelle's offensive should end; only if Nivelle failed could Haig then revive his own plan. Everyone knew that the full Flanders operation would thereafter take six to eight weeks to assemble. The French offensive began late and persisted on the Aisne until 20 May: only at that date did their troops take over the southern end of the British line and so permit the *start* of the northward movement of the 14 divisions needed for the northern offensive.

What if Allied policy had not gambled on Nivelle's formula and the British had not been thus tied to Artois in April and May? What if Haig had been free to move troops earlier so as to open his Flanders attack in late May or in June?[32] The daily weather reports from Vlamertinghe and adjacent stations tell us what might have been, and they are thought-provoking.

In May there were only three sunless days and 223 hours of sunshine (an average 8.25 hours per day on the 27 days): the sunshine factor is of course the inverse of cloud cover. In the whole month 30 mm. of rain fell, spread over 11 days and, of that, 6.8 mm. was accounted for by one day (the 14th). There were 20 days without any rain and a further 4 days when there was less than 1 mm. of rain per day. It was perfect campaigning weather.

June had one sunless day and 241 hours of sunshine (average 8.3 hours per day for the 29 days). There were 13 rainless days and 7 more when under 1 mm. fell per day. The total rainfall was 62 mm., with one day accounting for 14.3 mm. (the 18th). Again, good campaigning weather.

In July there were three sunless days and 195.4 hours of sunshine (average 7.0 hours across the 28 days). There were 18 rainless days and 6 more when under 1 mm. fell per day. The total rainfall was 80 mm.: in the first ten days 12.3 mm. (all on the 7th, 8th and 9th); in the second ten, 23.8 mm. (18.6 mm. on the 14th); and in the third period, 43.6 mm. (of which 33.3 mm. fell on the 29th and 31st). Haig had wished to attack on the 25th, but agreed to his subordinate commanders' requests for delays to ensure artillery supremacy. With hindsight we know that this six day delay was wasting the last of the invaluable fine weather. But what did the forecasts say?

The outlook at GHQ at this time was ably summarized in 1922 by Lieutenant-Colonel J H Boraston, who had served on Haig's staff at GHQ in 1916–18 and had access to the records. In a published account of Third Ypres he went into some detail:

the weather at the beginning of August was not merely exceptionally bad, it was also unexpectedly bad. On July 29, indications were neither strongly for nor strongly against good weather, but on the whole were rather more favourable for the development of anticyclonic conditions than for generally unsettled conditions. The beginning of August in Flanders is not generally, as the records show, a wet period. At Dunkirk the rainfall in August 1917 was 189 mm., against an average of 80 mm. over the whole previous period for which records are available. Since 1878 the August rainfall at Dunkirk had only once equalled that of August 1917, namely in 1897, when there was also a fall of 189 mm. The average number of August wet days at Dunkirk is 13 in the month. In 1917 there were 17 wet days; but while the number of wet days was thus considerably above the average for August, the frequency of the rain was not so outstanding a feature as were its intensity and the accompanying dull conditions which prevented the ground from drying even when no rain was falling. Such abnormal conditions constituted a misfortune which could not be reckoned with or remedied . . . [33]

Reverting to the "weather diary", we find that in August the total rainfall was 127 mm., with a punishing 84 mm. falling in five days (1st, 8th, 14th, 26th and 27th). Dividing the month into two 10-day and one 11-day periods we find the rain so spread across the dull and relatively windless month that the ground could not dry, the rain in those three periods being 53.0, 32.4 and 41.3 mm. respectively. More particularly, in the 96 hours between 1800 hrs on 31 July and 1800 hrs on 4 August no less than 63 mm. of rain fell, to add to the 12.5 of the preceding 61 hours. There were 3 rainless days in the whole month and 14 days when under 1 mm. fell per day. There were 3 sunless days and another day with only 6 minutes of sun. For the other 27 days there were 178.1 hours of sunshine (average 6.6 hours per day). In the light of Gold's and Griffiths's evidence we may surely grant Boraston's claim that August's weather was exceptionally and unexpectedly bad.

Haig noted on 1 August "a terrible day of rain. The ground is like a bog" and he repeated this in his published *Despatch* at the year end:

The low-lying, clayey soil, torn by shells and sodden with rain, turned to a succession of vast muddy pools. The valleys of the choked and over-flowing streams were speedily transformed into long stretches of bog, impassable except by a few well-defined tracks . . . To leave these tracks was to risk death by drowning, and in the course of the subsequent fighting on several occasions both men and pack animals were lost in this way . . . the resumption of our offensive was necessarily postponed until a period of fine weather should allow the ground to recover. [Local oper-ations were possible during brief slight improvements in the weather but] the month closed as the wettest August that had been known for many years. [34]

September improved, with one sunless day and two with 40 and 54 minutes' sun respectively The remaining 27 days had over 200 hours of sunshine (giving them an average 7.4 hours per day). The month's rainfall was 40 mm. – under one third of August's – with three days (5, 6, 19 September) accounting for 34.8 mm.. The three victories of the Menin Road Ridge, Polygon Wood and Broodseinde (20 September–4 October) were gained on hardening soil across which dust eventually began to blow: Henry Williamson remembered shells skidding on the dry ground.[35] At last the British weapons system began to crush the German defence and German tactics, but "the remedy which Ludendorff could not find was found for him by the weather. October saw a return of exceptional condi-tions".[36]

October had two sunless days and three when the sun showed for less

There has been another big battle on today & we have again done well: however it has started to pour with rain and it looks as though our offensive in this part of the world had come to an end until next year: the ground soon becomes impassable with a little rain.

(ix) Willoughby Norrie, Brigade Major, 90th Infantry Brigade, writes to his mother on 4 October about the rain: "it looks as though our offensive in this part of the world has come to an end until next year." [in fact not for another five weeks !] *(Lord Norrie, Liddle Collection)*

than an hour per day; the remaining 137.2 hours gave an average 5.3 hours' sunshine per day. The total rainfall was 107 mm. (compare 1914: 31 mm, 1915: 32 mm., 1916: 69 mm.), with 5 rainless days, and 5 days of under 1 mm. of rain each. Writing to his wife on 14 October, Haig admitted that "the rain has upset our arrangements a good deal, but I still hope that the weather may take up *before long* and the ground become as dry as it was in 1914 at the *end* of October" [my italics].[37] But although his recollection of 1914 was accurate, the next fortnight brought no improvement and he noted the awful conditions in his diary with entries such as: "The 7th Division were really engulfed in mud in some places when they attacked Gheluvelt. Rifles could not be used" (28 October), while his published *Despatch* wrote of men struggling "through mud up to their waists". But who now can say whether or not the cratered mud might have dried sufficiently if ten days' clear, windy weather had come in mid-October? It may have been unlikely – was it impossible?

As for the first ten days of November, there were a mere 9 hours of sunshine – the 1st, 2nd, 3rd, 6th and 10th were sunless – so that the comparative lack of rain did nothing to dry the ground: up to and including 9 November 7.5 mm. of rain fell, with 3 rainless days and 2 with less than 1 mm. of rain each, though on the 10th 13.4 mm. were recorded.

To conclude. Major campaigns in the lowlands of North-West Europe, against a resolute enemy in strong defensive positions, inevitably create harrowing conditions which will progressively worsen so long as battle continues: the battles for Walcheren and the Rhine crossings in the autumn and winter of 1944–45 were in similarly awful conditions. When the BEF consolidated its Passchendaele position on 11 November 1917, it had to summon up all its reserves of grit and stubbornness. Yet after another year of titanic struggles it was not the BEF which sought an armistice. The mud, rain and horrors of Third Ypres did *not* break the British Army.

Modern analysis shows clearly that in 1917 Major Gold and the British high command could reasonably expect weather in Flanders which would be generally favourable to British plans. It was never in Haig's mind that there would be "no rain" or that the battle would be in a "rainless" season, but he did believe that in a normal summer, sun and wind would offset the effects of any rain. The British commanders were fully informed of the weather history and the meteorological prospects, and the operational plans were drawn up in the light of that information. August 1917 was abnormally bad and the meteorological records could give no warning of this. Late September 1917 showed what could be achieved on ground which had begun to dry, and had October not been abnormally wet, progress could still have been made then.

The campaign was not a reckless gamble on a rainless autumn. But it is plain that if Nivelle's plan had been abandoned or his campaign had ended in mid or late April the Flanders offensive could have begun sooner, during a nearly perfect mid-summer. At the very least, in Haig's words at the year end:

> what was actually accomplished under such adverse conditions is the most conclusive proof that, given a normally fine August, the capture of the whole of the ridge, within the space of a few weeks, was well within the power of the men who achieved so much. [38]

ACKNOWLEDGEMENTS

I wish to thank the Controller of HM Stationery Office for permission to quote from Crown copyright material in the Public Record Office (CAB and WO series) and from the British *Official History*. Despite written enquiries through the University of Birmingham's alumni office, neither they nor I have been able to trace Mr Philip Griffiths, author of a most able paper on the weather conditions of mid 1917, and I wish here to make full acknowledgement of his copyright. My thanks go also to Lord Haig and the Trustees of the National Library of Scotland for quotations from the Haig papers, to the Commonwealth War Graves Commission, Dr B D Giles of the University of Birmingham, Captain C L W Page RN and Dr Paddy Griffith, all of whom provided much assistance. Aspects of this chapter appeared in my article on the history of the "1917 Monsoon", published in the *Journal of the Society for Army Historical Research* in 1996, and I thank the Society's Council for permission to adapt it here.

APPENDIX I: MUD AND RAIN

Third Ypres may have been uniquely horrible, but bad weather and armies have always produced similar conditions across the centuries and in diverse theatres – and national policy has usually claimed precedence over meteorology. Napoleon commented during his 1807 Polish campaign that he had encountered "the fifth element, mud", but this warning has not stopped the Germans fighting several major campaigns there in this century. Here are three examples of weather affecting British campaigns, the first from Mesopotamia in 1915–16, the next from Palestine in 1917 and the last from Flanders in 1707.

> "It is difficult for anyone who has not seen the effect of rain upon the flat alluvial desert of the Basrah delta to form any idea of the resulting abomination. A particularly glutinous kind of mud is evolved in which it is almost impossible to stand upright, and in which cars and carts stick fast, and horses and camels slide in every direction". [Major Sir Hubert Young, *The Independent Arab* (1933) p.44]

On 19 November 1917, during Allenby's advance upon Jerusalem, the 157th Brigade of the 52nd Division was on the Ramle–Lydda road. At 5.45 p.m. "it was pitch dark and the rain began to fall in sheets. The road was now, if it can be said to have existed at all, over long stretches indiscoverable. The few limbered wagons brought forward had to be divided and man-handled. The camels slipped in the wet, cut their feet on the rocks, in some cases broke legs, in others fell into ravines. Many of the men had their boots so torn that they had to take them off and bind their putties round their feet". So late was the transport that no blankets could be issued and the troops "had to pass the night in their drill jackets and shorts". Christmas in the mountains, under pouring rain, meant minimum rations: "the only luxury added to the dinner – for most, of biscuits and cheese – consisted of Jaffa oranges" – as heavy seas had interrupted supplies. Under the rains Sdud, a major depot in the plain of Philistia, became "an island in a brown sea". [Captain Cyril Falls, *Military Operations, Egypt & Palestine*, ii, pp.192–93, 279, 292–93]

"Never did Marlborough's men toil to less purpose than in the 1707 [Flanders] campaign, when the rains descended and the floods rose till all movement was impossible. In August of that year Marlborough wrote that they had so much rain that he *'could scarcely stir out of his quarters, the dirt being up to the horses' bellies, which is very extraordinary in this month'*, and, when he did get a chance of moving and chased [the French Marshal] Vendôme back from Nivelles behind the shelter of the French lines round Mons, such was the state of the roads that many of his infantry actually perished in the sloughs". [C R L Fletcher and C T Atkinson, 'The Flanders Battleground', in *Army Quarterly* vol.i, Oct 1920, p.155.]

APPENDIX II: COLONEL E GOLD'S LETTER TO THE SPECTATOR, 17 JANUARY 1958
(reproduced by permission of the Editor of the Spectator*)*
On 15 November 1957 Liddell Hart wrote an article on Passchendaele in the *Spectator*; a furious debate raged in its correspondence columns until 24 January 1958. In particular, a letter from Brigadier Desmond Young (who had not been at Ypres since he was then in England recovering from wounds) made a series of highly critical assertions many of which were disputed by survivors of the battle. Among the rebuttals was one from Colonel Gold, and I quote him in full and with his italics:

Sir – In his letter about Passchendaele (*Spectator* December 27) Brigadier Desmond Young states 'In fact the monsoon conditions of August, 1917, were no worse than in the three previous years'. This statement needs correction; it is quite contrary to the evidence of the actual records which show that the weather in August, 1917, in and behind the battle area, was exceptionally bad. The rainfall directly affecting the first month of the offensive was more than double the average; *it was over five times the amount for the same period in 1915 and 1916.*
The period is July 29 to August 28. The rainfall at Vlamertinghe was 157 mm. (6.18 inches) in 1917 and 29 mm. in 1916; at St Omer it was 30 mm. in 1915 (there was then no rain gauge at Vlamertinghe). The quite exceptional heavy rain from July 29 to August 4, 1917, was followed by

muggy, stagnant weather which prevented the drying by evaporation, normal in the intervals of fair weather at that time of the year.

Brigadier Young may have been misled by an unconsidered statement of Charteris that in Flanders the weather broke early in *August* with the regularity of the Indian monsoon. This statement is so contrary to recorded facts that, to a meteorologist, it seems too ridiculous to need formal refutation. In 1915 there were twenty-two days in August without any rain and in 1916 there was no rain from the middle of July to the middle of August and then only small amounts until the end of the month. The official record for Lille, 1878 to 1913, showed that the first ten days of August had had 40 per cent. less rain than the last ten days of July.

Yours faithfully,

E GOLD.

Formerly Commandant Meteorological Section R.E., France 1915–19

8 Hurst Close, NW 11

Notes

1 Charles Douie, *The Weary Road* (1929, repr 1988), p.181: the *intended* speed of advance is equal to seven full 5-foot paces in one minute. Reichsarchiv, *Der Weltkrieg 1914–1918*, band xiii (1942), p.86, the quotation being from the actual Fourth Army report.

2 The British *Official History, Military Operations, France and Belgium, 1917*, vol.ii (1948) [henceforth *OH*, with campaign year and volume] contains a certain number of references (see 'Rain' in its general index) and is superior in this respect to the Reichsarchiv's generalized treatment in its band xiii. John Terraine's fine study *The Road to Passchendaele* (1977) the stature of which grows as newer accounts appear, gives copious weather quotations from contemporary diaries and related works in his sections entitled 'The Invincible Enemy'. Chris McCarthy, *The Third Ypres, Passchendaele, The Day-by-Day Account* (1995) gives temperature, cloud and rainfall figures at the start of each day's account, starting on 31 July. Robin Prior and Trevor Wilson, *Passchendaele, the Untold Story* (1996) give some weather information.

3 John Terraine's *The Road to Passchendaele* shows conclusively the importance of the Flanders naval bases to British thinking: Jellicoe, First Sea Lord, wrote to the War Cabinet on 18 June 1917 of "the absolute necessity of turning the Germans out of Northern Belgium at the earliest possible moment. It must be done during the present summer" (quoted in the CIGS's memo of 23 June, CAB.27/7 and WO.106/1513). *Der Weltkrieg*, xiii, 85, records that on 18 October 1917 the German Fourth Army opposed withdrawal from the Passchendaele ridge to a rearward position because "if this [rearward] line were broken *then the U-Boat bases could no longer be defended*" [my italics].

4 Liddell Hart always referred to Ypres as being "little above sea level" (e.g. *RUSI Journal*, Nov 1959, p.433), but I should call the 66 feet contour rather more respectable than that.

5 *OH 1914*, vol.ii, pp.128–31.

6 Mud and rain were so awful on the Somme and at Third Ypres that we may forget how often armies across the centuries and across theatres have endured them: see Appendix I.

7 *OH* 1917, ii, p.126. Edmonds gives his reasons for the two last sentences and invokes further testimony on pp.374–78. The image suggested by "divided into zones" seems all too neat for what undoubtedly became a featureless battlefield, and the memoirs of those who were in trenches and shell-holes scarcely reflect his view. But the reader should study Edmonds's comments in full.

8 On 29 July 1917, when the Vlamertinghe (Ypres) weather station recorded 11.6 mm. of rain, Cap Gris Nez had 18 mm. and Melbourn, Cambridgeshire, 83 mm.. Two days later, when Vlamertinghe had 21.7 mm., Canterbury had 50 mm., quoted in Philip Griffiths, *The Effects of Weather Conditions on the Third Battle of Ypres, 1917*, The University of Birmingham School of Geography, Working Paper No.51 (1989), p.14 [hereafter Griffiths].

9 Sir Reginald Blomfield wrote: "I was suspicious of the ground, and enquired of my friend Mr Koomans, architect to the town of Ypres, what sort of subsoil I should find, and was assured that I should find a solid layer of clay extending from Ypres to Tournai [as the Belgian geological maps of 1897–1901 indeed show]. This was cheering news, but I had one or two trial holes dug to make sure, and found to my horror running sand, the worst possible ground for foundations. I think I must have struck a bad patch in view of the fact that the immense tower of the old Cloth Hall had stood for centuries without failure": *Memoirs of an Architect* (1932), pp.186–87.

10 I am most grateful to the staff of the Commonwealth War Graves Commission for their prompt and detailed answers to my questions and for providing scientific soil analyses from 1993. The names of Arnhem, the Rhine cemeteries, Berlin – let alone Walcheren – remind us that generals cannot always pick and choose which soils to fight on.

11 Railway Dug-outs cemetery is just south of Zillebeke lake. Data from the CWG, which adds that the heavy clay, despite its relatively low percentage in the soil mixture, becomes a hard, cracked and impenetrable mass when dry.

12 The nearby station at Lille recorded for the entire months of October and November 1914 no more than 31 and 39 mm. rainfall respectively (1.2" and 1.5"). Vlamertinghe, just outside Ypres and 18 miles from Lille, recorded 107 mm. (4.2") in October 1917 and 43 mm. (1.7") in November (sources: Griffiths p.9; Gold's weather reports, cited below).

13 Haig's words come from his OAD.538 of 5 July, cited in Terraine, *Road to Passchendaele*, pp.185–87; Lloyd George, *War Memoirs* (1934), vol.iv, p.2207 (and Odhams ed, p.1306); Liddell Hart, *History of the Great* (later, *First World*) *War* (1934), pp.427–31 (originally published as *The Real War* in 1930); Leon Wolff, *In Flanders Fields* (1959), p.81 (Penguin ed, p.112); G J De Groot *Douglas Haig 1861–1928* (1988), p.336.

14 Denis Winter, *Haig's Command, a Reassessment* (1991), p.91, quoting a GHQ "I" paper of about 4 May 1917; I have not seen this document and Winter's reference is imprecise; moreover his ascriptions, textual accuracy and soundness of dating are not always reliable. Would GHQ's statements be unreasonable if written about Bedfordshire or the vale of Severn?

15 See John Charteris, *Field-Marshal Earl Haig*, 1929, pp.272. Everyone seems to have ignored Charteris's comment on the next page that 1917 saw the wettest August in thirty years.

16 Ernest Gold CB, DSO, OBE, MiD, FRS and medallist of several learned societies (1881–1976), the grandson of a farm labourer, Third Wrangler of his year at Cambridge and then a Fellow of Trinity College, became an

outstanding figure in international meteorology, "a world architect" of a fore-casting service to aviation. There is a perceptive notice of him, "warts and all", in the *Biographical Memoirs of Fellows of the Royal Society*, vol.23, 1977, though it might have dealt more fully with his Great War work. Denis Winter depicts Gold in a somewhat dismissive fashion (p.92).

17   *Meteorological Magazine* [hereafter *MM*], vol.84, p.177. This data is now preserved in Gold's monthly weather reports among GHQ's war diary files at the Public Record Office, WO.95/14 and 15 (for 1917).

18   Even if all the basic data were not flawed the chain of reasoning involves assigning a "probability" to each link: no individual step need be wrong in itself and yet the end result may be astray. Much of this paragraph draws on *Forecast for Overlord* (1971), pp.22–23, by Dr J M Stagg (1901–75), who as a temporary Group Captain was Eisenhower's chief meteorologist in 1944 [hereafter Stagg].

19   E Gold, 'Weather in War' in *Army Quarterly*, vol. 47, (Oct 1943), pp.83–91 [hereafter Gold *AQ*]: this passage is on pp.88–89. See also *OH 1917*, ii, p.251.

20   Gold *AQ*, p.89. In 1935 Harington, recalling the bad weather after 4 October, wrote that "it is easy to say now that everyone knew it was going to rain like that except those at GHQ and that the whole operation was an 'unjustified gamble'. I do not know how any operation of war can be anything but a gamble unless the enemy tells you what he has got the other side of the hill and in what state his troops are" (*Plumer of Messines* (1935), p.130). *OH 1917*, ii, pp.338–45 gives an unsparing account of the conditions and fighting on 11–12 October. For German relief at the awful weather see Crown Prince Rupprecht's war diary entry (*Mein Kriegstagebuch*, ii, 271) quoted at the head of this chapter.

21   Gold, *AQ*, 86. Should, therefore, a forecast be formulated in words to encourage generals to act so as to gain a tactical advantage and surprise the enemy? Stagg concluded that he should provide the best weather advice about alternatives and to suppress any views he might have "as an amateur tacti-cian": how the advice was used must be a matter "solely" for the military commander (Stagg, pp.59–61).

22   Dr H. Cotton, 'Memoirs of a Meteorologist' in *MM* vols.108, 109, 1979–80, in six parts; the quotation comes from Part 5, Feb 1980, pp.58–59. I am indebted to Dr A J Peacock for drawing my attention to Dr Cotton's work. Synoptic features include the position and pressure readings at the centres of depressions, the sectors where pressure is rising and falling most markedly, cloud, rain areas, etc.

23   *Despatch* of 25 December 1917, para. 63, page 142 in J H Boraston (ed), *Sir Douglas Haig's Despatches* (1919). Haig's diary 30 and 31 July. His later entries are equally factual, e.g. 6 November 1917: "Sunrise was red and sky 'lowering'. But only a few drops of rain fell about 9 a.m. and then the day was fine. Glass began to fall late night. 'Meteor' prophesied wind but day was quiet. Glass steadied at noon". The diary shows Haig's continued reliance on the "weather prophet" in the days immediately preceding Cambrai later in the month.

24   Lloyd George's *War Memoirs* included a table of "Flanders" rainfall statistics for July, August and September as part of his condemnation of the Third Ypres plan (vol.iv, p.2207, or Odhams p.1306). No location or source was given and the figures were disputed by *OH 1917*, vol.ii, Note on pp.211–12. Lloyd

George's table cannot be reconciled with the daily Vlamertinghe statistics for 1917, and it is odd that he should have ignored October.

25 A Bryant, *Triumph in the West* (1959), p.205. The original 5 June date was deferred, but Admiral Ramsay and General Montgomery warned that operationally a 'go' or 'stand-down' decision would have to be made within a few hours. We now know that the next period for suitable moon and tides, 19 June, was a period of unexpected bad weather, cloud and gales. Hitler had insisted (18 March 1944): "once defeated, the enemy will never try to invade again. Quite apart from their heavy losses they would need months to organize a fresh attempt. And an invasion failure would also deliver a crushing blow to British and American morale." German troops would be freed from the west for the Russian front: quoted in J Keegan, *Six Armies in Normandy* (1982), p.65.

26 Stagg, p.127. He had previously said "the storms of June 1944 were abnormal in their severity. It is also now a matter of record that disturbed weather dominated the whole summer and autumn of that year. The only interval of reasonably quiet settled weather occurred in the first half of August" (p.126).

27 Griffiths, chapters 1 and 2 *passim*. See note 8 above.

28 From 1914 Lille was of course under German occupation, but BEF weather stations were established at St Omer (1915) and at Vlamertinghe (1916), 2½ miles west of Ypres, and provided detailed records thereafter.

29 Gold had intervened in a savage argument over Third Ypres which raged in the *Spectator* correspondence columns in 1957–58. I quote his letter in Appendix II. Wolff's publishers then joined in to assure readers that he was writing a study which would present "the whole [sic] background and story" of the campaign. Not one word of Gold's statement ever found its way into Wolff's eventual book.

30 What makes Charteris's comment (ostensibly the GHQ opinion on 26 July 1917) the more unbelievable is the daily weather diary for August 1916. This lists the Second Army (Ypres) area as *totally dry* 1–9 August, 0.1 mm. of rain on the 10th, 'traces' on 11–13 August, 18.1 mm. (0.7") between 14th and 20th, and 55.8 mm. (2.2") 21–31 August (of which the 29th and 30th accounted for 44.5 mm.): WO.95/6.

31 *Despatches*, para. 55, p.127.

32 It had originally been intended that the Western offensive should be *supported* by the Kerensky-ordained Russian offensive, which opened as planned on 28 June. Germany would thus have come under intense pressure all round. But as the western allies were not ready, the Russian early successes were unsupported and were wiped away in three weeks.

33 G. A. B. Dewar assisted by J. H. Boraston, *Sir Douglas Haig's Command, 1915–1918* (1922), vol.i, p.369. The Third Ypres chapter was by Boraston, and this quotation is almost certainly based on Gold's detailed report which Haig sent to the War Cabinet on 21 October 1917 – Hankey having written to the CIGS on the 17th that the Cabinet did not fully realize the effect that bad weather had had on operations! WO.106/407.

34 By the time Haig wrote that diary entry on the morning of 2 August there had fallen 55.3 mm. since the morning of the 29th. The summary is in *Sir Douglas Haig's Despatches*, pp.116–17, paras. 43, 45.

35 *OH 1917*, ii, p.284 says "the ground was now [26 September] so powdery and dry that the bursts of the high explosive shell raised a dense wall of dust and smoke". Williamson in *Time and Tide*, 21 March 1959, pp.340–42. The

success of the Menin Road battle which started on the campaign's 52nd day, on the day after 5.1 mm. of rain had fallen, in a September each week of which had seen rain, demolishes De Groot's accusation that "Ethiopian [i.e. extreme] drought" conditions were necessary and that "any" rain meant disaster.

36 Boraston in Dewar and Boraston, i, p.378.
37 Cited in Terraine, *Road to Passchendaele*, p.305. *OH 1914* vol.ii, provides daily comments on conditions in October 1914 (mainly dry, morning mist or fog, often fine later) and November (rain and frost, some snow). They are not indexed but appear on pp.131, 138, 165, 177, 185, 236, 251–52, 256, 265, 284, 303 and 349 for October and 356, 362, 379, 381, 393, 397, 404, 409, 420 and 448 for November. Keith Simpson's *The Old Contemptibles, a Photographic History* (1981) gives many pictures of the ground in those days. Haig's diary for October 1914 has one weather entry: "Rained on and off during day" (20 Oct); on 6 November he noted "fog"; these notes multiply after the weather began to deteriorate badly from the 12th onwards.
38 *Despatches*, p.133, para 61.

Chapter 11

The Royal Flying Corps and the Struggle for Supremacy in the Air over the Salient

Jack Bruce and Kevin Kelly

For the Royal Flying Corps in France, the early months of 1917 had been a grim period: April had been the grimmest of all, that month's losses of flying personnel, at 319, being the highest suffered in any month of the war up to that time. The spring of 1917 had seen the abject failure of the French offensive on the Aisne, a débâcle that had seriously damaged the morale of the French troops. These factors severely restricted the ability of Nivelle's successor as Commander-in-Chief, Général Pétain, to plan operations on any appreciable scale. The burden of the western offensive therefore, had to be borne in Flanders by the British forces.

In the Battle of Messines, which was an action of limited objectives and a preliminary to the Battle of Ypres, the British operations were initially an exemplary success. The battle began on 7 June 1917, its success assured by intense artillery bombardment. From noon on 1 June to noon on 10 June, 2,233 guns fired 2,843,163 rounds weighing a total of 64,164 tons. Second Army records noted that these figures represented 'a gun to every 4½ yards and 6½ tons of ammunition to every yard of front attacked'.[1] Vital to these guns was accurate observation, a duty which came to be an important role of the men and machines of the Royal Flying Corps, mostly the R.E.8's of Squadrons Nos 6, 21, 42 and 53. By 7 June, the R.F.C. had 18 squadrons in the battle area, a total that included single-seat fighter, fighter-reconnaissance and day-bomber units, with a total of 300 aircraft serviceable. A new scheme for monitoring and reporting enemy air activity had been introduced in May 1917, each Army being allocated one Aeroplane Compass Station and one Aeroplane Intercepting Station. Lack of radio communication with the aeroplanes made the scheme cumbersome, but it proved useful in several ways.

Artillery observation was well-organized and efficient, and aerial photography was extensively used, as were strategic aerial reconnaissance and bombing. Contact patrols, flown at perilously low level, monitored the progress and positions of the troops; fighter aircraft harassed the enemy's troops and attacked his aerodromes, which were also bombed by day and by night.

All of this was done by an R.F.C. that was severely stretched. On 10 June, its GOC, Major-General H. M. Trenchard, wrote in a memorandum to his Brigade Commanders:

> ... that it is of the utmost importance that the Flying Corps should avoid wastage in both pilots and machines for some little time. My reserve at present is dangerously low, in fact in some cases it barely exists at all, and the supply from home is not coming forward sufficiently freely to enable us to continue fighting an offensive in the air continuously. It is just as impossible for the air forces to fight a continuous offensive as it is for the infantry, and as we have no reserve squadrons it is necessary to do everything to avoid losses . . . It is of the utmost importance, however, that the offensive spirit is maintained in the Flying Corps.[2]

Training in the R.F.C. had been inadequate throughout the war, and the expansion of the Corps approved early in 1917 made matters worse. With a further expansion, to a total of 200 squadrons, decided upon in July, the statistics alone became daunting, the logistics overwhelming. In terms only of pilots, it was calculated that during the six months ending 31 December 1917, no fewer than 3,252 trained pilots would be needed, plus a further 2,199 from January to 31 March 1918.

The towering difficulties notwithstanding, a massive expansion of the entire training organization was initiated, extending beyond essential flying training to embrace Officers' Technical Training Wings, new Schools of Aeronautics and Cadet Wings, an Equipment Officers' School, and greatly expanded arrangements for the practical training of men.

Most historically significant for the entire future of flying training, not merely in the R.F.C. but worldwide, was the establishment in August 1917 of the first School of Special Flying at Gosport under Major Robert R. Smith-Barry, an officer of unique talent and personality. In the history of aviation it was a milestone of massive importance. He turned flying tuition from a haphazard and dangerous 'Black Art' into a sound and safe system which forms the basis for all flying instruction even today.

Overdue and invaluable though these great changes were, they came about too late to avail the men of the R.F.C. who had to bear the burden of the intensive flying, fighting, bombing, reconnoitring, photographing and artillery spotting that was demanded of them during the Third Battle of Ypres which began on 31 July 1917. On that date, the strength of the British air services on the Western Front comprised 45 R.F.C. squadrons, five Royal Naval Air Service fighter squadrons attached to the R.F.C., one squadron newly arrived and not yet ready for action, one Special Duty Flight, and 44 Balloon Sections. Of serviceable aeroplanes, the squadrons had a total of 858. Reserves, if indeed there were any, must have been minimal.

The strength [and disposition] of the Corps from the coast down to Second Army's border with First Army near Armentières was as follows:

Ninth (HQ) Wing	Machines	Airfield
19 Squadron	Spad	Liettres
27 Squadron	Martinsyde Elephant	Clairmarais
55 Squadron	DH4	Boisdinghem
56 Squadron	SE5 and SE5A	Liettres
66 Squadron	Sopwith Pup	Liettres
70 Squadron	Sopwith Camel	Liettres
Special Duty Flight	BE12, BE12a, BE2e	Clairmarais

Fourth Brigade
Third Wing

34 Squadron	RE8	Bray Dunes
52 Squadron	RE8	Bray Dunes

Fourteenth Wing

6 RNAS Squadron	Sopwith Camel	Frontier Aerodrome
9 RNAS Squadron	Sopwith Camel	Leffrinckhoucke
48 Squadron	Bristol Fighter	Frontier Aerodrome
54 Squdron	Sopwith Pup	Leffrinckhouke

and 2 Balloon Sections

Fifth Brigade
Fifteenth Wing

4 Squadron	RE8	Abeele
7 Squadron	RE8	Proven
9 Squadron	RE8	Proven
21 Squadron	RE8	La Lovie

Twenty-second Wing

10 RNAS Squadron	Sopwith Triplane	Droglandt
23 Squadron	Spad	La Lovie
29 Squadron	Nieuport Scout	Poperinghe
32 Squadron	DH5	Droglandt
57 Squadron	DH4	Boisdinghem

and 9 Balloon Sections

Second Brigade
Second Wing

6 Squadron	RE8	Abeele
42 Squadron	RE8	Bailleul
53 Squadron	RE8	Bailleul

Eleventh Wing

1 Squadron	Nieuport Scout	Bailleul
1 RNAS Squadron	Sopwith Triplane	Bailleul
20 Squadron	F.E.2d	St Marie Cappel
45 Squadron	Sopwith 1½ Strutter & Camel	St Marie Cappel

and 9 Balloon Companies

First Brigade serving the First Army supported the battle to their North with their aircraft:

First Wing	Machines	Airfield
2 Squadron	Armstrong Whitworth AWFK8	Hesdigneul
5 Squadron	RE8	Acq
10 Squadron	AWFK8	Chocques
15 Squadron	RE8	La Gorgue
16 Squadron	RE8	Camblain-l'Abbé
35 Squadron	AWFK8	Savy
Tenth Wing		
8 RNAS Squadron	Sopwith Triplane & Camel	Mont St Eloi
25 Squadron	DH4 and F.E.2d	Auchel
40 Squadron	Nieuport Scout	Bruay
43 Squadron	Sopwith 1½ Strutter	Auchel
100 Squadron	FE2b and BE2e	Treizennes
and 12 Balloon Sections		

Further South the R.F.C. had another Brigade (Third) with a squadron of Morane Parasols, two with B.E.2es, two with R.E.8s, two with Bristol Fighters, two with D.H.5s, one converting from Nieuport Scouts to SE5s and another converting from F.E.2bs to D.H.4s plus twelve balloon sections.

In addition, 101 Squadron, F.E.2bs, had only been in France five days and was not yet operational and the R.F.C. could call upon the R.N.A.S. squadrons around the Dunkirk area for support. The R.N.A.S. fighter squadrons actually attached to the R.F.C. Wings were an indication that the Navy had spare planes and pilots above their normal requirements and an admission on the part of the R.F.C. that it could not carry out all the fighter patrol work it wanted to from its own resources.

Not all of these squadrons were viable in the combat conditions of late Summer 1917. The Sopwith Pup single-seat fighter was an agile and delightful aeroplane, but under-powered and under-armed with only a single Vickers gun regulated by the Sopwith-Kauper synchronizing mechanism. There were still Sopwith 1½ Strutters with Squadrons Nos 43 and 45, slow and hard to manoeuvre; and No 27 Squadron's Martinsyde Elephants, although made gallantly to do some useful work as day bombers, were ponderous and vulnerable. Also in the bomber category were the F.E.2bs of Squadrons Nos 18, 100 and 101; while No 20 Squadron had the F.E.2d, a more powerful development of the F.E.2b with the Rolls-Royce Eagle engine. Pilots' devotion to their aircraft, even in obsolescence, could be strong. At the time, Arthur Gould Lee, later Air Vice Marshal Arthur Gould Lee MC, was in No 46 Squadron, flying Sopwith Pups. No 46 Squadron shared St Marie Cappel with Squadrons Nos 20 (F.E.2d's) and 45 (Sopwith 1½ Strutters). Of the former squadron, Lee wrote, in his excellent and evocative book, No Parachute: "We've pitched

1. The Prime Minister, David Lloyd
   George. (From a set of
   contemporary postcards, Liddle
   Collection). Chapter 2.

2. Field Marshal Sir Douglas Haig, a
   water-colour, by Major Alfred
   Kingsley Lawrence, RA RP,
   Northumberland Fusiliers
   (Tyneside Scottish). (Print held in
   Liddle Collection). Chapter 3.

3. Sir Douglas Haig conferring with
   General Anthoine, in command of
   the French troops at Third Ypres.
   (French War Office official
   photograph). Chapters 3 and 7.

4. Field Marshal Paul von Hindenburg at a conference of senior German military and naval officers on the Belgian coast. (E.L.Berthon, Liddle Collection). Chapter 4

5. An oblique view of the Ypres battlefield in June 1917, looking East-Northeast towards Kitchener's Wood and St Julien, before the commencement of the offensive. (Liddle Collection).

6. The problem: British gunners attempting to drag a field piece through the mud into a new position. (G.M.Liddell, Liddle Collection)

7. The effects of German counter-battery fire. Disconsolate British gunners inspect their weapon. (G.M.Liddell, Liddle Collection)

8. Admiral Sir John Jellicoe, First Sea Lord at the time of the Third Battle of Ypres. (Lady Jellicoe) Chapter 6

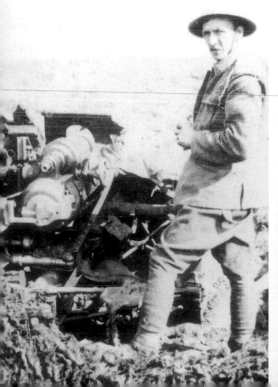

9. German submarine pens on the Belgian coast. (E.L.Berthon, Liddle
   Collection) Chapter 6

10. After the 31 July attack, French infantry make a detailed study of the terrain.
   (French magazine *L'Illustration*, 11 August 1917) Chapter 7

11. The battlefield between the second and third German lines after the attack of 31 July. (French magazine *L'Illustration*, 11 August 1917) Chapter 7

12. French troops beside the Yser canal, 4 August 1917. (French magazine *L'Illustration*, 11 August 1917) Chapter 7

13. German prisoners crossing the Yser canal in the aftermath of the 31 July attack. (French magazine *L'Illustration*, 11 August 1917). Chapter 8

14. The Bull sound-ranging apparatus as used by the British, based on the Einthoven string-galvanometer and a 35 mm cine-film recorder. (The Royal Engineers Institution) Chapter 9

15. A temporary flash-spotting post during an advance. Various observation instruments were used. (The Royal Engineers Institution) Chapter 9

16. A topographer of a corps topographical section resecting a field battery position by plane table; heavy batteries were fixed by observers of field survey companies using the theodolite. (The Royal Engineers Institution) Chapter 9

17. Triangulation with the 5-inch theodolite and Lucas daylight signalling lamp. Rough alignment was first obtained with the plane-table. (The Royal Engineers Institution) Chapter 9

18. II Corps Topographical Section (Lieut. R.B.Beilby MC) in a hut in the grounds of La Lovie Château during Third Ypres. (The Royal Engineers Institution) Chapter 9

our camp next door to No. 20 Squadron, who have F.E.2ds, and for some strange reason don't seem to mind them . . . "³

For all that, No 20 Squadron must have been relieved when the replacement of their sturdy old pushers by Bristol Fighters had begun that August, during the Battle of Ypres. No 46 Squadron had to wait until November 1917 for the start of its own re-equipment with Sopwith Camels.

To work with and for the Fifth Army, extensive re-disposition of squadrons gave to the V Brigade, R.F.C. (Brigadier-General C A H Longcroft), four R.E.8 Squadrons which formed the HQ Fifteenth (Corps) Wing, while the HQ Twenty-Second (Army) Wing had one D.H.4 squadron and four single-seat fighter squadrons. [No 10 Naval Squadron, No 23, No 29 and No 32]. The Fifth Balloon Wing added a total of nine Balloon Sections provided by Companies Nos 8, 13, 17 and 20.

For co-operation with the Fourth Army on the coast, the IV Brigade, R.F.C., (Brigadier-General J. H. W. Becke DSO) had two R.E.8 Squadrons, Nos 34 and 52 of the Third (Corps) Wing; the Brigade's HQ Fourteenth (Army) Wing comprised two Camel squadrons (Nos 6 Naval and 9 Naval), No 48 Squadron, and No 54 Squadron. No 9 Balloon Company provided Balloon Sections Nos 7 and 21. The Ninth Wing of the R.F.C. had already moved north to participate in the Battle of Messines, and had on its strength, six further squadrons, viz. Nos 19, 27, 55, 56, 66 and 70.

The numerical strengths, in aircraft, of these wings were:

Ninth Wing	111
Fourteenth Wing	102
Fifteenth Wing	172

To these could be added the 123 aircraft of the seven squadrons of the 11 Brigade, and on 31 July 1917, there were, in all, 508 British aeroplanes between the Lys and the sea.

The French aerial support consisted of approximately 200 aircraft with 50% of this total being fighters, mostly Spad 7's similar to those used by 19 and 23 Squadrons R.F.C. These fighters were arranged into 'Groupe de Combats', [Fighter Wings], of four squadrons each, including the élite G de C 12, 'Les Cigognes' [The Storks], which numbered in its ranks many of the best fighter pilots the French possessed. The most famous of these was Capitaine Georges Guynemer, France's leading 'ace' with over 40 victories. Another fêted unit in the area was N124, the 'Lafayette Escadrille', whose pilots were nearly all Americans, volunteering to join the French cause long before the entry of the U.S.A. into the war in April 1917. Allied airpower was further strengthened by the small Belgian air service which contributed about 40 artillery observation aircraft to the total. Moreover, as there were over 100 R.N.A.S. aircraft at Dunkerque the potential Allied air strength was in the region of 850 aeroplanes.

The aerial strength of the Germans was mostly concentrated in the Fourth Army area which extended from the North Sea inland for a distance of some 50 miles. The Battle of Messines had influenced the German command to increase the aircraft available in this area from around 300 on 7 June to double that amount when the Ypres offensive opened. Some 200 of this total were single-seater fighters organized into Jagdstaffeln [Jastas: 'hunting squadrons']. Four of the best Jastas had been combined into an elite group, Jagdgeschwader 1 [Fighter Wing 1] commanded by Rittmeister Manfred von Richthofen, the leading German fighter pilot. To the British with their air of flippancy, he was simply 'The Red Baron' and his unit, 'The Flying Circus', both soubriquets referring to the unit's painted appearance.

The main equipment of the Jagdstaffeln was the Albatros D111 and DV Scouts, twin-gun fighters which were capable of dealing with most R.F.C. aircraft, although the newer types, such as the Sopwith Camel, S.E.5, Bristol Fighter and the Navy's Sopwith Triplane, were gradually wresting aerial superiority from German grasp. Albatros pilots continued to score successes but these were increasingly the result of pilot skill and experience, coupled with the advantage of fighting over their own territory rather than their accustomed technical superiority.

A serious drain on Trenchard's resources began with a daylight raid on 13 June. On that day, a force of German Gothas, large twin-engined aircraft based in Belgium, bombed London and the subsequent outcry from the press, public, and politicians led to a major review of the country's aerial defence which up to then had been geared towards the menace of the night-flying Zeppelin airship. Despite his protests, Trenchard had to release 66 Squadron to be posted to Calais and 56 Squadron to Kent to intercept future Gotha raids. In order to prepare for the Battle of Ypres, these fighters returned after a couple of weeks but the Gothas raided London for the second time the day after 56 Squadron had left England. This compelled the War Cabinet to order the return of a Scout squadron. On 10 July, 46 Squadron's Sopwith Pups duly left the battlefront for the inactivity of England, not returning until 30 August.

Worse was to follow for the Commander in the Field. On 13 July, he was informed that 24 Sopwith Camels, vital to the re-equipment programme for his Sopwith 1½ Strutter squadrons, were to be retained in England for Home Defence duties, as well as four D.H.4s. The plans to re-equip the Sopwith squadrons under his command, the Pups, Triplanes and 1½ Strutters, with the potent Camel, all fell behind schedule.

The political will to seek reprisals on Germany expressed itself later on in the year. In October, Trenchard had to release 100 Squadron and 55 Squadron (arguably his best night-bombing and day-bombing squadrons respectively) to form 41 Wing together with an RNAS squadron of Handley Pages also for night-bombing. They were based in the French sector, out of reach of Trenchard. All three squadrons were based at Ochey, and the 41st Wing's first attack was made on 17 October 1917 by eight D.H.4's of No 55 Squadron; their target was the Burbach works near Saarbrücken. The first night raid, again principally on the Burbach works, was made on 24 October by nine Naval Handley Pages and fourteen

F.E.2b's of No 100 Squadron. From this modest beginning arose eventually the Independent Force, R.A.F.

The Gotha raids therefore had a series of consequential effects which even extended to the later cabinet decision to amalgamate the R.F.C. and R.N.A.S., into the Royal Air Force, but, for the moment, Trenchard's mind was focussed on the present offensive.

The first preparatory orders for co-ordinated aerial action were issued on 7 July by Major-General Trenchard. These defined the reconnaissance, offensive-patrol and bombing areas of the various Wing commands from the Lille-Armentières railway to the sea, and came into force at midnight on 8 July. The general air offensive was to be initiated on, and was to develop fully from, that date. Considerable importance attached to bombing by day and night, and to destroying German observation balloons.

Although the Battle of Messines had been favoured with – and helped by – good weather, poor conditions on 7, 8 and 9 July severely hampered flying. The German attack at Lombartzyde inflicted serious damage and casualties; and German artillery fire from batteries concealed by smoke screens made counter-battery work even more difficult. A method of close co-operation between aeroplanes and balloon observers proved successful, as did an ingenious form of wireless co-operation between aeroplane observers and sound-ranging sections of the Royal Engineers.

Air combats increased sharply in number from mid July; on 26 July, some 94 fighters clashed in a long but inconclusive battle near Polygon Wood, but this allowed four German two-seaters to penetrate British air space and carry out a vitally important reconnaissance of the area around Ypres without interference. Next day, the outmoded F.E.2b's, played the part of bait in a trap and lured 20 Albatros scouts into an ambush of 59 British fighters. The fight lasted over an hour with additional British, French and German aircraft joining in. The British claimed nine Albatros destroyed for the loss of two of their own, earning a letter of praise from Sir Douglas Haig the following day.

After two postponements, from 25 and 28 July, the Ypres offensive opened at 3.50 a.m. on 31 July. British squadrons did much low flying, the two-seaters in contact-patrol operations, the fighters in attacks on ground targets. The weather was bad, but reports by aeroplane observers helped the infantry materially, while in attacks on enemy aerodromes all specified targets were bombed, notably by the Martinsydes of No 27 Squadron. Fighter aircraft dropped 25-lb Cooper bombs on targets of opportunity; an innovative measure on their part.

Typical of the Corps squadrons taking part in the battle was 6 Squadron, flying R.E.8's from Abeele. Their commanding officer, Major Archibald James, has recalled his unit's duties:

> All the Corps Squadrons that were to take part in the battle were made up to 24 machines thus making each up to 24 Pilots, 24 Observers, 2 N.C.O. Air Gunners, a total flying personnel of 50. Squadron

Headquarters comprised the C.O., Recording Officer, (Adjutant), Intelligence Officer, 2 Wireless Officers, an Armament Officer and, attached from Corps, an Artillery Liaison Officer. Some of their functions require explanation. The Intelligence Officer had a small skilled staff to develop and interpret air photographs. Upon his skill depended identifying German Artillery positions for our Artillery to bombard, and to detect dummy positions. From air photographs too, the intricate German trench systems had to be interpreted on to maps. A second Wireless Officer was necessary because a Squadron had some 50 Wireless Operators attached to Batteries which had to be visited and their technical needs supplied. The duties of Corps Squadrons were ranging batteries, photography as aforesaid. Artillery observation was ordinarily carried out from between 5,000 and 6,000 ft. and most photographs were taken from this level, and what was called Contact Patrol, a difficult, dangerous, and nearly always unrewarding activity. It involved flying at some 1,500 ft. over the supposed advancing troops during an attack with the object of reporting progress and thus enabling our artillery barrage to be moved in front of them. At this time every Corps machine crossing the line carried two 20-lb. bombs. These it dropped whenever convenient, not that it was expected that they would hit any particular object but to make the Germans dislike having our machines over them. This would also have the effect of making them the more critical of their own Air Force for not giving them further protection. To aid spotting the Front Line, the troops were issued with small, about coffee-cup size, flares which they were supposed to light when the contact plane flew over them to show their position. But this they were extremely reluctant to do because the smoke from the flares would probably also indicate their position to the opposing Artillery Forward Observing Officers. Quite frequent combats with German aircraft were incidental in the Corps Squadron's tasks".[4]

From 1 to 5 August, rain set in and turned the battlefield into the ghastly quagmire that characterized so much of the battle. R.F.C. squadrons contributed to the success of the Canadian Corps in the taking of Hill 70 on 15 August. In preparatory bombing attacks during the night of 13/14 August, the Armstrong Whitworth F.K.8's of No 10 Squadron bombed railway junctions and billets at Carvin, Berclau and Oignies; this last-named place was bombed again on 14 August by the D.H.4's of No 25 Squadron. These aircraft were again in action that evening, bombing the German aerodrome at Dorignies; and also on 14 August Phalempin aerodrome was bombed by No 27 Squadron's Martinsydes. In the early hours of 15 August, No 10 Squadron's Armstrong Whitworths again flew as night bombers, attacking rest billets of the German troops that were due to meet infantry attack that day.

The German response went further than just ordering extra Jasta patrols:

Hauptmann Wilberg, the Kofl [Kommandeur der Flieger: Commander of all Flying Units within an Army] of the 4th German Army in Flanders arranged the flying units at his disposal well and made wide use of the Ifl [Infanterieflieger: Infantry co-operation aircraft] aeroplanes. An important change in the use of these machines was the introduction of wireless telegraphy to actually control the aircraft over the fighting area, and to receive reports on their observations by this means. They were thus saved from shuttling backwards and forwards between the front-line and the communications centres to drop message bags and read ground signals, and could spend their flight endurances in a more productive manner over the fighting area. The losses suffered by these machines were high and in an attempt to reduce the hazardous nature of this work, the armoured Ifl aeroplanes made their appearance. There was a marked improvement immediately on the introduction of the first few armoured Infanterieflieger aeroplanes.

The Schusta [Schutzstaffel: Unit of two-seater aircraft for the protection of other low-flying two-seaters] were now being increasingly used to support infantry and to attack enemy reserves and artillery batteries from a low height with hand grenades and machine-gun fire. Flying ordinary machines in the C category at this time the losses to these formations were high and this position was not to improve until the end of 1917 when the first Schusta were equipped with light high performance aircraft of the new CL category.[5]

To keep the skies clear of low-flying German aircraft, an advance landing ground was set up at Mazingarbe, some three miles from the front line and a flight of Nieuport Scouts of No 40 Squadron was sent there. Messages were sent in from an advanced anti aircraft observation station near Loos. These prompted 30 flights by the Nieuports, which destroyed two German aircraft, sent down three out of control, and drove off many others. This helped R.F.C. artillery-spotting and reconnaissance aircraft to work unmolested, the R.E.8 crews of No 16 Squadron earning the specific commendation of the GOC 1st Canadian Division. During the Battle of Langemarck (16 to 18 August), No 9 Squadron also won praise, in this case from the GOC Royal Artillery, XIV Corps, for its accurate reporting.

Ground-attack sorties were flown by No 32 Squadron, No 23 Squadron and No 29 Squadron. The success of No 29 Squadron's Nieuports was the more meritorious because their only weapon was a single Lewis machine-gun mounted on the upper wing. As a result, they had to dive at a steeper than normal angle when ground-strafing, in an aircraft which was rather tiring to fly at low level. The weather remained obstinately unhelpful, yet on 16 August, Squadrons Nos 27, 55, 56, 66 and 70 of the HQ Ninth Wing flew a total of 230 hours. In particular, Nos 66, 70 and 56 put up offensive patrols for the battle area continuously from dawn. In various local infantry actions (e.g. Guillemont Farm, Bohain, Cologne Farm Hill) concentrated ground-attack sorties by D.H.5s, F.E.2bs and S.E.5as preceded the infantry attacks to good purpose.

This was also a day of low-level activity for the French Scouts for although Groupe de Combat 13 had left the Salient, the remaining Spads

(x) From the flying logbook of Lieutenant B.U.S.Cripps, No 9 Squadron RFC (operating RE 8s and based at Proven). On 10 September, Cripps' two seater is engaged by an enemy aircraft while attempting to photograph enemy positions at Langemarck. On the following day, Cripps was on artillery co-operation duties, assisting in the direction of fire of 8" howitzers but he also had to drop propaganda pamphlets over the German lines. While engaged on a patrol to assist in the neutralization of the fire (N.F.) of enemy batteries on 12 September, his sporting instincts – some might say unsporting – lead him to attempt to machine-gun ducks on the Yser marshes. (B.U.S.Cripps, Liddle Collection)

flew to some effect. 2nd Lt. J Chaput attacked an Albatros Scout but was unable to watch it crash due to a second Albatros on his tail. Two of his colleagues bombed Handzaeme airfield hitting a hangar, while others buzzed around Houthulst Forest bombing and machine-gunning batteries in action, hutments, and vehicles on the roads. Future ace, Sgt A. P. J. Cordonnier, circled Lichtervelde at 4.45 a.m. and from 900 ft observed a moving train at which he aimed two bombs. When he looked back the locomotive was seen to be derailed. He also bombed Staden later the same day. The Storks scored two victories over the Forest, one being the eighth victory of Lt René Fonck, destined to be the highest scoring Allied pilot by the end of the war with an exceptional 75 enemy aircraft shot down.[6]

The man he beat to become France's top scorer was Georges Guynemer who, the next day, raised his total to 52 when he downed a pair of two-seaters, again near Houthulst Forest. Despite this 'double', Guynemer was by now living on his nerves, a pale thin figure only kept going by his intense devotion to duty. He scored only once more before 11 September, when he failed to return from a patrol. His body was located by British troops but the force of subsequent artillery barrages pounded the earth beyond recognition and his grave was lost. The loss was indeed a national one as he was fêted in France like no other soldier in the war, and in death he passed into the realm of romantic legend. Subsequent generations of French schoolchildren were told he had flown so high that he could not come back down.

The deaths of other heroes were more accurately reported. The German pilot said to have killed Guynemer was himself killed by an S.E.5 pilot of 56 Squadron R.F.C. on 28 September and, five days prior to that, No 56 was involved in a fight of Homeric proportions. Over the Salient, a patrol from 56 Squadron noticed a pair of S.E.5's of 60 Squadron under attack by a Fokker F1 Triplane, which was flown by Lt Werner Voss, one of Germany's most outstanding pilots. Voss's fire was so accurate that the 60 Squadron aircraft had to withdraw due to combat damage and the German gave 56 Squadron the same treatment, shooting holes in all seven S.E.5a's, yet remarkably not wounding any of the British pilots. His defiant fight and brilliant flying won the admiration of all his opponents because he did not pull out of an unmatched fight as in fact he could have done. The unequal combat ended in Voss's death but he had served notice on the R.F.C. that Germany had a new and formidable single-seat fighter.

One of Voss's opponents was Capt J. T. B. McCudden, whose combat flying was a remarkable blend of dedication, enthusiasm and skill. He had joined the Royal Engineers aged 15 and secured a transfer to the Royal Flying Corps in 1913, as soon as he reached 18. By 1915 he was flying as an observer, later becoming a pilot before gaining his commission. He had barely started on the compilation of his impressive list of combat victories at the time of the Voss fight. Voss's triplane was finally shot down by 2nd Lt A. P. F. Rhys Davids, who, like his opponent, was only 20 years of age.

A former head boy of Eton with a brilliant future forecast for him after the war, he was destined to outlive Voss by little more than a month.

September had brought with it a spell of drier weather, and a fresh attack was planned to start on the 20th. Twenty-six R.F.C. and R.N.A.S. Squadrons were directly involved, and some of the preceding night's bombing was assigned to the Handley Page bombers operating from Coudekerque. The reconnoitring, artillery spotting, bombing by day and night, fighting, ground attack and photography continued, despite difficult weather, through and beyond the German counter-attack and the Battle of Polygon Wood. Heavy losses were inflicted on the German troops, some being struck down before they even reached the front line. The official historian wrote:

A study of the reports of the low-flying fighting pilots makes it clear, also, that the German troops brought up for counter-attack suffered casualties before they had to meet the British artillery fire. As was done for the attack on the 20th, tactical maps were supplied showing the enemy assembly points and routes of approach, and the area was divided into sections which were specifically allotted for the special attention of the low-flying patrol pilots. Many parties of German infantry marching behind the battle-front were found and scattered with light-weight bombs and machine-gun fire. Other targets included active batteries and machine-guns, and troops entrenched or holding strong-points in the forward areas.[7]

Enemy aerodromes were strafed but with an economy that suggested that the R.F.C. was still critically short of reserves. When low-flying attacks on nine German airfields were ordered on 26 September, each was to be attacked by one fighter pilot only. The day bombers of Squadrons Nos 27 and 55 also targeted aerodromes. In combat, "The Bristol Fighter and the S.E.5 had the measure of the best of the enemy's fighters" wrote the official historian.

The month of September 1917 had seen a substantial increase in night flying and the night attacks made by the F.E.2bs of Squadrons Nos 100 and 101 were supplemented by raids flown by R.E.8s and Armstrong Whitworth F.K.8s of the Corps Squadrons. German night raiders now risked interception by the Bristol Fighters of No 48 Squadron, and, in England and France, pilots found that even the tricky Sopwith Camel could be flown at night.

Bad weather hampered many of the R.F.C.'s activities in early October, although things picked up on the 20th, in a quite spectacularly successful attack on Rumbeke aerodrome. This was made by no fewer than 45 aeroplanes: eleven Camels of No 70 Squadron, each carrying two 25-lb bombs, with eight more Camels of the squadron as close escort; 19 Camels of the recently arrived [8 October] No 28 Squadron were to come in from the rear to attack any German aircraft which managed to get airborne; and seven Spads of No 23 Squadron which were to fly as high cover. Much damage was done, not only by the bombs but by subsequent machine-gun attacks made at a height of only 20 feet: indeed, the wheels of two of the Camels touched the ground. The escorting Camels of No 70 Squadron drove down four German fighters out of control; those of No 28 Squadron defeated three more similarly. This type of combined operation would be one the British would refine and employ in 1918 to the detriment of the German air service.

Fine weather on 27 October gave the artillery an excellent opportunity, which they seized. Ninety-five German batteries were destroyed, twenty-one more neutralized. Many aerial photographs were taken; over 250 Cooper bombs and twenty-three 112-pdrs were dropped; and over 6,000 rounds of ammunition were fired by low-flying pilots at troops and gun emplacements. The R.F.C. suffered twenty casualties including 2nd Lt A. P. F. Rhys Davids of No 56 Squadron.

On 30 October, just when the infantry advance on Passchendaele had started, rain set in. After a brief dry period, the weather broke again on 6 November, but the Canadians attacked anew and captured Passchendaele and the high ground to the north and north-west of the village. It was in the malevolent morass of that martyred place that Third Ypres ended on 10 November 1917. The War Cabinet's Report for the Year 1917 understated what had been endured:

This battle has secured for us eleven miles of the main ridge east of Ypres, including the village of Passchendaele and the high ground to the north of it. Our progress has been achieved in spite of every disadvantage due to quite exceptional weather, the rainfall of August being nearly 2½ times the normal, and the water-logged nature of the ground has imposed an extremely severe strain on the troops.

In these operations we captured, between July 31st and November 18th, 24,000 prisoners and 64 guns.[8]

Conspicuously absent from the Olympian detachment of that note was any intimation of the price. It could be argued that the pilots and observers of the R.F.C. had been detached from the ground conditions where, principally, that price had been paid, yet they had seen the state of the battlefield from their 'privileged' viewpoint and were thankful they were not sharing the hardships of the troops on the ground. Sir Archibald James, formerly O.C. 6 Squadron, wrote of the perspective of the airmen:

1917 was an exceptionally wet summer and autumn. The constant rain on the shell-pitted ground of the battle area reduced everything to a swamp, the water-filled shell-holes giving the impression from the air of more water than dry land. Under these depressing conditions the Battle of Passchendaele dragged [on] . . . During that time we had in the Squadron 52 flying casualties, killed wounded and prisoner. These losses in no way affected the morale of the Squadron. We were all very young.

When I took over the Command I was 2 months under my 24th birthday. It was with such pliable material that Trenchard created the R.F.C.

The R.F.C.'s honourable part in Third Ypres might have been greater if it had had more aircraft of the calibre of the Bristol Fighter, D.H.4, S.E.5a and Sopwith Camel, and larger quantities of reliable aero-engines to power them. When the Battle of Cambrai began on 20 November, the R.F.C.'s strength had increased slightly to a total of 52 squadrons with, despite the losses sustained between July and November 1917, a total of 961 aeroplanes. Although No 46 Squadron had not yet completed its re-equipment with Camels, No 54 Squadron still had Pups and two Squadrons of R.E.8s and three of Camels were in process of being transferred to the Italian Front, No 43 Squadron did have Camels in place of its Sopwith 1½ Strutters, No 8 Squadron now had Armstrong Whitworth F.K.8s having shed its B.E.2es and No 12 Squadron had R.E.8s.

At home in Britain, intensive work on development of aircraft, aero-engines, armament and on-board equipment went on unceasingly, most notably at the Royal Aircraft Factory at Farnborough, at Martlesham Heath and at Orfordness. The greatest difficulties lay in the field of aero-engines, the design and development of which were slower than corresponding work on aircraft design. The combination of the Bristol Fighter and its Rolls-Royce Falcon engine was one of the most successful of the war. And yet, incredibly, the Air Board rejected a Rolls-Royce proposal to purchase an existing factory that could have substantially increased the production of Rolls-Royce engines. One suspects the dead hand of a militarily and aeronautically illiterate Treasury.

The aero-engine situation was always critical. In the case of the Bristol Fighter, greatly increased orders were placed without assured availability of enough engines. Output of the Falcon had been restricted by the inept decision mentioned above and could not possibly match the production of airframes, consequently alternative engines had to be sought. The one eventually chosen, the Sunbeam Arab, gave endless trouble and was never satisfactory. Its shortcomings led to a crisis in S.E.5a production, for the Arab had been chosen as an alternative power unit for that important type also. A similar case was the Siddeley Puma engine chosen for the D.H.9, development of which was started during the Battle of Ypres. The Arab-powered Bristol Fighter was supposed to replace the R.E.8 and Armstrong Whitworth F.K.8 in the Corps squadrons but never really did; and the D.H.9 bomber, although built in very large numbers, was no replacement for the much superior D.H.4, especially in that latter type's Rolls-Royce-powered form. The Sopwith Aviation company was working on the prototypes of two fighters, the Snipe and Dolphin, that would see service in 1918. The Dolphin proved to be very successful but another promising single-seater fighter the Martinsyde F.3, in its production form as the F.4 Buzzard, was too late to reach the squadrons before the Armistice.

By late 1917, technical development in several fields was carefully monitored by the Technical Department, and extensive liaison with manufacturers was maintained. Communication between Departments in Britain and the R.F.C. in the Field was not always as efficient as it should have been, and R.F.C. Headquarters occasionally expressed understandable displeasure when major changes were introduced without prior advice or consultation.

In the category of heavy bombers, the Handley Page o/100, originally created for the Royal Naval Air Service, was developed into the o/400 and was first ordered in quantity in August 1917, thus creating greatly increased demands for Rolls-Royce Eagle engines. On 10 September 1917, Sir Douglas Haig wrote to the War Office, asking that 25% of future additional bombing squadrons which were to operate in France should be night-bomber units.

From Trenchard's viewpoint, any new aircraft, any new engine, any new technical improvement, was welcome. His Corps had made great strides in the modernity of its equipment since the black days of 'Bloody April'. The 'lame ducks' were being phased out, while the replacement airmen were slowly benefitting from a higher standard of training back home. The work of the R.F.C. in assisting the Army was all that had been asked of it, weather permitting, and several new aspects of aerial warfare had been developed such as night flying of fighters in France, the use of bombs by fighter planes and the multi-squadron attack on an enemy aerodrome. These were all tactics that would be successfully refined in 1918, and indeed before, as the Battle of Cambrai saw a great deal of ground strafing by the R.F.C.'s fighter squadrons, as well as the improving two-seater air to ground co-operation.

Despite the weakening of his forces due to the political interference that saw three squadrons detached for the bombing of Germany, another five sent to Northern Italy and, most galling of all, the retention in England of front line aircraft and their crews, Trenchard's forces in the B.E.F. were consolidating their strength in numbers and in experience.

The German air force was not the source of worry to Trenchard that it had been in the Spring of 1917, for whilst new types of infantry co-operation aircraft and tactics were under development, the Jastas main equipment was still the Albatros Scout which no longer enjoyed a technical superiority over the Allied fighters. The new German fighter, the Fokker Dr1 Triplane, might have posed a threat in the hands of the Jagdgeschwader pilots, but following a series of wing failures the type was withdrawn until the New Year. Meanwhile, the British were settling on a range of aircraft types which were reliable, types which in the main were good enough to see them through to the end of the war and beyond. The British flying services emerged from the Battle of Ypres with great credit. Building on their hard won experience and developing all that was being learned, they applied their accumulating human and material resources to Cambrai with some effect and then went into the stern tests of 1918 with their tails up.

Notes

1 Official History: *The War in the Air*, Vol IV, H A Jones O.U.P. 1934, p. 113, footnote 2.
2 ibid, pp. 133–34.
3 Arthur Gould Lee, *No Parachute*, Jarrolds, London, 1968, p. 103.
4 Wing Commander Sir Archibald James, Typescript recollections, Liddle Collection, Brotherton Library, the University of Leeds.
5 Alex Imrie, *Pictorial History of the German Army Air Service 1914–18*, Ian Allan, London, 1971, pp. 47–48.
6 Data drawn from Royal Flying Corps Communique No 102, 26.8.17, p. 10, Liddle Collection Brotherton Library, the University of Leeds.
7 Source cit., p. 193.
8 War Cabinet: Report for the Year 1917 [Cd 9005, 1918] H.M.S.O., p. 142, para 5.

Chapter 12

Third Ypres – Casualties And British Medical Services: an Evaluation

Ian Whitehead

The duty of the Royal Army Medical Corps (R.A.M.C.) was threefold: sanitary; therapeutic; and military. This classification of its duties reflected the critical role to be played by the medical services in the prosecution of modern warfare. First amongst these functions was that of sanitation; the maintenance of the highest possible standards of hygiene in order to prevent or minimize the incidence of infectious diseases. Not only did such measures enhance military effectiveness, by reducing wastage, the prevention of sickness was also an important element in the maintenance of morale. Second, was the importance of providing immediate and skilled curative treatment of injuries and diseases. This involved the organization of an efficient system for the evacuation of the sick and wounded, and the provision of appropriate treatment as near as possible to the fighting line. The sanitary and therapeutic responsibilities of the R.A.M.C. were inextricably linked with the third part of its duty, the military role. It was the duty of the medical services to preserve the Army at its maximum fighting strength; to ensure that those soldiers who became ineffective, due to sickness or wounds, were cured and returned to their units in quick time; and that the treatment given was appropriate, recognizing the importance of maintaining morale and a soldier's fighting spirit. It is the intention of this chapter to examine the performance of the British medical services during the Passchendaele offensive, in the light of this threefold mission of military medicine.

Disease prevention was undoubtedly the most important challenge facing the R.A.M.C.. The wastage from preventable diseases during the Boer War had taught the military authorities the need for an efficient sanitary organization. Prior to 1914, the R.A.M.C. improved its training in preventive methods,[1] and the Army introduced measures for the strict observance of sanitary discipline. With the outbreak of war, it is clear that the medical authorities on the Western Front were cognisant of the lessons of South Africa. The sanitary organization of the B.E.F. proved to be highly

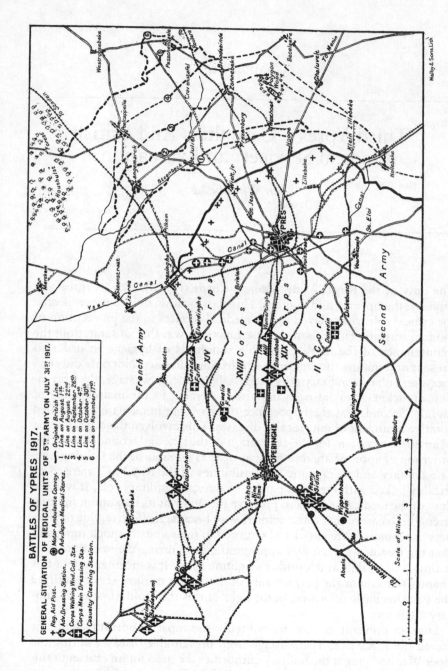

(xi) The medical network for Fifth Army on 31 July 1917. (source: "W.G. MacPherson (ed) Official History of the War: Medical Services – General History Vol III" London HMSO)

efficient, and simply expanded to meet the requirements of a growing force. The guiding principle of the sanitary organization was that the responsibility for the sanitary conditions of the quarters or localities of units and formations lay with the officer in command, who took all measures necessary for preserving the health of his men. The Director of Medical Services (D.M.S.) was the Commander-in-Chief's adviser on all medical and sanitary matters, and his representatives were similarly the advisers of the commanders to whose headquarters they were attached.

Each unit had a regimental personnel for sanitary duties, which consisted of one N.C.O., and between two and eight men, depending upon the strength of the unit. Also, one corporal, and two to four trained R.A.M.C men, were attached for water duties. A sanitary section was attached to every base, and sanitary squads to each railhead and advanced base. Sanitary squads were also allotted to each permanent post on the lines of communication. It was possible to subdivide sanitary sections into squads, or increase their size by the addition of further sanitary squads. The personnel of a sanitary section consisted of one officer of captain's or subaltern's rank, two staff sergeants or sergeants, and twenty-three rank and file; while that of a sanitary squad was one sergeant and five rank and file. By 1917, however, the increasing shortage of R.A.M.C. officers and other ranks had produced changes within the staffing of sanitary sections. R.A.M.C. personnel were often replaced by regimental personnel; and it became more common for them to be placed under the command of non-medical men, who nevertheless had experience in sanitary engineering or related fields.[2] The Deputy Assistant Director of Medical Services (D.A.D.M.S.) responsible for sanitation in the Fifth Army during the Passchendaele offensive, observed that the employment of highly trained non-medical officers in no way compromised the efficiency of the sanitary sections:

Officer Commanding no. 34 [sanitary section] though not a medical man struck me as the most capable.[3]

The initial success of the sanitary sections in improving and enforcing the sanitary standards of towns and base areas led to their deployment with the field army. Divisional sanitary sections were established in October 1914. These units followed the division to which they were attached, and were responsible for cleaning up recently occupied ground, incinerating rubbish, filling in latrines, disposing of manure, disinfecting clothing, supervising the sanitary arrangements of local towns, purifying water and ensuring that sources of drinking water were carefully monitored.[4] Such work ensured that sanitary standards in the B.E.F. were high, and made them the envy of the French Army, which lagged behind in the establishment of an efficient sanitary organization.[5]

Even so, the British arrangements were not problem-free. During the Somme campaign in 1916, the constant movement of divisions meant that sanitary sections were unable to settle down to their work. As a consequence, sanitary measures were neglected and, according to one observer, the Somme became "easily the messiest, untidiest and most insanitary (though not the muddiest) battleground of the war."[6] A memorandum to the Director General of the Army Medical Service (D.G.A.M.S.), dated 19 November 1916, concluded that a sanitary section could not fulfil its role successfully unless it was "well acquainted with the sanitary circumstances and requirements of the area in which it is working."[7] Prior to the Flanders campaigns of 1917, it was therefore decided that sanitary sections should become extra- divisional troops, and so carry out the constant sanitary supervision of a fixed area.

The importance of the work undertaken by these units is clear from the record of No. 4 Sanitary Section during the Passchendaele campaign. In August 1917, a slight epidemic of dysentery occurred in the forward area of the IX Corps, with approximately fifty cases being reported. The highest incidence was found in 124th Brigade R.F.A., 37th Division. The sanitation of this unit was considered defective, and the O.C. no. 4 Sanitary Section took a number of steps to remedy the situation:

> I visited formally all units affected and traced all cases of diarrhoea which were investigated by order of the Assistant Director of Medical Services 37 Division. The chief defects in sanitation noted were
> 1. Imperfect chlorination of water.
> 2. Defective latrines – not fly proof.
> 3. Imperfect measures against access to food by flies.
> 4. Exposure of excreta awaiting incineration.
> A memo issued on this subject stimulated units to renewed efforts to remedy defects. A hospital for the investigation of dysentery cases was opened . . . near Bailleul, at the request of the Director of Medical Services. I supervised the sanitation of the hospital which was formerly an internment camp.[8]

Flies caused a particular problem in August 1917, and it was essential that measures, similar to those outlined above, be employed in order to minimize the risks of disease. W. R. Ludlow, an Area Commander attached to the X Corps found that he had to "put the fear of God into the C.Os. about the disposal of manure and disinfecting it, as the flies are becoming a real nuisance this weather and an epidemic is feared by the Principal Medical Officer."[9]

Lapses in sanitary discipline, similar to that recorded in the 37th Division were noted by the D.M.S. of the Fifth Army, Surgeon-General Skinner.[10] But, it would appear that in all instances during the course of the Passchendaele campaign, an effective system for sanitary inspection ensured that these deficiencies were remedied, thus preventing them from reaching crisis proportions. The success of the sanitary arrangements for Third Ypres was indicated by the fact that the majority of the work undertaken by the sanitary sections was described as routine. The sickness rate was slight, and the cases sufficiently trivial to allow the vast majority to be treated in the forward area, thus minimizing wastage.[11] In pursuit of the R.A.M.C.'s duty to prevent the incidence of infectious disease, the continuity of the often dull routine of sanitary inspection cannot be exaggerated in its importance. Indeed, given that inoculation against infection remained voluntary in the British Army,[12] high standards of sanitary discipline were of paramount importance in the fight against disease.

Preventive measures were an important constituent of the duties of medical officers serving with the forward units. The Regimental Medical Officer (R.M.O.) had to act as a medical adviser to his unit, and inspect the health of the men at daily sick parades. He had to be fully acquainted with the mental and physical condition of each individual and, on the basis of this information, had to take appropriate measures to uphold the effective fighting strength of the unit. The importance of this role was noted by the British Medical Journal (B.M.J.) in August 1917:

> Bearing in mind that the sole reason why the men are in his charge at all is in order that they might fight, and fight effectively, he treats them much in the spirit of the medical attendant of a racing crew. Hence he is always endeavouring to tackle small evils early, and to winnow out the sick to whom he can afford all necessary treatment himself from those who must be sent elsewhere.
>
> Everything that can in any way affect the health of his unit comes within his purview.[13]

It was the responsibility of the R.M.O. to ensure that routine measures were employed to prevent the onset of conditions such as trench foot. The heavy rains that occurred, during the course of Third Ypres, ensured that trench foot remained a cause of sick wastage. However, the adoption of a standard programme of treatment ensured that there was no repeat of the incidence during the severe winter of 1914–1915. Army Routine Order 554, issued in January 1915, recommended that, before going into the trenches, boots should be wiped inside and outside with whale oil. Feet were to be washed regularly in cold water, dried and fresh, dry socks put on. When feet had become chilled, massage and gentle rubbing with oil were the best means of relief. On no account were chilled feet to be held near a fire. The difficulty of carrying out these procedures in the trenches was recognized, and it was recommended that men should be kept in trenches for the shortest possible time. Obviously, in times of battle the difficulties were exacerbated. But, the attempts to abide by the above regulations do appear to have prevented the occurrence of large numbers of severe cases. The D.D.M.S. XIX Corps noted that many men simply developed "spongy feet" and did not reach the stage of full-blown trench foot.[14] The O.C. 47 C.C.S. noted that all cases of trench foot admitted on 4.8.17 had been able to have a change of socks and boots, and consequently the cases were "not severe."[15]

Alongside his work as 'health officer' to his unit, it was also the responsibility of the R.M.O. to make arrangements for the initial evacuation and treatment of the wounded. In preparation for an attack, the R.M.O. had to establish a Regimental Aid Post (R.A.P.), finding a location that was both close to the firing line and offered suitable protection for the wounded.[16] He had, under his command, sixteen men from the regiment who acted as stretcher bearers, although in heavy fighting, such as Third Ypres, this number might be doubled. In July 1917, the Fifth Army made arrangements for 200 additional stretcher bearers to help clear the battle-field. Because of the growing strain on R.A.M.C. manpower, it was also decided that personnel from medical units should be pooled to undertake work in rest stations, thus releasing more men for work in the forward areas.

The stretcher bearers were trained in first aid, so that some basic treatment could be applied to the wounded, prior to their removal to the Aid Post. It was important that they then be placed in the care of the R.M.O. as soon as possible. In the best of circumstances, the task of retrieving the wounded was an arduous one; given the constant danger from enemy fire, and the difficulties of carrying the stretchers in confined spaces. During the Passchendaele campaign, these problems were exacerbated by the poor weather conditions, which turned the country into a quagmire, causing severe difficulties for the bearers.[17] The conditions were such that some of the wounded actually drowned in waterlogged shell holes and mud, before medical assistance was able to reach them.[18] R. L. MacKay, who was temporarily assigned to a bearer section, recorded that his party "could scarcely move one foot after the other. Our job was to carry down wounded. This is my first job as a bearer. I hope to goodness it is my last – prefer going over the top."[19] Evidently, these conditions contributed to a delay in the collection of wounded from the trenches:

> Very few stretcher cases have been brought down [to No. 33 Field Ambulance] today. This is owing to the difficulty which the regimental stretcher bearers have in getting them back from near the front line owing to the sniping . . . The conditions were very bad owing to the heavy rain today.[20]

The regimental bearers were assisted in their task by the bearer divisions of the Field Ambulances. To ease the work somewhat, as the battle progressed, the wounded were increasingly brought back to the R.A.P. via a series of relay posts, separated by distances of between 500 and 800 yards.[21] By transferring the wounded between these posts, "the rescue work continued until dusk with relays of men bearing stretchers right down to B.H.Q. and thus a great number of men were got safely away."[22] When the weather conditions permitted, bearers were also sent out at dusk to search for wounded, thus ensuring that many more men were collected.[23] The Official Historian observes that, despite the undoubted difficulties, the evacuation of the wounded was sufficiently rapid to ensure that the Casualty Clearing Stations were occasionally overwhelmed by the number of cases being admitted.[24]

On arrival at the Aid Post, the wounded were attended by the R.M.O., who classified them for evacuation, carried out any emergency treatment that was required, and implemented measures to prevent the onset of shock. More extensive treatment was discouraged, the role of the regimental personnel being to fit the wounded for evacuation down the line.

In ideal circumstances, the stretcher cases would be taken by motor or horse-drawn ambulances to the Advanced Dressing Station (A.D.S.)[25]. However, as noted above, the conditions during the course of Third Ypres were far from ideal. For most of the period the majority of the roads remained impassable, for both motor ambulances and horse-drawn wagons. Continuous transport of the wounded along trench tramways and light railways was disrupted by the effects of enemy shellfire; whilst the poor condition of the terrain prevented the extension of the railways as the line advanced.[26] Thus, for the most part, relays of bearers remained the only viable option for effecting the removal of stretcher cases from the R.A.P. to the Field Ambulance (F.A.).

A Field Ambulance usually served around three or four battalions at once, and, in order to fulfil its duties properly, it was divisible into three sections (A, B and C) capable of independent action. These sections were of similar composition, except that Section A (the headquarters section) had four motor ambulance cars (or horse-drawn wagons), whilst B and C had only three. Each of these sections A, B and C was, in turn, subdivided into a stretcher bearer section (for collecting the wounded) and a tent section (for treatment of the wounded). The bearer sections brought the wounded down from the R.A.P., via an A.D.S. to a Main Dressing Station (M.D.S.), formed by the tent subdivision.[27]

The functions performed by the F.As. on the Western Front were, however, significantly different from those envisaged prior to the War. Designed for conditions of mobile warfare, it was intended as the unit where initial emergency surgery was to be conducted. Yet, by 1917, the comparatively static nature of trench warfare had enabled the transformation of the Casualty Clearing Station (C.C.S.), originally designed as a mobile unit, to facilitate the evacuation of wounded, into a large settled hospital. Under these conditions it became the primary role of the F.A. to ensure that the wounded were fit for their journey down the line. A Field Ambulance subsection would be placed in the forward area to run an A.D.S., where dressings and splints were inspected and adjusted; and any essential early treatment, such as the splinting of fractures, that had not been possible at the R.A.P., was undertaken here.

An indication of the general organization and work of a F.A. can be seen in the record of 1/1 South Midland F.A., during the Passchendaele campaign. This unit assumed control of an A.D.S. at Duhallow on 5 August 1917. The A.D.S. was established on the banks of the Yser canal, approximately one and a half miles north-west of Ypres. It consisted of thirteen dugouts, which were organized to perform a variety of functions. The first acted as a dressing room, where the wounds of stretcher cases received initial attention; and the second was a reserve dressing room, where such cases could be similarly dealt with during periods of particularly heavy fighting. In the third dugout, there was a dressing room for walking cases; whilst the fourth was an evacuation ward, where cases remained until a full lorry load had been amassed. A buffet, providing refreshment for all suitable cases was established in the fifth, and the sixth acted as Medical and Quartermaster Stores. All remaining dugouts provided billets for the Officers, N.C.Os. and men of the unit.[28] The working conditions, afforded by this accommodation, were far from easy:

[the A.D.S.] was rather cramped, two lying cases could only be dealt with at a time in each Dressing Room in case of a rush especially in inclement weather. This meant casualties lying in the open awaiting treatment, two large shelters were erected one being solely to keep casualties in awaiting treatment and the other to keep them in after being dressed and awaiting removal to different hospitals by Motor Ambulances. These proved quite useful both from the medical and patients point of view.[29]

From the A.D.S. the wounded were taken by motor ambulance or horse wagon down to the M.D.S.; whilst in some corps areas, such as that of XIX Corps, light railways were employed for this purpose.[30] On arrival at the M.D.S., the cases were classified, ready for distribution to other units. It was essential that this administrative role be performed carefully, so as to avoid the evacuation of cases that were easily treatable near the front; and to ensure that casualties were directed to medical units where appropriate specialist treament was available. David Rorie, describing the work of the XVIII Corps M.D.S., at Gwalia Farm, referred to the care taken to ensure that cases requiring evacuation were sent to the correct hospital:

Here came in much work for the Dispatching N.C.Os.: head cases and chest cases going to one C.C.S., fractured thighs to another, gas cases to a third, general cases to a fourth, and so on. As the nature of the casualties taken by the various C.C.Ss. occasionally changed at short notice, every one had to be alert and on the look-out to see that each class of case reached its proper destination. To make such things easier of remembrance, a large diagram of the human body was at one time hung up in the receiving room with arrows pointing from each part – head, chest, thigh, etc – to the name of the C.C.S. whither each special case should go.[31]

Within each corps, certain F.As. were detailed to establish Rest Stations and specialist treatment centres, where easily cured diseases, such as scabies, could be dealt with. Surgeon General Skinner, D.M.S. of the Fifth Army, anxious to avoid wastage, emphasized throughout the course of the campaign the importance of retaining and treating trivial cases within the corps area. It was decided that the F.As. should look after all cases likely to be fit for duty within fourteen days.[32]

However, the role of the M.D.S. was not solely administrative in nature. It was not always possible for casualties to be evacuated immediately, and the M.D.S. might have to retain cases for some time; in such instances further treatment, including dressing or re-dressing of wounds, might be given. At all times, provision existed to rest, dry, warm and feed the patients; and to ensure that they had received anti-tetanus serum. But, medical personnel of the M.D.Ss. were discouraged from anything other than essential treatment; extensive operative work was considered inadvisable. The priority remained evacuation to the relative security of the C.C.S., where the prospects for successful surgery were much brighter.[33]

Prior to the campaign, arrangements had been made for the wounded to be brought down to the C.C.Ss. by motor ambulances. However, during the opening day of the operations these plans were not adhered to, causing significant disruption, particularly for the group of C.C.Ss. at Remy Siding. Vast numbers of wounded were brought back by broad-gauge trains, arriving in large batches; in contrast to the smaller and steadier supply of wounded that the planned road transport would have provided. The decision to use broad-gauge trains was delaying the evacuation of wounded to the C.C.Ss., as cases were kept waiting to be placed upon the four- hourly trains; a delay which was feared to be "prejudicing their surgical chances."[34] This delay, in turn, held up the removal of cases from the C.C.Ss. by the temporary ambulance train based at Remy Siding; instead of being filled by a steady flow of patients from motor ambulances, it had to await the arrival of the broad-gauge train. The impact of this disruption was described by the O.C. No. 2 Canadian C.C.S., which was one of the four C.C.Ss. that comprised the Remy Siding group. Its crisis accommodation was judged to be 1,000, yet the estimated number of admissions for 31 July 1917 was put at over 1,400. The wounded came in so quickly that considerable numbers could not be put under shelter, and had to be placed outside, covered with blankets and rubber sheets:

> Last night's work will not be soon forgotten by those who took part in the work at this station. The steady rain – the rapidity of arrival of casualties with the delay (in the early hours) of our evacuation trains created a difficult problem. Fortunately, relief came at just the right time and all our casualties were got under shelter. A few had to remain outdoors for a short time but were well protected and did not suffer in any way. The worst problem was in dealing with the cases that came in at the rear from the shuttle trains. In the dark it was very difficult to keep them separated from the Walking Cases admitted at the front.[35]

Approval for the use of the broad-gauge trains was given by the Deputy Adjutant and Quarter Master General (D.A.Q.M.G.), without Surgeon General Skinner being consulted. The latter "would not have allowed these trains," and was frustrated by a growing sense of his own lack of authority.[36] The Edwardian army reforms had left the R.A.M.C. under the control of the Adjutant-General's branch, and no medical representative

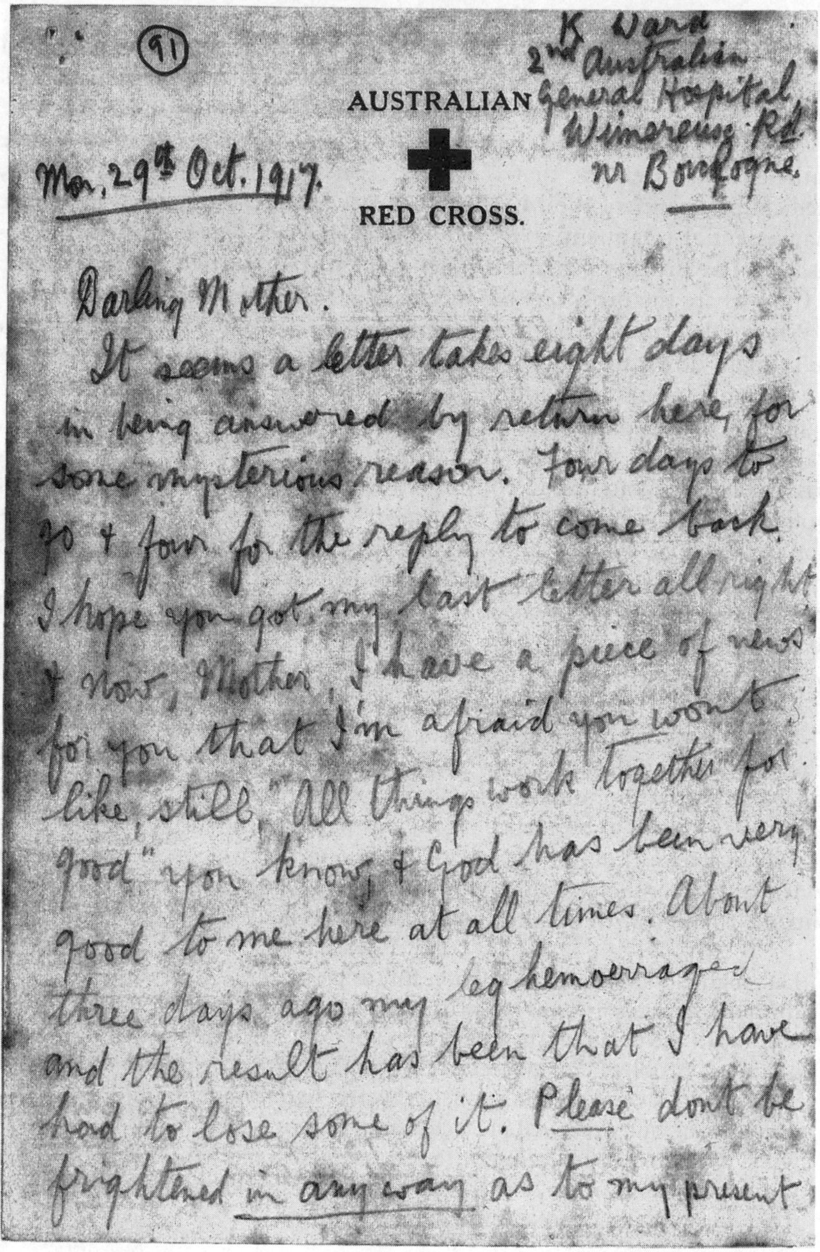

(91)

AUSTRALIAN

RED CROSS.

B Ward
2nd Australian
General Hospital,
Wimereux Rd
nr Boulogne.

Mon, 29th Oct. 1917.

Darling Mother.

It seems a letter takes eight days
in being answered by return here, for
some mysterious reason. Four days to
go & four for the reply to come back.
I hope you got my last letter all right
& now, Mother, I have a piece of news
for you that I'm afraid you wont
like, still "All things work together for
good" you know, & God has been very
good to me here at all times. About
three days ago my leg hemorrhaged
and the result has been that I have
had to lose some of it. Please don't be
frightened in any way as to my present

(xii) "now Mother, I have a piece of news for you that you won't like ...", Pte
C.G.Joss, 2nd Bn H.A.C., writes home with the news that his wound has
necessitated amputation. *(C.G.Joss, Liddle Collection)*

was placed upon the Army Council. The Esher Committee had justified this omission on the grounds that experts, immersed in detail, would slow down the decision-making process; whilst, in any case, the Council was not intended to be a representative body.[37] The B.M.J. had feared that this decision signified a dangerous complacency; that a return to the conditions of the Boer War (when a good deal of the medical disasters were attributable to the R.A.M.C.'s lack of authority) would be the result.[38] The history of the Army Medical Service on the Western Front suggests that such fears were unwarranted. But, the difficulties experienced by the D.M.S. Fifth Army, during this campaign, demonstrates that the administrative structure could pose problems for the R.A.M.C.. Indeed, earlier in 1917, Lord Esher himself had arrived at this conclusion:

> How much of the suffering undergone by our soldiers since the war began has been due to the shortsightedness of my committee, and notably of myself, will never be known. Certainly the control of the adjutant-general's branch over the Royal Army Medical Corps was and is responsible not only for the early failure to grip the medical factors of the war, but they hampered conditions under which the surgeon-general has worked. His triumphs and those of the Royal Army Medical Corps have been achieved in spite of obstacles that the subordination of science to ignorance and of elasticity to military discipline explains but can not justify.[39]

The immediate problem of congestion in the C.C.Ss. at Remy Siding was relieved by diverting the wounded to units elsewhere; admissions to No. 2 Canadian C.C.S. were halted at 3 pm on 1 August 1917. This decision greatly eased the pressure, and, at 1.15 am on 3 August, admissions were resumed. By the end of the month, this unit had taken in a total of 11,141 cases, making this, in the view of its O.C., "by far our busiest month."[40] During September, when these units came under the control of the Second Army, the scheme for evacuation was altered. A light railway was now in place, linking Remy Siding with the A.D.Ss. on the Menin Road, thus enabling the wounded to be sent direct from an A.D.S. to a C.C.S.. The purpose of the new scheme was to hasten the evacuation from the front line, and to prevent the patients from unnecessary handling and re-dressing of their wounds. Pressure on Remy Siding was further relieved when, on 4 October 1917, the first ambulance train was run from Ypres since 1914. This train evacuated stretcher cases to the Godewaersvelde group of C.C.Ss..[41]

The D.M.S. Fifth Army had ensured that extensive medical preparations had been made, in readiness for the offensive. Altogether sixteen C.C.Ss. were placed at his disposal. This number included the groups of C.C.Ss. at Remy Siding and Mendinghem (which had been transferred from the Second Army), and the establishment of new groups of C.C.Ss. at Brandhoek, Bandaghem and Dozinghem. Those at Remy Siding were returned to the Second Army when its front was extended; it also had groups of C.C.Ss. at Godewaersvelde and Bailleul.[42] Skinner's primary concern was to ensure that these units were situated as far forward as possible, to facilitate surgical treatment of wounds at the earliest possible moment. However, doubts were expressed concerning the vigour with which he pursued this policy; concerns were voiced that C.C.Ss. were being sited too far forward, and these appeared to be justified by numerous instances of C.C.Ss. coming under heavy fire.

Skinner was evidently heeding advice that the sooner cases were operated on, so the greater were their chances of survival. The surgical staff at No. 32 C.C.S., Brandhoek, were, according to Skinner, enthusiastic about the results of placing their unit further forward; arguing that many cases would have died had they been forced to endure a longer journey.[43] However, this forward position exposed the Brandhoek group to enemy fire, receiving a devastating bombardment on 21 August 1917, as outlined by the O.C. no. 44 C.C.S.:

> The shelling was continued all day with intervals of about half an hour between each group of three or four shots. D.M.S. Fifth Army ... ordered the evacuation of all patients, nurses to be sent to 62 and 63 C.C.S. The remainder of the personnel to move to No. 10 C.C.S.[44]

Thus, according to the Official History, the Brandhoek group was shelled out before it "had been of any material value."[45] This assessment was evidently contrary to the views held within the Fifth Army command, and supports the concerns expressed by Sir Arthur Sloggett, the Director General of the Medical Services (D.G.M.S.). At the beginning of July 1917, the latter had circulated all Ds.M.S., highlighting the dangers of siting C.C.Ss. too near to the front line:

> They [Ds.M.S.] must realise that the Casualty Clearing Stations have now become an unwieldy unit, chiefly because of the necessity of making every preparation for extensive surgical work and post-operative treatment in them, and that a unit of that nature is out of place in the zone of Main Dressing Stations, and must in the interests of the majority of the wounded be kept further back in a zone of comparative safety. The main object in having Motor Ambulance Convoys allotted to Armies is to enable wounded to be brought back to positions of safety without delay, and positions of comparative safety can always be found within ½ hour to 1 hour's journey from the zone of hostile artillery fire.[46]

Quite apart from the obvious danger, there came a point where proximity to the front might have a negative rather than a positive impact on the patients. Colonel Soltau, Consulting Physician, pointed out that chest cases performed better in quieter, more settled conditions. Skinner was concerned that evacuation further down the line would reduce the chances of survival for such cases. Soltau disagreed, arguing that careful work at the F.As. was adequately preparing casualties for the longer journey.[47] In fact, the longer journey involved little danger; whereas a location further away from the noise and danger of enemy shelling brought great advantage in terms of more speedy recovery. Yet, even after Brandhoek had been abandoned, and Nos. 44 and 3 Australian C.C.Ss. transferred to a new site at Nine Elms, Skinner kept up the pressure for a forward surgical unit to deal with abdominal cases. However, plans to establish a new forward C.C.S. at Elverdinghe were abandoned.[48] Whilst early surgery undoubtedly aided recovery, it is clear that the Fifth Army's pursuit of this aim began to be counter-productive. C.C.Ss. performed at their best when they provided their patients with the safe and stable conditions that were essential to the survival of serious surgical cases.

It was not, however, only the C.C.Ss. at Brandhoek which were the target of enemy action; during the course of the Passchendaele campaign, and the month preceding, there were a number of attacks on medical units. The Official History notes that the concentration of attacks during this period was so exceptional as to suggest that they were deliberate.[49] On 6/7 July there was an apparently deliberate attack on No. 11 C.C.S., at Bailleul, which left twenty-seven dead and sixty-eight wounded; of whom all but nine were patients. According to a report by the D.M.S. Second Army, the planes flew sufficiently low to recognize that their target was a medical unit.[50] Later in the War, under the heading Blackguard Nation, an article in the B.M.J. strongly implied that German activity against C.C.Ss. was a calculated measure.[51] But, the evidence was not clear-cut:

> Until this month [August] the C.C.Ss. have been left almost entirely alone. That four groups in this area should have suffered in the last month seems more than a coincidence. Of course two groups, viz. Brandhoek and Dozinghem are pretty far forward and not far removed from guns and dumps which may account for their trouble. It seems difficult to place C.C.Ss. in this area without having an ammunition dump, a battery, a railhead or an aerodrome in close proximity. Even here [Remy] where we were fairly well isolated, they began parking ammunition lorries on all sides of us until we registered a protest and had them removed.[52]

It was such difficulties which highlighted, during the campaign, not only the problems of placing C.C.Ss. too far forward; but also the need to ensure that medical sites were sufficiently distant from legitimate targets, such as ammunition dumps, aerodromes and the like. In any case, the nature of its role ensured that the site of a C.C.S. ordinarily remained only just beyond the reach of enemy fire. Thus, regarding the issue of enemy attacks on hospital units, it is difficult to separate accident, suspicion and propaganda; and the accusations of deliberate targeting remain not proven.

The pressure of heavy casualties meant that cases needed to be evacuated, from the C.C.Ss. to the Base hospitals, as soon as suitable rail or motor transport became available. In readiness for Passchendaele, Nos. 7, 58 and 59 General Hospitals, at St Omer, were made available to the Fifth

Army. It was also allocated Nos. 4 and 7 (Canadian) Stationary Hospitals, located at Arque, and No. 4 (Canadian) Stationary Hospital, which opened near St Omer. To reduce the pressure on ambulance transport, and on the capacity of the Base hospitals, Armies not involved in the offensive were asked, wherever possible, to retain sick and wounded within their own hospital units.[53]

However, whilst the C.C.Ss. had to be kept clear for the receipt of new cases, it was important that casualties were not evacuated to the Base if the journey were liable to endanger their recovery. Chest cases remained at the C.C.S. until there was no chance of haemorrhage; and abdominal cases were retained until they were fit for evacuation to a U.K. hospital. In general, however, the priority was to avoid evacuation to Britain. All patients likely to recover within three weeks were to remain at a Base hospital. Convalescence depots existed in the Base area, to ensure that full recuperation could take place on the continent.[54]

Examining the system of evacuation, the extent to which the military and therapeutic duties of the R.A.M.C. were intertwined, becomes clear. The system had to ensure that the sick and wounded were treated as soon as possible; but it also had carefully to check the men, to prevent their being sent further down the line than was necessary. The prime objective was to return fit men back to the front at the earliest possible opportunity. However, 1917 had opened with renewed concern about the ability of the R.A.M.C. to achieve this objective, following Sir Almroth Wright's assertion that the evacuation procedures were preventing efficient medical treatment, and so undermining the Army's fighting strength.

In a memorandum, based on his experiences as Consulting Physician on the Western Front, he fulminated against the R.A.M.C. administration for contenting itself with claiming credit for evacuating record numbers of wounded to the bases and home hospitals, when "it ought to lay emphasis on good service done in saving lives and healing the wounded." Whereas a system based entirely on concern with the speed at which huge numbers of men were passed down the line was clearly convenient, from an administrative point of view, he claimed that it operated "as a damper upon all good and an encouragement to all unconscientious professional work."[55] He believed that the system of evacuation interfered with the basic principle of wound treatment: that operation should take place at the earliest possible opportunity; that every wound should be closed up by surgical operation, as soon as bacterial infection had been overcome; and that compound fractures, especially those of the leg, should be retained in hospital until union had taken place. The emphasis on rapid evacuation meant that treatment was delayed, and that fracture cases were moved whilst still in a delicate state. Wright saw the consequences in large numbers of amputations, with accompanying danger to life, performed on men who had been moved too early. He felt that more could have been done to facilitate rapid front-line surgical treatment, and he deplored the policy of passing wounded from one unit to another.[56]

Particular criticism was directed at the F.As., which he saw as obstacles in the path of early treatment. He also claimed that they were wasteful of medical manpower, because the work undertaken by doctors was professionally undemanding. Wright's criticisms were by no means isolated. H.W. Bayly condemned the F.A. as a "harmful . . . waste of time," and during the course of the War, numerous complaints were levelled against it.[57] However, the Commission on Medical Establishments, which gathered evidence during the course of the Passchendaele campaign, largely rejected these criticisms. It concluded that the employment of doctors with F.As. was not wasteful, arguing that it was essential for these units at all times to be prepared for the possibility of mobile warfare. In such circumstances, the M.D.Ss. would have to undertake a substantial amount of the surgical work currently performed by the C.C.Ss..[58]

Even in trench warfare, the F.A. had an important role to play: cleansing wounds and taking measures to prevent the onset of shock. Moreover, the M.D.S., in its role as a sorting centre, not only prevented troops from being unnecessarily evacuated from the divisional area; but also ensured that the patients received appropriate treatment as quickly as possible. The insistence, throughout this offensive, on the importance of providing treatment for trivial cases in the divisional area, does not comply with Wright's image of a service obsessed with passing patients down the line. Nor does the evidence support the notion that inflexible evacuation schemes stood in the way of proper treatment. Indeed, the medical services sought to ensure that patients requiring urgent treatment were evacuated as rapidly as possible from the A.D.S. to the C.C.S.. As outlined above, the employment of light railways meant that wounded could be brought direct from Ypres to the C.C.Ss., thus by-passing the M.D.S.. But, in battle conditions, direct evacuation was frequently impracticable; and, in these circumstances, the treatment available at the M.D.S. became vital. If the line extended, it was difficult for the increasingly unwieldy C.C.Ss. to move forward. Consequently, since the Somme, in 1916, it had become the practice for F.As. to establish Advanced Operating Centres which provided surgical treatment for emergency cases, such as abdominal wounds, where delay was potentially fatal. Such units proved useful during the Passchendaele offensive, especially given the difficulties concerning the siting of C.C.Ss.:

In ordinary times 2 surgical teams would be necessary at each [Advanced Operating Centre] (no sisters) where large shell proof dugouts would be available. Cases should be sent on to C.C.S. as soon as practicable after operation. The distance back to C.C.Ss. will lead to many more deaths en route, unless some such measure is carried out. Directly a C.C.S. is shelled it has to move back, and as all our C.C.Ss. are in range of H.V. guns there is no telling where this movement will lead to as long as the enemy is sure to shell others when he feels inclined to do so.[59]

Such operating centres were increasingly placed under the command of a C.C.S., and in periods of general pressure were reinforced by M.Os. from the C.C.Ss.. By the time of Third Ypres, it was also the practice for similar centres to be established by advanced units from the C.C.Ss..[60]

Moreover, the development of the C.C.S. as a surgical unit demonstrated the commitment of the R.A.M.C. to providing expert surgical treatment, as near to the front-line as was practical and safe. Indeed, it is clear that in the Fifth Army, during 1917, the commitment to surgery in the forward area was so zealous that the latter considerations were, on occasion, being ignored. A balance had to be struck between Wright's demands for immediate surgery, and the practicalities of locating the C.C.Ss. in relatively safe areas. In any case, by 1917, the organization of the C.C.Ss. was such that significant surgical developments were taking place.

The work of the C.C.Ss., during the earlier battles of 1917, led to their further expansion in preparation for Passchendaele. On the advice of the consulting surgeons, it was decided that:

1) Each casualty clearing station should provide arrangements for eight operating tables, instead of four as previously.

2) Six surgical teams should be supplied to each casualty clearing station, and should each include an orderly used to operating theatre work.

3) Extra medical officers should be supplied to bring the total medical officers of each casualty clearing station up to a minimum of twenty-four.

4) Twenty additional orderlies should be allotted to each casualty clearing station, as well as additional stretcher bearers.

5) The number of nursing sisters should be increased to twenty- five.

6) Each casualty clearing station should be supplied with additional equipment of surgical instruments, operating tables, gowns, towels and other articles in proportion to the increase of the staff and according to schedules supplied for the purpose.[61]

As a consequence of this expansion, more operations now took place in the C.C.Ss. than were undertaken in the general and stationary hospitals. Between 31.7.17 and 16.11.17 the C.C.Ss. of the Second and Fifth Armies admitted a total of 201,864 cases and carried out 61,423 operations. This work was facilitated by the deployment of additional surgical teams. As well as reinforcements from the C.C.Ss. of other armies, the Second and Fifth Armies received thirty-two additional surgical teams from the general and stationary hospitals. Furthermore, they were assisted by teams from the United States, such as that of Colonel Harvey Cushing.[62] Each team comprised a surgeon, an anaesthetist, a sister and a couple of theatre orderlies, all accustomed to working together.[63] Three teams, working eight hour shifts (eight hours on and four hours sleep) could keep two operating tables running continually as long as a week. The reinforcements prior to Third Ypres meant that it was possible, in certain C.C.Ss., to plan for as many as eight tables to be working simultaneously. The deployment of these additional teams was evidence of the growing effectiveness of planning to deal with the expected heavy casualties, and an ability to adjust the available medical skill to meet the situation. The results from both the Second and Fifth Armies suggested that the work was successful. Fewer operations had to be carried out at general hospitals; and the benefits of early surgery were a lack of surgical complications and a high rate of recovery. The Official History notes that "the condition of the wounded from a battle of the same magnitude had never been so good".[64]

Possibly the most important surgical development to occur during the War was the adoption of blood transfusion. In the course of the Passchendaele fighting, transfusion became established as a routine measure in the C.C.Ss., with the establishment of standardized methods and a system for the classification of donors.[65] There were also improvements in the use of anaesthetics:

> Major Gask operated on several chest cases under gas and oxygen using the special apparatus employed by the U.S.A. Medical Service. The results are splendid – the patient keeps a perfectly natural appearance and breathes quietly. He comes out without nausea as soon as the anaesthetic ceases. There is no shock or bronchial irritation.[66]

The procedures for blood transfusion, and the use of nitrous oxide and oxygen anaesthesia, were not war induced but, as a consequence of war surgery, both became widely known and employed. However, there were some new surgical discoveries during the War, particularly with regard to the treatment of wound infection, which became one of the greatest medical concerns. Prior to the conflict, developments in first aid and wound disinfection led to an expectation that the incidence of wound infection would be slight. This belief was shattered by the impact of modern artillery. Shrapnel drove infecting organisms, from the rich agricultural soil and from the men's clothing, into the wounds; thus wounding and infection took place simultaneously. Consequently, first aid dressings actually contained these organisms within the wound, and many became infected with the gas bacillus. Guidelines were issued highlighting the need to avoid applying dressings too tightly; and the opening and drainage of wounds at the front helped to reduce the incidence. The development of the C.C.S., during 1917, greatly contributed to a reduction in the incidence of gas infection. It was now possible for wounds to be subject to careful operation and excision; and for innovations, such as the Carrel-Dakin method for the surgical toilet of wounds, to be more widely employed.[67] The latter was the most widely used technique for treating wound infection, but it was not without its critics. Whilst the method worked well in stationary hospitals, it was not always practicable in the C.C.Ss., as became evident in the Passchendaele campaign:

> During recent operations the B.I.P.P. treatment has largely suppressed the Carrel-Dakin method in this area for the following reasons.
> a) more easily and quickly performed.
> b) cases require less after care and attention.
> c) C[arrel]-D[akin] only satisfactory when cases are kept under continuous supervision by the same surgeon.
> d) Reports from the base show that B.I.P.P. cases do well.[68]

In this method, the bismuth-iodoform-paraffin-paste (B.I.P.P.) was applied to the surface of the wound, which was only loosely sutured. The subsequent performance of cases indicated that treatment was a success.[69] However, the standard of surgical treatment was also improved by a growing realization of the need to ensure that specialists were effectively employed. This was facilitated by arranging that the treatment for particular classes of injury was concentrated at specialist centres. The Fifth Army's plans for Passchendaele involved provision for all head injuries to be dealt with by the Mendinghem group of C.C.Ss., and for all abdominal cases to be treated at Brandhoek.[70] The provision of specialist centres also had particular advantages for dealing with shell shock and cases of gas poisoning.

Early in the War, the British system for diagnosing and treating shell shock was characterized by confusion and inconsistency. The term 'shell shock' was in itself problematic. It suggested an organic causation, resulting from the effects of a shell explosion. In fact, the vast majority were functional disorders; nervous conditions brought on by the emotional strain of modern warfare. Once this became apparent, the diagnostic terminology was altered. Organic cases were to be labelled 'shell shock (w[ound])', signifying that they were to be given the same status regarding pensions as other wounded cases. Functional cases were to be known as 'shell shock (s[ick])', and were considered to be psychiatric disorders consequent upon predisposing factors in an individual's personal or family history. The latter were the subject of a great deal of prejudice, with many seen as malingerers, or court-martialled for cowardice.

Difficulty also arose because few medical officers possessed the knowledge of psychiatry that was necessary to distinguish between 'shell shock (w)' and 'shell shock (s)'. Because of the stigma attached to the latter, combined with their own uncertainty, many medical officers chose to label these cases as 'shell shock (w)'. This led to the unnecessary evacuation of men suffering from functional disorders, who could have been more effectively treated in a forward hospital; the consequent delay in treatment led to a deterioration of these conditions. There was no separate organization for dealing with psychiatric casualties. As they were transferred down the line, the patients were the subject of further hurried and inconclusive medical examinations. This series of uncertain diagnoses contributed to a fixation of the patient's symptoms; frequent medical inspection giving the impression that his condition was serious, and that the doctors were unsure about the appropriate treatment:

> ... the duration and persistence [of the neuroses] may be prolonged indefinitely by repeated changes from one hospital to another and by inevitable and misguided methods, by which is meant a therapy promoted to suggest to the patient that he is suffering from a minor disability of organic nature.[71]

It was standard practice for these cases to be evacuated to specialist hospitals in the U.K.. In terms of the R.A.M.C.'s military duty, this system was a failure, as it led to an unnecessary loss of manpower. First, it caused numerous cases to become far more severe than they would otherwise have been; had there been provision for specialist treatment in the forward area, a greater proportion of men would have been returned to duty. Second, once these cases had been exposed to the comforting atmosphere of a home hospital, they were unlikely to return to the front as capable soldiers; those who did, often experienced a recurrence of their condition.[72]

The military and medical deficiencies of this method of evacuating psychological cases were quickly recognized by both the French and Germans who, in early 1915, instituted more systematic arrangements. The principal development was the creation of separate psychiatric hospitals, no more than a few hours away from the firing line. These allowed for rapid treatment and avoided the fixation of symptoms caused by delay and unnecessary evacuation to the Base. To deal with severe cases, which required evacuation from the advanced psychiatric hospitals, special centres were established at the Base.[73]

Lieutenant-Colonel C.S. Myers, Consultant Psychiatrist, was at the fore-front of pressure to have the British system for handling psychiatric casualties re-organized along similar lines.[74] However, there was strong resistance from both the British military and medical authorities. There was a reluctance to recognize emotional shell shock as an illness, since many military and medical officers continued to believe that its supposed sufferers were either malingerers or men of poor calibre. There was also the widely held opinion that the creation of special treatment centres would encourage the incidence of such ailments, thus opening up "a floodgate of wastage."[75]

The D.G.M.S. argued that the treatment of 'mental' cases in the Army Area was impossible; his concern was that Myers should prevent the evacuation of shell shock and nervous exhaustion cases from the Base to the U.K.. This task was complicated by the absence of a proper system, at the Front, for supervising the transfer and treatment of these patients. Many men suffering from functional nervous disorders were being despatched to the U.K., wrongly labelled as cases of organic neurological disease. But, with shell shock cases dispersed across the various hospitals at the Base, it was impossible to trace the source of these diagnostic mistakes.[76]

The Battle of the Somme had produced a shift in the thinking of the British authorities on this matter. The Somme witnessed a vast increase in the incidence of psychiatric casualties, and this weight of men had exacerbated the difficulties involved in administering the system of evacuation to Britain. The need could no longer be ignored for a separate line of evacuation for these cases; for the provision of special treatment centres; and for clearer diagnostic guidelines. In response to this need, a new system for dealing with shell shock cases was developed, in readiness for the Passchendaele campaign.

In June 1917, a General Routine Order was issued which sought to minimize the employment of the term 'shell shock', and so avoid wrongful diagnosis. No definite diagnosis was to be made by the R.M.O. who first dealt with the case. Instead, all such cases were to be sent to a specialist hospital, with the letters N.Y.D.N. (Not Yet Diagnosed Nervous) marked on their field medical card.[77] The D.M.S. Fifth Army exercised vigilance regarding adherence to these new regulations.[78]

The initial proposal was for No. 47 C.C.S. to be the N.Y.D.N. centre for the Passchendaele campaign. But, there was some confusion about the suitability of its location. The D.G.M.S. suggested that this site was too far forward, but Surgeon General Skinner claimed that the Consultant Psychologists, Lieutenant-Colonel Myers and Lieutenant-Colonel G. Holmes, had considered this unit to be ideal. However, it would appear that this advice was reconsidered:

> D[irector] G[eneral] forwards another report from Lt. Col. G. Holmes to effect that 47 C.C.S. is now too noisy. Previously he said the sound of the shell near the treatment centre made recovery more permanent, or recovered cases then returned to duty accustomed to the noise. Also that the French were adopting this system.[79]

As a result, No. 62 C.C.S. was appointed as the N.Y.D.N. centre for the forthcoming operations. The success of the new arrangements is clear from the fact that only 16% of the approximately 5,000 cases, dealt with by No. 62 C.C.S., required evacuation by specialist Base hospitals,[80] whilst thereafter evacuation to the U.K. was only necessary for 10% of cases. A separate line of evacuation now existed for psychiatric casualties, so the fixation of symptoms that had resulted from the more haphazard system, in operation earlier in the War, was avoided. Patients reached the Base in a condition that was far more amenable to treatment.

The British Army's attitude to shell shock remained open to criticism. Functional cases tended still to be looked upon with scepticism, or as individuals lacking in moral fibre; whilst some observers suspected that the new guidelines were primarily motivated by a desire to minimise diagnosis, and so keep down the pensions bill. Nevertheless, it is possible to see developments during Passchendaele as representing "the first tentative

19. The effects of prolonged rain in the Ypres
    Salient - the battlefield viewed from an aid
    post, looking toward Wallemollen after its
    capture, around November 1917.
    (G.R.Bromet, Liddle Collection)
    Chapter 10

20. A few days before his death, the French
    aviator Guyncmer with his aircraft in
    Flanders. (French magazine *L'Illustration*, 29
    September 1917) Chapter 11

21. The F.E.2ds of No 20 Sqn featured
    prominently in a number of the actions
    fought during the Third Battle of Ypres. The
    subject of this photograph is A6516, heavily
    armed with three Lewis guns; its occupants
    are Captain F.D.Stevens (pilot) and
    Lieutenant W.C.Cambray MC (observer).
    (J.Bruce/G.S.Leslie Collection) Chapter 11

22. An important aspect of the work of the RFC over the Salient was photo reconnaissance; this oblique aerial photograph shows Belgian Wood in the German sector near Hollebeke, August 1917. The wing of the aircraft is visible, somewhat out of focus, on the right hand side. (L.Beaumont-Tansley, Liddle Collection) Chapter 11

23. Perhaps the best known British single-seat fighter of the First World War was the Sopwith Camel. No 45 Squadron was much involved in the fighting during 1917 around Ypres, and this photograph is said to record 'A' Flight's last operation before the Squadron was transferred to Italy. (J.Bruce/G.S.Leslie Collection) Chapter 11

One of the most successful fighters on the Allied side was the SE5A; B4863 was first allocated to the RFC in France on 23 August 1917 and was first flown by Captain J.T.B.McCudden of No 56 Squadron on 6 September 1917. It was in this aircraft that he took part in the combat of 23 September 1917, which ended in the death of Werner Voss. (J.Bruce/ G.S.Leslie Collection) Chapter 11

25. The DH4 was widely used as a day bomber, and was most effective when powered by a Rolls Royce Eagle engine. This example, A7583, was an aircraft of No 57 Squadron and is here seen in German hands after being forced down in combat over Roulers on 2 October 1917. Its pilot, 2nd Lieutenant C.G.Crane, was made a prisoner of war, but his observer, 2nd Lieutenant W.L.Inglis, was killed in the combat. (J.Bruce/G.S.Leslie Collection) Chapter 11

26. The wreckage of a German aeroplane in Houthulst forest, Autumn 1917. (L.H.Matthews, Liddle Collection) Chapter 11

27. A narrow-gauge railway being used to convey wounded to the rear. (A.Medcalf, Liddle Collection) Chapter 12

28. German prisoners of war acting as stretcher bearers at an advanced dressing station on the Menin Road, September 1917. (R.S.Goodman, Liddle Collection) Chapter 12

29. The extreme northern end of the trench system on the Western Front: sand dunes around Nieuport. German positions viewed from the Belgian lines. (Liddle Collection) Chapter 13

30. Barbed wire entanglements among the dunes at Nieuport - the sea
    visible in the distance. (Liddle Collection) Chapter 13

31. Men of the 11th Battalion South Wales Borderers, 38th Welsh Division,
    behind the lines in the Ypres Salient, late summer 1917. The 38th
    Division were popularly known as 'Lloyd George's Welsh army'.
    (E.S. Nevell, Liddle Collection) Chapter 14

32. Men and pack mules bound for the front line rounding Idiot Corner, on
Westhoek Ridge, on 5 November 1917. To follow the duckboard and
corduroy track here was to be silhouetted against the skyline, both from
the Australian position and from that of the enemy before he was driven
from Broodseinde Ridge. However, passage over any part other than the
top of the ridge was impossible owing to the mud, and consequently
numbers of guns and vehicles were destroyed here by the constant
shellfire. (Australian War Memorial, negative E01480) Chapter 15

33. A photograph taken on 10 October 1917, on the railway embankment beyond Zonnebeke station. Stretcher bearers and dressers of the 9th Australian Field Ambulance, utterly exhausted, have fallen asleep in the mud, in total disregard of the cold, the drizzling rain which had just started to fall, and the harassing shell fire of the enemy in the area. (Australian War Memorial, negative E941) Chapter 15

34. Australian troops manning improved shell craters at Polygonveld, on 21 September 1917, the morning after the positions had been captured. (Australian War Memorial, negative E971) Chapter 15

35. Dead and wounded Australian and German soldiers in the railway cutting on Broodseinde Ridge, 12 October 1917. The Australian soldier, wearing a tin hat, slightly left of centre is Pte. Walter Radley, 60th battalion AIF. (Australian War Memorial, negative E03864) Chapter 15

36. Five Australians, members of a Field Artillery unit, passing along a duckboard track over mud and water in the ruins of Château Wood, 29 October 1917. Left to right, Cpl. Reid of South Grafton, Lieutenant Anthony Devine, Sgt. Clive Stewart Smith, and two others. (Australian War Memorial, negative E01220) Chapter 15

foundations of an understanding psychiatric approach to nervous cases."[81]

During the Flanders operations of 1917, the Germans introduced mustard gas, the effects of which posed a new challenge to the British medical services. The new gas proved to be particularly dangerous as a consequence of its insidious nature, as noted by J. Campbell, 6th Battalion Cameron Highlanders:

> Yesterday our C Company got badly gassed . . . Seemingly, they didn't know they were gassed at all as this new gas of the Germans does not take effect for some time after. For that reason it seems a dangerous thing and will be difficult to avoid.[82]

Mustard gas caused particular problems, because its odour was not particularly strong. As the men grew accustomed to its smell, many were failing to wear their masks. On the first night of its use, the new gas led to nearly 5,000 British casualties. This prompted orders to be issued that "the wearing of respirators in alert position during gas shell attacks is to be enforced nightly."[83]

The steady increase in the incidence of gas casualties had led to the development of special procedures for handling their evacuation and treatment. Measures evolved similar to those outlined above for dealing with shell shock. N.Y.D. Gas Centres were formed within each Army area. Here, the nature and severity of the gas poisoning could be assessed; treatment and convalescence provided for the less severe cases. The more serious cases would be classified, and then evacuated to those C.C.Ss. designated as the specialist centres. The arrangements in the Fifth Army, prior to Third Ypres, were for numbers 12, 46, 47 and 64 C.C.Ss. to admit gas cases.[84] It was at these units where the specialist personnel and equipment were located. However, the Official History admits that in periods of heavy fighting, when the incidence of gas and other casualties was at its highest, the segregation of cases was not always entirely possible. It was therefore important that all C.C.Ss. had trained personnel and adequate equipment to deal with possible intakes of gas casualties.[85]

These procedures applied to all cases of gas poisoning, but the handling of mustard gas casualties did differ in certain respects. In particular, it was usual for gas cases to be evacuated as 'lying' cases throughout their journey, in order to reduce the risk of respiratory complications. The delayed onset of mustard gas symptoms, however, meant that these cases could initially be evacuated as 'walking' cases, and then transferred to the C.C.Ss. as 'sitting' cases. It was then usual for most treatment of mustard gas poisoning to take place at a C.C.S.. Such cases could not be evacuated to the Base in their later stage of development, as there was a risk of fatally aggravating the symptoms of broncho-pneumonia. But, these were lessons learnt from painful experience, as knowledge of mustard gas poisoning had been limited during the earlier attacks.[86] These differences from other gas cases highlighted the importance of careful classification of casualties in the gas centres.

Mustard gas placed an additional strain on the medical services because of the extent to which it lingered on clothes and equipment. The victims of this gas had to be stripped of their clothing, bathed in soda solution and provided with fresh attire. Facilities for bathing the men, providing clean clothes, and decontaminating clothing, therefore had to be provided at the gas treatment centres. The less severe cases were treated here, and the more serious ones sent on to a C.C.S..

The results of this examination of the British medical services suggest that, whatever the debates concerning the political and military handling of Passchendaele, from a medical perspective, the campaign can be judged a success. The attention of the R.A.M.C. to sanitary discipline ensured that wastage was kept to a minimum. Considerable attention was given to the provision of immediate treatment. The evacuation system was motivated by a recognition that treatment should be provided as far forward as was appropriate and practicable, to allow the early return of men to their units.

" *Yellow Cross*," containing Dichlorethyl Sulphide, the so-called "Mustard Gas," a liquid which boils at 217° C. and has a faint garlic-like smell. Although the vapour produces no immediate discomfort, it is highly lethal and in addition attacks the eyes. The ill effects are not noticeable until some hours after exposure. If the skin comes in contact with the liquid or is exposed to the concentrated vapour, no pain is felt at the time, but blisters are developed about six hours afterwards. Washing with soap and water removes the liquid from the skin, and if done immediately, may prevent blistering.

Dichlorethyl Sulphide is very persistent, and may remain in the ground for several days after a bombardment. During this period it is necessary to post sentries to warn troops about to enter the affected area (Standing Orders, 4 (iv.)).

The absence of immediate discomfort forms one of the chief dangers of Dichlorethyl Sulphide. Care must be taken that respirators are put on at once and men should be specially warned of the danger of exposing the eyes to the gas. In order to avoid blistering of the skin every effort should be made to avoid contact with earth contaminated with the liquid. Clothes and equipment which have been in contact with the liquid should be removed and submitted to treatment for removing the liquid, or, if this is not practicable, exposed to the air for 48 hours, or longer if the weather is cold.

(xiii) "Defence against gas": after the German introduction of mustard gas, the official pamphlet giving information on the gases being employed by the enemy was updated as shown here. (*C.A.Birnstingl, Liddle Collection*)

This consideration was evident in the measures adopted for dealing with shell shock, which demonstrated an appreciation of the military and medical advantages of careful sifting of cases. The development of the C.C.S. reached its apogee during the Passchendaele campaign,[87] leading to improved standards of medical and surgical provision in the Army area. Of course, the medical situation on the Western Front was not without its problems. Passchendaele had shown that the control of the R.A.M.C. by the Adjutant-General's branch still created difficulties. Meanwhile, criticisms continued to be made that specialist medical skills were inadequately employed. Nevertheless, the performance of the medical services supported those who believed that such concerns were exaggerated. At Passchendaele the R.A.M.C. achieved its threefold mission, with significant advances in the emergence of a highly organized system for preventing sickness, and evacuating and treating the wounded. Thus, whatever criticism may, justifiably, be made of Sir Hubert Gough's command in the battle, his assessment of the R.A.M.C. appears sound:

> ... the manner in which [the medical work] has been performed reflects the greatest credit on all concerned. The evacuation of the sick and wounded from the C.C.Ss. has been most carefully organised and successfully carried out, while the professional skill and attention displayed at the C.C.Ss., together with increased comfort provided for the patients, has led to highly satisfactory results being obtained.[88]

Notes

1   Christopher Childs, *Prevention of Typhoid In Our Home Camps*, British *Medical Journal* (B.M.J.), 1914 (II), p. 1087.
2   *The Duties Of A Sanitary Section In The Field*, B.M.J., 1916 (I), p. 215.
3   WO 95/533, *Public Record Office*, Kew (P.R.O.), D.A.D.M.S. (Sanitation) Fifth Army, War Diary, 18.8.17.
4   W G MacPherson, *Official History Of The War – Medical Services – General History*, II, London, H M S O, p. 61.
5   *French Sanitary Squads*, B.M.J., 1916 (II), p. 665.
6   L. W. Batten, *Liddle Collection*, Brotherton Library, University of Leeds (L.C.,) letter to son, 18.3.70.
7   MacPherson, *General History*, (II), p. 62.
8   WO 95/350, P.R.O., O.C. No. 4 Sanitary Section, War Diary, August 1917, pp. 2–4.
9   W. R. Ludlow, L.C., Diary, 21.8.17, p. 107.
10 WO 95/532, P.R.O., D.M.S. Fifth Army, War Diary, 20.7.17; 7.8.17; 16.8.17; 20.8.17; 20.9.17.
11 MacPherson, *General History*, III, p. 171.
12 Humphrey Humphreys, *Some Medical Memories of Two World Wars*, *Journal Of The Royal Army Medical Corps* (J.R.A.M.C.), 101, 1955, p. 238.
13 *The Royal Army Medical Corps And Its Work*, B.M.J., 1917 (II), p. 217.
14 WO 95/969, P.R.O., D.D.M.S. XIX Corps, War Diary, 7.8.17.
15 WO 95/500, P.R.O., O.C. no. 47 C.C.s., War Diary, 4.8.17.
16 I. R. Whitehead, *British Regimental Medical Officers In The Field*, in H. Cecil

& P. H. Liddle (eds), *Facing Armageddon*, Leo Cooper/Pen & Sword, 1996, p. 470.

17 WO 95/2550, *P.R.O.*, O.C. 131 Field Ambulance, War Diary, 1.8.17.

18 V.F.S. Hawkins, *L.C.*, Diary, Passchendaele Section, p. 2; H.G.R. Williams, L.C., Memoir, Third Ypres – 1917, pp. 297–298.

19 R.L. MacKay, *L.C.*, Diary, 1.8.17.

20 WO 95/1805, *P.R.O.*, O.C. 33 Field Ambulance, War Diary, 27.8.17.

21 MacPherson, *General History*, III, p. 159.

22 D.F. Stone, *L.C.*, Diary, 27.10.17.

23 WO 95/1805, *P.R.O.*, O.C. 33 Field Ambulance, War Diary, 29.8.17.

24 MacPherson, *General History*, III, p. 159.

25 The Royal Army Medical Corps And Its Work, *B.M.J.*, 1917 (II), p. 220.

26 MacPherson, *General History*, III, pp. 144–145.

27 The Royal Army Medical Corps And Its Work, *B.M.J.*, 1917 (II), pp. 220–223. Macpherson, General History, II, pp. 22–24.

28 WO 95/2752, *P.R.O.*, O.C. 1/1 South Midland Field Ambulance, War Diary, 5.8.17 & Appendix II (August 1917).

29 WO 95/2752, *P.R.O.*, O.C. 1/1 South Midland Field Ambulance, War Diary, 6.8.17.

30 MacPherson, *General History*, III, pp. 144–155.

31 D. Rorie, *A Medico's Luck In The War*, Aberdeen, Milne & Hutchison, 1929, pp. 143–144.

32 WO 95/532, *P.R.O.*, D.M.S. Fifth Army, War Diary, 15.7.17. WO 95/659, P.R.O., D.D.M.S. II Corps. 13.7.17.

33 *Manual of Injuries And Diseases Of War*, London, H.M.S.O., 1918, pp. 3–6. WO 95/532, P.R.O., D.M.S. Fifth Army, War Diary, 7.8.17.

34 WO 95/532, *P.R.O.*, D.M.S. Fifth Army, War Diary, 31.7.17; 2.8.17.

35 WO 95/346, *P.R.O.*, O.C. No. 2 Canadian Casualty Clearing Station, War Diary, 31.7.17; 1.8.17.

36 WO 95/532, *P.R.O.*, D.M.S. Fifth Army, War Diary, 2.8.17; 3.8.17; 6.8.17.

37 *Report Of The War Office Reconstruction Committee*, Cd. 1968, 1904, VIII, p. 128. *Report Of The War Office Reconstruction Committee*, Cd. 2002, 1904, VIII, p. 166.

38 *The Medical Service Of The Army*, *B.M.J.*, 1904 (I), p. 445.

39 Lord Esher, *The Times*, 3 February 1917, p. 7.

40 WO 95/346, *P.R.O.*, O.C. No. 2 Canadian Casualty Clearing Station, War Diary, August Remarks.

41 WO 95/346, *P.R.O.*, O.C. No. 2 Canadian Casualty Clearing Station, War Diary, 9.9.17; 13.9.17; 4.10.17. MacPherson, *General History*, III, pp. 161–162.

42 MacPherson, *General History*, III, pp. 116 & 155.

43 WO 95/532, *P.R.O.*, D.M.s. Fifth Army, War Diary, 2.9.17.

44 WO 95/345, *P.R.O.*, O.C. No. 44 Casualty Clearing Station, War Diary, 22.8.17.

45 MacPherson, *General History*, III, p. 155.

46 WO 95/532, *P.R.O.*, D.M.S. Fifth Army, War Diary, July 1917, Appendix.

47 WO 95/532, *P.R.O.*, D.M.S. Fifth Army, War Diary, 25.8.17; 1.9.17.

48 MacPherson, *General History*, III, pp. 156–157.

49 *Ibid.* pp. 162–165.

50 WO 95/45, *P.R.O.*, D.G.A.M.S., War Diary, 17.7.17.

51 *The Blackguard Nation*, *B.M.J.*, 1918 (II), p. 202.

52 WO 95/346, *P.R.O.*, O.C. No. 2 Canadian Casualty Clearing Station, War Diary, August Remarks.

53 MacPherson, *General History*, III, p. 142.

54 *The R.A.M.C. And Its Work*, B.M.J., 1917 (II), pp. 255; 259.

55 Sir A. Bowlby, *Wellcome Institute For The History of Medicine* (W.I.H.M.), R.A.M.C. 365: *Memorandum on the Necessity of Creating at the War Office a Medical Intelligence and Investigation Department to get the best possible Treatment for the Wounded, diminish Invaliding and return the men to the Ranks in the shortest time*, by Colonel Sir A. Wright (henceforth the Wright Memorandum) pp. 1–2.

56 Bowlby, *W.I.H.M.*, R.A.M.C. 365: *Wright Memorandum*, pp. 3–4.

57 H.W. Bayly, *Triple Challenge: War, Whirligigs And Windmills: A Doctor's Memoirs*, Hutchinson, 1935, p. 151. *Report Of The Commission On Medical Establishments In France*, W.I.H.M., R.A.M.C. 1165, pp. 5–6.

58 *Report Of The Commission On Medical Establishments in France*, W.I.H.M., R.A.M.C. 1165, pp. 58–61; 120–121; 126–133.

59 WO 95/532, *P.R.O.*, D.M.S. Fifth Army, War Diary, 4.9.17.

60 WO 95/345, *P.R.O.*, O.C. No. 44 Casualty Clearing Station, War Diary, 6.9.17. MacPherson, *General History*, III, pp. 20–21.

61 W G MacPherson, *Official History Of The War – Medical Services – Surgery Of The War*, I, London, H.M.S.O., 1923, p. 222.

62 WO 95/532, *P.R.O.*, D.M.S. Fifth Army, War Diary, 24.7.17. MacPherson, *General History*, III, p. 165. William C. Hanigan, *Neurological Surgery during the Great War: The Influence Of Colonel Cushing*, Neurosurgery, Vol. 23, no. 3, 1988, p. 287.

63 Owen Richards, *The Development of Casualty Clearing Stations*, Guy's Hospital Reports, LXX, 1922, p. 117.

64 MacPherson, *Surgery*, I, pp. 221–223.

65 MacPherson, *Surgery*, I, p. 224.

66 WO 95/346, *P.R.O.*, O.C. No. 2 Canadian Casualty Clearing Station, War Diary, 3.9.17.

67 J.S. Haller, *The Great War: Its Impact On The British And American Medical Communities, 1914–1918*, New York State Journal of Medicine, Vol. 91, no. 1, 1991, p. 23, J.S. Haller, *Treatment of Infected Wounds During The Great War, 1914 to 1918*, Southern Medical Journal, Vol. 85, no. 3, 1992, pp. 305–313. J.D.C. Bennett, *Medical Advances Consequent to the Great War, 1914–1918*, Journal Of The Royal Society Of Medicine, Vol. 83, 1990, p. 738. MacPherson, *Surgery*, I, p. 223.

68 WO 95/346, *P.R.O.*, O.C. No. 2 Canadian Casualty Clearing Station, War Diary, 16.10.17.

69 WO 95/500, *P.R.O.*, O.C. No. 53 Casualty Clearing Station, War Diary, September 21 – 30 1917.

70 MacPherson, *General History*, III, p. 143.

71 W.A. Turner, *The Bradshaw Lecture On Neuroses And Psychoses Of War*, J.R.A.M.C., XXXI, 1918, p. 411.

72 A.F. Hurst, *Medical Diseases Of War*, Baltimore, Arnold, 1943, p. 163.

73 E. Miller, *The Neuroses In War*, MacMillan, Cambridge, 1940, p. 164.

74 C.S. Myers, *Shell Shock In France*, Cambridge University Press, Cambridge, 1940 p. 90.

75 Miller, *Neuroses*, p. 171.

76 Myers, *Shell Shock*, p. 91.

77 WO 123/200, *P.R.O.*, General Routine Orders (G.R.O.), G.R.O. 2384.

78 WO 95/532, *P.R.O., D.M.S.* Fifth Army, War Diary, 3.8.17; 6.8.17.

79 WO 95/532, *P.R.O., D.M.S.* Fifth Army, War Diary, 1.7.17; 3.7.17; 18.7.17; 19.7.17; Appendix III, July 1917.

80 L. MacDonald, *The Roses Of No Man's Land*, Penguin, Harmondsworth, 1993.

81 L. Gameson, *Imperial War Museum* (I.W.M.), Memoirs, pp. 179–180.

82 J. Campbell, *L.C.*, Diary 2, 13.7.17.

83 WO 95/532, *P.R.O., D.M.S.* Fifth Army, War Diary, 13.7.17.

84 WO 95/659, *P.R.O.*, D.D.M.S. II Corps, War Diary, Appendix 2, "Z" Scheme of Medical Arrangements, pp. 24–25. MacPherson, General History, III, p. 143.

85 W.G. MacPherson, *Official History Of The War – Medical Services – Diseases Of The War*, II, London, H.M.S.O., 1923, pp. 499–500.

86 MacPherson, *Diseases*, II, pp. 498; 511.

87 The return to mobile warfare in 1918 was to restrict the work of the C.C.S.

88 *The Work Of The A.M.S. In The Recent Flanders Operations*, B.M.J., 1917 (II), p. 666.

Chapter 13

The Planned Amphibious Assault

Andrew Wiest

In most works of history concerning the Third Battle of Ypres, the British plan to stage an amphibious landing behind German lines on the Belgian coast receives scant notice. After a few cursory sentences admitting that such a plan did indeed exist, historians rightly turn their attention back to the prosecution of the battle itself. There is little belief that the landing plan was important to Haig, who did not believe in such "shallow trickeries."[1] The landing never took place and as a result there has been little speculation concerning its possible importance. New research indicates, however, that Sir Douglas Haig considered the amphibious landing in conjunction with a proposed assault along the coast to be a vital component of his Ypres offensive. Planning for an amphibious landing originated with Winston Churchill in 1914 and remained part of British plans for an offensive in northern Belgium throughout the conflict. Haig readily accepted the idea of a landing upon taking command of the British Expeditionary Force in late 1915. His approval of a combined operation on the Belgian coast preceded and had an effect on his planning of Third Ypres. By 1917, the plans and preparations for a landing were complete. The planners themselves had learned much from the harsh experience of Gallipoli, and their plans represent a leap forward in amphibious warfare, closely resembling the amphibious operations of World War II. Haig believed that the landing and coastal operation would be successful. He hoped that their implementation would force an enemy, already battered at Ypres, to crack. He retained this belief throughout the Battle of Passchendaele.

In October 1914, the Germans seized the Belgian ports of Ostende and Zeebrugge and provoked an immediate reaction from the First Lord of the Admiralty, Winston Churchill. He realized that German possession of ports at the eastern end of the English Channel would, in time, become a grave threat. The Admiralty continued to see the ports as a threat to the British war effort throughout the conflict. As a result, denial to the Germans of use of the Belgian ports became a central concept in British strategic thinking. Indeed the Admiralty, and its demands regarding recapture of the Belgian coast, played a pivotal role in the inception and governmental approval of Haig's planning for Third Ypres.[2] On October 26, 1914, Churchill first brought the threat posed by German possession of the ports to the attention of Sir John French, then the Commander-in-Chief of the British Expeditionary Force. Churchill wrote to French, "But my dear friend I do trust that you will realize how damnable it will be if the enemy settles down for the winter along lines that comprise Calais, Dunkirk or Ostende . . . We must have him off the Belgian coast."[3] During the next few months Churchill placed increasing pressure on French to consider an offensive in northern Belgium. The First Lord of the Admiralty promised French that the army, augmented by naval fire power, could turn the German flank off the coast. To French this seemed to offer the chance to use the BEF in a decisive manner and restore a war of movement. Understandably, French was enthusiastic about the idea of a combined offensive and adopted it as his main plan of action for 1915.

French and Churchill worked together to develop detailed plans for an offensive designed to recapture the Belgian coast. Sir John proposed to launch his main attack between Dixmude and the sea. His forces would advance down the coast using naval gun fire to offset their lack of sufficient artillery support. To augment this forward movement the Admiralty planned to undertake a surprise amphibious landing in the vicinity of Zeebrugge. The landing forces (presumably one to three divisions depending on availability) would wade ashore on the beach four miles to the west of Zeebrugge under the cover of a naval bombardment. The amphibious forces would then advance to join with the men advancing down the coast. Such a movement, French speculated, would dislocate the German right flank.[4] In the end the British government rejected French's planning for an offensive in Belgium in favour of operations in the Dardanelles. However, the strategic design that would lead to Third Ypres was in place, and an amphibious landing was at its heart. By the end of the year both French and Churchill lost their positions. However, new proponents of operations in Belgium stepped forward, and an amphibious landing would remain an important part of their scheme.

In December 1915, Haig replaced Sir John French in command of the BEF. He was well aware of the plans regarding an offensive and amphibious landing in northern Belgium. Soon after Haig assumed his new post, Rear Admiral Reginald Bacon, the Commander of the Dover Patrol, visited him. Bacon warned Haig of the dangers posed by the Germans at Ostende and Zeebrugge. The two men then went on to discuss co-operation between the fleet and the army in an effort to recapture those ports. At a second meeting in January 1916, Haig gave Bacon his approval for an amphibious landing and asked the admiral to develop detailed plans for the operation.[5] It is doubtless that Haig needed little prodding to consider an offensive in Flanders. He had always seen that area as strategically vital. Naval considerations, then, did not cause Third Ypres. However, approval for an amphibious landing predated Haig's own planning for an offensive in Flanders. The landing would remain part of his plan, and indeed affect his thinking and the outcome of the battle itself.

Haig appointed Lieutenant-General Aylmer Hunter-Weston, experienced at Gallipoli, to work with Bacon on the landing plan. By March 1916 the two men were ready to present their findings to Haig. However, by this point, Haig's Passchendaele plans had begun to develop. He had decided to make his main thrust in the area of Ypres instead of along the coast. The landing would be secondary and would not take place until the main advance had made considerable gains. Bacon proposed to use 6 monitors and 100 trawlers to land an initial force of 9,000 men in Ostende harbour. A total of three divisions would land in Ostende, in conjunction with a coastal assault from Nieuport. Bacon hoped that the troops participating in the landing would link up with forces from Nieuport and Ypres and complete the "overthrow of the enemy's right flank."[6]

Bacon planned several deception measures to ensure surprise including feints toward Zeebrugge and Middelkerke. Naval forces and a minefield would block any German interference with the operation. The landing itself would take place under cover of a phosphorous smoke screen with the 1st Division having the honour of landing in the van. Its duty was to effect a surprise landing and capture the harbour to enable two additional

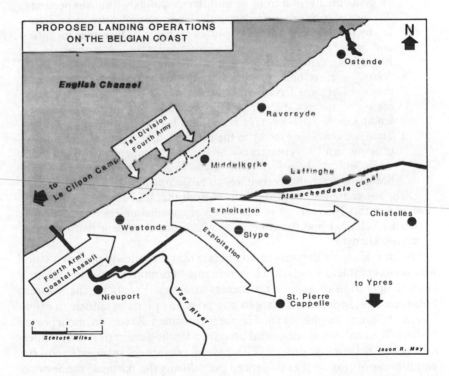

(xiv) Proposed Landing Operations on the Belgian Coast. *(Jason R.May/Andrew Wiest, University of Southern Mississipi)*

divisions to land safely. Also the 1st Division was to seize a bridgehead across the Plasschendaele Canal. The troops were to use their initial surprise to capture a variety of assigned locations. Of primary importance were the German coastal batteries, which had to be eliminated before the reinforcements could land. For this purpose Bacon included fast cars, cycles and 16 tanks in the landing force. Most supplies for the landing divisions would accompany the coastal advance from Nieuport.[7]

It was up to Hunter-Weston to advise Haig on whether or not Bacon's plan could actually succeed. In his report to Haig, Hunter-Weston stated: "Nothing is impossible in war, and this landing, if successful, and made in sufficient strength . . . co-operating with a British advance from the vicinity of Ypres, would have a very great effect on the war."[8] What follows in Hunter-Weston's report is a very lengthy, detailed account of various problems with the existing landing plan and suggestions to improve upon it. The critique of the landing plan is important because it forms the basis of the revised plan for 1917. It also demonstrates that Hunter-Weston had learned much from the problems of the Gallipoli campaign. Hunter-Weston informed Haig that the plan was too risky because:

1 One of the essentials for a successful landing in force is that it shall be made on a broad front or at different points within supporting distance of each other, so that, if the landing or advance be held up at any locality, our advance at other points may turn that locality and prevent the whole enterprise from failing . . . A landing on a broad front cannot be made at Ostende under present conditions.

2 A landing, therefore, can only take place in the harbour . . . The fact that the Germans have a 16.5 inch howitzer well inland . . . gives reason to suspect that all proper precautions to prevent our . . . landing in the harbour have been taken by our methodical foe . . .

4 Time is a governing factor in the problem, and vigour and rapidity of action in all directions is essential . . . Unfortunately except to the south and southeast, all roads away from the harbour lead past houses or through streets likely to be occupied by the enemy . . .

The above are the principal of the reasons that lead me to the conclusion that this enterprise is not to be recommended unless the German defence collapses and the conditions which can at present be foreseen entirely change.[9]

The critical report demonstrated to Haig that the landing plan as it stood was unacceptable. However, Haig remained committed to the idea of a landing operation to augment a success at Ypres. Events on the Western Front, though, soon forced Haig to postpone any plans to launch an offensive in Belgium during 1916. He then informed Bacon to incorporate Hunter-Weston's suggestions and prepare a landing operation to be undertaken the following year.[10] That Haig remained interested in the amphibious operation was evidenced even during the Battle of the Somme. On 18 September, 1916, three days after the battlefield debut of the tank, Haig had a meeting with Bacon. "I spoke to Admiral Bacon regarding his preparations for landing on the Belgian coast. In view of the successes obtained by the tanks, I suggested that he should carry out experiments with special flat-bottomed boats for running ashore and landing a line of tanks on the beach with the object of breaking through wire and capturing the enemy's defences."[11]

Bacon began detailed planning for landing one division on the coast near Middelkerke soon after his meeting with Haig. A beach landing would avoid the congestion that Hunter-Weston had feared in the proposed Ostende operation. In addition Bacon proposed to land the division in three separate but supporting landing areas. Lieutenant-Colonel C. Macmullen worked with Bacon and acted as Haig's advisor regarding the new planning. Macmullen warned Haig that the landing and coastal operation should be strictly subsidiary to a general advance from Ypres. Placing troops on the shore behind enemy lines was a risky business. He wanted there to be no chance that the Germans could isolate and destroy the amphibious force.[12] Haig agreed, and decided that the landing would not take place until British forces advancing from Ypres had reached Roulers. At this point the Germans would be reeling from a major defeat and the landing forces would have the greatest effect.

Bacon first had to devise a method safely to place at least one infantry division on the beach behind enemy lines. He knew from Hunter-Weston's previous comments that speed was the key to any successful amphibious operation. The Admiral believed that existing methods of landing troops on shore, as used at Gallipoli, were inadequate. He decided that what was needed was a flat-bottomed landing craft that could be beached. A ramp would then enable men and tanks to disembark at speed. He designed and developed such a craft and called it a pontoon. The wooden vessel was 200 yards in length and was sturdy enough to carry both men and tanks. The vessel was lashed between two monitors. The momentum of the monitors would drive the pontoon ashore. Three monitor-pontoon groups were sufficient to land one entire division and nine tanks because the monitors themselves could carry additional men.

Bacon began to test his rather awkward landing craft as early as March 1917. At first there were numerous problems with the system. However, after a period of trial and error, the crews of the monitors became adept in getting the pontoons ashore. The pontoons themselves survived every test which suggested that they could be used to land reinforcement divisions as well. To facilitate the landings, Bacon had aerial photographs and submarine readings taken to ascertain the exact depth of the water in the Middelkerke area. In addition, Bacon practised night landings using wire stretched between buoys and the shore to guide the pontoons to within 100 yards of their intended onshore location.[13]

After staging practice landings with both men and tanks, Bacon was convinced that he had the problem in hand. However, a new difficulty emerged, for there was a sea wall in the proposed area of the landing near Middelkerke. Planners feared that the tanks might have trouble surmounting the incline of the wall. By April, replica sea walls had been constructed at tank headquarters in France and in Dover. The tanks could climb the initial slope of the wall of about 30 degrees. However, the top of the wall was perpendicular and about two and a half feet in height. The tanks could not climb over this obstacle. After many failed attempts the tanks began to carry special ramps that would enable them to climb over the perpendicular portion of the wall. By late May, tanks were surmounting the wall with ease.[14]

On 10 May, 1917, General Sir Henry Rawlinson received orders that he would command the forces used in the landing and the coastal assault. The choice of a senior commander like Rawlinson, with his valuable experience from the Somme, demonstrates the level of importance Haig placed on the operation. Rawlinson met with Bacon and reviewed and approved of the Admiral's planning. Rawlinson was understandably concerned with the complicated pontoon system. However, after witnessing trial landings and tank training, the General became convinced that the scheme was feasible. He commented, "I really rather like it [the landing plan] . . . With a really strong battery of guns and the command of the air we shall, I think, at least get possession of Middelkerke if not Ostende in the first round."[15] In June, Rawlinson reported on the progress of planning to Haig's Chief of Staff. At this meeting, Rawlinson learned how his coastal operation related to the forthcoming Flanders offensive as a whole. The conference also demonstrates the importance that Haig placed on the landing. Rawlinson summarized the conference in his war journal:

> I gather that the Nieuport attack is to be considered subsidiary in so far as the initial operations are concerned, but if things go well and we gain possession of Ostende that port will be made the base of further extensive operations with a view to advancing on Bruges from the north west and clearing the enemy out of the whole coastline up to the Dutch frontier . . . [If the main force reaches Roulers] and the Boche seem to be inclined to give way Haig will then put in the Nieuport attack and possibly make that the main line of advance.[16]

Bacon and Rawlinson presented Haig with a very detailed plan of action. They had decided to land one division on the beach near Middelkerke. The landing would take place at dawn, under the cover of a heavy naval bombardment. Eighty small vessels would take part in the operation to provide a smoke screen as additional cover. Trawlers would carry telephone cable to keep the landing force in constant contact with Rawlinson. The division would land in three parties of roughly 4,500 men with the total number of troops landed to be 13,750 officers and men. The tanks would exit the landing craft first. They would then climb the wall and provide cover for the infantry disembarkation. For artillery support the landing parties carried four 13-pounder guns and two small howitzers. Each wing of the landing also included a motorized machine-gun battery and transport for ammunition. Finally, each landing party had over two hundred bicycles and three motorcycles to facilitate speed in expanding the landing areas.[17]

The northernmost brigade of the landing force was to send a flying column to deal with the German guns at Raversyde for securing sea communications. The column contained engineers especially trained to deal with the German battery. Upon completion of the mission, the column was to return to the landing area to advance east or southeast with a view to threatening the German line of retreat to the south, which would effectively isolate Ostende. All landing parties were to exploit their surprise and push patrols toward Leffinghe and Slype to occupy the bridges over the Plasschendaele Canal and various road junctions. The landing division would not be able to advance much past this point without additional transport. The transport would arrive with the XV Corps advancing down the coast from Nieuport. Thus any major exploitation of the landing would depend on the speed of the coastal assault.[18]

The XV Corps was to launch its attack to coincide with the landing. A force of 300 guns supported by a naval bombardment would lay a barrage across the 3,500 yard frontage of the advance. Two divisions, each with two brigades in the line, would carry out the initial assault. A further three divisions were held in reserve to exploit any success. The German defenders had two brigades readily available in two lines of defences. The plan called for the XV Corps to advance 1,000 yards and then rest for one hour while the artillery prepared for the next phase of the attack. Four such advances, taking an estimated six hours, would take the XV Corps to Middelkerke, where they would link up with the landing force.[19] Rawlinson believed that the landing plan and the coastal assault would facilitate turning the Germans out of their strong coastal positions. Such an event would have hugely beneficial consequences. The Fourth Army's summary of the plan makes clear the relationship between the landing and the coastal assault. The landing was, "designed to cut off the retreat of the enemy's artillery about Westende, to turn his second and third positions and to penetrate as far inland as possible." The XV Corps would support the landing forces, "and assist them in exploiting their success to the utmost."[20]

Haig witnessed both practice landings and tank training. He was convinced that the plans would work, and could convert a hard won victory at Ypres into a strategic success by completing the process of turning the German right flank. On June 18, 1917, Haig met with both Rawlinson and Bacon. He gave the planning his final approval, and allowed Rawlinson to begin to train his troops for their complex operation.[21] Rawlinson chose the 1st Division to undertake the landing. On 16 July, the 1st Division entered a special, isolated camp at Le Clipon to begin its training. In order to explain the seclusion of the division, the British reported that it had been afflicted by the outbreak of an epidemic. Engineers built a replica sea wall in the camp so men could practise climbing its rather sharp incline. Also they constructed a scale model of the invasion area so that each section could study its task from all possible standpoints.[22] An important new development complicated planning for the coastal assault, when, on 10 July, the Germans attacked in the Nieuport area and forced the northern portion of the British line back to the Yser River. Elements of the XV Corps involved in the coastal assault would now have to cross the river and seize additional ground. As a result Rawlinson believed that the operation would be considerably more difficult.[23] It was Haig's opinion, however, that the loss of ground would be a minor inconvenience. The Germans would, after all, be nearing their breaking point before the operation began. He informed his commanders that the coastal assault would proceed as planned.[24] As a result of the new situation, the XV Corps command did add an attack on the town of Lombartzyde scheduled to take place one day before the coastal advance, which would cover the right flank of the forces crossing the Yser.[25] By the beginning of the Third Battle of Ypres, Bacon and Rawlinson had completed the planning and preparation for the landing and coastal operations. The ships were gathered and ready, and the crews and landing forces were trained. The British had learned from the failure at Gallipoli. Bacon and Rawlinson had left little to chance.

They decided that 8 August was the day with optimum tidal conditions for the dawn landing. However, the initial advance from Ypres yielded little, and Rawlinson realized that Haig would not implement the landing as planned. Haig, however, refused to abandon the plan. He still expected to reach Roulers, and suggested the first week of September for implementation of the landing and coastal assault. Both Bacon and Rawlinson agreed that on 6 September conditions for the landing would be favourable.[26] The fate of the landing plan rested on the success of the 16 August attack at the Battle of Langemarck. The Fifth Army, under General Sir Hubert Gough, had made little progress at Ypres. The II Corps had failed on 10 August in an attempt to capture the critically important Gheluvelt plateau. Such an event should have forced Gough to postpone the main offensive, until he had launched another attempt to clear the plateau. Indeed subordinates within the Fifth Army made that very suggestion. However, Gough realized that any further delay of the offensive would affect the landing, which had to catch the high tides at the end of the month or face an additional postponement of four weeks. Thus, at least partly due to the requirements of the landing plan, Gough rushed his main offensive.[27] The landing and coastal assault were having an impact on the prosecution of the Third Battle of Ypres, demonstrating once again the importance Haig placed in them.

The Battle of Langemarck achieved little, helping to hasten Gough's downfall. As a result it became clear to Rawlinson that the landing and coastal assault were in jeopardy. On 22 August, Rawlinson and Bacon met with Haig to discuss the future of the operation. Rawlinson suggested three alternatives to Haig: he could wait for a major advance at Ypres and carry out the operation as planned at a later date; the landing and coastal operation could take place independently of the main advance; or, many of the troops could be removed from the coast to reinforce Fifth Army.

Rawlinson believed that his troops were doing little good languishing on the coast. He proposed that Haig allow the landing and coastal assault to take place independent of the main advance. He suggested that his forces would at least capture the coast to Middelkerke, bring Ostende under British fire, and force the Germans to counter-attack. As a result the operation would draw German forces away from the main advance. Rawlinson contended that, "The chances of the success of this attack are distinctly favourable if the wind and weather are good. It would come as a surprise . . . The troops are very confident of success, and the means at our disposal are adequate to deal with any opposition that may be encountered . . . I have every confidence that, with reasonable luck, it will succeed."[28]

Rawlinson's arguments did not move Haig, who believed that the attack from Ypres was still going to be successful and wanted to retain the coastal operation and the landing plan in their original form. Haig noted that during the first week of October the tides would be favourable for a night landing. When Rawlinson and Bacon agreed that the landing could be undertaken in the light of the full moon, rather than at dawn, the landing was again postponed until the first week of October, unless the speed of advance from Ypres quickened and necessitated an earlier landing.[29]

During September, Rawlinson and Bacon began to despair and believe that their part in the offensive might never take place. Haig, however, was more optimistic. He remained firm in the belief that his forces could reach Roulers and the landing and coastal operations would come off as planned. The beginning of the attacks of the Second Army under General Sir Herbert Plumer on 20 September served to convince Haig of impending success. Haig, however, realized that hoping to implement the landing during the first week in October was too optimistic. As a result, he wrote to Rawlinson and informed him that the landing had once again been postponed. He went on to instruct Rawlinson to have everything in readiness for operations by mid month. Haig wrote that the Second Army would launch major assaults at Ypres during the first two weeks of October. He expected these assaults to have great results, and instructed Fourth Army to stand ready to undertake its part in the campaign to augment any disintegration of the German positions. Rawlinson recorded his conclusions regarding Haig's statements in his war journal: "If only the weather will last till then [October 10] we shall do a big thing and I may possibly come into it too if the Boche break, as is quite possible – anyway D.H. is quite optimistic."[30]

The success of the Battle of Broodseinde on 4 October convinced Haig that one more blow might well force the Germans to break. As a result he again informed Rawlinson to have the entire coastal operation in readiness. Even after the relative failure of the Battle of Poelcappelle on 10 October, Haig's optimism did not waver. Once again Haig sent word to Rawlinson to be ready for action. However, Haig did admit that now the landing and coastal operation might not take place until the end of October.[31] The fate of the landing plan hinged on the next stage of the Flanders campaign, which began on 12 October and is known as the First Battle of Passchendaele.

The results of the battle were minimal. The Second Army, advancing through the mud, could make but little forward progress against stubborn German defence. Rawlinson now realized that Haig's optimism had been misplaced and that his Fourth Army would not be called upon to undertake its dramatic part of the offensive. He recorded in his war journal, "things have not been running at all smoothly – It is now clear that we shall do nothing on the coast here."[32]

Two days later, Rawlinson and Bacon learned that Haig had indeed called off and not merely postponed the landing plan. Haig's Chief of Staff informed them that:

Persistent ill-luck in weather conditions has delayed our advance so much that there is no possibility of our being ready for the combined operation this month . . . [The army still hoped to make great advances, but the weather then would be too rough for a sea landing.] It is very disappointing, especially for you after all you had done to ensure success – but you know we have done our best and the weather has not been kind. From our experiences we are convinced that with good weather the full programme would have come off.[33]

The 1st Division left its camp at Le Clipon on 21 October officially marking the end of the landing plan. The remainder of the Fourth Army departed from the coast on 3 November leaving only a covering force that later turned the area over to the French. The landing plan never took place.

The question of whether or not the landing plan would have succeeded is moot. Detractors such as Admiral Roger Keyes contend that the 1st Division would have met disaster, while supporters such as Admiral John Jellicoe suggest that the innovative plan would have met with great success.[34] The most important proponent of the landing's success was Haig. He perceived it to be the important final blow that would force a shaken German army to break. Haig's actions demonstrate his perception of the landing's relative importance to his overall plan. He had never considered undertaking an offensive from Ypres without an integral landing plan. As the campaign developed, he insisted on retention of the landing at all costs. Although he needed every available man to press the attack from Ypres, Haig allowed the Fourth Army to remain on the coast during the most desperate times of the struggle, awaiting its special operation, instead of fighting at Ypres. Haig had to allow some of the Fourth Army to remain on the coast to cover the line, but, in the case of the Fourth Army, there were far more divisions present than necessary to defend the area. Rawlinson had even suggested to Haig that many of the divisions of his army ought to be transferred to Ypres if Haig did not plan to undertake the landing and coastal offensive. Haig had refused.

The landing plan, though never undertaken, was an imaginative effort to circumvent the front lines and possibly restore a war of movement. The planning for the operation represents a clear step forward in amphibious warfare. Indeed the use of flat-bottomed landing craft and tanks foreshadows the landing operations of World War II. The imagination demonstrated in the landing does Haig credit. However, circumstances surrounding the landing serve to prove that Haig still had much to learn about the very nature of the Great War. He had wisely decided not to allow the landing to take place until British forces had reached Roulers. Both Bacon and Rawlinson had requested an independent landing, but Haig had refused. It was to be an integral part of a great victory. To that end he retained the landing as part of his overall planning until mid October. It is obvious that until then Haig believed that the Germans were about to crack. Only on 12 October did Haig realize that his forces would not break through the German lines and capture Roulers. Only then did he cancel the landing plan and only then did he accept that 'breakthrough' was impossible.

Notes

1   Leon Wolff, *In Flanders' Fields* (New York: The Viking Press, 1958), 27.
2   For a full discussion of naval influence concerning Third Ypres see, Andrew Wiest, *Passchendaele and the Royal Navy* (Westport, CT: Greenwood Press, 1995).
3   Winston Churchill to Sir John French, October 26, 1914, Sir John French Papers, Imperial War Museum, London.
4   Admiral Sir Roger Keyes, "Notes on the possibilities of a landing on the Belgian Coast near Zeebrugge," February 2, 1915, Admiral Sir Roger Keyes Papers, British Museum, London, 6/1, C.F. 89.
5   General Sir Douglas Haig, Diary entry, January 7, 1916, Haig Diary, Public Record Office, London.
6   Letter received by Flag Captain Bowring, April 29, 1916, Admiralty Papers, ADM 137/2103, Public Record Office, London.
7   Admiralty Papers, ADM 137/2103. That Bacon planned to use tanks in his landing before they had even seen battle is somewhat surprising and testifies to his imaginative mind.
8   Aylmer Hunter-Weston, "A note on the projected landing at Ostende," February 24, 1916, Hunter-Weston Papers, British Museum, London, ADD MSS 48357.
9   Ibid.
10 Notes on a conference between Haig and Bacon, June 12, 1916, Admiralty Papers, ADM 137/2103.
11 John Terraine, *The Road to Passchendaele* (London: Leo Cooper, 1977), 15–16.
12 Lieutenant-Colonel C. Macmullen, Ypres plan, January 15, 1917, Fourth Army Records, Imperial War Museum, London.
13 Admiral Sir Reginald Bacon, *The Dover Patrol* (London: Hutchinson and Co., 1929), 231–232.
14 General Sir Henry Rawlinson, Appendix Z, Fourth Army Records, 19:3.

15 General Sir Henry Rawlinson, Diary entry, May 25, 1917, Rawlinson War Journal, Churchill College Archives, Cambridge.

16 Ibid., June 22, 1917.

17 Instructions for the Belgian coast operation, Fourth Army Records, 19:71.

18 Colonel William Dobbie, "The Operations of the First Division on the Belgian Coast in 1917," *Royal Engineers Journal* 38, no.2 (June 1924):203–204.

19 Plan of attack of the 32nd Division, July 5, 1917, T. S. Lambert Papers, Imperial War Museum, London.

20 Instructions for the Belgian coast operation, Fourth Army Records, 19:104–5.

21 Rawlinson, Diary entry, June 18, 1917.

22 Dobbie, "First Division," 188–89.

23 Rawlinson, Diary entry, 15 July, 1917.

24 Haig to French, 21 July, 1917, French Papers, Imperial War Museum, London.

25 Archibald Montgomery, Diary entry, 20 July, 1917, Montgomery Papers, Imperial War Museum, London.

26 Rawlinson, Diary entry, August 6, 1917.

27 While concern for the landing was not Gough's only reason for continuing his unsuccessful offensive, in Edmond's estimation it was uppermost in Gough's mind. J.E. Edmonds, *Military Operations, France and Belgium, 1917* (London: Macmillan and Co. 1948), 189–190.

28 Rawlinson to Haig, August 22, 1917, Fourth Army Records, 209:231–33.

29 Launcelot Kiggell to Rawlinson, August 28, 1917, Fourth Army Records, 20:241–42.

30 Rawlinson, Diary entry, September 29, 1917.

31 Ibid., October 10, 1917.

32 Ibid., October 13, 1917.

33 Kiggell to Bacon, October 15, 1917, War Office Papers, WO 158/239, Public Record Office, London.

34 For a full discussion of the landing plan and its chances of success see, Andrew Wiest, *Passchendaele and the Royal Navy*.

Part III

Military Effectiveness, Identity and Experience

Chapter 14

The British Divisions at Third Ypres

John Lee

The British army in the autumn of 1917 was the product of three years of fighting on the Western Front. It had been learning and disseminating the lessons of 'trench to trench' warfare ever since the deadlock had developed in November 1914. In particular the long experience of the 1916 fighting in Picardy had resulted in the codification of the lessons of infantry – artillery – air (and later tank) co-operation in a series of important training pamphlets that would transform the battle performance of the British divisions.

These improvements in attacking technique had already produced two stunning first-day successes, on 9 April, 1917 (at Arras, which is, of course, usually remembered exclusively for the 'Canadian' success on Vimy Ridge) and 7 June, 1917 (the storming of the Messines Ridge). On 9 April, two divisions in particular, the 9th (Scottish) and 34th, had made spectacular advances behind near perfect 'creeping' barrages against formidable enemy defences.

The pause in the offensive after Messines was, in hindsight, particularly regrettable. As early as May 1917, Haig had decided that the offensive would be continued, not by Plumer's Second Army, but by Gough's Fifth Army, designed to break out of the Ypres salient proper and capture what passed for the high ground in Flanders. The six week delay did allow the massing of an unparalleled attacking force, supplied with unprecedented quantities of artillery and ammunition. All the assault divisions had time to rehearse their attack over replica models of their objectives.

The divisions assembled for the great attack on 31 July 1917, were in a high state of confidence. Twelve British divisions, plus one brigade, were to open the offensive – the Guards and 8th Divisions; the 51st (Highland) and 55th (West Lancashire) Divisions; and the 15th (Scottish), 19th (Western), 24th, 30th, 37th, 38th (Welsh), 39th and 41st Divisions, and a brigade of the 18th (Eastern) Division. The New Zealand and 3rd Australian Divisions were to make supporting attacks to the south; two French divisions went in on Gough's left. All the British divisions – two of

Regulars, two of the Territorial Force, and eight of the New Armies – had fought on the Somme in 1916, five of them again at Arras; three of them were at Messines (one – the 24th – had been through all three major battles).

Knowing, as we do, that the ambitious objectives set for the Battle of Pilckem Ridge were not achieved because of the atrocious weather that set in that afternoon and the punishing German counter-attacks that forced withdrawals in several places, it is easy to forget what a sweeping advance was made at the outset by divisions on the left and in the centre. Admittedly this included the very deep German outpost line, which they had no intention of defending in detail. But the following account, from the narrative of operations of the 39th Division, shows an infantry tackling powerful enemy defences in a thoroughly efficient way:

"On the resumption of the advance at 7.10 am, 'Alberta' and 'Regina Cross' proved main centres of resistance. Both places were very strong positions with concrete emplacements and dugouts which survived our artillery bombardment."

'Alberta' was captured by the 17th Sherwood Foresters as follows:

Lewis guns, rifle bombers and Stokes guns opened a heavy fire on the enemy machine-gun emplacements. Two tanks also opened a heavy fire at very close range and one of them (G.47) advanced through our barrage

Tomorrow the 38th (Welsh) Division will have the honour of being in the front line of what will be the big battle of the war.

On the deeds of each individual of the Division depends whether it shall be said that the 38th (Welsh) Division took Pilckem and Langemark, and upheld gloriously the honour of Wales and the British Empire.

The honour can be obtained by hard fighting and self sacrifice on the part of each one of us.

"GWELL ANGAU NA CHYWILYDD."

C. G. BLACKADER, Major-General.

The above will be distributed to all Officers and read by them to their men.

H. E. ap RHYS PRYCE, Lieut.-Colonel,
G.S.O. 1,
38th (Welsh) Division.

(xv) Welsh divisional identity and morale, as communicated by Divisional Command to the men of the 38th (Welsh) Division on the eve of battle. (*T.S.Richards, Liddle Collection*)

and rolled out a lane for the infantry in the uncut wire. Meanwhile, rifle sections worked round the flanks of the position and, on the barrage lifting, assaulted from both sides and captured the garrison which had been driven into their dugouts.

'Regina Cross' was attacked and captured in the same manner by the 16th Rifle Brigade, but without the assistance of tanks as the latter did not get up on the left of the attack. 'Regina Cross' consisted of three separated strong points which were finally rushed by the infantry who bayoneted the machine gunners at their guns and killed or captured the entire garrison of thirty men with three machine-guns.

On the right the 13th Sussex, with a tank in close support, occupied St. Julien without serious opposition and took 17 officers and 205 other ranks prisoner in the cellars and dugouts of the village.[1]

The capture of 6,000 prisoners and 25 guns on the first day seemed to bode well for the campaign. Instead heavy rainfall and days on end of repeated German counter-attacks prevented any progress.

The August weeks that followed tested the British army more severely than anything it had hitherto endured. In atrocious weather, over ground that was a featureless swamp, utterly exhausting and very dangerous to move across, Gough insisted on renewing the attack. Gough had continued to set wide targets for his artillery and consequently never concentrated enough in one place to dominate the enemy guns massed behind the Gheluvelt plateau. On 10 August, the British 18th (Eastern) and 25th Divisions dragged themselves forward. The capture of Westhoek village by the 25th Division was the only success of the day. The 18th Division stormed Glencorse Wood and got into Inverness Copse, but German counter-attacks bundled them back almost to their start line, a rare defeat for the justly-renowned division which, under the inspired leadership of Sir Ivor Maxse, had been unbeatable on the Somme.

Even the Official History says that the failure to secure the above objectives should have logically been followed by the postponement of the next great attack scheduled for 14 August. Gough still had it in mind that he had to get on and meet an amphibious operation planned along the Belgian coast; he would brook no delay. Allowing a one day extension of the preliminary bombardment, and forced to delay again because of torrential rain, the next big effort was on 16 August – the Battle of Langemarck – a truly depressing day for the army.

Eight British divisions went in, supported by the French on the left. Two of regulars (the 8th and 29th), two of the Territorial Force (48th and 56th), four of the New Armies (the 11th, 16th, 20th and 36th) – all veterans of the Somme and of earlier fighting in 1917, three of them fresh from victory at Messines. Once again any progress made was on the left; the Germans were giving no ground that threatened the key to their defences on the Gheluvelt plateau.

The French, the 'Incomparable' 29th and the 20th (Light) Divisions all took their set objectives for the day, despite the atrocious conditions.

According to the history of the 20th Division, "in many places the only possible formation for the troops was a series of small columns which wound their way in single file between the pools of mud and water".[3] A real tragedy occurred where the 16th (Irish) and 36th (Ulster) Divisions went in side by side, for the second time in the war. After their shared triumph at Messines, many observers had hoped that friendships forged in the heat of battle would bode well for Ireland after the war. Instead both divisions endured a demoralizing defeat which seemed almost inevitable. In common with many divisions serving in the Fifth Army, they both complained that they had been kept far too long in the front line prior to the attack – thirteen days no less. The men were utterly exhausted; the units were very seriously depleted in numbers. Cyril Falls, a serving officer who wrote the history of the 36th (Ulster) Division, tells how the leading waves of the attack barely totalled three hundred rifles – "more like a big raiding party than anything else" according to one sergeant – of whom two hundred fell in half a minute.[4] The whole attack strength of the two brigades involved was some 2,000 men.

The most poignant accounts of the day come from the unit histories of the 56th (1st London) Division and they highlight the different styles of attack available to commanders of the day. The manual SS 144 "The Normal Formation for the Attack" allowed for two attack formations. In one the first objective line was taken and consolidated by designated units, and fresh units would pass through and take the next objective after a renewed bombardment, and so on. For those commanders who thought this was too cautious an approach, which might lead to opportunities for exploitation being missed, there was the option to let the leading battalions attack through to the final objective, with following units securing their rear. This latter method was preferred by Gough and the London Territorials elected to use it for this battle. Consequently the leading waves of the 2nd Londons (Royal Fusiliers) and 5th Londons (London Rifle Brigade) pressed boldly through Glencorse Wood and on into Polygon Wood and were, quite simply, never seen again. A similar fate befell the leading waves of the 8th Middlesex on their left. A company of men just disappeared. German counter-attacks thrust all other units back to their start line.

All the available divisional histories are scathing about this battle. For the 56th Division "it makes a sorry story in which the great gallantry of the London Territorials stands forth like something clean and honest in the midst of slime and mud".[5] Lack of time for preparation; difficulty of communications; fatigue of the men; the condition of the ground; the concentration of hostile guns opposite the front to be attacked – all these feature in the bitter reports of the day.

It could be argued that the morale of the British army on the Western Front fell to its lowest point in the war in this August of 1917. Even in the darkest days of the German offensives of March and April 1918, the fighting units never faltered in their duty. But a recent account of the London Rifle Brigade, an elite unit by anybody's definition of the word, shows that even this 'class' regiment was stupefied by its experience. "How could all these dashed hopes fail to dishearten us ? After seeing the pitiful remains of the battalion . . . something like disgust with the British tactics made itself felt".[6] Pride in their division helped the battalion keep the faith, but they never lost their loathing of Gough and his Fifth Army staff. Even the redoubtable Charles Carrington, an officer in the 48th (South Midlands) Division, noted how the partial attacks and inadequate gains meant that "generals grew angrier with their troops and troops with their generals".[7]

Small scale attacks continued. A brilliant example of infantry/tank/ artillery co-operation after a spell of good weather saw men of the 48th Division and 1st Tank Brigade seize powerful strong points on the St. Julien-Poelcappelle road on 20 August. The 14th (Light) Division battered its way into the forward edge of Inverness Copse, and it was when they were unceremoniously bundled back out of it by powerful German counter-attacks on 24 August that Haig seems to have lost patience with Gough's lack of progress.

Next day, the control of the battle was transferred to Plumer's Second Army and a completely new style of fighting the overall battle was instituted. A linked series of blows was planned, in which each stage of the advance onto the Gheluvelt Plateau and the Passchendaele-Staden Ridge would be by fresh divisions. Each battle would have limited objectives, and within it each attacking battalion would only be set tasks well within the physical limitations of the men involved. Plumer demanded, and obtained, a three week lull in the offensive to complete his preparations.

For the Battle of the Menin Road Ridge (20 September, 1917), Second Army committed four British and two Australian divisions, and Fifth Army used five British divisions. Four of the attack divisions –1st and 2nd Australian, 9th (Scottish)and 58th (2nd/1st London) – had not been used in a major battle since April or May 1917. Two more – 19th and 23rd – were 'fresh' from their success at Messines in June. The other five divisions – 20th (Light), 51st (Highland) and 55th (West Lancashire) of Fifth Army, and 39th and 41st of Second Army – had all seen hard fighting in the Salient during the current autumn campaign. All attacking formations received extensive training over models of the defences to be assailed; all adopted the 'leap frog' system of relieving attacking battalions with fresh ones, behind lengthy standing barrages, before proceeding to the next objective. All had it impressed upon them that they were to follow the crushing, five-layered barrage of shrapnel, high-explosives and machine-gun fire onto their objectives, which were to be immediately prepared for defence to face the inevitable German counter-attacks.

The ensuing battle was a great success. Not only did most divisions take all their objectives (there were local difficulties which denied complete success to all) but, more importantly, the Germans were goaded into a series of counter-attacks which were totally smashed by the power of

British artillery and machine-gun fire. The recent work by Prior and Wilson on this campaign has failed to recognize the importance of this aspect of the battle. In particular, the weather had been very good to the attackers. An early morning mist had assisted the infantry in getting in amongst the defenders. The rest of the day was bright and clear, which made the crucial role of the Royal Flying Corps – the tracking minute-by-minute of the forward movement of the German counter-attack divisions – quite perfect. The ground gained, tactically important as it was in denying observation posts to the enemy artillery, was as nothing to this clinical destruction of the specially-trained German counter-attack divisions, three of which were absolutely ruined by this day of fighting. The Germans had been forced to fight this battle on Plumer's terms; their predictable tactics had been turned against them with devastating effect. British morale soared after such a clear success. The battle is replete with examples of a very skilled attacking infantry, going forward in widely-dispersed formations, and capable of using the inherent firepower of the platoon to overcome local points of resistance. Even where local difficulties of terrain (it had rained heavily the night before after a long, dry spell, leaving the ground slippery) meant that the infantry fell behind the creeping barrage (which guaranteed success over much of the field), the fire and movement tactics of the four sections of the platoon usually overcame enemy resistance. In one astonishing example of the infantry's confidence in themselves and their artillery comrades, a company of the 6th King's Own Scottish Borderers (9th Division) advanced in a gap left inside the shrapnel belt of the creeping barrage, enabling them to bypass Hanebeek Wood while the garrison cowered in their dug-outs, and to storm the formidable defensive position from the rear.

Plumer's second great blow hit the Germans on 26 September, the Battle of Polygon Wood. Five British and two Australian divisions again wrested important tactical features from the enemy and, in line with the new policy, heavily defeated the subsequent counter-attacks. In the centre, the 3rd British Division actually pushed beyond its final objective to secure most of the village of Zonnebeke, aided by the success of 59th (2nd North Midland) Division on its left and the Australians on its right. The preparations of 33rd Division for the attack had been seriously disrupted by massive German counter-attacks on the previous day and their subsequent failure to get forward made things very difficult for the 5th Australian Division. The British Official History ruefully comments that the 'natural ill-feeling' of the Australians did not take into account the extent of the fighting endured by their British neighbours. (Not for the first or last time in the war). All the attackers, however, spent the afternoon cheerfully massacring the hapless German infantry as they routinely counter-attacked and were routinely swept away.

Lloyd George later called the Battle of Broodseinde (4 October, 1917) a 'manufactured victory'. He overlooks the fact that to Ludendorff the defeat suffered by his troops was one of the 'black days' of the German army.

Having seen Plumer turn the 'new' German defensive tactics, with their reliance on organized counter-attacks to restore defensive positions, against them, the Germans only response had been to thicken the garrisons of their lines (to the delight of the British artillery) and to move the counter-attack formations closer for a quicker response. In this third of Plumer's measured blows, it merely created horrendous losses for a German army reeling from a string of tactical defeats.

This is the first battle in the campaign where one can say that the Dominion troops (three Australian and one New Zealand divisions) played the principal role, but they were supported by eight British divisions – the 4th, 11th (Northern), 29th and 48th (South Midlands) on their left, and the 5th, 7th, 21st and 37th on their right. Once again vital ground was captured. Tyne Cot Cemetery stands on the Broodseinde ridge and any visitor will appreciate the tactical importance of this dominating position. Tanks did great service on this day; 4,000 prisoners flowed into the cages, bringing the total for the 'three steps' to over 10,000. Ludendorff admitted to extraordinarily severe losses; many British observers said they had never seen so many German corpses on a battlefield. The so-called counter-attack divisions had to be fed into the German line to stop it cracking wide open.

A sense of excitement mounted at the headquarters of the B.E.F. and both Second and Fifth Army. The cavalry divisions were put on the alert; other reserve divisions were closed up. The Germans were generally considered to be on the edge of collapse and preparations for the next blow were pushed ahead. And then the true price for the delay in opening the campaign in the summer had to be paid. The weather broke on the evening of 4 October and got steadily worse. The troops forming up for the next attack were thoroughly drenched and exhausted before they began.

Though II ANZAC Corps was the main attack formation for this Battle of Poelcappelle (9 October), it went in with one Australian division (2nd) and two British divisions – 49th (West Riding) and 66th (2nd East Lancashire). They were supported by a further seven British divisions – the Guards, 4th, 5th, 7th and 29th of the Regular Army and the 11th (Northern) and 48th (South Midlands). The artillery programme, fired by guns on increasingly unstable platforms and with shells exploding ineffectually in saturated ground, was a serious disappointment to infantry well used by now to walking onto their objective lines behind crushing barrages. No previous attack organized by the Second Army in the war had such an unfavourable start. The attackers were shocked to see the extent of new German barbed-wire entanglements, larger and more complex than anything previously encountered. Many divisions barely made it to their first objective. The supporting divisions of Fifth Army (Guards, 4th, 11th, 29th and 48th) did slightly better, but that is a relative term in this unhappy development of the campaign.

The First Battle of Passchendaele fought on 12 October was meant to be the last big effort to secure the high ground in and around the village of that name (if one is to take the three objective lines set for the day at all seriously, that is). In the pouring rain, which rendered the artillery singularly ineffective, the main attack by Australians on the right broke down completely. In the centre three justly-proud and famous formations – the New Zealand, 9th (Scottish) and 18th (Eastern) Divisions – barely progressed a hundred yards and all fell woefully short of their first objectives; for all of them a uniquely unpleasant experience. Only on the left was progress made to fulfil much reduced objectives – the Guards and 4th British Divisions doing most of what was asked of them, and in between them that splendid, unsung 'workhorse', the 17th (Northern) Division, actually pushing beyond its final target. (In the featureless swamp to which the battlefield was reduced they probably couldn't recognize any of these 'lines' at all !) This depressing picture should not blind us to the fact that the German army was also suffering greatly in these appalling conditions. The state of their morale is illustrated by the incident in which, having been by-passed unnoticed by the first attacking wave, ninety Germans emerged from a concrete shelter and surrendered to three unarmed soldiers of the 7th Lincolns (17th Division) who were carrying forward baskets of messenger pigeons !

Three more British divisions were in action on 22 October, a day of drizzle rather than heavy rain. All the commanders in the Salient understood that their men were nearing the limit of their endurance; any objectives set were very modest in nature. The 18th (Eastern), 34th and 35th Divisions each made small gains, usually to clear out particularly troublesome machine-gun nests in their sectors; all provoked fierce enemy counter-attacks.

Having gone so far towards securing the highest ground overlooking the Ypres salient, it is understandable why the British high command wanted to make one last effort to gain a position from which the campaign could be 'safely' shut down for the winter. With this in mind, the Canadian Corps was brought up from the Lens area and was used as the principal attack formation in the series of actions between 26 October and 10 November known collectively as the Second Battle of Passchendaele.

They got off to a difficult start on 26 October, a day of unrelenting rain. On the right, the 5th and 7th British Divisions attacked down the Menin Road towards the village of Gheluvelt, making very little progress into this, the very heart of the German defensive system. Two Canadian divisions made slight advances on the main axis of the attack. To the left, four more British divisions attacked, all employing only one brigade, as if they realized that the infantry were in for a hard time and it was best to conserve as much of their strength as possible. The 63rd (Royal Naval) Division alone made some small gains. The 58th (2nd/1st London), 57th (2nd West Lancashire) and 50th (Northumbrian) Divisions ended the day back on their start lines. The 57th reported being stopped by an 'impassable morass', which tells us all we need to know about the conditions these men had to endure.

On 30 October, a day entirely free of rainfall, two Canadian divisions made important gains and they were well-supported by the 58th and 63rd Divisions on their left. It should be pointed out that, during these terribly difficult days of battle, we do know from the important after-action reports that most formations prepared carefully, there were many examples of the infantry using their well-rehearsed battle drill, the skilled integration of the 'firepower' and 'manoeuvre' sections of the platoon, to reduce powerful enemy strong points even in the absence of good artillery support.

On subsequent and still rain-free days, the 50th and 63rd Divisions kept up the pressure on the Germans and, by small scale, limited operations, seized further strong points. On 3 November, the 63rd Division made small gains but the two Canadian divisions could not hold their ground. It was on 6 November that the Canadians (two divisions) finally cleared the village and eastern crest of the Passchendaele ridge, well-supported by the 5th British Division on their left. It might be noted in passing that these two days were the only ones in the whole campaign where the number of Dominion divisions attacking exceeded those of the British.

The last day of the campaign was symbolic in various ways, with the 1st Canadian and 1st British Divisions attacking side by side, in torrential rain. They just about took their first objectives; further progress was impossible. The sorry state of the attacking infantry is conveyed in a famous incident concerning the 2nd Royal Munster Fusiliers. They were falling back under powerful German counter-attacks and their firearms were hopelessly fouled with mud. The 'fighting Irish' resorted to pelting the enemy with balls of mud, which, mercifully, the Germans mistook for hand grenades, causing them to go to ground long enough for the Munsters to fall back and consolidate their defences !

The lasting impression of the 44 British and 10 Dominion divisions engaged in this protracted campaign is of their extraordinary ability just to keep going, no matter how difficult the conditions could be. While their French allies were being nursed back to operational efficiency after their 'acts of collective disobedience' earlier in the year, and long before the Americans would make any meaningful contribution in the chief theatre of war, the British Army kept up an offensive that sucked 88 German divisions into battle. In a proper awareness of what was endured by the attackers, we should not underestimate the punishment to which those Germans were subjected.

Of the British Expeditionary Force, there were engaged eight divisions of the Regular Army, twenty three of the New Army and thirteen of the Territorial Force (eight of these were 'First Line', and five of the 'Second Line'). These included three Scottish, two Irish, one Welsh and thirty English divisions, the latter including three of Londoners alone. For the record we should note that eight of the infantry divisions serving on the Western Front were not used in the autumn campaign – 2nd, 6th, 12th (Eastern), 31st, 32nd, 40th, 46th (North Midland) and 62nd (2nd West Riding). Five of these were subsequently engaged in the Cambrai fighting.

The 44 British divisions were involved in a total of 103 days of battle;

an average of 2.3 per division. The ten Dominion divisions were engaged 27 times in all; an average of 2.7 per division. This hardly suggests that the latter shouldered an undue share of the battle or that they were seen as elite assault formations whose presence on the field guaranteed success. Rather it is interesting to see how the British divisions seemed to go into these battles with their usual steady disposition, all but two of them veteran formations with several marked successes to their credit. (This was the first major battle for the 57th and 66th Divisions). Typical is the self-assessment of one of the component battalions of the 55th (West Lancashire) Division, the 1st/4th Loyal North Lancs in their battalion history: "We enjoyed our stay at Andrehem, knowing that our last battle had raised us to the status of Storm Troops and that when we moved up again it would be for another attack and not back to the demoralizing influences of trench life".[8] It is interesting that they select a 'Germanic' phrase to describe their status but this is clearly a unit that sees itself as inferior to no one on the Western or any other Front. The battle narratives show just how well the attacking divisions could perform even under the most difficult circumstances. On many occasions all the officers and warrant officers leading an attack were killed or wounded, and the sergeants and corporals took over the leadership of their companies and platoons and carried out the tasks assigned to the battalion. This shows how the strictures of the new training manuals, that all the men should know and understand the plan of attack, were taken to heart and put into practice by an increasingly-confident army.

The ethos of the whole army was that of the old Regular Army; the pre-war Territorial Force subscribed to it; the volunteers of the New Army, made up of 'service' battalions of the old regiments, aspired to it. The primary (some would say 'primal') loyalty was to the regiment, which the British army had always fostered but had become especially important since the Cardwell reforms of the 1870's when all the regiments were paired and named, and allocated to a specific region or locality for recruiting and identification. While its critics might say that the regimental system made the army too rigid and prey to a seething mass of resentments towards 'other cap-badges', there can be no doubt that intense loyalty to the regiment and its traditions made for a fighting force of quite extraordinary doggedness and determination.

But the soldiers of 1914 – 1918 had another organization to which they belonged which could, under various circumstances, command a certain sense of loyalty. The units were organized into divisions, were moved about as divisions and committed to battle as divisions. Apart from a spell in 1915 when five Regular divisions swapped a brigade with five New Army divisions, and the great upheaval early in 1918 when the infantry component was reduced from twelve to nine battalions, the division was a fairly stable organization, which men could think of as 'their own'. The first six infantry divisions of the B.E.F. had served together for some years before 1914; the fourteen divisions of the Territorial Force all had very strong regional connections reflected in their names. The first twelve divisions of the New Army, in two groups of six, were given names to foster a sense of identity but the idea was dropped subsequently. It is doubtful if men could relate to general names like 'Northern' (11th and 17th), 'Eastern' (12th and 18th), or 'Western' (13th and 19th). The two 'Light' divisions (14th and 20th), made up of light infantry and rifle battalions, were clearly intended to hark back to the days of Wellington. Where the designation was purely national, 'Scottish' for the 9th and 15th, 'Irish' for the 10th and 16th, the sense of belonging was considerably enhanced. Lloyd George's bid to create a Welsh army corps may only have produced one 'Welsh' division, the 38th, but it fostered its 'Welshness' through its insignia, mascots and the like. A very special case was the mass-embodiment of the Ulster Volunteer Force into the army as the 36th (Ulster) Division. Perhaps the division that fostered its own image most assiduously was the Highland Division (the 51st, T.F.), which even went to the extent of spreading a story about a captured secret German document putting the 51st at the head of a list of British divisions to be most feared ! This list has never been produced in any printed work or archive !! Tommy Atkins' sardonic sense of humour insisted that the HD of the divisional badge stood for 'Harper's Duds' !!!

This opens up two other aspects of 'belonging' to a division. Most divisions designed their own badge to enhance unit cohesion. Where the badge was actually worn by all units, it seems to have added to the self-esteem of the men. We have references to this effect in the 17th, 29th, 30th, 36th, 38th, 40th, 51st and 55th Divisions. Of particular interest is the way the 19th Division awarded the right to wear the 'White Butterfly' to battalions that had performed a fine feat of arms. An individual commander could also become an object of affection or regard. Official unit histories tend to suggest that all commanders were 'beloved', and individual memoirs do not often mention a figure as lofty as the Major-General, G.O.C. But the 41st Division certainly had time to get used to Sidney Lawford (it is the only division in the B.E.F. never to change its commander throughout the war); the Highland Division did like 'Uncle Harper'; even after he had left the 18th Division, his soldiers still tried to do things the way Sir Ivor Maxse would have liked.[9] We are, of course, reminded by Frank Richards that the teetotaller general who denied the rum ration to the men of the 33rd Division was not a figure of great affection to his soldiers.

In the final analysis, the test of battle would determine the sense of self-worth of the division, and how it was perceived by G.H.Q. A great deal of new research work is being conducted into the battle performance of the divisions of the B.E.F.[10] It is already clear that certain divisions had a consistently high reputation in the army. (Such a list would include the Guards, 9th, 18th, 29th and New Zealand Divisions, to which most veterans would add the division in which they served.) Most divisions were thoroughly reliable, but we are still left with the mystery as to why several of them never produced a divisional history to celebrate their deeds. (The

1st, 3rd, 21st, 24th and 58th [2nd/1st London] Divisions all fall into this category). Some divisions do not seem to have been used in battle as often as others. How significant is their terrible experience on the 1 July 1916 that both the 31st and 46th (North Midlands) Divisions should fall into this category ? Much research remains to be done in this field.

We are left with an army, initially of volunteers, later conscripted, that rarely gets the credit it deserves for its ultimate victory. Faced by the single most powerful military machine in the world, the men of 1914–1918 fully understood the dire consequences of defeat and determined to see the war through to the end. Their ordeal at Third Ypres is much talked of; the ordeal they inflicted on the enemy is not. Whether these men should have been asked to attempt some of the things they were expected to do, or why the battle was delayed at the start and persisted with at the end, lies outside the remit of this essay, and is taken up by other contributors. The clear victories of late September and early October showed what they could achieve when they had good preparation, good artillery support and good weather.

Notes

1 WO95/2566 39th Division General Staff report on Operations of 31st July, 1917. PRO Kew.
2 Edmonds, J. *Military Operations: France and Flanders 1917 Vol. II* p. 189.
3 Ingelfield, V. *The History of the 20th (Light) Division* p.159.
4 Falls, C. *The History of the 36th (Ulster) Division* p.116.
5 Ward, D. *The 56th Division (1st London Territorial Division)* p.160.
6 Mitchinson, K. *Gentlemen and Officers: The Impact and Experience of War on a Territorial Regiment 1914–1918* p.170.
7 Carrington, C. *Soldier From the Wars Returning* p.190.
8 Anon. *The War History of the 1st/4th Battalion the Loyal North Lancashire Regiment* p.81.
9 Simkins, P. *The War Experience of a Typical Kitchener Division*, in Cecil, H. & Liddle, P.H. *Facing Armageddon: The First World War Experienced* p.302.
10 The SHLM (Simkins-Hammond-Lee-McCarthy) Battle Assessment Project recruits volunteers to study the performance of individual divisions on the Western Front. Those interested in assisting this work should contact Bryn Hammond or Chris McCarthy at the Imperial War Museum, Lambeth Road, London SE1 6HZ.

37. The 'Anzac Express' – a light train loaded with Australian and New Zealand troops (A.Bayne, Liddle Collection) Chapter 12, 15, 17

38. Canadian soldiers of 100th Bn CEF at a training camp in the UK, many of them destined to serve at Third Ypres. Sgt A.D.Wills (seated 2nd left) went on to serve with the 78th Battalion, which, as part of 4th Canadian Division, took part in the second assault on Passchendaele village. (A.D.Wills, Liddle Collection) Chapter 16

39. Canadian platoon attack training demonstration, Shorncliffe, Sussex, in September 1917. (National Archives of Canada [PA 4773]) Chapter 16

40. Canadian wounded being brought in, Passchendaele November 1917. (National Archives of Canada [PA 2086]) Chapter 16

41. A Canadian field dressing station, with a large calibre shell bursting in the distance. (A.D. Wills, Liddle Collection) Chapter 16

42. This sturdily constructed German pillbox, reinforced with pieces of railway track, now shelters New Zealand troops in Polygon Wood. (A. Bayne, Liddle Collection) Chapter 17

43. This publicity photograph for 'New Zealand at the Front', the NZEF annual for 1917, does not mask the evident tiredness on the faces of the stretcher bearers. (H series, NZ Official, QE II Army Memorial Museum, Waiouru). Chapter 17

44. German prisoners evacuate the wounded, escorted by New Zealanders carrying empty water cans from the line, near Spree Farm, Gravenstafel, 4 October 1917). (H Series, NZ Official, QE II Army Memorial Museum, Waiouru). Chapter 17

45. The price of the October fighting, a New Zealand aid post, Gravenstafel, 4 October 1917. (H Series, NZ Official, QE II Army Memorial Museum, Waiouru). Chapter 17

46. A New Zealand Brigade rehearsing the worm formation for an attack in May 1917. Note the Light Trench Mortar team nearest the camera. Each formation and unit rehearsed all aspects of the attack so that on zero hour 'every individual taking part in the attack was thoroughly conversant not only with his own task, but with those of the others working on either flank.' (H Series, NZ Official, QE II Army Memorial Museum, Waiouru) Chapter 17

47. Major-General Sir Andrew Russell inspecting New Zealanders. Russell knew that success in war demanded professionalism and that is what he imposed on the New Zealand Division. (H Series, NZ Official, QE II Army Memorial Museum, Waiouru) Chapter 17

48. A sector of the battlefield near the Menin Road. (A.H. Simpson, Liddle Collection)

49. Men of the South African Scottish in support trenches, September 1917. (South African National Museum of Military History, Johannesburg. T2925) Chapter 18

50. A South African working party, in the rear constructing duck boards. (South African National Museum of Military History, Johannesburg. T2781) Chapter 18

51. South African troops crossing duck board tracks, September 1917. (South
African National Museum of Military History, Johannesburg. T2923)
Chapter 18

52. A shell bursting in
Polygon Wood,
September 1917.
(A. Bayne, Liddle
Collection)

Chapter 15

The Australians at Passchendaele

Ashley Ekins

In late October 1917, a regimental medical officer recorded his experiences in the unsuccessful assault on Passchendaele Ridge on 12 October. Writing from London, where he was convalescing from a bullet wound received during the attack, he described in harrowing detail how his unit of '750 men went over the top and less than 50 came back'.[1] First, he recalled the painful progress of his unit towards the front line, the men heavily laden under extra bandoliers, bombs, picks and shovels and struggling through the heavy mud: 'No one looked forward to it, the weather had turned very bad and there was no time to reconnoitre the ground'. They marched in single file through the pitch black night for five miles across a 'trackless bog'. This freshly captured ground was, 'simply a mass of shell holes and everlasting mud, raining most of the time, shelled at intervals, never going 20 steps without a halt, occasionally striking duck boards, but soon knee deep in the mud again'.

Finally they reached the front line, only to discover that 'there were no trenches and the Huns and ourselves were facing each other along a line of shell holes'. The rain was almost continuous for much of that day and through the following night as companies began forming up along their jumping-off tape for the attack the next morning. His unit went over the top at zero hour, 5.25 a.m. on 12 October. Within the first few minutes most of the officers and N.C.O.s were killed or wounded, leaving few to lead the men. The writer, waiting in the front line to establish a regimental aid post in a captured pill box, described the attack as:

> The most terrible thing I have ever seen for you could see them fall, see them blown high into the air and still pressing on, taking cover where possible, and then a bayonet rush again ... I waited for three quarters of an hour nearly for the barrage to lift and then it became obvious that we were being held up and were not advancing – and those cursed machine guns had not ceased.

He closed his letter with a personal revelation of the anguish he still suffered from the experience: 'Oh! I wish it would all finish – all the good fellows going, and the end not yet in sight ... Since the 12th all that ridge we fought so hard for has been taken but at a price'.

This first-hand account epitomizes the popular perception of both the battle of Passchendaele and Australian involvement in it. The name became 'one to shudder at' in the words of the Australian official historian.[2]

The five divisions of the Australian Imperial Force (AIF) were all engaged in the campaign and, like the four divisions of the Canadian Expeditionary Force and the single division of the New Zealand Expeditionary Force, the Australians were increasingly used as shock troops. In the eleven major attacks of the Third Ypres campaign, five were spearheaded by Australian divisions and four were spearheaded by Canadian divisions. This honour carried a price. The Australians suffered a total of 38,000 casualties, half of them in the final, gruelling eight weeks of the campaign.[3]

The Australian divisions, like the New Zealanders, were exhausted when they were relieved by the Canadians in mid-October.[4] Passchendaele was their final round in the battles of 1917, a year considered by historian Bill Gammage, 'the low point of the war' for Australian soldiers on the Western Front.[5] In 1917 Australian troops spent their longest period, eleven months in total, in the front line. They suffered their worst defeat and lost their largest number of prisoners in the twin battles of Bullecourt in April and May. Then they suffered their largest number of casualties in a single battle during the attacks on Passchendaele Ridge in October and by the end of the year the Australians had incurred more battle casualties than in any other year of the war.[6] Another historian has claimed: 'The most sustained fighting in the AIF's experience occurred in 1917 and accounted for 40 per cent of Australia's dead in the whole war'.[7] Third Ypres seemed the dismal culmination of this experience.

Yet the Australian official historian Charles Bean considered that Third Ypres was for the Australians, 'in the main a successful offensive, at one stage brilliantly so'. Australian divisions attacked successfully in the battles of Menin Road, Polygon Wood and Broodseinde Ridge. Their losses were heavy, but lower than for the initial battles on the Somme in 1916, and in Bean's judgement, 'far more had been effected, with less agony to those who achieved it'.[8] Bean acknowledged however, that Australian losses in Third Ypres led to serious misgivings by the end of 1917 about the future of the AIF: there were concerns that the exhausted Australian force might have 'passed its zenith of achievement'; that 1918 'might find the Australian soldier past the zenith of his quality'; and, that without sufficient reinforcement with fresh troops there would be an inevitable deterioration in Australian soldiers' morale.[9]

In the event, these misgivings were not borne out by the events of the following year. Yet 1917, and Third Ypres in particular, continue to be viewed as the low points of the war for the Australians. Clearly, several questions require re-examination. Was Passchendaele in fact the lowest point of Australian soldiers' morale? If so, how did this affect the Australians' combat performance, especially during their final, hapless assaults on Passchendaele Ridge? And what brought about the recovery of the Australian divisions from these depths to play their important part in the victorious battles of the second half of 1918? The starting point in exploring these issues must be to ask, what was the state of morale amongst Australian troops on the eve of the Third Ypres battles?

Australian soldiers had experienced a remorseless initiation into the realities of warfare on the Western Front in the second half of 1916. In their first battles on the Somme, four AIF divisions had suffered over 38,000 battle casualties in five months from July to November; most notably, in seven weeks during July and August the Australian divisions had suffered over 28,000 casualties in their assaults at Fromelles, Pozières and Mouquet Farm.[10] The morale of Australian soldiers plummeted in late 1916 as the final attacks on the Somme waned in the deteriorating weather of November. Some men sought escape through malingering, desertion to the enemy lines, self-inflicted wounds and even suicide.[11] Through the harshest winter in northern France in 40 years, the Australians experienced a sharp increase in sickness rates as they held their sector of the front line – over 20,000 Australian soldiers were evacuated suffering from trench feet, frostbite and exhaustion.[12]

The battles of the first half of 1917 exacted a further toll on the Australians. The first battle of Bullecourt in April cost the AIF 3,000 casualties – the heaviest proportionate loss by any Australian formation in a single action – mostly inflicted upon the Australian 4th Division, 'a magnificent instrument recklessly shattered in the performance of an impracticable task', in Charles Bean's words.[13] Another three Australian divisions were flung against the Hindenburg Line in the second battle of Bullecourt in May. Despite the rout of some 400 men in one Brigade, the Australians captured their objectives, but at the high cost of 7,500 casualties.[14] The Bullecourt battles had three immediate impacts upon the strength and morale of the AIF. First, the blood-letting in the four Australian divisions involved forced them to draw heavily on their reserves, leading directly to the disbandment of the 6th Australian Division then forming in England. Second, their unhappy experiences at Bullecourt, in Bean's view, 'shook the confidence of Australian soldiers in the capacity of the British command'.[15] Third, the three hard-worked Australian divisions of I Anzac Corps, which had held front line positions almost continuously from July 1916, were withdrawn for four months' well-deserved rest, refitting and training from mid-May until September.[16] The 4th Australian Division, which had been under the same long strain, received only one month's rest before it was transferred to II Anzac Corps. This Corps was committed to the Battle of Messines in June.[17]

The capture of the Messines Ridge by Plumer's Second Army secured the British right flank for the forthcoming Flanders operations; this overture to Third Ypres is generally regarded as one of the greatest set-piece victo-

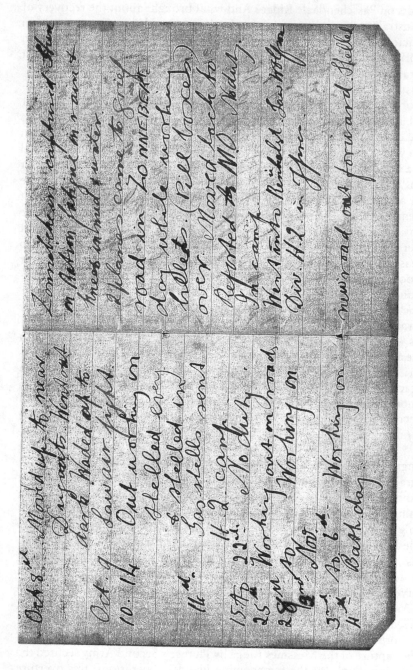

(xvi) 8 October: "Went out on ration fatigue in rain and dark. Waded up to knees in mud and water". The diary of Private Hickman, 2nd Pioneers, 2nd Australian Division. (*L. Hickman, Liddle Collection*)

ries of the war.[18] Plumer's thorough preparations, an effective artillery barrage, and the detonation of nineteen huge mines which annihilated the enemy front lines, all contributed to the success. But Messines was still a costly operation with losses almost equal on both sides. Of the 26,000 total British casualties, more than half were incurred by II Anzac Corps. The two Australian divisions in II Anzac together suffered almost 7,000 casualties, 2,677 in the already depleted 4th Division and 4,122 in the fresh but previously untried 3rd Division.[19] The latter, which had trained in England for six months and had been nurtured in the quiet Armentières sector since February 1917, suffered 500–1,000 casualties from a German gas bombardment on the night before the assault; consequently, some of its battalions went into the Messines attack ten per cent under strength. The 3rd Division also, like most of the other divisions engaged, suffered the additional strain and casualties from both German and misdirected British artillery bombardments.[20] Despite its success, Messines pointed to the need for closer co-ordination of artillery and infantry assaults and revealed the limitations of even the most thoroughly prepared attack.[21] The later phases of the battle also gave a foretaste of the ferocious fighting to storm German pill boxes which would characterize Third Ypres.[22]

The overall state of morale amongst Australian soldiers on the eve of the Third Ypres battles can be fairly accurately gauged. Three divisions (the 1st, 2nd and 5th) had been rested from combat and brought up to strength with reinforcements. Months of vigorous training and refitting had brought them to the peak of preparedness. But even in these divisions Charles Bean estimated that 'the troops had seen too much hard fighting to welcome the prospect of more'. Moreover, there was a belief growing amongst Australian soldiers that their divisions were being overworked in comparison with some British divisions.[23] The freshly-blooded 3rd Division was considered the most 'tamed and tractable' of all the Australian divisions and was said to suffer from fewer of the problems of indiscipline which plagued Australian formations.[24] But the loss of over 4,000 casualties at Messines had been a heavy blow and it was compounded when the 3rd Division lost a further 550 casualties in a single brigade during a feint attack on 31 July in support of the opening of the Third Ypres battle.

The morale of the 4th Australian Division remained the least certain. The 4th had the reputation of being 'the toughest of all the Australian divisions', but on the eve of Third Ypres it was, according to Bean, 'at its lowest ebb'.[25] The exhausted 4th Division had gone through more heavy fighting in 1917 than any other Australian division. It had been rested for one month after its disastrous attack with tanks at First Bullecourt and it was again briefly withdrawn to the rear area after Messines. To make good its losses the division had been 'heavily diluted with new reinforcements', 3,400 men after Bullecourt and 6,000 after Messines, bringing its strength up to the level of most British divisions – but still below that of the other Australian and dominion divisions. As an indicator of low morale in the

4th Division, Bean records that the problem of absence without leave, then 'troublesome in all Australian divisions', was especially acute in the 4th at this time.[26] On the positive side, in late August the 4th Division was transferred to I Anzac Corps, joining the three rested Australian divisions, so that Anzac divisions could be sent into battle in pairs – a first step towards attaining the aim sought by the Australian government of creating independent Australian formations under Australian command.[27]

The Third Ypres campaign opened in mid-July with a preliminary bombardment of unprecedented scale. Over 3,000 guns – one gun for every 6 yards of front – fired over four and a quarter million shells on the German defences over fifteen days. The infantry assaults delivered by Gough's Fifth Army steadily tackled the lower features east of Ypres, beginning with Pilckem Ridge on 31 July, the Gheluvelt Plateau on 10 August and Langemarck on 16 August. But British artillery support proved inadequate either to cover further advances or to suppress German artillery resistance. The offensive stalled on 27 August as heavy rains combined with the artillery destruction of the Flanders drainage system to cause extensive flooding, reducing the battlefield to a quagmire.[28]

Aside from the brief feint attack by the 3rd Division on 31 July, the Australian infantry were not involved in this first month of the offensive, which was predominantly an artillery battle. However, most of the Australian divisional field artillery and heavy batteries were deployed in the Fifth Army in this opening stage. They incurred heavy casualties, exposed as they often were to intensive German counter-battery fire. At the end of August the Medical Officer of the 7th Australian Field Artillery Brigade recorded the strain on the gunners during this period: 'all ranks are showing effects of constant strain ... men have been parading to me of late from Debility and evident inability to stand shell-fire any longer. The Officers are showing the effects of the constant tension'. At the same time, the Medical Officer of the 8th Australian Field Artillery Brigade reported:

> Cases are becoming increasingly frequent of men breaking down in health and becoming nervous, due to the long and continuous strain they have been under. Number[s] of them are being constantly sent to the Wagon Lines by their Officers because they have been unable to stand shell fire and perform their duties ... this state of affairs is due to the long and continual nervous and bodily strain to which these men have been subjected. As an example, at the sick parade of one Battery to-day there were 12 men whose only ailment was as above mentioned, and this is typical of all Batteries.[29]

Total British casualties by the end of August amounted to almost 70,000. The artillery suffered over 9000 casualties in the first 23 days of the battle.[30] The opening phase of the Third Ypres campaign had failed utterly by late-August and Gough's vision of 'semi-open warfare' was soon caustically derided as 'Semi-Immobile Operations' by one corps commander.[31] Gough had acquired the reputation of being profligate with the lives of his troops, providing insufficient artillery cover for their attacks, and even exhorting against relieving divisions in the line too frequently in order to avoid unnecessary waste of fresh divisions.[32]

Australian infantry divisions entered Third Ypres after Haig passed control to General Plumer of the Second Army in late-August. During this period the campaign entered its more hopeful second phase and the Australians achieved their greatest victories. Plumer conducted a series of comparatively successful attacks against the higher ridges of the Gheluvelt Plateau through the dryer weather of September, employing his methodical 'step by step' tactics: under copious artillery support, the infantry attacked limited objectives in advances of no more than 1,500 yards at each step; they then consolidated their gains against enemy counter-attacks while waiting for the artillery to advance to new positions to support successive advances.

German developments of 'elastic defence' in depth had made these 'bite and hold' tactics the only tenable offensive option. In late 1916, the Germans had begun to thin out their front lines and deepen their defence zones in response to British improvements in artillery techniques and the emergence of the tank on the battlefield.[33] By mid–1917, the German defences consisted of a thinly held front outpost line established on reverse slope positions. In the muddy wastes of Flanders they largely abandoned their flooded trench lines and occupied a chain of fortified strong points, concrete blockhouses and pill boxes, with small groups of men from platoon to company strength. These strong points were arranged to give mutual support through interlocking fields of machine-gun fire. Barbed wire was deployed to funnel attacking troops into these zones of fire. The German artillery was located far back in the rear lines and protected by gun emplacements; the main reserves of infantry were also massed out of shell range ready to be employed in counter-attacks.[34]

On 20 September, in the first of his 'steps', Plumer launched his assault on the Menin Road. The attack was preceded by a five-day artillery bombardment which delivered a concentration of shells on the German lines two to three times that of the opening bombardment of 31 July.[35] The infantry then advanced under the protection of an intense barrage of five different belts of fire 1,000 yards deep. The 1st and 2nd Australian Divisions attacked side by side in the centre of eleven divisions of the Second and Fifth Armies. This was the first time two Australian divisions had attacked side by side and, according to Bean, they 'were consequently elated with a confidence and enthusiasm which British leaders did not, at that time, understand'.[36] The attack was an overwhelming success.[37] The Australian battalions 'leap-frogged' one another at particular stages in order to maintain the momentum of their attack which consisted of short, rapid advances, briefly halted by bloody incidents of pillbox storming.[38] Within three hours almost all the objectives were captured across the entire eight-mile front of the British advance. German counter-attacks were rapidly crushed by artillery fire. But even this carefully orchestrated victory

15th Sunday after Trinity.

W. Gambles: S.R. Snow; Simpson
were killed.

THURSDAY 20th.

Hop out, and lads done well. Hogg
pushed up to a pill box in Glencorse
Wood. Collected some fine souvenirs
there; Lachmatory gas in one
Pill Box. Two wounded Fritze
in one; + helped them to the
dressing station.

FRIDAY 21st.

Heavy shelling at night. S.O.S
went up; and it was a grand
sight to see all the flashes.
+ hear the roar of the Artillery
Left the Pill Box at 3 pm for
Dickybusch. Rode back in a
Motor Lorry.

SATURDAY 22nd.

Fair amount of work in the
Office. Lads relieved
at night time; + were in
great spirits. Letters from
D.Cameron + McPam

(xvii) "Hop out, and lads done well". The September diary of Private Radnell,
8th Bn A.I.F. up in the front line – a pillbox – in between battalion office work
duties. *(G.A.Radnell, Liddle Collection)*

234

still carried a high cost – 21,000 British casualties (probably equalling German losses) for the capture of less than six square miles of ground.[39] The two Australian divisions together suffered over 5,000 casualties, almost one-quarter of this total.[40] But fed on victory, the morale of the Australians remained high.

The offensive was resumed with Plumer's second step on 26 September. Two Australian divisions, together with five British divisions, attacked at Polygon Wood. In a repeat of the attack one week earlier, the paired 4th and 5th Australian Divisions (who had together relieved the 1st and 2nd Divisions) comprised the central apex of the assaulting wave. On the eve of the attack, the commander of the 5th Division endeavoured to heighten his troops' aggressive spirit with the news that they were attacking a German division which had committed atrocities in Alsace.[41] But the 4th Division was not so easily roused. In some battalions of this heavily-worked division, the announcement of their commitment to the Ypres offensive had been greeted with jeering.[42] The tensions within one battalion, the 14th (4th Brigade) were perhaps typical: when the battalion was informed on 4 September that their promised rest had been cancelled, 'the news that they would be going back into battle so soon was not well received at any level'.[43] Shortly before the battle, the Brigade commander further inflamed the officers and men of the 14th with his tactless criticism that, 'the whole bloody battalion were dopey'. Most officers of the battalion immediately sent in letters of resignation in protest and the commander was forced to apologise publicly. As the battalion had merely two weeks' further training before their move forward to the attack, such disharmony came at a critical stage in their preparation.[44] The 14th Battalion went into the Polygon Wood battle seriously riven, relationships between the commanding officer and his company commanders having almost totally broken down. From one officer's account, it seems that the company commanders effectively led the battalion and held it together during the attack, so ensuring its success.[45]

At Polygon Wood the attackers were assisted once again by intensive artillery preparation and a creeping barrage which was, for the Australians, the most effective that had ever protected them.[46] An Australian officer of engineers observed:

> We have been in again though the recent fighting is entirely different to the Somme last year. There the Germans fought hand to hand and the assault was only the beginning of a swaying bayonet and bomb fight lasting with intervals for a couple of days. Now our artillery is so perfect and so tremendous that we practically catch all the Germans who surrender at once or are too dead to do so.[47]

Once again victory was swift. Nearly all the objectives across the five-mile attack front were captured by mid-morning. German counter-attacks were destroyed by artillery and machine-gun fire. The morale of Australian troops was boosted by their capture not only of their own objectives, but also the ground assigned to British units which had not kept up with the attack.[48] But, as on the Menin Road, victory at Polygon Wood was costly: total British losses were over 15,000 casualties, over one-third of them in the Australian divisions, for the capture of less than four square miles of ground.[49] Moreover, the shallow advances made in Plumer's step by step tactics did not permit the capture of the German artillery which continued to take its toll on the concentrated attacking forces; and the British guns remained unavailable for counter-battery fire while being moved forward to support the next step.[50]

That next step, Plumer's attack on Broodseinde Ridge, was launched on 4 October. The 1st, 2nd and 3rd Australian Divisions together with the New Zealand Division assaulted at the centre of a twelve division attack. This was the only occasion when four Anzac divisions attacked side by side and according to Bean, 'the already high spirit of these troops was greatly enhanced by this concentration'.[51] The men of the 1st and 2nd Australian Divisions in particular, in contrast to their experience in the Somme battles in 1916, were buoyed by their success at Menin Road, and again, wrote Bean, they 'advanced to this second operation in exuberant spirits'.[52] However, misfortune struck the 1st and 2nd Divisions on the morning of the attack when a heavy German bombardment fell on their crowded front lines – about one man in seven was killed or wounded before zero hour. The Australian battalions then attacked straight into an enemy counter-attack but quickly shattered the Germans.[53] In places the Australian units encountered fierce German resistance and the fighting was of the nature of vicious hand-to-hand conflicts and bombing duels.[54] Despite inadequate artillery cover in some quarters, the advancing troops captured most of their objectives across an eight-mile wide front. Due to the German decision to hold their front line in greater strength just prior to the battle, their losses were heavy, including some 5,000 taken prisoner.[55] Total British casualties were also high at over 20,000 in return for a 1,000 yard advance of the front line; Australian casualties, over 6,400, were again almost one-third of the total.[56]

The battle of Broodseinde has generally been considered a resounding victory, sometimes with the qualification that the opportunity to exploit it was lost due to the deteriorating weather.[57] However it was, according to Trevor Wilson, 'in every sense a limited success': the Germans still held much of the ridge; the casualty bill was mounting relentlessly; and the Germans were successfully modifying their tactics in response to Plumer's attacks.[58] In fact, Broodseinde demonstrated the limitations of Plumer's 'bite and hold' operations. Successes had to be followed up by periods of consolidation as guns and ammunition were brought forward and re-ranged, units were replenished with reinforcements and communication and supply were re-established. These thorough preparations between attacks were not possible under the pressures of Haig's schedule for rapid advances; moreover, they relied upon continuing fine weather.[59]

As to the morale and performance of Australian soldiers, Bean con-

sidered that the Australians at Broodseinde, 'had never fought better'.[60]
One man's experiences provide some confirmation of this view together
with some insights into what the battle entailed for an ordinary
infantryman. A Lewis gunner, Private William Vincent of the 21st
Battalion AIF, laconically recorded in his diary his unit's experiences in the
attack of 4 October: 'At 5 AM a very heavy artillery barrage started and we
went forward about 2 miles, our lads falling in dozens and German prisoners coming in hundreds. We got as far as we were supposed to go and
dug in for our lives and held it ... we lost heavily'.[61]

Adding to their discomfort, rain had begun to fall on the night of 3
October and a steady drizzle continued during the attack. There was no
respite for his section on the following day:

We were under a heavy barrage all day. One shell burst on the parapet
and knocked 6 of us down. We were shaky for some time, otherwise no
harm done. In the afternoon two of us with my [Lewis] gun went about
50 yards in front of our trench and made a strong post. We were
surrounded by m[achine]/guns and caught in our artillery so we got back
the best way we could, then we got relieved to fall back to [the] rear.

An apparent victory like Broodseinde Ridge could seem double-edged to
men at the sharp end of battle. On 6 October, in the aftermath of the battle,
Vincent mused on the cost:

We made dugouts for ourselves for the night. I was left to carry the
[Lewis] gun back by myself and had to go through mud up to my knees
Wet through and nothing to change [into] but had a little sleep. We
stopped in our dugout out of the rain. It cleared up in the afternoon so
I had to clean my gun. It was in a terrible state. Then I had some tea and
had a look round for some of my mates. Very few left this time.

In the three step by step attacks, the five Australian divisions lost a total
of almost 17,000 men – a casualty rate, notes Bill Gammage, equalling that
at Pozières in 1916, in return for a total advance of about 4200 yards.[62]
Thirteen Australian battalions lost over 200 casualties and two lost over
300 at Broodseinde.[63] One Australian soldier recalled that his battalion
came out of the Broodseinde battle only 150 strong, his company
numbered only 25, and there were merely two men left in his own
platoon.[64] An anger grew amongst some, at the near impossible difficulties
the terrain and weather now presented for the men ordered to carry out
these attacks. Australian official photographer, Captain Frank Hurley,
who followed the Australian advances to the crest of Broodseinde Ridge,
left a vivid written record which complements his photographs of the
battlesite. He recorded in his diary:

This shelled embankment of mud [along the route to Zonnebeke] was a
terrible sight. Every 20 paces or less lay a body. Some frightfully

mutilated, without legs, arms and heads and half covered in mud and slime ... The terrain had become one great slough. One dares not venture off the duckboard or he will surely become bogged, or sink in the quick-sand-like slime of rain-filled shell craters ... God knows how those red-tabbed blighters at headquarters (60 miles from the front) expect our men to gain such a strong position when they have to drag themselves through mud. Curse them! I'll swear they were not within 20 miles of the firing line when this attack was arranged, the ground is impassable ... The battlefield on which we won an advance of 1500 yards, was littered with bits of men, our own and Boche, and literally drenched with blood.[65]

Despite such dispiriting scenes, it seems that the morale of many soldiers was lifted by victory. A soldier in the 2nd Australian Battalion wrote home triumphantly about Broodseinde on a postcard bearing a cartoon illustration of a British tank crushing a mass of terrified German soldiers:

I am still alive and well and came out in one piece after the Battle of Oct 4 which we took part in. It was awful in the trenches on account of the rain but nevertheless we gave Fritz all we could give and as you know we pushed him back up in Flanders ... On the 2nd of Oct before we hopped over Fritz counter attacked and we all stood up on the parapet and we simply mowed them down. They ran away from us something like on the other side of card but more of it.[66]

Some soldiers were not so apparently unmoved by the slaughter of their enemy. A nineteen-year old private with the 8th Australian Battalion was so deeply shocked by the sight of the three German soldiers he killed while assaulting a pillbox at Broodseinde Ridge on 4 October, that the memory still haunted him nearly fifty years later. He recalled that, 'a German left the pillbox and began walking in my direction ... I aimed point-blank at his stomach and pressed the trigger. Down he went, on his right knee, and covered his face with his hands.'[67] He killed two more enemy soldiers in similar fashion as they emerged. After the pillbox had been rushed and captured, he examined the men he had shot and was depressed to find two of them appeared younger than himself while the first man he had shot, was still propped on one knee, with his hands covering his face.

Overall, the step by step advances had provided tangible victories and lifted the spirits of Australian soldiers. No such claims could be made about the final two assaults by the Australians in the Third Ypres campaign, the two unsuccessful attempts to capture Passchendaele Ridge on 9 and 12 October. In unceasing rain, the campaign was pressed, beyond realistic expectations, for a further month in an attempt to capture Passchendaele village and the ridge. Due mainly to the weather and its effects upon the battlefield, this last phase of the offensive, 'involved a quality of misery that almost beggars description'.[68] Australian soldiers were committed to this hapless venture almost to its closing days.

On 9 October in the first attempt (subsequently named 'the battle of Poelcappelle', after its secondary objective), the 2nd Australian Division, together with two British divisions, assaulted the slopes below Passchendaele village.[69] Continuous rain since 4 October had by now turned the battlefield into an impassable morass. Mud had also rendered most British offensive weapons useless: guns and tanks became bogged in it; infantrymen's weapons were clogged by it; high explosive shells were buried and smothered in it; mortars and guns sank in it when fired; and the impassable wasteland presented almost insurmountable difficulties in hauling matériel across it.[70]

Charles Bean, as Australian official war correspondent, attended a briefing given by Major-General Harington, Plumer's Chief of Staff, on the eve of the assault and recorded in his journal:

I believe the official attitude is that Passchendaele Ridge is so important that tomorrow's attack is worth making whether it succeeds or fails. Also Harington having fixed a day for the attack intensely dislikes going back on it especially once the troops are in position ... I suspect that they are making a great bloody experiment – a huge gamble and more than that: a deliberate attempt to see how it works. I think they are playing with the morale of their troops. Harington said that the top of the Ridge is sandy and as "dry as a bone'. I feel, and most of the correspondents feel, awfully anxious – terribly anxious – about tomorrow. They don't know the fight there was for the last ridge, those Major Generals back there; they don't know how nearly the Broodseinde crest held us up. They don't realise how much and desperately hard it will be to fight down such opposition in the mud, rifles choked, LG's [Lewis Guns] out of action, men tired and slow – and a new division like the 66th amongst them! Every step means dragging one foot out of the mud ... I shall be very surprised if this fight succeeds. They are banking on their knowledge of the German troops' "demoralisation" ... They don't realise how very strong our morale had to be to get through the last three fights.[71]

Bean's forebodings proved prescient – especially his comments on the physical condition and morale of the Australians. The attacking Australian battalions, which had held the front line since Broodseinde, were 'exhausted, wet and under strength'.[72] The commander of the 5th Australian Brigade reported that his men 'were "so fatigued and worn out through exposure and exhaustion" that he doubted their fitness for battle'.[73] The men of the 6th and 7th Australian brigades had worked in appalling weather through the previous week, laying cables and building tracks and tramways. Hundreds of exhausted men, defeated by labouring in these conditions and with no dry shelter, had simply melted away to the rear; some were suffering from trench feet but many others, in Bean's words, had 'temporarily deserted'. By 9 October, the 7th Brigade had dwindled to 800 men and the 6th to 600.[74] The result was that the

Australian battalions went into the attack with an average strength of only 7 officers and 150 men.[75]

The British divisions, due to attack on the Australians' flanks, had to struggle overnight through nearly four miles of bog simply to reach the front line positions. Added to these difficulties, the artillery support was wholly inadequate due to the weather and ground conditions.[76] The 2nd Australian Division and the previously untested 66th (2nd East Lancashire) Division doggedly advanced to their first objectives, only to be driven back by heavy enemy fire from their flanks. By the end of the day the survivors of the 2nd Australian Division had withdrawn to their original front line positions, having incurred over 1200 casualties.[77] Nothing was achieved for these losses.[78] The battle of Poelcappelle represented the sorry climax to the 'steadily diminishing yield' of Plumer's step by step operations.[79]

Their failure at Poelcappelle acutely disheartened the Australians. The experiences of one Australian soldier and his section were probably typical. On 7 October Private Vincent of the 21st Battalion AIF wrote in his diary: 'What is left of us have to go back up the line this afternoon. We started soon after dinner got heavilly shelled on the way'.[80] On the following day, he wrote, 'We walked up to our knees in mud and have been wet through now for four days but have to do another hop over first thing in the morning. We had to crouch down in a trench all night out of the road of shells'. On 9 October they attacked, but the results were disappointing: '[We] Started off 5 AM chased the Germans back a long way. One Sargent [sic] and eight of us found ourselves alone in front with Germans on three sides of us. We dug in and kept them back until dark then got back with another battalion and dug in again and kept watch'.

His unit was relieved around 2.30 a.m. on the following day and the men slowly wound their way through the dark to dugouts in the rear – a five hour trip which left them exhausted. They then walked on to Ypres, where, he noted with obvious pleasure, 'we washed our feet and put on clean sox'.

An Australian junior infantry officer described, in dejected tones, his similarly inconclusive experiences in attempting to storm a German pillbox at Poelcappelle on 9 October:

I had orders to establish a forward command Post ... [we] couldn't get near it because it was held very strongly and it took one and a half hours to surround it. There were six guns and 30 Bosch in it ... [we] stayed only a few hours as we were compelled to get out. I came back with only two men and they were both wounded, one in the eye and the other in the hand. All my men are gone now and it will take some time to get used to the new reinforcements.[81]

The demoralization of Australian soldiers after their fruitless attack on Poelcappelle was also recorded on film. Official Australian war photographer, Captain Frank Hurley, wrote in his diary how he found and photographed a group of exhausted Australians near the shattered Zonnebeke railroad: 'Under a questionably sheltered bank lay a group of dead men. Sitting by them in little scooped out recesses sat a few living; but so emaciated by fatigue and shell shock that it was hard to differentiate'.[82]

The second Australian assault against Passchendaele Ridge on 12 October proved even more futile than Poelcappelle. The 3rd Australian and New Zealand Divisions together comprised the apex of the attack with the 4th Australian Division on their right flank and five British divisions on their left. Conditions all along the front of the attack were appalling; the battlefield had been turned into a quagmire by heavy rain which continued right up to the morning of the attack. Plumer rushed the attack on the mistaken premise that the Poelcappelle operation on 9 October had

'From a pillbox on the ridge in front a machine gun opens up – the earth flies off our parapet. Despite warning our men will not keep down – until – there is a thud + a man standing up – no one of my men – collapses – stretcher bearers quick! too late – clean thro' the head. The earth that comes out of the trench covers him covers him to day almost where he fell, also one or two others whom we found lying about. It is a lesson + for a few minutes the men keep down – but they are strange fools these Australians + it seems part of their nature to court danger. In ten minutes they are walking about again as they would in their garden at home. It seems infectious for both you + I are doing the same thing condemn it as we may.
Continually the Hun planes are over us – low down so that we can see the observer leaning out – can see his goggles

(xviii) Lieutenant Cyril Lawrence (Australian Engineers) writes to his sister of his fellow Australians: "they are strange fools these Australians and it seems part of their nature to court danger." (C.Lawrence, Liddle Collection)

captured a 'sufficiently good jumping off line' from which the Anzacs could be launched to capture Passchendaele, over 2,000 yards distant. But intelligence reports indicating that the front had scarcely advanced on 9 October appear to have been ignored by the high command.[83] The 3rd Australian Division, on relieving the British 66th Division on 10 October, discovered that the 66th was not holding a consolidated front line position at all.[84]

Artillery support for the attack on 12 October was deplorably inadequate. The weather and muddy terrain had produced almost insurmountable difficulties in moving guns and setting them up and many batteries were unable to reach their appointed positions. One Australian artilleryman described how his battery's guns were bogged for three days in the mud, 'until at last we put 26 horses onto each gun and then proceeded on our way to the position, ploughing through the mud up to the horses' stomachs'.[85] On the day of the attack, 'many guns still lay temporarily abandoned or out of action and unreplaced'.[86] Those batteries in position found it difficult to bring forward sufficient shells, the journey taking up to 17 hours from the waggon lines to the guns. Added to these problems, were those of manning, ranging and firing the guns in the flooded positions. The recoil of the guns drove them into the mud, making it impossible to register them accurately on targets. Moreover, casualties were high among the artillery units as they were exposed to German counter-battery fire, the waterlogged ground making the digging of protective gun pits impossible.[87] The artillery units at this time, according to one observer, 'lived and fought in conditions of constant physical distress. Guns sank in the mud till they became useless and ultimately disappeared beneath the surface; till our battery positions were dotted with little red flags marking the positions where guns had sunk from view'.[88]

Given the conditions, it is hardly surprising that the preliminary artillery bombardment failed either to suppress German batteries or to destroy enemy strongpoints and barbed wire. The creeping barrage was so feeble that it could not be distinguished from the enemy's shells and it advanced too quickly for the infantry who soon fell behind it. But the planners, not the artillery, were responsible for these failings. As Charles Bean was led to ask caustically in his official history, 'were any of the higher commanders aware that in these operations their infantry attacked virtually without protection?'.[89]

The Australian battalions came under persistent enemy shelling during the approach march and through the night as they huddled in their jumping-off positions. They attacked at dawn under the thin barrage. The 3rd Australian Division troops slowly advanced through the heavy mud of the Ravebeek valley to take their first objective, but were forced to fall back under enfilade fire from their exposed flanks. They suffered over 3,000 casualties. The 4th Australian Division on their right failed to make any progress for the loss of over 1,000 casualties. The New Zealanders on the 3rd Division's left advanced straight into a thick belt of uncut wire on the

Bellevue Spur where they came under deadly machine-gun fire from German pill boxes. The morale of the New Zealanders was already low due to 'their exposure to miserable weather in undrained shellholes, the sight of the unbroken wire, and the knowledge of the previous failure'.[90] Their loss of almost 3,000 dead and wounded on Bellevue Spur was calamitous.[91] Overall, the attack against Passchendaele Ridge produced a total of 13,000 British casualties, the equivalent of a division of troops, for which expenditure there was no significant gain of ground; it failed utterly in its objective, the capture of Passchendaele.[92] Australian casualties amounted to over 4000.[93] The futility of these later attacks is reflected in the comparison of numbers of casualties with the amount of ground won. The 3rd Australian Division had captured its objectives on Broodseinde Ridge for the cost of less than one man per yard gained, Passchendaele cost this single division over 35 men for every yard of ground taken.[94]

The character of the fighting involved in the assault on Passchendaele Ridge is graphically conveyed in an Australian infantry officer's account:

on the 10th we had miles to go to the assembly point and had a hell of a time in the rain and mud. On the night of the 11th we marched off at 6.30 p.m. and walked till 5 a.m. of the morning of the 12th. The Bosch had got news of us through a deserter and he gave us a gruelling. Before 5 a.m. we had lost men like rotten sheep those who survived had the most marvellous escapes. I nearly got blown to pieces scores of times. We went through a sheet of iron all night and in the morning it got worse. We attacked at 5.25 and fought all day at times we were bogged up to our arm pits and it took anything from an hour upwards to get out. Lots were drowned in the mud and water. The Bosch gave us hell but we managed to hold on to the little we had taken till night when we dug in. We remained in the new country till the 20th eight days of absolute hell and then we were relieved.[95]

The memories of men drowning in the mud remained with survivors for many years. Lieutenant Russell Harris of the 27th Battalion considered this his 'worst recollection' of all his memories of Third Ypres:

The feeling of frustration at having been unable at times to go to the help of men trapped in those mudholes is still a painful memory. It was impossible to shut one's ears to their cries, and when silence came it was almost like a physical blow, engendering a feeling bordering on guilt.[96]

The task of clearing hundreds of wounded from the battlefield on the following days was formidable. On the 4th Australian Division front the full strength of three bearer divisions was not sufficient even with the addition of infantrymen. On the 3rd Division front the bearers were quickly exhausted from carrying across the barren wastes of shell craters filled with soft mud; many emergency bearers deserted and further numbers were gathered from depots around Ypres.[97] The Australian official history records that 'the stretcher-bearers' "carry" was a nightmare, and the pillbox aid-posts, around which the wounded lay in crowds on their stretchers, were a magnet for shell-fire'.[98] A report from the 3rd Australian Division War Diary conveys the gruelling nature of the stretcher bearers' tasks: 'The total carrying from the R.A.P.'s to the loading post for horse ambulances was over 3,500 yards and the tracks were all very difficult, being covered with shell holes knee deep and in some places waist deep in mud'.[99]

This ordeal was slightly relieved by a local cease-fire. A medical officer with a British regiment recorded how on the morning of the attack on 12 October all but three of his stretcher bearers were killed as he led them out to tend the wounded. Through that and the following day, the dug-in Germans extended an informal truce to the stretcher parties to allow them to collect the large numbers of wounded. Many of the Germans, he noted, 'pointed to where wounded were lying – Hun snipers pointed to where their victims were. It was a most extraordinary experience, and as a result, I have a respect for the Hun I never had before'.[100]

The failed second attack on Passchendaele Ridge marked the last full-scale involvement of the Australians in the Third Ypres campaign. The exhausted and demoralized Anzac divisions were relieved on 18 October by the Canadian Corps, who replaced them as the shock troops for the final attacks on Passchendaele. The previous phases of the campaign had clearly demonstrated the futility of sending infantry into attacks with inadequate artillery protection. The commander of the 3rd Australian Division, concluded from the unhappy experience of his division's assaults, that 'Passchendaele could be won only if the defences were deluged with artillery fire'.[101] This lesson was subsequently applied by General Currie, commander of the Canadian Corps. Currie planned his offensive meticulously, employing massive artillery preparation and slowly moving barrages to protect his infantry in a series of limited advances which recalled Plumer's earlier, successful 'bite and hold' tactics.

In their first attack on 26 October the Canadians succeeded in capturing one of the spurs on Passchendaele Ridge, despite driving rain and at the cost of over 3,000 casualties. The 6th Australian Battalion provided flanking support for the Canadians in what was the final Australian participation in the campaign.[102]

The Australian divisions remained in the Ypres salient until they were withdrawn in mid-November. They continued to suffer casualties from German shelling, including their new mustard gas, even in the rear areas. But, according to one account: 'Conditions on the Broodseinde ridge were tolerable; those in rear were barely so, although most people who served there seemed to agree that things were not quite as bad as at Flers a year before.'[103]

From every physical and morale aspect the last months of the Third Ypres campaign also represented the lowest point of the war for Australian soldiers. The five Australian divisions finished the campaign war-weary and depleted having suffered a total of 55,000 casualties in 1917, over 38,000 of them in Third Ypres.[104] In September 1917, the AIF had reached its maximum strength in France.[105] But, by the end of the year, the high wastage from casualties, combined with a dwindling supply of reinforcements, had left the AIF with a manpower crisis as the flow of reinforcements appeared insufficient to maintain the divisions in the field at fighting strength.[106]

As the year 1917 came to a close, the Australian brigade commander, 'Pompey' Elliott, reflected on the changes the Third Ypres campaign had wrought in the Australian soldiers' morale: 'They have not the same spirit at all as the old men we had. The difficulty once was to restrain their impatience for action ... now we find men clearing out to avoid going into the line at all'.[107] The disciplinary records of the Australians in France broadly confirm Elliott's perception.[108] The total number of British soldiers reported absent in France rose steadily during the Third Ypres campaign to reach a peak of almost 2000 men absent in December 1917.[109] Absent Australian soldiers constituted 10 per cent of that total.[110] But these figures do not reveal the whole scale of the absentee problem. Most of the men reported absent were in fact apprehended and charged for this offence. Absence without leave was the most frequent court-martial offence in both the Australian army and the British army during the war. Significantly, the monthly frequency of courts-martial charges against Australians in France for absence, as well as the more serious offence of desertion, both peaked for 1917 in October, the final month of Australian involvement in the Third Ypres campaign.[111] The peaks were telling indicators of the state of morale amongst the Australians.

The monthly frequencies of courts-martial of Australian soldiers for all offences show the same trends, especially when compared with that other large group of dominion troops in France, the Canadians. Monthly totals of Field General Courts-Martial of Australian soldiers in France in 1917 were, on average, double the monthly totals in the Canadian force.[112] Australian courts martial rose to a peak of over 400 cases per month in October and November 1917, almost double the peak of about 220 Canadian courts martial in September and October 1917.[113] The serious nature of these offences and the correspondingly severe punishments awarded to Australians by the military courts is revealed in the sharp rise in the numbers of Australian soldiers in British military prisons in France by the end of 1917. In July 1917, at the start of the Third Ypres campaign, the numbers of Australians (per thousand strength) in military prisons in the field was already four times that of British and other Dominion soldiers. During the second half of the year the numbers of Australians in prison rose steeply. By December 1917, after their involvement in Third Ypres, the rate of imprisonment of Australian soldiers was over six times that of all the other dominion troops combined (New Zealand, Canadian and South African) and eight times the rate in the British army.[114]

The disciplinary records clearly reflect a decline in Australian soldiers' morale and fighting spirit through 1917. However, despite this slump, many still considered the Australians' combat performance, at least in the first phase of Plumer's operations, to be their best. Bean judged 'the three battles of Menin Road, Polygon Wood and Broodseinde . . . the cleanest and most decisive victories [the Anzacs] had yet fought'.[115] Nevertheless, the final, fruitless attacks on Passchendaele Ridge had left the Australian divisions battered and weakened; and there were already signs that the harshest test for the Australians would emerge in 1918 when their reduced battalions, without hope of adequate reinforcement, would be committed to help oppose a massive German offensive. The Australian divisions had truly reached the depths in late 1917; but three positive factors were already working to assist their recovery.

First, in November 1917, the Australian divisions were brought together with the formation of the Australian Corps. Initially this comprised four divisions, the depleted 4th Division being withdrawn into reserve as a 'depot' division to supply reinforcements to the others and to be rotated with them as required. The creation of this unified corps gave a tremendous boost to the Australians. Commanders had consistently claimed that Australian soldiers' morale was highest and they fought best when their divisions were paired. Now with this arrangement, one of the greatest strengths the Australian force possessed, their homogeneity, was confirmed. Second, the Australian divisions were moved to the quiet Messines sector for rest, refitting and training from the middle of November 1917 until March 1918. Through a comparatively mild winter, the Australian divisions were nurtured back to strength. The health and morale of the troops recovered rapidly.[116] Third, the Passchendaele campaign had revealed within the British army the beginnings of a growing technological and tactical proficiency which would flourish into the final victories in the summer of 1918.[117] But these developments would not come quickly. Through the Third Ypres offensive, British infantry battalions remained 'oppressed by the treadmill to which they had been consigned and from which there seemed to be no escape'.[118]

Third Ypres demonstrated that high morale in troops was no longer a major determinant of combat success. Provided enough men retained sufficient fighting spirit to go forward behind the artillery barrage, storm enemy strong points and mop up behind the advancing assaulting waves of troops, success would come to whichever side possessed the capacity to direct massive artillery damage onto their enemy's front and provide artillery cover to enable their own infantry to advance. The crucial factor was no longer the infantry, or their strength, condition, training, morale, or state of discipline. Victory now depended upon the number of guns and shells and the intensity of shelling which could be applied to the chosen area of attack. This was the lesson the British army would take into 1918.

Notes
1 This account and the quotations are from an anonymous medical officer, in a letter to his parents in Australia, dated 26 October 1917, Item 68, PR84,

Australian War Memorial (hereafter AWM). [The provenance of this item is unclear. It is wrongly attributed to Driver Alexander Birnie, 12th Field Company Engineers, Australian Imperial Force (AIF), but from internal evidence it appears likely that the writer was an Australian serving with a British division in XVIII Corps.]

2 C.E.W. Bean, *Anzac to Amiens* (first published 1946), Canberra, Australian War Memorial, 1983, p. 376.

3 There were 36,500 casualties in the five Australian divisions, an average of 7,300 casualties per division; Australian and Canadian divisions incurred slightly higher casualties proportionately than most British divisions, see C.E.W. Bean, *The Australian Imperial Force in France 1917* (first published 1933), vol. IV, *The Official History of Australia in the War of 1914–1918*, 12 vols. Sydney, Angus & Robertson, 1943, pp. 946–8, 948, n. 129.

4 Prior and Wilson, *Passchendaele: The Untold Story*, p. 171.

5 Bill Gammage, Introduction to University of Queensland Press edition, 1982, C.E.W. Bean, *The Australian Imperial Force in France 1917* (first published 1933), vol. IV, *The Official History of Australia in the War of 1914–1918*, 12 vols. Sydney, Angus & Robertson, 1943, pp. xxiii, xxv.

6 In 1917 the AIF suffered 76,836 AIF battle casualties on the Western Front, almost double the 1916 AIF total of 42,267 battle casualties. Similarly, the AIF total of 89,084 non-battle casualties in 1917 was almost double the 1916 total of 45,657. In 1918 the AIF suffered 60,352 battle casualties and 73,237 non-battle casualties, source: A.G. Butler, *The Western Front*, vol. II, *The Australian Army Medical Services in the War of 1914–1918*, 3 vols., Melbourne, Australian War Memorial, 1940, p. 492, Graph No. 7.

7 Denis Winter, *Making the Legend: The War Writings of C.E.W. Bean*, St Lucia, University of Queensland Press, 1992, p. 161. In 1917 the AIF suffered 20,036 deaths from battle casualties on the Western Front (about one-third of total AIF deaths in the First World War), about 45 per cent of the total 44,764 battle casualties in the AIF on the Western Front; the equivalent totals were 12,541 in 1916, and 12,187 in 1918, A.G. Butler, *Special Problems and Services*, vol. III, *The Australian Army Medical Services in the War of 1914–1918*, 3 vols., Melbourne, Australian War Memorial, 1943, p. 912, Table No. 41.

8 Bean, *The Australian Imperial Force in France 1917*, pp. 946–7. Bean here ignored his own calculations which indicate higher losses in Third Ypres: AIF casualties for Third Ypres averaged 7,300 per division engaged (see note 9 above); the four Australian divisions which served in the battles of Fromelles, Pozières and Mouquet Farm in 1916, averaged about 7,000 casualties per division, see C.E.W. Bean, *The Australian Imperial Force in France 1916* (first published 1929), vol. III, *The Official History of Australia in the War of 1914–1918*, 12 vols. Sydney, Angus & Robertson, 1942, pp. 862–3, n. 2.

9 Bean, *The Australian Imperial Force in France 1917*, p. 948; C.E.W. Bean, *The Australian Imperial Force in France during the main German offensive, 1918* (first published 1937), vol. V, *The Official History of Australia in the War of 1914–1918*, 12 vols. Sydney, Angus & Robertson, 1943, pp. 1–2.

10 Butler, *The Western Front*, pp. 102–3. Casualties in AIF divisions on the Somme were high but no higher than those in British divisions similarly engaged, see Bean, *The Australian Imperial Force in France 1916*, pp. 862–3, n. 2.

11 Bean, *The Australian Imperial Force in France 1916*, pp. 940–1.

12 Bill Gammage, *The Broken Years: Australian Soldiers in the Great War*, Ringwood Vic, Penguin, pp. 174–9.

13 Bean, *The Australian Imperial Force in France 1917*, pp. 342–4, 354. In the 4th Australian Brigade, battalion losses averaged two-thirds of those who attacked in First Bullecourt. 1,170 of the 3,000 casualties were taken prisoner, the greatest number of Australians taken prisoner in a single action during the First World War.

14 Bean, *The Australian Imperial Force in France 1917*, pp. 541–5. The 1st, 2nd and 5th Australian Divisions were engaged in Second Bullecourt. For the rout of the 5th Brigade (2nd Division) troops see *Ibid.*, pp. 433–5.

15 Bean, *The Australian Imperial Force in France 1917*, p. 544, Bean's perception of Australian soldiers' attitudes reflected his judgement that British commanders were alone responsible for Bullecourt; but the inadequacies of Anzac commanders and poor Australian staff work undoubtedly contributed to the débâcle, see Eric Andrews, 'Bean and Bullecourt: Weaknesses and Strengths of the Official History of Australia in the First World War', *Revue Internationale d'Histoire Militaire*, no. 72, Australian Commission of Military History, Canberra, University College, University of New South Wales, 1990, pp. 25–47.

16 I Anzac Corps (1st, 2nd and 5th Australian Divisions) received 'probably the longest, most complete, and most pleasant rest ever given to British infantry in France', Bean, *The Australian Imperial Force in France 1917*, pp. 683, 730–4.

17 Bean, *The Australian Imperial Force in France 1917*, pp. 579–80. The 4th Division rejoined I Anzac Corps in late-August 1917 to take part in Third Ypres.

18 A solitary dissenter is Denis Winter who cites records purportedly showing that the Messines mines were detonated under empty front line positions, the Germans having withdrawn a week before the attack, Winter, *Haig's Command*, p. 96.

19 Bean, *The Australian Imperial Force in France 1917*, pp. 681–2, n. 129.

20 Prior and Wilson, *Passchendaele: The Untold Story*, pp. 62–3; also Bean, *The Australian Imperial Force in France 1917*, pp. 638–9, 673–4.

21 Prior and Wilson, *Passchendaele: The Untold Story*, p. 65.

22 Bean, *The Australian Imperial Force in France 1917*, pp. 623–9, 771–2, n. 115; for a graphic example of the savagery of this fighting see Prior and Wilson, *Passchendaele: The Untold Story*, p. 63–4.

23 Bean, *The Australian Imperial Force in France 1917*, pp. 683–5, 733–4, n. 148.

24 Bean, *The Australian Imperial Force in France 1917*, pp. 561–3.

25 Bean, *Anzac to Amiens*, p. 349; see also Bean, *The Australian Imperial Force in France 1917*, pp. 579–80, 734, n 149. The strain of the 4th Division's long exposure to combat was perhaps reflected in instances of panic during withdrawals in the battle of Messines, see Bean, *The Australian Imperial Force in France 1917*, pp. 662–3, n. 59.

26 Bean, *The Australian Imperial Force in France 1917*, p. 734, n. 148, 149.

27 Bean, *The Australian Imperial Force in France 1917*, p. 733.

28 Prior and Wilson, *Passchendaele: The Untold Story*, pp. 107–8.

29 Reports by Regimental Medical Officers, 7th and 8th Australian Field Artillery Brigades, War Diary of Administrative Staff, HQ 3rd Australian Division, August 1917, Item 1/4/79, AWM 4.

30 GHQ calculated that in the first 23 days of August 1917 there were 9177 casualties in British artillery units, David Horner, *The Gunners: A History of Australian Artillery*, Sydney, Allen & Unwin, 1995, p. 154. There were 1375 casualties in Australian artillery units in July–August 1917, Butler, *The Western Front*, pp. 191–2.

31 Major-General Ivor Maxse (commander 18th Division and later commander XVIII Corps), cover note to 18th Division tactical plan, 28 September 1917, quoted in Paddy Griffith, *Battle Tactics of the Western Front: The British Army's Art of Attack, 1916–18*, New Haven & London, Yale University Press, 1994, p. 237, n. 17.

32 Gough at commanders' conference, 17 August 1917, quoted in Prior and Wilson, *Passchendaele: The Untold Story*, p. 105.

33 Shelford Bidwell & Dominick Graham, *Fire-Power: British Army Weapons and Theories of War 1904–1945*, London, George Allen & Unwin, 1985, pp. 127–8.

34 On the German defensive network at Third Ypres, see Prior and Wilson, *Passchendaele: The Untold Story*, pp. 71–3, 87–8.

35 Bean, *The Australian Imperial Force in France 1917*, p. 744, n. 28; Prior and Wilson, *Passchendaele: The Untold Story*, p. 115.

36 Bean, *Anzac to Amiens*, p. 366. Bean comments that British commanders seemed initially unwilling to recognise the benefits to morale in pairing the Australian divisions, see Bean, *The Australian Imperial Force in France 1917*, pp. 759–60.

37 However, the preliminary artillery bombardment did not achieve the success that is generally claimed, as it failed to neutralise the German batteries, Prior and Wilson, *Passchendaele: The Untold Story*, pp. 116–18.

38 For examples see Bean, *The Australian Imperial Force in France 1917*, pp. 761–72, n. 82, n. 115.

39 Prior and Wilson, *Passchendaele: The Untold Story*, p. 119. This amounted to 3,800 casualties per square mile, over double the rate of 1500 casualties per square mile expended on 31 July to capture 18 square miles, *Ibid.*

40 Total Australian casualties at Menin Road were 5013 (1st Division: 2754; 2nd Division: 2259), Bean, *The Australian Imperial Force in France 1917*, p. 789, n. 169.

41 Suzanne Welborn, *Lords of Death: a people, a place, a legend*, Fremantle, WA, Fremantle Arts Centre Press, 1982, p. 126.

42 Bean, *The Australian Imperial Force in France 1917*, p. 734, n. 148; and Ian Grant, *Jacka, VC: Australia's Finest Fighting Soldier*, South Melbourne, Macmillan in association with the Australian War Memorial, 1989, pp. 132–3.

43 Grant, *Jacka, VC*, p. 132.

44 Grant, *Jacka, VC*, pp. 134–5, 138–41. The commander of the 4th Brigade, Major-General Brand, burnt the letters of resignation but the officers immediately resubmitted them, thus forcing him to apologise; subsequently, battalion training was carried out largely under the direction of the company commanders.

45 Account of the battle of Polygon Wood, written by Captain Albert Jacka, VC, MC, in 1931 for the author of the 14th Battalion unit history, see Grant, *Jacka, VC*, pp. 141–7. Jacka's account, most of which is corroborated by other sources, condemned the CO and his Adjutant for locating the Battalion headquarters in a safe area in the rear and remaining out of contact with the

advancing companies. Jacka steadied the troops when they began to withdraw after running into their own barrage and he led them forward onto their second objective, Bean, *The Australian Imperial Force in France 1917*, p. 828.

46 Bean, *Anzac to Amiens*, p. 368; Horner, *The Gunners*, p. 157.

47 Major Consett C. Riddell, DSO, 12th Field Company Engineers, AIF, letter dated 9 October 1917 (describing the attacks of the step by step battles), from a collection kindly lent to the author by Dr John Riddell.

48 Prior and Wilson, *Passchendaele: The Untold Story*, p. 129–30; Bean, *The Australian Imperial Force in France 1917*, pp. 821–4, 832, n. 140.

49 Prior and Wilson, *Passchendaele: The Untold Story*, p. 131. This amounted to 4400 casualties per square mile, 50 per cent higher than at Menin Road, *Ibid*. Total Australian casualties at Polygon Wood were 5452 (4th Division: 1729; 5th Division: 3723), Bean, *The Australian Imperial Force in France 1917*, pp. 831–2, n. 139.

50 Prior and Wilson, *Passchendaele: The Untold Story*, pp. 126, 131.

51 Bean, *Anzac to Amiens*, p. 369.

52 Bean, *The Australian Imperial Force in France 1917*, p. 840.

53 Bean, *The Australian Imperial Force in France 1917*, pp. 843–8.

54 Prior and Wilson, *Passchendaele: The Untold Story*, p. 136. German morale showed no sign of decline and in places the Germans stood and fought tenaciously at their pill boxes, Bean, *The Australian Imperial Force in France 1917*, p. 849.

55 In an attempt to counter the successful British step by step tactics, the German high command had partly reversed their defence in depth policy before the Broodseinde battle by strengthening their front line positions and packing counter-attack divisions close behind the front line. Bean, *The Australian Imperial Force in France 1917*, pp. 857–9.

56 Total Australian casualties at Broodseinde Ridge were 6432 (1st Division: 2448; 2nd Division: 2174; 3rd Division: 1810), Bean, *The Australian Imperial Force in France 1917*, p. 876, n. 130. The New Zealand Division incurred 1700 casualties.

57 Many at the time considered Broodseinde 'the most complete success so far won by the British Army in France', a view apparently later confirmed by the German official history which refers to 'the black day of October 4th', see Bean, *The Australian Imperial Force in France 1917*, p. 875–7. Bean had earlier described Broodseinde as a strategic and tactical victory: he wrote that the 'vital heights' (of Broodseinde Ridge) were one of the most important enemy-held positions in the Ypres sector, which 'for over two years had enabled the Germans to turn the Ypres Salient into a graveyard of British troops'. C.E.W. Bean, 'The Australians at Broodseinde', in *The Battle Book of Ypres*, compiled by Beatrix Brice (first published 1927), Stevenage, Herts, Spa Books edition, 1990, pp. 72–3.

58 Trevor Wilson, *The Myriad Faces of War: Britain and the Great War, 1914–1918*, Oxford, Basil Blackwell, 1986, p. 476.

59 Prior and Wilson, *Passchendaele: The Untold Story*, pp. 137–9.

60 Bean, *The Australian Imperial Force in France 1917*, p. 875.

61 This account and quotations from Private William Percival Vincent, 21st Battalion (6th Brigade, 3rd Division) AIF, diary entries dated 4–6 October 1917, Item 261, PR84, AWM. Vincent was No 2 on his Lewis gun team.

62 Gammage, *The Broken Years*, p. 190.

63 *Bean,* The Australian Imperial Force in France 1917, p. 876, n. 130.

64 Dudley Jackson, MM, 'Flanders, 1917', *Stand-To* (Journal of the Canberra branch of the Returned Services League), vol. 11, no. 3, July–September 1967), pp. 6–13, esp. p. 7. Private Dudley Jackson served as a Lewis gunner with the 20th Battalion (5th Brigade, 2nd Division) AIF. The 20th Battalion was not one of the battalions suffering the highest losses at Broodseinde.

65 Frank Hurley, diary, 4 October 1917, quoted in *Hurley At War: The Photography and Diaries of Frank Hurley in Two World Wars*, Introd. by Daniel O'Keefe, Annandale NSW, Fairfax Library, 1986, pp. 52–4. Hurley photographed the Australians through most of their involvement in Third Ypres, see also David P. Millar, *From Snowdrift to Shellfire: Capt. James Francis (Frank) Hurley 1885–1962*, Sydney, David Ell, 1984, pp. 46–61. Bean records the admiration many soldiers felt for Hurley's bravery in exposing himself to danger in order to take his photographs, Bean, *The Australian Imperial Force in France 1917*, p. 800, n. 27.

66 Lance Corporal Robert Otto, 2nd Battalion (1st Brigade, 1st Division) AIF, postcard dated 10 October 1917, Manuscript ML A2661, 'Letters written on active service 1914–1919', Mitchell Library, State Library of New South Wales, Sydney.

67 W.J. Bradby, 'Polygon Wood and Broodseinde', *Stand-To* (Journal of the Canberra branch of the Returned Services League), vol. 8, no. 5, September–October 1963), pp. 19–22, 27–28, esp. pp. 21–22. Walter James Bradby served as a Private with the 8th Battalion (2nd Brigade, 1st Division) AIF.

68 Wilson, *The Myriad Faces of War*, p. 478.

69 The British 49th and 66th Divisions had replaced the 3rd Australian and the New Zealand Divisions in II Anzac Corps: I Anzac Corps consisted of the 1st and 2nd Australian Divisions, see Butler, *The Western Front*, p. 232. The Australian Official History gives the names, 'First battle of Passchendaele' to the attack on 9 October (Poelcappelle), and 'Second battle of Passchendaele' to the attack on 12 October, however, the British official nomenclature attributes, 'First battle of Passchendaele' to the attack on 12 October, and 'Second battle of Passchendaele' to the Canadian attacks which began on 26 October and concluded on 10 November with the capture of Passchendaele, *Ibid.*, p. 185, n. 6.

70 Griffith, *Battle Tactics of the Western Front*, pp. 88–9.

71 Charles Bean, diary entry, undated (probably 8/9 October 1917), Item 89 (pp. 29–32), 3DRL 606, AWM. Partly quoted also in: Bean, *The Australian Imperial Force in France 1917*, pp. 884–5; and with some transcription errors, in: Dudley McCarthy, *Gallipoli to the Somme: the story of C.E.W. Bean*, Sydney, John Ferguson, 1983, p. 300; and Winter, *Making the Legend*, pp. 186–7.

72 Prior and Wilson, *Passchendaele: The Untold Story*, p. 162.

73 Australian Brigade 'Report on Operations', quoted in Prior and Wilson, *Passchendaele: The Untold Story*, p. 164.

74 Bean, *The Australian Imperial Force in France 1917*, p. 890; 40 men 'went astray during the night' in a single battalion (the 20th), *Ibid.* 891, n. 31.

75 Bean, *The Australian Imperial Force in France 1917*, pp. 891, 895.

76 Prior and Wilson, *Passchendaele: The Untold Story*, pp. 161–3.

77 Total 2nd Australian Division casualties were 1253 in this first assault against Passchendaele Ridge. Bean, *The Australian Imperial Force in France 1917*,

p. 900, n. 80. The 1st Australian Division sent 85 men into a minor feint and only 14 returned unwounded, *Ibid.*, pp. 899–900.

78 'The Battle of Poelcappelle had not advanced the British line a yard towards Passchendaele Ridge', Prior and Wilson, *Passchendaele: The Untold Story*, p. 165.

79 Plumer's preparations for successive operations had become increasingly rushed and less thorough, under the pressure of Haig's conviction of an imminent German collapse, see Prior and Wilson, *Passchendaele: The Untold Story*, pp. 164.

80 The following account and quotations are from Private William Vincent, 21st Battalion AIF, diary entries dated 7–10 October 1917, Item 261, PR84, AWM. Vincent was wounded by shellfire on 8 November and evacuated to England on 17 November 1917; he returned to Australia in May 1918.

81 Lieutenant G.M. Carson, MM, 33rd Battalion (9th Brigade, 3rd Division) AIF, letter dated 3 December 1917, Item 185, 2 DRL, AWM. Carson and his surviving party were strafed and bombed by German aircraft as they withdrew. The German block houses and pill box defensive structures of reinforced concrete were very difficult and costly to capture, proving resistant to anything but direct hits by heavy artillery fire or daring bombing assaults by infantry.

82 Frank Hurley, diary entry dated 12 October 1917, describing the aftermath of Poelcappelle, quoted in *Hurley At War*, p. 64.

83 Bean, *The Australian Imperial Force in France 1917*, p. 901; Prior and Wilson, *Passchendaele: The Untold Story*, p. 165. Major-General Monash, commanding the 3rd Australian Division, also ignored these reports and he did not personally reconnoitre the front, see P.A. Pedersen, *Monash as Military Commander*, Melbourne, Melbourne University Press, 19895, pp. 200–1.

84 'The 66th Division front was found by the 3rd only after perilous scouting across the mudfield . . . posts were found full of dead and dying men cut off from any contact with the rear', Butler, *The Western Front*, p. 236, n. 7; see also Bean, *The Australian Imperial Force in France 1917*, pp. 906–7.

85 Bombardier Frederick Corder, 7th Australian Field Battery, October 1917 (PR86/043, AWM), quoted in Horner, *The Gunners*, p. 162.

86 Bean, *The Australian Imperial Force in France 1917*, pp. 906, 902–6; and Prior and Wilson, *Passchendaele: The Untold Story*, pp. 166–7. The combined batteries of three Australian Divisional Artilleries, which were deployed to support the 4th Division's attack on 12 October, lacked over one-fifth of their guns, due to their being 'either out of action or stuck in the mud in moving', Horner, *The Gunners*, p. 160.

87 Horner, *The Gunners*, pp. 151–4.

88 Lieutenant Colonel J.H. Boraston, quoted in John Terraine, *White Heat: The New Warfare 1914–18*, London, Sidgwick and Jackson, 1982, p. 220. A Canadian soldier recalled that his infantry unit assisted engineers and artillerymen to make gun platforms at Passchendaele by 'transporting tons of bully beef and pouring it into the mud until at last it had sunk deep enough to give a solid foundation for an eighteen-pounder gun', anecdote in William D. Mathieson, *My Grandfather's War: Canadians remember the First World War 1914–1918*, Toronto, Macmillan, 1981, p. 123.

89 Bean, *The Australian Imperial Force in France 1917*, pp. 912, 911–12.

90 Col. H. Stewart, *The New Zealand Division 1916–1919: A Popular History Based on Official Records*, Auckland, Whitcombe and Tombs, 1921, pp. 281–2.

91 Stewart, *The New Zealand Division*, p. 291. A New Zealand officer condemned the high command's deficient planning for this loss: 'Exhausted men struggling through mud cannot compete against dry men with machine guns in ferro-concrete boxes waiting for them', diary entry quoted in *Ibid.*, p. 292.

92 Prior and Wilson, *Passchendaele: The Untold Story*, p. 169.

93 Total Australian casualties in this second assault against Passchendaele Ridge were 4217 (3rd Division: 3199; 4th Division (12th Brigade): 1018), Bean, *The Australian Imperial Force in France 1917*, p. 928, n. 87.

94 Calculations in Pedersen, *Monash as Military Commander*, p. 203.

95 Lieutenant G.M. Carson, MM, 33rd Battalion (9th Brigade, 3rd Division) AIF, letter dated 25 October 1917, Item 185, 2DRL, AWM. Carson was killed in action at Mont St Quentin in August 1918.

96 Russell H. Harris, 'The 27th in the Menin Road Battle', *Stand-To* (Journal of the Canberra branch of the Returned Services League), vol. 10, no. 3, January–March 1966), p. 4. See also the horrifying personal accounts by: Captain E.S.C. Vaughan, quoted in Prior and Wilson, *Passchendaele: The Untold Story*, p. 98; and Major C.A. Bill, quoted in Wilson, *The Myriad Faces of War*, p. 473.

97 Butler, *The Western Front*, pp. 237–40.

98 Bean, *The Australian Imperial Force in France 1917*, p. 927.

99 From War Diary of Administrative Staff, HQ 3rd Australian Division, October 1917, Item 1/47/11, AWM 4. Australian Army Medical Corps soldiers of the 3rd Division evacuated 610 wounded men over two days, 12, 13 October during which time their losses were 26 killed and 61 wounded; the Divisional Burials Section buried 253 dead during these two days, 'while the area was being shelled'.

100 Account by an anonymous regimental medical officer, letter dated 26 October 1917 (wrongly attributed to Driver Alexander Birnie, 12th Field Company Engineers, AIF), Item 68, PR84, AWM. The informal cease-fire by the Germans to allow collection of the wounded is confirmed in Bean, *The Australian Imperial Force in France 1917*, p. 927.

101 Report by Major General Monash, dated 12 October 1917, cited in Geoffrey Serle, *John Monash: A Biography*, Melbourne, Melbourne University Press in association with Monash University, 1982, p. 298.

102 Bean, *The Australian Imperial Force in France 1917*, pp. 933–5.

103 Ronald McNicoll, *The Royal Australian Engineers 1902–1919: Making and Breaking*, Canberra, Corps Committee of the Royal Australian Engineers, 1979, p. 110; see also Bean, *The Australian Imperial Force in France 1917*, pp. 931–3.

104 Total AIF losses in 1917 were 54,353 (1st Division: 9082; 2nd Division: 12375; 3rd Division: 13315; 4th Division: 12110; 5th Division: 7471); total AIF losses in Third Ypres were 38,093 officers and men, see Bean, *The Australian Imperial Force in France 1917*, pp. 683–4, n. 2, 936.

105 The average daily strength of the AIF in France was 118,454 in 1917, 86,163 in 1916, and 110,031 in 1918, source: Butler, *The Western Front*, p. 539. The peak average monthly strength of the AIF in France was 123,842 in September 1917, source: Butler, *The Western Front*, p. 246, n. 18.

106 The AIF remained a volunteer army as the Australian people rejected conscription in two national plebiscites on 28 October 1916 and 20 December 1917. Throughout 1917 voluntary monthly enlistments were only one-quarter to

one-fifth of the level of 16,500 per month deemed necessary by the government; in the aftermath of Third Ypres they fell to 2,247 in December 1917 and in February and March 1918 enlistments fell below 2000 monthly, the lowest levels of the war, see Joan Beaumont, 'Australia's war', Joan Beaumont, ed., *Australia's War, 1914–18*, St Leonards, NSW, Allen & Unwin, 1995, pp. 19–20, 23; and Ernest Scott, *Australian During the War*, vol. XI, *The Official History of Australia in the War of 1914–1918*, 12 vols. Sydney, Angus & Robertson, 1936, pp. 871–3, Appendices 3, 4.

107 Brigadier General H.E. Elliott (commander 15th Australian Brigade, 5th Division), letter dated 31 December 1917, quoted in P.A. Pedersen, 'The AIF on the western front: the role of training and command', in M. McKernan and M. Browne, eds., *Australia Two Centuries of War & Peace*, Canberra, Australian War Memorial in association with Allen & Unwin, 1988, p. 183.

108 The following summary of discipline within the AIF in 1917 is condensed from the author's study of AIF discipline and punishment currently in progress.

109 Total numbers of British Soldiers reported absent in France monthly during 1917: 1,540 in July; no figure recorded in August; 1,651 in September, 1,764 in October, 1808 in November, and 1957 in December. Figures from Adjutant General GHQ, War Diaries, January 1916–December 1919, Item 26, WO95, PRO.

110 A total of 199 Australian soldiers were reported absent in France at the end of December 1917. Figures in Assistant Provost Marshal Australian Corps, War Diaries, November 1917–October 1918, Item 13, WO154, PRO.

111 Australian courts martial figures from author's database collated from AIF courts martial proceedings files under conditions of Special Access granted under the Australian Archives Act.

112 The Field General Courts Martial was the least formal and most common court martial used in dealing with the majority of serious charges arising in France. Australian courts martial figures from author's database; Canadian courts martial data collated by author from Nominal Roll of Court Martial Proceedings, Canadian Expeditionary Force, Item 45, WO93, PRO.

113 Australian courts martial figures from author's database; Canadian courts martial data collated by author from Nominal Roll of Court Martial Proceedings, Canadian Expeditionary Force, Item 45, WO93, PRO.

114 See chart, 'Military Prisons in the Field, B.E.F. France', in War Office 'Most Secret' publication, *Statistical Abstract of Information regarding the Armies at Home and Abroad*, War Office, London, 1st October 1919, facing page 596, IWM 83558, Imperial War Museum.

115 C.E.W. Bean, *Anzac to Amiens* (first published 1946), Canberra, Australian War Memorial, 1983, p. 376.

116 Butler, *The Western Front*, pp. 241–2, 613–5.

117 For example, advances in the techniques of sound ranging, flash spotting and the use of aerial observation made British artillery counter-battery fire more effective. During the latter stages of Third Ypres the British artillery developed field survey and calibration techniques which enabled batteries to fire accurate barrages without previous registration fire – a technique used to achieve surprise in the successful attack on Cambrai on 20 November 1917, see Travers, *How The War Was Won*, pp. 20–21; also Horner, *The Gunners*, p. 164.

118 Bidwell & Graham, *Fire-Power*, pp. 117.

Chapter 16

The Canadians at Passchendaele[1]

Dean Oliver

*"Again and again personnel from private soldiers up asked each other if
the Higher Authorities had ever made a survey of the fighting area, for it
was incredible that men equipped with even fewer than average brains
could ever send troops into such terrain."*[2]

Passchendaele occupies an uneasy niche in most Canadian accounts of the
Great War. Falling awkwardly between the triumph on Vimy Ridge in
April 1917 and the unprecedented success at Amiens the following August,
it is generally perceived as a waste of life and energy unequalled in the
Canadian Corps' distinguished history and, as such, is depicted in the same
mournful, tragic, angry prose endemic to British accounts of the battle. The
Corps was already well advanced in its professional development by the
time Sir Douglas Haig's long-anticipated Flanders offensive finally
commenced, the literature implies, and the long fight up Passchendaele
Ridge offered few unique tactical lessons to units already acclaimed for
their sterling performances at Vimy and Hill 70. Many, if not most, of
the key developments in the Corps' doctrinal maturation dated from the
previous winter.

At Passchendaele, as well, GHQ demanded speedy execution in an
environment hardly conducive to the Canadian tactical 'system'. The
Corps staff came to the ridge reluctantly, altogether certain of the carnage
likely to ensue. The rank and file shared their foreboding. Having had their
fill of the Ypres salient in 1915[3] grizzled veterans knew a raw deal when
they saw one; newer men were easily convinced of the survivors' wisdom.
This was bad ground, and heavily defended. It was low and wet, and overlooked from north to south by well-sited enemy positions, including dozens
of concrete pillboxes. A good portion of the battlefield was fully or
partially submerged, and most of the rest had been pulverized beyond
recognition by weeks of uninterrupted artillery fire from both sides. Sir
Arthur Currie's famous prediction that the operation would cost 16,000

of his countrymen dead and wounded would overshoot the mark by a mere 346.

That the Canadians succeeded at wresting the nearly featureless, shell-ravaged ridge from German grasp was a military feat of the first order. Acknowledged – indeed, trumpeted – by nearly every national commentator since 1917, the success brought honours and accolades from all sides to the troops and to their corpulent, decidedly unmilitary-looking commander. But the casualty rolls tainted the victory and brought stern reproaches to Currie from hostile Canadian politicians and newspaper editors. In the run-up to the December 1917 federal election, fought mainly over the government's conscription programme, Currie was accused of wasting lives and for acquiescing all too readily in the designs of Britain's apparently luckless, if not incompetent, generals. However impressive the victory from a technical and tactical standpoint, it had not changed the strategic balance on the Western Front, and the heavy losses had aggravated the manpower crisis. With the General firmly in the pro-conscriptionist camp, his vilification by the government's opponents was as inevitable as it was indecent. That he could scarcely have refused to participate in Haig's floundering offensive was largely irrelevant to such critics; that he had wrangled numerous concessions from a desperate GHQ was not known; that he had ultimately accomplished the well-nigh impossible was utterly beside the point.

But if the success of Canadian arms at Passchendaele remained tarnished, the feat itself was irrefutable evidence of the Corps' professional competence. There thus emerged from the débâcle a second impression: that Passchendaele was a battle only the Canadians could have won. "No one ever contemplated that the Flanders offensive would end without the Canadians figuring in it," recalled one battalion historian.[4] After Vimy, a brilliant operation to be sure, the popular imagination from Halifax to Victoria had been seized by the notion that Canadians were elite troops, called upon in the toughest operations to succeed where other troops, frequently British, had failed. The fact that the Corps commander, Lieutenant-General Sir Julian H.G. Byng and many of the key staff officers responsible for Vimy, were British affected Canadian smugness hardly at all. A glorious image was a wonderful tonic to induce young lads to the colours at a time when the recruitment system had largely broken down, particularly when it was not the forced creation of government propaganda. The Corps had evolved into a highly effective fighting force by mid–1917, arguably the best similarly-sized formation on the Western Front, and the record of its exploits fed the public's appetite for good news from the front. Success, of course, had little to do with the innate martial qualities allegedly imbued in all Canucks by their northern, frontier upbringings, but, like Australia's "digger" myth, it made excellent copy.[5] Good officers, sound planning, technical expertise, and innovative tactics, were the real keys to Canadian success, as well as the immeasurable luxury afforded the contingent by its remaining unified as a national formation.

Academic historians are still grappling with the outlines of this professional development,[6] but for most contemporaries the answer was obvious and emotionally satisfying: in the clash of arms, the Empire's best had not been found wanting.[7]

As a victory, therefore, Passchendaele added lustre to a long-standing and hopelessly outmoded militia tradition just as it darkened indelibly the image of both British troops and British generals. Currie did not escape censure. The Corps commander, whose wartime treatment by the political caste amounted to an unmitigated national disgrace, would later be vindicated fully by both the historians and the courts,[8] but his difficulties with detractors and political opponents typified the country's painful peacetime adjustment. By the mid–1930s, the appearance of David Lloyd George's memoirs had helped cement Currie's reputation as one of the war's finest generals, but premature death in 1933 at the age of fifty-seven meant he would never bask in the nation's thanks. Two of his three biographers, Urquhart (1950) and Dancocks (1985), are unrestrained in their praise of Canada's greatest soldier; the third, Hyatt (1987), is more balanced and more critical but still unreservedly sympathetic.[9]

The precise circumstances of the battle added to the national legend and removed the Canadian contribution, ever so slightly perhaps, from the charge of mindless slaughter levelled at the British high command. In the historiography of the campaign, this surely is the key difference between Canadian and non-Canadian accounts. Not at all enthused at the prospect of returning to Flanders; for instance, Currie had consented only after receiving from Haig solid assurances of adequate preparation time, extra artillery, and logistical support; Currie's men then proceeded to gobble up the ridge, piece by methodical piece, following a carefully scripted and manifestly intelligent plan, stymied occasionally by the weather, the mud, and the failure of the British on their left to keep up the pace. Stories of individual heroes, especially the Victoria Cross winners, added extra spice to this mix, while the physical condition of the battlefield itself highlighted the impressive accomplishment.[10] The Canadians had, in short, come, seen, and conquered.

This inspiring tale, despite the casualty returns, contributed in no small measure to Canada's gradual assertion of its national independence in the post-war period. The Canadians had not saved the Empire on a cold November morning in 1917, but they had certainly helped the national case for sovereign recognition, and even the grander myth, that the Corps had rescued Haig, the British Expeditionary Force, and the entire Allied coalition by its determined performance, nevertheless, died hard.[11] Sir Robert Borden's failure even to mention Passchendale in his memoirs must place the battle's political significance in a more restrained context,[12] but from Vimy onward, successive Canadian governments sought to atone for the battle's sacrifices (and the war's) by positing the achievement of nationhood at the graves of its war dead. Individual citizens, meanwhile, honoured their loss in the righteous defence of Christianity and traditional ideals. "The Armistice allowed Canadians to return to the comforting belief that the war had indeed been a crusade", Jonathan Vance has argued, that "because the war had been won, they could now rest easy in the certainty that they had been fighting God's battles."[13] Passchendaele, inadvertently, was a Canadian Calvary.

That God had demanded such offerings of his dutiful flock in the Flanders mud, was a bitter pill, but arguably no less so than the war itself. For this reason, Third Ypres became short-hand for the conflict's futility, in Canada as elsewhere, despite the important – in fact, crucial – qualifier that, for the Canadian Corps, most of the operation's objectives had been achieved.[14] It was not the virtuous triumph of reluctant amateurs, however, but the grim endurance of polished professionals. The Corps learned much from its horrific ordeal in October and November 1917, just as it had studied carefully its experiences on the Somme and at Vimy. The fight, however frightful the outcome, contributed to the Corps' long, costly learning curve just as the bitter victory at Third Ypres had resulted from it. If "military lessons" is perhaps too whiggish and clearsighted a term for such incremental progress (despite the "lessons learned" documents pouring forth from GHQ and its sub-formations by 1917), it still comes closest to describing the Corps' accumulation and assessment of raw data and the transformation of tactical doctrine that resulted. Passchendaele proved for reluctant Canadians a testing ground for Canadian proficiency but the force fielded so successfully at Amiens one year later benefited handsomely from the effort.[15] As they had at the Somme and at Vimy, all levels of the Corps command structure studied assiduously the experience gained to improve performance in future operations.

This evolution in tactical methods must be the starting point for any discussion of the Canadian Corps' effectiveness at Third Ypres. The formations that inched towards Laambeek and the Woodland Plantation on the morning of 26 October were vastly different from those that had fought along the Somme the previous September, much less those that had been 'blooded' at Second Ypres in 1915 or Mount Sorrel the following year. Long gone were the monotonous masses of riflemen plunging blindly ahead in the aftermath of the artillery's preparatory fire. In their place had emerged well-co-ordinated, diversely armed infantry sub-units supported by thousands of technical specialists and hundreds of scientifically co-ordinated guns and mortars. Re-trained to advance in short bounds and to overcome strongpoints by manoeuvre and firepower, not overwhelming force, Canadian infantry battalions had also been rearmed with a plethora of support weapons which were familiar to them and with which they were well trained, making them infinitely more capable of attaining modest objectives after a short advance. Co-ordinating artillery fire with infantry movements had become a secular gospel, to save lives with technical solutions its first commandment. Engineers had also assumed a crucial role in Corps operations, with careful pre-battle preparation Currie's most

IN LOVING MEMORY

OF

Private W. Kennerley

(9th Batt., Ches. Regt.),

WHO WAS KILLED IN ACTION WHILST FIGHTING IN FRANC
ON SEPTEMBER 20th, 1917 ;

Aged 30 years ;

AND WAS INTERRED AT POLYGAN WOOD.

Into the field of battle
He bravely took his place,
He fought and died for England
And the honour of his race.

He sleeps not in his native la
But 'neath a foreign sky,
Far from those who love him best
In an Hero's grave he rests.

53. A casualty of the fighting near Polygon Wood – an *In Memoriam* card from the relatives of Pte W.Kennerley. Remarkably, his place of burial, and that he had fallen at the Third Battle of Ypres, were known to his family very soon after his death. (H.Humpage, Liddle Collection) Chapter 19

54. A view from a pillbox near the Schuler Galleries, captured in September 1917. (M.F.T.Baines, Liddle Collection).

55. Officers of the German Nr 162 Infantry Regiment are able to pose, before the battle, on a Gheluvelt strongpoint. (G. Werth) Chapter 20

56. A German photograph of the sector of the Gheluvelt plateau defended during the battle by Infantry Regiment Nr 162. (G. Werth) Chapter 20

57. Interrogation of British prisoners in the Gheluvelt sector, held by Infantry
    Regiment Nr 162. (G.Werth) Chapter 20

58. A photograph taken from a German prisoner captured in Eagle Trench near
    Langemarck, showing the burial of forty German soldiers killed in a British
    bombardment on 6 September 1917. (J.Lindsay-Smith, Liddle Collection)
    Chapter 20

59. German troops and supplies moving through Moorslede towards Passchendaele during the batt. (W.C.Smith, Liddle Collection) Chapter 20

60. Mending a break in a telephone wire, exposed and under fire; the work of a signaller. (J.C.Williams, Liddle Collection) Chapter 21

61. A German unit photograph of a German cemetery near Passchendaele village, shortly before its capture by Canadian troops. (W.C.Smith, Liddle Collection) Chapter 20

62. Tank crew on parade: clothing and equipment worn here include overall trousers, and revolvers with ammunition pouches. (N.V.H.Symons, Liddle Collection) Chapter 21

63. A British tank wrecked on the Ypres battlefield, the breech of its six pounder gun exposed in the right hand sponson. (L.H.Matthews, Liddle Collection) Chapter 21

64. A British Tommy demonstrates the correct procedure for throwing the Mills hand grenade; with the pin removed but still held in the left hand, the grenade is then hurled overarm from the right hand, in a fashion similar to the way one might bowl a cricket ball. (A Campbell, Liddle Collection) Chapter 21

65. Small Box respirator being worn in the Ypres salient by a British Officer, G.M.Liddell, September/October 1917. (G.M.Liddell, Liddle Collection) Chapter 21

66. Exponent of the art of the machine gun - Pte James Paling, Machine Gun Corps, 1917. (J.Paling. Liddle Collection) Chapter 21

67. Agriculture: a factor in the manpower equation. Men and boys haymaking near a Gloucestershire village; unskilled agricultural labourers were vulnerable to military conscription. (Liddle Collection) Chapter 24

68. Lance Corporal W.C.Cordery, Military Police. (W.C.Cordery, Liddle Collection) Chapter 22

69. Essential or non-essential? Workers at Hunslet Glass Works, south Leeds. To what extent would the call-up into the armed forces of semi-skilled industrial labourers, like these men, impede the nation's war effort? (Liddle Collection) Chapter 24

70. *Battle Wood, Ypres Salient*. A watercolour by J.W.Parkes. (J.W.Parkes, Liddle Collection) Chapter 25

71. *German pillboxes, Passchendaele* by Olive Mudie-Cook. (O. Mudie-Cook, Liddle Collection) Chapter 25

72. *White Chateau, Hollebeke, showing plank track over Messines Ridge* by G.A.A.Willis (G.A.A.Willis, Liddle Collection) Chapter 25

73. A continuing artistic legacy. *Products*, painted by Terry Atkinson in 1975, showing a Thornycroft 3 ton J Type truck, knocked out by a Krupp manufactured German shell, on the Menin Road, September 1917. (University of Leeds) Chapter 25

famous dictum. The general's less than charismatic personality would earn him few admirers during the war, but a concern for saving lives and avoiding senseless operations were among his most endearing leadership qualities. His bite-and-hold approach at Passchendaele, with four, short, sharp operations separated by careful preparation and the rotation of assault units, was simple but effective. It was also as much as any Corps commander could have done under the circumstances to ensure success while limiting losses.

Many of these changes had been heralded long before October 1917. Many of them, in fact, long pre-dated Vimy. All ranks in an attack should "thoroughly understand and frequently rehearse" the mission, wrote L.J. Lipsett of 2nd Canadian Infantry Brigade in a typical report nearly a full year before the Somme.[16] Closer infantry-artillery co-operation, improved communications at all levels, and a greater emphasis on platoon tactics featured prominently in Canadian battle drills and "lessons learned" documents by mid–1916. While many of these assessments bore the imprimatur of parent British formations, it was at least clear that the Canadians were taking to heart the need to learn from one's own mistakes and from those of others. After the battle for the St. Eloi Craters in March-April 1916, for example, 2nd Canadian Division concluded that "all subordinates must be prepared to act on their own initiative. The one unforgivable sin when in difficulties is to do nothing and wait for orders."[17] Neither von Hutier nor his subsequent scholarly admirers could have said it better.[18]

Byng, who had replaced Lieutenant-General Sir E.A.H. Alderson as Corps commander on 29 May, 1916, was instrumental in this process.[19] Jeffery Williams's fulsome praise of Byng for the Vimy operation is only slightly overstated and many of the more famous incidents in the Corps' doctrinal evolution were a direct result of its British commander's intervention or guidance.[20] It was he, for example, who, in the spring of 1917, ordered Currie, at the time a division commander, to visit the French in the Verdun sector to assess the lessons of recent fighting. The resulting report remains one of the best known and most important tactical documents in the Canadian Corps' professional development.[21] Byng "paid particular attention to the training of junior officers", Williams notes, "and, in the infantry, reorganized the basic unit, the platoon, to give it more independence. In doing so, he began a trend toward the more flexible tactics which proved so successful later in the war."[22] Incremental change reaped its reward at Mount Sorrel in June 1916, the Corps' most impressive success to date and a triumph of close artillery-infantry co-operation, preparation, and the judicious employment of specialists and their weapons within infantry platoons.[23] By this time, Bill Rawling notes, "in both the battalion and the platoon, tactics were slowly changing to take into account the destructive potential of barbed wire, artillery, and machine-gun."[24]

As at Passchendaele the following year, the Canadian Corps on the

Somme was granted the luxury of not having been committed early in the campaign, a lull which permitted the almost leisurely analysis of ongoing operations, German defence systems, and the evident weaknesses in British attack doctrine. Having had their German opponents pounded by British and other colonial formations for two and a half months was an additional benefit of arriving late to the party. "Lessons learned" pamphlets circulated widely during this period and everything from GHQ's translations of German documents to staff reports on British and French methods made the rounds of corps, division, brigade, and battalion staffs with ever increasing frequency. The benefits of the creeping barrage, of rapidly crossing No Man's Land, and of providing sufficient weight to the attack to enable consolidation on the objective, had all been assimilated by the Canadians well before their September insertion into the maelstrom along the Albert-Bapaume road. "The infantry should be taught to follow the artillery barrage as closely as a horse will follow a nosebag filled with corn", Currie wrote on 15 August in one such document. "Unless they do this the enemy are sure to get a few machine-guns into action, and two machine-guns will stop a whole battalion or a brigade. It is far better to lose a few of our men from our own artillery fire than to sacrifice hundreds by hostile machine-gun fire."[25]

Still, advancing in long straight lines fifty to one hundred yards apart laden with up to a hundred pounds of kit, "a load-to-weight ratio greater than that of a mule",[26] Canadian infantry suffered heavy casualties in a series of grinding battles from September to November 1916. The operations of 2nd Infantry Brigade were typical. Attacking from Courcelette towards several German trench lines on 26 September, the brigade initially found its supporting artillery and machine-gun barrage "very effective" and the forward battalions reached their first objective in less than ten minutes, seizing it from stunned and badly shot up defenders.[27] The Canadians moved in "successive waves as orderly and calmly if not even better then they ever did on the parade ground", noted a 5th Battalion observer with evident pride;[28] by nightfall the following day such tactics had cost the battalion 465 men killed, wounded, and missing from its pre-battle strength of roughly 700.

Despite a quick success in the early going, German artillery and small arms fire had so thinned out the attackers, however, that the first and second assault waves combined to move on the next objective, Hessian Trench. The counter-barrage, meanwhile, decimated the third and fourth waves moving up in support before they had even entered the fray. The handful of unwounded men who struggled into Hessian Trench (and captured most of it) would go no farther that day. Blasted by carefully registered German guns, prevented from advancing by uncut wire on a reverse slope to their front, and swept from the left by German machine-guns after the failure of British troops to secure their flank, the brigade began to consolidate and to prepare for relief. The third objective, Regina Trench, would not fall to Canadian troops until November.

The stark simplicity of this attack with long lines of infantry in successive waves advancing slowly behind a creeping barrage was replicated in Canadian formations throughout the Somme campaign. Counter-battery fire remained largely ineffective, German wire all too frequently remained uncut, and the assault battalions generally ran out of men before the final objective had been reached. Leaning on 'the creeper' was at least better than the 'fire-then-advance' tactics employed previously, however, and the search continued for other improvements. Most after-action reports highlighted the necessity of adding both firepower and manoeuvrability to the infantry platoons. Currie's report on French offensive tactical doctrine, as well as battle rehearsals, detailed staff studies, and intensive training in platoon tactics, all contributed to the radically altered attack doctrine that had emerged by the spring of 1917.[29] The search for answers originated at Corps level and permeated all echelons of the command structure. "The Corps commander is anxious to obtain the opinions of Divisional, Brigade and Battalion commanders as to the lessons to be derived from operations on the Somme", one headquarters document noted, "in order that the valuable experience gained there by the Corps may be turned to the best account in future operations."[30]

Platoon tactics was not the only object of Canadian attention in this period but it was certainly the major one. Because the platoon was "the largest unit that, under modern circumstances, can be directly controlled and manoeuvred by one man", training for infantry companies should henceforth be based on "the combined action of self-contained platoons and that of the battalion on the combined action of self-contained companies."[31] The infantry would advance quickly, bypassing pockets of resistance if possible, but outflanking and overwhelming them with their own firepower if necessary. This was fire and movement, a philosophy well articulated in *Instructions for the Training of Platoons for Offensive Action*, a GHQ document issued in February 1917 which proposed the reorganization of infantry platoons into four sections: bombers, Lewis gunners, riflemen, and rifle grenadiers.[32] Canadian documents on the new system indicate clearly that old ideas staggered on into 1917, despite the Somme. 'Pushing on to the objective at all costs' and similar phrases punctuate tactical reports with alarming regularity,[33] yet the move towards greater flexibility and the intelligent use of supporting arms and small unit manoeuvre is equally clear.

Other changes completed the picture. Artillery doctrine shifted from the destruction of enemy guns and positions to their neutralization or suppression; elaborate preparation on scale models and taped practice areas preceded most attacks; a reformed training establishment incorporated the lessons of recent fighting in new courses with battle-hardened instructors; vastly improved artillery range-finding, flash-spotting, and fire control techniques increased exponentially the effectiveness of counter-battery fire;[34] and Canadian machine-gunners perfected the technique of the indirect machine-gun barrage. Rawling has noted that by 8 April, 1917:

The men were trained in the tactics of the platoon and the movements of the battalion, having learned or relearned the use of bomb, rifle, rifle-grenade, and machine gun not only on the training ground but in raids against their entrenched enemy. Whole divisions had gone over the taped course time and time again until the men became somewhat disgruntled with their officers' silly games, but they had learned every detail of the job at hand. The gunners had practised cooperation with the infantry in one raid after another and were adopting new technology and practices to engage the enemy's wire, trenches, and guns. The engineers had made their direct contribution to the battle in constructing or reconstructing tunnels which sheltered those members of the Canadian Corps who would be the first to move across no man's land . . . [35]

This was the "set-piece attack", notes another recent scholar, the product of doctrinal ingenuity that left even the vaunted German Army somewhat behind.[36]

Vimy, along with the Hill 70-Lens campaign four months later, demonstrated beyond doubt the utility of the Corps' improved methods. The details of both battles are well covered elsewhere;[37] both, suffice it to say, exemplified the wisdom in a bite-and-hold approach executed by highly trained infantry and supported by well-equipped and well-co-ordinated artillery. By mid-summer, the Corps had also learned to counter the German preference for immediate and (usually) highly effective counter-attacks by consolidating quickly and by bringing down artillery concentrations on German assembly areas before the assaults had fully developed. "Our gunners, machine-gunners and infantry never had such targets", Currie noted of the firepower directed at German counter-attack formations on Hill 70.[38] Not only had the Corps perfected the techniques required to seize German defensive positions by the time of its deployment to the Passchendaele sector, but it had also figured out how to hold them. The cost of such operations remained high (more than 10,000 casualties at Vimy, another 9200 at Hill 70 and Lens) but the tactical results were deemed to be worth it. Canadians still died in swathes as they struggled towards the next pillbox or roll of wire, but they were no longer dying so obviously in vain.

This almost unbroken record of costly victories (Vimy, Arleux, Fresnoy, Hill 70) continued at Third Ypres. With the sensible habits developed in the aftermath of the battles of 1916, the Corps was tactically and, perhaps more importantly, intellectually prepared for the challenge of Passchendaele Ridge, even if everyone from Currie and then down the command chain laboured under no illusions as to what would be required. "Every Canadian hated to go to Passchendaele", the Corps commander wrote after the war in a famous passage. "I carried my protest to the extreme limit . . . which I believe would have resulted in my being sent home had I been other than the Canadian Corps Commander. I pointed out what the casualties were bound to be, and was ordered to go and make the attack."[39] "Nobody wanted to go there", Lieutenant-Colonel A.G.L.

McNaughton, Currie's Counter-Battery Officer, reiterated. "You don't want to be paralyzed by poor terrain and mud before you start."[40] They would be reluctant saviours indeed.

The appalling physical condition of the Passchendaele battlefield needs little elaboration, though its tactical importance to Currie's battle plan must be emphasised. The impenetrable swamp that radiated outward from the Ravebeek astride the Corps' axis of advance, for example, divided the battlefield into two sections and narrowed considerably the front on each side of the stream. This left little room for manoeuvre and provided inviting targets for German machine-gunners and for their artillery. It would also slow the pace of advance to a near crawl until drier ground had been reached, and limited the effectiveness of supporting artillery fire as shells would bury themselves harmlessly in the mud before exploding. This worked both ways, of course, but coupled with the difficulty of supplying the Canadian guns with ammunition, of moving them into firing positions, and of keeping them from sinking once the barrages had commenced, it limited considerably the effectiveness of their artillery support. Maintaining communication with the guns and simply identifying physical targets in the nearly featureless bog, also presented exceptional difficulties.

To help overcome the sector's tactical obstacles, Currie despatched a pair of senior officers to reconnoitre carefully the terrain before the Corps moved into the area. He also protested vigorously lest his troops be assigned to Gough's Fifth Army, whom Currie believed incompetent.[41] In addition, he demanded from GHQ, and received, extra time to help prepare for the impending battle. There was much to be done, including the construction of gun platforms, roads, and light railways, the laying of telephone lines, harassing fire, feint artillery barrages, and the systematic destruction of German pillboxes, wire entanglements, and point defences. The infantry used this period to rework the techniques that had proven so successful in the recent past: understand the objective, study the terrain, build models and training areas, and practise. By the time the first phase of the battle opened in the early morning hours of 26 October, some of the assault battalions had been rehearsing for weeks.

Currie's tactical philosophy at this time was as simple as it was bold. "The great lesson to be learned from these operations", he had written after Vimy, "is this: if the lessons of the war have been thoroughly mastered; if the Artillery preparation and support is good; if our Intelligence is properly appreciated; there is no position that cannot be wrested from the enemy by well-disciplined, well-trained and well-led troops attacking on a sound plan."[42] In proving his point, the next two weeks provided as severe a test of Canadian endurance as anyone could have imagined. Even in the preparation phase, German artillery, machine-guns, and snipers killed and wounded thousands. Moving by short bounds on 26 October, 30 October, and 6 November, with a more limited attack on 10 November, the Canadians slogged across No Man's Land and up the ridge, pausing on each objective to rotate battalions, brigades, and (for

6 November) divisions, to remove the wounded, and to prepare the artillery for the next push. It was a fierce, bitter fight. War diaries, battalion histories, and the recollections of participants make for sombre reading and Nicholson's official history, in one of that fine volume's rare inadequacies, fails utterly to capture its nature. It "plumbed the depths of horror", Desmond Morton has noted,[43] grinding up platoons, companies, and battalions, often in a matter of minutes. Dancocks' battle history is superb in its recreation of the vicious, confused fighting and his account, relying on the papers and recollections of combat infantrymen, presents a perspective contrasting strikingly with the dry, official reports and most campaign histories.

Still, the battle developed more or less according to plan. There were numerous setbacks but the degree to which the Canadians met their commanding general's schedule under possibly the worst conditions they would face during the war is nevertheless remarkable. It is easy with hindsight to allow Corps headquarters too much of the credit for this. The elaborate artillery preparations, careful infantry training, and attention to logistical and topographical details that were among the lessons of previous battles each played a role in the result, but success at Passchendaele was equally the product of hard fighting, individual bravery, and collective determination. As much as the Corps depended for its success on the artillery, in fact, Passchendaele was an infantry battle. Ever astute in his assessments, Currie would write on November 20 that the number one reason for the success of the attack was the "fighting spirit of the men."[44]

The artillery, which, for some of the reasons already mentioned, did not have its best outing at Third Ypres, was still reasonably effective first in suppressing German positions and in shooting the battalions on to their objectives, and then in disrupting German counter-attack efforts as it had done to even greater effect at Hill 70. Dancocks is unnecessarily harsh on the gunners in his account, pointing repeatedly to deaths from friendly fire and to the ability of German machine-gunners to emerge unscathed after the barrage had passed to harrass the assault waves from the rear and the support waves from the front. Most of the battalion, brigade, and division after-action reports are more forgiving, despite occasional complaints. The Corps summary of operations from 2–9 November, which includes the capture of Passchendaele village on the 6th, notes that in the 1st Division's sector "the barrage was excellent, and the enemy's defences were so demolished as to form no serious obstacle to our advance." The situation of 2nd Division's front was similar, where "our barrages have been prompt and effective on all occasions."[45] Enemy artillery, however, was extremely active and effective during most phases of the battle, having been registered on its own front lines prior to the Canadian assault. On 30 October the German guns took eight minutes to reply to the Canadian attack, a fatal delay during which the infantry had moved well beyond their start line, but on 10 November the shells were falling on 2nd Division just four minutes after Zero hour; on 6 November, it had taken only three.

The new German defensive system[46] with a lightly held forward zone, numerous pillboxes and machine-gun posts, and a reinforced defence line 500–1000 yards behind their front line, caused serious problems, especially in the initial attacks, though none that the Canadians could not overcome. Platoon tactics had emphasized flexibility, manoeuvre, and individual initiative since the fall of 1916, leaving platoon and company commanders well-prepared to handle the defence in depth which confronted them on the ridge. There appears to have been no echo in Canadian formations of the criticism levelled occasionally (and unfairly) at British infantry for its continuing to possess a 'trench warfare mentality', digging in at every opportunity and relying on the artillery to do the lion's share of work.[47]

Currie's headquarters was well aware, prior to the attack, of the nature of German defences. Third Division's intelligence files, for example, offer a remarkably accurate picture of what the Canadians would face: trenches in various states of repair; pillboxes organized in depth, some with loopholes; a proliferation of wire, some of which would likely remain uncut by Zero hour; and bolstered machine-gun strength in the forward positions.[48] "The enemy's defences in this area consist principally of isolated posts in short lengths of trench which are connected by wire entanglements," a 1st Division assessment noted three days before the battle.

> Many of these isolated posts are round concrete 'pill boxes'. Those 'pill boxes' appear to have been constructed usually only for protection and not for defensive purposes (though some recently captured have loopholes for enfilade fire), the machine gun garrisons coming out from them to take up their positions in shell holes nearby. There is no definite trench line in the area opposite this Corps, and there are no signs of very recent activity, except in the repair and construction of wire entanglements . . .[49]

The problems created by such an irregular defence system for mopping up and consolidation on the objective were also fully appreciated and divisional commanders ordered that specific formations be detailed to secure each area of ground captured.[50] Based on intelligence reports, field officers had preached incessantly the need for movement, manoeuvre, and flanking operations to dispose of pillboxes and strong points. Speed of movement, tactical depth in the attack, co-ordinated firepower, and initiative on the part of junior officers, NCOs, and enlisted men would be essential. First Division's operation order offers a classic example of the Corps' response to the tactical conditions of Third Ypres and a manifestly sensible application of the lessons of recent fighting.

> Present conditions call for a large degree of initiative and resource on the part of all unit commanders. To enable them to use their initiative all such commanders from the platoon upwards must have a reserve in their

own hands capable of being quickly put in to fill a gap, to form a front to a flank or to work round the flank of some hostile centre of resistance which is holding up the advance of their own or an adjoining unit.[51]

Topographical conditions, the weather, the restricted attack frontages, and the effectiveness of the German artillery, all militated against the text book application of such principles, as did the number of German machine-gunners who survived the preparatory bombardment. The attitudes instilled by several months of intensive training nevertheless ensured that, from the initial assault to the final operations in November, a familiar scene played itself out across the ridge with Canadian Lewis gunners and rifle grenadiers holding the attention of German pillboxes while riflemen and bombers manoeuvred into position to deliver a close-in attack.

Again, with hindsight, it is easy to exaggerate the regularity of such minor successes and to ascribe to Canadian tactical doctrine a level of coherence and effectiveness that it clearly did not possess. To ascribe victory solely to doctrinal innovation, in fact, ignores the course of the battle itself and the specific, difficult circumstances in which it was fought. The 3rd and 4th Divisions struggled towards their objectives inch by labo-rious inch after overcoming brutal ground and weather conditions and a surprisingly skilful and determined enemy.[52] Ninth Infantry Brigade, attacking towards Bellevue and Lambeek, very nearly failed altogether. If not for the actions of Lieutenant Robert Shankland, 43rd Battalion, who rallied the survivors of several platoons in clinging to a small position on the Bellevue Spur, the centre of the Corps' great offensive might have bogged down before it had truly begun.[53] Shankland was awarded the Victoria Cross for his efforts. Similarly, the capture of Meetcheele by the Princess Patricia's Canadian Light Infantry (PPCLI) on 30 October swung largely on the actions of two men, both of whom won the Victoria Cross. So too did George Pearkes of the 5th Canadian Mounted Rifles (CMR), whose struggle on the far left in an exposed position against vastly supe-rior numbers is one of the epic chapters in Canada's military past.[54] It was on this flank that British units repeatedly failed to keep up the pace, forcing first the 5th CMR and later units of the 1st Division to refuse their left in defence against uncaptured German positions.

By 6 November, as the 1st and 2nd Divisions moved off in the assault, having replaced the 3rd and 4th Divisions respectively, most of the Corps' objectives were well within reach. Fierce fighting still ensued, but a week's preparation time, fresh troops, drier ground, and the weakened German defences helped ensure that this phase of the attack was quickly success-ful. On the right, for example, Passchendaele was taken by 6th Brigade in roughly three hours. The Canadians expanded their hold on the position again on 10 November, but by this time the battle was all but over. German artillery continued to inflict heavy casualties as the Canadians dug in along the battered ridge and Allied gunners helped prevent the German infantry from counter-attacking. Working with the aid of the Royal Flying Corps, the tired gunners repeatedly scattered enemy infantry concentrations before serious attacks could develop.

Passchendaele demonstrated beyond any doubt that the lessons of the Somme, Vimy, and Hill 70 had been well learned. More important than the application of any specific insight or method, however, it highlighted the extent to which the Canadian 'system' had become an effective battle-field weapon. The same process of tactical analysis, assessment, and doctrinal change that carried the Corps to Passchendaele would now carry it beyond, through Amiens and the Hundred Days to Mons and victory. The 'lessons learned' reports began to emerge immediately, Currie's own coming on 20 November.[55] In the long period between Passchendaele and Amiens, the Canadians would build on the techniques and tools available to incorporate the lessons of open warfare, current in the BEF by late 1917, but driven home with Teutonic precision by the Ludendorff offensives the following spring. Amiens, like Passchendaele, would be a triumph of tactical doctrine, sound leadership, and, as always, hard fighting.

It may indeed be true, as Paddy Griffith and others have argued, that the tactical and technical innovations generally attibuted almost solely to the Canadians and ANZACs during the First World War were the products of BEF-wide developments, and that the much-maligned British corps and divisions performed creditably, if not in fact brilliantly, from early 1917 onwards when presented with suitable opportunities for a set-piece attack. CEF records and the private papers of Currie, McNaughton, and other Canadian officers pay ample tribute, explicitly more often than not, to their British counterparts in this regard, and the innovations of several British senior officers are well known. Nevertheless, the Canadian record of tactical achievement stands almost unique. One need not conclude from this that Canadians, alone among the Empire's contingents, had unlocked the mysteries of trench warfare, but merely that revisionist accounts of British performance still have some explaining to do.

Part of the explanation for Canadian success was timing. They were late in being committed on the Somme, had months of planning for Vimy, attacked a badly shaken foe at Passchendaele, and would move against poorly prepared German defences at Amiens. But this hypothesis can only be stretched so far. Hill 70 and the later battles of the Hundred Days cannot be accounted for so easily, nor, in truth, can Passchendaele, and yet the Canadians persevered each and every time. Currie's leadership weighed heavily in this balance, although the Corps was well on its way to success at Vimy (under Byng) while Currie was still a divisional commander. Granting luck, leadership, and timing their due, tactical skill and its concomitant, individual courage, remain as the cornerstones of the Canadian Corps' military accomplishments from 1916 onwards and nowhere were both qualities better displayed than Passchendaele.

Having well earned its reputation by October 1917, the Canadian Corps approached Third Ypres as an operational problem to be overcome in the same manner as Vimy and Hill 70 had been: by careful planning, all-arms co-operation, close artillery support, and innovative tactics. No plan could hope to survive first contact with the enemy and Currie's was no exception, but more noteworthy from a doctrinal perspective than the Homeric struggles by individual sections and platoons as they moved up the ridge was the degree to which Passchendaele represented the studied application of a military organization's applied learning. So well had these military lessons been internalized, in fact, that the Corps adapted smoothly to the German's new defensive system, ploughing through it across the entire front. The artillery too, despite the frightful conditions of its gun pits and supply routes, succeeded in aiding the infantry advance and in dissuading the Germans from many counter-attacks. Artillery support was not ideal at Passchendaele but it was remarkably good.

Success here, as elsewhere in 1917 and 1918, elevated the image of the Canadian Corps to that of an elite formation in the minds of the troops, the Canadian public, and a great many foreign observers. The Germans, who ought to have known something of the effectiveness of Allied units, in no small measure shared this view. Far from being, to paraphrase the cynicism of a modern expression, "legends in their own minds", the Canadians appeared as legends in virtually everyone's mind. The huge casualty lists, the brutal nature of the struggle, and the Corps' thoroughly incremental doctrinal progress, were largely irrelevant to this construction, as was the extent to which the Canadians had benefitted from British leadership, British staff work, British tactical innovation, and – in the peculiar allowances made by GHQ for the often troublesome colonials – British forbearance.[56] Still, the aura of Canadian invincibility served as a grand salve to the collective conscience in ways, one suspects, frequently denied the citizens of other combatant nations. Nothing succeeds in the making of national myths quite like success.

And victory cast a long shadow. It contributed directly, for example, to an unbounded popular faith in the citizen-soldier which parsimonious post-war governments would utilize with devastating effect to forestall the development of a viable regular army. Sam Hughes, Canada's controversial Minister of Militia and Defence for much of the war and the epitome of militia arrogance, was well pleased in the event. Somewhat paradoxically, victory – or, more accurately, Canada's contribution to it – also supported the sustained and equally successful assertion of Canadian sovereignty, as much by its effects on the national psyche as by the cold reference to raw statistics that it continued to invite. That the country's enviable wartime record might be rewarded by London with greater independence was certainly appropriate, and perhaps to be expected; that it would contribute as well, under the oppressive weight of the militia myth, to the speedy undoing of the professional military system ultimately responsible for such victories must rank as one of the Canadian Corps' most confounding and unfortunate legacies.

Notes

1   The following article is not a battle study. Rather, in accordance with the editor's instructions, it attempts to measure the Canadians' performance at

Third Ypres against the closely related factors of military identity and military effectiveness.

2   W.W. Murray, *The History of the 2nd Canadian Battalion (East Ontario Regiment), Canadian Expeditionary Force in the Great War, 1914–1919* (Ottawa: Mortimer Ltd., 1947), p. 224.

3   See Daniel G. Dancocks, *Welcome to Flanders Fields: The First Canadian Battle of the Great War: Ypres, 1915* (Toronto: McClelland and Stewart, 1988).

4   Murray, *The History of the 2nd Canadian Battalion*, p. 207.

5   See Jane Ross, *The Myth of the Digger: The Australian Soldier in Two World Wars* (Marrickville: Hale and Iremonger, 1985). For the Canadians, see Jean-Pierre Gagnon, *Le 22e bataillon (canadien-français), 1914–1919: Étude socio-militaire* (Montréal: Les Presses de l'Université Laval, 1986).

6   See Bill Rawling, *Surviving Trench Warfare: Technology and the Canadian Corps, 1914–1918* (Toronto: University of Toronto Press, 1992).

7   Canadian exceptionalism flourished in the late nineteenth and early twentieth centuries, leading some to predict a dominion-led empire in the decades to come. See Carl Berger, *The Sense of Power: Studies in the Ideas of Canadian Imperialism, 1867–1914* (Toronto: University of Toronto Press, 1970).

8   Currie had sued successfully a minor Ontario newspaper after it had run an article on June 13, 1927 accusing him of incompetence and inhumanity over the Canadian Corps' occupation of Mons, Belgium on the last day of the war. The case completely vindicated the general. See A.M.J. Hyatt, *General Sir Arthur Currie: A Military Biography* (Toronto: University of Toronto Press, in collaboration with the National Museums of Canada, 1987), pp. 140–2.

9   Hugh M. Urquhart, *Arthur Currie: The Biography of a Great Canadian* (Toronto: J.M. Dent & sons, 1950); Daniel G. Dancocks, *Sir Arthur Currie: A Biography* (Toronto: Methuen, 1985); and Hyatt, *General Sir Arthur Currie* (1987).

10 Future general, lieutenant-governor, and minister of national defence, George R. Pearkes won his VC at Passchendaele. See Reginald H. Roy, *For Most Conspicuous Bravery: A Biography of Major-General George R. Pearkes, V.C., Through Two World Wars* (Vancouver: University of British Columbia Press, 1977), pp. 56–63.

11 This is a pervading theme in Daniel G. Dancocks, *Legacy of Valour: The Canadians at Passchendaele* (Edmonton: Hurtig Publishers, 1986).

12 Henry Borden, ed., *Robert Laird Borden: His Memoirs, Volume II: 1916–1920* (rep.; Toronto: McClelland and Stewart, 1969).

13 Jonathan F. Vance, "Sacrifice in Stained Glass: Memorial Windows of the Great War", *Canadian Military History* 5/2 (autumn 1996), p. 17.

14 The extensive debate over Passchendaele has, for the most part, not been reflected in Canadian accounts, though most have been critical. The official history was highly sceptical of most claims for the campaign's beneficial effects, but nevertheless concluded that in terms of attrition it had "produced important results." G.W.L. Nicholson, *Canadian Expeditionary Force, 1914–1919: Official History of the Canadian Army in the First World War* (Ottawa: Queen's Printer, 1962), p. 330. Dancocks, *Legacy of Valour*, the only reliable Canadian monograph on the battle, is far more judgmental, arguing that those who view the battle as 'pointless' are, quite simply, "wrong" (p. ix).

15 On Amiens, see Brereton Greenhouse, "'It Was Chiefly a Canadian Battle':

The Decision at Amiens, 8–11 August 1918", *Canadian Defence Quarterly* 18/2 (autumn 1988), pp. 73–80.

16 National Archives of Canada (NA), Records of the Department of Militia and Defence, Vol. 4051, folder 19, file 2, "Report on Enterprise at La Petite Douve by 2nd Canadian Infantry Brigade, November 17, 1915", p. 4.

17 Militia and Defence, Vol. 4141, folder 4, file 10, "2nd Canadian Division, 12 April 1916".

18 See, for example, Bruce I. Gudmundsson, *Stormtroop Tactics: Innovation in the German Army, 1914–1918* (New York: Praeger, 1989), especially pp. 114–20. Also Timothy J. Lupfer, *The Dynamics of Doctrine: The Changes in German Tactical Doctrine during the First World War* (Fort Leavenworth, Kansas: US Army Combat Institute, 1981).

19 Alderson commanded the Canadians from September 13, 1915. Currie replaced Byng on June 9, 1917 and led the Corps until its disbandment in August 1919.

20 Jeffery Williams, *Byng of Vimy: General and Governor General* (London: Leo Cooper, 1983), p. 128.

21 Rawling, *Surviving Trench Warfare*, p. 89–90.

22 Williams, *Byng of Vimy*, p. 128.

23 D.J. Goodspeed, "Prelude to the Somme: Mount Sorrel, June 1916", in Michael Cross and Robert Bothwell, eds., *Policy By Other Means: Essays in Honour of C.P. Stacey* (Toronto: Clarke, Irwin & Co., 1972), pp. 147–61.

24 Rawling, *Surviving Trench Warfare*, p. 66.

25 Militia and Defence, Vol. 4051, folder 19, file 8, Currie to 2nd Canadian Infantry Brigade, 15 August 1916.

26 Rawling, *Surviving Trench Warfare*, p. 71.

27 Militia and Defence, Vol. 4051, folder 19, file 6, "Report of 2nd Canadian Infantry Brigade".

28 Militia and Defence, Vol. 4053, folder 24, file 20, "5th Battalion Report, October 2, 1916."

29 In addition to Rawling, *Surviving Trench Warfare*, pp. 87–113, see also William Stewart, "Attack Doctrine in the Canadian Corps, 1916–1918", MA thesis, University of New Brunswick, 1982.

30 NA, E. Jones Papers, Vol. 1, folder 5, Canadian Corps to divisions, 3 November 1916.

31 Militia and Defence, Vol. 3864, folder 99, file 3, Canadian Corps to divisions, 27 December 1916.

32 Rawling, *Surviving Trench Warfare*, p. 97.

33 Militia and Defence, Vol. 3864, folder 99, file 8, "Platoon Organization: Revisions", February 1917, for example.

34 John Swettenham, *McNaughton: Volume I, 1887–1939* (Toronto: Ryerson Press, 1968), pp. 49–84; G.W.L. Nicholson, *The Gunners of Canada: The History of the Royal Regiment of Canadian Artillery, Volume 1, 1534–1919* (Toronto: McClelland and Stewart, 1967), pp. 311–17.

35 Rawling, *Surviving Trench Warfare*, p. 112–13.

36 Ian M. Brown, "Not Glamorous, But Effective: The Canadian Corps and the Set-piece Attack, 1917–1918", *Journal of Military History*, 58/2 (July 1994), pp. 424 and 425.

37 Both are covered in detail in Nicholson, *Canadian Expeditionary Force*, and in the other key surveys, including John Swettenham, *To Seize the Victory: The Canadian Corps in World War I* (Toronto: Ryerson Press, 1965), and

Desmond Morton and J.L. Granatstein, *Marching to Armageddon: Canadians and the Great War, 1914–1919* (Toronto: Lester & Orpen Dennys, 1989). Vimy was the first action in which all four Canadian divisions had fought simultaneously and is interpreted in most accounts, both military and non-military, as marking the emergence of a distinctive Canadian identity. See D.E. Macintyre, *Canada at Vimy* (Toronto: Peter Martin Associates, 1967) and Pierre Berton, *Vimy* (Toronto: McClelland and Stewart, 1986).

38 Currie Diary, 15 August 1917, cited in Brown, "Not Glamorous", p. 427.

39 Cited in Hyatt, *General Sir Arthur Currie*, p. 79.

40 Cited in Swettenham, *McNaughton, Volume 1*, p. 110.

41 Hyatt, *General Sir Arthur Currie*, p. 80.

42 Militia and Defence, Vol 3846, folder 52, file 5, "1st Division Report on Vimy Ridge."

43 Desmond Morton, *When Your Number's Up: The Canadian Soldier in the First World War* (Toronto: Random House of Canada, 1993), p. 189.

44 Militia and Defence, Vol. 3854, folder 71, file 7, "Causes of Success and Failure – Passchendaele", by Lieutenant-General A.W. Currie, 20 November 1917.

45 Militia and Defence, Vol. 3860, folder 89, file 3, "Canadian Corps Summary of Operations, Nov. 2nd to Nov. 9th, 1917", 9 November 1917.

46 Nicholson, *Canadian Expeditionary Force*, pp. 316–18.

47 Militia and Defence, Vol. 4051, folder 19, file 12, "Notes on Recent Operations", General Staff, Fourth Army, nd (cApril 1917). See also Shelford Bidwell and Dominick Graham, *Fire-Power: British Army Weapons and Theories of War, 1904–1945* (Boston: George Allen and Unwin, 1982), pp. 112–22.

48 Militia and Defence, Vol. 3853, folder 68, file 7, "3rd Canadian Division, Intelligence File – Passchendaele Sector No. 1", 16 October 1917.

49 Militia and Defence, Vol. 3853, folder 68, file 1, "1st Canadian Division. Instructions for the Offensive. Passchendaele No. 1," 23 October 1917, p. 4.

50 Militia and Defence, Vol. 3853, folder 68, file 5, "3rd Canadian Division Operation Order No. 135", 28 October 1917, p.1.

51 Militia and Defence, Vol. 3853, folder 68, file 1, "1st Canadian Division. Instructions for the Offensive. Passchendaele No. 1," 23 October 1917, p. 6.

52 Echoing GHQ's suspicions, several Canadian reports based on interviews with prisoners allude to weakening German morale and disciplinary problems in the units defending the ridge.

53 Nicholson, *Canadian Expeditionary Force*, p. 319 20.

54 Roy, *For Most Conspicuous Bravery*, pp. 56 63.

55 Militia and Defence, Vol. 3854, folder 71, file 7, "Causes of Success and Failure – Passchendaele", by Lieutenant-General A.W. Currie, 20 November 1917. See also Vol. 3853, folder 68, file 3, "1st Canadian Division Report on the Passchendaele Ridge Operations, November 4–12, 1917", December 1917, p. 29, "Lessons and Deductions from the Operations."

56 The most recent account of the campaign disputes this. Robin Prior and Trevor Wilson, *Passchendaele: The Untold Story* (New Haven: Yale University Press, 1996), p. 172. It is also critical of Currie, noting (p. 173) that his plan to capture what amounted to "a most pronounced salient" was "not sensible at all."

Chapter 17

The New Zealand Division at Passchendaele

Christopher Pugsley

On 7 November 1917 Major-General Sir Andrew Russell commanding the New Zealand Division wrote to James Allen, the New Zealand Minister of Defence and briefed him on the results of his division's part in the October fighting before Passchendaele during the Third Battle of Ypres:

> The Division figured in two separate attacks, one on the 4th October and the other on the 12th. In the first we were entirely successful and at a very moderate cost... We went out of the line almost at once and a British Division made another attack on the 9th, which was, for whatever reason, an entire failure. We were brought in on the 11th to renew the attack on the morning of the 12th. This though not an entire failure, was very nearly so. Uncut wire was the cause of our failure. It is true that the Artillery barrage was quite inadequate, owing to the difficulty which had been experienced in getting guns forward, so reducing the number available, and also to the fact that with no stable platform from which to shoot, their registration was faulty and guns were frequently out of action owing to the trails or wheels shifting their position in the mud and soft ground, but, be the barrage good, bad or indifferent, I am confident that our men would have got forward excepting for the insuperable difficulties of the wire. You cannot fight machine-guns plus wire, with human bodies. Without the wire to check them the men would have tackled machine-guns in spite of their losses. As it was, they tried heroically to tackle both. This was humanly impossible.
>
> The Division only took over at 10 o'clock on the 11th and attacked at dawn on the 12th. Whatever the obstacles might have been on our front, it was too late to deal with them by Artillery preparation. We as a Divisional Staff, assumed that the wire had been cut. Assumption in war is radically wrong if by any means in your power you can eliminate the uncertain . . .
>
> In this case I got sufficiently accurate information as to the state of affairs, but 24 hours too late to be of any use. Had it been received 24

hours earlier one would have been in a position to ask for an extension of time before attacking to deal with the difficulty . . .

We cannot always expect to succeed, but I feel very sorry about it all when I think of the numbers of men who were lost. My chief fear is that the men may lose confidence in the arrangements made for them as they had always been taught that, provided the Staff arrangements are good, they are able to do anything that is asked of them.

I am happy to know to-night that, where we failed, the Canadians have succeeded, but with the advantage of three weeks preparation and twice the number of troops.

In these days of Parliamentary criticism, questions may be asked as to the operations I refer to. The somewhat bald and concise statement I have made above accurately represents the position.[1]

This correspondence between a divisional commander and his defence minister would be unusual in most armies on a number of aspects. First it is a frank admission of failure and acceptance of blame by Russell. But it also shows the particular nature of this division which, with the exception of a mounted rifles brigade in Palestine, was New Zealand's national army. It was a citizen force raised in wartime and disbanded in peace. Russell was well aware that on his division's survival and success rested the hopes and aspirations of the one million inhabitants of New Zealand. Unlike any other divisional commander he was answerable both to his superior head-quarters which at Passchendaele was that of Lieutenant-General Godley's II ANZAC Corps, but also to Godley again in his role as Commander of the New Zealand Expeditionary Force (NZEF). This was distinct from the operational chain of command and involved matters of national administration concerning the provision and training of reinforcements, appointments and promotions, pay, mail, and welfare. Similar national command structures existed in the much larger Australian Imperial Force (AIF) of five infantry divisions, and the Canadian Expeditionary Force (CEF) of four infantry divisions. This provided a buffer for the divisional commanders of the AIF and CEF, but in New Zealand's case the division was the sole focus of national attention, and political concern. Everything that happened within it and to it was the subject of press and public interest. Because of this both Godley and Russell were expected to write regularly and in detail to James Allen, Minister of Defence and also acting Prime Minister for much of the war. Godley reported on NZEF matters which also included training and hospital establishments in Britain and France, and Russell on his division, but it was the affairs of the division which not surprisingly became the primary focus of both.

The Godley/Russell relationship is an important one if one is to understand the New Zealand experience at Passchendaele. From 1910 to 1914, Godley had commanded the New Zealand Defence Forces and implemented the introduction of the Territorial system based on universal compulsory military training. The New Zealand Government appointed Godley to command the NZEF, and on its arrival in Egypt he joined his force with Australian formations to form the New Zealand & Australian Division as part of Birdwood's Australian and New Zealand Army Corps (ANZAC). Godley succeeded Birdwood as commander of the ANZAC Corps on Gallipoli, and in 1916 with the expansion of the ANZAC forces in Egypt, he was appointed commander of II ANZAC Corps, but retained command of the NZEF for the duration of the war. A sound administrator and trainer, Godley was an aloof man who never courted popularity with his citizen soldiers. He was hated by Gallipoli veterans and this reputation lingered on in France.[2]

The New Zealand Division was formed as an uniquely New Zealand formation in Egypt on 1 March 1916. Its commander, Andrew Russell, was born in New Zealand in 1868 to an old-established New Zealand family. He followed in the family traditions and was educated at Harrow and Sandhurst and graduated in 1887 as a lieutenant in the Border Regiment. He saw five years service in Burma and India before resigning his commission in 1892 to return to the family sheep station in the Hawkes Bay in the North Island of New Zealand. Russell had to make a success of farming for his financial survival. He was a practical man who hated waste and these factors are evident in his approach to command. Active in the Volunteers and Territorial Force on the outbreak of war, he commanded a Territorial Mounted Rifles brigade. Godley, whose natural preference was towards professional soldiers, saw in Russell the only New Zealand Territorial officer capable of commanding a brigade on active service. Godley invited him to command the New Zealand Mounted Rifles Brigade which, together with the New Zealand Infantry Brigade, formed the initial NZEF. Russell confirmed this ability both as a brigade and divisional commander on Gallipoli and was the logical choice to command the New Zealand Division on its formation in 1916.

Committed to France in April 1916, Russell had little time to forge his raw division into a fighting unit. It grew in skill and professionalism by trial and error. On the Somme, as part of XV Corps in September 1916, the New Zealand Division earned a reputation as an outstanding fighting formation. Haig commented that "for 23 consecutive days" which was the longest single tour by any British division in this battle, it carried out "with complete success every task set... always doing more than was asked of it."[3] However Russell knew that it was his "diggers", as the New Zealand soldiers became known after the Somme, rather than his work and that of his staff that had achieved this success.[4] This had been at a cost of 7408 casualties, and reinforced Russell's belief that men were his most valuable asset, and a resource to be husbanded. His priorities became 'the men's comfort and safety first, the rest nowhere.'[5] Russell's ambition was to have the best division in France. He was always conscious of how much he and his staff did not know, and believed that this could only be overcome by detailed preparation and planning, and sound training at each level of command.

Meticulous planning and attention to detail became his hallmark for every operation. Russell by nature and background was a man who had to see things for himself. The daily inspection of units in and out of the line was part of his routine. Little escaped his attention. Every visit would lead to written suggestions and conference items with his brigadiers and commanding officers. In the same way he insisted on detailed rehearsals which were then discussed by his staff, brigade commanders and commanding officers, and attack plans modified accordingly.

In 1917, the Division had four infantry brigades, each of four battalions. Three of them, 1st, 2nd and the newly formed 4th Brigade, consisted of battalions of the Auckland, Wellington, Canterbury, and Otago Regiments.[6] The exception was the 3rd (Rifle) Brigade with its four Rifle battalions. The strong provincial links added to the character of the Division, and for many it was home town first and New Zealand second. Russell disliked and opposed this four brigade structure, but was overruled by Godley and a War Office that happily accepted a fourth brigade as a compromise when it pressured New Zealand to form a second division. To fit in with other divisions in the line meant that one of the brigades was always detached on Army labouring tasks which Russell believed affected both its state of training and administration, and inevitably its discipline and morale.

Russell was fortunate in having a guaranteed supply of trained reinforcements. New Zealand introduced conscription for overseas service with the Military Service Act of 1916. Two thousand personnel marched in each month to meet the reinforcement quotas for the NZEF. Universal compulsory military service was already in force for all 18 year olds in New Zealand, and by the time an individual reached enlistment age of 21 he had a veneer of military experience. On marching into camp, his draft spent three months on basic and corps training in New Zealand before sailing to England for further training. Reinforcements to France went through the "Bull Ring" at Etaples before joining the Division. A New Zealand reinforcement could spend ten to fourteen months in training and travel before reaching the front line; by this time he had fired the musketry course at least twice, and had few illusions about army life. This guarantee of trained men in sufficient quantity throughout the war was a cornerstone to the success of the New Zealand division. It is customary to talk of the natural ability of the Anzac soldier who disregarded the norms of saluting and discipline out of the line, but was ferocious in battle. This has become part of the Anzac myth. Russell knew from bitter experience on Gallipoli and in France that success in war demanded professionalism, and that is what he imposed on the New Zealand Division. He insisted that his men conform, and demanded equally high standards in leadership and training.

Russell's preparations for the Battle of Messines exemplified this. This was Godley's II ANZAC Corps' first major offensive. Russell's Division was the left assault division, with Major-General John Monash's newly arrived 3rd Australian Division on the New Zealand right. Both men had served as brigade commanders under Godley on Gallipoli, and the allocation of the capture of the town of Messines to the New Zealanders reflected Godley's faith in Russell's ability and the greater experience of the New Zealand Division.[7]

Russell rehearsed and refined his plan in the two months leading up to the Messines' offensive on 7 June 1917. Divisional training emphasized junior leadership and platoons were organized to reflect the doctrine outlined in S.S. 143 *Instructions for the Training of Platoons in Offensive Action*. Russell wanted every one of his soldiers to 'be able to throw a bomb, fire a Lewis gun, rifle or rifle grenade and use a bayonet.'[8] Paddy Griffith's study of the evolution of small unit tactics in the British Armies on the Western Front shows that, from 1916 on, sound advice on tactical doctrine was issued by the General Staff, but most divisions never got organized enough to implement it. Time out of the line was filled with absorbing reinforcements and rudimentary repetitive training.[9] Russell's strength is that he made time, and ensured organizational and tactical improvements were implemented at every level. He was conscious that the cost of a success like the Somme inevitably demanded the rebuilding and retraining of the formation if it were ever to succeed again.

Before Messines, each section commander had gone forward to vantage points with his platoon commander and viewed the ground over which they were to attack. Each battalion and brigade rehearsed all aspects of the assault and reorganization and, as one battalion report noted, by Zero Hour: 'every individual taking part in the attack was thoroughly conversant not only with his own task, but with those of the others working on either flank'.[10]

On 7 June 1917, Messines was outflanked by the two attacking New Zealand brigades, Clearing parties entered the town to mop up German defenders in the cellars and bunkers in which they themselves then sheltered during the German artillery counter-bombardment. In a pre-attack briefing, Haig thought Russell's plan too bold and one that would produce 'an awkward salient prematurely' and suggested a more deliberate advance in 'three jumps'.[11] Russell kept to his original plan. The rapid seizure of Messines by the New Zealanders led to the crumbling of German resistance on both flanks and played an important part in giving Haig his most outstanding success of the war to that time. Haig noted that Russell 'was holding Messines with many machine-guns in great depth, all our troops being in positions around the outside of the village to avoid shell-fire'.[12] It is now recognized that one of the weaknesses with the Messines offensive was that too many men were pushed onto the ridge to fall victim to German artillery fire.[13] Russell had anticipated that in his planning and wanted to withdraw one of his two attack brigades, as well as evacuating Messines itself. He carried out the latter, but was directed to keep both brigades forward, and as he feared, it was this that led to the majority of the 3666 New Zealand casualties.[14] Messines was an outstanding success for Plumer's Second Army and Godley's II ANZAC Corps. There had been weaknesses in co-ordination by Godley's headquarters, but this was understandable in his Corps' first major offensive role on the Western Front. However, as Passchendaele would show, while his divisional commanders, Russell and Monash, evaluated and improved on the tactics used at Messines, success blinded Godley to the deficiencies in his staff's performance.

After Messines, Russell had to rebuild the strength and fighting effectiveness of his division. In July 1917, his units concentrated on individual soldier skills during their spells out of the front line. Ernest Langford, a signaller in the 2nd Otagos, wrote of 'extended order work and gas drill. In afternoon rapid loading etc' – the latter 'a tedious job Heartily sick of the business.' Two days later Langford's battalion was 'put through individual assault which consists of a run, bayonet two men fire 5 rds and throw live grenade.' This was a 'Good day. Bayonet Instructor takes us in afternoon. Go thro orders as L[ance] Cpl.'[15] This was repeated throughout the division.

Russell also reviewed the fitness of his unit commanders and weeded out his "empties" as he privately termed those commanding officers who had given everything, but who now needed to be rested. Those who did not recover combat fitness were posted back to New Zealand with the tacit understanding of the New Zealand General Staff that they would not return.

On 20 August 1917, Russell wrote in his diary that he had been warned that his division was 'to go North' but first would ' go out to rest and train.'[16] His division went into reserve in September for a period of intensive training for three of his four infantry brigades; 1st, 2nd and 4th Brigades, while the 3rd(Rifle) Brigade was detached from the division to work under Second Army, burying cable south of Ypres.[17] The divisional training followed the pattern that Russell had established in his build-up to the Messines offensive in June. 'Full advantage was taken of the good facilities for training in the Reserve Areas, platoon, company, battalion, and Brigade training being carried out, and attacks practised from the trenches, as well as Wood and Village fighting and open warfare. Musketry training received attention and full use was made of the ranges available.'[18] Training was designed to counter the 'new Bosche tactics of shell holes and disposition in depth.'[19] Platoon organizations were adjusted to reflect the latest recommendations from General Staff, and platoon training schools were set up in each brigade.[20] In the first week, Russell carried out daily battalion inspections and viewed his battalions in training at company and battalion level attended by the brigade commanders. Training then progressed to formation level with brigade inspections and brigade attack rehearsals.[21] It was hard and demanding. Private Langford of the 2nd Otagos wrote that on 6 September the day started with a battalion parade. 'Then proceed to top of hill for start of attack. Gen Godley, Gen Braithwaite [Brigade Commander 2nd Brigade] etc on the scene. Advance over rough country for about three miles... Home about 5 pm very tired.'[22]

On 14 September, Haig inspected the New Zealanders and wrote in his diary:

> The 1st, 2nd, and 4th Brigades were on parade. The men were well turned out and handled their arms smartly. They are a sturdy, thick set type of man. After my inspection the troops marched past by platoons. A very fine show indeed. Every man seemed to be trying to look his best and the whole went past in fine style. Mr Winston Churchill accompanied me and seemed much impressed.[23]

Training and planning continued throughout September with divisional conferences on 6 and 19 September to discuss points arising from II ANZAC Corps conference on the previous days. Russell spent 20–21 September 'studying map of our projected attack.'[24] Changes to the plan were then discussed with Godley the following day. Attack plans were rehearsed by each brigade. On 24 September, Russell watched an attack by Brigader-General Hart's 4 Brigade which was 'fairly well carried out, rather amateurish', and Russell then critiqued it with Hart and his commanding officers. Russell met with Plumer and Harington his Chief of Staff on 25 September and also Major-General Smyth, VC, GOC 2 Australian Division with whom he discussed the Australian attack of 19–20 September 'details of which are useful.'[25] The next day was spent going over maps, and reconnoitring the ground for the attack before motoring to Godley's Corps Headquarters for the latest orders.[26]

On 28 September, Russell met Lieutenant-General Maxse 'who commands the adjoining Corps to discuss matters, or rather to be talked to; he is full of his own ideas, which are good.'[27] Russell already practised much of what Maxse preached, and deserves inclusion in Griffith's "elite" who were those individuals whom he classes as the truly effective individual commanders within the BEF.[28] Russell spent the last two days of September talking to Corps, visiting flanking divisions, and discussing the plan in detail with his brigade commanders. Finally on 30 September, he visited Plumer 'to explain plans'.[29] On the same day, the advance elements of the division moved forward to the Ypres area. It concluded an impressive planning and training process that left little to chance. On 2 October, Russell met with his brigade commanders and commanding officers. 'I fancy we have got most of the work done and everyone seems confident.'[30]

Godley was keen to build upon his Corps' success at Messines, and was confident that Russell and Monash would repeat this for him on 4 October. Haig visited Godley on 1 October and spoke to him:

> of the importance of making his arrangements so as to be able to exploit any success gained without delay. Thus guns should be placed behind Gravenstafel Hill (as soon as it is captured) for dealing with

Passchendaele – and the reserve brigades of the attacking Divisions should be used *at once* to exploit a success, if the enemy counter-attacks and fails.[31]

Godley's faith in his divisions was not matched by the performance of his own headquarters. Too much of what was Corps' responsibility was left to the divisional staffs to solve. The major problem was the lack of Corps' co-ordination of engineer effort. There was only a single road forward from Ypres and this was so congested that there was no room for the engineers to get their road building stores forward except by carrying parties on the duckboard tracks on either side. 'The road was so congested by heavy guns moving along it before it was ready to take them, and by poor traffic control at first, that it was impossible to get horsed wagons along it.'[32] Despite constant complaints to Corps, this never improved. It worked for 4 October, but not for the attacks that followed on 9 and 12 October, Godley and his staff showed no understanding of the time it took to move guns and ammunition forward for a Corps battle, and made no effort to see that the necessary preliminaries were achieved. His was a lazy headquarters with little tactical or administrative skills and got by on the strength of Russell and Monash's detailed preparation. They were unable or not prepared to assist the two attached British divisions on 9 October and a tragedy ensued.

The attack on 4 October 1917 was the single occasion when the two ANZAC Corps attacked side by side on the Western Front. Birdwood's I ANZAC's objective was the Broodseinde Ridge while on its left II ANZAC was to seize Gravenstafel Ridge. The New Zealand and 3rd Australian divisions attacking alongside each other with the New Zealanders as always on the left. Gravenstafel was the New Zealand objective. This was divided by the Wieltje-Gravenstafel road which passed over the valley of the Hanebeck stream up the imperceptible rise to the road junction at Gravenstafel with the hamlet of Korek to the left of the road and the slight rise known as Abraham Heights on its right. Beyond this, the road continued into the valley of the Stroombeck and its continuation the Ravebeck Stream before climbing up Bellevue Spur and continuing along it north west of the village of Passchendaele. This was the scene for the attacks of 4, 9 and 12 October. The ground which pre war had been one of the richest farming areas of Europe had been turned into a wilderness of destruction and craters. The Hanebeck and Stroombeck/Ravebeck stream valleys had been turned into quagmires. It was a scene of total desolation where the brick remains of farms and villages had been turned into strong points in the German defensive line with reinforced concrete pillboxes standing out like islands in a sea of mud. This was difficult for infantry, impossible for tank and horse. Russell's divisional plan was to attack with two brigades, the 4th on the right against Abraham Heights and the 1st against Korek. Each would attack with two battalions to seize the immediate objectives this side of the ridge, then leap-frog through the remaining two battalions to seize the depth objectives, the furthest of which was just short of the Valley of the Stroombeck.

The 2nd Brigade initially held the divisional front until replaced by the assault brigades on the night of 2/3 October. Stakes were placed to mark the assembly areas for the attack and after dark on the night of 3/4 October, tapes were laid at right angles to the objective to mark each battalion's start line. The reality was mud-soaked men stumbling forward by night along the duck boards and paths, and then huddling in shell holes on the taped line as the rain that had held off, now came down as a clammy drizzle and a strong westerly wind chilled them to the bone. It was a quiet night with little activity until 5.30 am when German artillery began a strong bombardment on the New Zealand front. It fell behind the assembly areas, and casualties were few. Unknown to the waiting New Zealanders, the Germans too were in their assembly areas waiting to attack. To counter the success of the British attacks, the German forward battle zone had been reinforced with machine-guns and the support and reserve battalions moved forward, together with the leading regiment of the counter-attack division. In addition, the German 4th Guards Division had moved into its assembly areas in front of the two ANZAC Corps to counter-attack and recapture the Grote Molen spur lost on 26 September.[33] It was this mass of German infantry that was caught in the open at 6 am when the British artillery bombardment began.

There was no preliminary bombardment for this attack, only a "hurricane" of fire at Zero Hour. Ten brigades of artillery organized in two groups, including the 1st and 3rd Brigade NZFA,[34] supported the division. Exclusive of medium and heavy guns, this numbered one hundred and eighty 18-pounders and sixty 4.5" howitzers on a frontage of 2000 yards and to a depth of 1000 yards. The Artillery programme had the heavy guns concentrating on strong points and counter-battery fire while the attacking infantry were protected by four lines of fire. A creeping barrage was provided by the field guns advanced in front of the infantry. Beyond that, three stationary lines of fire were put down in turn by field guns and howitzers, the medium 6-inch Howitzers, and, furthest out, 60-pounders, 8-inch and 9.2-inch howitzers. Smoke was fired to mark each objective, and a curtain of smoke and high explosive masked the advance from German observers on Bellevue Spur.[35]

At 6 a.m., the bombardment started, followed five minutes later by a barrage of 60 machine guns. The infantry moved forward, each battalion on a two company frontage. As the photograph shows, they 'moved in sections in single file covered by a screen in extended order like beaters.' The leading platoons advanced in extended order while behind them came platoons with sections in single file along the ridges of earth that lipped the shell holes. As the leading elements struck opposition so the following sections could either change formation to extended order and give fire support, or remain in file and move to attack the pillbox from the flank. It was this tactical flexibility that ensured success. Within two hundred yards, they came across the remnants of the first line of the 4th German Guards Division, the second was two hundred yards in rear. Both had been destroyed in the artillery barrage. 'On the 1st Auckland front alone were about 500 corpses, and generally along the whole line every shellhole held 1 to 4 dead Germans.'[36]

Each battalion was supported by light trench mortar teams moving with the infantry. At any strongpoint or machine-gun post that gave opposition, a trench mortar brought down fire while the infantry deployed and attacked. The New Zealanders found that one or two well-placed mortar rounds was enough to bring the machine-gunners out with their hands up. Despite pockets of determined German resistance, both brigades consolidated on the Blue Line or final objective while patrols pushed forward to the edge of the Stroombeck. Observers flying overhead picked up, through the wind and rain, the line of red flares that marked II ANZAC's objective.[37] Russell was pleased with what had been achieved:

> We got off first and his losses must have been heavy – Anyhow we gained all objectives advancing our line some 1900 yards on NZ front and this division captured some 1100 prisoners. Our casualties I estimate at 1500/2000, the others make it less – All battns. (1st and 4th Bde) fought well, especially latter – More rain fell during day and ground will become bad.[38]

German prisoners taken by the Division numbered 1159 from four different divisions, while New Zealand casualties totalled 330 killed and 1323 wounded.[39] On the evening of 4 October Russell wrote to his Minister of Defence:

> We've been having one of our periodical battles today: and so far have done well. Casualties not so heavy as at Messines, nor nearly so heavy as on the Somme which was the biggest battle, and the heaviest fighting that we shall ever see I hope. The more I see of it the less I like it. These long casualty lists, with all they mean, do not lose their effect through familiarity. It seems so futile, tho' one knows it isn't. Unfortunately it is raining, and the sun hasn't the power to dry the ground so late in the year. We've got a very muddy time in front of us, and that means a lot. The mud is a worse enemy than the German who did not, today, put up much [of] a show of resistance, tho' I shall not be surprised if he tries to get in tomorrow. I believe we have the luck to start first as he was going to make a big counter attack: if true he must have lost heavily. We got over 1000 prisoners in this Division alone.[40]

Heavy rain set in and turned the valley of the Stroombeck into a quaking morass. Russell thinned out his forward elements, and leaving his artillery, engineers and Pioneers in place, was relieved by 49th British Division on 6 October. This division with 66th Division was to continue the II ANZAC attack on 9 October. Russell had serious doubts that a further attack was possible in the conditions: 'Genl. Percival, my successor, and I walked up to Spree Farm – wanted him to see roads.'[41]

Godley was keen to continue, but it is clear that he had no conception of the difficulties his divisions faced in the mud and the rain. Birdwood knew his Australians had done all they could and even Gough expressed doubts on continuing the battle, but Godley had no such qualms. On 8 October, Haig was told by Plumer that Godley's II ANZAC 'had specially asked that there should be *no postponement.*' Haig wrote on the day of the attack: 'a gale blew all night... A general attack was launched at 5.30 am today... The results were very successful... the 66th Division advanced without barrage and took all objectives. 49th gained all except small piece on the left.'[42] Godley's headquarters reported an advance equal to that achieved on 4 October, and planned to exploit this success with the New Zealand and 3rd Australian divisions. It was all wishful thinking, and only the next day these achievements were qualified to Haig's Headquarters. 'Reports from Second Army show that progress on 2nd Anzac Corps front yesterday was not so great as first stated! The 66th Division on the right advanced a mile; the 49th Division on the left about 500 yards on an average.'[43] Even this report greatly exaggerated what had been achieved. Both divisions were stuck on their start lines with little or no gain in ground. Russell wrote on 9 October that the II ANZAC attack that morning was a failure . . . 'troops held up early and arrived at Assembly point exhausted.'[44]

For Godley it now became a point of honour to seize Passchendaele. On 10 October he briefed Haig that the '3rd Australian Division and the New Zealand Division go into the line again tonight. Godley told me that they are determined to take Passchendaele in the next attack and will put the Australian flag on it! The advance will be then over 2000 yards. But the enemy is now much weaker in morale and lacks the desire to fight.'[45] There was no consideration given by Godley and his staff as to why the attack had failed, only a determination to attack again as quickly as possible to fulfil promises given to his Commander-in-Chief.

On 10 October, the New Zealanders moved back into the line and took over from 49th Division. Russell designated 2nd and 3rd (Rifle) brigades as the attack formations, with 4th Brigade in reserve, and 1st Brigade relieving the 3rd as a labour force for Second Army. The relief in line was a nightmare. Private Leonard Hart of the Otago Battalion wrote of the five mile approach march through the mud.

> We struggled on through this sea of mud for some hours and everyone was feeling pretty well done. It was quite common for a man to get stuck in the mud and have to get three or four to drag him out . . . Well, we at length arrived at our destination – the front line and relieved the worn out Tommies. They had not attempted to dig trenches but had simply held the line by occupying a long line of shell holes, two or three men to each hole.[46]

The New Zealanders had no sooner taken over the line than:

we were surprised to hear agonised cries of "stretcher bearer", "help", "For God's sake come here" etc. coming from all sides of us... and were astonished to find about half a dozen Tommies, badly wounded, some insane, others almost dead with starvation and exposure, lying stuck in the mud and too weak to move.[47]

These were some of the 127 stretcher cases left behind by 49th Division, many more had died. Evacuation 'was extremely difficult, involving a 3 and a half mile carry over tracks under heavy fire from artillery, machine-guns, and snipers, and rendered a quagmire by the heavy rain.'[48] Hart mirrored feelings of most New Zealanders in writing to his parents: 'still the fact remains that nothing was done until our chaps came up, and whoever is responsible for the unnecessary sacrifice of those lives deserves to be shot more than any Hun ever did.'[49]

Evacuating the wounded of the outgoing division was only one of the problems facing the New Zealanders. It was soon apparent to Russell and his staff that neither 49th Division nor Godley's Corps Headquarters had any idea of the location of the front line, nor of the state of German defences on Bellevue Spur. With less than 24 hours to zero hour, the artillery fire plan had yet to be confirmed, and the condition of the single road forward had worsened since 4 October. Brigadier-General Napier Johnston, Russell's CRA, reported to Russell in the early afternoon of 11 October that the 'guns are all forward but he evidently feels uneasy about the attack – says preparation inadequate.'[50] Johnston had reported his concerns to Godley and his staff: 'it surely does not seem excessive to expect the road and narrow gauge railway authorities to push on almost contemporaneously with the advance of the troops.'[51] He was assured that it was a Corps' priority, but nothing was done.

The constant rain made it impossible to get guns forward to the new battery positions. 'Guns out of action were in every case either completely bogged or else blocked on the road'.[52] The Wieltje-Gravenstafel Road was littered with guns and ammunition desperately needed forward. 'Men and horses worked incessantly till they were tired out when the battle of the 12th took place. Heavy and Field guns were constantly bogged, and it must be remembered that it is not only necessary to get guns forward, it is necessary to put them on stable platforms, and to make side roads by which ammunition may be brought up. Many officers seem to think that it is sufficient to get the guns forward; this is a mistake: it is equally important to have them mounted on stable platforms, ammunition clean, and the equipment in good order. The fine shooting necessitated by the modern barrage necessitates the most thorough preparation.'[53] This was never achieved. All was reported to Corps, but Godley had promised Haig the village of Passchendaele, and despite rain, mud, and congestion, any delay was unthinkable. Godley obviously took faith in the fact that the New Zealanders and 3rd Australians had never yet failed in an attack.

Godley's attack was the Second Army effort on 12 October while XVIII Corps of Fifth Army attacked on its left. II ANZAC attacked with, as always, the New Zealand Division on the left, and 3rd Australian Division on the right. The New Zealand objective was the Bellevue Spur a low ridge that dominated the approach across the swampy morass that was the valley of the Stroombeck and Ravebeck. Monash's 3rd Australian Division had Passchendaele as its objective, but getting there would be largely determined by the speed with which the New Zealanders secured Bellevue Spur to a depth of some 2000 yards to a point north-west of Passchendaele at Meetcheele. The attack was made with 3rd (Rifle) Brigade on the left, and 2nd Brigade on the right. The depth of the objective saw each brigade attack with a single battalion in turn to seize each of three objectives, battalions leap-frogging through each other once each objective had been seized. Bellevue Spur was a formidable position strongly defended with pillboxes and strongpoints. The barbed wire entanglements had been further strengthened since 9 October. This was discovered on the night of 10/11 October by a patrol led by Sergeant Travis from 2nd Otago, and the 'formidable nature of the wire entanglements' detailed.[54] Artillery fire on 11 October made little impression and information on the extent of the wire did not reach Divisional Headquarters until the evening of 11 October. Russell believed it was now too late to request a postponement of the attack, but warned his brigades not to expect too much from supporting artillery. That night, as the brigades moved into their assembly areas, 'a drizzling rain started making the ground very difficult; this rain continued throughout the day becoming very heavy in the evening.'[55]

As on 4 October, there was no preliminary bombardment. Ernest Langford a runner with 2nd Otago cryptically recorded in his diary: 'Barrage started 5.25 am. Boys hopped bags 5.29 am… attack a failure on acc[oun]t of wire encountered. Casualties extremely heavy. Hun machine guns and snipers play havoc. Absolute hell… Bde practically wiped out. Only 2 runners left.'[56]

Hart of the Otagos was in the assembly area when the barrage, instead of falling 150 yards in front of the taped line, 'opened right in the midst of us. It was a truly awful time – our own men getting cut to pieces in dozens by our own guns.'[57] The artillery, which was so important to success on 4 October, now disrupted the New Zealand attack. A shell landed on the headquarters of the 1st Canterbury Battalion killing Lieutenant-Colonel G A King, the Commanding Officer, and making casualties of his headquarters. It also destroyed the limited supply of trench mortar ammunition that had been laboriously carried forward by the Light Trench Mortar teams. Attacking battalions now lacked the indirect fire support that had been so effective in dealing with strong points on 4 October. Ironically the barrage was at its most effective on the New Zealand assembly area and then became 'weak and patchy' as it advanced 'and at places it was almost impossible to see the barrage.'[58]

Hart was with the leading elements who 'made a rush for the ridge:

> What was our dismay on reaching almost to the top of the ridge to find
> a long line of practically undamaged German concrete machine gun
> emplacements with barbed wire entanglements in front of them fully fifty
> yards deep. The wire had been cut in a few places by our artillery but
> only sufficient to allow a few men through at a time... Dozens got hung
> up on the wire and shot down before their surviving comrades eyes. It
> was now broad daylight and what was left of us realised that the day was
> lost. [59]

By 5.50 a.m., 'enemy machine gun fire had become so heavy that, after
this hour, no further combined advance was made'. Many isolated
attempts were made to get through 'uncut wire running practically along
the whole front' and silence the machine-guns. But at '10 a.m. both
Brigades reported being held up by uncut wire and machine guns, that the
barrage was lost, and that they were digging in on the line gained.'[60] The
3rd Australian Division had made good progress on their right but were
held up on their left by enfilade fire from Bellevue Spur. The artillery
barrage was brought back to protect the infantry line on the lower slopes
of Bellevue Spur, and at noon, a warning order was issued for both brigades
to continue the attack at 3 pm. At 1.45pm, Brigadier-General W G
Braithwaite of 2nd Brigade informed Russell that 'it is impossible for this
Brigade to continue the attack without incurring abnormal additional
losses. Re-organisation is absolutely out of the question in daylight owing
to snipers and machine gun fire and my men are so closely dug in under
the enemy wire that the heavy bombardment of the Pill Boxes is also impossible.'[61] At 2.50 pm, the attack was cancelled. The men scrabbled for cover
in the shell holes on the lower slopes of Bellevue Spur as German snipers
picked off anyone who moved. Braithwaite had no doubts about why the
attack had failed.

> The failure of this Brigade to reach its objectives was entirely due to want
> of artillery preparation in destroying broad belts of wire in front of the
> Pill Boxes NORTH and NORTH EAST of the RAVEBECK and not to
> the Pill Boxes themselves which are comparatively easy of capture
> provided the wire is cut by artillery beforehand.[62]

Both brigades hung on to what they had gained, and Russell moved
forward 4th Brigade to assist if the Germans counter-attacked. Losses were
heavy in both brigades. 'They had poured out their blood like water. The
bodies of 40 officers and 600 men lay in swathes about the wire and along
the Gravenstafel road.'[63] Of the two attacking brigades, the 2nd Brigade
lost 1500 men and the 3rd Brigade 1200, a total of 2700 casualties in four
hours. It is New Zealand's blackest day. Russell wrote in his diary:
'Attacked this morning at daybreak – we, and indeed all other divisions,
were held up at the start by M.G. Evidently the artillery preparation was

insufficient, the barrage poor, and it goes to show the weakness of haste – our casualties are heavy, Geo. King amongst others – I am very sad – Weather conditions bad.'[64]

The rain and mud made the evacuation of the wounded a nightmare. Langford wrote on 13 October 'Wounded coming in galore. Great difficulty in getting them away thro mud, six men to a stretcher. Practically an armistice on all day both sides carrying in wounded. See Huns everywhere carrying in wounded... A hellish experience coming out thro mud arrive in middle of night.'[65] Eventually 1200 men from 4th Brigade, a battalion from 49th Division, as well as artillery and transport personnel, were employed as stretcher bearers to get the wounded out on 13 and 14 October. Braithwaite signalled Russell on 14 October. 'In spite of frequent appeals to every branch of the Staff and to the A.D.M.S. three times the 75 stretcher cases at WATERLOO ... are still lying there. 40 of them have been lying out in the open under shell fire the whole night. I am powerless to do more than I have done. As a last extremity I appeal to you personally.'[66] For many it was too late; gas gangrene had set in or they drowned in the shell holes. Passchendaele broke the spirit of the New Zealand Division. It destroyed Braithwaite who had commanded 2nd Brigade since its formation. He like many veterans had reached the limits of his endurance. A New Zealander wrote of Passchendaele:

The sights and experiences out here in Flanders are awful at times in fact unless he saw them [one] could not believe them. I have seen human bodies used as temporary rly sleepers and as fascines for moving guns over. I have seen bodies and parts of bodies scattered all over the place lying and decomposing. I have seen roads along the side of which men – horses and wagons have been lying in broken tangled masses. I have seen men killed by shells, fall in the mud of the road and the traffic go on just the same... Men are smashed and patched if possible to be sent back to be smashed again. Ambulances and dressing stations are smashed, railways and trains and motor lorries and guns both great and small are smashed and so it goes on... But enough of this it's "Just the War"[67]

On 16 October, Russell took Godley forward to Gravenstafel Heights:

from where a good view is got of Bellevue, wire shows on the forward slope plainly, and the ground looks an easy slope with practically no shell holes – Our front trench just discernible – forward pillboxes stand right out... It is plain we attacked a strong position, stoutly defended with no adequate preparation, nor was the supporting barrage or covering barrage such as to help us over the difficulty – Genl. Plumer came in to see me and expressed his entire satisfaction with the way our men had fought – and attributes no blame for our failure.[68]

Russell did. On 24 October, he held a divisional conference for his commanders and staff.

Explained as well as I could what appeared to be the obvious lessons of 4th and 12th. The chief one, applying more especially to Div[isiona]l. Staff and Self, is that under no circumstances in war is one justified in assuming anything which can possibly be verified – and that where there are certain known conditions necessary to success it is a great risk, however justifiable, to attack before they are fulfilled.[69]

On 31 October, he reinforced these lessons again at a divisional conference 'at which I drew attention to our failure and [its] lessons – Notably the crime of the Division in assuming the wire to be cut which ought to have been verified.'[70] Russell accepted that the artillery barrage had failed, but he knew that had the wire been cut beforehand, his men would have succeeded, because of their training with or without the supporting barrage. He blamed himself for committing his men to an impossible task, and wrote accordingly to Allen.

The New Zealanders wintered in the Ypres Salient and Russell's task was to rebuild the strength and spirit of his Division. Careful administration and attention to the welfare of his men restored the division's faith in itself. Russell weeded out his "empties" and instituted a training programme that placed emphasis on open warfare and practised his commanders in being able to react to a rapidly changing situation. Because of this, 1918 was a year of outstanding achievement for Russell's New Zealanders.

Passchendaele was the last ANZAC battle. The Australian Corps was formed on 1 January 1918, and Godley's II ANZAC, including the New Zealand Division, became XXII Corps. Circumstances saw the New Zealanders detached from the Corps for all of 1918 so that the defeat before Passchendaele was the last major battle the New Zealanders fought under Godley's command. For the Division it left the bitter taste of defeat, but Godley, writing to Allen, saw it differently:

The New Zealand Division had another big fight on the 12th October. It had to attack a very difficult piece of country on the way to Passchendaele, crossing the Ravebeck stream, and attacking the Bellevue Spur, which is one of the outlying spurs of the Passchendaele Ridge. They were successful in crossing the river and establishing themselves on part of the Spur, but did not quite succeed in getting it all. Altogether we gained about 500 yards and took nearly 600 prisoners, so, though not such a big success as Messines or the battle here on the 4th, it was a very good day's work and the Division again did it excellently. The casualties were about the same as last time, and the two added up together, though not unduly heavy, necessitate the provision of a good many reinforcements.... A German officer, being brought back as a prisoner, when he saw where the foremost guns had got to, and saw the roads, exclaimed in astonishment that no troops in the world would have attempted an offensive with such facilities of approach.[71]

No troops should have, and it was Godley's failure that they did.

Notes

1   Major-General Sir Andrew Russell to James Allen, New Zealand Minister of Defence dated 7 November 1917, Allen Papers, National Archives.

2   Pugsley, *Gallipoli The New Zealand Story*, Auckland, 1984 p. 348.

3   Colonel H Stewart, *The New Zealand Division, 1916–1919*: Christchurch, 1921 p. 119.

4   CEW Bean, *The Australian Imperial Force in France 1917*, Sydney, 1938. See also Pugsley "Putting the NZ in ANZAC", *New Zealand Defence Quarterly*, No.3, Winter 1994, pp. 732–733.

5   Major-General Sir Andrew Russell to James Allen, New Zealand Minister of Defence dated 25 December 1916, Allen Papers, National Archives. See also Pugsley, *On the Fringe of Hell*, and Russell Diaries, 21 and 30 October 1916, pp. 167–184.

6   Originally each brigade consisted of one battalion from each province: e.g. 4th Brigade (3rd Auckland, 3rd Wellington, 3rd Canterbury, and 3rd Otago) However in December 1916 Russell reorganised his brigades to disperse better his war-weary Gallipoli veterans concentrated in 1st Brigade, and grouped 1st and 2nd Auckland and Wellington Battalions into 1st Brigade, and 1st and 2nd Canterbury and Otago Battalions into 2nd Brigade. See Pugsley, *On the Fringe of Hell*, Auckland, 1991, pp. 168–170.

7   This is discussed in some detail in my paper, 'A Comparison Between Russell and Monash, the Divisional Commanders of II ANZAC Corps in 1917': 1989 Australian War Memorial History Conference.

8   Organization of a Platoon, 3 NZ (Rifle) Brigade dated 4 May 1917, WA 22/6/17, National Archives.

9   Paddy Griffith, *Battle Tactics of the Western Front*: New Haven and London, 1994, pp. 76–77.

10 Report on the Capture of Messines by 4th Battalion, 3 NZ (Rifle) Brigade, NA 20/3/13, National Archives.

11 Diary, 24 May 1917, Haig Papers, Volume XVI, May 1917, National Library of Scotland. Quoted in Pugsley, 'A Comparison Between Russell and Monash, the Divisional Commanders of II ANZAC Corps in 1917': 1989 Australian War Memorial History Conference.

12 Diary, 7 June 1917, Haig Papers, Volume XVII, June 1917, National Library of Scotland. Quoted in Pugsley, 'A Comparison Between Russell and Monash, the Divisional Commanders of II ANZAC Corps in 1917': 1989 Australian War Memorial History Conference.

13 Paddy Griffith, *Battle Tactics of the Western Front*: New Haven and London, 1994, p. 86.

14 Russell to Allen dated 19 June 1917, Allen Papers. Casualty figures from Operations of the New Zealand Division, 1 May – 30 June 1917, WA 20/3/8, National Archives.

15 24 and 26 July 1917, War Diary 1917, Private Ernest Harold Langford, Signaller, 2nd Otago, MS Papers 2242, Alexander Turnbull Library.

16 Russell Diaries, 20 August 1917, The Russell Family Saga, Volume III, Russell Family.

17 The four brigade structure made the New Zealand Division the odd one out, and one of its brigades was always detached to Army on labouring tasks. Russell believed that the detached brigade always suffered through losing out on proper administration and training, and for this reason was strongly against having a four brigade division.

18 Operations of the New Zealand Division, Period September 1st to October 31st 1917. New Zealand Division War Diaries.

19 Russell Diaries, 5 September 1917, The Russell Family Saga, Volume III, Russell Family.

20 S.S. 143, *Instructions For The Training of Platoons For Offensive Action 1917*: Issued by the General Staff. Reprinted with Amendments, August 1917. See Russell Diaries, 21 and 24 August 1917, The Russell Family Saga, Volume III, Russell Family.

21 Russell Diaries, 5–11 September 1917, The Russell Family Saga, Volume III, Russell Family.

22 6 September 1917, War Diary 1917, Private Ernest Harold Langford, Signaller, 2nd Otago, MS Papers 2242, Alexander Turnbull Library.

23 Field-Marshal Sir Douglas Haig Papers, Friday 14 September 1917, Volume XX, National Library of Scotland.

24 Russell Diaries, 20 September 1917, The Russell Family Saga, Volume III, Russell Family.

25 Russell Diaries, 25 September 1917, The Russell Family Saga, Volume III, Russell Family.

26 Russell Diaries, 27 September 1917, The Russell Family Saga, Volume III, Russell Family.

27 Russell Diaries, 28 September 1917, The Russell Family Saga, Volume III, Russell Family.

28 Paddy Griffith, *Battle Tactics of the Western Front*: New Haven & London, 1994, p. 83.

29 Russell Diaries, 30 September 1917, The Russell Family Saga, Volume III, Russell Family.

30 Russell Diaries, 2 October 1917, The Russell Family Saga, Volume III, Russell Family.

31 Field-Marshal Sir Douglas Haig Papers, Monday 1 October 1917, Volume XXI, National Library of Scotland.

32 Narrative of the Ypres Offensive, [CRE Report] WA 151/42, National Archives. See also Russell Diaries, 3 October 1917, The Russell Family Saga, Volume III, Russell Family.

33 Captain G C Wynne, *If Germany Attacks*: Westport, Connecticut, 1976, pp. 306–307.

34 Narrative of Operations of New Zealand Divisional Artillery. From 1 to 20 October, 1917, WA 50/4/32, National Archives.

35 Colonel H Stewart, *The New Zealand Division, 1916–1919*: Christchurch, 1921, pp. 261–262.

36 Colonel H Stewart, *The New Zealand Division, 1916–1919*: Christchurch, 1921, p. 262.

37 Colonel H Stewart, *The New Zealand Division, 1916–1919*: Christchurch, 1921, p. 269.

38 Russell Diaries, 4 October 1917, The Russell Family Saga, Volume III, Russell Family.
39 Colonel H Stewart, *The New Zealand Division, 1916–1919*: Christchurch, 1921, p. 271.
40 Major-General Sir Andrew Russell to James Allen, New Zealand Minister of Defence dated 4 October 1917, Allen Papers, National Archives.
41 Russell Diaries, 5 October 1917, The Russell Family Saga, Volume III, Russell Family.
42 Field-Marshal Sir Douglas Haig Papers, Friday Tuesday 9 October 1917, Volume XXI, National Library of Scotland.
43 Field-Marshal Sir Douglas Haig Papers, Friday Wednesday 10 October 1917, Volume XXI, National Library of Scotland.
44 Russell Diaries, 9 October 1917, The Russell Family Saga, Volume III, Russell Family.
45 Field-Marshal Sir Douglas Haig Papers, Friday Wednesday 10 October 1917, Volume XXI, National Library of Scotland.
46 Jock Phillips, Nicholas Boyack and E P Malone, (Ed.) *The Great Adventure*: Wellington, 1988, p. 144.
47 Jock Phillips, Nicholas Boyack and E P Malone, (Ed.) *The Great Adventure*: Wellington, 1988, p. 144.
48 Operations of the New Zealand Division, Period 1 September to 31 October, 1917. New Zealand Division War Diaries.
49 Jock Phillips, Nicholas Boyack and E P Malone, (Ed.) *The Great Adventure*: Wellington, 1988, p. 148–149.
50 Russell Diaries, 11 October 1917, The Russell Family Saga, Volume III, Russell Family.
51 Comments on Operations 4 to 12 October, 1917, included in Narrative of Operations of New Zealand Divisional Artillery. From 1 to 20 October, 1917, WA 50/4/32, National Archives.
52 Narrative of Operations of New Zealand Divisional Artillery. From 1 to 20 October, 1917, WA 50/4/32, National Archives.
53 Comments on Operations 4 to 12 October, 1917, included in Narrative of Operations of New Zealand Divisional Artillery. From 1 to 20 October, 1917, WA 50/4/32, National Archives.
54 New Zealand Division, Narrative of Operations for PASSCHENDAELE attack, 12 October, 1917. WA 151/42, National Archives.
55 New Zealand Division, Narrative of Operations for PASSCHENDAELE attack, 12 October, 1917. WA 151/42, National Archives.
56 12 October, Ernest H Langford, 2nd Otago, War Diary 1917, MS Papers 2242, Alexander Turnbull Library.
57 Jock Phillips, Nichals Boyack and E P Malone, (Ed.) *The Great Adventure*: Wellington, 1988, p. 145.
58 New Zealand Division, Narrative of Operations for PASSCHENDAELE attack, 12 October, 1917. WA 151/42, National Archives.
59 Jock Phillips, Nicholas Boyack and E P Malone, (Ed.) *The Great Adventure*: Wellington, 1988, p 145.
60 New Zealand Division, Narrative of Operations for PASSCHENDAELE attack, 12 October, 1917. WA 151/42, National Archives.
61 Brigade Headquarters to NZ Division, 1.45 p.m. BM 28, Second New Zealand Infantry Brigade, Messages Despatched from 10 October 1917, WA 151/42, National Archives.

74. Portrait of Wilfred Ewart, aged
    about thirty, by Nora Cundell.
    (Hugh Cecil) Chapter 26

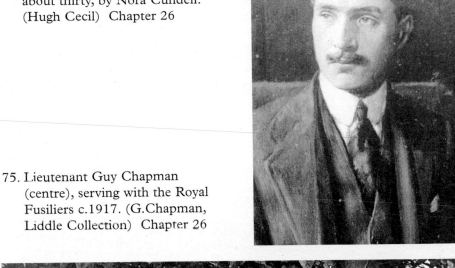

75. Lieutenant Guy Chapman
    (centre), serving with the Royal
    Fusiliers c.1917. (G.Chapman,
    Liddle Collection) Chapter 26

76. Ernest Raymond, a padre in the British Army in the Great War. (Hugh Cecil) Chapter 26

77. An engraving on glass in memory of Edmund Blunden, by the artist Laurence Whistler. Whistler, a friend of Blunden, describes his work for this commemorative window as '... the interpenetration of two worlds - not the solace of healing and forgetting, but the barbed wire as a living briar, and the shell burst as a tree in bloom.'(Laurence Whistler) Chapter 26

78. The watch worn by
Captain Harry Oldham,
West Yorkshire Regiment
during the Third Battle
of Ypres. It is still caked
in the mud from which
Oldham was pulled after
being buried in October
1917. (H.Oldham,
Liddle Collection)
Chapter 28

79. Lieutenant Gerry Brooks of
the Tank Corps was wearing
this helmet in action in
August 1917 - as his tank
became ditched and the crew
was forced to abandon it, the
hole at the front of the
helmet was caused by a shell
shard flying upwards from an
explosion. (G.Brooks, Liddle
Collection) Chapter 28

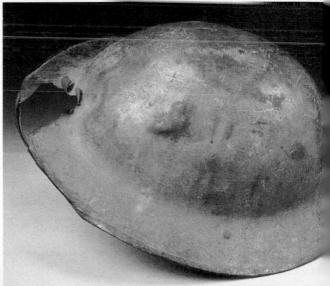

80. The Cloth Hall at Ypres, as it stood at the end of the First World War.
    (H.C.Eccles, Liddle Collection) Chapters 27, 29

81. The Menin Road at Inverness Copse, shortly after the Armistice.
    (G.D.Fairley, Liddle Collection) Chapters 27, 29

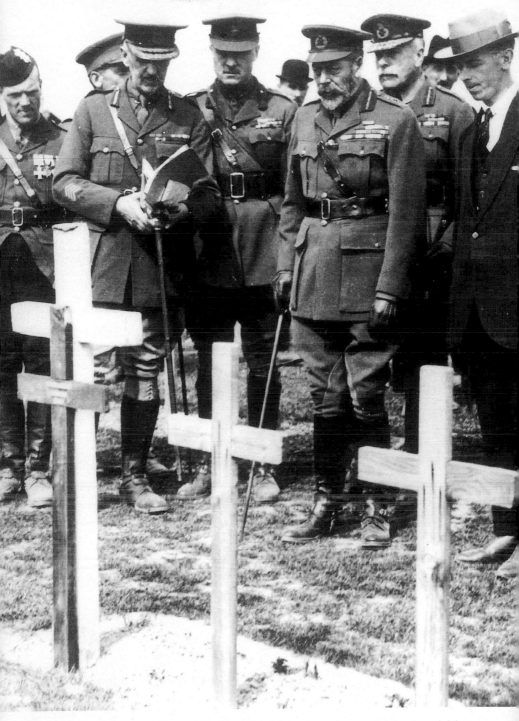

82. H.M.King George V and Sir Douglas Haig are among dignitaries visiting a
British war cemetery near Passchendaele, shortly after the war. (H.C.Eccles,
Liddle Collection) Chapters 27, 29

83. The Menin Gate at Ypres under construction in the early 1920's. (L.Mills, Liddle Collection) Chapters 27, 29

84. British veterans returning to Ypres in the 1930's. (A.E.Smith, Liddle Collection) Chapter 29

85. The original group of battlefield burials, dating from 1917/18, at Tyne Cot cemetery Passchendaele. (Alasdair Cheyne/Liddle Collection) Chapter 29

86. 'A division on parade': uniformity at Tyne Cot. (Alasdair Cheyne/Liddle Collection) Chapter 29

87. Concrete bunkers at Broodseinde Farm, as they are today. (Ed Skelding) Chapter 29

62 Brigade Headquarters to NZ Division, 5.20 p.m. BM 38, Second New Zealand Infantry Brigade, Messages Despatched from 10 October 1917, WA 151/42, National Archives.

63 Colonel H Stewart, *The New Zealand Division, 1916–1919*: Whitcombe & Tombs, Christchurch, 1921, p. 291.

64 Russell Diaries, 12 October 1917, The Russell Family Saga, Volume III, Russell Family.

65 13 October, Ernest H Langford, 2nd Otago, War Diary 1917, MS Papers 2242, Alexander Turnbull Library.

66 Braithwaite 2nd Brigade Headquarters to Russell, NZ Division, 5.20 p.m. BM 38, Second New Zealand Infantry Brigade, Messages Despatched from 10 October 1917, WA 151/42, National Archives.

67 Letters of C S Alexander to his cousin, dated 20 December 1917, quoted p. 251, Pugsley, *On the Fringe of Hell*.

68 Russell Diaries, 15/16 October 1917, The Russell Family Saga, Volume III, Russell Family.

69 Russell Diaries, 24 October 1917, The Russell Family Saga, Volume III, Russell Family.

70 Russell Diaries, 31 October 1917, The Russell Family Saga, Volume III, Russell Family.

71 Lieutenant-General Sir Alexander Godley, GOC, 2 Anzac Corps and Commander NZEF to James Allen, Minister of Defence, dated 16 October 1917, Allen Papers, National Archives.

Chapter 18

South Africans in Flanders: *Le Zulu Blanc*

Bill Nasson

By the time the South African Infantry Brigade trundled across from the Somme region to detrain at the Ypres salient in September 1917, the Union's volunteer contingent had been meeting German forces on the Western Front in more or less continuous combat for more than a year. Moreover, for some men of the South African Scottish 4th Battalion, Flanders was already an old digging ground. In late 1915 and early 1916, South African troops had undergone initial trench warfare training in Belgium, an experience which had given them a slightly misleading notion that this was a war which was going well. For one Lance-Corporal, that instruction had suggested that it would be 'quite safe to walk anywhere behind the front line without fear of being hit'.[1] Others found social contact with Flemish civilians enjoyable, as South Africans had been welcomed by Flaamsche as cultural novelties. They must certainly have seemed an extraordinary colonial phenomenon: white men from Britain's African Empire whose Dutch-Afrikaans vocabulary enabled them to communicate easily with Flemish-speakers and to read and understand newspapers from Ostend or Antwerp. There were, of course, also local misconceptions. Many soldiers had found either baffling or preposterous the expectation of some welcoming Flanders inhabitants that 'South Africans should be black men'.[2] With many of them raised on rugby, Latin classics and college school Christianity, it was not for nothing that most of these bronzed and large-framed infantrymen were rather more inclined to see themselves as Africa's European elect, or archetypal 'colonial supermen', to use Paddy Griffith's vivid phrase.[3]

By the time of their arrival in the reserve trenches of the Ypres battlefield, the 149 officers and 2790 combat troops of the four battalion-strong South African Brigade had minted a quite distinctive form of soldiering self-identification, refracted through the assertion of a vaulting 'Springbok' national identity. Martialled behind the laurelled springbok head emblem of the South African Brigade, with its encircling motto, 'Union Is Strength – Eendracht Maakt Macht', Pretoria's expeditionary force was viewed as the living embodiment of a sharp-looking, superbly disciplined Dominion Army.[4] As a shared identity between officers and rank-and-file, Springbok motivation and conditioning derived from a fairly idiosyncratic combination of assumed characteristics and underlying values. At one level, a singularly powerful sense of diaspora 'Scottishness', bound together South African Brigade soldiers, many of whom had been recruited through the Transvaal Scottish, Cape Town Highlanders, the Cape-based Duke of Edinburgh's Rifles, and a vibrant network of Caledonian societies.[5] And now at Passchendaele, as earlier on the Somme, unit attachment to the highly-regarded 9th (Scottish) Division helped to blend the social camaraderie of colonial 'Jocks' with the old warrior guilds of the Royal Scots or the Argylls.

Equally, kilted Springboks brought their own sense of what it was to be Transvaal Scottish. 'Bonnie Highland' marching songs as men wobbled across the engulfing mud east of Ypres, were invested with vocal imagery which celebrated the imagined bonds of affection and respect between Celtic colonists and subject African societies recognized as having notable military talents. 'Zulu Gaelic', 'Basuto Gaelic' and even Rhodesian 'Matabeleland Gaelic' (evidently rendered as *ena palili, Zomkie Palili mangie*) underscored the distinctiveness of the South Africans as an empire presence within an Old World 9th Scots Division.[6] What reinforced this further were the customary trench cries to raise the spirits of exhausted men; rooted in the discourse of an imitative African tribalism, exhortations commonly took the shape of Zulu war cries or mock Zulu war dances. This drove home a simple message: the regimental spirit of the 4th South African Infantry could match that of a nineteenth century Shakan impi. Lastly, in snatched recreation periods, some of the South African Brigade's white Springboks engaged in self-parody as *le Zulu blanc*, blackening their faces with soot. 'We put candles in tins and covered the top with our hands', recalled one ninety-nine year old Rand Rifles veteran, and 'we then rubbed the soot over our faces and necks. The boys loved that chance to mess about and shout *Usuthu*.[7] In this respect, playing at Zulus provided a fleeting imaginative haven from the horrors and arduousness of the war.

Passchendaele's South African force was also tightly-knit at two other levels. One was its overriding middle class English and loyalist anglo-Afrikaner orientation, which fostered common patriotism and social closeness between officers and men. A further contributory factor was its localized recruitment pattern, drawing officers and men from schools, merchant houses, and mining company offices where they frequently knew one another in peacetime. Another was the Brigade's heavy 'blood sacrifice' in the ferocious July 1916 Battle of Delville Wood, where it fought with great distinction and at terrible cost, losing 2,536 men from a complement of 3,153 troops.[8] Almost a quarter of the surviving 700-odd rump of the original Brigade which survived the 'Devil's Wood' ordeal would die later in the war, including those who were now to drown in the engulfing mud of Passchendaele shell holes.[9] After the Somme, it was the impetus of

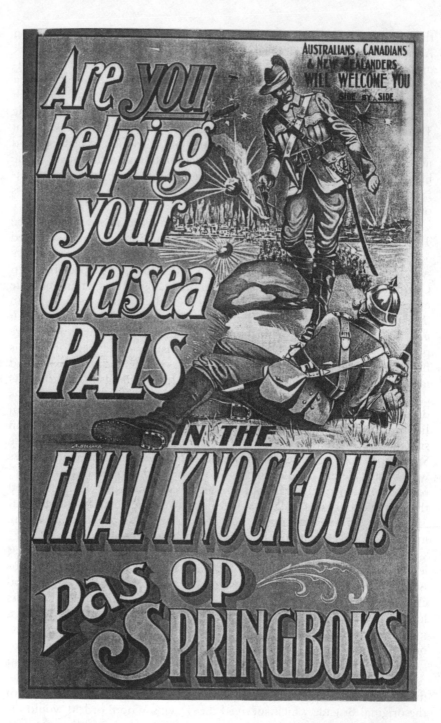

(xix) A recruiting poster for the "Springboks" – in English and Afrikaans.
(South African National Museum of Military History, Johannesburg)

Delville Wood which continued to provide the essential moral lubricant of the South Africans' perceived fighting attributes on the Western Front. Through an unprecedented discharge of fierce courage, gritty sacrifice and disciplined endurance, the conduct of South Africa's colonial volunteers would go on, to quote Trevor Wilson, 'to become legendary'.[10] Here, the presence within the reconstituted post–1916 Brigade of a seasoning of decorated Delville Wood veterans helped to keep up the stock of a resurrectionist Somme battle inheritance through operational service between July 1916 and September 1917. This included operations at Vimy, Butte de Warlencourt, Arras, Fampoux and Menin Road.

But the level of South African courage and elan by 1917 should not be exaggerated. For, as Third Ypres approached, the bile of recent engagements had left increasingly raw wounds. Their toll was a serious blow to Brigade strength; while continuing losses had not necessarily weakened its mobilizing Springbok spur, casualty rates after Arras and Fampoux by July 1917 had left it 'a shadow' of the 5,708-strong force which had embarked for Britain in 1915.[11] What this all amounted to was that the South Africans commenced July training for the Ypres onslaught not only considerably under strength but showing signs of growing strain and rocky morale. For even the most motivated Cape Town Highlander, the immense hardships of prolonged Western Front campaigning and accumulating personal tragedies made a further trek from Arras to Ypres a miserable prospect. South African soldiers had come so far; they were now less ready than ever before to go further when there was little sense of decisive victory in sight.

Suggestive anecdotal evidence reveals a growing cluster of widely-shared feelings amongst both officers and men. One, for the first time, was open anger in May 1917 at what was perceived as incompetent British generalship. At Fampoux, despite inadequate advance reconnaissance and misgivings from South African command, the Brigade was prodded into highly risky action. Heavy losses for a 200-yard territorial gain now saw soldiers grimly dubbing themselves, 'the suicide Springboks'.[12] Another was rising resentment at having to 'go into the trenches again, quite sickening'[13] to train new recruits, and the intensifying ghoulishness of the unauthorized parts of that induction. Third, there was a sometimes bilious disdain for new batches of higher-paid 1917 recruits, viewed as mercenary 'three shillings a day' bodies to replace original 1915 'bob a day' Somme campaign patriots, a sacrifice which the Union government seemed thereby to have cheapened.[14] Fourth, the use of companies of South African infantry combatants in mass burial parties after the end of the Somme offensive brought into the Brigade a gnawing sense of gloom at the war's seemingly endless carnage. One officer was prompted to conclude that for his soldiers to tramp into further battle in Flanders, 'with the reek of death still in their nostrils . . . these memories would be distressing to even the hardest . . . [and that] this misuse of fighting troops was cruel and useless'.[15] Finally, by August and September, the tone of ordinary soldiers' songs, ditties, and doggerel verse in Eyre Camp, near Poperinghe, where the Brigade underwent training for Third Ypres, had become in turn sharply sombre or biting, and suffused with longing for transcendence. 'Please take me back across the sea/Where the blasted Allimans won't drop bombs on me', was one typical diary entry; other lines such as, 'Now where will my favourite girl be/To Hell with France and Blighty/They aren't so mighty/Africa's the place for me', seemed a South African equivalent of the popular Australian Imperial Force refrain, 'Blighty is a failure/Take me to Australia'.[16]

As these men began to prepare for battle in mid-September, performing assault-party manoeuvres and practising advance movements amidst the clay models and tape lines which simulated German strong points and barbed wire contours, there was undoubtedly a diminishing desire to see the war through to its still uncertain fruition. Yet, at the same time, in the view of the prominent South African imperial hand, Sir Lionel Phillips (who enjoyed visiting Brigade trenches in a tin hat and gas mask), this remained a disciplined and resilient body of soldiers who knew what to do, knew how best to take care of themselves, and most of all knew how to keep going.[17] And they still seemed to have few doubts about the right-eousness of their particular cause.

This reputation was now again to be tested. On 17 September, the South African Brigade was trucked from a Poperinghe railway siding to occupy deep dugouts along the canal bank west of Ypres. Although their original commander, Major-General Henry Timson Lukin (commonly dubbed 'Tim' or 'Little Tim') had been given overall command of the 9th Division in December 1916, he now revisited his contingent to speak to both officers and men. A veteran of nineteenth century Southern African colonial wars as well as the 1899–1902 South African War and the recent 1914–15 conquest of German South West Africa, Lukin appears by all accounts to have been an able and much-liked leader – robust, brave, and also espe-cially attentive to the welfare needs of his troops. To this, he added personal prowess with horses and bushcraft, and a courageously insou-ciant style – although gassed at Delville Wood, he still continued to decline gas mask protection when visiting frontal positions.[18] Lukin announced that the Brigade would be joined by Brigadier-General Frederick Maxwell's 27th Brigade in an attack on a section of the front which had already been subject to several costly and fruitless assaults by other British divisions.

Extending on a segment of the battlefield running on a front some 2,000 yards north of the haunting Menin Road to a depth of about one mile, the terrain ahead 'presented a horrible appearance. Derelict tanks lay shattered and engulfed in mud. The ground was torn and churned by shellfire. Not a blade of grass was to be seen. No trenches remained except a shallow excavation in the front line. Communication trenches did not exist'.[19] According to Private Kenneth Earp, 'the sight was hard to believe . . . it simply had the look of an indescribable hell. You faced this end of the earth and wondered if you or your chums would make it. It felt like hard lines'.[20] In exhorting his infantry to maximize their efforts, Lukin took his cue from the suffocating sight of the Ypres battlefield: if the going looked perilously forbidding, who better to 'win through' than South African Springboks? Had they not been acknowledged as among the best troops in the British Army, with a toughness and offensive inclination to match that of the Anzacs? The Union's 'commando' military tradition was also invoked. Lukin reminded his old Brigade of its creative blending of British Union Defence Force discipline and cohesion with Boer-Afrikaner burgher fighting traditions long on small unit initiative, tactical boldness, and swift firing movements. This special pedigree would work greatly to the advantage of assaulting South African infantry. They would be closing on German positions not in shoulder to shoulder formations, but more as independent, darting 'commandos', to which specific enemy targets had been assigned. Able to wheel as decisively as any herd of *Springbokken*, Brigadier-General Frederick Dawson's irregular line of foot commandos had the nerve and 'national' character to rout the German defensive cordon.[21] This was a great leap forward of the optimistic imagination. It was less clear that it could be matched by South African Scottish boots.

The nights of 17 and 18 September set the infiltrationist 'commando' thrust for the advance of a 4th South African Infantry platoon spearhead on the left, and 3rd platoons on the right. Following careful reconnaissance, safe pathways from reserve trenches to attack assembly areas were marked with white tape to funnel troops along duckboard-covered ground to identified battalion positions. Even as his troops paddled their way across 'water and evil-smelling slime', Dawson fretted over the risks of night movement in terrain wholly unfamiliar to most men, and was not hopeful of the capacity of his soldiers, many of them newer recruits, to concentrate safely and rapidly at key points. In one respect, he had no reason to worry unduly. 'Except for the occasional crash of a heavy shell', suggests Peter Digby, 'progress through the ghostly town of Ypres, along a slow and devious route with many halts, was unusually easy'.[22] In fact, the South African advance was a model execution of Herbert Plumer's new offensive tactics of thinning out troops aimed at first objectives,[23] and maintaining the protectiveness of wide gaps between moving units. Moreover, widely schooled and experienced scouts, braced by both the desert sands of German South West Africa and the murderous mud of the Somme and Ypres, proved reliable guides through the blackness to forward positions.

In another respect, however, the state of battle preparedness looked anything but rosy. In pitch darkness, with few if any physical bearings within sight, some men stumbled off duckboards and were nearly smothered in muddy shell holes. Troops were having to assemble, 'soaked through and shivering constantly', with nerves not helped by the knowledge that in view of the British failure of August, the defending force confronting them was extremely formidable. Alert to the dread fear around him, Second Lieutenant Geoffrey Lawrence risked distributing an over-generous measure of rum.[24] A more senior fellow officer pondered that 'sjamboks' might be handy: he imagined emulating turn-of-the century republican Boer Generals, having to flog recalcitrant soldiers into turning out for combat.[25] Indeed, even a company commander here and there became a stammering liability. One, Captain Albert McDonald, 'shivering with cold and nerves', pressed a subordinate to take over his command. As recalled by this sympathetic officer, 'he was in a terrible state of nerves and fear which he seemed unable to fight down. He appeared to dread the coming of the dawn . . . I could do nothing to comfort him'.[26] The extent of such stomach-churning immobility within the 3rd and 4th South African Infantry is corroborated by several other accounts, including that of an NCO who yearned for an issue of those quintessentially masculine South African comforts, *biltong* (dried meat) to still chattering teeth, and potent *witblits* or *skokjaan* as a pre-battle narcotic.[27] What is undoubtedly striking about this heightened moment for South African combatants, is the immense gulf between the robust and rhetorical 'Jock', 'Springbok', or 'Zulu' warrior spirit which obviously gave the Brigade its national pride

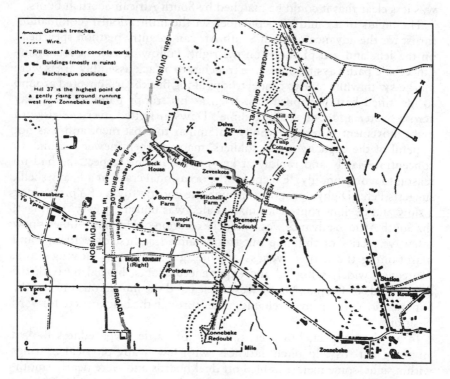

(xx) The South African Attack at the Third Battle of Ypres (Official History: Union of South Africa and the Great War 1914–18, Government Printer, Pretoria, 1924); identical copy in John Buchan, The History of the South African Forces in France (Nelson, Edinburgh, 1920) p. 133

and identity, and the small change of individual thinking, feeling, and survival rituals into which it ended up being translated. Equally, the pre–1916 combat idiom of the war as a European playing-field, which had originally animated so many middle-class South African volunteers,[28] had by now lost its meaning. The measure of infantrymen's mental equipment was an ever more sardonic resort to a colonial white South African cultural vocabulary. This craggy self-expression now seemed to become an increasingly emotive code of national character for many soldiers who had probably come to believe by September 1917 that they lived their lives purely by luck or chance.

With the supporting 1st and 2nd South African Infantry having threaded their way through to bunch up close behind the vanguard 3rd and 4th, the 532-strong 4th battalion surged into action on 20 September, advancing in dawn darkness over 'slimy' and 'swampy' ground lit only fleetingly by gun-flashes, shellbursts, and ominously erratic signalling flares. While attacking in file, section commanders often found themselves having to stop and assemble men in shell holes, in order to try to establish accurate direction or just their exact whereabouts.[29] Yet advance on the left was still rapid. Within a few hours, a time in which attacking troops had to dodge a British artillery barrage, their assigned objectives of Beck House, Borry Farm and Mitchell's Farm had been taken. A simultaneous onslaught against enemy outposts on the Zonnebeke Stream also saw German defenders reeling back, leaving behind a substantial number of corpses and wounded as well as prisoners and weapons to be scooped up by the South Africans. When deployed frontally, there was still plenty of fight left in *le Zulu blanc*. On the right front, the 3rd battalion of 676 men was no less ferociously on the offensive. Led by a gritty Delville Wood veteran, Lieutenant-Colonel Edward Thackeray, the 3rd seized the fortified Vampir Farm, their principal target, and fanned out with skill and system to overrun other German defensive positions north of Potsdam and south of Borry Farm. Like the 4th, the 3rd battalion relied on the shock of a surprise attack which heaved forward not merely right on the heels of the creeping British barrage, but risked jinking through it to hammer away at startled German defenders. One Springbok later recalled being repelled by what seemed to him to be the indiscriminate bayonetting of bleeding and bewildered German soldiers, and the whooping 'war cries' which accompanied this, 'they were hardly able to stand their ground and it was quite sickening, poor devils . . . this was not a part that I enjoyed'.[30] While some undoubtedly felt squeamish about such excesses, these minor 'bush' attacks suited South African inclinations, kindling recent memory of bayonet-driven night ambushes over the rough ground of German South West Africa. In such frontal operations, the Passchendaele experience breathed life into a style of fighting at which South Africans, like Australians,[31] seemed particularly adept: tactics which put a premium upon stealth, patience, a high level of individual initiative, and closing ferocity.

So breakneck had been the pace of the South African rush on the left that the 3rd Transvaal ran into enfilading machine-gun fire from the Potsdam pill box strongpoint on the right, as it crossed open ground. In effect, these infantrymen were ambushed during their advance, and began to falter. Then, in a creditable display of courage and promptness, companies were rallied by officers and swung against the Potsdam Redoubt. Under covering Lewis gun fire, and using shell holes as defensive pits, the South African force pressed forward an attack in controlled stages. And, once more, troops vaulted through their own barrage, then waded across the Zonnebeke Stream, seized some German buildings and bombed others, and routed the Potsdam garrison, killing or capturing German defenders and snatching weaponry and stores.

These actions were, of course, minor skirmishes. But they were psychologically crucial. Their effect must have been a tremendous boost to South African morale. No longer were troops under the strain of nervous expectation of what lay ahead; with considerable *élan*, they had struck the first decisive blows and proved their continuing military effectiveness. 'After all the suspense, the fine haul gave us real excitement', crowed Corporal George Shaw.[32] Thrown off balance, German forces withdrew southwards towards the Ypres-Roulers railway line. In order to maintain pressure while extending its present advance towards the northern railway embankment, the South African force was split into small parties to attack various points simultaneously, aimed roughly at hounding opponents from pillar to post. But their German enemy was neither intimidated nor without teeth. Rearguard machine-gun counter-attacks, accompanied by the incursion of German aircraft which mowed down exposed infantry, produced a bloody crop of killed and wounded. After a costly push, Lieutenant Geoffrey Lawrence's platoon picked off a railway embankment dugout. He recalled how hard it was to impose a moral curb upon vengeful impulses towards surrendering Germans. 'Our tempers were up with our losses', disclosed Lawrence, who battled to restrain his men 'from shooting the enemy as they came out'.[33] As Richard Holmes has pointed out generally, the death of friends provides a common reason for soldiers not to accept enemy surrender, to say nothing of the uncertain luck accompanying surrender in actual battle.[34] Yet what perhaps also underlay such an incident was the pulsating level of murderous hatred which the war had reached by 1917: even in a Brigade which gloried in the battlefield reliability, efficiency and discipline of its troops, there were elements of bristling savagery.

The second stage of the South African advance sent men floundering through that most dreaded of Passchendaele campaign conditions, sucking mud. Soldiers encountered a quagmire the nature of which they had never before experienced, sinking in chest-high and losing equipment. Parallel co-ordination with the Royal Scots proved extremely difficult. Yet, once dug in and concentrated defensively, the 1st was able to hold its ground against German counter-strikes. The 2nd, while subjected to heavy bombardment from the steep ground of Tulip Cottages and Hill 37, successfully charged the bastions of the Bremen Redoubt, Zevenkote and Waterend Farm, taking some seventy prisoners and abandoned arms. In this attack Lance Corporal William Hewitt won a Victoria Cross for single-handedly eliminating a pill box.[35] The South Africans then entrenched their 20 September front line positions, checking German assaults with frontal and flanking fire, and calling up artillery to pulverize assembling assault parties. A crack 2nd Regiment Corporal who 'really enjoyed' the experience of 'decent sniping' wrote of the horror of this bombardment, 'one of the most awful sights I have ever seen . . . you could see nothing but bodies and bits of bodies, equipment, and trees flying up into the air'.[36]

At night on 21 September the South African Brigade was relieved in the front line by the 7th Seaforths and 5th Camerons. Having gone into battle 2,576-strong, it emerged with a harrowing casualty list of 1,255 killed, wounded or missing. 'We carried our front and stuck it out, although with no time to do anything at all for those who were drowning or being cut up . . . we were played out, and should've been finished had we been left there any longer', recalled Joe Samuels.[37] With more equanimity, the Brigade's official historian, John Buchan, declared that if Delville Wood had been the South Africans' 'most heroic episode in the War', the September Ypres offensive was 'its most successful achievement' up to that point, leaving men tired but exultant.[38] Jan Smuts wrote to congratulate Lukin on the 'brilliant advance' of South African boys, seeing in it the seeds of the inevitable British victory.[39] This was nothing if not a touch premature.

After spending just over two weeks away from the battlefront, the South African force left the warm food and clean blankets of billets on farms as the 9th Division re-mobilized for action east of Ypres. Between 10 and 12 October, the Brigade was ordered up to occupy trenches near to the foot of Passchendaele ridge. Continuing deterioration of the terrain now imposed crippling difficulties. South African infantry in the frontal area were more or less immobilized, their vital duckboard tracks continuously shelled by well-directed German artillery, their communications constantly cut, and their heavier weaponry claimed by the mud. Save for one tortuous pin-prick advance on 13 October which saw the village of Wallemolen fall to South African troops, Lukin's Springboks shared the fate of almost all other soldiers at Passchendaele: that of hapless, scrabbling victims of its appalling quagmire. For Geoffrey Lawrence, life had boiled down to a 'war machine' which 'was geared up and just could not stop'.[40] Others felt that they were barely clinging to existence, finding it miraculous that they were not drowning or 'all down with pneumonia', while yearning for the heavy heat and dusty landscape of Southern Africa.[41]

With communications barely operational, and Lewis guns and artillery pieces bogged down in mud, exhausted infantrymen were reduced to killing time. As prospect of any further advance receded, infantrymen floundered between reserve positions and front line relief with an almost tidal regularity. Soldiers who were relieved just to be alive found some outlet for their dour mood in auxiliary tasks. A large South African infantry contingent was attached to the Royal Army Medical Corps and South African Ambulance for four days, as stretcher bearers and dressing station orderlies. As a Duke of Edinburgh Rifles officer reflected, 'this was death's work and an awful business', but also found deep within himself some consolation that good would come from secondary duties of comforting stricken men, providing Dutch-Afrikaans interpretation for British doctors tending wounded Afrikaners, and stiffening those who would pull through.[42] Contact between the South African Brigade and Germans huddled nearby in their shell holes and shallow trenches now consisted largely of mutual vigilance against any risky exposure to sniper fire and the common fear of random shelling. An officer recorded the spontaneous surrender of several 'weary and dejected' Germans and inwardly wondered whether some of his more worn Springboks might not contemplate something similar.[43] For all the Zulu battle cries which still floated up intermittently, there was a sense of slithering debilitation, of aching for respite from Ypres hostilities. On 23 October, the Brigade was withdrawn from the Salient, having lost a further 261 troops killed or wounded. Union Springboks were not to be there at the final taking of Passchendaele ridge.

After Ypres, the Brigade was replenished by new drafts of men fresh from the German East Africa campaign. From another heat of war, they brought a chemistry and mission of their own to blend with the sacrificial witness of Delville Wood and the more immediate legacy of Passchendaele: some small skirmish achievement in a numbing landscape which for South African imagination remained largely barren of anything profoundly poetic or literary. For those few soldiers who tried their hand at expressing 'Ypres', the borrowing of a commonplace Victorian religious and moral vocabulary was pervasive. So, for Private Shaw of the South African Scottish, to leave behind the atmosphere of 3rd Ypres was to be free of some cold contagion:

> The thunder of the drums of death
> Is hushed; the autumn air
> No longer blights with poisoned breath
> The City of Despair[44]

From similar literary stock, a homeland voice six thousand miles away depicted Passchendaele in December 1917 as a further spearpoint of a specific South African soldiering identity: Third Ypres was not some Delville Wood of Flanders, but it was a version of pioneer resilience to rally a recently constructed patriotic white South Africanism:

> Springboks
> You've heard of the great Canadians,
> Of Indians, and Famous Anzacs,
> But now more word of the Springboks,
> Who never turn their backs.

So let the sun sink on this land,
Where the sun burns brown and tan,
And always answer proudly if you're asked:
'Oh, me? I'm a South Aff-Rican'.[45]

Endnotes

1   *Rondebosch Boys High School Magazine*, 9 (48) 1916, p.19.
2   Cited in Bill Nasson, 'A Great Divide: Popular Responses to the Great War in South Africa', *War and Society*, 12 (1) 1994, p.48; see also, Ian Uys, *Rollcall: The Delville Wood Story* (Uys, Johannesburg, 1991), p.6.
3   Paddy Griffith (Ed.), *British Fighting Methods in the Great War* (Cass, London, 1996), pp.59, 177.
4   *Cape Times*, 17 August 1917; *Rand Daily Mail*, 22 August 1917; *Natal Witness*, 26 August 1917.
5   Nasson, 'Springboks on the Somme: The Making of Delville Wood, 1916', Seminar Paper, Institute for Advanced Social Research, University of the Witwatersrand, October 1996.
6   *Rondebosch Boys High School Magazine*, 9 (48) 1916, p.41.
7   Interview with Joseph Samuels (b. 4 November 1897), South African Brigade veteran, Cape Town, May, 1995; see also Nasson, 'Joe Samuels: A Springbok on the Somme', *Oral History*, Vol.26 (forthcoming 1997–98).
8   Uys, *Rollcall*, pp.192–95.
9   *Cape Times Annual* 1919, p.67.
10 Trevor Wilson, *the Myriad Faces of War: Britain and the Great War, 1914–1918* (Polity, Cambridge, 1986), p.334.
11 Peter K.A. Digby, *Pyramids and Poppies: The 1st SA Infantry Brigade in Libya, France and Flanders 1915–1919* (Ashanti, Rivonia, 1993), p.215.
12 *Diocesan College Magazine*, 145 (2) 1918, p.11.
13 *South African College Magazine*, 18 (6) 1917, p.43.
14 Joe Samuels interview, 1995
15 Cited in Digby, *Pyramids*, p.218.
16 See Bill Gammage, *The Broken Years: Australian Soldiers in the Great War* (Penguin Australia, Ringwood, 1987), p.209.
17 *Natal Mercury*, 7 October 1917.
18 R.S. Johnston, *Ulundi to Delville Wood: The Life Story of Major General Sir Henry Timson Lukin* (Maskew Miller, Cape Town, 1926), p.167.
19 Johnston, *Ulundi*, pp.177–78.
20 *South African College Magazine*, 19 (8) 1917, p.45.
21 *Diocesan College Magazine*, 12 (26) 1918, p.28.
22 Digby, *Pyramids*, p.227.
23 Wilson, *Myriad Faces*, pp.473–76.
24 Digby, *Pyramids*, p.227.
25 *Diocesan College Magazine*, 12 (24) 1918, p.9.
26 Cited in Digby, *Pyramids*, p.227.
27 *Rondebosch Boys High School Magazine*, 10 (52) 1917, p.63. *Witblits* ('white lightning') was a rough and highly potent spirit (or 'rotgut') and *skokjaan* an illicit, quick-fermenting and addictive African beer, popular amongst black mineworkers who often laced it with industrial additives such as methylated spirits or even calcium carbide. Appropriately enough for

wartime cravings, they were sometimes also known as a 'kill me quick': see Julie Baker, 'Prohibition and Illicit Liquor on the Witwatersrand, 1902–32', in Jonathan Crush and Charles Ambler (Eds.), *Liquor and Labour in Southern Africa* (Ohio University Press, Athens, 1992), p.143.

28 Nasson, 'War Opinion in South Africa, 1914', *Journal of Imperial and Commonwealth History*, 23 (2) 1995, p.255.

29 *South African College Magazine*, 18 (8) 1917, p.25.

30 *Rondebosch Boys High School Magazine*, 10 (50) 1917, p.33.

31 See Gammage, *Broken Years*, p.31.

32 *Diocesan College Magazine*, 12 (24) 1917, p.18; see also Lyn Macdonald, *They Called it Passchendaele: The Story of the Third Battle of Ypres and the Men who Fought in it* (Penguin, Harmondsworth, 1993), p.182.

33 Digby, *Pyramids*, p.239.

34 Richard Holmes, *Acts of War: The Behavior of Men in Battle* (Free Press, New York, 1989), pp.381, 385–86.

35 Digby, *Pyramids*, p.241.

36 *Our Boys: A City Tribute, Xmas 1917* (Cape Town, 1917), p.15.

37 Joe Samuels interview, 1995.

38 John Buchan, *The History of the South African Forces in France* (Nelson, Edinburgh, 1920), p.134.

39 *The South African Ambassador*, November, 1917, p.19.

40 Digby, *Pyramids*, p.253.

41 *The Selbornian*, 4 (6) 1917, p.17.

42 *The Selbornian*, 5 (2) 1918, p.22.

43 Diocesan College Archives, Bull Mss. Collection, W. Rogers diaries, entry for 17 October 1917.

44 Digby, *Pyramids*, p.256.

45 *Rondebosch Boys High School Magazine*, 19 (53) 1917, pp.8–9.

Chapter 19

Passchendaele Experienced: Soldiering in the Salient during the Third Battle of Ypres

Peter Liddle

"The Somme was a picnic and Arras a joke compared with Ypres now"[1] wrote Captain R L Mackay in his diary for 2 August 1917. He had served long enough to give weight to the comparisons he made. Sentences from another contemporary account, that of a Corporal Stone in the HAC, identify more specifically, constituent elements within Mackay's judgement. Stone wrote of "staggering from exhaustion and trembling with nerves"[2] and that "it was fatal to get into the mud".[3] Of that mud and of a further factor invariably associated with the image of Third Ypres, the German concrete pill boxes, Claude Worthington made mention in a letter written a day after the end of the battle in November: "You cannot conceive what the ground is like. The last sector we were in was a solid mass of shell holes practically touching each other and mostly full of water. The ground very low lying and sluggish streams, mostly mud and marsh, about a few Pill boxes scattered about which are concrete huts to hold a few men and a machine gun".[4] A little earlier, in October, Hugh Livingston wrote of the passing of "one more day in this hellish land".[5]

From such evidence a uniformly bleak image of the conditions under which the 3rd Battle of Ypres was waged has been engraved on the conscience of successive generations, bleak in physical detail and bleak in spirit as a man strove for the resolve to fulfil his duty. That there were men who recorded a different reaction, dissident voices as it were, is of course undeniable. There is, for example, a contemporary account of the first day of the battle in which the writer, W G Cameron, declares that it has been "the best engagement I ever was in . . . we were relieved two days later soaking through and covered in mud but feeling happy with a fag in your mouth and hoping a parcel is waiting for you from home until you get a good tightener".[6] Despite the subjective factors which must put qualification upon any general judgements made from such evidence, there is no doubt where the balance of soldier reaction lay: the Autumn and early Winter of 1917 in the Ypres Salient was a supreme test for a soldier's mind and body. In this chapter, the intention is to look specifically at the ways in which that test was faced, not just by infantrymen and gunners, who indeed must command our attention, but by men involved in a much wider range of functional responsibilities. What needed to be done, how it was done, how men described their work and their reaction to it: the aim here is to use original letters and diaries to make this clear.

Enemy shelling, the sun, the wind, rain and temperature variation, daytime and night, changing ground conditions, they were all of course supremely important to the soldier in the front line or at his battery position, but they also conditioned the circumstance under which men worked to get ammunition, rations and other supplies brought up the line, their working environment if in the rear or indeed out of the line. From this attempt to widen our vision of soldiers enduring their Ypres experience, more will be learned about what was required of them. Their adaptability was impressive, as was their capacity to improvise. The extent to which men made themselves 'comfortable', or their living conditions more bearable, is remarkable. In the case of those in the most demanding circumstance, as with those 'just' doing a dirty, dangerous, tiring, monotonous job, contemporary evidence shows that for few men the reservoir of resolve ran completely dry.

There can be little doubt that the vast proportion of the three million shrapnel and high explosive shells fired by the B.E.F. in France and Flanders in the week ending 5 August 1917 was from guns and howitzers in positions in the Ypres Salient. Developing the logistical implication of this by a small point of detail, it might be added that the total of ammunition expenditure included 592 x 15 inch howitzer shells, each weighing 1400 lbs. A less daunting statistic, though one which is still impressive, is that at this time, B.E.F. establishment included as many as 68,000 railway personnel.[7] Supply factors demand our consideration.

By rail and road, the Ypres share of the weekly total of ammunition had to be conveyed up to and then within the Salient. Trains on differently gauged lines, vehicles, horses and mules on different types of roads which sometimes needed construction and always needed maintenance, hauled, additional to munitions, all that was required, to answer the needs of more than a million men in the battle area.

These needs ranged from rail-mounted guns and the full range of artillery pieces with their distinctive ammunition, to vehicles including tanks and then food for the men, fodder for horses and mules, petrol, coal, construction materials, timber, road stone, trench and general stores. All this and goodness knows what else, together with the men involved in loading, conveyance, unloading, were essential to the battle. This is the wider context of the Ypres experience. Efficient organization from bases, along the lines of communication into the rear areas and expedition in dealing with all that was required, were not easily to be achieved.

The scale of the problem is shown in the diary of Xth Corps Area Commandant, Brigadier-General W. R. Ludlow and, as it happens, he also records something recognized less than it should be, that men of the Chinese Labour Corps indispensably served the men in forward positions.

12.8.17 – McHenry of the Canadians
took us on his trench railway drawn by a petrol engine round the whole of the positions. There was a good deal of shelling going on, and at times it is quite exciting for a pleasant Sunday afternoon. The railway, which is Decauville, is frequently destroyed and at intervals of about half a mile or even less in places are dugouts for the men repairing the line, and when a shell strikes any part they rush out and lay a half circle section round the excavation made by the explosion of the shell and fill it in afterwards by night and re-lay the line straight, so that there shall be no break in getting up the supplies. We went round the whole of the positions in the rear of the balloons and guns starting at Vermoiselles.

29.9.17 –
Rode to Reninghelst and inspected the new destructor and incinerator. Issued orders as to the employment of the Chinese. They are doing well in making duckboards and work in gangs, each with a Native overseer who brought them over from China.

6.10.17 – Re Anzac and Canadian base area administration:
Their organisation is perfectly wonderful and they have unlimited money sent to them from the Colonials, . . . before an attack they send up tea coffee and chocolate and biscuits also soup in huge containers like thermos flasks strapped to a man's back.[8]

There are many references in diaries to improvization on the Decauville railway lines and also the high degree of professional organisation entailed in running these railways with all the points and junctions staffed and with teams of signallers manning the railway telephone system. In one instance it seems a Ford car was converted to run with wheels adapted to the lines and bringing up shells for three batteries. However, it came off the lines so frequently that the fun of hitching a ride paled beside the regular task of lifting the vehicle bodily back onto the rails.[9]

The roads of course suffered from shelling, over-use, inappropriate though necessary use and weather conditions. In a letter written on 9 October, artillery officer M. B. Donald wrote: "It is pretty rotten taking stuff up to the guns though as the roads are shelled and are so full of ditched waggons, dead horses that we are having to rely on packs".[10]

Another gunner, Claude Chavasse, later recorded a moving account of trying to get his mules to cross a shell hole on planks bridging the gap in a timber road. He lost one mule which took fright, fell in the mire and, almost immersed, had to be shot.[11] This was a tragically common fate for horses and mules in the periods of heavy rain though desperate efforts seem always to have been made to prevent such an occurrence. The muddy wasteland on either side of many supply routes claimed soldier lives too

307

though every endeavour was made to save an unfortunate parachuting balloonist precipitately vacating his basket as a German aircraft approached. He fell into Dickebush Lake, the parachute forming a sail and dragging him into the centre. Four or five men stripped and swam out to the rescue, the fastest swimmer, a Channel Islander called Davey, getting nearest to the man before he was finally dragged under.

> Davey located the body and after several attempts succeeded in getting it up but it was weighed down by all the paraphernalia of the parachute attachments and ropes and the man's heavy leather coat. Eventually we got a rope out to him and Davey tied it on. It was only about 20 fathoms long, so it was hard pulling in such a weight; the parachute was partly bellied out and the rope was hard to [detach] even if we [had] had a knife.[12]

Above the Salient or above the River Ancre on the Somme in the previous year, the decision as to whether or not to jump from the balloon basket on the approach of an enemy aircraft was particularly difficult for the inexperienced Observer. Andrew Clark, remembered his first occasion as he cowered in fear at the bottom of the basket quite unable to follow over the side into free flight the Balloon Corps officer in command who had wasted no time in abandoning ship. Ironically the failure of the German aircraft in pressing home the attack led to ribald comments shaming the professional and words of praise for the amateur who had stayed his post.[13]

In a letter to be published in the newspaper for which as a civilian he worked, Private J. D. Urquhart of the Royal Scots described well the hard labour which could fall to the soldier anticipating having to 'fight' in the Salient. "We went up first to do some road-mending. This was no ordinary road-mending, however. Reveille at 4 am, four hours march, five hours work with pick and shovel, and four hours' march home again, with no meals in between". Urquhart, entering the Salient for the first time, found villages which were, "literally mounds of rubbish and brick dust. Long lines of duckboards stretched away across this dreary waste, winding round or crossing myriads of shell-holes". He reached Langemarck having passed debris of every description, "all lying in mud a foot deep". Under shell fire they did their job which consisted of "searching among the mounds for bricks and broken stones . . . and making a road for the big guns to advance over".[14]

At night, rations would be travelling the same road, bread, bully beef, tins of stew, biscuits, bundled in muddied sacks carried by ration parties in single file bumping into each other sliding off the duckboards, the Guide peering down into the gloom to discern a discoloured white tape laid to show a route. When Gunner Fraser received his food, he recorded his disgust with small allowance for the via dolorosa of the ration party. "Then our stew arrived but most of mine went into a ditch. Vile muck". [15.8.17] Tea was made on site and was more appreciated. "Then tea was made and an officer went out and fetched it from the cook's dugout. Had good feed.

Jam, butter, cheese and tea. Heavy shells dropping all round us and the dugout was shaking". [19.8.17] Fraser must soon have forgotten the satisfaction of this meal because later in August he recorded sardonically, "Had very good tea – don't know what's the matter – we must be winning". If there were to have been a skein of optimism beneath the mordant wit, it would not last because in early November he recorded another dinner finding its last "resting place in a shell hole. Awful stuff".[15]

It ought not to be forgotten that for the soldier in the Salient there was another world, and yet still within reach of the battle front – "out at rest". Here, football, concert parties, playing cards, writing letters, better meals, undisturbed sleep, may not have been as good as a spell of home leave but how welcome they must have been. The diary of Signaller W B Kitching [R.G.A.] for July 1917, contained graphically detailed description of danger which in juxtaposition with his account of rest illustrates perfectly the restorative effect of a period out of the line. For 23 July:

On our way back the enemy started shelling the road. He is using a very peculiar type of shell which bursts in mid-air and sends out in the form of a downward spray a stream of white smoke or gas which stays in the air without losing its form, for a considerable time. Our nights have been very troubled by the enemy shelling around the camp. Sunday has been a black letter day for us for we have had 6 casualties, two wounded by shell fire and four by the bursting of a gun. Penton and myself tossed a coin in the morning as to who should go back for our empty drum: Penton lost and on his way to join us was wounded by a fragment of a shell which burst close by him.

To set against this there is the soothing tranquillity of the scenes described in the diary, written a few miles from Hazebrouck from 21 September. They represent so idyllic a rest period that we must simply recognize the principle of the healing influences of days such as this rather than seeing here the general picture of life out of the line. There was a quality gradation in rest periods and accordingly in their benefits.

It is a pretty spot right away in the country and we are billeted in a farm. Everything is so peaceful and beautiful, no sign of war or even of the army, it is like a little bit of heaven itself after what we have been accustomed to. In the evening I took a stroll to Vieux Berquin, a village about two miles away. It was a perfect evening, the sunset was glorious and everything so quiet and peaceful that it was like a soothing balm to the mind.

22 September: "The day was beautiful and sunny, a perfect September day; we paraded at 9.30 and had the rest of the day off. I spent the day in writing and walking". The perfect weather continued and on the following day, also free, he enjoyed, "breathing the fresh pure air of the countryside

barrage opens out at 5 A.M.
Thurs 16th, up 3 o'm & breakfast
& away up the line, just reached
A.D.S. as the British barrage
fire opened, a terrific fire,
had a splendid view of the
bursting shells, 29th Division
gained all objectives & advanced
over 2,000 yods, barrage lasted
4½ hrs. over 8,00 German
prisoners taken. helping
to carry the wounded in,
Battle of Langemarck
crossed Steenbecke river,
many stretcher-cases, a long
way to carry them in, "Fritz"
sending heavy stuff over, all
3 Ambulances bearing, morroon,
Anderson, Martin hove, & some of
8 & Y 88th wounded, our squad
partly buried by a big shell
at Hants Aid Post, concrete
wall saved us, all of us badly
shaken & partly deafened, a
terrible experience, never as
near to death as to day, thank'd
Almighty God for being safe,
a miracle we were not blown
to pieces, sent down to A.D.S.
by feet, & seen by Capt. Stgassey
there, & he sent us for a rest
down to Boesinghe, had
some tea down there & glad of a
lay down, dead beat, been
a great battle to day

(xxi) Private Frank
Ridsdale, in his diary,
thanks "Almighty God
for being safe" after
his experiences during
the Battle of
Langemarck.
*(F. Ridsdale, Liddle
Collection)*

and listened to the carolling of the birds. I felt so joyous and thankful to be alive and well".

From a distant church nestling amidst trees came the sound of bells, Sunday-dressed villagers bade him friendly 'good day' and then a breakfast of new-laid eggs and ham led him to feel "ready for anything". Small wonder that with orders coming for his unit to move back up the line, he wrote on 24 September: "Did ever one have such a disappointment?"[16]

It is for the authors of other chapters in this book to explain how and why an offensive for strategic objectives in the Summer of 1917 became *une bataille d'usure*. Here, what must be appreciated, is one consequence of this for gunners at their batteries. When their positions were vacated and movement of guns and howitzers had to be attempted, the difficulties were appalling, but, for lengthy periods, men worked from the same positions, in action far more demandingly than usual, often under heavy counter-bombardment but living simply under a stepped-up routine, a new demanding normalcy.

Personal diaries make this quite clear. The big howitzers crushed the timber roads or slid off them, sank up to their axles and beyond in the embrace of mud, were jacked up and hauled back onto the trackway, again and again in wearisome repetition but if they were to reach their ordained destination what we must then envisage is described well in the diary of Gunner Fraser.

From August well into October, each day he was on duty, seems to have a similar pattern. On 2 August:

In the morning made a dugout, out of an old gun pit and made it very nice. Had dinner and went up to the guns. There's a big push on tonight. Worked very hard until eleven then turned in. Then Fritz began. First of all he tried gas and we lay in our dugouts with helmets on. I was coughing and sneezing terribly. At last the gas moderated a little and we went to sleep. Called up at four and the Push began. I never heard such a terrible bombardment. Every gun for miles was blazing away. We could hardly hear each other speak even when we shouted. This went on till eight am when we just had time to drink our tea. Still we loaded and fired.

Meanwhile they saw a neighbouring battery being shelled out of action, ammunition set on fire and the men of that battery "running in all directions". Fragments of shell fell through their camouflage netting. "I picked up a piece that fell near me as I ducked and it was nearly red hot". Then they cleared out from their own positions such was the accuracy of the enemy fire. Casualties were suffered and all the men were "very tired and deaf by now". Dinner was brought up to them and it was hastily downed and "they keep on firing as we had since 4 am. Then the relief came up".

Day after day, when up with the guns, similar details are recorded. The strain on the nerves could scarcely be more clear, sometimes spelled out as for 26 August: "What an existence here. All the time we are on the qui vive and it is worst when we are firing, for we can't hear the shells coming".

Strikingly, this Gunner too, wrote of exhaustion diminishing the will and capacity to take emergency action under danger. 27 August: "the captain shouted at us to take cover. I never felt so completely reckless and I was cold and wet and hungry. We packed up our tea and very slowly took refuge in a trench".[17]

The constituent, inter-acting elements in the sustenance of morale and the Army's encouragement of unit and individual performance, its effort, to deter failure in fulfilling duties and to bring offenders to book when it occurred, are central to Peter Scott's chapter in this book. All that need be stated here, if contemporary description of Ypres battle experience were to lead some readers to the border of bewilderment that men could endure without breakdown into incapacity or mutinous refusal to obey orders, is that surviving personal diaries show morale holding up. Occasionally it dips dangerously.

Signaller Kitching [R.G.A.], on the first anniversary of his engagement to his 'dear girl', and with wistful memories of a peaceful country scene when his ring was presented and accepted felt "caged like a bird" in the Salient. "I want to get away from all this continual strife and desolation. Each day the same roaring of the guns, the same hard work: then a push and a stop, but the end seems no nearer. Will it ever end? Is there any sense in prolonging this awful struggle". He wrote this on 2 September even adding the thought that "some wise conference would at least be useful and might be the means of bringing about a satisfactory termination". There is no denying that his recording of such an idea raises his cri de coeur above the average but within days he was exulting in a "very successful aeroplane shoot today", had found a gas course "very interesting and instructive" and then that "sitting round the little stove watching the bacon sizzle and listening to the splutter of the eggs, at the same time sniffing the good aroma, produces a most pleasant feeling, a feeling that life out here with all its dangers and hardships has its bright side".[18]

There are common assumptions about the experience of the soldier at Third Ypres: he was always in mud which threatened to engulf him; his lot was never to earn satisfaction from the gaining of his objective; he was never far from abject misery and was nearer and nearer to complete disillusionment with the ideals which had so cruelly deluded him and drawn him to this test beyond his imagination. Not least, he was simmeringly resentful of all military authority, the more senior, the more bitterly this resentment was felt. These assumptions were founded on the undeniably foul and often fearsome 1917 reality but the variable truths and falsehoods they contain tell us more about post-war attitudes to "Passchendaele" than battlefield reaction itself. Now to the men in tanks . . .

The diary of Gunner R O Arscott, G Battalion, M.G.C. (H.S.), offers a sparse, yet by implication, revealing account of the nature of a Tank crew's daily life in the Salient during the first month of the battle. For the opening day, 31 July, tank No. 43 "moved forward over our lines [to] ditch in enemies [sic] front line. Got out. Afternoon dug ourselves in. Rendezvous

6 PM". 1 August: "Arrived back at starting point between 12–1 AM. Returned to camp 2 AM. Wet, dirty, tired and hungry. Wrote Horace, Beat [Beatrice] and Bert. Letter from Beat". Then for over two weeks his days were filled with resting, reading, physical jerks, writing letters, greasing and cleaning the tanks, a map lecture and then on 17 August, moving up ready for action. On 18 August, he was preparing for action; on the following day his predictably terse note stated: "Wounded 6 AM. Taken to 61st Div. Hospital".

In fact, the attack had been launched from St Julien at 4.45 AM and in the report of the commander of No. 43 tank, Second Lieutenant H. G. Coutts, he related that he had met with heavy machine-gun fire from North, East and South and had replied vigorously. Approaching their objective, a massive concrete strongpoint, they had seen and fired on more than thirty Germans who were running from the position. The tank then got badly ditched and the crew got out taking the Lewis guns to operate them from nearby shell holes. A message by pigeon was sent back to tell the infantry to come forward and occupy the position vacated by the enemy. It would not be expected that such a report would comment upon the noise, the heat, the vibration, the lurching jolts, the danger of burns or injuries from touching, moving or hot engine parts though falling unconscious from the fumes is mentioned in some reports.[19]

Arscott's experiences on 31 July and 19 August can only be drawn within our vision by reference to sources other than his own record; for Gerry Brooks, there survives a remarkable document which allows us to feel close to what he went through. Brooks, in command of a tank named Fay, wrote of his experience as he awaited medical attention for the wound he had just received in an action two days after Arscott received his wound:

> The fun began when the tape which we were following led through some very swampy ground. It was so wet we found it hard to swing. The four of us [tanks] got rather bunched and the Foam received a couple of direct hits and Harris her commander and two more of his crew were wounded. Harris was in great pain having his left arm nearly blown off from the elbow and also armour plate and rivets in his leg. He came round to the front of my tank in great pain and called to me. His men bound him up and put him on a door and eventually got some German prisoners to carry him back. All the time we were being heavily shelled. We got on a little further and got ditched so I got out with my two gearsmen and put on the unditching gear – we had to get out through the roof as we were in so deep. Shells were bursting so near us that they covered us with mud and water. We got out without any difficulty and took off the unditching gear and proceeded on our way. We left the Foam knocked out and the 'Fiara', with her unditching gear broken, stuck in the mud. (She got out too late to be of any use.) The 'Fairy' followed me shortly afterwards. The next part of our journey was over good ground and the sun got up and we felt very bucked at getting out of the bog we had just left. I could

with a terrific barrage.
The next hour was
a very great nerve strain
as we did not know at
what moment we might
be rushed up & fling in some
gap of the line - however
the Scots got there and at
7 am prisoners began
coming down. Most of them
were in a terrible plight.
it is ghastly to see
human beings either
friend or enemy so mangled
and torn, how men could
live in that fire of hell
cannot be imagined. Four
counter attacks were made
by the enemy but were
unsuccessful and 4000
prisoners were taken.
One could not attempt
to estimate what the
cost of such an attack

(xxii) Digby Stone records in his diary the "fire of hell" on 4 October. *(D.Stone, Liddle Collection)*

see the buses of the other section on ahead. We were driving by looking out of the flaps as our periscopes were broken and our prisms covered with mud thrown up by the shells. We had one or two shells close which blew dirt into our faces but otherwise we were having quite a good time. We passed a good many dead who had fallen on July 31st. Soon we came up to our infantry who were hiding in shell holes with very heavy machine gun fire. This pattered against our armour and some came through in fine spray so that we were all soon bleeding from small cuts. We were now doing some good as every bullet that hit us meant one less for the infantry. The ground was now a mass of shell holes and I had the greatest difficulty in guiding the bus as the bullets were getting too near my flap. I noticed that there was a nice round hole just in front of me guided the bus in the direction of where I thought the bullets were coming from – where there was a ruin. After a bit Arnold told me to turn as they were getting very uncomfortable behind. Soon after we had turned, the old bus stuck. We could not put on the unditching gear as we were under such heavy machine gun fire. Arnold led the way out. I left last handing out the guns and some ammunition. My N.C.O. Cpl Rea was killed as soon as he got outside a bullet through the arm and another through the heart almost simultaneously. We crawled back for some way towards the infantry who had gone back some way. Our guns got full of mud and became useless. We had to keep very low as we could see the bullets hitting up the earth all round us. We got covered with mud and wet through as we had to practically swim through shell holes. We soon got separated up. I looked round and saw the Boches advancing with the bayonet not more than 100 yards away. I got up and ran and shouted to two of my men to do the same. Just then I got hit in the head and fell down hoping that I should not lose my senses. I got up and then saw the Boches were all round me. I saw it was no good running and I had lost all my revolver ammunition crawling back so I stood still and waited to see what would happen next.

The extraordinary sequel which allowed this particular tank commander to evade capture and live to fight another day is kindred to that which might have fallen to an infantryman cut off from his section in a raid or full scale assault. It is not appropriate that it should stand representative of service with the Heavy Section M.G.C.[20]

Before dealing with the infantry soldier striving in his sector to win more ground or kill more of the enemy, mention must be made of the Sappers' constant responsibility under fire to deal with a whole range of practical problems including draining positions held by Gunners or the infantry. Of course, such responsibility also fell to the beleaguered troops on site but the know-how of the Sappers was likely to retrieve something from the most unpromising situation.

The improvisation talents of the Engineer was not limited to drainage as mat bridges were constructed and laid successfully to help cross a canal deeper in mud than in water according to Harry Ridsdale. Ridsdale's diary describes his varied duties – wiring, cleaning up captured concrete emplacements, giving them sand-bagged parapets because of course they faced the wrong way for use against their recent occupants. In trenches which they were attempting similarly to clear, they were sometimes working in mud up to the waist. Putting pontoon bridges over water courses under shelling resulted in casualties to one section of their Field Company.

Road mending and tree felling were further tasks but he was "violently cursed" by the Divisional Commander Royal Engineers for minor irregularities in road construction and for allowing the work to be interrupted by enemy shelling. Camouflage screens, making dugouts gas-proof, tramway construction, carrying up materials for all this work, constructing a range, there were constant demands upon the expertise and imagination of the Sapper and it still left time for football and a 2-0 beating by the Irish Guards.[21]

There is a precision about the contents of the diaries written by Sappers: lists are made, explanatory sketches are there and when things are not done properly, it is clear that professionalism is affronted. G. MacLeod Ross was furious that a Pioneer Battalion had just hurled into new defensive positions timber taken from German trenches. It had not been bedded in nor nailed and only here and there had the useful hurdles of brushwood been employed. "Such an important job should never have been left to a Pioneer Bn especially one as gloriously irresponsible as ours". MacLeod Ross's journal assault sought more senior targets too.:

> The hopeless decentralisation of control is another awful snag and the pity of it is that this was to be the push that was going to succeed because we had learnt all our lessons before . . . Then people come along crying and saying, 'if only the weather . . .' etc. 'who would have reckoned for such weather?' Well it doesn't need a soldier (and they all profess to be professional soldiers) to tell them that you can't leave too little to chance or that the element of chance in war is so great that you can't do too much by prevision to counter it.

It should be remarked that this was written as early as 2 August. MacLeod Ross was, in a sense, exercising prevision himself and it has a melancholy ring to it. However, he does seem to have been something of a stickler for things being right. Two months of the Ypres Salient later, with a few hours away from his duties and looking forward to a game of billiards, he accepts that there can be no thought of playing, "as the cues have no tips".[22]

And now to turn to the men at closest contact with the enemy: infantry attempting under small arms fire and shell fire to move forward through a boggy wasteland, the flat landscape exposing them as easy targets, the morass, like an undertaker at a sick man's door, ready to take the soldier out of this world. These are the most familiar images of Ypres and they hold much truth. We need to remember that there were days on drier ground, days as we have learned in other chapters, of success, days of extraordinary achievement like that of Sergeant E Cooper of the 12th Bn Kings Royal Rifle Corps who captured a concrete blockhouse with forty-five prisoners and no less than seven machine-guns.

Cooper's deed required more than courage; soldierly acumen and composure were essential elements in his success. In his response to the author's questions, Cooper set out the scene and the sequence of events on 16 August:

The blockhouse was on the left of my advance and was causing us very heavy casualties because it was firing into our flank. The officer ordered the men to take what cover they could. We knelt down and there was a lone tree. There had been a hedge there but there was only one lone tree standing at this stage and of course everybody when they came into view they immediately went to stand against this tree to look and see what was holding up the advance and of course the Germans were using this as an aim for their guns and that was where we had all the casualties. At this particular spot I lost my company commander, my platoon commander, the colonel was wounded, the Lewis gun officer was killed, the intelligence officer was killed and the sergeant major was killed. At this particular spot I should think we had roughly 50 to 70 casualties out of our company strength, then about one hundred and fifty, much below strength.

I was left now without an officer so I took my officer's revolver and his maps and I gave my men orders to fire at this blockhouse and try and put the machine-guns out of action. This proved useless. To save ammunition I told them to stop firing. I immediately called on some of them to follow me and I jumped up and rushed towards this blockhouse. I suppose I had something over a hundred yards to cover, skirting shell holes and I made off to the flank of the blockhouse. When I got there I called on them to surrender. I just put my head through the door [at the back] and called on them to surrender and come out. I shouted in English and of course I was excited.

Cooper ran to each of the three doorways of the blockhouse, shouting at those inside to come out. In brandishing his newly-acquired unfamiliar revolver at the first man to emerge, the German was accidentally shot:

of course they immediately rushed back in and started fighting again. I had to go through the whole procedure again getting them out. By this time I had put the revolver in my belt and I had my gun across my shoulder and the next man out, as soon as he got out I clipped him across the ears and kicked him up the backside and they all came out. I lined them up alongside the rear of the blockhouse and waved my men on. By the time my men joined me these Germans were getting very excited.

They were lined up against the wall facing their own lines. Then they were talking amongst themselves and I could hear the word 'corporal' and they were pointing some distance away and all of a sudden the Germans opened up again on us and of course by this time I had been

317

Serial No. of Grave.	No.	Rank.	Name & Initial.	Unit.	Date of Death.	Map Location of Grave.	Any further information indicating position of Grave.
	27880	Pte	C. London	} 9ᵗʰ L.N. Lancs	31 - VIII - 17	Zillebeke Sheet 28 N.W. 4 & E.3 ½ of	from the left hand side of the Ypres - Menin Rd
	35710	—	H. Freedman			I 17. b. 86. 77.	50 yds beyond Bn⁰ H.Q. marked with a cross.
	30046	—	F.W. Jackson				
	34041	—	W. Lawrence				
	34540	Capt	R.E. Morgan				
			W.I.E. Edmunds M.C.	11ᵗʰ Lancs Fus	5 - VIII - 17	Sheet 28 N.E. 1/10,000 J. b. 4.3.	in front of Concrete dug-out marked with rough cross.
		2/Lt	G.M. Carruthers	11ᵗʰ Lancs Fus	10 - VIII - 17	J.1.d. 65. 80	
	29485	Pte	J.E. Green	" "	7 - VIII - 17	J.1.d. 4. 8.	
		2/Lt	R.E. Rushmore Rushmer	" "			
	34098	Pte.	M. Nugent	" "	} 7 - IX - 17	J.7. d. 9. 9	

(xxiii) Padre M.S.Evers records the locations of various battlefield graves including that of a Military Cross holder, Captain W.E. Edwards. As the battle continued, the graves of many of these men would be lost in later fighting. They would subsequently be commemorated on the Menin Gate at Ypres, or on the Memorial to the Missing at Tyne Cot Cemetery. (M.S.Evers, Liddle Collection)

318

joined by some of my men. Two or three of them were wounded and several of the Germans [also] when this machine-gun opened fire on us and then I realised what the Germans were trying to tell us. That this corporal had left the blockhouse with a machine-gun and set it up in position and started to fire on us and his own men. So I called on one of my snipers to see that man off which he successfully did and we collected this machine-gun as we advanced.

No doubt the Germans surrendered because they thought they were surrounded. They got the shock of their lives when they found that there was only me there but my men were then coming up very quickly and of course the Germans came out unarmed so they couldn't offer any resistance. I told them to come out unarmed, drop your rifles and come out and anyhow eventually we got them lined up and there was no need to tell them what they had to do they knew the ground as well as we did. I just pointed to the rear and the officer led them off. They picked up their wounded and our wounded and carried them out.[23]

Cooper's account is not a contemporary source but it has been carefully evaluated. It carries the ring of truth and it also provides useful insight into the special character of infantry combat against strongpoints with overlapping fields of fire rather than the more linear framework from which attacks south of the Salient had been launched and defence of positions maintained. Outflanking initiatives by well-led small groups may have operated against great disadvantage but such opportunities were there as indeed was the threat of being cut off. The Ypres battlefield offered prizes, perhaps to be bought dearly, but also held the menace of a potentially disastrous isolation.

The strongpoints, even with their low profile, were obvious enough, otherwise so much of the landscape was featureless that we need not be surprised at individuals, groups, even platoons being lost. Frequently reliefs or reinforcements failed to turn up in time. To some extent this was due to dependence on the undamaged presence or adequacy of direction posts but also to the overcrowding and danger of communication routes. Ten minutes before zero hour on 20 September, Major Shakespeare of the 8th Bn. North Staffs told Lt Firstbrooke Clarke that "2 platoons of A Coy had failed to turn up and that he would need 2 platoons of D to take their places". Clarke had already experienced over crowding as he tried to get his men in their support positions and then had found he did not know the way to the front line despite diligently having studied the maps beforehand and having use of his compass. He had found further units within his battalion lost too. Not surprisingly the men got seriously mixed up when they did move forward. German counter-attacks against the somewhat disorganized but successful British advance came to a halt in waterlogged ground and under heavy shelling. The North Staffs "sat tight for 2 days and 1 night" before being relieved. Clarke was full of praise for his platoon runner who had repeatedly carried messages through heavy fire. As for himself, his feet were very sore through standing so long in water and it is abundantly clear he was glad to be out of the line.

I suppose that to people at home it is a fine victory. Well so it is, but they don't see the dead and wounded lying out and they don't have 9.2's bursting 10 yards away, machine gun bullets scraping a parapet. I lost 17 of my platoon (4 killed) besides the casualties in the rest of the Coy. I was so sick of it and upset that I cried when we got back.[24]

Three weeks earlier, men of the 8th Battalion Suffolk Regiment were lost for hours under the guardianship of a Signals Officer with a "trench map of this sector which apparently is no good or he cannot read same". Instead of moving to new positions forward they ended up near their battalion H.Q. They had, however, still to get forward and in artillery formation [parties of about thirty], they did so under shelling. It was "an awful trip [we] cannot stop as we have to get through somehow".

During these days of attempting to battle forward, this N.C.O., Corporal Crask, was witness to a nightmare experience for the crews of four tanks which they had seen that morning getting to "within 50 yards of the embankment and there they have stuck, they cannot move forwards or backwards owing to the state of the ground, the mud is just like a huge bog and shells are dropping into it as fast as they can and when the Boche realise that they are stuck every bally gun round about seems to be trained onto them". The crews attempt to exit and shelter under the embankment. The diarist adds with surely a touch of bleak humour that the "cheeriness" of the situation is not helped by the fact that it is "raining as hard as it possibly can".[25]

Returning to battle experience of infantry in the assault, the nervous excitement of battle does not necessarily extinguish a sense of mercy for the vanquished but it can diminish it to the faintest flicker of recognition. There are also the practicalities of ensuring that a beaten enemy stays beaten as his positions are over-run. The account of Captain G B Riddell (13th Bn Northumberland Fusiliers), of his battalion's attack on 4 October, makes uneasy reading. It lays bare an essential essence of war:

The Boche simply hid in shell holes, waiting to be killed. 'Remember 16th of June' was a kind of Motto for that day and the Germans killed must have been greater than our casualties. Our first objective was passed with ease. 'This is grand' said a new draft to Graham. I went up and down the line with Crooks as a runner, carrying a supply of S.O.S. signals and my revolver. I jumped into one trench and found it full of Bosche. Clarke, one of my Lewis Gunners was quicker than they though, and gave them a whole magazine at 20 yards before they had time to fire or surrender. We did not want prisoners. Sergeant Brewis brought his section into action and put a deliberate volley into one Bosche who was trying to get away.

The village of Rentel was the objective and Riddell moved further towards it, trusting "to everyone else to follow. The fire from the Bosche was now terrific and several men fell. A shell knocked out all my section except myself and the man with me. Then I was hit in the shoulder with a bullet. While this lad was looking to see whether I was badly hit, another shell burst close by and killed him but did not touch me".[26]

The provision of medical attention on the field and then back down the line to base hospitals and, where necessary, across the Channel to hospitals in the U.K. is the subject of another chapter in this book so Riddell must be left at the stage of his wounding during his infantry experience of 3rd Ypres but he provides evidence of two facts which deserve our recognition: first of fairly free physical movement over the ground at certain stages of the battle and relatedly of successes being achieved by certain units on certain days.

As a Private in the 2nd Battalion H.A.C., Digby Stone has no such satisfaction to report in his diary. 28 October he recorded as, "the most terrible day of my whole existence . . . we were shelled and machine gunned from three directions". He was detailed as a guide to bring up men of the Cheshire Regiment relieving his own unit in their outposts. A shell killed some men with him and dazed him. "We were all in a highly nervous state and did not know which direction to take . . . my great fear had been that we should get into the enemy outposts". Stone completed his mission and set off for the rear. "It seemed terrible to leave men in such a place".[27]

Exhausted men fell asleep in what may have seemed an acceptable position to awaken later standing or lying in sucking, stinking mud, their uniform sodden with either new rain or from the liquid squalor in which they were sinking. When the temperature dropped and wind sought to freeze the last vestiges of warmth pathetically nourished by breath on hands or near futile swinging of arms, then misery to a new degree of awfulness had to be endured. Feet already distended, calves ridged as they swelled against the constriction of puttees, the knees and the inner thighs sore and chafed by rough wet serge, these areas of discomfort would all now feel the penalty of circulation being still further reduced and the onset of a new pain induced by freezing conditions. Fingers, nose, lips, ears, could all fall victim to chillblains. Rum might temporarily ease the suffering but, 'in the line', under such conditions, real alleviation through dry clothes and boots, a source of warmth and hot food would almost certainly lie beyond reach.

While there were soldiers who in such conditions still made the best of things sustaining their own spirits in so doing as well as encouraging others, there were men like Corporal Robert Chambers whose mordant thoughts were expressed pungently in his diary. 27 August: "Raining like fury. Everywere a quagmire. Fancy fighting Germans for land like this. If it were mine I'd give them the whole damn rotten country".[28]

Of course it was not Chambers's country to give back but his comment encourages thought today about the human cost involved in refusing to concede the Salient and the rest of Belgium to the invaders and then of fighting to throw those invaders out. Many from the list of fallen do have a voice in the expression of their feelings, attitudes or opinions in letters or diaries written before their fateful day – some have been quoted here. They are always in the mind in any consideration of the experience of serving at 3rd Ypres – when everything is said and done, they had in fact given their all, or, differently expressed, they had everything taken away from them. Accordingly, the last words in this chapter will be from the papers of Padre Evers of the 74th Infantry Brigade. The burial registration sheets he compiled showed that, "in front of Concrete Dugout marked with rough cross" [map reference Sheet 98 NE 1/20,000 J.I.b. 4.3] he had buried Captain W I Edwards MC, 11th Battalion Lancashire Fusiliers, killed in action on 5 August 1917. In the same week, Privates J E Green and H Nugent and 2nd Lt G M Carruthers of the same battalion were buried by the chaplain. In response to the Padre's letters of condolence, Captain Edwards' father wrote of his son's identification with "the battalion he loved so much"[29] and in this we may have a key to understanding the vital element in making the Ypres experience just endurable, for both officers and men.

Notes

1   Captain R. L. Mackay, 11th Bn Argyll and Sutherland Highlanders, Diary 2.8.17, Liddle Collection, The Library, University of Leeds [hereafter Liddle Collection].
2   Corporal D. F. Stone, 2nd Bn H.A.C., Contemporary Account 2.10.17, Liddle Collection.
3   ibid 28.10.17.
4   Major Claude Worthington, 6th Manchester Regiment, Letter 2.11.17, Liddle Collection.
5   2nd Lt Hugh Livingston R.G.A., Letter 6.10.17, Liddle Collection.
6   Private W. G. Cameron, 6th Bn Black Watch, Contemporary Account ["tightener", it may be presumed, was a good meal tightening one's belt], Liddle Collection.
7   Statistics of the Military Effort of the British Empire during the Great War 1914–1920, HMSO London, 1922 pp. 401, 413, 601.
8   Brigadier-General W. R. Ludlow, Xth Corps Area Commandant, Diary August–October 1917, Liddle Collection.
9   W. A. Rigden R.G.A., Retrospective Account, Liddle Collection.
10   Lt M. B. Donald R.F.A., Letter 9.10.17, Liddle Collection.
11   C Chavasse R.F.A., Retrospective Account, Liddle Collection.
12   Lt G. L. Reid R.E., Diary 18.8.17, Liddle Collection.
13   Andrew Clark R.F.A., Retrospective Account, Liddle Collection.
14   Pte J. D. Urquhart, 15th Bn Royal Scots, Letter published in *The Northern Scot* 22.12.17, Liddle Collection.
15   Gunner P. Fraser R.F.A., Diary August 1917, Liddle Collection.
16   Signaller W. B. Kitching, 283 Siege Battery R.G.a., Diary 21–24 September 1917, Liddle Collection.
17   Gunner P. Fraser R.F.A., Diary August–November 1917, Liddle Collection.
18   ibid 2–16 September.

19   Gunner R. O. Arscott, G Bn M.G.C. (H.S.), Diary 31 July–19 August [and related papers provided by his son], Liddle Collection.
20   2nd Lt G. H. Brooks M.G.C. (H.S.), Contemporary Account, August 1917, Liddle Collection.
21   Lt H. Ridsdale R.E., Diary August–October 1917, Liddle Collection.
22   Lt G. MacLeod Ross R.E., Diary 2 August and 11 October.
23   Eric Cooper, formerly Sgt 12th Bn K.R.R.C., Edited Transcript of Tape-Recording, Liddle Collection.
24   Lt Firstbrooke Clarke, 8th Bn North Staffs, Letter 24.9.17, Liddle Collection.
25   L Cpl V. C. Crask, 8th Bn Suffolk Regiment, Diary 31.7.17, Liddle Collection.
26   Capt G. B. Riddell, 13th Bn Northumberland Fusiliers, Account written in hospital June/July 1918, Liddle Collection.
27   Pte Digby Stone, 2nd Bn H.A.C., Diary 28 October, Liddle Collection.
28   Cpl R. Chambers, 6th Bn Bedfordshire Regt, Diary 27 August 1917, Liddle Collection.
29   Papers of Captain M. S. Evers CF, Chaplain to 74th Infantry Brigade. Letter 29.9.17 to Evers from S. W. Edwards, Liddle Collection.

Chapter 20

Flanders 1917 and the German Soldier

German Werth

The grim, costly sameness of Western Front fighting from 1915 to late November 1917, when Cambrai broke the mould, offers the temptation to dismiss these central years of the war and their offensives as without distinctive character or significance. And yet, the battles of Champagne in 1915, Verdun 1916 and the Somme in 1916, or Flanders in 1917, should not be reduced to the same denominator despite the absence of a break-through, nor can the German soldier of 1916 be compared with that of 1917 or with that of the first struggle at Ypres in 1914. Indeed, just as the British would not consider the Third Battle of Ypres to be a "second Somme", the Germans could not regard Flanders in 1917 as a defensive battle along the lines of the one they had fought the previous year on the Somme.

The 3rd OHL (Oberste Heeresleitung) under General Ludendorff did not want to commit the same fault as on the Somme where the rigid "clinging" to the ground had caused heavy unnecessary losses. A new elastic method of defence was to "spare blood".[1]

Even so, the Reichsarchiv was not willing to revise the publication of the Official History of the Third Battle of Flanders, edited in 1942 in the middle of World War II, because of its "monotony in the defence although the battle had lasted longer than others and an enormous amount of forces had been wasted".[2] But this attitude was in conformity with the opinion of the commanders of the German Wehrmacht at that time who were set on the spirit of the offensive rather than on defence and its methods. On 1 December 1916, the new "Principles on Directing the Defensive Battle in Trench Warfare (Grundsätze für die Führung der Abwehrschlacht im Stellungskrieg) had been published containing the following points:

- mobile defence from troops held behind the line
- defensive zones instead of lines
- support of the troops in line by counter-attack divisions
- counter-attacks when losing or abandoning positions

- concentrated gun fire on changing targets
- artillery observation aircraft to direct the fire of artillery batteries
- infantry observation aircraft to assist the troops on the ground

This tactical revision was of course for a front of mud and water desolation – a continuous trench system was impossible and dug-outs could not be installed. Isolated concrete bunkers served as the focal points of defence.[3] The huge crater-area necessarily led to such methods of defence.[4]

The loss of the Salient at Wytschaete in June 1917 had warned the OHL and Crown Prince Rupprecht's Group. "I expect the new British offensive to take place on a small front in order to drive us back by snatches with overwhelming concentration of artillery leaving dents in our lines which can easily be blown up afterwards",[5] the heir apparent to the Bavarian throne wrote, full of misgivings. The target of the enemy was clear, too: the submarine-bases on the Belgian coast. Tactical withdrawal was rejected by the 4th Army – "never has an army been in a better position before a defensive battle", so General v. Lossberg, Chief of the General Staff of the 4th Army under Sixt von Armin declared.[6] The 4th Army was subdivided into 3 groups: Dixmuide, Ypres, Wytschaete including 10 divisions in line and 6 counter-attack divisions but despite their preparations, the Germans had underestimated the weight of the gunfire when the offensive started on 31 July. By the end of that day, the British had penetrated the defensive line of the 4th Army to a depth of 3 kilometres on a 16 kilometre front. Bixschoote was lost and the enemy almost broke through here.[7] Langemarck, St. Julien, Zonnebeke for the moment held and the tactic of the counter-attack divisions, had proved itself. For instance, the Infantry Regiment No. 41 which had been introduced to the new fighting procedure in June 1917 had been able to reconquer the Steenbeke terrain on the opening day of the battle.[8] The losses of the 4th Army amounted to 30,000 men and nearly 50% of the heavy guns. However, constant rain now proved invaluable to the defender. The commanders regarded the ground conditions as an ally whereas of course the soldiers took the mud as a second enemy.[9] The fear of an extension of the large-scale attack was unfounded: for the moment, the battle of Flanders went on with local attacks, counter-attacks, improvements of positions; above all it continued as an artillery duel.

The offensive on and after 16 August, led to the loss of Langemarck, St Julien and Hooge. In view of the bad ground conditions, a counter-attack for their recapture could not be considered. Poelcappelle changed hands more than once. Again, the losses were high. For instance, the companies of the 15th Infantry Division, each starting with a fighting strength of 80 men, were reduced to around 16 men at the end of August.[10] In the middle of September, Group command thought that the mud and rain period had conclusively ruined the offensive.[11] For a short time, the 4th Army even drafted two divisions and thirteen artillery batteries to another front and what was worse, several squadrons of aeroplanes.[12] But the increasing gunfire on 19 September, pointed to the continuation of the offensive. The

(xxiv) Flanders, as depicted in a German magazine, even before the commencement of the British offensive in the Ypres Salient in 1917. *(German Werth)*

4th Army was surprised by the new tactics of the enemy[13]: restricted attacks on limited targets, sealing off the new front attacked by box-barrage fire so that the German reserves could not come to their comrades' aid, a proof that strengthening of the front lines had been tactically mistaken.

On 20 September too, there was only one counter-attack division at the disposal of the Wytschaete group near Gheluvelt. The fights for Polygon Wood and the southern border of Houthulst Forest near Poelcappelle, lasting for days, had worn out the troops. On 4 October, the drum-fire of the enemy hit precisely those German troops who were prepared for the big counter-attack. The enemy again succeeded in penetrating the front to a depth of 2 kilometres on a 10 kilometre front, Poelcappelle finally falling under British control. The 4th Army had used an immense amount of ammunition, exhausted divisions in the line were even used as counter-attack divisions. This led to a vehement discussion between v. Lossberg, Chief of the General Staff of the 4th Army, and Albrecht v. Thaer, Chief of the General Staff Wytschaete Group, during the course of which v. Lossberg declared that he was unable to relieve a totally exhausted division in the line.[14]

On the other hand, a new tactic, elastic defence, conceding ground when necessary and in a measured way, was introduced to reduce German losses. Consolidating an area of the immediate front with a thin cordon, and allowing elastic withdrawal of the forward troops to the main fighting zone approximately 1,000 metres behind and with no stubborn holding of the ground; this would mean area defence in the purest form.[15] Army Group and 4th Army fixed the furthest defensive position for a withdrawal. Crown Prince Rupprecht however, criticized such tactical advice as confusing, a *cure-all* did not exist, hard and fast rules would be "harmful".[16]

The large-scale attacks of 9 and 12 October, with a loss of 2 kilometres on a 6 kilometre front, jeopardized Passchendaele for the first time, and produced a crisis in command. It was not just troop losses, 159,000 men by that time, which might lead to a breakdown of the front but also the impact on the remaining troops of the 'mental shock'[17] they were enduring. There was a divergence of view: according to 4th Army command, only a big counter-offensive could reanimate the morale of the infantry, whereas OHL and Army Group counselled for a withdrawal; it was a question of playing for time[18]. The enemy would be forced into a new concentration of his artillery by such disengagement and this would be very problematic in the swampy terrain. Furthermore, the mud excluded the enemy's use of tanks. Since no adequate forces were available for an offensive, only the divisions in line were relieved and it was ordered that the troops in line and in reserve be changed every six days. On 6 November, Passchendaele fell, but as it was possible to seal off the salient at this place, the 4th Army gave up the attempt to recover the ground especially as the more elevated positions remained under German control.

Like the 1916 battle on the Somme, the Flanders-offensive "suffocated

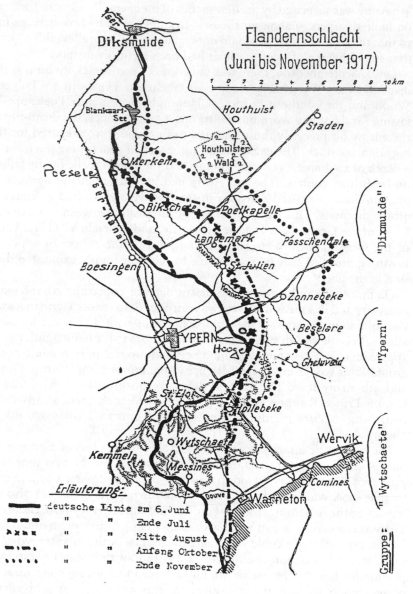

Flandernschlacht
(Juni bis November 1917.)

Iser
Diksmuide

Blankaart-See

Houthulst

Staden

Houthulster
Wald

Poesele

Merkem

"Dixmuide"

Bikschote

Poelkapelle

Langemark

Pässchendale

Boesingen

St. Julien

Zonnebeke

Beselare

YPERN

Hooge

"Ypern"

Gheluvald

St. Eloi

Hollebeke

Wervik

Wytschaete

Wytschaete"

Kemmel

Messines

Comines

Warneton

Gruppe

Erläuterung:

deutsche Linie am 6.Juni
" " Ende Juli
" " Mitte August
" " Anfang Oktober
" " Ende November

(xxv) The Battle of Flanders: a German Perspective. *(Adapted by German Werth from a published German source)*

in swamp and blood".[19] No breakthrough into the Flemish plain took place. It was however, for the first time that the enemy had observation of the German artillery positions. Only 5 kilometres separated him from where his long-range guns could have hit the submarine bases.

The 4th Army endured and refused to break. 73 German divisions took part in the Third Battle of Flanders, the casualties amounting to 216,000 men. British shelling was considered to be the most dreadful of the whole war. The Germans themselves had fired 18 million shells. Despite all this, v. Thaer declined to make a comparison with the Somme: this time, the heavy losses had been limited to the days of the major battles.[20]

"I always had a horror of the name "Flanders",[21] a German soldier who later fell at Langemarck, wrote on 30 July 1917. He had written this remembering 1914 and 1915 fighting there. The well-known frontispiece of the "Simplicissimus" dated 19 June 1917 shows Death, a skeleton with a coat around the shoulders sitting on a pile of corpses in a field of carcasses; he has put his scythe aside, covering his eyes with his hands: it is the "death of Flanders" which cannot cope with the rapidity with which people are producing dead bodies: "You people stop – I can't take any more".

This was even before the Third Battle of Flanders. The association between death and Flanders, inspired by the medieval "danse macabre" of the Flemish artists, was still proverbial when Otto Dix painted his picture, " Flanders" (1934–1936), understood to be a protest and opposition to the heroic myth of the Langemarck ideal upheld by the National Socialists in Germany. Dix had fought as an artilleryman at the front in Flanders and had at the time, produced a graphic illustration of the battlefield, "Langemarck". "Lice, rats, wire-entanglement, corpses, blood, schnapps, gas, guns, rubbish – this is the war"[22], he noted in his diary. His painting, which was declared "degenerate" by the Nazi regime, shows a statuesque soldier, submissive to his fate, in the midst of a lunar landscape of craters, a wasteland of water and mud. It is no more possible to differentiate between the living and the dead. This was to correspond to the general impression of soldiers longing for the end of the war but, nevertheless, fulfilling their duty.[23]

And yet, Dix did not show the full reality. Numerous war letters document the intensive fighting which, no doubt, demonstrates the spirit of the counter-attack divisions. In regimental histories, in letters and then in novels, we read of a far from passive response to one's fate.[24] Flanders had above all been a battle of artillery, *matériel* was dominant. The soldier felt himself a victim of the "great Flemish human mill".[25] For half an hour on a day of a major battle it was possible "to fight, the rest was unconsciousness lying in the puddles of mud, occasionally endeavouring to get into areas less fired upon, being killed".[26]

In countless letters, complaints are made of the unbearable hardship and "bloody losses being suffered", as a staff officer noted; huge numbers of soldiers on leave reported at home on the "increasing superiority of the enemy".[27]

A letter seems to prove that a remark by Ludendorff was well-founded, that is, in Flanders even "the horror of the crater-area of Verdun was surpassed".[28] "The hard times experienced here exceed everything which we have gone through before. It is horrible. You often wish you were dead, there is no shelter, we are lying in water, everything is misery, the fire does not cease for a moment night and day, our clothes do not dry. The worst, however, is the setting in of vomiting and diarrhoea".[29] Officers of the general staff admitted that the commanders were no longer successful in making the soldiers see the purpose of the struggle because some sectors seem to be held for no good reason, as the soldiers at the front complained.[30]

The new tactics to avoid contact with the enemy required disciplined and independently operating combat troops but many units could not comply with this demand, "not even the bravest troops".[31] Certainly life in the concrete bunkers or pill-boxes was appalling.

In a contemporary account, Company Commander Lubinski of the 74 Infantry Regiment wrote:

Life in the cement block is hell. We are eleven men living here. Officers and other ranks share the lousy plank beds. Others are sitting on planks and chests, snoring by day and night. The plague of flies is terrible, the more so since the water-logged shell craters are still full of cadavers. Attracted by [this] the flies gather here by the thousands, invade the shelters, creep over hands and faces, settle down on foodstuffs. One cannot risk being seen outside . . . and worst of all is the unbearable air.

In his memoirs Colonel Lubinski wrote:

It is no use denying that the old military discipline was gradually slackening for in almost every single order of the day warrants were issued for deserters. The unexpected prolongation of the war, the shortage of reserves often resulting in overburdening front-line troops, the poor food conditions, particularly at home, the inexperience of young wartime officers and similar shortcomings, all that added to the deterioration of morale.

The regimental historian of Lubinski's unit also drew attention to the impact on the health of the men at this period. "Numerous cases of enteritis are affecting practically everybody in the front line. Within the last eleven days 5 officers and 165 other ranks have been sent to hospital because of enteritis. In addition to this there were 40 other ranks in the sick bay."[32]

There was a further potential ordeal for men holed up in the pill boxes and it is described in the memoirs of another officer, Kalepky in the 86th Infantry Regiment:

The bunkers were reasonably strong and could withstand even direct hits from shells of a calibre up to 6 inches but owing to ground conditions in the area they could not be erected over a strong foundation. When a heavy shell opened a crater close to them, they would lean over, sometimes with the entrance down, with the soldiers trapped inside. There was no way of rescuing them, of course, and we suffered rather heavy casualties this way, not to speak of the painfully slow death of those trapped inside.[33]

Since the reserves were nearly at an end, a loss of combat capability was unavoidable in this the fourth year of war. Offences against superiors, refusal to move into a position, these serious military crimes increased.[34] Even Nazi-orientated authors referred later to the symptom of "disintegration", to their own feeling of "grey desperation"[35] although they celebrated the German soldier as a hero. The Bavarian heir apparent did not do justice to the terrible fatigue of his men in noting on 11 October 1917, the: "Distressing fact that our troops are getting more and more inferior".[36]

Flanders in 1917 means somehow more than Verdun or the Somme; in every respect, a collective trauma, as the author Carl Zuckmayer, a gunner at the front in Flanders, wrote later. "We were stigmatized, marked, either to die or to live with the burden of a scarcely bearable, non-communicable memory".[37] The flood of war reminiscences in Germany lasted till the mid–1930s. Remembrance of the "old death of Flanders"[38] did not fit into the concept of the new total mobilization of the nation by the Nazis.

Notes

1 Deutsche Militärgeschichte in sechs Bänden. Hrsg. v. MFGA. Taschenbuchausgabe Hersching 1983, Bd. 6, 512f; Kritik des Weltkriegs. Das Erbe Moltkes und Schlieffens im großen Kriege. Von einem Generalstäbler (d.i. Hptm. Hans Richter), Leipzig 1921, 50ff.

2 Der Weltkrieg 1914 bis 1918. Im Auftrage des Oberkommandos des Heeres hrsg. v. d. Kriegsgeschichtlichen Forschungsanstalt des Heeres. 13. Band: Die Kriegsführung im Sommer und Herbst 1917. Berlin 1942, V.

3 Werner Beumelburg: Die stählernen Jahre. München 1929, p. 369.

4 Kritik des Weltkriegs, pp 52 u. 197.

5 Kronprinz Rupprecht von Bayern: In Treue fest. Mein Kriegstagebuch. Hrsg. v. Eugen v. Frauenholz. München 1929, 2, Bd., p 202.

6 Der Weltkrieg, p 55.

7 Otto von Moser: Ernsthafte Plaudereien über den Weltkrieg. Stuttgart 1925, p 192.

8 Geschichte des I.R. von Boyen 5. Ostpreuß. Nr. 41. Berlin 1929, pp 194–211.

9 Albrecht von Thaer: Generalstabsdienst an der Front und in der OHL. Aus Briefen und Tagebuchaufzeichnungen 1915–1919. Göttingen 1958, p 141; Franz Wallenborn: 1000 Tage Westfront. Die erlebnisse eines einfachen Frontsoldaten–Leipzig 1929, p 228.

10 Das Ehrenbuch der Rheinländer. Die Rheinländer im Weltkriege. Stuttgart o.J., p 514.

11 Kronprinz Rupprecht, p 260.

12 Darstellung der Flandern–Schlacht nach: Der Weltkrieg, pp 53–100; Schlachten des Weltkrieges. In Einzeldarstellungen, bearbeitet und hrsg. i.A. des Reichsarchivs. Bd. 27. Flandern 1917, dargestellt Werner Beumelburg. Oldenburg–Berlin 1928; Peter Graf Kielmannsegg: Deutschland und der Erste Weltkrieg. Frankfurt a.M. 1968, pp 339–357; Hermann Stegemann: Geschichte des Krieges, Stuttgart–Berlin 1921, 4.Bd., pp 466–485. Fritz v. Loßberg: Meine Tätigkeit im Weltkriege 1914–1918. Berlin 1939.

13 Kielmannsegg, p 355.

14 Thaer, p 141.

15 Kritik, p 52.

16 Kronprinz Rupprecht, p 270.

17 Der Weltkrieg, 86; Kritik, p 174.

18 Kronprinz Rupprecht, p 271

19 Wir Kämpfer im Weltkriege. Feldzugsbriefe u. Kriegstagebücher von Frontkämpfern aus dem Material des Reichsarchivs. München 1929, p 394.

20 Thaer, p 140.

21 Wellenborn, p 228.

22 Otto Dix – Zum 100. Geburtstag 1891–1991. Katalog. Galerie der Stadt Stuttgart. Nationalgalerie. Stuttgart 1992, 51 u. 268f; weiterhin: Reinhard Dithmar (Hrsg.): Der Langemarck–Mythos in Dichtung und Unterricht. Neuwied 1992, XXX.

23 Kriegsbriefe gefallener deutscher Juden, Stuttgart 1961 [reprint].

24 Erich Hoinkiss, Nacht über Flandern. Berlin 1933, p 29; Wellenborn, p 238; Das Bayernbuch vom Weltkriege 1914–1918. 2. Bd. Stuttgart 1930, pp 317 und 441; weiterhin: Der deutsche Soldat. Briefe aus dem Weltkrieg, München 1937.

25 Das R.I.R., Nr. 80 im Weltkriege 1914–1918. Wiesbaden 1935, p 248.

26 Beumelburg, Jahre, p 381.

27 Moser, Plaudereien, p 192.

28 Erich Ludendorff: Meine Kriegserinnerungen. Berlin 1919, p 391.

29 Der deutsche Soldat. Briefe aus dem Weltkriege. Vermächtnis. München 1937, p 337.

30 Moser, Feldzugsaufzeichnungen 1914–1918. Stuttgart 1928, p 322.

31 Kritik, p 198.

32 K. Lubinski, Contemporary reports, memoir and extracts from regimental history, Liddle Collection, University of Leeds.

33 L. Kalepky, Typescript recollections, Liddle Collection, University of Leeds.

34 Rupprecht, p 262; Wellenborn, pp 228 u. 213.

35 H. Zöberlein, Der Glaube an Deutschland. München 1931, 722ff (wenn auch ohne Verständnis registriert).

36 Kronprinz Rupprecht, p 262.

37 Carl Zuckmayer: Als wär's ein Stück von mir. Erinnerungen. Frankfurt/M. 1969, p 193.

38 Hoinkiss, pp 18, 36, 233, und andere Autoren, die an der Flandern–Schlacht teilgenommen haben.

[The author and the editor gratefully acknowledge the assistance of Anita Werth in translating this chapter.]

Chapter 21

The Weapons and Equipment of the British Soldier at Passchendaele

Matthew Richardson

Since the days when Marlborough's army campaigned in the wet fields of Flanders, the British Army has been traditionally defined in terms of the equipment it carried or the uniforms it wore. To cite but one example, the Brown Bess musket will forever be associated with Wellington's victories and the footslogging soldiers whom the Iron Duke called "the scum of the earth". In the same way, the Tommy of the First World War will always be defined by his trusty Short Magazine Lee Enfield (SMLE) or his rakishly worn "gorblimey" cap. The intention in this paper, mindful of the fact that, in the past, military historians of the First World War seem to have been drawn from two quite separate camps, is to analyse that equipment within the confines of the Third Battle of Ypres. With regard to those two camps, there are historians who approach 1914–18 warfare from an academic position, who have tended to look down upon the "nuts and bolts" of their subject, and have seldom given serious consideration to rifles, bayonets, and equipment and there are the "militaria buffs", often equally insular, content with the knowledge that bayonets are stamped with a pattern number and manufacturer on the ricasso, but often not looking any further than this fact into the First World War experience associated with that artefact. It should be possible to unite these two factions, by offering a survey of the arms and equipment of the British soldier at Third Ypres, with an analysis of their background, how they operated in practice, and how, if at all, they impinged on the conduct of the battle. The question of tactical employment of infantry bearing the arms discussed here is looked at elsewhere in the book but in this chapter will be seen what it was like to use the weapons and equipment examined, first and foremost the arms and equipment of the British front line soldier and officer, but with some reference to the equipment of the support arms. Following on from this understanding, an attempt is made to draw some reasonably based conclusions about weapons and equipment of the British soldier, and how well they served him at Third Ypres.

All British other ranks went to France in 1914 wearing the 1902 khaki Service Dress. This was a tough and hard wearing suit of khaki serge tunic and trousers, designed to be worn in all weather conditions likely to be encountered in the temperate zone, the season or daily temperature having its influence on what undergarments were worn underneath it, or whether a greatcoat were to be worn over the top. It had brass general service buttons, which were sometimes exchanged for regimental ones, or in the case of those units which followed "rifle" traditions, black horn buttons with the hunting horn motif. "Carried" within the tunic was an item of

Description of the Box Respirator (Fig. 1).

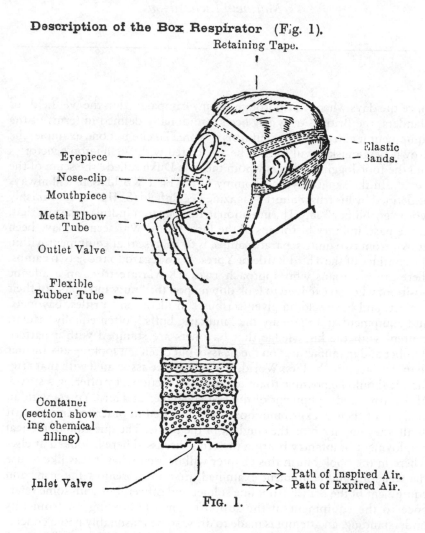

Retaining Tape.

Eyepiece

Nose-clip

Mouthpiece

Metal Elbow Tube

Outlet Valve

Flexible Rubber Tube

Elastic Bands.

Container (section showing chemical filling)

Inlet Valve

⟶ Path of Inspired Air.
⟶⟶ Path of Expired Air.

FIG. 1.

(xxvi) The Small Box Respirator: an illustration from a training manual (SS534). *(Liddle Collection)*

special significance: R.W.F.Johnson remembered that "Every soldier in the infantry carried, sewn inside the front of his tunic, on the right hand side, a first aid dressing consisting of a bandage, an ampoule of iodine and a safety pin all inside a cotton envelope. By 1917 the first aid dressing had been increased in size and was styled a shell dressing."[1] During the Third Battle of Ypres, there is evidence to suggest that troops were ordered to divest themselves of brass regimental shoulder titles prior to an attack, and certainly by late 1917 cloth battle insignia worn on the tops of sleeves or the centre of the back were coming into vogue, as a means of distinguishing units within brigades or divisions, but depriving this information from the enemy. An operation order issued by the 7th Battalion Leicestershire Regiment in March 1917 states that: "All ranks will hand in to stores on the morning previous, identity discs, titles, all private letters and cut away any unit names on the inside of clothing . . . On the inside corner and on the right hand side of the service jacket, all ranks will pin a small card marked with their squad number and letter."[2] It is interesting to note that the same order makes reference to the Brodie pattern or "battle bowler" steel helmet in universal wear among British and Empire troops, stating that in the event of snow they are to be camouflaged with whitewash. General Jack comments that his 2nd Battalion West Yorkshire Regiment went into action on 31 July 1917 with their helmets deliberately dulled by coating them with mud to cut down on give-away reflections from the smooth surface.[3]

So, with his khaki serge uniform and his steel helmet the soldier now needed some sort of harness with which to carry his other impedimenta. This was known as his "equipment", and that worn in the ranks by infantrymen was generally one of two types – either the 1908 Mills webbing pattern, or the 1914 leather pattern – a stopgap intended at first only for troops in training, but which many soldiers in France were still wearing in 1917. The Mills set was the product of extensive trials to determine the best way to distribute the load that an infantryman had to carry, and was probably superior to the personal equipment in use by any army (except perhaps the US) engaged in the First World War. It was made of tough cotton belts and straps fastened together by adjustable brass buckles, and was treated with "blanco" to waterproof it. This usually left it with a lightish green tint. The 1914 pattern by contrast had dumped most of its predecessor's advantages in the name of speedy production, and the very fact that it was made of leather was a retrograde step.[4] Empire troops almost exclusively wore the Mills pattern equipment, with the exception of some Australian troops who wore a set which emulated the 1908 pattern but which was made of kangaroo hide [5] Hung at various points on a soldier's equipment as he went into action were his essential items: on his back a webbing haversack containing perhaps spare socks and iron rations. Below that hung his mess tin, shaped like a half-circle, and over the small of the back the head of the entrenching tool in a webbing or leather cover. At his left hip hung the haft of the entrenching tool and the bayonet, at the right hip hung his waterbottle, made of enamelled steel and with a khaki-felt cover to avoid reflection and to muffle sound. From his knees down to the tops of his hobnailed boots, his trousers were bound close to the leg by a four inch wide length of woven cloth, his puttees (the Urdu word for bandages). While this helped to prevent the trousers snagging on wire, the constriction of swollen legs by sodden or frozen puttees sometimes affected the circulation of the blood and varicose vein or frostbite problems could develop.

Highlanders still went into battle wearing the kilt – however, it was covered front and back by canvas khaki skirts, in the interests of camouflage. This was particularly important in certain units such as the Cameron Highlanders whose tartan was predominantly red in colour, as well as in some Canadian Highland units. The merits or otherwise of the kilt at Passchendaele are still the subject of some dispute. Some have argued that, unlike his Lowland counterpart, the Highlander was not forced to spend an inordinate amount of time standing around in sodden trousers, and indeed could hitch his kilt up around his waist at certain times. Others however maintain that the Highlander was in fact more likely to suffer as a result of the kilt. Highland troops in particular were vulnerable to Mustard Gas, which burns on contact with the skin [6]

Officers, both lowland and highland, purchased their own kits, resulting in some variety of shades and styles. The officers' tunic was distinctive and easily recognizable – most were of a sturdy herring-bone twill-type material. So-called "Cuff ranker" tunics displayed the officer's rank prominently on the cuffs of his khaki service dress, by means of white piping and pips, which made him a prime target for snipers. Much has been made of the preference for "wind-up" tunics over "cuff-rankers" as the war progressed: popular opinion suggests that by 1915 or 16, officers in the front line had taken to wearing their pips on their shoulder straps, leading to suggestions from more cynical quarters that these officers had "the wind up".[7] However, photographic evidence suggests the cuff ranks were still widespread in certain battalions in 1918, and were certainly in use at Passchendaele. Furthermore, examples of officers actually wearing other ranks' tunics to deceive snipers seem to be rare, and examples of them wearing 1908 pattern webbing for the same reason are only slightly less so. Most still preferred the "Sam Browne" rig (a leather belt and braces arrangement, designed by a one-armed Indian Army officer in the Nineteenth Century), and borrowed items of the 1908 equipment such as haversacks where necessary. Trench macs (gabardines) were also popular.

By the Summer of 1917, the British soldier at Ypres was almost universally [8] equipped with the Lee-Enfield Mk III or Mk III* rifle – one of the most robust weapons ever made. It weighed around 9lbs, a noteworthy drag on the line of march but which helped to absorb recoil on firing. It was introduced in its Mk III form in 1902 – a shortened version of the long Lee-Enfield Mk I* which had been used in the Boer War, the new rifle being intended for use by both infantry and cavalry. To compensate for the shortened barrel, the length of the bayonet was now increased to 18 inches – the general view was that an overall "reach" of 6 feet was needed to stop a charging Zulu or Dervish. In the previous 30 years, most British wars were colonial, and for the same reason the Webley revolver chambered a huge .455 round, for "knock-down" effect. It was not until the 1930's that the more manageable .38 round was adopted. Both officers and some other ranks were armed with the revolver – it was issued to machine-gunners and Lewis gun teams who would otherwise be encumbered by a rifle, although of course anyone who really wanted one could lay his hands on a pistol or revolver without too much difficulty, either British or German.[9] A bewildering variety was available on the British side, with wartime contracts being placed in the USA (with Samuel Colt & Co) and in Spain and elsewhere. Edward Cooper who, as a sergeant with the King's Royal Rifles was to win the Victoria Cross at Third Ypres, had an encounter with one such weapon during the battle: "I had the officer's revolver. I hadn't had a revolver in my hand before and it was a Spanish revolver, what they call a Spanish Webley, which was a self cocking type, which when you pulled the trigger the thing went off straight away. You hadn't to cock it . . . Well, the first man out [of the blockhouse] I pointed the revolver at him and the thing went off – killed the man – and, of course, they all rushed back in and started fighting again. I had to start the whole procedure again getting them out."[10] Eric Watts-Moses took part in a rifle and bayonet fight with German troops near Houthulst Forest in September 1917, and described the scene: "Three or four of us got tangled up with a rather bigger bunch of Germans. I think we had the advantage of them because they were surprised to see us but they all had their bayonets fixed which I found was fairly unusual on that terrain. We went in with our rifles without bayonets fixed or with bayonets only. Using bayonets in the form of a dagger and rifles as clubs and they were much more effective that way. Although a shorter reach of course. We really got into a tangle, that is the only expression one can use – rather like the old fashioned warfare I should think at Agincourt, where, if one of your men went down wounded you promptly tried to protect him – you stood over him . . . "[11]

The Mk III* Lee Enfield was introduced in 1916, and did away with the complex magazine cut-off (a shutter which could be inserted over the top of the magazine, making the weapon effectively single-shot and saving the rounds in the magazine for an emergency), the wind-gauge and the long range sights of its predecessor. This move was partly to simplify the rifle for easier mass production, but also reflected the fact that conditions of trench warfare (along with an overwhelmingly war-service army with a minimum of training in musketry) negated the need for these marksman's features. The two rifles served side by side at Third Ypres, and by 1917, there was a considerable array of appendages available – telescopic sights, wire cutters, and above all, rifle grenade dischargers.

The British Army had begun the war deficient in grenades, and early types had included home-made jam tins packed with nails, or the Battye

6. **MACHINE GUNS.** One section Machine Gun Company will support attack on and consolidation of GREEN LINE by this Battalion and the 12th East Surrey Regiment.

7. **TRENCH MORTARS.** One Stokes Gun under 2/Lieut. W.G.Leishman will be in support of and follow the Battalion.

8. The following Light Signals will be used within the Brigade during the attack only:-

(a) To be fired by an Officer only:-

Single White Very Light fired towards our original line to signify an Objective gained.

(b). May be fired by any rank:-

Single Red Very Light fired in direction of suspected enemy Strong Point or Machine Gun holding up part of our line, for information of immediate supports.

(xxvii) Machine-guns, trench mortars and signals working in conjunction, Operation Orders, 11 September 1917. (D.J.Dean VC, Liddle Collection)

bomb, designed in 1915 by Major Battye of the Royal Engineers. However, by late 1915 and early 1916, the Mills bomb, or No 5 grenade, was in widespread use. In a confined space it was truly deadly, its pineapple-like casing being designed to fragment and fly in all directions. In fact its lethal range was further than it could usually be thrown, making it dangerous to the thrower. At least two per man were on general issue during assaults in late 1917. However, the prevalence of the grenade over the rifle in infantry training during the second half of the war, could be a cause for some concern, as Frank Richards noted, "Everybody at this time [Spring 1917] seemed to be bomb mad. The Mills bombs were wonderful for throwing into shell holes, trenches and dugouts but were absolutely useless for holding up attacks. The distance one could be thrown was only between twenty and thirty yards . . . the young soldiers that were now arriving had been taught more about the bomb than about the rifle."[12] A new and even deadlier development, introduced towards the middle of the war by the British Army, was the "P" or Phosphorous bomb which was also used to dramatic effect in clearing out strongpoints, by setting either strongpoint or occupants on fire. A battalion report on operations east of Polygon Wood on 4 October 1917 describes a number of "hostile concrete fortresses" as actually being set alight by these weapons.[13] The adaptation of grenades into rifle grenades increased their range and effectiveness considerably, although the amount of stress placed on the rifle in this procedure was extraordinary. One contemporary report suggested that firing a rifle grenade produced stresses equivalent to dropping the rifle 13 or 14 feet onto its butt,[14] and sometimes weapons set aside for rifle grenade firing by a platoon can be seen bound with wire, to try to prevent splitting of the woodwork. The versatility of this weapon is indicated in an operation order issued in October 1917 by Lt. Col. A.B Beauman DSO, CO of 1/S.Staffs: "14 (iii) the SOS signal by day or by night will be the rifle grenade parachute signal (RED over GREEN over YELLOW)".[15]

In 1915 Vickers machine-guns had been taken out of battalion control and grouped together in machine-gun companies at brigade level, with the formation of the Machine Gun Corps (MGC). The Vickers gun was a formidable weapon. Developed from Maxim and Vickers-Maxim precursors, it was capable of a cyclical rate of fire in the region of 600 rounds per minute, a rate of fire that could literally cut a man in half if he were caught in a burst of several seconds. The gun in action, under the hands of the gunner, felt like a living animal as the blowback of gas from the preceding round discharging drew in the next. Stoppages were common if the ammunition belts were not fed in carefully and horizontally, and she could be a cruel mistress – grazed and bloody knuckles were part and parcel of the machine gunner's lot. Machine gunner James Paling remembered that "the gun was loaded by passing the metal tag of the belt through the feed block, right to left, turning the metal crank twice and pulling the tag. The firing of the gun was done by raising a pawl and pressing the thumb piece which was between the handles, at the back of the gun. The firer sat above the rear leg of the tripod [with] his elbows between his knees, giving a tight control."[16] When going forward into a new position, often with attacking infantry, one man would carry the enormously heavy barrel over his shoulder (Paling estimates 52 lbs), while another carried the equally heavy tripod. Other members of the team would move forward with ammunition, a can full of cooling fluid for the water jacket, and perhaps maintenance equipment such as cleaning rods. So encumbered were the men of a machine-gun team, that it was not unknown for officers to pitch in and help with the carrying.[17]

The MGC tried hard to push for machine-gun tactics to emulate those of artillery. After all, the Vickers was not a weapon best used from the front line. It worked best when sited some way back, perhaps firing indirectly on a fixed line. As Paddy Griffith points out, it was no coincidence that machine-gun clinometers and ranging devices resembled those used by the artillery.[18] The infantrymen were compensated for their loss of firepower with the introduction of the Lewis gun (strictly speaking to the purist not a machine-gun at all, but an automatic rifle, the distinction between the two lying in the fact that a true machine-gun has some form of tripod or carriage arrangement, allowing it to be fired on a fixed line). The Lewis carried a 47-round drum magazine (as opposed to the belt-fed Vickers), and this rather small magazine in action could be rattled off in around 6 seconds. A Lewis gun team was typically of six men – two men, gunner and loader, operated the weapon. The other four were there simply to carry the spare magazines. Like any other weapon of moderately innovative technology, it had to be kept clean in order to function properly, but in the mud of the Salient, Lewis guns could be dropped end on into flooded shell holes or buried entirely if a shell happened to pitch among a Lewis gun section.[19] R.W.F.Johnstone describes a pause in his battalion's advance on 21 October, in which "Fox stripped and cleaned [the two Lewis guns] in the rain. They were choked with mud. So were the drums of ammunition and these too were cleaned by the men".[20] Stoppages were a problem, but, as Griffith comments,

in the specific case of tackling pillboxes, the SS 143 manual of February 1917 was already urging that the platoon Lewis be used as a major source of covering fire, and there was also apparently a very impressive high command recommendation of around November-December 1917 for Lewis guns to be used as pillbox busters. In the event they were undoubtedly often used in this role in 1917 and 1918, alongside trench mortars or volleys of rifle grenades.[21]

The 3 inch Stokes Mortar was one of the most versatile of infantry support weapons, and it was widely used at Third Ypres. It was light enough to move forward with the infantry in an attack, and a platoon or section from each battalion was detached to form the brigade trench mortar battery. Stokes gun rounds operated on a simple principle – the base of the projectile contained a sporting cartridge which went off when it struck a spike at the base of the barrel, propelling it out. Extra range was obtained by fitting extra charges to the base of the round. The business end of the projectile comprised either an impact fuse, which went off when it struck something substantial, or a time fuse. This latter resembled a Mills bomb in that it had a fly-off lever. Having pulled the pin, the confines of the barrel held the fly-off lever in place until the projectile was airborne. The Stokes also came in a heavier 4 inch version, which was widely used for putting down smoke barrages to mask an infantry attack, or a gas barrage. As Griffith comments, mortars provided an extremely useful way of giving infantry commanders some direct control over artillery, and giving them some on the spot artillery support, without having to go up the lengthy and tortuous chain of command required to bring field artillery into play.

Telephones of various forms were the main source of communication between battalions and brigades during an assault, but so frequent were the breaks in the line that often the only messages to get through, once an attack had begun, came by runner.[22] Signalling in action by methods other than field telephones in the flat open plain of the Salient was a difficult and dangerous occupation – heliographing (using mirrors on a fixed stand to flash Morse code messages) might well have worked on the sun-baked plains of central India, but in the often overcast conditions of Belgium it was seldom used. "Flag-wagging" – signalling in semaphore using flags – was an extremely hazardous operation when under fire as the signaller and his comrade reading out the message were required to take up position on high ground in order for their message to be read by an observer with a telescope.

Artillery batteries of the Royal Field Artillery, behind the lines, mainly operated the 18 pounder quick-firing field gun. It was so called because at the time it was one of the few guns for which rounds came as a single unit. Shell and shellcase containing the charge were manufactured as one piece, enabling higher rates of fire to be achieved. When loading most other artillery pieces, gunners had first to load the shell, and then, in behind it, either a bag charge or a brass cartridge containing the propellant. This latter was the case with the 4.5 inch howitzer, the RFA's other main work-horse. Richard Blaker, in his book *Medal Without Bar*,[23] alludes to the propensity of the 4.5 inch howitzer to detonate rounds prematurely in the breech, although problems with faulty ammunition had, it seems, largely been corrected by July 1917.

18 pounder gun drills from the period of the Third Battle of Ypres state:

Number 1 [the senior NCO] is responsible for the entire service of the gun. He commands, attends to the traversing lever, but will not touch it once the gun is layed. He orders deflection for difference in levels of wheels. He assists in passing orders down from the battery where necessary. He will occasionally examine the settings on the sight clinometer, range and fuse indicators. He is responsible for the application of the gun correction and corrector correction. When the gun is layed for elevation by means of the field clinometer, he will remove it from the clinometer plane before giving the order to fire.

Number 2 attends to the breech mechanism, range indicator, clamping gears, and brake, lowers and raises the shield, attends to the fuse indicator on the shield when required, and mans the right wheel forward when the trail has to be lifted. When laying with the field clinometer, he is responsible for setting it at the elevation ordered and for levelling the bubble .

When an order is given to "add" or "drop", the elevation for his gun he will make the necessary alteration on his range indicator and call out the new elevation loud enough for number 6 to hear.

Number 3 lays, fires, attends to the releasing lever of the brake, and assists number 2 to raise and lower the shield. When laying direct he will level the sight clinometer as soon as possible.

Number 4 loads, assists in setting fuses when required, attends to aiming posts if in use, and mans the left wheel forward when the trail has to be lifted.

Number 5 sets fuses and supplies ammunition.

Number 6 attends to the fuse indicator, and assists in supplying ammunition.[24]

It might be added, if the above were not to seem sufficiently taxing, that in a well-trained and efficient battery, each member of the crew was also trained to take over the tasks of any of the other five in the event that they should become a casualty. A subaltern might in turn command a section of two guns, with perhaps eight guns making up a battery. The precise number in any given battery could vary because of guns having been damaged or destroyed in action and awaiting replacement, and others away receiving attention or maintenance from armourers.

Larger guns and howitzers were much in evidence at Third Ypres, being necessary to deal with concrete installations and underground shelters so favoured by the Germans. The Royal Garrison Artillery operated 6 inch howitzers, 8 inch howitzers, 9.2 inch howitzers, as well as larger weapons mounted on railway carriages, and naval guns were operated by the Royal Marine Artillery. Such was the prolific rate of fire achieved by some guns during the October stage of the fighting that accuracy was actually lost as recoil springs and barrel linings wore out.[25]

Artillery ammunition was moved by rail up to the various rail heads, from which it was moved by light railway to the ammunition dumps. From this point, limbers would draw up to take it to the various batteries. In some cases mules or men were used for this stage – mules could have a pannier lashed over the saddle enabling them to carry 8 x 18 pounder rounds apiece. The First Canadian Division records that during the period 3–12 November 1917, its field batteries were issued with 116,125 18 pounder shells, and 17,868 4.5 inch howitzer shells, and that transport of this ammunition represented a total of 18,990 animal trips.[26] Men could also be utilized in the transport role, and could carry 2 or 4 rounds in a pannier over the shoulder. Rations were moved forward in a similar way, as were men coming into the line, travelling by light railway in open trucks until they reached the support or reserve positions from whence they would advance on foot. Decauville light railway was one of the most versatile and indispensable links in the chain required to keep the army ticking over. Additionally, the Army Service Corps made extensive use of 3 ton lorries, and these were also used for moving ammunition and rations. Big guns like 8 inch howitzers were moved using Holt caterpillar tractors, and varieties of civilian and agricultural traction engines and tractors were employed by the Royal Engineers and Royal Artillery.

Some of the best evidence, for arms and equipment actually in use during those months July – November 1917 in the Ypres Salient, comes from photographs, but also, archaeologically from the items turning up in the fields and when major excavations are undertaken. Photographic evidence is interesting and revealing, as most official photographs are actually dated precisely. For example, a study of troops moving up to the line shows picks and shovels in abundance – almost as many being carried as rifles in fact. Canvas breech covers are also strongly in evidence, testifying to the conditions likely to be encountered in the line, and indeed some men can actually be spotted with complete canvas covers for the entire rifle. Trench waders, made of rubber and reaching the thigh, are also frequently seen in photographs and turn up in surprisingly large numbers today in the Salient in abandoned blockhouses or when dugouts are uncovered. In most photographs too, the box respirator is seen in the "alert" or "ready" position on the chest – testimony to the fact that barrages often contained gas and the Germans made extensive use of Mustard Gas at Third Ypres.[27] Private J.Campell of the Cameron Highlanders, in his diary for 22 August 1917, describes moving up to the front line south of Ypres, which was reached at about 4am: "The Germans were putting over gas shells all the time and we had to wear our respirators for two hours or more . It was no joke stumbling up a rough track unable to see owing to the eyepiece of the respirator getting clouded, and keeping touch with the man in front as best you could".[28] Again, revealingly, numbers of men can be seen in photographs still with the old PH gas hood in its pouch slung over the shoulder, in use as a back-up gas mask. Another interesting piece of evidence concerns the large numbers of men wearing shorts during the middle part of the battle, and this serves as a useful reminder that far from being the stereotypical mud bath, there was some hot, dry weather, particularly in September.

Finally, this survey would not be complete without some appraisal of Tanks at Third Ypres. Although space is limited here, a brief look at both men and machines is necessary. By late 1917, the Tank Corps was widely operating the newly introduced Mk IV tank. It was a dramatic improvement on both the Mk I (used on the Somme in September 1916) and Mk II (used at Arras in April 1917). The "female" tank was armed only with Lewis guns, but the "male" version mounted two cut down naval six

From:- The Adjutant.

To:- All O.C. Companies.

In the Field,
29th Sept. 1917.

The following is a provisional list of the articles to be carried into action by N.C.Os. and men:-

1. All Riflemen.

Equipment. (Less haversack and entrenching tool).
Iron Rations.
Rations for Z. day and Z. plus 1 day.
220 rounds of S.A.A. (ends of extra bandoliers hanging outside
                          left of pack.)
2 Mills Grenades with rods (in breast pockets).
Pick or shovel.
5 Sandbags (right side of pack).
Washing material.
Waterproof sheet.
Pair of clean socks.
5 rounds of blank for rifle grenades by each N.C.O.(in right
                                  hand tunic pocket).
1 ground flare per 2 men (in left tunic pocket)
All gas appliances.
Oil tin and 4 x 2 in pack.
Mess Tin.

2. Rifle Grenadiers.

50 rounds of S.A.A.
8 rifle grenades per man.
Spare sticks and cartridges in right tunic pocket.

3. Lewis Gunners.

1 & 2 (revolvers.)
3, 4, 5 & 6 50 rounds S.A.A.

4. Signallers & runners.

50 rounds of S.A.A.

Companies carry the following articles:-

Very Pistols, 1", 2 per platoon, one with P.Commander & one with
                                                              (L.G.
    do.   1½" with O.C.Company.
Very Lights pro rata of pistols.
Wire cutters on rifles distributed over leading platoons.
Wire Cutters carried on belts with rear platoon.
Tape with Coy.Headquarters.
S.O.S. grenades:- Coy. and Platoon Commanders.
Compasses and Binoculars all officers and N.C.Os.

(xviii) Equipment to be taken into action, Operation Orders, 29 September 1917
(K.A.Oswald, Liddle Collection)

pounder guns, as well as Lewis guns. Contemporary sources give a rate of fire for the six pounder as 15–20 rounds per minute, but this seems extraordinarily high.

Weighing around 26 tons fully loaded, the Mk IV could attain a top speed in 4th gear of 4 miles per hour. However, on rough ground necessitating use of 1st gear or 2nd gear, speed was reduced to between 3/4 mile per hour and 1½ miles per hour.[29] Bob Tate, a Tank Driver in 1917, recalled that:

> Just the officer beside you [was seated] and the other men were standing up. There was a place, a bit of a platform between the two sides at the back of the engine where we used to put a starting handle in . . . and of course you could sit on there . . . but in action nobody sat down because you had your number one gunner in heavy tanks, you had your number two gunner and you had your third man who was handing the ammunition up. Number 2 gunner was putting in the breech block and he tapped the gun layer on his shoulder to say that the gun was loaded and then the gun layer got in his objective and fired.[30]

The Mk IV had a vacuum driven fuel pump, which enabled the fuel tank to be moved to the rear of the tank where it was better protected. This was a vast improvement over the Mk I's gravity driven system, which had depended upon two fuel tanks placed high up in the front "horns" of the machine, where they had been extremely vulnerable. Inside the tank, space was at a premium. It was basically an armoured box constructed around a huge Daimler or Riccardo engine, and crew comfort had not been a design priority. Much of the available stowage space was taken up with either racks of six pounder shells, or small arms rounds, several thousand of which were carried loaded into Lewis magazines. Six pounder rounds were generally of two types – high explosive, intended for use against strongpoints, and also a kind of canister round for use against enemy infantry. This comprised a number of lead shrapnel balls, packed in wax, and when fired, it acted like an enormous shotgun blast.

The armour plate hull of the tank rendered it impervious to most small arms fire unless a lucky shot were to hit the intersection of two plates or a loophole – it should also be noted that the Germans were quick to issue armour-piercing ammunition to their infantry, and this could also cause problems when it was encountered. However, the real tank killer during the First World War was artillery. An artillery round could easily penetrate the hull, and the slow moving leviathans were easy targets for field gunners. A tank having been hit and set ablaze, a crew stood practically no chance of escape, the entry and exit hatches being extremely small. Tank Corps crewman Jason Addy was witness to one such incident at Third Ypres:

> I have seen them [catch fire] and I have been in to try and help the others that have been wounded in tanks and tried to get them out, but you couldn't do anything about it because once the shell struck the tank . . .

in a six pounder [ie Male] tank it was worse. In fact, if you went into a six pounder tank you just asked for it . . . because [of] the shells . . . one side set the other side going because they were in racks you see at each side. They were shocking. Once a tank got hit there was no hope of getting inside to help.[31]

Machine-gun bullets striking the outside of the hull produced what was termed "splash" inside – tiny fragments of metal would fly off in all directions, and so to counter this, chainmail and leather masks were issued. Whether or not they were ever worn in action is a matter of conjecture. As they would have seriously hampered visibility, it is perhaps doubtful, but they certainly seem to have been carried as a badge of honour by tank crews, and Tate asserted that he wore his in action.

A brown canvas boiler suit was also standard issue to tank crews in 1917, but the sweltering heat inside a tank meant that more often than not shirt sleeves and shorts were the order of the day. Personal weapon for officers and men was the Webley revolver. The confined space inside the tank made anything else impractical, and the Webley was well suited for holding off attackers by firing through the numerous loopholes cut into the armour plate for just this purpose. Before leaving the Tank crew's experience, a final and little known aspect is well worth considering: some crews were withdrawn from the battle to practise for the projected seaborne landing on the Belgian coast. In training, an attempt had to be made to get a tank over a sea wall. Jason Addy recalled: "We had a lot of preparation beforehand . . . they were thinking of climbing a wall [near] a sea somewhere . . . it was this side of a place called St Pol where we did all this practising . . . but we never did it because the sea wall was too steep, it jutted out at the top, you know how a sea wall juts out. We put a ramp on there but there was a danger of tipping over. Nearly every tank that tried it went over [on its side]."[32]

Thus, by the late Summer of 1917, the weapons and equipment of the British soldier had evolved to meet the terms dictated by battlefield conditions and the British soldier was arguably the best prepared for his task of all the combatant nations. Having advanced under the protection of artillery support until within "hand to hand" range of the enemy, that is until contact was made with live and actively resisting German troops – perhaps at 30 to 100 yards – and encountering concerted small arms fire from blockhouses, infantry would engage the enemy using the appropriate weapons. Having gone to ground, mills grenades were an effective weapon to be used from the cover of shell holes. For slightly longer ranges, there was a number of types of rifle grenades which could be fired from Lee-Enfields, where appropriate, fitted with a suitable adapter. For stiffer opposition, they could call upon Stokes gun fire. A light and immensely portable weapon, the Stokes was capable of being moved up quickly. It could put numbers of bombs into the air at once, and deluge a target with high explosive or gas or smoke rounds, with timed or impact fuses.

While the rifle platoons sniped at targets which showed themselves, further mobile support came in the form of the company Lewis gun sections, used to increase the firepower of a battalion and acting as a mobile reserve of fire. Longer range support generally came in the form of the Vickers guns of the MGC, often firing from fixed positions on fixed lines.

As the historian John Bourne has commented, the front line infantryman of this period appears in many ways as a well equipped industrial worker[33] The Brodie steel helmet gave some protection against shell fragments and splinters to troops peering over the edge of shell holes or trenches. The sturdy Mills webbing (or its leather counterpart) contained his ammunition, his waterbottle, his bayonet slung at his side, and the head and haft of his entrenching tool. On his back was the small haversack, containing iron rations, spare socks etc. Hung at convenient points on the webbing were typically a pair of wire cutters, the mess-tin at the small of the back, and perhaps a couple of bombs.

It could be strongly argued then, that by late 1917 and early 1918, the British soldier's equipment in terms of personal small arms, the stowage of vital implements around the body, and right up to equipment like tanks, had reached a zenith of efficiency and suitability for the purpose before it, which it would not see again until 1944 or 1945. A sobering thought indeed for those who still see the British soldier of the First World War as a lumbering beast of burden, not only ill-led but inadequately equipped.

Notes

1   R.W.F.Johnson papers typescript recollections, Liddle Collection, The Library, University of Leeds (hereafter shown as LC). See also D.B.Eliot papers, typescript recollections (LC).
2   S.W. Clarke, papers, Operation Orders, March 1917, LC.
3   Terraine, J. (ed.) *General Jack's Diary*, London, Eyre & Spottiswoode, 1964. p239.
4   Chappell, M. *British Infantry Equipments 1908–80*, London, Osprey, 1980.
5   I am indebted to Mr Paul Reed for bringing this to my attention.
6   In view of this it seems very surprising that a number of regiments still went into battle wearing the kilt in 1940 (see for example H.V.Dawson, tape recording 1089, September 1996, LC).
7   See for example R.Graves, *Goodbye To All That*, London, Cape, 1929 p109.
8   Exceptions would be various hunting rifles, usually of .303 calibre, which were used in sniping. Some Canadian units may also have retained one or two of their old Ross rifles for this purpose as it was reputedly a more accurate weapon than the Lee.
9   Richards, F. *Old Soldiers Never Die*, London, Faber & Faber, 1933, p122.
10 Cooper, E. tape recording 30/32, August 1970, LC.
11 E.Watts-Moses, tape recording 204, January 1974, LC.
12 Richards, F. *Old Soldiers Never Die*, opus cit, p233.
13 K.A.Oswald papers, Operation Report, 4 October 1917, LC.
14 Bull, S. *British Grenade Tactics 1914–18*, Military Illustrated No7 June/July 1987.
15 K.A.Oswald papers, Operation Orders, October 1917, LC.
16 J.Paling papers, typescript recollections, LC.

17 D.Crockatt papers, original letters and diaries, Operation Orders, LC. These contain extensive contemporary references to the use of machine-guns, in particular numbers in use and methods of employment during the Third Battle of Ypres.

18 Griffith, P. *Battle Tactics of the Western Front*, London, Yale University Press, 1994 pp 120–129.

19 See for example the copy of a note sent by Lt-Col J.Walker, 1st/4th Bn Duke of Wellington's West Riding Regt, to his brigade commander describing just such an incident in October 1917 (J.Walker papers, LC).

20 R.W.F.Johnson papers, typescript recollections, LC.

21 Griffith, P. *Battle Tactics of the Western Front*, opus cit p134.

22 Richards, F. *Old Soldiers Never Die* opus cit p253.

23 Blaker, R. *Medal Without Bar*, London, Hodder & Stoughton, 1930.

24 *18 Pounder QF Gun Drill*, HMSO 1918, LC.

25 Edmonds, J.E. *Military Operations France & Belgium 1917* Vol II HMSO 1948, p300.

26 Edmonds, J.E. opus cit, p 353.

27 Edmonds, J.E. opus cit. See for example pp. 137–138, p. 347.

28 J.Campbell papers, diary 22 August 1917, LC.

29 Stern, A.G. *Tanks 1914–18 The Logbook of a Pioneer*, London, Hodder & Stoughton, 1919.

30 R.Tate, tape recording 202, February 1974, LC.

31 J.Addy, tape recording 278, January 1975, LC.

32 J.Addy, tape recording 278, January 1975, LC.

33 Bourne, J. "The British Working Man In Arms", in *Facing Armageddon* ed. H Cecil & Peter H.Liddle, London, Leo Cooper, 1996 p. 336.

Chapter 22

Law and Orders: Discipline and Morale in the British Armies in France, 1917

Peter Scott

Early in April 1917, when the strength of the British Armies in France stood at 1,893,874 all arms and all ranks,[1] Brigadier-General John Charteris, head of the Intelligence branch at General Headquarters, noted that, after two-and-a-half years of war, virtually every aspect of civilian life now had its counterpart in the organization and administration of such a huge muster of military manpower:

> Food supply, road and rail transport, law and order, engineering, medical work, the Church, education, postal service, even agriculture, and for a population bigger than any single unit of control (except London) in England.[2]

Of these services, the one at the very core of the administration of all the British forces in France and Flanders (and around the world) was the one Charteris had placed third on his list: the maintenance of military law and order.

However, unlike the role of British civil law as the keystone of the administration of a system of justice, almost the sole purpose of British military law was as the keystone of the administration of a system of discipline. In military law, justice as a civil concept (assuming that it was considered at all) was wholly subordinated to the exigencies of command and discipline.[3]

Since 1881, the legality of a standing army in Britain had rested on the Army Act (previously the Army Discipline and Regulation Act 1879 and prior to that the twin Mutiny Act and Articles of War) that was given force each year by the Army (Annual) Act. The Army Act consolidated the retained disciplinary provisions of the earlier legislation and, although competently drafted in parliamentary terms, it was no finely honed legal instrument, but rather a broad-headed sledgehammer to be brought down smartly and with great force on any military delinquent. After all:

acts and omissions which are mere breaches of contract in civil life – e.g., desertion or disobedience to orders – must, if committed by soldiers, even in time of peace, be made offences, with penalties attached to them; while, on active service, any act or omission which impairs the efficiency of a man in his character of a soldier must be punished with severity.[4]

The Army Act and its associated *Rules of Procedure* formed the centrepiece of the official *Manual of Military Law*[5] that, together with Section VIII of *The King's Regulations and Orders for the Army*,[6] constituted the main repository of the laws by which the discipline of the army was to be maintained. But there were other orders and instructions, such as the Pay Warrant[7] for details of punishment by stoppage or forfeiture of pay, that could provide additional pitfalls for even the most legally competent regimental officer, of whom there appear to have been all too few.

According to one informed observer, the military law education of some 90 per cent of young officers commissioned in the regular army, left them "quite unfitted" to sit as members of a court-martial[8] and, even allowing for some degree of exaggeration, it would seem that a similar percentage almost certainly held good for the temporary officers of Kitchener's New Army. In military law, just as in so many other aspects of their training, these (mostly) young officers were often left in a teach-yourself vacuum that specialist and general publishers hastened to fill with pocket manuals, cribs and guides to the mysteries of military law in general and courts-martial in particular.

Among the best known and apparently well regarded pre-war commercial military law manuals revised and reprinted during the war were Lt.-Colonel S.T. Banning's *Military Law Made Easy* (Gale and Polden)[9] and Lt.-Col. Sisson C. Pratt's *Military Law, its procedure & practice* (Kegan Paul, Trench, Trubner).[10] To these were added a large number of wartime publications such as F.J.O. Coddington's *The Young Officer's Guide to Military Law* (Gale & Polden)[11] and Major T.F. King's *What to Do and How to Do It!: Field General Courts Martial* (Foster Groom).[12] Thus equipped, the junior officer in France in 1915 and 1916 was expected to take his full part in the day-to-day maintenance of discipline and the administration of military law in his unit and the formations to which it belonged.

By the summer of 1917, the officers who had survived the harsh noviti-ate of the Western Front were well versed in the disciplinary practicalities of active service. Moreover, a steadily increasing number of new officers was being commissioned from the ranks. The men brought with them not only their own hard-won practical expertise, but also experiences of discipline and morale which could never have been shared by those who had not seen active service in the ranks.

The coming of the Military Service Acts[s] in 1916 meant that on the eve of the Third Battle of Ypres the ranks of the British armies in France were made up of a steadily increasing proportion of conscripts. It appears that

GENERAL ROUTINE ORDERS

BY

FIELD-MARSHAL SIR DOUGLAS HAIG,

K.T., G.C.B., G.C.V.O., K.C.I.E.,

Commander-in-Chief, British Armies in France.

General Headquarters,
December 5th, 1917.

ADJUTANT GENERAL'S BRANCH.

2906—Court-Martial.—No. S/17688 Private .... Cameron Highlanders, was tried by Field General Court-Martial on the following charge:—

" Misbehaving before the enemy in such a manner as to show cowardice."

The accused, having been warned to go over with his company on a bombing raid, remained behind in the trench, in circumstances which showed that his conduct was due to cowardice. The sentence of the Court was " To suffer death by being shot." The sentence was duly carried out at 6.50 a.m. on 23rd November, 1917.

(xxix) The ultimate sanction: A General Routine Order notifies the fate, after Field General Court Martial and confirmation of sentence, of a soldier charged with "Misbehaving before the enemy in such a manner as to show cowardice." *(Liddle Collection)*

351

the almost universal opinion in the army was that these pressed men tended to dilute the loyalty, courage, self-sacrifice and patriotism that, it was believed, continued to animate the surviving volunteers of 1914 and 1915. Additionally, the conscripts' manifest unwillingness to come forward voluntarily clearly signified a lack of patriotism allied to a deep-rooted aversion to the rigours and dangers of army life in general and its discipline in particular. Moreover, the conscript was perceived as "a being of progressively declining intelligence, physique and ability".[13] [Of course it might be observed that conscription denied the opportunity of voluntary 'for the duration' enlistment for those newly arriving at military age.]

As early as 28 July 1916 Captain J.C. Dunn, medical officer of the 2/Royal Welch Fusiliers (19th Brigade, 33rd Division), noted of his battalion that whether "Volunteers, Derbyites or Conscripts the average physique was good enough, but the total included an astonishing number of men whose narrow or misshapen chests, and other deformities or defects, unfitted them to stay the more exacting requirements of service in the field".[14] Standards continued to deteriorate and when Siegfried Sassoon joined the same battalion in March 1917 he found that a "recent draft had added a collection of under-sized half-wits to the depleted battalion".[15] Physical condition appears to have improved somewhat when the new annual class of conscripts came forward, but they lacked training. Dunn records of a draft of 70 eighteen-year-old conscripts in October 1917: "With a few exceptions their physique is good for their age, but they are no better trained than their predecessors of the last 18 months. How will they stand an average winter? According to Napoleon they won't". [16]

Initially, there was friction between conscripts (whether Derbyites or Military Service men) and the old sweat volunteers. W.V. Tilsley, a Derbyite, recalled that even his 1917 draft to the 4/Loyal North Lancashire (164th Brigade, 55th Division) was "still despised by the dwindling originals" and that in their turn Tilsley and his chums felt "volunteers to the later Derby groups".[17]

However, as Ian Beckett points out, since "the way in which conscription was applied was such that there was no material change in the social composition of the army after 1916",[18] there was a predisposition to cohesiveness which to a large extent meant that any friction was lubricated away in a common background and then by shared service experiences. In other words, the new boys became old sweats and in their turn looked askance as drafts of green conscripts filled the gaps in their ranks. In general, therefore, conscripts were accepted and absorbed, producing a reasonably homogeneous force that was no more and no less difficult to discipline that its undiluted Regular, Territorial or New Army predecessors. The view of Major-General Sir Wyndham Childs that as a result of conscription "crime became more prevalent, especially that of desertion"[19] is not supported by the published statistics or by recent surveys of unpublished Judge-Advocate- General records. The increase in the total number of crimes appears proportionate with the increase in the size of the army and continuing analysis of court-martial records has, as yet, failed to provide unequivocal evidence that any particular class of British soldier[20] had an especially poor disciplinary record.

As Keith Simpson tells us: "Ultimately, the British soldier obeyed his officers and military authority out of a combination of habit, social deference, the fear of the consequences of disobedience, and personal loyalty and respect".[21] Moreover, it was precisely the personal loyalty that the soldier gave, not just to his superiors but most particularly to his immediate comrades, his mates in the section or platoon, that was the crucially important factor for the state of his individual morale and cumulatively for that of his group and his unit.

Military morale – defined, at least in part, as the mental state of the soldier as regards spirit and confidence – was subject to many influences, both internal by way of self-respect, self-control and self-discipline, and external by way of peer pressure, military authority and discipline, and particularly physical well-being. Indeed, the interdependence of morale and discipline almost to the point of symbiosis makes it virtually impossible to mark where the one ends and the other begins. Slack discipline could affect morale just as adversely as a harsh regime and as Wavell wrote: "The soldier does not mind a severe code provided it is administered fairly and reasonably".[22]

For many officers the very responsibilities of their rank appear to have helped sustain their own morale while "setting a good example, promoting confidence and enthusiasm, and in taking an active and personal interest in the welfare and comfort of those they command".[23] A commanding officer's personality certainly marked the discipline and morale of his unit, even in the very shortest time. Colonel W.N. Nicholson tells of a Manchester battalion that suffered heavy casualties on the Somme, including the loss of its commanding officer killed in action. Morale slumped and then they did "wonderfully well" at Arras under a new commanding officer, but he also was killed. "Then came bad times again; till eventually a New Army officer was posted to the command. Once again the battalion became as good as any in the division. The stuff was there all the time; but the right leader was essential. It had to be the right man; for every battalion varied somewhat in its requirements".[24]

Underpinning any natural authority and qualities of leadership that a commanding officer might possess was the authority given him by his rank and appointment. For those under his command, his summary power of punishment was the most visible display of that authority. For minor offences not subject to court-martial, a commanding officer could award equally minor punishments, such as limited periods of confinement to camp or barracks. Where the degree of offence was such that the accused might elect trial by court-martial rather than accept his CO's award, a commanding officer's summary powers were strictly limited by the Army Act and King's Regulations. They included detention and field punishment (neither exceeding 28 days) and allowed forfeiture of or deductions from ordinary pay (also not exceeding 28 days) and a fine of up to 10 shillings for drunkenness.[25]

Within the unit, policing was carried out by the Regimental Police, identified by their black armlets with the letters RP in red. Outside the commanding officer's bailiwick, and on occasion within it, the policing of the British army in France was the responsibility of the Provost Marshal's section of the Adjutant General's branch at GHQ. The Provost Marshal was Brigadier-General W.T.F. Horwood,[26] a re-employed retired officer who had been the Chief of Police of the London and North Eastern Railway between 1911 and 1914. Each Army Headquarters had its own Provost Marshal and during Third Ypres the Provost Marshal at Second Army was Lieutenant-Colonel W.H. Trevor[27] and at Fifth Army Lieutenant-Colonel H.S. Rogers,[28] both career regulars. Each Corps and Division had its own Assistant Provost Marshal, as did the various bases and administrative districts on the Lines of Communication.

At the divisional level, the one with which a soldier would be most familiar, the APM (usually a Captain but occasionally a Major) was assisted by four sergeants and 21 rank and file of the Military Mounted Police and a detachment of either the French or Belgian gendarmerie. A provost marshal and his MMPs had the power to arrest, without warrant, any person of any rank subject to Military Law and "carry into execution any punishment to be inflicted in pursuance of a court-martial, *but shall not inflict any punishment on his or their own authority*".[29] In addition to these disciplinary duties the divisional APM's little unit was responsible for the control and regulation of traffic, collection, control and disposal of battle stragglers, custody and disposal of POW's, issue and validation of passes, surveillance and control of "followers" (British civilian workers with the Red Cross, YMCA, etc.), protection and evacuation of local inhabitants and their property, control of civilian movements, security against espionage, regulation of estaminets and "Out of Bounds", control of venereal disease by indentifying infected women, and searches (perquisitions), often for stolen British army property and sometimes for deserters. During active operations, the APM's main responsibility was the establishment of battle straggler posts with his MMPs and selected Regimental Police. Battle stragglers were defined as NCOs and men who, without reasonable excuse, straggled from the immediate fighting line or from their units when they were moving up to the line.

Although unlikely to be entirely typical of a British infantry division, the statistics of the New Zealand Division's APM for 1917 do have the merit of having survived intact. During the year, the division's MMPs brought a total of 2,558 charges, made up of: absence 1,186, failure to salute 529, drunkenness 105, improperly dressed 244, disobeying orders 288, and miscellaneous 206. Two hundred and twenty-eight cases of venereal disease were brought to the APM's attention.[30] The divisional Field Punishment Compound was in use on 305 days and 189 cases of FP No.1 and 246 cases of FP No. 2 were carried out there.[31]

While the Provost Marshal's branch, its APMs and the military police represented the executive arm of military law, the army's senior legal adviser and jurisconsult was the Judge-Advocate-General, Felix Cassel, KC.[32] He had been recalled from front line service with the 19/London in August 1915 to join the JAG's Department and had been appointed to the senior post in October 1916. The JAG's representative in France was the Deputy Judge-Advocate-General, Lieutenant-Colonel Gilbert Mellor, CMG,[33] a barrister since 1896, who had his office and staff at GHQ. Although he advised the Commander-in-Chief on all aspects of military, martial and international law, his particular concern was the review of court-martial proceedings, especially those requiring the C-in-C's confirmation, to ensure that they were regular and legal. It was later said that "Mellor performed his difficult and often unpleasant duties with tact and consideration".[34]

It was Mellor who introduced Courts-Martial Officers to France shortly before the start of the Third Battle of Ypres.[35] This innovation came in the wake of "constant allegations of acts of injustice committed by military tribunals at the front"[36] and "as a consequence of the want of experience of many officers whom it is necessary to appoint members of [Field General] Courts-Martial".[37] "It was ... not regarded at first with unqualified favour, but Mellor combined with an insistence on the fundamentals of criminal justice, which never lapsed into mere legal pedantry, a high sense of the necessity of maintaining discipline".[38]

These legally qualified CMOs (usually practising barristers) were allotted to Armies and then attached to Corps Headquarters with the intention that, working six days a week, they should serve as a "member of every Field General Court-Martial" within the Corps area "save in circumstances which render such a course impracticable". The CMO sat as a full member of the court and rendered a verdict with other members as well as "advising the Court on all points of law and procedure" and recorded the evidence. However, he would "in no circumstances take part in preparing a case for trial".[39]

Arthur Page was a barrister and a Lieutenant in the Royal Marine Artillery when he was appointed as a CMO, a job that he later described as "one of the most delightful ... in the Army".[40] As an officer from Corps HQ, the CMO received "respect and consideration as belonging to a higher formation, and as a specialist there is no one to supervise his work; with the happy result that, so long as he attends his courts, the CMO is his own master in a sense seldom realisable in the service". A FGCM might be held anywhere, in a tented camp, or in a Nissen hut, or in a dug-out and the CMO might expect to find that a "table with a blanket over it, and some upturned sugar boxes, usually did service for the court equipment; and, as I entered, I invariably received what is perhaps the best thing that can come one's way – a genuine welcome", the President of the court being "profoundly relieved when the weight of responsibility for the course of the trial is taken off his shoulders". Page described a typical court-martial scene as one of the "dim light of a few sputtering candles throwing into relief the forms of the accused and his escort; the tired and drawn faces of the witnesses under their tin helmets; and the accused himself, apparently taking only a languid interest in the evidence as it accumulates against him".[41]

Lieutenant A. B. Ashby, 3/4 The Queen's (Royal West Surrey Regiment), was appointed the CMO of XVIII Corps. After his first court-martial resulted in an acquittal he wrote home of the accused "I think he would certainly have been convicted if I had not been there".[42] A comforting thought. However, although the appointment of CMOs may have had an improving effect on the manner in which FGCMs were conducted, it certainly had no effect in improving an accused soldier's chances of an acquittal. In the twelve months ending 30 September 1917, there were 32,830 FGCMs on British soldiers outside the United Kingdom of which 3,720 (11.33 per cent) resulted in acquittals. In the twelve months to the end of September 1918, the number of FGCMs increased by nearly 27 per cent to 41,668 while the number of acquittals declined to 10.38 per cent (4,327).[43] The numbers of death sentences carried out on other ranks remained stable at 94 in the year ending 30 September 1917, and 95 in the following twelve months.[44]

Executions were regarded by senior officers not merely as the ultimate punishment but, quite mistakenly, as an important means of stiffening the backbones of any waverers. Early in the war Sir Douglas Haig had recommended that a death sentence should be carried out in the following terms: "I am of the opinion that it is necessary to make an example to prevent cowardice in the face of the enemy as far as possible".[45] A few months later a brigade commander in the 1st Division wrote: "The execution of a man has a salutary effect on the bad and weak characters (in resisting temptation)".[46]

The promulgation of death sentences at parades following their publication in General Routine Orders, Army Routine Orders and Lines of Communication Routine Orders was intended to bring them to the widest possible notice in the ranks, but it is almost inconceivable that these terribly repeated examples did dissuade men from going absent or deserting. The sense of personal invulnerability – "It won't happen to me" – that is so strong in all humans and that fortified the soldier in the trenches also fortified his deserting mate as he evaded capture by the Military Police. As for those terrified, confused and exhausted men who had come to the end of their tether and simply "walked away from the guns", no examples, no matter how harrowing, or how often repeated, would have had the slightest effect on them. Death was a commonplace of soldiering, capital punishment was an accepted and acceptable part of the civil law code and for the vast majority who heard or read the promulgation of a death sentence the overwhelming reaction was undoubtedly a short-lived one of "But for the grace of God there go I".

As has been noted, among those things which did bear on the morale of the individual soldier, and particularly on the infantrymen, was a number of external forces and this was especially true of those that directly and cumulatively affected his immediate, individual physical comfort and well-being: food (his chief concern and whether sufficient and palatable), tobacco (ranked with food), sleep (invariably in short supply), shelter (primarily from the weather rather than from enemy fire), sanitation and medical attention (and, in some instances, spiritual care), rest (well behind the lines and not treated as a euphemism for fatigues), contact with family and friends by a reliable postal service, and regular leave. As long as these elements remained in some kind of equilibrium and allowing for the "haggard element of fear", the individual soldier could face his life with at least some degree of equanimity.

All these elements were well appreciated by regimental officers and, contrary to popular myth, also by the gilded staff, many of whom in 1917 had seen front line regimental service and knew full well the value of the "care of men" in the maintenance of morale. For example, when the rain-sodden and muddied men of the 113th Infantry Brigade (38th (Welsh) Division) came out of the line during the night of 4/5 August 1917, they were met by the divisional AA & QMG, Lieutenant-Colonel H.M. Pryce-Jones, and his staff, busily supervising reception parties at Elverdinghe Chateau. They ensured that as well as receiving a "complete clean change of khaki", clean underclothing, whale oil to rub into their feet, matches and candles: "Each man in addition to his rations was given 10 cigarettes, a piece of chocolate & a packet of biscuits, also hot tea by my Divisional canteen show". The same process was repeated the following afternoon and evening when the 114th and 115th Brigades were relieved and later with individual battalions: "16th Welsh came out of the line last night [28/29 August] – about 290 strong! I arranged for each man to have hot tea or soup, packet of biscuits, 10 cigarettes & box of matches". Events such as these were more commonplace than some personal accounts allow.

So, if individuals were content then their unit tended to be collectively content, but this broke down rapidly in units where the casualty rate was so high that its ranks had to be filled up quickly with drafts from other regiments. In a lecture on "Mutinies and Discontent" given at the Staff College, Quetta, in November 1939, Colonel A.F.P. Christison[47] drew on his first-hand experiences of Third Ypres as an officer of the 6/Cameron Highlanders (45th Brigade, 15th (Scottish) Division) when describing the results of just such a set of circumstances to a new generation of officers:

> By 11 August [1917] it was clear that there was to be no breakthrough, and the 5th Army Commander [Gough] held a parade of survivors by Infantry Brigades of the battles of 31 July – 6 August, at which he said he would shortly fill up the ranks and send units in again to avenge their comrades. This tactless speech was received sullenly.

Units were made up to strength by 21 August with all sorts of details from the bases; units sometimes receiving drafts belonging to three

(xxx) A Military Policeman's notebook for 17 September 1917 includes details of "two suspicious characters", one dressed as an officer. There is also a reference to Etaples in the same month as the disturbances there. Later in the month, Lance Corporal Cordery searches for a man charged with "cruelty to a horse". *(W.C. Cordery, Liddle Collection)*

different other regiments to make up. In some cases units went into action without even nominal rolls of their men, and platoon commanders did not even know their men by sight.

> The attack on 23 August [sic] in many places was a complete fiasco. Some men flatly refused to go over the top, saying they were not going to fight under officers they'd never seen, and in strange units; that their commanders were deceiving them and that no break through was possible. Some men lay down and refused to move, others arranged with their pals to shoot each other in cushy parts in the first shell hole. The troops had been bluffed and knew it.[48]

On 24 and 25 August the survivors were withdrawn, and on 27th were paraded for the Army Commander who asked for grievances.

> He said he wanted frank speaking. He got it from the troops all right. It was then he was called a 'bloody butcher'. Afterwards he saw senior regimental officers, and a certain C.O. said 'Why don't you and your staff go and have a look at the ground over which you have been ordering these attacks?' The Army Commander promised to do so....[49]

With obvious approval Christison then went on to quote selectively from a relevant passage in John Buchan's history of the war. Buchan's complete text is as follows: "For almost the first time in the campaign there was a sense of discouragement [abroad on our front]. Men felt that they were being sacrificed blindly; that [every fight was a soldiers' fight, and that such sledge-hammer] tactics were too crude to meet the problem. [For a moment] there was a real ebb of confidence in British leadership. [That such a feeling should exist among journalists and politicians matters nothing; but it matters much if it is found among troops in the field]".[50]

Just how far was Buchan's an accurate assessment of the mood of the Army in France in late 1917? Extracts from just two contemporary evaluations of morale are preserved in the Cabinet records.[51] Both surveys drew their evidence from the censorship of the letter mail, though the methods of sampling differed. The first, a brief "Note on the Moral [sic] of the British Troops in France disclosed by Censorship", dated 13 September 1917 and submitted to the Cabinet by the Director of Special Intelligence, Brigadier-General G.K. Cockerill, was based on the examination of 4,552 letters in "Green Envelopes".[52] These were a restricted special issue which enabled soldiers to write letters about "private and family matters" that "need not be censored regimentally", thus avoiding any possible embarrassment by having them read and censored within their unit. They were still liable to examination by the Base censor, but those in this sample had not been examined until they reached the hands of the censor in Britain. If, as seems probable, they were written by British troops (rather than by British and Imperial troops) the sample represented about 0.26 per cent of the total number of British troops of all ranks serving in France and Flanders on 1 September 1917.[53]

The examination revealed that only 28 letters or 0.61 per cent of the sample "contained any expression of complaint or war weariness". Moreover, since seven of the 28 letters "contained specific complaints that had no relation to war weariness, the number of letters showing weakening of moral is less than 21 or under 0.46 [per cent of the sample]". The DSI was able to report that "No serious breaches of the censorship regulations were found" and summed up this concise report: "The examiners report that the general impression gathered is that the British troops in France are very cheerful and determined and that love of fighting has eradicated the peace-time habit of grumbling". One doubts that this smug, self-satisfied analysis took any account of the inherently special nature of "green envelope" letters, or the habit of many soldiers in minimizing their fears and discomforts to spare the feelings of their loved ones at home.

The other surviving report was submitted to the Cabinet by the Chief of the Imperial General Staff, General Sir William Robertson, on 18 December 1917, and comprised an "extract from the report of the Censor in France" covering October and November 1917. Some 17,000 letters were specially read having been "carefully selected from the mails of the fighting troops". This then was not simply a somewhat larger statistical sample but one drawn from a more narrowly defined target group: the fighting troops. On 1 September 1917, 77.7 per cent of the British other ranks in France were classified as fighting troops and a sample of 17,000 letters would therefore represent 1.32 per cent of those men.[54]

However, the report was not based exclusively "on the specially read mail but on the general impression gained from the last three months working ...". There then followed this analysis:

MORALE
The Morale of the Army is sound. ... there is ample ground for the belief that the British Army is firmly convinced, not only of its ability to defeat the enemy and its superiority man to man, but also of the dangers of a premature peace.

There is a very striking difference between the results of the examination of the Second Army which at the time was bearing the brunt of the fighting, and that of the other Armies, and it must be admitted that in the former the favourable and unfavourable letters were almost evenly balanced; but taking into consideration the stress both mental and physical under which letters were written by men who are in the thick of the struggle it would be an injustice to the men to suggest that no mental reaction will take place under less strenuous circumstances, any more than that the high morale of troops in the quieter sectors would die away when they are moved to more lively positions. In the other Armies the favourable extracts greatly exceeded the adverse. In all Armies a very large proportion of the letters specially examined contained no passage directly bearing on the subject, but were merely cheery ordinary letters which taken as a whole may be regarded as a favourable sign. It is not desired to gloss over or minimize the unfavourable aspect of this all important subject. War weariness there is, and an almost universal longing for peace but there is a strong current of feeling that only one kind of peace is possible and that the time is not yet come."

In that part of his Quetta lecture dealing with mutinies in general and specifically the so-called mutiny at Etaples in September 1917, Colonel Christison observed "that there were so few mutinous incidents speaks volumes for the British soldier." Now this could be quite simply Christison's tribute to the qualities of the British soldier, but could also be a remark indicating this officer's judgement that the British soldier had more than sufficient reasons for mutiny on a number of occasions. Whatever may be the case in this matter, Christison believed the root causes of the Etaples incidents to be:

> "(a) the monotony and unsuitability of the training.
> (b) the restrictions on recreation and amusement.
> (c) the bullying by the 'red caps' or military police."

In his opinion (and with his emphasis retained):

> The training *was* most monotonous, and what I saw of it was *badly organised* and hopelessly *out of date*. Squads marched out to sandy arenas known as *"bull rings"* and there for *six hours a day* they sweated away at individual training or made *short rushes* in the open. The same officers seldom took the same squads and the permanent staff was inadequate, generally inefficient, and bored. No attempt was made up to that time to bring reinforcements up to date in tactical doctrines. There was a base commandant and staff, an A.P.M. with a large squad of 'red caps', many of them *bullies* of a bad type.[55]

The course of the five days of the Etaples "mutiny" is too well known to need rehearsal here.[56] It was the most serious disciplinary disturbance to afflict the British army in France and Flanders throughout the war. Its causes were much as Christison laid them out in his lecture and most significantly it was an entirely *ad hoc*, short-lived protest born out of those immediate causes rather than as expression of a deep-seated malaise that affected the entire British army on the Western Front. It did not even affect the working of the majority of the Infantry Base Depots which made up the Etaples Base and they continued to function normally with drafts coming and going and training continuing. Unlike the French army, not one unit or formation of the British Army in France and Flanders suffered an act of premeditated collective indiscipline.

Indeed, mutiny was an uncommon court-martial indictment. Between 17 September and 12 November 1917, the Judge Advocate General's department in London registered the receipt of the details of approximately

5,720 Field General Courts-Martial held throughout the Army on all the fronts. Of these only 21 included the charge of Mutiny and all of these were courts-martial held in France.[57]

The Etaples disturbances resulted in four courts-martial for mutiny, all them held at the base. The first took place on 12 September, while the disturbances were still in progress. No. 626 Corporal J.R. Short, 24/Northumberland Fusiliers (103rd Brigade, 34th Division) – "a reinforcement and available for the front" – was found guilty of mutiny on 12 September, the day after he committed the offences with which he was charged. The President of the court, Major K.R. Balfour,[58] commanding No. 38 Infantry Base Depot, noted on the trial papers that "owing to urgent necessity of bringing the accused to trial having regard to the present disturbances amongst a portion of the troops in this command" they could not delay the trial by giving the accused the 24 hours notice called for by the Rules of Procedure. Short was sentenced to death, Haig confirmed the sentence on 30 September and the execution was carried out at Boulogne on 4 October.[59]

The second Etaples "mutineer" to be tried was Private R. McIntosh, Royal Scots Fusiliers. He was tried on 18 September, found guilty and sentenced to 10 years penal servitude; the sentence was not commuted or suspended. Private J.F. Davies, Australian Machine Gun Corps, was also tried on 18 September. He was found guilty of mutiny, violence to a superior officer and resisting or escaping his escort. He also was sentenced to 10 years penal servitude, but in his case the sentence was commuted to two years hard labour and then suspended. Fourth and last was Trooper G.H. Flint, Canadian Light Horse, who was tried on 19 September. He was found guilty of mutiny and also sentenced to 10 years penal servitude but, like Private Davies, his sentence was commuted to two years hard labour and suspended.[60]

The remaining 17 of the 21 mutiny courts-martial noted above, divide into two groups. Of twelve privates of the 2/Otago Regiment, New Zealand Expeditionary Force (2nd NZ Brigade, NZ Division) court-martialled on 1 and 2 September, seven were charged with mutiny. All seven were found guilty and sentenced to 10 years penal servitude; the sentences were not commuted or suspended. In the midst of a strike and "riot" by men of the Egyptian Labour Corps in Boulogne early in September ten labourers were charged with mutiny and court-martialled on 6 September. All were found guilty and sentenced to 8 months hard labour; the sentences were not commuted or suspended.

Although they could not be described as relating to acts of collective indiscipline, there was a handful of courts-martial at this time which pointed to small groups of men acting in concert. It is difficult to imagine what horror can have overtaken a Lance-Corporal and three privates of the 2/5 Gloucestershire (184th Brigade, 61st Division) which resulted in them all being charged with cowardice and the 'catch-all' s.40 of the Army Act which covered "any act, conduct, disorder, or neglect, to the prejudice of good order and military discipline" not specifically covered by the other sections of the Act. The four men were tried in Ypres on 10 September and found guilty. The Lance-Corporal was sentenced to six years penal servitude, two of the privates to four years penal servitude and the third private to one year hard labour. None of the sentences was commuted or suspended. Similarly, one can only wonder at the reasons for a Lance-Corporal and three riflemen of the 15/Royal Irish Rifles (107th Brigade, 36th Division) being charged with quitting their posts. The courts-martial were held on 5 October and all the accused were found guilty and sentenced to death. The sentences were commuted to five years penal servitude but not suspended.[61]

From the outbreak of war to 31 March 1920, courts-martial imposed 3,080 death sentences of which 346 or 11.23 per cent were carried out. Ninety-one of those executed were under suspended sentences, of those, forty had been previously sentenced to death and one was under two previous death sentences.[62]

Despite a number of applications by Haig, all death sentences passed on Australian soldiers were commuted as a matter of course, the Australian government having refused to allow the full writ of the Army Act to run in the Australian Imperial Force. For example, a private of the 4th Australian Pioneer Battalion (4th Australian Division) tried on 29 August for desertion and twice escaping confinement, was sentenced to death, a sentence which was later commuted to penal servitude for life.

According to one administrative commander, it was commonly believed that: "All the trouble with the Anzacs arises from the fact that no capital punishment can be inflicted upon them", but there is no direct evidence that this freedom from the supreme penalty increased the prevalence of disciplinary crime in the AIF. It certainly deserved its reputation as the most indisciplined element of the British Armies in France, indeed the Australians seemed to revel in their reputation. "The Anzacs are very brave men, but they are simply a mob in uniform" was the October 1917 appreciation of the same commander who had suffered (literally) at the hands of Australians on more than one occasion,[63] showing that even then the AIF's reputed fighting prowess was used to excuse its appallingly high rate of indiscipline which, in its turn, was justified as an expression of something peculiarly Australian, the myth of the Digger and the psychology of "mateship". "In the first six months of 1917 ... out of 677 convictions for desertion in the whole B.E.F. (62 divisions), 171 were in the five Australian divisions. The average number convicted in each Australian division was 34.2, and in each of the other divisions, British and dominion, 8.87".[64]

The JAG's receipt of the proceedings of 33 AIF FGCMs on one day in October 1917 gives some further indication of the disciplinary problems presented by the Australians. The cases came from eighteen different battalions and the total of 47 charges included twelve of absence, seven of desertion, six of disobedience, five of escaping confinement, four of insubordination and one of theft, while the remaining eleven were "miscellaneous" charges, mostly from s.40 of the Army Act. The Australians also present the only case that might be described as approaching collective indiscipline when eleven men of the 52nd Australian Battalion (13th Australian Bde., 4th Australian Div.) were tried on 15 September on charges of disobedience. Each man was found guilty and sentenced to 60 days Field Punishment No. 1.[65]

For the period of the Third Battle of Ypres, only Fifth Army records provide a reliable statistical disciplinary overview based on its monthly courts-martial convictions. These show that as the Fifth Army expanded (to 540,964 in July 1917) and then contracted again (to 212,260 in November) the numbers of convictions remained in proportion with the strength of the Army and that there were no great fluctuations in the individual charges.

Self-inflicted wounds were seen as symptomatic of declining morale (witness Christison's comments on pals arranging to "shoot each other in cushy parts") and yet, even at their most frequent, there were only 30 convictions per month for self-inflicted wounds in July, August and September, representing at their greatest 6.8 per cent of monthly convictions and 5.5 per cent of total convictions, June to December, 1917. In the same period, there were 190 convictions for desertion and 591 for absence, representing 8.2 per cent and 25.66 per cent of total convictions respectively. Convictions for desertion peaked at 50 in August and for absence at 137 in July, in other words around 0.009 and 0.025 per cent of the Fifth Army's total strength in those months, hardly the statistics of an Army in disciplinary crisis.[66]

Throughout the war the overwhelming majority of the British troops on the Western Front accepted the discipline which ordered every aspect of their lives. Largely drawn from the working class with its habit of deference and ingrained distrust of radical change, let alone revolution, they simply obeyed orders and got on with the task at hand, whether in a combatant or non-combatant role. But this did not make them merely unthinking, biddable, submissive or tractable. The British soldier was above all things resilient, his apparently dour acceptance of his lot leavened by a ceaseless grumbling and grousing that acted as a safety-valve, making the intolerable tolerable through a stoic, clownish dismissal of anything that did not affect him directly.

In January 1918 a government report on the labour situation in Britain concluded that the "overwhelming bulk" of the workforce was "loyal and temperamentally conservative",[67] a description that could be applied with equal force to their brothers in the Salient during the Third Battle of Ypres.

Notes

1   Includes Australian, New Zealand, Canadian, South African and Indian (British and Indian) troops. The total of those drawn from the home countries alone was 1,597,172. *Statistics of the Military Effort of the British Empire during the Great War.* HMSO, [1922].
2   Charteris (Brigadier-General John). *At G.H.Q.* Cassell, 1931. p.208.

3   *Manual of Military Law.* War Office/HMSO, 1914. 6th Edition. Chapter II (by Lord Thring), para. 2.

4   *Manual of Military Law.* Ch.II, para. 2.

5   *Manual of Military Law.* War Office/HMSO, 1914. 6th Edition.

6   *The King's Regulations and Orders for the Army 1912. Re-printed with Amendments published in Army Orders up to 1 August, 1914.* War Office/HMSO, 1914. Section VIII dealt with Discipline, Courts-Martial, Military Prisons and Detention Barracks, and Courts of Inquiry.

7   *Royal Warrant for the Pay, Appointment, Promotion, and Non-Effective Pay of the Army. 1914.* War Office/HMSO, 1914. See also: *Regulations for the Territorial Force, and for County Associations, 1912.* War Office/HMSO, 1912. *Regulations for the Allowances of the Army 1914.* War Office/HMSO, 1914.

8   Page (Arthur). "Courts-Martial in France" in *Blackwoods Magazine*, June, 1919, p.794.

9   Lieut-Colonel S.T. Banning (1859–1935) had been an instructor in military law at the Royal Military College, Sandhurst, 1896-1903. He was re-employed in 1914 as an Assistant Adjutant General in Eastern Command and in 1917 was on the staff of the Judge Advocate General's Department. His *Military Law Made Easy* was first published in 1901 and went through its 8th to 11th revised editions during the Great War. It was regularly updated after Banning's death and the final edition, the 25th, was published in 1954.

10   The 19th and final edition of Lieut.-Colonel Sisson C. Pratt's *Military Law, its procedure & practice* was published in 1915.

11   F.J.O. Coddington (1881–1956) was a barrister in Sheffield from 1913 to 1934 and then became the Stipendiary Magistrate of Bradford until his retirement in 1950. His *Young Officer's Guide* remained in print through twenty-two editions until the close of the Second World War.

12   Major T.F. King was a retired officer without apparent legal qualifications. Another similar manual was *The A.B.C. of Military Law; a concise guide for the use of officers, N.C.O.'s and men* (T. Fisher Unwin, 1916), the first book by Captain F.D. Gierson, then on the staff of MI7b(1), the War Office press and publicity section, and later better known as the author of numerous crime and thriller novels.

13   Dr. Ian F.W. Beckett, "The Real Unknown Army: British Conscripts 1916–1919", in *The Great War*, vol. 2, no. 1, November, 1989, p.4.

14   Dunn (Captain J.C.) comp. *The War the Infantry Knew 1914–1919: A Chronicle of Service in France and Belgium.* Jane's, 1987 (New ed., with an introduction by Keith Simpson), p.245.

15   Sassoon (Captain Siegfried) "A subaltern's service in camp and in action", in Dunn, p.306.

16   Dunn, p.412.

17   Tilsley (W.V.). *Other Ranks.* Cobden-Sanderson, 1931. p.173. Quoted in Beckett, p.9.

18   Beckett, p.9.

19   Childs (Major-General Sir Wyndham). *Episodes and Reflections.* Cassell, 1930. p.139.

20   On 1 August 1917 there were 1,654,664 British other ranks (Regular, Territorial, Kitchener, Derbyite and Conscript) on the Western Front.

21   Simpson (Keith). "The British Soldier on the Western Front". In *Home Fires*

and Foreign Fields: British Social and Military Experience in the First World War. Ed. P.H. Liddle. Brassey's, 1985. p.151.

22 Quoted in: Richardson (Major-General F.M.). *Fighting Spirit: A Study of Psychological Factors in War.* London, Leo Cooper, 1978. p.90.

23 *Report of the War Office Committee of Enquiry into "Shell-Shock".* [Southborough Committee]. HMSO, 1922. Cmd. 1734. p.151.

24 Nicholson (Colonel W.N.). *Behind the Lines.* Strong Oak Press/Tom Donovan Publishing, [1987]. New Edn. p.152.

25 A company commander's summary powers of punishment were very limited. NCOs below the rank of sergeant could be reprimanded or admonished and private soldiers could be given up to seven days C.B. for minor offences, extra guard duty, fines for drunkenness, etc.

26 Brigadier-General Sir William Thomas Francis Horwood, GBE, KCB, DSO (1868–1943). Provost Marshal, BEF, 16/12/15 – 27/10/18.

27 Colonel William Herbert Trevor, DSO (1872–1936). Provost Marshal, Second Army, 9/2/15 – 13/11/17.

28 Brigadier-General Hugh Stuart Rogers, CMG, DSO (1878–1952). Provost Marshal, Fifth Army [later Fourth Army], 2/7/15 – 28/10/18.

29 SS 414: *Regulations for the use of the Provost Marshal's Branch, British Armies in France.* GHQ, February, 1917. Second Edition. p.9. Emphasis added.

30 Some 46 per cent of all 1917 fresh admissions for venereal disease in France were contracted in the United Kingdom.

31 Public Record Office: WO 154/104: War Diary, Assistant Provost Marshal, New Zealand Division [Captain D. Kettle, DSO, Wellington Regiment]. The charges would have included a number brought against men of other divisions.

32 Rt.Hon.Sir Felix Cassel, PC, KC (1869–1953). Judge Advocate General, 1916–1934.

33 Brigadier-General Sir [J.] Gilbert [S.] Mellor, KBE, CB, CMG, KC (1872–1947). He had served in the CIV(MI) during the South African War, as secretary to the Royal Commission on Martial Law Sentences (South Africa) and as British Agent on the Venezuelan Claims Commission before being appointed as Legal Assistant to the JAG in 1907. He remained a DJAG until 1932.

34 *The Times.* 18 April 1947.

35 The first appointments of Courts-Martial Officers for Home Service had been made in September 1916.

36 Babington (Anthony). *For the Sake of Example: Capital Courts Martial 1914–1920.* London, Leo Cooper, 1993. "Revised" Edition. p.119.

37 B/2305: *Circular Memorandum. Employment of Court-Martial Officers on Field General Courts-Martial.* Lieut.-General G.H. Fowke, Adjutant-General, General Headquarters, 28 July, 1917.

38 *The Times.* 28 April 1947.

39 B/2305: *Circular Memorandum...*

40 Sir Arthur Page, KC (1876–1958). Served in France and Flanders as an AB RNVR and later commissioned in Royal Marine Artillery; Captain, 1917. Chief Justice of Burma, 1930–1936. Page: "Courts-Martial in France", p.793.

41 Page: "Courts-Martial in France", p.795.

42 Liddle (Peter H.). *The Soldier's War 1914–18.* Blandford Press, 1988. p.87.

43 *Statistics of the Military Effort of the British Empire during the Great War...* p.666.

44 *Statistics of the Military Effort of the British Empire during the Great War...*
    p.666. But see p.648 for slightly different figures.
45 Babington, p.7
46 Babington, p.19.
47 General Sir [Alexander Frank] Philip Christison, Bt., GBE, KBE, CB, DSO,
    MC & bar, psc (1893–1993). Temp. 2nd -Lieutenant, Cameron Highlanders,
    5th September 1914; Regular commission, 4th May 1915. Served with
    6/Cameron Highlanders as MG Officer until wounded 26 September 1915,
    rejoined 30th September 1916 and served until he was returned to England 3
    November 1917. At the outbreak of war in 1939 he was commanding the 4th
    (Quetta) Brigade, was then appointed Commandant of the Staff College,
    Quetta, and between November 1942 and February 1946 commanded first
    the XXXIII and then the XV (Indian) Corps.
48 The attack actually opened at 4.45am on 22 August. This was the state of the
    battalion immediately prior to the assault: "The name 'battalion' was a
    misnomer, for it had been reduced to a skeleton of its normal strength, and
    the prospects of a continuation of the fighting were not too bright when it was
    discovered that large proportions of the fresh drafts absorbed into the ranks
    were only partially trained and had but little experience of trench warfare.
    Many of them also belonged to other units". – *Historical Records of the
    Queen's Own Cameron Highlanders.* Vol. IV. Blackwood, 1931. p.199.
49 Christison: "Mutinies & Discontent". [Lecture at Staff College, Quetta, 13
    November 1939]. Liddle Collection, Brotherton Library, Leeds University
    Library.
50 Buchan (John). *Nelson's History of the War.* Vol. XX: *The Summer
    Campaigns of 1917.* Nelson, [1918]. p.95. Also: Buchan (John). *A History of
    the Great War.* Vol. III: *From the Battle of Verdun to the Third Battle of Ypres.*
    Nelson, 1922. p. 592. In the context of his history, Buchan's observation
    constitutes remarkably unrestrained criticism, even for one first published a
    year after the events to which it refers.
51 It is possible that as Great War intelligence records are released to the Public
    Record Office they may be found to contain further material relating to the
    quality of British troop morale.
52 Public Record Office: CAB 24/26: GT2052. 13 September 1917.
53 Percentages drawn from *Statistics of the Military Effort...* table facing p.64.
54 Public Record Office: CAB 24/36: GT3044. 18 December 1917. Percentages
    drawn from *Statistics of the Military Effort...* table on p.65.
55 Christison: "Mutinies & Discontent".
56 See particularly: Gill (Douglas) and Dallas (Gloden). *The Unknown Army
    [Mutinies in the British Army in World War I].* London, Verso, 1985.
57 Public Record Office: WO 213/17: [Register of FGCM's]. Courts-martial
    proceedings were registered as they were received in London and delays
    between the date of the court-martial and the date of receipt in London varied
    between a few days and several weeks. The majority of the trials logged in this
    register took place between late June and late October, 1917.
58 Lieut.-Colonel Kenneth Robert Balfour, J.P. (1863–1936).
59 Public Record Office: WO 71/599.
60 Public Record Office: WO 213/17. As regards suspended sentences, the Army
    (Suspension of Sentences) Act of 1915 and the amending act of 1916 had been
    introduced as manpower saving measures for troops on active service to
    discourage "certain types of men [who] would commit crimes solely to avoid

duty at the front" and to ensure that any convicted soldier sentenced to penal servitude or imprisonment but with a previous good record could be returned to his unit for further service. If he kept out of trouble the sentence would be reviewed with the chance of full remission, but the slightest misdemeanour could activate the sentence immediately and the soldier find himself in a Military Prison in the Field.

61 Public Record Office: WO 213/17.
62 *Statistics of the Military Effort...*pp. 648 and 649.
63 Brigadier-General Sir Walter Robert Ludlow, KCB. DL, VD, TD (1857–1941). Area Commandant, Flanders, 1917–1918. Carbon typescript diary. Liddle Collection, Brotherton Library, Leeds University Library. With regard to the behaviour of Australian troops see particularly Ludlow's entries for 13, 17 and 18 October 1917. For example, on 18 October he found a café in Bailleul under siege from Australians demanding more liquor: "I went in with my man Bradshaw and stood behind the bar with my revolver, and I threatened to shoot the first men who came inside. They howled and swore and refused to clear out". It took half an hour of "intense excitement" to clear the place without any assistance from the APM or his police.
64 Bean (C.E.W.). *The Australian Imperial Force in France during the Main German Offensive, 1918.* [The Official History of Australia in the War of 1914–1918. Vol. V]. Sydney, Angus and Robertson, 1937. p.28.
65 Public Record Office: WO 213/17.
66 Public Record Office: WO 95/525 and 526: War Diaries, Deputy-Adjutant and Quartermaster-General, Fifth Army. Self-Inflicted Wounds were classified as "wilful", "negligent", "without negligence" and "accidental". In total only twelve officers and 3,892 men were tried throughout the army for Self-Inflicted Wounds between August 1914 and March 1920. Medical statistics indicate that they accounted for 0.13 per cent of wounds, that 9.16 per cent of self-inflicted wounds admitted to hospital died and that 77.66 per cent were returned to duty.
67 Wilson (Trevor). *The Myriad Faces of War: Britain and the Great War, 1914–1918.* Cambridge, Polity Press, 1986. p.654.

Part IV

The British Home Front

Chapter 23

Images of Battle: The Press, Propaganda and Passchendaele

Stephen Badsey and Philip Taylor

If news, as Lord Reith later put it so memorably, is the shocktroops of propaganda,[1] and war reporting has come to provide the 'first rough draft of history', then by the summer of 1917 these two ostensibly contradictory axioms were found wanting by the British. Modern warfare has been accompanied by the need to address morale from the battle front to the home front and, as the twentieth century has unfolded against the backdrop of the communications revolution, governmental propaganda has had a profound effect on the media 'record' of events such as battles. The Third Battle of Ypres was an exception, but not in any obvious or straightforward sense. The official wartime British organisations for the release of news, and thereby for the conduct of official propaganda, had by that time achieved their most important initial objective, namely the entry of the United States into the war on the Allied side, but, as a result, they were undergoing a major re-organization of both their aims and their structure. This was not completed until several months after Third Ypres had ended, and so they were unusually poorly placed to influence public perceptions about 'Passchendaele'. Consequently, the media record – which might be assumed to have affected public understanding of the battle down to the present day – in fact says far more about the propaganda performance within the wider political context of the time than providing a useful historical record of the battle itself.

This is only apparent with hindsight. The campaign against American neutrality had been chiefly conducted, with great success, by a clandestine organization based at Wellington House in London (sometimes referred to as the War Propaganda Bureau) and headed by the Liberal M.P., Charles Masterman. This body worked under close Foreign Office supervision. Even though its approach had been a news and information-based strategy rooted in a commitment to 'factual' information, the careful selection (and therefore omission) of which facts would help the Allied cause, while damaging that of the Central Powers, gradually emerged as a professional

371

wartime responsibility of government – and the way the British developed it was to earn the admiration of friends and enemies alike.[2] It must be remembered that the term 'propaganda' had not been widely used before the First World War, and it did not acquire its largely negative connotations until more than a decade later. Its pioneers saw themselves not as purveyors of lies or distortion, but as professional persuaders trying to attract potential supporters through the force of their convictions and arguments. The guiding principle, described by Masterman himself as 'the propaganda of facts', was the presentation of a reasonable case for British wartime policies and actions, as distinct from those of Germany.[3] Wellington House's methods were politically sophisticated, chiefly indirect, and very much in the Liberal political tradition, focusing on elite opinion in neutral countries largely through written articles and pamphlets and personal contacts. In other words, this was not a direct appeal to public opinion itself, but rather to the opinion-makers, including the newspaper men and the newly-emerging cinematographic professionals, whose coverage of events would shape the wider public impression of what was going on. But by 1917, the third summer of the war, the military stalemate was such that no news was better for the military than the good news desired by the politicians; bad news was what all wanted to avoid. Military censorship, or the absence of news, had become the shocktroops of propaganda. As a result the media record was nothing like 'reality', but rather an illusion of reality in that what was not being said counted for far more in shaping popular perceptions than the type of positive campaign that had been tried and tested in the United States. It would be for the historians to re-write the resultant flawed first rough draft, to fill in the enormous gaps, and for hindsight to expose the real horrors of the war.

After the United States' declaration of war against Germany on 6 April 1917, Wellington House and its successor organizations continued their attempts to strengthen American support for the war and to influence other countries. The scale of this activity was phenomenal, even though it was to be minimized subsequently by those who were to take charge of the official propaganda machinery in the months that followed. In any given months of 1917 (such as July when the Third Ypres offensive began), Wellington House in London was producing about 150 different book and pamphlet titles in various languages, with a print run of around 2,500,000 copies, of which half a million were despatched abroad. A monthly print run of a further million books and pamphlets was produced in overseas branches, together with ten illustrated newspaper titles. By the time of the Third Battle of Ypres, the New York outlet for Wellington House material, the British Information Bureau, was sending out pamphlets regularly to a mailing list of 170,000 influential American citizens (rising to 260,000 by the war's end). Nonetheless, the precise extent of British propaganda directed overseas remains hard to estimate since, in keeping with its indirect style, Wellington House was to commission or produce work which in most cases appeared to have originated with independent citizens or informal committees. Positive propaganda was masqueraded by patriotism. For example, throughout 1917 every Catholic priest in the United States and Canada received a monthly letter from an apparently independent British Catholic committee, while a Protestant committee sent similar letters to pastors in the United States, the Netherlands and Scandinavia. Cloaked in such anonymity, a considerable amount of British propaganda material also managed to circulate within Germany. Later, this type of activity would be defined as 'black' or covert propaganda, namely that which appears to originate from a source different from its true origin.

At home, British propaganda aimed at domestic audiences, emerged in a far less planned manner. It was more the result of official initiatives to encourage the work of the numerous local or unofficial patriotic organizations which sprang into existence at the start of the war. The semi-official Central Committee for National Patriotic Organisations (CCNPO), with the Prime Minister as the honorary president and the editor of *The Pall Mall Gazette*, Henry Cuts (also a former Unionist MP) as its chairman, functioned as a central co-ordinating body.[4] Whereas an important part of the British governmental approach to propaganda was the trustworthiness and general respectability of official pronouncements, such unofficial or semi-official propaganda, often in the forms of newspaper reports and editorials, was characteristically much more outspoken. Indeed, it was a principle of British propaganda from the outbreak of war that the press should be largely self-regulating. Much of the 'hate propaganda' of the war, therefore, was the product not of deliberate government policy, but of an almost spontaneous outburst of emotions on the part of wide and disparate segments of the population.

It is a widely held belief about the war on the Western Front generally, that no contemporary civilians understood its reality. In the strictest sense this is true, as many veterans felt a reluctance or inability to describe their experiences to those who had not shared them. However, given the relatively positive nature of British government news and propaganda policies, an average working class adult, newspaper-reading and cinema-going, with friends or relatives in the Army, would have had to have been remarkably obtuse not to have had some idea about the likely course and effects of a major British offensive by July 1917, or the conditions in which it would be fought. The basic structure of Western Front reporting had been in place since roughly a year after the war's start. In June 1915, the Press Section was established at GHQ in France, with a group of five reporters, uniformed as captains, who were joined by two American reporters after April 1917. Inevitably, the sense of mutual identification which these arrangements created, encouraged the phenomenon of what would later be termed 'bonding', namely an increased media awareness of, and empathy for, what the soldiers were going through, their hopes and fears, which had a tendency to undermine the journalistic ideal of objectivity.

The first two official Western Front cinematographers (who wore uniforms but were technically civilians until 1918) arrived at GHQ in

SAFE PASSAGE FOR ALLIES' HOSPITAL SHIPS

The Daily Mirror

CERTIFIED CIRCULATION LARGER THAN THAT OF ANY OTHER DAILY PICTURE PAPER

No. 4,302.

Registered at the G.P.O.
as a Newspaper.

WEDNESDAY, AUGUST 8, 1917.

One Penny.

THE BATTLE OF FLANDERS—TOMMY GIVES FRITZ A LIGHT

A badly-wounded German asks a British soldier for a light.—(Official photographs.)

Two German prisoners looking at a dead comrade.

Photographs taken at the time of the battle in Flanders. There was nothing of outstanding importance operations at present. Colonel X., however, writes that the pro-special interest to report yesterday; the ground being so soaked that it is impossible to hibitions for the new effort of the British troops augur well for new success.

November 1915 and the first official Western Front photographer, with the rank of second lieutenant, arrived in March 1916. Putting these reporters in uniform, again increased the sense of shared destiny even though all forms of war reporting remained subject to field censorship at GHQ. The members of the Press Section soon worked out what was acceptable practice to the Army as well as to their employers. The reporters continued to work directly for their respective newspapers. The cinematographers, of which two filmed the Third Ypres offensive, were from November 1916 employed directly by the War Office Cinema Committee (WOCC). The still photographers, of which two photographed Third Ypres, worked for Wellington House. In addition, Australian involvement in the offensive was covered by two still photographers and one cine-cameraman employed by the Australian War Records Section. The Canadian involvement in the last stages of Third Ypres was covered by one still photographer and one cine-cameraman employed by the Canadian War Records Office. The New Zealand Division had its own cameraman who took both still pictures and cine film.[5]

This was an elite group, and one which was hardly an adequate number of reporters and cameramen to do justice to any Army of more than sixty divisions. It has to be said, however, that if it had been left to most senior officers in 1917 there would have been even less of a press presence or, better still, none at all. Stories of William Howard Russell of *The Times* during the Crimean war still rankled amongst officers who saw the press corps as a potential enemy within its gates, capable of undermining civilian support by exposing the true nature of modern war. They need not have worried. The Press Section came under the Intelligence Branch at GHQ and Brigadier-General John Charteris, who viewed its members with barely concealed disdain. Charteris' view was that the role of the Press Section was to provide a 'steadying' effect on the home population, and he expected and encouraged the kind of upbeat purple prose which by the end of 1916 had in fact brought the reporters into disrepute with many serving soldiers.[6] Although the Press Section's senior conducting officer, Major the Honourable Neville Lytton, hoped to encourage more realistic reporting in 1917, he also expected the reporters to help promote good relations with the French.[7] Field Marshal Haig does not appear to have issued either specific instructions or a briefing to the Press Section for Third Ypres, but he undoubtedly remained true to his basic press principles, issued before the Somme offensive of the previous year.[8] In keeping with Haig's own quiet but formidable determination, these principles were that the press should explain the justice of the British cause to the Home Front and the Army alike, together with the need for a hard struggle and victory going to the side with the greatest endurance. This was to be the real task of the

Opposite page:
(xxxi)"There was nothing of special interest to report yesterday, the ground being so soaked that it was impossible to anticipate important operations at present." *The Daily Mirror 8 August 1917.*

war correspondents, and they duly obliged in their lavish French châteaux billets ('châteaux warriors'). Haig's state of mind during Third Ypres is perhaps reflected by the fact that, quite unusually, he sat (on horseback) for official photographs twice during the offensive, on 12 September and again on 11 October. Significantly, he never lost his high opinion of the reporters of the Press Section for what he saw as their unflinching support throughout the period of his command, and at the war's end he conferred on each of them the reward of his handshake and a small Union Jack flag.[9] Haig appreciated that the realities of Passchendaele would never reach the public via a press corps that identified so patriotically and co-operatively with the high command.

With the United States in the war, the chief role of the British propaganda organizations changed from trying to influence elite opinion overseas to maintaining popular support for the war (described as 'high morale') on the Home Front and in the Army. Britain may have been in advance of other Great Powers in her parliamentary system but she was by no means fully democratic. Mobilizing 'public opinion' in support of the war was a complex equation for the Lloyd George government in which the influence of various elites weighed very heavily. Other than their own instincts, politicians and propagandists had virtually no means of measuring opinion in the mass – and would not have until the introduction of opinion polls shortly before and particularly during the Second World War. Being used mainly to communicating their ideas to the public through newspaper contacts, they tended to give disproportional influence to editors and owners of the major national newspapers in assessing public attitudes. With popular morale deemed to be falling after three years of Total War, the age of the 'Press Baron' was about to flower.

By the time of Third Ypres, the need for propaganda to strengthen morale on the Home Front was self-evident. The low point in wartime morale came between March 1917 and February 1918, and there were only limited actions that the government could take to redress this decline, which had all the appearance of being related specifically to the events of the war, rather than to the influence of propaganda on either side. Although the entry of the United States into the war held out the promise of victory in the long term, this was offset by the initial Russian collapse in February 1917, the costly and limited victory of Arras in April, the failure of the Nivelle offensive, and the early successes of the German submarine campaign. To state the obvious, the government's problem would have been more than solved by a successful breakthrough in Flanders of the kind originally promised by Haig.

Winter 1916–1917 had been unusually cold and harsh, making severe demands upon domestic fuel and affecting food production. The impact of the war on the home economy, including rising prices and taxes, and food shortages as the German submarine campaign began to take effect, was felt particularly by craftsmen and skilled workers in reserved occupations. The first serious wave of unofficial strikes since 1914 began at the end of March

1917, particularly among munitions workers, spreading to 58 towns and involving 200,000 men before it died away at the end of May, with the loss of 1,500,000 working days. Industrial relations remained poor, and a fresh outbreak of strikes took place beginning in August.[10] In September, King George V paid an official visit to 'Red Clydeside' in an attempt to ease the situation, an event which was turned into a thirty minute official propaganda film, 'HM The King on the Clyde'. An analysis of complaints by the government in April gave the worsening food shortages as the strikers' major grievance, along with profiteering. Government actions against this problem, including the introduction of the convoy system in June and the establishment of proper rationing, would require some time to have any obvious effect.

The state of morale of the Army on the Western Front was harder to judge, despite being better documented through the military censors' analysis of soldiers' letters home. The factors which make up a soldier's morale (not unlike a civilian's) frequently have far more to do with his immediate surroundings and conditions than with wider considerations, and could fluctuate considerably over short periods. Nevertheless, there was a marked and general drop in Army morale in May, increasing war-weariness during the period July-August, and by October an almost universal longing for peace. The only serious disturbance of any size suffered by the British Army on the Western Front and in fact one relating to local and not wider circumstances, was at Etaples in September 1917, although a final and thorough censor's analysis in December concluded that the morale of the Army was still basically sound, in the sense that large scale mutiny was not likely.[11]

Again, self-evidently, British official propaganda policy for 1917 had as its principal objective the raising of morale both on the Home Front and in the Army in France and Flanders, while attacking German morale. The characteristic 'propaganda of facts' approach that year can be seen from the emphasis of certain themes in official press statements, cinema film and photographs. These were the arrival of United States' forces into the war, British successes against German submarines, improved Home Front food production and organization, and continuing good relations with the French – but not necessarily the promise of a great victory on the Western Front.

The propagandists and their close associates were themselves Whitehall politicians, and they directed their policies accordingly, rather than in keeping with the views of GHQ in France. Historians have noted Lloyd George's distancing of himself from the Third Ypres offensive in Autumn 1917.[12] The most plausible explanation of Lloyd George's behaviour, apart from his limited freedom of action, is that he was resigned to the offensive's failure, and was preparing the political ground for Haig's dismissal at the end of the year, as well as that of Sir William Robertson. But, in challenging Haig even indirectly after the Nivelle fiasco, Lloyd George's own position as Prime Minister was at risk, and Whitehall was full of manoeuvres and shifting alliances by ambitious politicians and kingmakers waiting to see which way the wind would blow. Unfortunately, if inevitably, at the critical time of Third Ypres, British propaganda also got caught up in the internal political games.

For the first two years of the war the main organizational problems facing British propaganda derived from the familiar turf wars of Whitehall ministries, in this case the Foreign Office, Home Office and War Office (and to a lesser extent the Admiralty) each claiming the right of control. Given that the main propaganda effort during this period was overseas, the Foreign Office tended to win. But the inter-departmental in-fighting had produced the curious arrangement that the official cine-cameramen and photographers, who worked together in pairs on the Western Front and shared GHQ transport facilities, came under the separate organizations of Wellington House and the War Office Cinema Committee. As Prime Minister in December 1916, Lloyd George had just come from the War Office and was inclined to back its position that a completely new organization was needed. With Lloyd George himself very much on the populist wing of the Liberal Party, his supporters also included newspapermen[13] and entrepreneurs who portrayed themselves as populists and professionals in the art of propaganda, in contrast to what they saw as the elitist amateurism of the civil servants who dominated the machinery until 1917. Lloyd George's determination to wrestle influence from the Foreign Office has been well documented.[14] One of his first actions as Prime Minister was to commission Robert Donald, editor of the *Daily* Chronicle, to print a highly critical report into British propaganda. Evidence suggests that Donald's findings had already been largely pre-determined by the new Prime Minister. Another report on reorganization was commissioned, this by Lieutenant-Colonel John Buchan, a protégé of Lord Milner and already famous as a propagandist and author.[15] The result was the formation in February 1917 – a few days before the notorious Calais Conference – of the Department of Information (DoI) under Buchan. Although technically still a branch of the Foreign Office, the DoI (which absorbed Wellington House) had far greater independence, and Buchan reported directly to the Prime Minister. The DoI also greatly increased overt propaganda directed at enemy countries and their armed forces, including the use of balloons on the Western Front to distribute propaganda leaflets over the German rear areas. By the time of Third Ypres, it appears that British trench raiding parties on occasion left behind pamphlets in German describing the advantages of surrendering and the good treatment given to prisoners of war.[16]

As an important part of the move towards a more overt and populist propaganda style (and also as a way of bypassing Whitehall), Buchan pressed for centralized direction of the domestic informal and regional patriotic committee structure. This culminated on 4 August 1917 – a few days after the start of the Pilckem Ridge battle with which Third Ypres commenced – in the formation of the inappropriately named National War Aims Committee (NWAC) with Lloyd George as its chairman and Buchan on its executive committee, absorbing the CCNPO and the multitude of smaller committees which went with it, and with them the overall direction of rallies and public speeches at a regional level. In one fourteen day period during Third Ypres (25 September to 10 October, the height of the British successes at Polygon Wood and Broodseinde) a total of 889 meetings took place around the country under NWAC auspices.[17] The same populist style was reflected in the NWAC's employment as a touring speaker of the former Liberal MP and demagogue, Horatio Bottomley, who was sent to visit both the Army in France and the Grand Fleet. In the same spirit, in May, the WOCC invited the famous Hollywood film director, D.W Griffiths, to visit the Western Front in order to gain inspiration and scout for locations for the planned anti-German war film 'Hearts of the World'.[18] It is perhaps a reflection of the same policy change that, also in May 1917, for the only time in the war, the British government broke its own rules by promoting a propaganda atrocity story, the notorious 'German Corpse Factory' affair. The idea that the Germans, starved by the Blockade, were so desperate that they were prepared to melt

"ARE WE DOWNHEARTED ?—NO."

British soldiers cheering as they go forward on light railways to take part in the great battle in Flanders. The conditions at the front are reported to be improving, and the roads are drying rapidly.—(Official photograph.)

(xxxii) "Cheering as they go forward"; *The Daily Mirror 8 August 1917.*

down the corpses of the fallen for recycling into other war substances such as soap, was so ludicrous – until World War Two – that most soldiers would have laughed at it. Back home, however, the climate of hate propaganda was sufficiently unreal that even the Foreign Secretary, Arthur Balfour, upon reviewing the 'evidence', wrote that 'there does not, in view of the many atrocious actions of which the Germans have been guilty, appear to be any reason why it should not be true'.[19] Masterman, who remained in charge of Wellington House despite the fact that he and it had been reduced in status to a printing operation, reluctantly went ahead with producing the resultant four page pamphlet.[20]

One of Lloyd George's supporters in December 1916, had been the Canadian-born Unionist MP, Sir William Maxwell Aitken, millionaire owner of the *Daily Express* and other newspapers, who was rewarded with the title of Lord Beaverbrook in the new year. Beaverbrook had organized and controlled all Canadian propaganda, including cine film and photographs, through the Canadian War Records Office (CWRO). He was also the instigator of the WOCC, which consisted of himself, the War Office Permanent Secretary, Sir Reginald Brade, and William F. Jury, owner of Jury's Imperial Pictures. This body controlled British and Imperial (including Australian) official filming on all fronts. Beaverbrook's dual responsibility for Canadian propaganda meant that there were constant complaints from both the Australians and some British officers that the Canadians on the Western Front were getting a disproportionate amount of publicity.

The overwhelming majority of motion pictures shown between 1914 and 1918 were fictional, and were intended to provide relief from the war rather than information about it. However, from the start, British government policy had been keen to market the official films of the Western Front as a commercial operation, with any profits going to War Office charities. This policy had succeeded far beyond expectation in 1916 with the spectacular triumph of a series of documentary films of an hour or more in length. Beginning in July 1916 with the famous 'The Battle of the Somme' (the final Home Front audience for which may have been more than half the population), followed by 'The Battle of the Ancre and the Advance of the Tanks' in January 1917, these films, like most films of the era, were shot without sound and in monochrome, but shown tinted in colour to musical accompaniment. This 'big battle format' continued until the five-part series 'Sons of our Empire', released in Britain in March and April 1918. However, by that point, the bottom had fallen out of the market. 'The Battle of the Somme' and 'The Battle of the Ancre' had together earned the WOCC at least £65,000 in their first three months of release. But from January 1917 to June 1918, domestic revenues from all other British official films came to only a further £35,000.[21] The last of the 'big battle' documentaries, 'The German Retreat and the Battle of Arras', released in June, was a commercial failure.

There are numerous possible explanations for this collapse in popularity, including the combined impact of a new Entertainment Tax for cinemas and the cutbacks in domestic spending, which also produced the May 1917 strikes. While audiences had flocked to see the first 'big battle' films probably out of some degree of curiosity about what the Western Front looked like, that curiosity had by 1917 been more than satisfied. Also, just as the big offensives themselves had failed to produce correspondingly major victories, so the 'big battle' format no longer seemed appropriate to the matter of the war of 1917. But the explanation favoured by the British propaganda organizations was linked directly in the new populist policy. 'The public is jaded', wrote Beaverbrook, 'and we have to tickle its palate with something a little more dramatic in the future if we are to maintain our sales'.[22]

The WOCC continued to produce films of the Western Front throughout 1917, characteristically of between ten and thirty minutes in length. Although many of these have survived, lack of written documentation precludes our certain knowledge of their release dates, and in most cases they were probably shown to the British public a month or more after they were taken, robbing them of any immediate propaganda value. For example, though King George V remained a central figure in British official propaganda, the hour long film of his visit to the Western Front on 3–14 July was not released until September. For the rest, although British and Dominion cameramen filmed the Third Battle of Ypres from its first day, their approach to so doing marked an admission of failure on the part of the British propaganda authorities. It had been acknowledged almost from the start of the war that the difficulties and dangers of the front line made it quite impractical to film or photograph infantry fighting. The earlier 'big battle' films had concentrated quite heavily on scenes of the dead and wounded, which made up almost thirteen per cent of the content of 'The Battle of the Somme' and 'The Battle of the Ancre'. But these scenes virtually ceased to appear in official films after Spring 1917, being only two per cent of 'The Battle of Arras', with the implication that this was a deliberate change in propaganda policy.[23] By the end of 1917, the War Office had also issued orders to GHQ in France for still photographers not to take pictures of dead or seriously wounded.[24] From summer 1917, British official filming was confined virtually to the rear areas, with a new emphasis on the picturesque, the unusual, and the personal. This was typified by films of the overseas Labour Contingents from China, Egypt and South Africa (mainly Zulus), and particularly by what became known as the 'British Regiments' series' of more than twenty films, released between December 1917 and March 1918. Each of these lasted for about five minutes' duration and depicted an unidentified but supposedly typical battalion of each regiment at rest in the rear areas, with a heavy concentration on individual soldiers' faces.

This is not to denigrate the work of the Western Front cameramen, who got as far forward with their cumbersome equipment as often as they could. In that respect, their record is better than that of their print counterparts. One film in particular, possibly never released in the form in which it exists today, 'Ypres – The Shell Shattered City of Flanders' (with additional material added from a 1916 film of the same name) has provided later viewers with many of the classic images of the battlefield. While the in-fighting over propaganda organization continued in London, the cameramen were without anyone to support them effectively against the War Office back home and GHQ in France. Their first difficulty was getting transport from the GHQ motor pool, which they could usually manage only on two days out of five. There was little central direction and certainly nothing resembling a systematic policy on how to cover the battle. According to one cameraman, Bertram Brooks-Carrington, filming was largely at the discretion of the WOCC's operations manager at GHQ, Lieutenant-Colonel J.H.C. Faunthorpe:

> He'd say – 'Well, there's not much doing today. Just scout around and see what you can find' Or else 'There might be a bit of a show at So-and so. Go up there'. You went out, and if there was anything worth shooting you shot it; if there wasn't, you came back without anything at all. As soon as you got back, the war correspondents, *who had been sitting back there all the time*, would come up to the cameramen wanting stories. Quite a number of them used to do that, including some very famous names.[25]

Perhaps it would be too cynical to suggest that this was why, shortly after the start of Third Ypres, Buchan expressed concern to Brade that 'the [camera] operators on the Western Front need more direction than they got under present circumstances'.[26]

A further problem for the cameraman was that increasingly during 1917 the Army took the view that any man fit enough to serve on the Western Front should do so as a combatant and it proved difficult to recruit cameramen who were both technically unfit and willing to face the danger. By July 1917, the senior British cameraman, J.B. McDowell (who finished the war with a captaincy and the Military Cross for bravery), had been in France for more than a year. The other British cameraman to film Third Ypres, Harry Raymond, arrived as a replacement in March 1917. But Brooke-Carrington, who had arrived at about the same time, had to be sent home just before Third Ypres with shell shock.[27] The two still photographers, Ernest Brooks and John Warwick Brooke, faced a similar situation, with no apparent prospect of their being reinforced or replaced. Although they were all volunteers, it is hard to escape the conclusion that by the time of Third Ypres, like the rest of the Army, the cameramen and photographers were distinctly war-weary.

The major change in official film policy for 1917 – Beaverbrook's attempt to tickle the public's 'jaded palate' – was the establishment of a cinema newsreel to show British, Canadian and Australian official films. This was achieved by an arrangement concluded on 28 May between the WOCC and William Jeapes, owner of the Topical Film Company which produced the five minute 'Topical Budget' twice-weekly newsreel, and who accepted onto his staff Beaverbook's appointee, Captain William Holt-White of the CWRO. (Jeapes' brother Harold was sent out at the same time as the official cameraman to Egypt and Palestine). The WOCC also concluded a reciprocal arrangement with the French government for their official newsreel, the 'Annales de la Guerre'. Material from this was incorporated into the 'Topical Budget' newsreel, which, as a symbol of its new authoritative status, described itself from September as the 'War Office Official Topical Budget'. However, the arrangement proved a failure, with problems that were not solved until November when Beaverbrook bought the company outright for the WOCC and took complete control of the newsreel, by which time Third Ypres was virtually over.[28] One problem was the very low sales of the 'Topical Budget', which rose only from 78 to 82 issues sold between May and November, reaching an audience of barely 1,500,000. Another was a rapid breakdown in relations between Jeapes and Holt-White, who, in keeping with the new policy, stressed the need for the unusual and for material other than from the Western Front. More important was the newsreels' very topicality, which meant that it required film far faster than the official processing and censoring system between GHQ and London could possibly supply it. This, together with the limitations of a newsreel which showed four or five items, each of about a minute, in each issue, meant that the 'War Office Official Topical Budget' barely covered the Third Ypres offensive. The surviving run of the newsreel indicates that coverage began with an item released on 25 July showing the preliminary bombardment. But thereafter, the offensive received very little attention, except for occasional items on the difficulties of transport through the mud (released on 29 September, although presumably shot in August) and of Australians at 'Suicide Corner' (released on 3 November). Generally, the official newsreel made more use of French official film of the Western Front than British, presumably because of the novelty value.[29] Finally, the reality of the battle as recorded by the cameras was simply not dramatic enough for the new policy. D.W. Griffith, on his own visits to the Western Front, made exactly this point. 'It is too colossal to be dramatic', Griffith argued, 'You might as well try to describe the ocean or the milky way. A very great writer would describe Waterloo. But who could describe the advance of Haig? No one saw it. No one was a thousandth part of it'.[30] Certainly with the technology of the time, no one could record it adequately on film.

A similar pattern of limitations and problems beset the official still photographers, as can be seen by the use made of official photographs by *The Daily Mirror*, owned by Lord Rothermere and which claimed the highest daily circulation of any national newspaper of the period. Typically, the *Daily Mirror's* front page consisted of a major headline and up to five photographs, with the editorial and news inside. On 1 August, the paper duly announced 'Successful Opening to the Great New "Push"', but the accompanying photographs were all from earlier battles, including one showing soldiers with caps rather than helmets. The first British official photograph of the battle appeared on 8 August and the first Canadian official photograph on 3 September, followed by a front page dominated by Canadian photographs next day – despite the fact that Canadians were not involved in the battle at that stage! With Beaverbrook's protection, the Canadian official photographer, Lieutenant William Rider-Rider, frequently worked outside the Canadian area. It was also not unknown for Beaverbrook to see that British official cameramen went to cover Canadian operations.

The *Daily Mirror*, in fact, gave no further front page mention of Third Ypres or the Western Front until a spectacular front page given over to the battle on 6 September. Under the headline 'That Eternal Mud – Flanders: One Vast Quagmire' were four photographs including one that became an instant classic, taken by John Warwick Brooke on 1 August of seven men,

(xxxiii) The Times, 28 September 1917, "It is another lovely day, and the British Army would like you to know that it is in the best of spirits, thank you and enormously contented with the results of the last two days fighting – as it has a right to be" *War Correspondents' Head Quarters, 27 August 1917.*

with a stretcher, struggling up to their knees in mud.[31] The next mention of the battle was 22 September as 'Complete Success in Battle of the Pill Boxes', and two days later 'Hope Unfulfilled – Failure of the "Pill Boxes"', with a mixture of British and Canadian pictures of the Battle of Menin Road Ridge. The newspaper seems to have caught some of GHQ's optimism over the Battle on Broodseinde with its headline on 5 October, 'Third "Push" in a Fortnight Opens Successfully', including the first use of Australian official photographs taken by Captains Hubert Wilkins and Frank Hurley. The next day it ran with 'Haig's Smashing Blow – Splendid Welsh Troops', followed on 10 October with 'Haig strikes Another Blow – French Also Attacking' for the Battle of Poelcappelle. However, the headline for 13 October (after the resumption of the attack on the previous day) included a much larger caption than usual, set against a panorama shot of the battlefield, which illustrated both the openness and the limitations of reporting the battle:

> The public will be better able to realise the wonderful achievements of our Army, when they see this Australian official photograph. It shows the quagmires over which our troops advanced in Flanders, with what in the background is a German strong point which fell into our hands. Despite bad weather we made another advance yesterday.[32]

These were the only front-page references made by the *Daily Mirror* to Third Ypres while it was being fought. Other newspapers with smaller circulations were equally patchy. As for the *Daily Mirror*, after 16 October, with the headline 'Moving Forward in the West – A Wrecked Pill Box', the battle was never mentioned again. Other subjects which appeared on the front page in this period included the collapse of the Russian Army and riots in Petrograd, Allenby's capture of Beersheba, the brief mutiny in the German High Seas Fleet, and domestic news including a nine-day's wonder murder trial.

While Third Ypres was being planned and then waged, the Whitehall fight for control of propaganda also continued, with a strong element of black farce. Soon after the formation of the DoI, Buchan concluded that the only solution was a cabinet member to represent propaganda, for which Beaverbrook was the obvious candidate. Beaverbrook in turn alternated between manoeuvring for a ministerial post for propaganda and dropping it altogether for something better. Lloyd George, meanwhile, was determined to remove Admiral Sir John Jellicoe as First Sea Lord, not least for the Admiralty's apparent inability to deal with the submarine threat and for Jellicoe's deeply pessimistic performance before the War Policy Committee on 20 June.[33] In order to remove Jellicoe, Lloyd George first needed another post for his political protector, First Lord of the Admiralty Edward Carson, who was leader of the Ulster Unionists and a critical member of the coalition. Carson was appointed to the War Cabinet without portfolio, and in September took over control of propaganda, of which he had no experience. Within a month Buchan was pressing for another change.[34]

Buchan had already offered Beaverbrook control of photographs, in the form of a War Office Photographic Committee to run along identical lines to the WOCC, in order to improve the quality and distribution of photographs from the Western Front. From August through to the end of November – virtually the duration of Third Ypres – attempts were made to form such a committee, but the manoeuvre was firmly blocked by other press magnates, particularly Sir George (later Lord) Riddell, owner of the *News of the World*, chairman of the Newspaper Proprietors Association, and another crucially important supporter of Lloyd George's rise to power. Riddell had no intention of giving Beaverbrook such a monopoly, arguing that the press and 'certain interests' should be dominant in British propaganda.[35] After one more inconclusive meeting in which he had stressed the need for better coverage of the Western Front, Major Lytton of the Press Section recorded that:

> No one disagreed with our suggestions, but after the meeting I was informed privately that nothing could be done because Sir Reginald Brade was afraid to take any action independent of Lord Beaverbrook and that Lord Beaverbrook was expecting to be made Minister of Information (with portfolio) and until this appointment was ratified he refused to sanction any reforms no matter how urgently they were needed. It seemed to me a *non sequitur* that Sir Douglas Haig's armies should be kept short of photographers because Lord Beaverbrook wanted to be a Minister of the Crown.[36]

The issue was not resolved until the formation of a Ministry of Information in February 1918, incorporating the DoI with the WOCC, and the appointment of Beaverbrook as minister on 4 March. This was long past the date that British propaganda could have had any effect on morale during Third Ypres. It has even been suggested that the appointment was part of the price paid by Lloyd George for the silence of the Beaverbrook newspapers over the resignation of Sir William Robertson.[37]

It is easier to point to the failings of British propaganda during the Third Battle of Ypres than its successes, but it is extremely hard to evaluate its overall impact. Certainly, there is no evidence of German propaganda having any effect on British attitudes during this period, either on the Home Front or in the Army. No one in a position of authority attributed the low morale of the period to anything other than the circumstances of the war. Equally, there is no evidence of British propaganda having any visible effect either on the German Army or in Germany itself, where, by Autumn 1917, children were being taught by the sort of schoolmasters who functioned, 'in practice, as a propaganda agent of the state',[38] including in some cases reading the children the daily report of the Military High Command. Put simply, in Autumn 1917 both sides believed that Germany was winning the war, and neither side was prepared to negotiate. In these circumstances there was very little that propaganda aimed at an enemy could do.

There is also little evidence that British propaganda during Third Ypres had a measurable effect on Army morale in France and Flanders, but its impact on the Home Front is much more difficult to assess. It has been convincingly argued that, despite the belief that flourished in the 1920s and later, the power of film propaganda in particular was grossly overestimated by the British during the war, and that public attitudes would have been much the same had organizations like the WOCC never existed.[39] But the weak and disorganised nature of the British propaganda organizations at the time of Third Ypres prevented them from pursuing any coherent Home Front policy other than in very general terms. Without such guidance (or propaganda – with facts) the media record is therefore very patchy and erratic. Of course, we cannot be certain that a properly organized propaganda campaign might not have had a very different effect on Home Front morale, but the inescapable conclusion is that, like the Army in Flanders, the British propaganda organisations simply failed in their objectives at home in Autumn 1917.

As for the truthfulness and accuracy of reporting the Third Battle of Ypres from the Press Section at GHQ, Charles Masterman's wife recorded an observation by Lord Rothermere (brother of Lord Northcliffe) at a private dinner party on 8 November, just as the Canadians were securing their final positions on Passchendaele ridge:

> We haven't the pluck of these young lieutenants who go over the top. We're telling lies, we daren't tell the public the truth, that we're losing more officers than the Germans, and that it's impossible to get through on the Western Front. You've seen the correspondents shepherded by Charteris. They don't know the truth, they don't speak the truth, and we know that they don't. [40]

Apart from Rothermere's unconscious agreement with Bismarck's quip about humanity beginning with the rank of lieutenant, the implications of this remark were that 'the truth' about Third Ypres could be found not on the Western Front nor among the people at home, but within the closed circles of Whitehall and its associated corridors of power. The belief of the government, the newspaper proprietors and the propagandists was that the public was incapable of forming its own opinion and would take whatever perspective on the war it was given. Again, it was not until a decade or so later that such simplistic views of the value of propaganda within a democracy began to change – at precisely the time when 'propaganda' was being discredited as a useful function of government.

Finally, the claim has been made recently by cultural historians that the First World War saw a major change in representing war in art and literature, with an emphasis on the continuing personal experience of the lowly individual soldier rather than on the commander, the battle, or the army as a mass, and that this critical development in Modernist thought was the product of the work of alienated individuals protesting against the existing social and political order during or after the war.[41] This view neglects the impact on our understanding of the role played by the British official propagandists during the war, as they made a similar change to their approach shortly before the Third Battles of Ypres, for reasons that were largely political in nature. The priorities of propaganda had become mass persuasion rather than focussing mainly upon the elite. While there are entirely understandable technological, human and operational explanations for why the realities of war can never be portrayed contemporaneously by the mass media – by a hostile press corps let alone a co-operative one – the lasting image of Passchendaele as an event of tragic human suffering could not have come from the contemporary media record of 1917 – military control would have seen to that and perhaps that was why Sir Douglas Haig gave each of the correspondents his own Union Jack.

Notes

1   J.C.W. Reith, *Into the Wind* (London, 1949) p. 354.
2   See, for example, Adolf Hitler in *Mein Kampf*, Paul von Hindenberg, *Out of My Life* (London, 1931) and Erich Ludendorff, *My War Memories* (London, 1919). 'Admiration' is perhaps inappropriate in so far as the Americans were concerned; they were more alarmed at the skill of the British when post-war revelations showed the extent of the wartime campaign. See in particular H.C. Peterson, *Propaganda for War: The Campaign Against American Neutrality, 1914–17* (New York, 1939) and for a discussion of the impact of the earlier campaign on World War Two see N.J. Cull, *Selling War: the British Campaign against American 'Neutrality' in World War Two* (Oxford, 1995).
3   For further details, see M.L. Sanders & Philip M. Taylor, *British Propaganda during the First World War*, London, Macmillan, 1982).
4   Gary S. Messinger, *British Propaganda and the State in the First World War* (Manchester, 1993) p. 47.
5   N. Reeves, *Official British Film Propaganda in the First World War* (London, 1986) pp. 9–88; J. Carmichael, *First World War Photographers*, (London, 1989) pp 52–61; Roger Smither (ed.), *The First World War Archive, Imperial War Museum Film Catalogue*, Volume 1 (London, 1993).
6   Keith Grieves, 'War Correspondents and Conducting Officers on the Western Front from 1915', in Hugh Cecil and Peter H Liddle (eds.), *Facing Armageddon. The First World War Experienced* (London, 1996) p. 720.
7   Ibid., p. 728.
8   'Memorandum on Policy for Press', Haig Papers: Acc 3155.106 Diary May 1916 Note 100, National Library of Scotland, Edinburgh.
9   J. M. Bourne, *Britain and the Great War 1914–1918* (London, 1989) p. 208; Smither, op. cit., p. 134.
10 Bourne, pp 209–10.
11 Gary Sheffield, 'The Morale of the British Army on the Western Front 1914–1918', Occasional Paper 2, Institute for the Study of War and Society, De Montfort University, Bedford, 1996.
12 Robin Prior and Trevor Wilson, *Passchendaele, The Untold Story*, (London, 1996); John Terraine, *The Road to Passchendaele. The Flanders Offensive of 1917, a Study in Inevitability* (London, 1977).

13 J.M. McEwan, 'The Press and the Fall of Asquith', *Historical Journal*, 21 (1978) pp. 863–83.

14 Roberta Warman, 'The Erosion of Foreign Office influence in the making of Foreign Policy, 1916–18', *Historical Journal*, 15 (1972) pp. 113–59.

15 Both reports are in the Public Record Office, Kew, INF 4 1/B.

16 Andrew Steed, 'British Propaganda and the First World War', in Ian Stewart and Susan L Carruthers (eds.), *War, Culture and the Media: Representations of the Military in 20th Century Britain* (London, 1996) pp. 29–30; Stephen Badsey, 'The Trench Raid at Cherisy', *Imperial War Museum Review*, Number 4, 1989, p. 94.

17 Messenger, op. cit., p. 130.

18 Kevin Brownlow, *The War, the West and the Wilderness* (London, 1979) pp. 144–5; Smither, op. cit., p. 39.

19 Minute by A.J. Balfour, 26 April 1917. FO 395/147, Public Record Office, Kew.

20 *A Corpse Conversion Factory* (London, 1917).

21 Nicholas Reeves, 'Official British Film Propaganda – Myth or Reality?', *Historical Journal of Film, Radio and Television*, Volume 13, Number 2, (1993) p. 195.

22 Quoted in Reeves, *Official British Film Propaganda*, p. 64; Luke McKernan, *Topical Budget, The Great British News Film* (London, 1992) p. 39.

23 Reeves in *H.J.F.R.T.*, op. cit., p. 193.

24 Memo by M17a to Press Bureau, 5 December 1917, HO 139/42, Public Record Office, Kew.

25 Brownlow, op. cit., p. 67, emphasis added.

26 Buchan to Brade 13 August 1917, Beaverbrook Papers: Series E Box 'Cinema General', House of Lords Record Office, London.

27 Beaverbrook to Brade 9 July 1917, Beaverbrook Papers: Series E Box 'Cinema General', House of Lords Records Office, London.

28 McKernan, op. cit., pp. 38–47.

29 Smither, op. cit., pp. 496–508.

30 Brownlow, op. cit., pp 149.

31 Carmichael, op. cit., p. 64.

32 *Daily Mirror*, 13 October 1917.

33 Terraine, op. cit., pp. 154–58.

34 Steed, op. cit., p. 33; Reeves. *Official British Film Propaganda*, p. 291

35 Riddell to Beaverbrook 1 November 1917. IWM (Photo) Box 1, Imperial War Museum, London.

36 Neville Lytton, *The Press and the General Staff*, (London, n.d.) p. 118.

37 Steed, op. cit., p. 33.

38 Eberhard Demm, 'German Teachers at War', in Cecil and Liddle (eds.), op. cit. p. 709.

39 Reeves in *HJFRT*, op. cit. pp. 197–8.

40 Lucy Masterman, *C.F.C. Masterman, A Biography* (London 1929) p. 296.

41 See Modris Eksteins, *Rites of Spring: The Great War and the Birth of the Modern Age* (London, 1989); Paul Fussell, *The Great War and Modern Memory* (London, OUP, 1975).

Chapter 24

The 'Recruiting Margin' in Britain: Debates on Manpower during the Third Battle of Ypres

Keith Grieves

On 31 May 1917, the Adjutant-General, Lieutenant-General Sir Nevil Macready issued one of the most explosive and recriminatory documents on the subject of the supply of recruits for the army in the history of civil-military relations during the First World War. He reminded the War Cabinet that the War Committee on 30 November 1916 had agreed to the enlistment of 800,000 category 'A' men – who were fit for general service – and 140,000 men of lesser medical categories in 1917, of whom 570,000 category 'A' men would be available for the army by the end of May. Consequently, they would be recruited in sufficient time for the 'Great Offensive' which was widely expected in July 1917. In the first five months of 1917, 309,506 category 'A' men were recruited and British infantry divisions in France were described as below strength by 82,783 men. Macready was particularly critical of the failure to release men from protected industries by agreed quotas, for example, 20,000 men from coal mines and 21,000 from railways. The total quota negotiated for the period April-July 1917 was 215,000 men but, by 25 May, one man had been released for military service. The overall 'deficit' in category 'A' men was 250,000 men and Macready lamented the failure of recruiting in advance of the beginning of the great offensive and well before the euphemistically stated 'period of exhaustion which will supervene in early autumn'.

From the vantage point of the Army Council and General Headquarters (GHQ), British armies in France, this problem was unexpected and, moreover, was illogical, for how was the war to be won if the greatest number of fit men of military age could not be placed on the Western Front in sufficient time for the offensive envisaged for the Ypres salient? In 1916, conscription of single and married men had ensued with less difficulty than its advocates had expected. The acceptance of compulsion strongly implied that the notion of a 'large army first' prevailed. Macready saw no reason why this principle should be challenged and he argued for its clear expression in recruiting policy, namely, 'the simple basis that I can express in two words, "youngest first",' instead of advocating procedures which enlisted only the men who could be *conveniently* spared.[1] Macready's solution to the recruiting crisis was clearly stated; there were 830,000 men of 25 years of age and under in civil life. Two-thirds of them were required for military service. Urgent action would ensure that the problem was rectified without damaging British military plans.

For two and a half years of war, the *demands* of GHQ for manpower for decisive action on the dominant front, had subordinated all other claims for labour. In 1917 the problem of withdrawing men from essential war industries began to challenge the military assumption that all fit young men should be in the army.[2] Consequently, the period of preparation for the Third Battle of Ypres was accompanied by fierce struggles in Whitehall between the War Office and civil departments, which grew in intensity as the phases of the offensive unfolded.[3] In effect, the character of the British war effort underwent a transformation in which the military dimension became *part* of a more integrated and, eventually, transnational war effort. It was hastened by the political response to the final phase and immediate aftermath of Passchendaele. The complexity of the recruiting procedures in 1917, and the failure to obtain 940,000 men for military service, reflected the onset of a more total war effort in which delicate balances had to be struck between competing claims for manpower in a way that was barely comprehended two years earlier. The debates and negotiations appalled military high command because the fear of diminishing recruiting levels confounded the strategic direction of the war which assumed that its attritional features could be withstood by the continuous supply of new recruits. Field Marshal Sir Douglas Haig confirmed on 4 August 1917, in his report of the opening of the battle, that 'the total of his [German] casualties exceeds ours very considerably and not improbably by as much as 100%'.[4] His Chief of General Staff, Lieutenant-General Sir Launcelot Kiggell noted, one week later, that 'Boche killing is the only way to win', rather than territorial gain, and he had the sagacity to observe that 'moderate losses' would be an important element of any War Cabinet commitment to sustained offensive activity.[5] As *The Times* noted on 3 August 1917, well before it became critical of unavailing military activity on the Western Front, 'The public are perhaps inclined to be sceptical when they are told that the first stage of a mighty conflict has been cheaply won'.[6]

An intimation of concern about the effects of unrestrained military demands for men throughout the summer and autumn months of 1917, was evident in constant efforts to protect skilled ploughmen from recruiting officers.[7] Unrestricted U-boat warfare after February 1917 immediately emphasised the importance of the food programme. Bonar Law told King George V on 16 March regarding 'the arrangements necessary to secure the harvest this year, the government had decided that the need of the production of food must have priority over the need of supplying men [for the army]'.[8] The extended tillage programme required the retention of 177,000 men of military age in agricultural work. The Prime Minister, David Lloyd George, depended on the skill and energy of Lord Milner, who was effectively the War Cabinet's manpower expert and arbiter in inter-departmental negotiations. On 12 June 1917, Lord Milner instructed Lord Derby, Secretary of State for War, not to take any more men off farms in England and Scotland without the consent of county war agricultural committees. He stated that 'the withdrawal of further men just now is having a quite disastrous effect, and will give a death-blow to our whole agricultural policy'.[9] One month later Lord Milner demanded that ploughmen who had enlisted were lent to the farms; 'I find it hard to believe that, out of the whole 3.5 million under your control, 25,000 men knowing something of agriculture could not be found, and that without detriment to the Army as a fighting force'.[10]

Supplies of boy labour, uniformed women and German prisoners for agricultural work were insufficient. In continuous negotiations with the War Office in June and July 1917, the maintenance of food supplies curtailed recruitment in many rural areas and the War Office attempted to cope with the idea that it was in the national interest that agriculturists were released for harvesting. This problem continued throughout the offensive. On 26 October, as ploughs remained idle for want of men, the War Cabinet demanded 10,000 ploughmen from the army even if they had to be taken from divisions on the Western Front for a short furlough of two months.[11] This question of food supply or men for the army was raised in countless military service exemption tribunal meetings where individuals' contributions to the war effort were discussed and adjudicated in detail. A man from Hassocks appeared before the East Sussex Appeal Tribunal, having previously been rejected seven times by the army. He had a smallholding for pigs and chickens and acted as a mail carrier each night. His legal representative argued that 'his client was far more useful in a national sense where he was than he would be in the army'.[12] His temporary exemption certificate was renewed. Similarly, in September 1917, two blacksmiths, aged 30 and 38 years and both fit for general service, who regularly dealt with 100 horses for shoeing, were each exempted for a further period of six months. They worked in a certified occupation and Horsham Rural Tribunal noted that no proof of their 'non-necessity' was submitted.[13] Many military representatives were exasperated at this competing definition of the national interest. Sir Frederick Osborne Bt.J.P. told a farmer at Uckfield Rural Tribunal 'We are all sending our sons to the Front, and some come home and others do not. What are you going to do?'[14]

The quest for men for the army was undertaken in 1917 with increasing regard for the contribution they might make to the Allied war effort by *remaining* in civil life. In April 1917, there were four million 'eligibles' of military age of which two million were fit for general service. Of these, 1,530,000 men were badged or employed by government departments on essential war work, including 150,000 railwaymen, 150,000 agriculturists, 300,000 coal miners and 600,000 munition workers. In particular, the 'special demands' on available labour, apart from a continental-scale army, were the retention of command of the sea, the maintenance of a transport structure and the provision of coal and other commodities for the allies.[15] In 1916, 36% of British iron and steel production was for Allied countries which required an estimated labour force of 403,000 men and women. After the entry of the United States into the war in April 1917, the placing of foreign contracts with British firms became a prime example of the way that calculations for recruiting men were easily overtaken by new demands for supplies. In November 1917, the contracts placed by American, Serbian and Greek governments with woollen and worsted firms, was referred to by the Minister of National Service as of 'sufficient magnitude to engage the whole man-power of the Yorkshire textile trade, which has hitherto been on short time, and which I have regarded as an available source of supply of men for the Army'.[16] This example of a trade which was less vital after the clothing of the New Armies in 1915 and which had became more essential to clothe the American armies in 1917 suggested that the definition of essential work had to be constantly reviewed if the conduct of the war effort were to be characterized by the efficient management of manpower and material resources.

As the opening week of the great offensive unfolded in August 1917, the significance of shipyard labour, in addition to agricultural workers, was emphasized in response to the relentless attacks on British merchant ships.[17] Sir Eric Geddes, First Lord of the Admiralty, wanted an 'umbrella' over the shipyards to stop further recruiting but Lord Derby argued that it would be impossible to maintain divisions at the front because men whose exemptions were cancelled by tribunals would immediately obtain fresh protection as newly-employed Admiralty workers. Instead of allowing full protection, the War Cabinet avoided total exemption – unlike agriculture – by requiring the army to release skilled steel and blast furnace workers for merchant ship construction. In addition, 6,000 skilled shipyard workers were released by the War Office.[18] However, merchant ship-building failed to accelerate and on 8 October the War Cabinet decided to exempt all shipyard labour from military service. The War Office was gravely concerned by this development. Its attitude towards the favoured position of Admiralty manpower was encapsulated in Lord Derby's appeal for a reversal of this decision on 24 November: 'I am perfectly convinced that they have a large number of men which they could spare, and also in their dockyards there is a great opportunity of a far larger dilution than they have hitherto attempted'.[19]

The emergence of vital war industries where young skilled men were placed in scheduled occupations was clarified by the withdrawal of the trade card scheme in May, the end of the National Service scheme of substitution volunteers in July and the appointment of Sir Auckland Geddes as Minister of National Service soon after the opening attacks in August

1917.[20] In this month, and at a time of great strain, the administration of recruiting was entirely reformed to abolish the voluntary enrolment of substitutes who were older and unfit, alongside Neville Chamberlain's expectation, as Director of National Service, that *all* government exemptions in lower military ages would be cancelled and that men would be called up as required.[21] This scheme had foundered for want of effective centralized labour transfer procedures. In the context of the enlarging food and shipbuilding programmes, Auckland Geddes, as Director of Recruiting, had concluded, according to Lloyd George, that the 'only rational basis for recruiting is an occupation and not an age basis'.[22] Unlike Macready, who argued that 'freedom to consider individual cases leads to charges of corruption, favouritism and injustice',[23] Auckland Geddes recognised that a new authority for recruiting with responsibility for co-ordinating labour might help to rectify the deteriorating situation. Lord Derby emphasised the parlous recruiting position and informed Lloyd George on 9 August that 'the amount of reinforcements that we can send out in this month will barely cover the ordinary wastage'.[24] Five days later, Lord Derby looked forward with some optimism to Auckland Geddes's new ministerial role – having taken his khaki coat off – 'though it is very difficult to make bricks with as little straw as he will have'.[25]

In the absence of 'youngest first' and 'all for the army', the British High Command pursued the first phase of the Third Battle of Ypres in the *hope* that its appeals for more men would have an invigorating effect on the new schemes of labour and material co-ordination which were being debated, after much delay, by the War Cabinet.[26] Haig told Field Marshal Sir William Robertson, Chief of the Imperial General Staff, 'Many thanks for getting a hustle on about "drafts". The country, when it discovers what the Gov[ernmen]t has failed to do in this vital matter, will never forgive them!'[27] Robertson reassured Kiggell on 13 August 'you may rest assured that I am constantly giving attention to the question of drafts'.[28] Four days later, Robertson was in discussion with Macready on the subject of drafts but he warned GHQ that part of the response to the infantry deficit lay in 'combing' out more fit men from rearward jobs in the British armies in France for front line service. At the same time, Robertson astutely noted the difference between the net deficit of British infantry quoted by Kiggell at 58,000 men and the real deficit of 43,000 men, for which 33,100 men were promised in August.[29] He also had some sensitivity to the industrial context and, as the battles of August to October proceeded, Robertson recognised that the best that could be hoped for were periodic revisions of the Schedule of Protected Occupations. This allowed slight increases in the availability of men for the colours whenever the minimum age in specified trades could be raised to 23 or 25 or 31 years.

In September 1917, the influential "L" Committee at the Ministry of Munitions reaffirmed the principle of individual enlistment which was deliberately designed to forestall accusations of industrial compulsion. As there was no labour surplus, the process of dilution was supported by labour priority committees which understood that the process of enlistment was not 'recruitment of labour in the mass but is always recruitment of the individual workmen from the individual machine or an individual operation of some kind'.[30] The new emphasis of local boards, representing the ministries of Munitions, National Service, Admiralty and the War Office, to settle local recruiting and dilution disputes, acknowledged the intimate relationship between industrial unrest and the operation of military service legislation until the 'civilianization' of military recruitment in the autumn months of 1917.[31] Gradually, the capacity of departments of state to accede to relative priority claims for labour, brought some order to the distribution of manpower. The creation of the Aerial Operations Committee of the War Cabinet to recommend the level of priority which should be attached to the provision of a 200 squadron Royal Flying Corps, and the reconstitution of the War Policy Committee on 15 October to consider 'recruiting prospects and wastage', brought clarity of organization and procedure in the higher conduct of manpower policy.[32] A start was made in settling with statistical precision the competing claims of different departments, and more awareness was shown of the variety of programmes for aeroplanes, artillery, tank and machine-gun production which were previously subsumed by generalized references to munitions output.[33]

In this context, Robertson had access to a more cogent executive decision-making process. However, the argument for the front-line 62 division force in France, comprising 680,861[34] rifles, was thoroughly undermined by news of the battles in the second phase of the offensive which started on 28 August and continued through Menin Road Ridge, Polygon Wood and Broodseinde into the first week of October. Thereafter, despite appalling conditions, the offensive continued to the capture of Passchendaele on 6 November and ended four days later. These months marked the end of the British government's commitment to the 'large army first' principle as its confidence in Haig's purpose in the Ypres salient was progressively undermined. Instead, apprehension that the resilient, stoical home front might not withstand the costly and disillusioning outcomes of these continuous battles became of more urgent concern. The expression of wonder that such little sense of victory could follow such a substantial expression of 'continental commitment' ensured that, in December, replacement drafts were crossing to France at the rate of only 180 men per day.

As early as 23 August 1917, Lieutenant-General Sir Sydney Clive, head of the British mission at Grand Quartier General, concluded 'I see no chance of wearing out their reserves this year as to force them to go back at once without [wearing] ourselves out equally'.[35] Lloyd George put the same point, albeit with different semantic emphasis, to his confidant Lord Riddell: 'We are losing the flower of our Army, and to what purpose'.[36] Riddell's subsequent references to a 'wearing down contest' and conserving British forces on the Western Front in September 1917, reflected the War

Cabinet's extreme unease. Its profound anxiety was more vigorously stated in October and marked the beginning of more substantive political control over the military conduct of the war. Both Lord Milner and George Barnes drew the conclusion that more co-ordinated effort and a clearer sense of purpose was required to forestall future military plans and unlimited demands for men. On 17 October, Lord Milner – who was so important for his expertise on the priority allocation of labour – noted that 'the doubts ... about the probability of success in the policy of Hammer, Hammer, Hammer on the Western Front, are becoming increasingly strong in my own mind'.[37] Twelve days later George Barnes, representing Labour in the War Cabinet, informed Lloyd George that 'The absence of any marked strategical success is beginning to be commented upon in unfavourable terms and contrasts made as between actual achievements and the prospect held out from time to time by the Generals in the Field'.[38] In the last week of October, the casualty list numbered 26,000 men of whom 7,000 were dead and 1,000 were missing. Barnes commented on the 'serious risk' which attended the continuation of the offensive by which he meant that war weariness might be expressed in Britain in more disaffected ways.

October 1917 marked the last unconstrained 'wastage' return from the Western Front. The actuarial calculations on *normal* average casualties that month were entirely superseded by 'irritating over optimism that used to precede and accompany our offensives' as Maurice Hankey, Secretary to the War Cabinet, observed on 22 January 1918.[39] In October 1917, as the ruined village of Passchendaele was finally approached, British casualties amounted to 4,956 officers and 106,419 other ranks, but recruits numbered only 36,543 men of all medical categories. In his explanation of the casualty rate, the Director of Military Operations reduced the stark significance of the figures by drawing attention to normal average figures of 35,000 men per month; 'the actual casualties therefore, for the month of October due to the Third Battle of Ypres, were about 76,000'.[40] In December 1917, a new low of 24,923 recruits were obtained for the army. On 15 November 1917, Clive saw Haig at Bavencourt and subsequently noted 'D. H[aig] interested in the graphics of losses of resource. Looking at our figures he said very quietly: "Have we lost 500,000 men!"[41] Within three weeks of this conclusion, the War Cabinet was intent on formulating plans which were designed to reduce British casualty levels in 1918 by one-half. It also sought evidence from Marshal Pétain on French tactical planning, demanded the resignation of Brigadier-General Charteris as Chief of Intelligence at GHQ and, in January 1918, allocated only 100,000 new 'A' men for military service, which was one-sixth of the demand for manpower submitted by the War Office.[42] Hankey noted that military opinion was steady, but not unnaturally subdued.

In January 1918, timber, iron ore, food production, merchant ship construction, aeroplane and tank production and naval personnel were all accorded a higher priority for increased levels of labour allocation than men for the army. The notion of obtaining further large quotas of men from vital war industries for the British armies in France remained a chimera until the German spring offensive on the Western Front in March 1918. Consequently, in the discussions of manpower allocation for military, mercantile, industrial and agricultural purposes for 1918, the Adjutant-General, Army Council, GHQ and Secretary of State of War, were forced to recognise that the massing of men on the Western Front should not be at the cost of the diminishing output of essential materials. The supply of labour was finite and attempts to withdraw remaining fit men of military age from railways, ports, blast furnaces, arable farming, coal mining, saw milling and ship building caused severe shortages in vital occupational categories in the autumn months of 1917. Furthermore, in the course of 1917, dilution through substitution was advanced to the extent that the number of women employed in national filling factories and national shell factories reached 79 per cent and 72 per cent of the total workforce in these new government-sponsored munitions works.[43] In the production of all types of munitions, the number of men employed in the industry rose from 1,921,000 in January 1917, to 2,022,000 in October 1917. In the same period, the number of women employed in munitions work increased more markedly from 535,000 to 704,000 'munitionettes'.

In the circumstances, it was remarkable that 820,146 men of all categories were recruited for the army in 1917, but only 92,300 men were obtained in the last quarter of the year.[44] Alongside the final weeks of fighting of the Third Battle of Ypres, references to the recruitable margin, the limits of labour supply, the careful organization of the whole national effort and the avoidance of duplication, started to multiply.[45] In this period of great strain, the value of economic activity, in its widest form, continued to be reassessed. For example, retailers still placed advertisements in newspapers for non-essential commodities. Auckland Geddes bemoaned ladies clothing 'as the grave of an enormous amount of human energy. New hats alone absorb the work of millions of fingers, and whatever effect they may have, that effect certainly does not include helping to beat the enemy'.[46] The failure to restrict luxury trades by taxing higher incomes, sustained trades which did not employ fit men of military age but did diminish the pool of labour available for substitution. The continuing use of gun metal in the manufacture of cigarette lighters was a further example of the variable application of regulations which often fell short of rationing labour and materials in the economy.

These well-publicized examples of extravagance drew ample criticism from military representatives at local tribunals which reviewed individual circumstances and challenged men to justify their role in civilian life on grounds of occupation, personal hardship or conscientious objection. The work of the tribunals in adjudicating between the national interest and individual circumstances drew criticism from senior military officers in the summer and autumn months of 1917. The deliberations of the tribunals provided many sharply-focused examples of ways in which military assumptions about 'youngest first' for the army were overwhelmed by other considerations, not least of which was 'local feeling'. One of the most angry responses to the tribunal system was expressed by Lieutenant-General Sir Henry Wilson. He regularly provided Lloyd George with unofficial advice and was briefly side-lined, as General Officer Commanding, Eastern Command in the autumn of 1917, before he became Chief of the Imperial General Staff in February 1918. He noted that recruits for general service were available in his region at the rate of 450 per week or 24,000 per year which was sufficient for one day's battle on the Western Front. He perceived that the notion of the national interest was being redefined as the needs of specific districts because tribunals were 'composed of local men who owe their position to local popularity and local influences and who have had neither training in judicial or imperial matters nor that experience in official administration which develops the judicial facility and the instinct of placing the affairs of the Nation first and all other considerations in their proper perspective'.[47] Although tribunals were composed of councillors, other leaders of local opinion and representatives of labour, who had participated in recruiting meetings early in the war and supported military conscription in 1916, their perspective diverged from the War Office's demand for men in 1917.

Localism found expression in a variety of ways, according to socio-economic conditions, but the issue of one-man business recruiting became generally acute towards the end of the year. In December 1917, the Local Government Board published guidelines on the preservation of businesses of men released for the army by the co-operative action of men in the same trade which required surveys of essential needs for services in each district.[48] Consequently, as military representatives started to emphasise the great demand for men of 40 years of age, trades began to define the needs of towns in advance of grocers, butchers, greengrocers, bakers and dairymen appearing before tribunals as groups of traders. The preservation of local retail and workshop infrastructures finally became a prior claim on non-category 'A' men. Consequently, the individual circumstances of the applicant often coalesced with the specific requirements of the locality, not least in the distribution of food. One applicant to the West Sussex Appeal Tribunal in September 1917 for a review of his case, was a 39 year old master baker in Lancing. He was medically classified as B1 which meant that he was not fit for general (or front line) service but he could serve in France in a rearward unit. The military representative argued that there were ample supplies of bread in Lancing without this source. The baker argued that his one-man business was the largest of four bakeries in Lancing and he did the bread-making. He was given a renewal of exemption for a further period of four months.[49] Businessmen of C1 grade, who were fit for service at home only, also started to be claimed by the army on the grounds that, if they served in the Home Army, younger and fitter men could be transferred to France. However, even Lord Derby recognized that men might be of far greater value to the war effort in their civilian work than in joining the anti-invasion Home Army. On 24 August, he applied for exemption for a 40 year old C1 man who was a forester on his estate at Knowsley. He was the only man of military age on Derby's staff of foresters of 22 remaining men, and 29 class 'A' men had previously joined the army. Exemption was refused.[50] Consequent on the planning of the great offensive at Ypres was the assumption that from April 1917 tribunals would have been helping to locate 500,000 men for the army. But the ensuing level of 'wastage' halted the synonymous relationship between patriotic duty and service in the army for those who remained at home at the beginning of the fourth year of the war. Instead, the issue of the enlistment of 'Low Category Men', – which was often spelt out in tribunal petitions in upper case – clarified the widening gap or fissure between the interests of British high command in the short term and the long term requirements of the total war effort within a more frequently-cited Allied context.

The conundrum of unlimited recruitment levels and the retention of approximately 1,500,000 fit men of military age in vital war industries, presented itself on a daily basis in thousands of local centres where manpower needs were evaluated. On the subject of low category men, the Mayor of Stamford noted that 'in many cases to take them into the Army means closing small businesses, great hardships and loss and inconvenience to small Traders'.[51] East Grinstead Urban Tribunal issued a statement on 24 September which noted that a high percentage of cases under consid eration concerned low category men. At Cuckfield Rural Tribunal, the case of a 41 year old gardener who was classified C3 – fit for service at home on sedentary work – was erroneously discussed.[52] The military authorities had not (yet) reached the stage of recruiting men of 41 years who were in the lowest category of military fitness.

In the context of tribunal objections to the enlistment of low category men and government departments which protected skilled labour, recruiting officers depended on obtaining men under the Military Service (Review of Exceptions) Act of April 1917. It required the medical re-exam- ination of rejected or discharged men so that their exemptions could be individually reviewed, excluding all agriculturists or men wounded in battle or disabled in military and naval service. On the grounds that men were improperly rejected for military service early in the war and that 'counterfeit diseases', suggested by high percentages of pulmonary tuber- culosis, disorders of the heart and diseases of the ear, required renewed vigilance, re-examinations were undertaken by travelling medical boards.[53] At Leeds recruiting office, an old man with a white beard was called up for medical re-examination. He was aged 70 years and had served in the West Yorkshire Regiment for 22 years before being discharged in 1888.[54] In the Holbeach district of Lincolnshire a soldier blinded in the retreat from Mons reported for medical re-examination. In the period of two months he was required to report on three separate occasions.[55] Discharged soldiers and sailors became a further well-defined sectional interest which expressed firm opposition to the military manpower pre-suppositions on which the great offensive was based, as approximately 70,000 – 80,000 men were sought for the trenches under this statutory instrument.[56] Thereafter recruiting officers were forced to concede that there were men who would never be sufficiently fit for military service – however much the 'barrel was scraped' – just as there were fit men who would always be required as essential experts in the making of steel hulls, optical instruments, machine tools, aeroplane engines and other vital categories of war work.

Consequently, in the history of man-power allocation and control in the Great War, the casualty levels in the Ypres salient, for no obvious gain which could be clearly stated on the home front, brought a critical period of reflection and review which hastened the transfer of troops to Italy and the Anglo-French co-ordination of reserve armies on the Western Front early in 1918. The trend towards diminishing the claims of the War Office *vis-à-vis* other departments was reinforced by the military setback after initial success at Cambrai. Robertson noted that nineteen German divisions arrived to counter-attack at Cambrai which Haig believed were 'used up in [the] Ypres salient'.[57] The diminution of German morale and manpower in advance of Cambrai had apparently been overstated. Although Haig continued to argue that operations after 20 November made 'large inroads in German reserves'[58] they confirmed the government's growing tendency to give especial attention to morale in manufacturing centres by considering inequalities of food distribution and the wider political aspirations of the urban working class. At Lloyd George's secretariat, W. Ormsby Gore's briefing paper on the causes of industrial unrest noted 'The idea that the British Army in France after being encouraged to believe in great results from last autumn's offensive is now to go on the defensive, is getting generally known and produces a new outlook'.[59] The idea that the attacks should proceed because German permanent losses on the battlefield caused an infinitely greater strain on their manpower and economy was so lacking in tangible form, and so costly in human and material terms, that the War Cabinet firmly concluded that the British war effort required more total civilian control at the highest level.[60]

In particular, the lack of any direct relation between the objectives of the Third Battle of Ypres and the capacity and willingness of tribunals, industries, departments of state and individual politicians to maintain the flow of men for military service in France, seized the attention of Auckland Geddes. In August 1917, Lord Derby looked forward to Geddes's translation from a uniformed Director of Recruiting, with the temporary rank of Brigadier-General, to Minister of National Service with responsibility for surveying all available manpower for the War Cabinet. He hoped that Dr Auckland Geddes would be able to rectify recruiting procedures, assert the importance of men for the army and ensure that the 'combing out' of industries would retrieve men aged 18–25 years for military service. In effect, he hoped that this task of almost insurmountable difficulty would be proved possible (as if over two years of attritional industrialized artillery war had not taken place) and that the circumstances of 'all for the Army' of early 1915 could be simply reconstituted.

Auckland Geddes knew differently. In June 1918 he reflected on the impact, both apparent and real, of the battles of 1917 which required military and civilian experts on manpower to understand that in 1918 there would be no more Passchendaeles. In a review of the manpower situation he noted,

> With full knowledge of the general national position and of the impossibility of raising more than a limited number of men for service with the Army, the Military Authorities decided in favour of continuing the western offensive and of undertaking the subsequent operations at Cambrai. The heavy casualties which accrued and the impossibility of training the divisions fully after each infusion of new drafts, the effect of what was in common belief the unfruitful pouring out of life, upon the moral of the people and upon the willingness of men to serve dogged for many months the war effort of the nation.[61]

In the last year of the war, careful and sensitive monitoring was required of the 'general national position' in its broadest sense. Although the military conduct of the war reached an unprecedented scale and intensity of contest in 1917, Anglo-American co-operation in 1918 required an emphasis on naval and industrial resources in a more total war effort which few generals could begin to comprehend in the Ypres salient.

North Atlantic shipping traffic displaced the priority of maintaining British infantry establishment in France in the aftermath of Passchendaele. The threat of a 31 division force was less catastrophic than failure to improve steel production, increase shipping tonnage, create an effective home air defence programme and maintain coal output.[62] Alongside these industrial imperatives, the infantry deficit of 75,500 men was less perilous and Lord Derby's urgent references to the failure of recruiting were less persuasive.[63] No longer could national organization be defined as military conscription and generals left to define the scale and duration of offensive activity. The lessons of 1917 were immediate for, despite the perils of March 1918, the key to eventual Allied victory lay in a resolutely balanced distribution of labour across the diverse components of the war effort. Urgent attention to the supply of essential goods and services alongside a recognition of local and voluntarist dimensions of society at war, ensured that the social fabric of Britain survived the capture of Passchendaele. The war against Germany had, indeed, moved to its most total form. Consequently, it is little wonder that the loss of life in Flanders became one of the most enduring controversies of the Great War.[64]

Notes

Crown copyright material is reproduced by kind permission of the Controller of Her Majesty's Stationery Office. For permission to use quotations from other copyright material I am grateful to the Beaverbrook Trustees, the Clerk of the Records,

House of Lords Record Office, the University of Birmingham, the Trustees of the Liddell Hart Centre for Military Archives, King's College London, Lord Derby and Lord Haig.

1   Memorandum by the Adjutant General to the Army Council regarding the Position and Prospects of Recruiting, N. Macready, 31 May 1917, WO 162/28, Public Record Office (PRO).

2   Estimate of Number of Men of Military Age absorbed in Great Britain by special demands made upon it, section on Eligibles, unsigned but produced in Lloyd George's Secretariat and enclosed in W. Adams, National Service file, [April 1917] F/79/28/2, Lloyd George mss., House of Lords Record Office (HLRO).

3   *War Cabinet Report for the Year* 1917. Cd. 9005, HMSO, London, 1918, vii–viii.

4   Report on the battle of 31 July 1917, G.T. 1621, D. Haig, 4 August 1917, CAB 24/22, PRO.

5   L. Kiggell to H. Gough, 7 August 1917, V/III, Kiggell mss., Liddell Hart Centre for Military Archives, King's College, London (LHCMA).

6   *The Times* 3 August 1917.

7   P. Dewey *British Agriculture in the First World War* Routledge, London, 1989, p. 106.

8   A. Bonar Law to King George V, King's letters, 16 March 1917, 77/2, Bonar Law mss., HLRO. See also D. Lloyd George *Fact v. Fiction Mr. Lloyd George's Statement on Shipping and Food Supplies* Hodder and Stoughton, London, 1917, pp. 4–5.

9   Lord Milner to Lord Derby, copy, 12 June 1917, dep. 45, Milner mss., Bodleian Library Oxford (BLO).

10   Lord Milner to Lord Derby, 12 July 1917, dep, 45, Milner mss., BLO. See also H. Thornton's diary, 26 July 1917, dep 23/1, Milner mss., Major Hugh Thornton was private secretary to Lord Milner.

11   Minutes of the War Cabinet meeting, 26 October 1917, WC 258, CAB 23/4, PRO. For soldiers on the land see P. Horn *Rural Life in England in the First World War*, Gill and Macmillan, New York, 1984, pp. 93–111.

12   *Sussex Daily News* 29 September 1917.

13   *Sussex Daily News* 25 September 1917.

14   *Sussex Daily News* 18 October 1917.

15   Estimate of Number of Men of Military Age absorbed in Great Britain by special demands made upon it, [April 1917] enclosed in W. Adams National Service file, F/79/28/2, Lloyd George mss., HLRO.

16   The Acceptance of Foreign Contracts in Relation to Man Power, A. Geddes, 7 November 1917, CAB 24/31, PRO.

17   Minutes of War Cabinet meeting, 9 August 1917, W.C. 209, CAB 23/3, PRO.

18   Minutes of War Cabinet meeting, 8 October 1917, W.C. 246, CAB 23/4, PRO.

19   Lord Derby to D. Lloyd George, 24 November 1917, F/14/4/78, Lloyd George mss., HLRO.

20   Notes of Adjourned Conference with Trade Unions with reference to the Trade Card Exemption Scheme, Ministry of Munitions 10 April 1917, Box 70, Addison mss., BLO; D. Lloyd George *War Memoirs*, London, Odhams Press, 1938, Vol. 1, p. 812. See also C. Addison to D. Lloyd George, 21 May 1917, Box 70, Addison mss., BLO.

21   N. Chamberlain to D. Lloyd George, 19 July 1917, NC8/5/2/27, Neville

Chamberlain mss, Birmingham University Library (BUL). See also L. Amery to N. Chamberlain, 10 August 1917, NC8/5/2/5, N. Chamberlain mss.

22   D. Lloyd George to N. Chamberlain, 20 July 1917, F/7/1/2, Lloyd George mss., HLRO. For a response to this argument see N. Chamberlain to Hilda Chamberlain, 22 July 1917, NC18/1/120, N. Chamberlain mss., BUL.

23   Memorandum by the Adjutant General to the Army Council regarding the Position and Prospects of Recruiting, N. Macready, 31 May 1917, WO 162/28, PRO.

24   Lord Derby to D. Lloyd George, 9 August 1917, F/14/4/62, Lloyd George mss., HLRO.

25   Lord Derby to P. Sassoon, copy, 14 August 1917, 27/3, Derby mss., Liverpool Record Office.

26   On the phases of the Third Battle of Ypres I am grateful for the clarity of discussion in J. Bourne *Britain and the Great War 1914–1918*, London, Edward Arnold, 1989, pp. 73–78.

27   D. Haig to W. Robertson, 9 August 1917, I/23/46, Robertson mss., LHCMA. See also Haig's diary entry, 28 August 1917 in R. Blake (ed.) *The Private Papers of Douglas Haig 1914–1918*, London, Eyre and Spottiswoode, 1952, p. 252.

28   W. Robertson to L. Kiggell, 13 August 1917, IV/10/2, Kiggell mss., LHCMA.

29   W. Robertson to D. Haig, copy, 17 August 1917, I/23/45, Robertson mss., LHCMA.

30   Observations of 'L' Committee, Ministry of Munitions, on draft re. function of Ministry of National Service to W. Churchill, undated, [September 1917], MUN5/23/247. 2/3, PRO. W. Churchill, Minister of Munitions, responded to the discussion paper on 10 September 1917.

31   Board of Trade *Labour Gazette* Industrial Unrest, Vol. 25, No. 8, August 1917 pp. 273–4; *New Statesman* 6 October 1917, p. 2.

32   See minutes of War Cabinet meetings, W.C. 237, 21 September 1917 and W.C. 249, 15 October 1917, CAB 23/4, PRO.

33   Minutes of War Cabinet meeting, W.C. 246, 8 October 1917, Cab 23/4, PRO.

34   British armies in France, unsigned return, 13 September 1917, A4/2, Benson mss., LHCMA.

35   Diary entry, 23 August 1917, II/4, Lieutenant General Sir Sydney Clive mss., LHCMA.

36   Lord Riddell War Diary 1914–18, Ivor Nicholson and Watson, London, 1933, entry for 6 August 1917, p. 267. See also entries for 13 and 22 September 1917, p. 272 and p. 275.

37   Lord Milner to Lord Curzon, 17 October 1917, dep. 354. Milner mss., BLO.

38   G. Barnes to D. Lloyd George, 29 October 1917, F/7/2/14, Lloyd George mss., HLRO. See also Board of Trade Labour Gazette Vol. 25 No. 10, October 1917, p. 355.

39   M. Hankey to Lloyd George, 22 January 1918, F/23/2/11, Lloyd George mss., HLRO.

40   Minutes of the War Cabinet meeting, 2 November 1917, W.C. 263, CAB 23/4, PRO.

41   Diary of Lt. Gen. Sir Sydney Clive, 15 November 1917, II/4, Clive mss., LHCMA. For the wider context see P. Kennedy 'Britain in the First World War' in A.R. Millett and W. Murray (eds.). *Military Effectiveness: The First World War* Vol.1, Unwin Hyman, London, 1988, pp. 68–69.

42 W. Robertson to H. Plumer, 5 January 1918, I/34/46, Robertson mss., LHCMA.

43 *War Cabinet Report for the Year 1917*, Cd. 9005, HMSO, London, 1918, p. 69. See also Home Office and Board of Trade Pamphlets on the substitution of women in industry for enlisted men, 2nd ed., 1917, in the papers of Audenshaw Local Tribunal M138/67, Manchester Archives Department.

44 The Man-Power Situation 1917–1918, A. Geddes, 17 June 1918, G.T. 4874 in dep. 145. Milner mss., BLO.

45 For example on the 'recruitable margin' see the statements of D. Maclean MP, chairman of the House of Commons section of the London Appeal Tribunal, *The Times*, 1 August 1917.

46 *New Statesman* The Present Stage of the Man-Power Question, 15 December 1917, pp. 248–9.

47 H. Wilson, G.O.C. Eastern Command, to R. Brade, Secretary, War Office, unsigned, 27 October 1917, NATS 1/876, PRO.

48 R167 Circular, One Man Businesses: Cases of Hardship: Co-operation, Local Government Board, 17 December 1917, with papers of Audenshaw Local Tribunal M138/67, Manchester Archives Department.

49 *Sussex Daily News* 26 September 1917. For grades of fitness from Army Form W.3291 and other sources see K. Grieves The politics of manpower 1914–18, Manchester, Manchester University Press, 1988 pp. 219–220.

50 *The Times* 25 August 1917.

51 Statement by W.E. Martin, Mayor of Stamford, 30 August 1917 in the papers of Kingwinford Local Tribunal D585/187/1/1, Staffordshire Record Office.

52 *Sussex Daily News* 25 September and 29 September 1917.

53 Military Service (Review of Exceptions) Act 1917, Army Council Instruction No. 640 of 1917, War Office, 19 April 1917, in the papers of Audenshaw Local Tribunal, Manchester, M138/66. See also A. Bonar Law to King George V, 21 June 1917, 77/3, Bonar Law mss., HLRO.

54 *The Times* 5 July 1917.

55 *The Times* 17 July 1917.

56 G. Wootton The Politics of Influence. British Ex-Servicemen, Cabinet Decisions and Cultural Change (1917–57), London, Routledge and Kegan Paul, 1963, pp. 58–60.

57 W. Robertson to H. Plumer, 10 December 1917, I/34/41, Robertson mss., LHCMA.

58 Report summarising the operations between November 20th and December 7th 1917, D. Haig, 23 December 1917, WO 158/54, PRO.

59 The Labour Situation, W. Ormsby Gore, 1 January 1918 in M. Hankey to D. Lloyd George, 2 January 1918, F/23/2/1, Lloyd George mss., HLRO.

60 Review of the Military Situation in all theatres of war during 1917, Maj. Gen. F. Maurice to J. T. Davies, 18 December 1917, F/44/3/40, Lloyd George mss., HLRO.

61 The Man-Power Situation 1917–1918, G.T. 4872, A. Geddes, 17 June 1918, dep. 145, Milner mss., BLO.

62 N. Macready to W. Robertson, 27 November 1917, F/44/3/33, Lloyd George mss., HLRO.

63 Summary of the Recruiting Position, Lord Derby, I/11/12/2, attached to note by Lord Derby, dated 28 November 1917, I/11/12/1, Robertson mss., LHCMA. See also Memorandum to the Army Council by the Adjutant General on request by the Prime Minister for concrete proposals as to how

more Men are to be obtained for the Army, [N. Macready], 3 December 1917, WO32/9553, PRO.

64 For an early sense of the Third Battle of Ypres as a controversy about 'useless victories' see Haig's diary entry 26 December 1917 No. 120, Vol. 23, Haig mss., National Library of Scotland (NLS); Notes for Paris Speech. Inter-Allied Staff, 12 November 1917, unsigned, J. Smuts for D. Lloyd George, F/234, Lloyd George mss., HLRO; St. L. Strachey to H. Asquith, 16 November 1917, Strachey mss., HLRO; D. Haig to Lady Haig, 18 November 1917, No. 148, Haig mss., NLS.

Part V

Passchendaele: The Inspiration, Fascination and Discordance of an Enduring Legacy

Chapter 25

'An Epic of Mud':
Artistic Interpretations of Third Ypres

Paul Gough

> My first and last memories of Ypres were of a land pock-marked by a
> million shell-holes, wherein it was impossible to walk straight, each track
> or path twisting endlessly between these great sores, and in the silver
> mists the many battered trees of the salient seemed to belong to a dark
> primeval age. We crossed the canal which lay like a prison moat across
> the base of the salient, and everyone talked quietly and no lights burned.[1]

So wrote the artist Richard Talbot Kelly, recalling his time as an artillery
officer in 1917. With the keen sensibilities of a painter and illustrator,
Talbot Kelly identified many of the themes which would become the core
iconography of that battlefield: the disoriented spatial sense of the terrain
with its peculiar light and vaporous weather conditions; the atavistic reaction to the de-natured landscape, but above all, the shapelessness and
ubiquitous anxiety of the Salient. These will be the key concepts explored
in this chapter.

A considerable number of paintings, drawings and prints came out of
the Third Battle of Ypres: many of them are small, eye-witness images made
in sketchbooks or as illustrations in letters; others are modest attempts to
capture a significant moment or scene, often for private reflection. A
considerable body of work, though, was made by specially commissioned
artists – many of whom had served at the front – who painted large
canvases as part of a grand commemorative scheme that aimed to
memorialize the war in oils and bronze. Third Ypres would play a crucial
part in this pictorial commemoration because, by late 1917, the machinery
for commissioning artists was entering a new, and highly sophisticated
phase in governmental patronage.

Before looking at how artists actually responded to the battle, it is necessary to examine briefly the infrastructure for employing artists on the
Western Front.[2]

During September 1914, the British cabinet had set up a secret propaganda department – known as Wellington House, from its head-quarters near Buckingham Gate – to influence domestic and overseas press and opinion. In April 1916, as the propaganda value of visual imagery became recognized, a pictorial section was established to distribute war films and photographs. This soon burgeoned into a major activity: Wellington House's own all-picture publication, *War Pictorial*, for example, was produced in five different language editions with a global circulation of 300,000.[3] Such lavishly illustrated publications relied on a constant supply of front-line photographs that combined good tonal quality, interesting subjects and above all, could pass the censor. Wellington House could have resorted, as did many of the Fleet Street papers, to studio illustrators and cartoonists. Instead, driven by a number of reasons – not least the cultural capital to be gained – Wellington House chief, C.F.G.Masterman, and his colleagues argued for the employment of practising artists to be sent to the Front to record the war.[4] In May 1916, the forty year old Scottish etcher Muirhead Bone became the first official war artist, followed soon after by the portraitist, Francis Dodd. Neither had any soldiering experience and their work was stolid rather than spectacular, their artistic training prioritizing neutral observation over interpretation. In London, however, their graphic dexterity was well received and their war drawings were soon put to a range of propaganda uses. In February 1917, Wellington House was upgraded to a government department – the Department of Information under John Buchan – and numbers of artists, in sequence, were commissioned. Some, like Eric Kennington and Christopher Nevinson, had served on the Western Front or even further afield, and both had received widespread critical and public acclaim when their paintings and drawings of trench life had been shown in London in 1916. Nevinson's painting *La Mitrailleuse* was hailed by no less a figure than Walter Sickert as 'the most authoritative and concentrated utterance on the war in the history of painting'.[5]

In addition to the British government art scheme, the prospect for young artists with battle experience improved with the arrival in London of the Canadian entrepreneur, W. Maxwell Aitken.[6] In early 1916, he had established a Canadian War Records Office (CWRO) to record and publicise the work of the Canadian Forces. Using the profits accrued from his CWRO ventures, supported by the Canadian government, and with a zeal and flair sometimes missing from the Department of Information, Aitken began to sign up artists. His British counterparts were flabbergasted: 'The Canadian Government', wrote Masterman in 1917, 'alone seems willing to spend money on patronage of art in connection with war and are paying large sums of money for work by Kennington, Nevinson, Orpen and others'.[7]

Aitken (honoured in January 1917 as Lord Beaverbrook) recruited freely amongst the academies and arts clubs of the British art scene. His methods were direct and unorthodox. William Orpen ARA, recalled how he was poached from the British War Memorials scheme in September 1917:

About ten minutes past four up breezed a car, and in it was a slim little man with an enormous head and two remarkable eyes. I saluted and tried to make military noises with my boots. Said he: 'Are you Orpen ?' 'Yes, sir' said I. 'Are you willing to work for the Canadians ?' said he. 'Certainly, sir' said I. 'Well' said he, 'that's all right. Jump in, and we'll go and have a drink.'[8]

By early 1918, the CWRO was employing over fifty-five artists from six different countries, and in February of that year, Beaverbrook – having been instrumental in the elevation of Lloyd George to power – was appointed head of the new Ministry of Information (MoI). Using the Canadian War Art scheme as a model, Beaverbrook established the British War Memorials Committee (BWMC). It systematically set about recording the war not merely for short term propaganda purposes but for a long lasting record of the war on all fronts that would embrace every facet of war work – home and abroad, civilian and military.[9]

The apex of Beaverbrook's grand scheme would be the building of prestigious Halls of Remembrance, in London and Canada, which would house the collections and other specially commissioned paintings and sculptures. In the event, although both the Canadian and British War art collections were exhibited and well received, neither memorial hall was built.

Much of this frenzy of official artistic patronage had taken place as the Third Battle of Ypres was being fought. Many of the younger British artists, who before the war had formed the nucleus of the artistic avant-garde, were eventually commissioned by the MoI or its predecessor. Nearly all of them had some experience of the Salient. Paul Nash had already served there in the spring of 1917 and would return there as an official artist in November, Percy Wyndham Lewis and William Roberts had survived many dangerous months around Ypres with the Royal Artillery, and Ian Strang had worked just south of the area with the Camouflage Corps since early 1915. Christopher Nevinson had served at the front as an ambulance driver and later, as an artist, had earned a formidable reputation as 'a desperate fellow and without fear ... only anxious to crawl, into the front line and draw things full of violence and terror'.[10] In a typical gesture, he earned the ire of Army Intelligence when, on the eve of the battle for Passchendaele, he made a clandestine visit to the front line.

With the benefit of the Government's war art schemes, these artists and others were seconded from their regimental duties to the Ministry of Information or the Canadians. In the period 1918–1919, as they worked on their pictures for the proposed Halls of Remembrance they would each draw upon their memories of the Salient. Paul Nash and Christopher Nevinson focussed very specifically on the traumatic experience of Third Ypres as a basis for their very best, and most searing, war work. Nevinson's *Harvest of Battle* and *Paths of Glory*, Nash's *The Menin Road* and *Void* have proved to be amongst the most enduring and incisive visions of conflict ever painted.

There were though, many other soldier-artists at Third Ypres. Most were never commissioned as official artists and few had much involvement in the debates about modernist aesthetics, but their work also merits interest and much of it has survived largely unrecognized in national and other collections or museums. A typical case is the painter Louis Ginnett. Aged thirty-nine at the outbreak of war and a past President of the Modern (now Royal) Society of Portrait Painters, he had enlisted in 1915 with other artists from the St John's Wood Arts Club, London, and from 1916 served as a subaltern with 128 Siege Battery, RGA around Ypres. Stimulated by the scenery of the battlefield, he made a number of drawings which were exhibited and reproduced in publications on war art.[11] Immediately after the war, he painted *Ypres Salient, Dawn* – a large canvas that synthesized his memories of the desolated battleground. It is a strangely impassive rendition of devastation, the neutral language of the paint surface seems to abdicate from comment and the rising sun merely illuminates the wreckage rather than shed any symbolic light. It is as if the artist wanted to fix 'such strangeness'[12] in a cool, detached way without distortion or simplification; after all, this was a land that was already distorted and simplified enough.

Many of the images made on the Salient never aspired towards public display or to be set in expensive frames. Some of the most potent and evocative artworks from the Ypres campaign can be found in small, battered sketchbooks compiled by amateur painters with few of the artistic credentials of Louis Ginnett. A soldier-artist known only by his surname, Mason, had already served on the Somme in 1916 and at Messines earlier in 1917 when he arrived on the Salient later that year. During that period, if his collection of small but intense watercolours were to be taken as eye-witness evidence, he saw the battlefield at its most brutalized – crammed with massive artillery pieces, strewn with fallen trees, and violated by huge explosions – but also at its most strangely beautiful. One watercolour, *The Salient 1917* [13] depicts the customary dirty brown mudscape punctuated by waterlogged craters and punctured by artillery shellbursts. But the scene takes place under a livid ultramarine sky. A skilled colourist, Mason juxtaposes the cool blue against the warm brown of the land to striking aesthetic effect. Other sketches show a refined understanding of atmospheric effects, none more so than the quite tiny watercolour *K Track to Passchendaele*[14]. Painted some weeks after the end of the campaign, it describes a saturated, tonally dense landscape heavily scored by razor marks to indicate the incessant driving rain. It is one of the odd features of the Ypres campaign that it is often the smallest, most compact and modest images that manage to convey the vastness of the desolation. On this particular battlefield the vignette could speak more eloquently than the panorama.

Long before the Battle of Third Ypres, the Salient had earned notoriety as a hazardous place and it was dreaded by combatants. To the art world, however, Ypres was renowned and celebrated for its epic ruination. Few artists, amateur or professional, modernist or establishment, could pass the ruins of St Martin's Cathedral and the ancient Cloth Hall in Ypres without making a thumbnail sketch or a mental note for future reference.

There are so many images of these twin architectural icons that one could trace their gradual erosion from solid buildings to stumps of rubble by compiling a log of the dozens of drawings, watercolours and oils made week in, week out and from every conceivable angle, in styles that range from the architectural exactitude of Royal Engineer, William Ansell[15] to the sombre watercolours of David Baxter, a soldier-artist so fixated with the image of the gap-toothed Ypres sky-line that he painted it on more than twenty different occasions.[16]

This fascination with the city persisted undiminished throughout the war. Belgian artist-refugees in England, inundated the National Army Museum with extravagant claims to have been the 'last artist to have painted the famous Cloth Hall' before its destruction. Exhausted by many such bids, the museum's standard reply was that they would only be interested in purchasing pictures that showed 'the destruction of the buildings caused by bombardment'.[17]

The museum would not be short of offers. In the last months of the war, Belgian Flanders became a magnet for artists and sketchers eager to see the actual battlefield before it was cleared of battle debris and overgrown. In the months following the Armistice, frustrated 'war' artists, sketching clubs, students of picturesque ruination flocked to the Salient to record its key sights, some of which became celebrated during the Third Ypres campaign.[18]

Like the Cloth Hall and Cathedral of Ypres, numerous paintings were made of such subjects as Zillebeke Church, Woodcote Farm, Hellfire Corner, and the Menin Road. Of course, these places more often existed as names only. The delicate watercolour of Zillebeke painted by Royal Engineer officer, R.Cooper, shows little more than a cone of rubble and some fractured trees, brilliantly backlit by a radiant sky.[19]

Amateur soldier-artists seemed to have been magnetized by a few key locations. Invariably, these were the sites of once prestigious buildings, notorious hotspots in the Salient or places of symbolic import. The very absence of the motif was no deterrent, instead, the act of naming and drawing them in their 'absence', seemed to confer meaning and significance to these blank spaces. It is a curious reprise of a phenomenon identified by the archaeologist, Christopher Tilley, who has observed of megalithic sites that without 'the naming and identification of particular topographical features . . . culturally significant sites would not exist, [except] as a raw void'.[20]

The Ypres Salient, pushed back in primeval time to a highly fluid and raw landscape, confused this naming of parts even further. Most combatants understood that a local signage usually existed, a fragmentary cognitive map had to be learned daily. As Hugh Quigley wrote of the Salient in September 1917, it was a map made up of temporary 'features' to remember a road once shown, the oddest details must be noted – a solitary length of wire, a 'dud' shell, three stakes together, a fragmentary hedge, a deserted waterlogged trench, dead men lying at various angles, and the position of pill-boxes in relation to the track followed. The most exciting time I spent was in hunting 'B' Company headquarters across this monotony of mud and water.[21]

For those unversed in reading and translating this dispersed landscape, any attempt to paint it would be immediately frustrated. Even a relatively skilled draughtsman would find it difficult to portray receding space where there were few intermediate reference points between foreground and horizon. The limited range of colour might frustrate an amateur, and above all the sheer scale of unlimited, sprawling waterlogged terrain could deter an artist. Little wonder that many artists opted for sites with some semblance of order, a cross-roads or Aid Post perhaps, while so many others stuck to the formula of grand ruination with all its historical artistic precedents – a 'Modern Pompeii' as one described it.[22]

For artists, then, the Salient offered a number of challenges that were quite different from other parts of the Western Front. The shifting, amorphous condition of its waterlogged soil and the particular quality of the light – affected as it was by the proximity of the coast – would have a bearing on the way painters recorded and interpreted the face of this particular battle. Third Ypres, as we have seen, was to be especially well served by the leading British avant-garde painters, many of whom had military experience of the Salient. Their pre-war artistic experiments would add an important dimension to the interpretation of the battle. Amongst the phenomenological and artistic themes that would be explored we can list: an interest in the fracturing of multivalent space, the fragmentation of time and place, a revision in the understanding of light, a continued fascination with the spectacle of ruination, and the primacy of paint as an analogy for the deliquescent battlefield.

One of the real dilemmas for the younger, avant-garde artists trying to grapple with these complex issues was how to convey the actualities of war within the new, often geometric, abstract language that was the currency of modernism. Official war artists had also to operate within the strictures of the commissioning schemes which could be draconian but were also suprisingly tolerant of radical imagery.

What then were the basic pictorial issues facing artists on the Salient ? What stratagems did they employ to convert the experience of Third Ypres into a relevant and meaningful image ?

The first (rather basic) challenge lay in finding some sort of pictorial equivalent to mud. While historians still debate the finer differences between the chalky swamps of the Somme and the black slime of Belgian Flanders, most soldiers had little doubt that the Salient soil was a quite unique phenomenon. Charles Carrington recalled the 'sliminess, the stickiness of the mud . . . with its semi-solid filthiness, the smell of it, and the taste of it, and the colour of it'[23]. As the unseasonable August 1917 rain began to transform the solid Flanders earth into quagmire so combatants began to regard the flattened land as a new uncharted ocean.

In his bitingly ironic memoir, *Blasting and Bombardiering*, Wyndham Lewis takes a logical step and describes his period as an observation officer in the Salient as if he were a mariner. On one terrifying occasion under direct observation from a German spotter in a sausage balloon he describes his dilemma in 'this sea of mud' as he and his party struggle to reach 'terra firma' only to be bracketed by incoming artillery fire as they tried to work their way back to the distant 'shore'[24].

The Salient as ocean was a popular simile in war memoirs: it provided an imaginative bridge to explain how a once-solid world could seem so irreversibly drowned; how a battlefield could be transformed into a liquid morass of uncharted breadth and depth producing a zone that was transient, shapeless and 'without form'.[25]

In this liquified land, mortar fire would send ripples across the terrain; an officer, Carroll Carstairs, recalled how 'a direct hit on our pill box rocked the place like a boat caught in the trough of the sea'.[26] These physical experiences helped some artists to translate their sensations into image rooted in the marine world. It may explain why the soldier-artist, Robert Borlase Smart – a recognized expert at coastline painting – rendered the liquefied battlefield as a swelling, turbulent mass liberally dotted with wreckage and detritus, where exploding mines crash like gigantic breakers on the sandbagged breaker of a trench.[27]

Wyndham Lewis had described the Salient as 'all scooped out and very El Greco'[28] but he may also have derived some of his semi-abstracted language from the sea. His large canvas, *A Battery Shelled*, painted for the Ministry of Information in 1919,[29] represents the convulsed mud around a gunpit as crests and waves of grey-blue water rolling in and around groups of cypher-like bombardiers. Many of his preparatory drawings use the same device: in the ink sketch *A Canadian Gun Pit*[30] Lewis omits much of the stabilizing foreground and horizon. Instead, the Canadian battery seems to bobble precariously in deep troughs of liquid, while, to the right, two combatants gaze out as though from the deck of a sister-ship.

Whereas Lewis adopted a busy, rococo-esque line to describe the contorted earth of the Salient, others adopted a more painterly method derived from the very properties of the pigment. Glazing in oils was one such method. In this process, a painter adds a medium or varnish to the pigment and then lays repeated coats of thin transparent glaze onto the canvas; each glaze acts as a wash of colour subtly altering the underlying layer and adding a greater depth to the tonality and a richness to the colour that could not be achieved by alla primae or direct painting. Glazing is very much a studio activity, requiring painstaking preparation and a thorough knowledge of the nature of materials. It has an equivalent in watercolour painting whereby the artists sets down broad washes of diluted colour onto thick, sometimes dampened, paper. A spontaneous and highly fluid process, marks and shapes can be generated through an improvised method of looking and registering. As with glazing in oils, mistakes are difficult to conceal and it is a technique that requires experience and confidence.[31]

Both methods were to prove ideally suited to convey the atmospheric conditions and ubiquitous wetness that became the hallmarks of periods of the battles of Third Ypres. Glazing proved the perfect fusion of technique and content. Gilbert Rogers – an oil painter working with the Royal Army Medical Corps – used the technique to striking advantage in a series of large canvases depicting the role of stretcher bearers on the Front. In his painting *Gassed – In Arduis Fidelis*, [32] which shows a gas-masked British corpse gradually being reclaimed by a sodden landscape, the very pigment is heavily saturated in oils, the paint applied in a succession of loaded, unmodulated brushstokes. With its close tonal range and a palette limited to ochres and umber this is an image of utter bleakness. Rogers has deliberately excised any horizon line to emphasize the sense of immersion and the prone body is aligned along the customarily dynamic diagonal in a parody of action.

The watercolourist David Baxter, a sergeant in the RAMC, was perhaps one of the most prolific of the small section of painters commissioned to depict the work of the medical services in the Salient, but his many watercolours capture, in a way unparalleled by other painters, the phenomena of a land in a state of flux and liquidification. Applying the pools of pigment in pools of colour first to stain the thick paper, then, by rubbing back into the paint with his fingers, he drew out the few solid forms of the vaporous landscape. His refined technical abilities allowed him to play sophisticated formal games with his materials: in such large watercolours as *A Dirty Day in Flanders*[33] he 'floats' – both literally and metaphorically – the stretcher teams in the middle distance onto the diffuse and seemingly formless terrain. Large drops of water, puddles of unmodulated colour and pure washes of acidic yellow and purple become vital aesthetic equivalents to the conditions of the Salient.

Neither Baxter nor Rogers ever allowed their designs to collapse into total disintegration. Their training and, perhaps their affiliation to the human form, would have never permitted them to fragment the human body in the way that such German painters as Otto Dix and George Grosz were to do. Their faithfulness to a literal truth produced some evocative images but they lacked the modernists' understanding of distortion and their sense of abstract design to push their work beyond a traumatized realism. For artists to make this leap of faith meant a wholesale revision in their appreciation of pictorial space.

The concept of space as an undifferentiated, homogeneous void which uniformly surrounded solid objects, had been shattered by the French Cubists and Italian Futurists. Space had to be re-evaluated as a complex, multivalent and heterogeneous entity, no longer the blank all-pervading ether as presented by the 19th century artists. Cinema revolutionized the understanding of time and space; editing fractured continuous events; camera angles radicalized the fixed viewpoint that had dominated spatial order since Alberti; scientific research pioneered by Einstein argued for a number of distinct spaces equal to the number of unstable reference systems; the Cubist painters Picasso and Braque smashed the belief in a neat pictorial spatial system as though 'an earthquake had struck the precisely reticulated sidewalks of a Renaissance street scene'.[34]

Third Ypres was further proof that space was so torn asunder that it might never be re-constituted. The artist most able to capture this irreversible fragmentation was Paul Nash. Nash had first experienced the Salient during a quiet spell in February 1917. He returned to Ypres as an official artist during the closing stages of Passchendaele. A painter of gentle, fantastic landscapes before the war, Nash quickly developed a sensitivity to the topography of the battlefield. He was simultaneously enchanted and outraged at the violation of the natural order, and his artistic language matured remarkably quickly in the cauldron of the Salient. He wrote later of the 'ridiculous mad incongruity' that was all around him:

> where I sit now in the reserve line the place is just joyous, the dandelions are bright gold over the parapet and nearby a lilac bush is breaking into bloom; in a wood passed through on our way up, a place with an evil name, pitted and pocked with shells, the trees torn to shreds, often reeking with poison gas – a most desolate ruinous place two months back, today it was vivid green: the most broken trees even had sprouted somewhere and in the midst, from the depth of the wood's bruised heart poured out the throbbing song of nightingale.[35]

Such bizarre contradictions helped hone Nash's vision. During late October and November he made fifty drawings of 'muddy places on the Front'[36] visiting all the key sites of the battlefield – Hill 60, Gheluvelt, Inverness Copse, Zillebeke and Sanctuary Wood. He was often in real danger, at one time 'damn near killed – the bosche seems to have got wind of my coming & shelled me most rudely every time I opened my book'[37]

Unlike his Vorticist colleagues Wyndham Lewis and William Roberts, whose fascination lay in the mechanisation of war and the transformation of individuals into automata awash in a fluid world, Nash responded to the spatial dynamics of the conflict. By incorporating the angular geometric style of the Vorticists, he began to describe the idiosyncratic spaces of the Salient – the twisting, eccentric route of the duckboard tracks, the weird angles of shattered trees, the etched line of the driving rain as it pierced space from all angles.

Nash combined this brilliant graphic skill with a highly sophisticated sense of design. He was able to spread the elements of the composition to every part of the canvas; in so doing he devised an anti-hierarchy in which the corners and non-spaces of a design contain some of the most crucial (and often most harrowing) elements of the narrative. As was so often the case on the deepest darkest tracts of the Ypres Salient where every corner was crowded with possible danger, so Nash packs out the picture plane, littering the surface with the detritus and hazards of the scorched earth. On the other side of No Man's Land, the German painter and machine-gunner, Max Beckmann, would also experience this sensation of horror vacuii. His traumatized experience of the Western Front would in part lead to a lifelong terror of the void; his chosen method of dealing with the perils of this silent vacuum was to cram the foreground of his violent post-war images with a wall of objects to stop him from slipping into the blackness beyond, 'to defend myself against the infinity of space'.[38] Ernst Jünger had described the same physical sensation as the 'chaotic vacancy of the battle-field'.[39]

Nash seems to have understood how to graft the continental language of the avant garde onto his own skills as a colourist and decorative designer. In no painting is this more apparent than in his magnum opus of the war *The Menin Road*, painted for the Ministry of Information during 1918–1919.[40] At first sight it is the customary leitmotif of the Western Front – shell-holes, tree stumps, an endless vista of mud and water. But it is much more than an eleven feet wide panorama of chaos and despair; it shows a highly sophisticated reading of the spatial disjunctions and temporal dislocations of the empty battlefield of the Salient.

The canvas is divided into three territorial bands each containing its own directional properties. The foreground, as so often in Nash's war work, is crammed with insurmountable obstacles – pools of water, pyramidal concrete blocks, piles of debris – which frustrate any access to the road in the centre of the picture.

Between the concrete blocks and the pools, there is, however, a narrow strip of flat ground that comprises the sole pathway through the fore-ground mess. But here, instead of offering the spectator an entry point into the picture, Nash introduces a visual barrier – a single rectangular shape that looks like a window shutter – which seems to prevent any further movement through the gap. Furthermore this rectangular shape does not conform to the dominant diagonal which dictates virtually every other line in the picture. It rests uneasily in the general design of the painting as a deliberate compositional trick to 'trip' and frustrate the spectator, and a reminder of the secret language needed to decode this bastardized country.

These subtle games of pictorial movement persist into the central terri-torial band. Here the surface of the Menin Road is dealt with in broad sweeps of unmodulated paint, the shell-holes that punctuate it are spaced – like giant foot-steps in deep snow – at regular intervals, and the avenue of trees on either side lend it some lateral momentum. But again, Nash deliberately confuses the initial directional sense: on the left of the picture, sharp diagonal shadows distort the road surface, on the right, several trees are placed so as to offset the symmetry of the former avenue, debris constantly interrupts the decorative chaos of the middle band of the picture. Here, declares Nash, freedom of movement is no longer guaran-teed, mobility is severely controlled and progress is always hazardous and exposed – a spatial enforcement of the very real conditions of the infamous road.

In the third pictorial zone – the distance – a lesser artist might have drawn the battlescape as a series of parallel bands disappearing into the distance. But Nash understood that the Ypres battlefield was rarely so well ordered. Instead of parallel bands, Nash has drawn seven water-filled ditches; each one meanders sluggishly into the distance only to stop short of the horizon. Each of the ditches invites the eye to travel into the picture's fictive space, to explore the furthest reaches of the battlefield as though looking for some succour at the point where land meets sky. But each ditch in turn fails to open up the view and ends in either the lazy curve of an ox-bow lake or is abruptly ended by a terminal moraine. With a masterly understanding of the peculiarities of battlefield space, Nash has condensed into one painting three modes of spatial movement. As a closing coda, he heightens the agony by exposing the plight of two distant soldiers marooned in the mid-distance, while nearby, two huge explosions emit vast plumes of smoke that ironically mimic the form of verdant trees.

It is the glimpse of these tiny figures which reminds us how rarely the human form appears in paintings of the Salient. Earlier in the war, Nevinson had employed the figure as a mechanical element in a dynamic machine; established academic artists had portrayed the 'Tommy' as a stal-wart figure, whole in body and earnest in stance. Academicians such as J.B. Priest had adapted the language of hunting and stalking to validate the cowering postures of their hunched figures stooping in noisome trenches.[41]

By the time of Third Ypres, the painted figure had been reduced to an absolute immobility. In the hands of Wyndham Lewis, this posture took on an air of absolute weariness and indifference as his stone-faced bombardiers gaze carelessly into the middle-distance. In Nevinson's epic post-battle painting *The Harvest of Battle* [42] the endless column of walking wounded and German prisoners seems to seep into the muddy earth – the epitome of spent strength forever condemned to take an elliptical path within the confines of the picture frame.[43] No single image better conveys this idea of the soldier fixed permanently to the battlefield than Otto Dix's harrowing painting *Flanders*.[44] Painted two decades after the war, it shows a patrol of German soldiers immersed in the cloying soil of the battlefield, the resting figures calcified into place as if in the first stages of fossilization and in some grotesque parody of the military dictum of gaining and holding ground. Their stasis is further exaggerated by the near-apocalyptic skyscape with its fleeting cirrus formations and billowing cumulus clouds.

Dix's painting reminds us that the deserted battlefield of the Salient was not truly empty at all. Its very constituency was made up of the drowned and disintegrated bodies of both armies. Furthermore, the congealed and impasto surfaces of many of these large canvases suggest that many soldier-artists regarded the conflict as irresolvable, clotted in place. This is certainly true of the locked composition of *The Menin Road* which is filled to the very corners with incident and surface pattern.[45] This sense of wilful repletion came to manner much of the British painting after the war; the much heralded 'return to order' actually masking a stultifying exhaustion and loss of artistic nerve.

As an icon of the Salient, *The Menin Road* captures all that was inspiring and revolting about the area. Nash manages to combine modernist spatial distortion with a colour scheme derived from ancient Flemish tapestry – proof again of the weird incongruities of that 'phantasmagoric' land[46] and evidence that an aesthetic could be forged in the most miserable of surroundings, an experience summarized by Wyndham Lewis that 'ours, then, was an epic of mud'[47]

Notes

[IWM = Imperial War Museum, London, Department of Art]

1   Richard Barrett Talbot Kelly, *A Subaltern's Odyssey: A Memoir of the Great War, 1915 – 1917*, London, William Kimber, 1980, p63.

2   For a full account of the administrative history of the DoI, MoI and Wellington House see Sue Malvern, "War, as it is", *Art History* Vol.9, No.4, December 1986; W.P.Mayes, *The Origins of an Art Collection (First World War)* unpublished manuscript, Imperial War Museum (IWM); Meirion and Susie Harries, The War Artists, London, Michael Joseph, 1983.

3   *War Pictorial* was translated into five language editions – 'Latin', North European, Russian, Japanese and English (for the USA market).

4   Among Masterman's colleagues were Campbell Dodgson, Keeper of Prints and Drawings at the British Museum, Alfred Yockney, former editor of *Art Journal*, and Eric Maclagan, later Director of the Victoria and Albert Museum – all figures of real status in the London art world.

5   *Burlington Magazine*, September/October 1917.

6   For a full account of the CWRO and CWMF see Maria Tippett, *Art at the Service of War: Canada, Art and the Great War*, Toronto, University of Tornto Press, 1984.

7   CFG Masterman to Clement K Shorter, IWM Art, 20 December 1917.

8   William Orpen, *An Onlooker in France*, London, Williams and Norgate, 1924, p42.

9   As evidence of the systematic operation of the BWMC, it made a point of choosing the subject-matters needed to be painted first, then drawing up a list of artists and allocating each a relevant pictorial task.

10 CFG Masterman to John Buchan, 18 May 1917.

11 See Charles Holmes, Editor, *The War depicted by Distinguished British Artists*, The Studio, 1918.

12 IWM Department of Art (IWM Art) no. 5207. Letter to W. Mayes from Ginnett's daughter, 1 March 1960, artist's file, IWM Art.

13 IWM Art no. 15326, no. 7.

14 IWM Art no. 15326, no.11.

15 IWM Art no. 5204 a.

16 See for example IWM Art nos. 3535, 3558 3619, 3625. In 1922 a great many Baxter watercolours were transferred from the IWM to Royal Herbert, Netley, RAMC, and QAM Hospitals.

17 See for example correspondence between H.R.Carelli and Rt Hon Sir Alfred Mond, 12/25 February 1918, IWM Art file 151/4.

18 See for example correspondence between IWM and painter Rowland Hill,

January 1919 – January 1930, IWM Art file 156/5 part ii. See also Paul Gough, 'The Landscape at War', *The Independent*, 1st July 1991.

19 IWM Art no. 5571.

20 Christopher Tilley, *A Phenomenology of Landscape*, Oxford, Berg, 1994, p18–19.

21 Hugh Quigley, *Passchendaele and the Somme*, London, Methuen, 1928, p 126.

22 Inscription on drawing of St Martin's cathedral, Ypres by Emily Paterson, IWM Art 4759.

23 'Charles Edmonds', (Charles Carrington), *A Subaltern's War*, London, Davies, 1929, p130.

24 Percy Wyndham Lewis, *Blasting and Bombardiering*, London, Eyre and Spottiswoode, 1937, p173.

25 'Charles Edmonds', op.cit., p178.

26 Carroll Carstairs, *A Generation Missing*, London, William Heinnemann, 1930/Strong Oak Press, 1989, p103.

27 IWM Art no. 4478.

28 Wyndham Lewis op.cit., p170.

29 IWM Art no. 2747.

30 National Gallery of Canada no. 8357.

31 See Leslie Worth, *Working With Watercolours*, London, 1980, and Judy Egerton, *British Watercolours*, London, Tate Gallery, 1986 for a more detailed description of watercolour techniques.

32 IWM Art no. 3819.

33 IWM Art no. 3245.

34 Stephen Kern, *On the Culture of Time and Space 1880 –1918*, London, Weidenfeld and Nicholson, 1983, p140.

35 Paul Nash, *Outline: An Autobiography and Other Writings*, London, Faber, 1949, p187.

36 Nash to Masterman, 22 November 1917, IWM Artists file.

37 Nash to Masterman, 22 November 1917, IWM Artists file.

38 Max Beckmann, *Briefe im Kriege*, Munich, 1955, letter of 18 April 1915. For a full discussion of Beckmann's shift from an 'uncanningly beautiful depth' to 'empty, insane space' see Matthias Eberle, *World War I and the Weimar Artists*, Yale UP, 1985, pp 80–88

39 Ernst Junger, *The Storm of Steel*, London, Chatto and Windus, 1929, p30.

40 IWM Art no. 2242.

41 J.B.Priest, 'Got 'im', reproduced in *Royal Academy Illustrated*, 1918.

42 IWM Art no. 1921.

43 For an analysis of this movement see Jon Bird, "Representing the Great War", *Block* (3) 1980.

44 Staatliche Museen, Nationalgalerie Berlin.

45 My thanks to painter David Haste for these observations on Nash.

46 Herbert Read, *Paul Nash*, Penguin Modern Painters, 1944.

47 Wyndham Lewis, *op.cit.* p161.

Chapter 26

Passchendaele – A Selection of British and German War Veteran Literature.

Hugh Cecil

In the mythology of the Great War that has grown up since 1918, Passchendaele has been *the* definitive episode, outstripping in its awfulness even the first day on the Somme, or the blood-letting at Verdun. This most terrible of battles needed an exceptional writer – a veritable Dante – to do it justice, as, in 1928, the poet Edmund Blunden recognized : 'This chapter in the annihilating of any army's faith, this long and grotesquely cadaverous chapter, awaits an author. He should have the hand of a skeleton and scrawl in muck on one of those rolls of paper that are required by daily journals with million circulations.'[1]

Such a book, combining the highest literary skill with personal experience, has never been written. Many accomplished authors who went through the battle have attempted to describe it, but on the whole they have done so in poetry, or in only a chapter or two of their novels and memoirs. Some excellent reminiscences which do concentrate mainly on the battle, have appeared, such as P.J. Campbell's *In the Cannon's Mouth* and Norman Gladden's *Ypres 1917* ; but neither has artistic pretensions. The first shows an innocent at war, longing for acceptance from his R.F.A. fellow-officers. It was written after Campbell had been a schoolmaster for years, and is in many ways like a school story. Gladden, an infantryman, tells a thoughtful story, without frills, incorporating useful historical explanations of different stages of the battle, as one might expect of the efficient public servant he became.[2] Other memoirs which feature Passchendaele are mentioned later in this essay or in the bibliography. Though individually none of these constitutes the 'great book' about Passchendaele, collectively, their best passages, when combined with eloquent extracts from the poetry and novels, contribute to a 'literary' picture of considerable value.

What is striking is how few of the best-known literary names from the Great War are associated with Passchendaele. Many, of course, were dead before the battle: Rupert Brooke, Charles Sorley, Leslie Coulson, Julian Grenfell, Edward Wyndham Tennant, Arthur Graeme West, R.E.Vernède,

J.W.Streets and Edward Thomas; others – Wilfred Owen, Gilbert Frankau, Robert Graves, Ford Madox Ford and A.P.Herbert – were temporarily or permanently out of the war, or that part of the front. Siegfried Sassoon, too, was absent, though he was later the author of the most famous line of poetry about the battle: 'I died in hell – (They called it Passchendaele)', from his poem, ' Memorial Tablet', the pathetic tale of a man bullied by the local squire into going to the war. [3]

Of the other poets, Francis Ledwidge was killed on 31 July 1917, while Isaac Rosenberg and David Jones fought in Third Ypres but did not write specifically on the battle. Thomas MacGreevy's Flanders poems date from the winter of 1917/18, after the battle was over.[4] There was more good poetry about the Somme than about Passchendaele – and more good fiction, which included the best novels of the war, Sassoon's *Memoirs of an Infantry Officer* and Frederic Manning's *The Middle Parts of Fortune*.[5]

Published poetry about Passchendaele is, indeed, relatively sparse, even from minor poets.[6] Edmund Blunden M.C., in the verses printed at the end of his memoir, *Undertones of War*, [7] captured the horrors of the battle as well as any : 'Third Ypres' is a long poem recollecting, far from the line, an incident from which he barely escaped alive and 'a whole sweet countryside amuck with murder'. 'Pillbox' tells of a sergeant, after a minor injury, losing his wits and his will to live. In 'The Welcome' a tense, war-worn officer just returned to the battlefield from leave in England miraculously survives a direct hit on a pill-box, his nerves intact. 'Concert Party :Busseboom' juxtaposes, ironically, a musical variety show behind the lines, with another 'matinée' of gunfire and flame shortly after:

> To this new concert, white we stood;
> Cold certainty held our breath;
> While men in tunnels below Larch Wood
> Were kicking men to death.[8]

'The Prophet' is about reading at the Front an early 19th century guide-book to the Netherlands, containing phrases such as 'The air is reckoned unhealthy here for strangers', which give Blunden much amusement. Writing later, in one of several post-war reflections, he honours his battalion, the 11th Royal Sussex: 'Flanders Now', recalls both Passchendaele, where they took fearful casualties, and earlier memories of the Salient:

> They died in splendour, these who claimed no spark
> Of glory save the light in a friend's eye. [9]

The ardent, youthful-looking Blunden was eccentric and untidy, but a capable, courageous and loyal officer, keeping up with members of his battalion throughout his later life. After the war he was almost hysterical in denouncing both Robert Graves' *Goodbye to All That*, and Remarque's

All Quiet on the Western Front, feeling that both had betrayed their fellow-soldiers at the Front by sacrificing truth for sensationalism.[10]

Another Passchendaele poet, Herbert Read, was, oddly, a professed pacifist before and after the war. He served as an officer in the 7th, 10th and finally 2nd Green Howards and was an effective soldier, proud of his war record (he was awarded the M.C. and D.S.O.) He was determined not to shirk the test of war that faced his generation. On leave in the early days of Third Ypres, he felt guilt about not sharing his comrades' sufferings. He first saw action there in October as a company-commander near Zillebeke Lake, in heavy rain and under intense shellfire: 'We have had a terrible time' he told his fiancée, ' the worst I ever expected.' If only those at home knew the truth, he reflected, the war might end. Yet he was elated, as he told his fiancée, that his company had gained four Military Medals in one day, out of a total of seven for the whole battalion. His powerful poem, 'Kneeshaw Goes to War' with its theme of the effect of the war on an individual soul, contains a long passage about Third Ypres. [11]

Another poet, Ivor Gurney, joined the 2/5 Gloucestershires in February 1915 and fought in the later stages of the Somme battle. He was wounded in April 1917, and was mildly gassed at Third Ypres, in September . He spent the rest of the war in Britain. Growing mental illness led to his eventual discharge in October 1918 with 'delayed shell-shock'. By 1922 that he was committed to a lunatic asylum, though for many years he wrote verse and music. He died in 1937. In the poems that Gurney wrote before he was gassed and later, looking back on the Third Ypres battle, he dwelt on his fears of 'the fiery mouth of hell' and his guilt about having left his battalion. [12]

Of the novels about the war by war veterans, few concentrated exclusively on Passchendaele. Wilfrid Ewart's Passchendaele chapters in *Way of Revelation* (1921) take up only 24 pages out of 534 . They focus largely on the mortal wounding of the protagonist's company-commander, Eric Sinclair. This was based on a real tragedy during Third Ypres, the death of Lieut. Esmond Elliot, the younger son of a former Viceroy of India, Lord Minto. The book sold 30,000 within a few months. Its success owed as much to its sensational plot, its clichés and frequent sentimentality, as to its poetical descriptions and heartfelt patriotic message, drawn from the author's own experiences as an officer in the 2nd Scots Guards. [13]

There is a Passchendaele chapter in Robert Briffault's *Europa in Limbo* (1937), the second volume of a best-selling work. [14] It depicts the war as a sordid farce, fought to defend the interests of imperialism and big business. The chapter describes an inept plan of attack, a cowardly colonel, a fool of a staff officer, and heavy casualties. The author was attached as regimental M.O. to the 5th Yorks and Lancs Regiment. He was awarded the M.C. and Bar. Famous as as an anthropologist after the war, he became a communist, although he was never a Party member. Apart from purely descriptive passages, his racy vignettes of war and of debaucheries on various home fronts are unreliable: it was noted by fellow academics that to win an argument he often ignored inconvenient detail.

Ernest Raymond's *Jesting Army* (1930) has five Passchendaele chapters. Raymond was an army padre in the war, and later a very successful author. His most famous novel, *Tell England* (1922), was based on his Gallipoli experiences. Later he served in Sinai, the Western Front (including Third Ypres) Mesopotamia and Baku. *The Jesting Army,* though a patriotic celebration of the British soldier's stalwart courage, is not nearly as sentimental as *Tell England,* which is why, presumably, it sold less well. It is also more interesting.[15]

Patrick Miller's prize-winning *The Natural Man* has a chapter describing the Flanders battlefield in 1917, apparently at the time of Third Ypres. Miller (the pseudonym of George Gordon Macfarlane, M.C.) was a resourceful gunner officer who later had an adventurous career as a journalist. The theme of his book was the exhilarating nature of the war as a test of courage and enterprise. In the Ypres chapter, the protagonist, Blaven, takes over the battery when his superior officer loses his nerve.[16]

Many other war novels contain chapters on Third Ypres, such as Richard Blaker's truthful account of the R.F.A., a work of semi-autobiographical fiction, *Medal Without Bar* (1930).[17] One novel where the Passchendaele battle occupies most of the book is Thomas Suthren Hope's *The Winding Road Unfolds* (1937). This reconstructs the author's experiences as a 16-year-old boy in a London territorial battalion. He emphasizes futility, mismanagement and waste, while exalting the companionship. An undistinguished work, it gives a useful picture of Other Ranks' attitudes but the characters are neither attractive nor interesting.[18]

There are other novels dealing with Third Ypres, where the war veteran authors, without having been in the battle, applied their general knowledge of the war. *Pass Guard at Ypres* (1929), by Ronald Gurner, M.C., about the gradual wearing down of a young Kitchener army officer, has three chapters on Passchendaele. Gurner, a lieutenant in the 8th Rifle Brigade, was in hospital at the time of Third Ypres, but had served in the Salient during 1915–16. Throughout this dark little tale, he highlights the mutilated city of Ypres as the sacred symbol of the British Army's will to stand firm, whatever the cost to the individual soldier.[19]

Love and the Loveless (1958), the fourth war volume of Henry Williamson's multi-volume *Chronicle of Ancient Sunlight,* has nearly 150 pages about the battle. Williamson, though he served throughout the war (in a London territorial regiment and then as an officer in the Bedfordshire Regiment and the Machine-gun Corps), saw little action in the later part of it. He knew the Ypres area well and had an acute eye for rich and fascinating detail. These chapters, however, are principally a vehicle for his views: that there should have been an earlier, negotiated peace to end this ' fratricidal European civil war ' and that Haig is not to be blamed for the failure of the 1917 Flanders campaign, for he was not allowed to fight there earlier in the year, nor in the summer of 1916 – as he wished – when conditions would have been far better. Williamson conveys well the poor communications, misunderstandings and battlefield chaos that compounded the failures of Gough and others . [20]

Turning from novels to 'literary' memoirs, there is a powerful reminiscence in Wilfrid Ewart's *When Armageddon Came* (1935) a posthumously published collection of his articles. 'Three Days' traces a young officer's life from a wild party in Belgravia to the Front, thirty-six hours later. Joining an old friend, with whom he shares the gossip from town, he wades with the company through quagmires to 'the nether world' of the Ypres battlefield; subsequently the brave company-commander is mortally wounded. 'Give me morphia . . . and put an M on my forehead' he repeats pathetically again and again. It is an earlier version of the Eric Sinclair episode in Ewart's *Way of Revelation* . [21]

Hugh Quigley's *Passchendaele and the Somme* (1928), by an officer in the 12th Lancers, is eloquent about 'a land of horror and dread whence few return, like that country Morris describes in the *Well at the World's End*' but talks also of . . . 'a memory of great beauty caught by an awakened spirit and subtitilised to life itself!'[22]

One classic memoir, *A Passionate Prodigality* (1933), also has a Passchendaele section – about 40 pages out of 350 .The author, Guy Chapman, M.C., later became a distinguished historian. He served in the 13th Royal Fusiliers In his view, a splendid body of men – volunteers of the New Army – was needlessly wasted by a prodigal military system serving a cynical civilian leadership. The tone is forceful, angry but also affectionate. Bonamy Dobrée, his friend and colleague at Leeds University, said of him that 'he grumbles his way through life with indomitable gaiety.' The book is dedicated to his former commanding officer. [23]

Equally colourful, though less stylish, is the account given by A.M.Burrage, a professional writer aged twenty-seven when he joined the Artists' Rifles. He failed to gain a commission. His Passchendaele experiences occupy a hundred pages of his mocking and satirical memoir *War Is War* (1930) written under the pseudonym 'Ex-Private X'. He dwells mostly on the minor indignities, and sometimes on the tragedies and horrors, of army life.[24]

Carroll Carstairs M.C., author of *A Generation Missing* (1930), was an amorous, beau-monde American, who before the war worked in London for his father, a partner in Knoedler's, the picture dealers. At twenty-four, in 1914, he joined the Royal Artillery. He served at Second Ypres and subsequently transferred to the 3rd Grenadiers. His book is a romantic, valedictory work about companionship and love in time of war. There are thirty-five pages on Passchendaele . [25]

The most famous British recollections of Third Ypres are in five chapters of Edmund Blunden's *Undertones of War*, which finally appeared, after long gestation, in 1928. Blunden makes his points with a gentle, sometimes whimsical irony, though he does not shirk horror and tragedy and his conclusions, that the offensive was useless and the campaign eroded

1.8.17   It rained during the night —
& this morning the Downs usually.
2 feet wide & six inches deep is a
swollen torrent already spreading
over the fields with more & more
water coming down. Already it has
risen a foot. There is no fighting,
hardly a gun is fired. & the
wretched soldiers crawl about in
their shell holes sodden with rain.
unable to move — yet must die
of exposure if they don't. Trehearne-
son hit this morning. A bullet
caught him in the back as he came
back from LUMM FARM 2000 yards
behind the line & broke his back —
The futility of war — he was a delight.
All fighting has stopped. The luck of
Germany!

(xxxiv) Guy Chapman's diary for 1 August 1917, ". . . the wretched soldiers crawl about in their shell holes sodden with rain. Unable to move – yet must die of exposure if they do not." *(Guy Chapman, Liddle Collection)*

human feelings almost to nothing, are bitter indeed. Equally memorable are his often-expressed warmth for his comrades, his beautiful descriptions of countryside beyond the battlefield and his romantic encounter with a pretty teenage girl while waiting to go up to the front. [26]

From the opposing side, Ernst Jünger's memoir *Storm of Steel (In Stahlgewittern)* (1920) is the German warrior's testament. Lieutenant Jünger was one of the élite Storm Troopers – the advance force in major German attacks. A professional soldier before the war, at twenty-three, in 1918, he received the highest German military honour for courage, the *Pour Le Mérite*. 'It is not every generation that is so favoured', Jünger wrote of his war experience: 'Almost without any thought of mine, the idea of the Fatherland had been distilled by all these afflictions into a clearer and brighter essence.' His two action-filled Passchendaele chapters are told with panache and confidence, [27] contrasting interestingly with the Third Ypres passages in a novel by a compatriot, George Grabenhorst, *Fahnenjunker Volkenborn* (1928), where the gentle-natured teenage protagonist is 'white as chalk' and shaking, after mowing down British attackers with a machine gun .[28]

Another important German 'literary' testimony, Rudolf Binding's *A Fatalist at War,* is based on the writer's letters while an officer at the front. Binding first saw action in October 1914. By the time of Passchendaele, he was becoming war-weary: 'I am scared for the first time in this war,' he wrote on 29 July 1917. 'I have doubts whether we shall be able to hold out against the odds.' His account conveys the enormous damage inflicted on the German army by the British offensive, though not, he asserts, on German morale. [29]

In most respects there is a consonance between these different visions of Third Ypres, however dissimiliar their authors or their literary styles. All stress the strength of the companionship and the courage of fellow-soldiers in this grimmest of battles : Jünger writes, for example, of a fellow storm-trooper, Lieut.Brecht, 'one of those few who were encircled by an aura of romance, even in the most material of wars, owing to their insatiable dare-devilry. Men like him stood out from the common run; they laughed every time an attack was ordered.' [30] Blunden singles out the artist Lindsey Clarke, 'nowadays known for his imaginative sculptures, then for his hoarse voice, modesty and inexhaustible courage. He took charge of all fighting, apparently, and despite being blown off his feet by shells and struck about the helmet with shrapnel and otherwise physically harassed, he was ubiquitous and invincible.' [31] Again there is Carroll Carstairs' stolid Sergeant Wonnacott, D.C.M., who never ducks under shellfire[32] and Guy Chapman's 'calm and capable C.S.M. of no. 2, Edmonds, with his quiet persistent cheerfulness';[33] while in Burrage's account, another Edmonds, a married man with a business, drawn into the war against his will, is nonetheless 'one of the stoutest-hearted fellows in the whole crowd.' [34]

This is not to say that the 'literary record' depicts everyone behaving well all the time. Jünger has an interesting tale of a sullen N.C.O. who refuses to help him find his way in the middle of battle – mutinous behaviour more characteristic of the last stages of the war, as he observes, and very rare during actual fighting, crumbling morale being more likely to show behind the lines.[35] Surreptitious killing of prisoners, shattered nerves and momentary cold feet feature frequently in these accounts; Briffault and Williamson both have a 'windy' senior officer,[36] while Chapman speaks movingly of the many soldiers, from private to brigadier, still unbroken in nerve, and neither mutineers nor cowards, who find themselves at times at the limit of their endurance:

> From the line came those tired, desperate voices: "'E couldn't do it, Ser'eant, 'e's finished.": "The platoon's all in, old boy, we'll only make a balls of it": . . . "My battalion's been in the line for ten days, general; it's had 80 per cent casualties. We no longer exist." "Unless my brigade's relieved, I'll not answer for the consequence."[37]

Courage, loyalty, windiness, and exhaustion were all evident in the horrible conditions of Flanders in the autumn of 1917, but were also encountered in many other battles of the war. Other phenomena, however, which appear in nearly all the accounts mentioned here, belonged more distinctively to Passchendaele: one was the unprecedented scale of the artillery bombardments. On the eve of the battle, Rudolf Binding was extremely anxious about the huge weight of British ordnance that was harrying the Germans:

> If one reckons that the main offensive is being made on a front of twenty-five miles, that means a gun to every four yards. Imagine all these ten thousand muzzles hurling out not only projectiles of iron and lead but spreading poison gases as well; imagine only a fifth of this number of guns opposed to this concentration, all overworked pieces which fire, it is true, but not so accurately as on the first day; imagine an enemy airman cruising over each one of our batteries and directing on to it five times the fire which they can thunder, whereas they are perhaps unsupported by any air forces and simply have to sit tight: that is the picture which scares me. Verdun, the Somme, and Arras are mere purgatories compared with this concentrated hell, which one of these days will be stoked up to white heat.[38]

From the other side, Carroll Carstairs takes up the theme. Carstairs' narrative of the Front is usually low-key and unassuming (he never mentions getting the M.C.). When it comes to the guns, however, his excitement takes over:

> Through the long hours the nightmare persists until, at 5.40 a.m., the [Guards] division goes over the top to the tune of the most mighty cannonade conceivable, and my life reaches a peak of auricular experience. It is at last the whole world crashing about our ears. Gunfire has, at a moment, leaped into an intensity no human being could realize

without hearing. A veritable crescendo of sounds, so continuous as to merge and blend into a simple annihilating roar, the roar of a train in a tunnel magnified a millionfold, only the rattle of the machine gun barrage, like clocks gone mad, ticking out the end of time in a final breathless reckoning, rises above it, while the accelerating blasts of enemy shells add weight to the crowning catastrophe. One imagines the very air ripped and torn by the flight of numberless shells, the very sky to have become a tattered blue garment. [39]

'Our own guns shook me more than Fritzy guns with fear', wrote Ivor Gurney. [40] Ernst Jünger describes being on the receiving end of such unrelenting fury:

Hours such as these were without doubt the most awful of the whole war.

You cower in a heap alone in a hole and feel yourself the victim of a pitiless thirst for destruction. With horror you feel that all your intelligence, your capacities, your bodily and spiritual characteristics, have become utterly meaningless and absurd. While you think it, the lump of metal that will crush you to a shapeless nothing may have started on its course. Your discomfort is concentrated in your ear, that tries to distinguish amid the uproar the swirl of your own death rushing near. It is dark, too; and you must find in yourself alone all the strength for holding out. [41]

The landscape that this firepower and the rain had created was repeatedly described in all these works. Here is Robert Briffault, in *Europa in Limbo*, allowing himself a rare moment of seriousness amid his relentless scoffing:

Never probably had human eye looked upon such a vastness of desolation. Over the whole prospect was not one leaf or blade. Mile after mile the earth stretched out black, foul, putrescent, like a sea of excrement. Not a sign of animal and vegetable life; none of human life either, for it hid itself underground, and only the dirt-spouts thrown up by missiles of death, bursting like mephitic bubbles over the foulness, gave visible indication of its presence. But everywhere the detritus and garbage of the murderous madness. It was one vast scrap-heap. And, scattered over or sunk in the refuse and mud, were the rotting bodies of men, of horses and mules. Of such material was the barren waste that stretched as far as the eye could see. [42]

Despite a less 'anti-war' viewpoint, Wilfrid Ewart paints quite as sinister a picture:

In the nether world of Ypres, on its battlefields fought over again and again, in its grassless, grainless waste of stink-ridden soil and green slimy water – here are to be found the abomination of desolation, the world of which Dante wrote. Even the battle-field of the Somme will not compare with this or any other tract of ground on the Western Front unless it be Verdun. One has the feeling that whatever else befall this is hell.[43]

The pill-boxes, too, seemed to fascinate writers, those sinister German fastnesses, which, when captured, became squalid refuges and frequently death-traps for the attacking British. Robert Briffault describes a scene in one of them, where a group of British soldiers has taken shelter for the night. Two dead Germans are rotting in a waterfilled pit in the floor. The pill-box comes under fire. The passage sums up the claustrophobia, fear and filth in these concrete shelters round which the battle raged.

The last crump was quite near. They've got the range exactly. Then the next on the other pill-box. Three minutes, another nearer still. It must have hit the corner. The whole place shakes and rocks. One can hear the crumbling cement. A direct hit and all will be over. Three minutes. That one dropped a bit short. The next crash has hit the roof. Julian feels as if he had been struck on the head. The pill-box quivers and creaks. Another direct hit will finish it. Like that one they passed coming up, with the four German gunners. They will look like that. They will be all mixed up with the two Germans in the greenish-black water. It is inevitable.[44]

Unfortunately, given the state of the ground, digging holes for cover was usually impossible which was why pill-boxes, whose location was well-known to the enemy, frequently offered the only recourse; for as Richard Blaker puts it, in *Medal Without Bar* :

In the Salient, north of the cowering garbage that was the city, there was neither cover, nor possibility of cover. Any hole for man or gun, deeper than a single spit, was a water-hole. Dodging to right or left of the established, authorised, recognised, registered and duly punished road meant abandoning the deck of a raft for what was with equal probability water or slime, six inches deep or with a depth sufficient for drowning.[45]

Herbert Read, in 'Kneeshaw goes to War' focuses on this – one of the most horrific aspects of the Passchendaele battlefield : soldiers, overburdened with their equipment, stumbling into mud-filled shell-holes and becoming engulfed in the mire.

A man who was marching at Kneeshaw's side
Hesitated in the middle of the mud,
And slowly sank, weighted down by equipment and arms.
He cried for help;
Rifles were stretched to him;
He clutched and they tugged,
But slowly he sank.

His terror grew-
Grew visibly when the viscous ooze
Reached his neck.
And there he seemed to stick,
Sinking no more.
They could not dig him out –
The oozing mud would flow back again.
The dawn was very near.
An officer shot him through the head;
Not a neat job – the revolver
Was too close.[46]

Yet strangely, some writers (and perhaps many other soldiers) found beauty in the devastation. Hugh Quigley, a romantic-minded Scot who spent his later life in the regeneration of towns, industry and woodland, was awed by the 'haunting majesty' of a sunset landscape at the Canal Bank:[47] others were oddly exhilarated by the spectacle of the total annihilation of nature, and human order. The mystical, cranky and courageous 'Patrick Miller', speaking through his protagonist Blaven, as his battery approaches Lake Zillebeke, puts it thus:

> Everything else had been broken and changed, but the lake accepted no wounds, instantly healing itself, eternally smoothing its breast to receive the sky. Hills rose beyond – indefinite crumbling hills, cut into shapes Blaven had never seen before . . . you never got used to country like this; and he was glad of that.[48]

Ernest Raymond expresses the same view more analytically. His observations, from one of the Passchendaele chapters of *The Jesting Army*, go beyond even German writers like Jünger and Franz Schauwecker[49] in embracing the sublimity of war fought to extremes of destruction. Raymond was no proto-fascist; but he had a darkly imaginative side and sometimes, as here, he reached deeply into the mysteries of life:

> . . . beyond denial he could experience an intense aesthetic pleasure in the beauty of the Fact of War. and he could see this pleasure was something different from a mere youthful thrill in war's excitements; something different from a keen delight in the fine and lovely deeds that war enabled man to perform . . . To those who could look at the Fact only with their reason this pleasure must seem either foolishness or indecency; but to those who, standing in the detached position of the artist and placing an irrelevant morality aside, could observe it with a purely aesthetic eye, had it not its own sublimity? Why look: as he stood here on this higher ground and saw the vast wilderness of the Salient outspread before him, with all its harrowed mud-scape glistening beneath the moonlight – the ringed water in its shell-holes, and long, melancholy tarns reflecting sky – and never anywhere a sign of life, but all around, an horizon just luminous with morning, why, he was ready

to swear that it was at once as terrible and as beautiful a thing as he had seen or would ever see. Perhaps . . . Beauty had nothing to do with human pains and human values, but whenever there was perfection, it was there; and this was the perfection of desolation.[50]

Finally, on a less sombre note and coming down to earth with, as Edmund Blunden once put it, 'a splash like a 5.9. in the Ancre',[51] there is the matter of battlefield humour. We associate with Passchendaele, as with many extreme situations where people suffer together, a species of grim joke which does not stand much repetition, but was vital at the time – as P.J.Campbell put it, 'laughter was the only way of survival .' [52] Many of these 'literary' accounts provide examples, not necessarily the best.

Briffault's satire, which one might have expected to be rich in British army humour, is too continental (he was half-French), too barbed and didactic to get the note right. Burrage's War is War which is essentially a burlesque comedy in a British tradition from Smollett to the Carry On films, captures the spirit better. In one passage he describes advancing in an assault on the Passchendaele ridge with nothing to hold up his trousers save an improvised belt of pack-straps:

I was in the rear of the section . . . Edmonds kept on turning and waving me on, with the heroic gestures of a cavalry leader in the Napoleonic wars; I cursed him heartily, although he could not hear.Did the damned fool think I was funking it? No, my trousers were coming down.

My trousers seemed a positive curse, but I believe they were a blessing in disguise. They may have saved me from an extremity of terror. The human mind is not capable of concentrating on many things at once and mine just then was principally concerned with my trousers.[53]

Wilfrid Ewart's 'Pill-Boxes' is in the sardonic spirit of the B.E.F. trench Journal, The Wipers Times, and very characteristic of officer facetiousness:

You can't take a pill-box out of the medicine cupboard without being reminded of those handy little articles of circular shape etc, etc., and without there being recalled to your mind a deplorable afternoon on the banks of the Steenbeck when pill-boxes – even pill boxes – proved to be nothing but a delusion and a snare.[54]

Edmund Blunden provides many examples of soldier humour including his own: on one occasion he kept himself amused (and in his right mind) in a bombarded pill-box, by reading the solemn metaphysical meditations of an eighteenth century poet and finding lines unintentionally and comically appropriate to his predicament.[55] Jokes were generally less sophisticated, however. There was the old Third Ypres quip 'not altogether dismissed by junior officers, that the Germans could make it rain when they wanted it to.'[56] Often humour took the form of high jinks: Blunden

433

recalled the jocularity with which he was received at headquarters in a pill-box during a murderous bombardment. The adjutant :

> as though defying this extreme fury of warfare, was in an almost smiling mood, and quizzed me about "coming to dinner". Old Auger, the mess corporal, winked at me over the adjutant's shoulder and raised a tempting bottle from his stores. [57]

Blunden quotes Vidler, 'that invincible soldier' rushing into company headquarters' pill-box, between a series of violent explosions, observing merrily: 'That was a quick one 'Erb. I was feeling round my backside for a few lumps of shrapnel – couldn't find any though.'[58]

The infliction of indignities on intimate parts of the body was a regular theme of trench humour. Burrage employed this to cheer up a wounded comrade :

> a very old man of nearly forty and a Boer War veteran, had been shot sideways through the trousers. He was in considerable pain but responded quite happily to my badinage. I told him he couldn't possibly show his horrible scars to his lady friends.[59]

None of these or other, more unmentionable, jests were particularly witty, but the wonder was that people were capable of making any jokes at all, and far from some of the coarser jests about natural functions being a sign of degradation, they were rather, perhaps – as C.S.Lewis has suggested – a proof of human immortality. Bruce Marshall in his account of Buchenwald concentration camp in *The White Rabbit* argues that moments of bawdy humour even in that terrible place could do something to clean men of their misery.[60]

The 'literary heritage' from Passchendaele survivors is extensive though fragmentary. At its best, it provides some memorable impressions of the battle. Some of the works, Blunden's, Williamson's and Briffault's notably, do insist on the futility of the campaign; but, perhaps surprisingly, most of the literature is non-committal or expresses soldierly pride, despite the detestable nature of the conditions and the heart-rending lack of progress. These writers nearly all convey graphically the unearthly quality of the landscape and are agreed on the courage, humour and solidarity among so many of the combatants, despite the moments of black despair which Guy Chapman so well identifies.

Notes.

I would like to acknowledge and thank the present proprietors of the firms who originally published the works which are quoted here for purposes of criticism and comment ; also the staff of the Harry Ransom Humanities Research Center at the University of Texas at Austin; also Gary Sheffield and Neil Wilson for their help.

1   Blunden, Edmund, *Nation and Athenaeum*, 24 March, 1928, p.946.
2   Campbell, P.J., *In the Cannon's Mouth*, London, Hamish Hamilton, 1979;

Gladden, Norman,*Ypres 1917: a Personal Account,* London, Wm Kimber,1967.

3   Sassoon, Siegfried, *Collected Poems, 1908–56,* London, Faber & Faber, 1961.

4   Parsons, Ian, ed.,*The Collected Works of Isaac Rosenberg,* London, Chatto & Windus 1984.; Jones, David,*In Parenthesis,* London, Faber & Faber, 1937; Schreibman, Susan, ed., *Collected Poems of Thomas MacGreevy,* Dublin, Anna Livia Press, 1991.

5   Sassoon, Siegfried, *Memoirs of an Infantry Officer,* London,Faber & Faber, 1930; Frederic Manning' *The Middle Parts of Fortune,* London, Piazza Press, 1929.

6   See Powell, Anne, *A Deep Cry,* Aberporth, Palladour, 1993.

7   Blunden, Edmund,*Undertones of War,* London, R.Cobden-Sanderson,1928. My thanks to Mrs.Edmund Blunden for permission to quote his works.

8   Ibid., Penguin edn. 1938, p.

9   Ibid., Penguin edn. 1938, p.279.

10 See for example, Harry Ransom Humanities Research Center, (HRHRC), the University of Texas at Austin, Mss Sassoon, Blunden-Sassoon, 17 Nov.1929.

11 See Cecil, Hugh, *The Flower of Battle:How Britain Wrote the Great War,* S.Royalton, Vermont, Steerforth Press, 1996, ch.10.

12 See Hurd, Michael, *The Ordeal of Ivor Gurney,* Oxford, O.U.P., 1984, pp.101–15.

13 Ewart, Wilfrid, *Way of Revelation,* London, Putnam 1921, pp. 385–413.

14 Briffault, Robert,*Europa in Limbo,* London, Robert Hale, 1937, ch.13.

15 Raymond, Ernest, *The Jesting Army,* London, Cassell, 1930, Part III, chs. 3–10.

16 Patrick Miller,*The Natural Man,* Grant Richards 1924, ch.3.

17 Blaker, Richard, *Medal Without Bar* London, Hodder & Stoughton,1930, chs. 85 86.

18 Hope,Thomas Suthren,*The Winding Road Unfolds* London, Putnam, 1937.

19 Gurner, Ronald, *Pass Guard at Ypres,* London, Dent,1929, chs.29- 31.

20 Williamson, Henry,*Love and the Loveless: a Soldier's Tale,* London, Macdonald, 1958.,chs 13–18 .

21 Ewart, Wilfrid, *When Armageddon Came, Studies in Peace and War,* London, Rich & Cowan, 1933, pp.124–156 ('Three Days').

22 Quigley, Hugh, *Passchendaele and the Somme,* London, Methuen 1928, p. ix.

23 Chapman, Guy, *A Passionate Prodigality,* London, Ivor, Nicholson & Watson, 1933), chs.13–16; see also Chapman, Guy, *A Kind of Survivor,* London, Gollancz, 1975.

24 Burrage, A.M. ('Ex-Private X'), *War Is War,* London, Victor Gollancz,1930, pp.95–177.

25 Carstairs, Carroll,*A Generation Missing,* London, Heinemann,1930, chs.5–6.

26 Blunden, Edmund, op.cit., p.208,p.189.

27 Jünger,Ernst, *Storm of Steel,* tr. Basil Creighton, London, Chatto & Windus, 1929 (1st edn.1920), pp.161–89, 205–220.

28 Grabenhorst, Georg, *Zero Hour (Fahnenjunker Volkenborn),* tr. from German by A. Featherstonehaugh, London, Brentano's 1929, ch.3. (1st pub.1928)

29 Binding, Rudolf, *A Fatalist at War,* tr. Ian F.D.Morrow, London, Allen & Unwin, 1929, pp.177–197.

30 Jünger, op.cit., p.211.

31 Blunden, op.cit., pp.214–5.

32 Carstairs, op.cit., p.90.
33 Chapman, *Passionate Prodigality*, p.217.
34 Burrage, op.cit., p.128.
35 Jünger, op.cit.,p. 209.
36 Briffault, op.cit., pp. 306–7 ; see Williamson, op.cit. p.192.
37 Chapman, op.cit., p.253.
38 Binding, op. cit.,p. 178.
39 Carstairs, op.cit., p.103.
40 Hurd, op.cit., p.104.
41 Jünger, op.cit., p.180.
42 Briffault, op. cit., pp.311–12; see also Deeping, Warwick, *No Hero – This*, London, Cassell, 1936, p.251, another novel with a Passchendaele chapter
43 Ewart, *When Armageddon Came*, p.136.
44 Briffault, op.cit., p.313.
45 Blaker, op.cit., p.509.
46 Read,Herbert,'Kneeshaw Goes to War' in *Naked Warriors,* London, Art & Letters, 1919, pp.15–16. My thanks to Benedict Read for permission to quote this extract from his father's poetry. See also Sassoon, 'Memorial Tablet'.
47 Quigley, op.cit., 18 Oct.1917. The text is from Quigley's letters.
48 Miller, op.cit., p.117.
49 Schauwecker, Franz, *The Fiery Way (Der feurige Weg)*, London, Dent, 1929 (1st pub.Berlin, 1926).
50 Raymond, op.cit., pp.369–70. My thanks to Diana Raymond.
51 HRHRC, Mss Sassoon, Blunden-Sassoon, 20 Nov. 1926.
52 Campbell, P.J., op.cit., p.132.
53 Burrage, op.cit. p.132.
54 Ewart, *When Armageddon Came*, 'Pill-Boxes', p.180.
55 Blunden, op.cit., p.217.
56 Ibid., p.200.
57 Ibid., p.216
58 Ibid., p.201.
59 Burrage, op.cit., p.142.
60 Marshall, Bruce,*The White Rabbit*, London, Pan Books, 1954, pp.233–4.
61 Carstairs, Carroll, *Life and Death* (Poem, Ypres, 1917) *My Window Sill* London, Heinemann 1923 xiv.

Chapter 27

A Belgian Salient for Reconstruction: People and *Patrie*, Landscape and Memory

Mark Derez

'The first view of Ypres as one approaches it by the railway from Courtrai is most engaging, the gentle hill, over which the quiet old city spreads itself, being crowned with an architectural group unequalled in Belgium for grandeur'.[1] Here was a clear invitation to go and have a look at Ypres ('vaut le voyage' or at least 'mérite un détour'). The author, T. Francis Bumpus, connoisseur of cathedrals, wrote travel guidebooks in an age when tourists still sought cultural experiences and holiday-makers could take pleasure in 'the contemplation of the wonders wrought by man in bygone ages'. In 1908 he went pilgrim-like from cathedral to cathedral in Belgium. We do not know if his guidebooks were well-received. Scarcely six years later, thousands of his fellow-countrymen would follow the same path between Menin and Ypres, though in the opposite direction, and as soldiers, not tourists. With the taste of death in their mouths, they would pass through the old Menin Gate, the entryway to the trenches encircling Ypres, called by the soldiers 'the gate-way to hell'.

In November 1918, one week after the Armistice, Camiel Delaere, a clergyman in Ypres, travelled to Bruges. From Ypres to the rubble that was Elverdinghe, Houthulst, Staden, there was no trace to be seen along the way of the once flourishing villages of Boesinghe, Langemarck and Poelcapelle. He returned the same day, passing as Bumpus had done through Courtrai and Menin. Between Gheluwe and Ypres he found no remnant of any once-extant buildings: 'We descried nothing but puddles, shattered trenches, hiding-places, concrete reinforcements. Some tanks and canons, many shells, much artillery and barbed wire'.[2] Ten years intervened between Bumpus's enthusiasm and Delaere's dismay, and they made an unspeakable difference. The war they had brought had catapulted Ypres into the Stone Age. The war had once again given Ypres a place on the stage of history and had burned it into British collective memory for all time. Ever since, this same Menin road has been travelled by battlefield pilgrims.

To be precise, we must remember that Bumpus travelled by train. The Belgian roadways may have had a bad reputation at the beginning of the century, but in imitation of England, Belgium had an 'admirable railway system', and, as Bumpus remarked, 'the facilities which it affords of transit from one point of attraction to another, is in all probability one of the chief inducements'. That may have been one of the reasons why no other country on the Continent attracted as many of his compatriots 'desirous of seeking change of scene and climate'. Most of the British tourists were attracted by the sombre mysticism of *Bruges-la-Morte*, and under their influence that city grew ever more mediaeval. Ypres, the connoisseurs claimed, need take no back seat to Bruges, but it was too far off the well-travelled track to Saint Petersburg and Vienna. An inhabitant of Ypres could safely leave his doorstep without stumbling over a landscape-painter or being inserted into the picturesque street scene on the canvas of an English lady-painter. Bumpus had nevertheless found his way to Ypres, and from his train window he could see the same landscape which a contented Victor Hugo had earlier exclaimed that it made him think of paintings, not those produced by English ladies, but those of the Flemish masters. Hugo's *'petit enclos verts'*[3] were thickets in a park landscape so enclosed and partitioned by hedgerows and copses that they reminded the British of Devon and Yorkshire. West of Ypres, tobacco was grown, and to the east, round about Poperinge, there were hop-fields. Later, along the same Menin road which Hugo had found so appealing, the British would unfurl the canvas screens which were to hide their troop movements from observation by German artillery, a camouflage technique reminiscent of Turner and Kokoschka, and of low-cost theatre backdrops.

For ages now, Flanders had been seeing soldiers passing, between Menin and Ypres, so near greedy France. The flat countryside was a favourite locale for fighting out differences among the European powers. The traditional Scots *Will ye go to Flanders?* is from the time of the Duke of Marlborough's campaign in Flanders (Oudenarde 1708). Yet this ballad might just as well be from the Great War. However constant the theme of clanging weaponry may be in the history of the Low Countries, and however much it has penetrated the collective memory, in *la Belle Epoque,* war seemed distant indeed. Apart from some skirmishes with the Dutch, Belgium had known no battles since Waterloo. She had even managed to side-step the War of 1870. The burghers of Belgium had no grasp of geo-politics. They traditionally distrusted France, but the notion had escaped them that *Flanderns Küste* might be a link between *Mitteleuropa* and *Mittelafrika* for a Germany in need of *Lebensraum* and colonial expansion. And yet they were dangerously close, those North Sea ports which would ease communications with the colonies, a potential spearhead of *den Griff nach der Weltmacht*. In Ypres, however, they were undisturbed: 'fighting over Ypres seemed to us as inconceivable as a sudden snowstorm in Bombay'.[4]

Thus, when Francis Bumpus arrived in Ypres, he found a drowsy provincial city with exceedingly impressive mediaeval buildings. In the twelfth and thirteenth centuries, Ypres, with its thirty to forty thousand inhabitants, could compete with Bruges and Ghent to be capital of Flanders. But now the population was not even twenty thousand. Yet for some unfathomable reason it called itself *petit Bruxelles*, perhaps because in the mid-nineteenth century one of its mayors had actually become a Government Minister. It also vied with much smaller Poperinghe for the title, 'capital of the Westland'. When Ypres had been flattened, Poperinghe took on worldly-wise airs, if only because it had a Delousing Station and red and blue-light districts to solace the British soldiery. Ypres lay at the heart of one of Flanders' most fertile agricultural regions. Its principal contribution to the national economy was its renowned butter market, though here it had competition from that other city on the edge of the Salient, Diksmuide. There was no industry to speak of; only some textile establishments producing ribbons and cotton fabrics. There were distilleries, a soap factory and a gingerbread factory. There was also lace-making, a traditional home industry, which began to decline round the turn of the century. During the war, Ypres lace found a good market among the British soldiers. This being a border region, there were many who worked in neighbouring France. They commuted to the industrialized towns of northern France, or they found seasonal employment in agriculture. The Belgian cavalry had barracks in Ypres and a riding-school. The judiciary had its hands full with rabbit thieves and poachers. Earlier, the city had had its share of wealthy persons of the upper-class residing in *hôtels* aspiring to be French, the surrounding areas were sprinkled with castles such as Vlamertinghe Château, which Edmund Blunden came upon in 1917 still mainly intact, surrounded by 'poppies by the million'.[5]

Exchanges had been taking place between Flanders and England for centuries. In the early 1500's Thomas More stayed in Bruges regularly, and in the seventeenth century the recusants found a safe haven here. English Benedictine nuns established themselves in Ypres in 1665, succeeded by Irish nuns thirty years later. The Ypres bourgeoisie sent their daughters there to board for half a year to improve their English! Those who could afford it sent their children to England or to the aristocratic English convent in Bruges where Guido Gezelle, Flanders' greatest poet, breathed his last in 1899. Gezelle had translated Longfellow's 'Hiawatha's Song' and had close connections with English Catholicism. So had the Bishop of Bruges. He commissioned Welby Pugin to build a neo-gothic place of pilgrimage in Dadizeele, a three-hour walk from Ypres. A pinch of Anglophilia had no effect on the fact that the better bourgeoisie had become completely French, despite its Flemish roots. The educated middle class, however, was swept up by the Flemish Movement and its local variant: West Flemish Particularism. They were full-blooded romantics who desired the advancement of the local dialect and a revival of the glorious past. They opposed Frenchification, corruption and secularization. For them Flanders was a mythical land, the cradle of the Dutch language, the quintessential mediaeval territory above which the towers of Ypres soared. They considered it no accident that it was just here the German advance was halted. In this hinterland, Belgium's *roi chevalier*, at times depicted as a pre-Raphaelite St George,[6] would establish his mini-kingdom, ensconced behind the so-called 'fatherlanders', the sandbags of the trenches, filled with native soil.

Francis Bumpus's attention was engrossed by churches and cathedrals. Yet in Ypres he was struck first of all by a civic structure: the huge thirteenth century Cloth Hall, its facade 133 metres long, covering 4800 m², and having a belfry which had provided Sir Gilbert Scott with inspiration for the clock-tower of the Midland Railway Terminus Hotel in London. Bumpus was lavish with his praise. 'The whole effect of the building is inconceivably grand leaving behind it, in point of general effect, the Ducal Palace at Venice'. He found Ypres cathedral to be the most French church in all of Flanders, while he determined that the Sint-Jacobs church displayed a strong German influence. The history of art was then preoccupied with the national 'schools', and the tourist could still observe at his ease the encounter between Latin and Germanic influences in this tiny land which would soon be the setting for a dramatic confrontation between the two cultural spheres. Propaganda on both sides was similar in tone. The German author Eugen Lüthgen detected *Germanischen Einschlag* in the Cloth Hall's twin-naved interior.[7] In his view, trade halls in general were the most authentic achievement of Flemish architecture, and at the same time they expressed the *wirklichkeitsfreudiger Lebensbejahung der Belgier*. This was written in 1915. The Belgians would have no more joy of it, for on Sunday, 22 November 1914, Ypres had already been shot to pieces by the so-called cultivated German people (*Duitse Kultur-mensen*) as they were termed by the most respected local chronicler of the war.[8] After Louvain with its burnt library and Reims with its shelled cathedral, Ypres became the third *ville martyre* on the fragile borderline between civilization and *Kultur*. The German Emperor watched it all as he waited for the city to be taken so he could make his triumphal entry. Pastor Delaere and the Quakers of the Friends Ambulance Unit made daredevil trips to rescue works of art and church treasures. However, after the Second and the Third Battles of Ypres, scarcely any stone would be left upon another. The best preserved part of the town, ironically, was the municipal cemetery.

The lie of the land was decisive for how the military operations in and around the Salient were to be conducted. West-Flanders is on the whole flat and low-lying: a land like a sinking sheet, one poet has said. Ypres lies in a basin which connects with the Yser Plain, flooded by the Belgians. In ages past, Ypres was said to have been surrounded by marshes so unhealthy that the saying arose, 'looking like the Ypres death'.[9] The extremely fragile aquatic system of this now-drained soil was thoroughly damaged in no time at all by artillery fire. As a result, the offensives got stuck in the mud, 'Flemish porridge', *la boue des Flandres, die verdammte Flandrische*

Schlamm, mud that would become world-famous after the Battle of Passchendaele.[10]

There are countless descriptions of the lunar landscape which was left after military actions had ceased. In Belgium, a zone sixty kilometres long and ten to twenty kilometres wide had been levelled with the ground. In addition to the three cities of art – Nieuwpoort, Poperinge, Ypres – at least sixty villages had been wiped from the map. President Wilson came to visit the front, as did the Belgian Queen Elizabeth, who lost a shoe in the mud at Poelcappelle.[11] In their wake came disaster-watchers and battlefield pilgrims. Nature, however, reasserted itself. A plant-fancier of the romantic Flemish variety ranged through the battlefields with his specimen box, discovering all manner of foreign flora, the *Nachwuchs* of seeds dropped by armies from foreign lands on this godforsaken soil: the Our-Lady's-thistle, *Silybum Marianum* from England, which came along in the horses' oats, and turnips the size of a fist from Germany. Besides thistles – the accursed weeds – there were, especially along the trenches, the native poppies, *Papaver Rhoeas*. These were the poppies that Charles Lindbergh scattered by the thousands from his aeroplane over the Flanders' Fields American Cemetery in Waregem in 1927. They are also the poppies in the familiar poem by the Canadian Medical Officer, John McCrae, which made Flanders' Fields known everywhere – perhaps a necessary thing, given the number of British soldiers writing home from some village near Ypers and placing at the top of their letters, *somewhere in France*.[12] Our botanist, part-philosopher, saw how it was: 'people put their knowledge together with their science, and they managed to destroy what centuries of unremitting hard work had built up'.[13]

After the Armistice, the area which had been the front remained as it was for a year and a half. No one in authority seemed to pay it any attention. Not until those immediately concerned staged an alarming demonstration in Roeselare did the scandal make an impression in Brussels. Only then did the government put its hand to the plough as it were. In fact, even before the Armistice was proclaimed, the Minister of Agriculture had set up a special 'Service for the Devastated Regions' to study the problem. But in the local context there were neither inhabitants nor usable roads, and the Service, lacking both personnel and funds, was literally bogged down.[14]

In November 1919, funds were appropriated. The state took upon itself the task of restoration, but, only in the most severely affected areas – some ten sectors, 500 to 2000 hectares in size – did the authorities commission works. The state engaged one contractor for each sector. It was to the contractors' advantage to finish their jobs as quickly as possible. At one point there were some 30,000 workers clearing the ground, or so said official sources. However, by introducing fictitious payrolls for fictitious workers, unscrupulous Belgian contractors were able to squeeze extra benefits from the famous American contract. Elsewhere farmers and lease-holders cleared their fields themselves, receiving compensation from the state as their work progressed. This positive approach to private enterprise had a drawback however: the mountain of paperwork thrust upon the poor farmer. For just one contract, he had to sign no less than 85 documents.

By the spring of 1920, things began to move at last. The first measure to be taken was the redigging of hundreds of kilometres of channels to drain the sodden fields into which streams were emptying. There were corpses and dead horses everywhere, and the stench was nauseous. It was not always easy to find persons willing to do this sort of work. They were conveyed from the large towns to the field daily. Some remained all week long in a shed erected on the battlefield. The foreman and his family lived in a caravan. H. Bossier, who translated English war poetry into Dutch, worked at the time as a foreman when the Langemarck-Poelcappelle-Zonnebeke section was drained. He wrote: 'In Zonnebeke a gang was busy digging out a branch of the Hanebeek stream. They were continually encountering rat-chewed corpses. Judging by the boots and uniforms, they must have been Germans . . . I was reminded of that Hanebeek ravine, close to the Polygon Wood, while I was translating Herbert Read's collection of poems, *Naked Warriors*, some time later. In it there is a piece called *Killed in Action* about a group of English soldiers passing near the Polygon Wood on the way to the front-line. One of them falls into deep mud and sinks and sinks. No one can get him out, and finally one of his comrades mercifully puts a bullet through his skull'. . . .[15] The courses of the streams could hardly be recognized in the landscape, but their idyllic names were still there: Lekkerboterbeek, Palingbeek en Hanebeek (Tasty-butter-beck, Eel Beck, Rooster Beck) . . . Such names could suffice to start a whole process of anamnesis. Thus the collective war memories of the Flemings and the British sometimes intertwined.

In the aftermath of a war which valued the use of technology higher than valour and sacrificial dedication, it should surprise no one that the task of reconstruction was approached as a kind of *Materialschlacht*. In effect, the first approach considered was that of bringing in heavy machinery to level the ravaged earth. King Albert, fascinated by technology as were so many of the Coburgs, had even announced before the war had ended a 25,000 franc prize for the best restoration project. It was unfortunate that the winner had to be a Belgian; otherwise the prize would certainly have been carried off by a Mr Knox, an American engineer who had devoted all his energy to developing a huge 250 tonne dredge-like machine with a 600 h.p. capacity which, however, did not see completion until all the levelling work was already done. Mr Knox was nevertheless permitted to show his machine to the King, though the Treasury, given the budget restrictions, could offer him no remuneration for his having devoted his entire fortune and three years of his life to the cause.

Then there was the Belgian mechanic who tried to find financing for an even more monstrous machine which would not only smooth the ground and pick up shells, but also plough, harrow and sow, leaving the farmer nothing to do but harvest his crops. Another inventer proposed bringing in fresh earth by aeroplane and dropping it upon the trenches. This would at least have had the merit of solving the problem of the immobilization of each and every vehicle by the eternal mud. The solution was finally proffered by a simple farmer with a great deal of common sense. He wrote that to restore the front-line areas all that was needed was the diligent application of the shovel. Indeed, it was a shovel which many a farmer received upon his return, for Canadian farmers had donated 15,000 small agricultural implements as a gesture of solidarity.

The levelling work was done by hand. Modern agricultural machinery had far less importance than had been anticipated. Mechanization only made its entry when the time came for actual fieldwork, especially when the first ploughing began. Ford showed his admiration for 'poor little Belgium' by contributing an array of ten tractors. Initially these Fordsons encountered much suspicion among the rural populace, hostile as it was to anything newfangled and preferring the use of Belgian army horses. Enthusiasm grew quickly however, not least because the first ploughing was without cost, and the Ministry was soon obliged to purchase 120 additional tractors, whereby Ford also received proof that nobility and business were not mutually exclusive. With these motorized ploughs, more than 20,000 hectares were worked, including the small plots of many a cottage, and even the vegetable patch of the village priest who now succumbed to the blessings of technology as readily as his parishioners.

Needless to say, digging up a battleground with all its explosives – shells, grenades, missiles – was a perilous undertaking. There were places where as many as five unexploded shells were located within one square metre. During the first years some ten serious accidents occurred. Still, this was far less than the insurance companies had predicted. They demanded high premiums, as much as 8% of wages paid out. For that matter, it was the state which assumed responsibility for risks involving explosions. Levelling operations unearthed as much as 5000 kilos of shrapnel and detonators per hectare, not counting the shells and the larger pieces. Yet that was but the tip of the iceberg. Even today ploughing still turns up munitions. These are said to be mostly grenades left from the 1917 offensive, the Third Battle of Ypres; they are the projectiles which did not explode as they were expected to do. Not far from Passchendaele is Houthulst Wood where during the final offensive of 1918 the fighting was intense. The recovery of scrap and munitions gave rise to a small enterprise at the edge of the wood run by a British veteran, Pickett. After a few years, the business passed into the hands of the Belgian army which established a military domain with a munitions depot, a barracks and a mine-clearing service. To this day it continues to defuse munitions from the Great War. In recent years, the harvest has even increased as a result of the many new roads which are being laid. Annual collection totals can run as high as 250,000 kilos. Each day, at noon and again at four-thirty in the afternoon, old munitions are exploded. First the sirens wail; then comes the muffled thunder of the explosions. The sound can be heard in the surrounding villages: an echo of the Great War which has continued to reverberate these eighty years.[16]

In the beginning it was questioned whether the battle-zones would ever be cultivated again. The sea-salt deposited in the flooded areas of the former Belgian front would, it was feared, forever impede the growth of vegetation. A German expert had declared that all soil containing one per mil of sodium chloride or ordinary salt would be totally barren. Belgian researchers found salt content up to 20 per mil and aligned themselves gloomily with their German colleague. In the end, it was experimental fields which were able to demonstrate the opposite to the farmers, always a distrustful breed. A prophet of doom announced that in the British sector of the Ypres Salient agriculture would be impossible. The only solution would be to plant an enormous forest. This solution was not unwelcome in a Flanders where few forests stood, but then it was realized that this would deprive Belgium of one of its most fertile agricultural regions, covering about a twentieth of the country, and would force permanent emigration on the rural populace. The farmers however did come back. In no time the battlefields were transformed into green expanses. Now one spoke of 'the miracle of Flanders' partially brought about by the solidarity of the Allies, and one could almost believe that the biblical words had been fulfilled and that swords had been turned into ploughshares.

A dealer in seeds, the firm of P. Johnson in Boston, England, provided seeds sufficient for 7000 vegetable gardens. Animal husbandry too was revived, in the main through donations distributed to the earliest returning inhabitants of the front-line areas. The Queen herself, who had just returned to the Laken Palace near Brussels from which she had been banned for four years, presented the afflicted farmers with presents from her poultry farm. Each family received three hens and a cock, selected from the best strains of laying chickens. This royal contribution toward livestock replenishment may appear modest, but it provided an example to be followed. The Agricultural Relief of Allies Committee, which was under the exalted patronage of H.M. King George V and the Duke of Portland sent not only many goats and cows but also 3072 hens and 2035 unhatched eggs![17] Dairy-Shorthorn and Ayrshire cattle were especially appreciated by the Flemish farmers. The cattle-breeders immediately established a co-operative association to maintain a first-class bull, thereby sharing both costs and benefits. The Herdbook was scrupulously kept. The 'Service for the Devastated Regions' organized competitions which were attended by representatives from Agricultural Relief. The British benefactors were received with generous Flemish hospitality, and the festivities made a marked contribution toward heartening the populace.

The people were certainly in need of encouragement. However flourishing agriculture and animal raising might be, housing long remained a sorry affair. Since not one stone was left upon another in the combat areas and every returning inhabitant was in principle and in fact homeless, temporary shelters were needed.[18] To this end the government had set up the King Albert Fund as early as 1916 with a planned endowment of ten million francs. During the war, few of the promised subsidies arrived. The Allies only furnished credit to the Belgian government in exile for military purposes. The British and French governments refused credit for the post-war housing project despite the fact that King Albert was its patron. Nor did individual benefactors produce adequate support, and an international campaign for contributions had poor results. Not until October 1919 did the Fund receive from the government the long-awaited sum.

Financial constraints obviously dampened the creativity of those in authority who were supposed to come up with temporary housing solutions. Just two types of wooden sectional pavilions were considered, the first type had three rooms and an area of 6 by 6 metres while the other had two rooms and 4 by 4 metre area, i.e. small and still smaller. Having done this, the Albert Fund planners considered their work complete. The overwhelming predicament of housing tens of thousands of families of all sizes and varying work patterns, in the country and in the city, was reduced to constructing and transporting two types of standardized wooden shacks to be deposited everywhere. On the architect's drawings, these dwellings were charmingly shuttered gingerbread houses shown amidst greenery, the ideal setting for a *roman de retour* where a faithful Penelope awaited her returning hero. Reality in the grim war-torn areas was quite different. No thought had been given to public facilities such as schools, churches and hospitals. The temporary shelters were conceived of as encampments. The planners, who had doubtless imbibed the reigning military atmosphere, clearly took their inspiration from an army camp's monotonous rows of barracks. There was also a marked resemblance to the camps for Belgian refugees in Holland. Returnees therefore found little difference – if, that is, they were lucky enough to obtain a shack from the Albert Fund. After two years of planning, the Fund had distressingly little to show for its efforts. At the time of the Armistice, the 150 barracks which Belgium had erected in the Netherlands were still inhabited by Belgian refugees, whereas in France, Belgium had only assembled two such barracks.

When the winter was past, many refugees returned home, and by early 1919, the ravaged zones had recovered almost 30% of their prewar population. These pioneers had no choice but to take shelter in primitive squatters' shelters, pieced together from ruins and material left behind by the German army. Thus did the inadequacy of the emergency programme become painfully apparent. The government did bring some administrative measures to bear in an attempt to maintain some control over population movements. In February 1919, the construction of 2000 barracks was commissioned, but the contractors could not deliver the necessary lumber, and a half-year delay resulted. The majority of the shelters erected after August 1919 was of a metal dome type, the so-called Nissen Huts, 4500 of which had been purchased from the British army following difficult negotiations. The people were furious: "Nissen Huts? Pits with metal roofs not fit for farm animals!"[19] Rumours that, at last,

445

barracks had been erected somewhere or other, would cause new waves of migration which the government tried in vain to stem. At the end of October 1919, when the Albert Fund was to have completed its task, only 850 dwellings had been assembled.

The numerous petitions which the homeless and displaced, including many veterans, sent to their 'Very Dear Queen', are tragic. But no queenly succour ensued. The Fund which bore the name of her consort was so despised that those it was intended to help called it not *le Fonds du roi Albert* but *le vol du roi Albert*. Brussels was worlds away from the front. So the afflicted from Flanders' fields betook themselves to the capital where the good citizenry, still flushed with victorious patriotism, had little sympathy for these peasants screaming out their discontent at 'the government's shameful neglect of the Flemish people' (*De Standaard*, 9 July 1919). By February of 1920, requests for 7,721 barracks had come from South-West Flanders, the region of the Ypres Salient, but less than 2,000 had been erected. The housing crisis was at its dramatic peak: only 25,000 more or less habitable dwellings were available for the returning 45,000 families. Thus, thousands of families had to endure the winter of 1919–1920 in grievous conditions. In the Salient it seemed that the miseries of the war would never end.

Emergency housing was of course not enough. The owners were impatient to rebuild their houses, preferably upon the old ruins. Immediately after the war a law had been passed to the effect that everyone who had suffered damage during the war would be reimbursed. Special courts were instituted for this purpose. In practice it was impossible to deliberate on the hundreds of thousands of damage claims in the course of a few months. 62,400 claims had been filed with the court at Ypres alone, yet, by 30 August 1920, only 136 decisions had been handed down.[20] This scheme of damage-compensation for individual owners was paralysing. Private initiative could not meet the need by itself. Rapid reconstruction would require more commitment on the part of the authorities. Moreover, the war years had actually caused a rapid increase in the number of households; many couples were eager to marry. Demographically speaking, there was a compensatory trend in nuptiality exacerbating the housing crisis. Thus the country was faced with a gigantic construction task, and the government realized that the respective municipalities could not meet the need on their own. A law of 8 April 1919 permitted such municipalities to be adopted by the state, on the condition that they establish general plans and building regulations. The Ypres region received special attention, acquiring its very own High Royal Commissioner. Thus reconstruction became a state matter, which was in itself no guarantee of success. Reconstruction was officially terminated in 1926. In reality the last reconstruction work was not completed until 1960. Each time a new government took over in Brussels, policy was modified. At times the authorities took the lead, at other times private initiative was given free rein. 'The Service for the Devastated Regions' had a plan whereby the government would build 2000 leasehold farms and 2000 workers' houses; this was halted by a new minister in early 1920 before it ever got started. In the prevailing liberal climate in Belgium, state intervention was systematically watered down. The comprehensive, durable policy of reconstruction, which progressive urbanists had envisioned during the war, never got off the ground

Conservative elements had long been at work. Such was the City Council of diminutive Diksmuide which met in Paris in 1917 to make plans for reconstruction. Here, in the metropolis, they decided how their mini-city would be reborn in the old style. (The architect, Huib Hoste, who had himself fled to the Netherlands, commented that those City Councillors ought to know that one cannot treat an ill person 'by telephone'.)[21] Meanwhile, the modernists were also making themselves heard. Their approach was more functional, more social and economic, and they thought in terms of town and country planning, industrial development, communications infra-structure. Huib Hoste envisioned a role for Ypres as an industrial centre, connected with the ports of Zeebrugge and Oostende. It was modernists such as Hoste who were the great planners while the war was on. They were all isolated to some extent, being either abroad or far from the scene of battle and the resulting devastation. They did, however, come into contact with the newest developments and received much theoretical help from their Dutch, French and especially British colleagues.

In England, as early as 1914, the International Garden Cities and Town Planning Association had taken Belgium under its wing, for Belgian urban planning was still in its infancy.[22] There was an element of condescension in this patronage; Belgian engineers in London, for example, were given training in how to accommodate Belgium's infamous cobbled streets to automobile tyres. Much of the planning was of course more far-reaching, and naturally a vision of a new Belgium arose. Wars provide urbanists with great opportunities, and here was a chance to build model towns in a model country which might perhaps have to do without many of its glorious monuments, but which would be a healthy place to live in. It seemed that never since the Great Fire of London in 1666 had there been such an opportunity. What Christopher Wren had wrought in old London would pale next to what the idealists of the early twentieth century planned to do in Flanders. But would all this be accepted by the country it was intended for? Not that their modernism was all that extreme; rather, they underestimated the *genius loci*, the historicity of the region and of the people's sentiments. A major conference on the reconstruction of Belgium was held in London's Guild Hall from 11 to 16 February 1915. More than 300 Belgians participated. During a visit to Letchworth Garden City, where an ample colony of Belgian refugees was installed, the conference participants were even addressed by Ebenezer Howard, the promoter of the Garden City idea. The garden neighbourhood concept was highly fashionable in Belgium after the war. But these were neighbourhoods, not towns or cities. The idea of reconstructing Ypres as a large garden city never got off the drawing-board. The few unassuming garden neighbourhoods that did get started, remained half-finished, without public utilities, though the designers seem to have done their best to recast the British model in accordance with a patriotic Flemish 'beguinage' concept.

The *beguinage* model would have been too modest for city fathers contemplating reconstruction. Early enthusiasm over German reparation payments – *le boche paiera!* – spread to every city, and the plan was to rise immediately from the ashes, handsomer and above all richer than ever. *Resurgam!* So it was in devastated Ypres, though there was some doubt whether the completely levelled city should be reconstructed on the old site. The more affluent bourgeoisie had moved to the big cities of the interior, and at times they seemed to be obstructing reconstruction. The municipal authorities, however, never doubted: Ypres would rise again! There was a small obstacle to be faced: the ruins and their defenders. While 4000 workmen cleared the ruins month after month, intelligentsia throughout the land was still agonizing over the question whether or not the ruins in the heart of the city should be preserved. Even in 1916, at the *Exposition de la Cité reconstituée* in Paris where Ypres' Municipal Architect Jules Coomans had presented the first reconstruction plans, Mayor René Colaert had vehemently opposed preserving the ruins. He brought economic, aesthetic, patriotic and archaeological arguments to bear, and cited the Minister of Public Works, Georges (Joris) Helleputte: '*La Belgique n'a pas besoin de conserver ses ruines pour se souvenir de ses malheurs*'.[23] This minister had in fact made allowances for rare exceptions, but there the mayor kept cannily silent. However, at the end of the war, the entire discussion did indeed come to centre upon whether Ypres should be seen as such an exception or not.

Many from Britain dreamed of keeping part of the city's ruins and even making a large cemetery there. *The Graphic* of 15 November 1919 wrote about *Ypres as a British War Memorial*. The British town-major of Ypres, Beckles-Wilson, prohibited the rebuilding of the city's houses for reasons of respect, enforcing this as long as possible. There was a sign set in the rubble of the Cloth Hall stating, 'This is holy Ground'.[24] Yet it could not prevent the Saturday egg market from swiftly reestablishing itself within the shattered walls of this holy hall. Proposals were put forth to enclose the cathedral and Cloth Hall ruins with fences, to encompass them with wide zones of greenery where silence would be enforced, and to make of them perpetual places of pilgrimage. Less noble but certainly understandable were the anti-German sentiments. One could hear, as it were, the cry of indignant tourists, 'May these ruins be maintained for they are the most eloquent witness of Teutonic vandalism'.[25]

Going against the British, right after the war, was almost inconceivable. Their prestige in Ypres was immense and one would not wish to make open opposition such as that voiced by the architect Albert Roosenboom (no son of Ypres, to be sure) with the uncouth words: *Au lieu d'y laisser des ruines, pour en faire un ossuaire, que Messieurs les Anglais nous aident donc à l'oeuvre de résurrection; qu'ils fassent des Halles reconstruites leur musée de guerre, s'ils le veulent, mais qu'ils ne nous obligent pas à être les gardiens de leur cimetière et les fossoyeurs de notre cité.*[26] That was a view not shared by the architect Eugène Dhuicque, highly respected in Ypres for all he had done during the war to save what could be saved, and who had buttressed what was left of the Cloth Hall. He was indignant that the municipal authorities had done nothing more since the war to strengthen what still stood, whereas, everywhere commerce in war souvenirs was flourishing and makeshift structures sprouted up with names such as *café de la paix* and *rendez-vous des alliés*. Indeed, he virtually divested the citizens of Ypres of any proprietorial right over their own city: *Et pourtant, ces ruines nous appartiennent. Ce n'est plus à la ville à décider de leur sort. Trop de sang a coulé pour les défendre. Elles sont aujourd'hui au Pays tout entier. Elles appartiennent au monde coalisé contre la barbarie et pour lequel elles resteront un éternel symbole. Elles appartiennent à l'Histoire. Elles appartiennent à ceux qui sont tombés tout autour d'elles, à ceux qui dorment, enveloppés dans un linceul de gloire, aux versants des côteaux de Flandre.*[27]

Of course there were aesthetes, too, who favoured preserving a landscape of ruins. Their reasons were sentimental and stemmed from a romantic worship of the picturesque. Most artists and intellectuals, however, advanced more serious arguments on behalf of the archaeological preservation of certain important ruins, in particular because they considered historicizing reconstruction to be absolutely insufferable.[28] Huib Hoste received confirmation of this view among the Dutchmen he queried. Almost no one advised rebuilding the Cloth Hall. Piet Mondriaan was the lone exception. This pioneer of geometric abstraction found it essential that in the midst of all that was new a few very good examples of older art be retained. He found the reconstruction desirable from both the national and international points of view.[29] Architect Jan Stuyt, who favoured the gothic style, cautioned against rebuilding in the new style for he found that Dutch modern architecture was quite German in character, and would be a catastrophe in beautiful, distinctive Belgenland. Ypres was not at risk. The clergy from the surrounding villages even accused Hoste himself of cubism and 'hollandism'. In any event the Dutch intelligentsia showed little enthusiasm for reconstruction. An abstract painter and a neo-gothic architect were almost the only intellectuals who were in tune with Ypres' municipal architect who had made plans for a full, identical and if necessary improved historic reconstruction.

The mayor, having previously earned his spurs in the struggle for women's suffrage, now launched a crusade against the 'picturesquers' and the 'aesthetes', whereas the modernists did not seem to perturb him. He criss-crossed the country collecting funds to rebuild his Cloth Hall. Nieuwpoort had already rebuilt its Cloth Hall (a much smaller structure, it is true), utilizing the heavy oak beams which the Germans had transferred to Zeebrugge for military purposes.[30] Ypres must not lag behind.

The mayor won out, as was to be expected. The reconstruction of the Cloth Hall proceeded in fits and starts, and was finally completed in 1967.

Neither the moral might of the British nor the opposition of the intellectuals could stand against the single-mindedness of the city fathers for whom the rebuilding of Ypres' chief landmark was as much a matter of civic pride as of prestige. And it is certain that they had a good portion of the people on their side, people who had already erected a number of facades exactly as they had been. Instead of modern town-planning there was much pre-war town-scaping giving consideration to open spaces, picturesque passageways, viewing-points and planned vistas, façades that conferred a special character on streets and squares and the relevant ornamental detail – Bruges gothic, and Veurne renaissance windows! – which were to bring Ypres back to its prewar appearance. The people of Ypres had chosen to resume normal life in a familiar setting, a bit of banality in a sublime civic decor, albeit an ersatz replica of what was lost forever. It would not be fair to repudiate all of the reconstruction architecture as a pastiche. Ypres did not become an operetta theme-park. Allusions to the city that had been were integrated as part of the present. The private citizens who had already erected the proud structures on the market square were well aware that they had done something new. They did not try to mask the caesura which the Great War had created; on the contrary, they emphasized it by placing the year of construction proudly visible in the gables, a remembrance of the catastrophe and a starting point toward a new era.

The British Empire, however respectable its claims, had to give way to a small city's nostalgia for its magnificent past. The British were not to have the 'sacred zone' round the ruins of Ypres Cloth Hall, although they were permitted to extricate one of its stones for their field of honour near Canterbury Cathedral. However, just a few hundred metres away, there arose a monumental arch of triumph where the old Menin Gate had stood, the gateway through which young men from Britain and the Empire marched for four years, on their way into the Flemish inferno. The Menin Gate Memorial was inaugurated on 24 July 1927 by Lord Plumer, the former commander of the British forces in Flanders. King Albert reminded his hearers that Ypres was for the British what Verdun had been for the French, and that for fifty months Ypres had been the threshold of the British Empire. Yet it was just this imperial aspect of Sir Reginald Blomfield's construction which called forth so much opposition, as when Siegfried Sassoon, on passing the new Menin Gate, was inspired to compose his famous invective. Sassoon had been in the crowd, and he wrote his poem damning the 'sepulchre of crime' the next day in his Brussels hotelroom.[31] The Flemish were impressed by the long procession of soldiers' mothers (who so resembled their Flemish counterparts), widows and orphans invited to the ceremony by the Ypres League. How different was the contemplative, religious atmosphere of the British ceremony from the hurrah! patriotism of Belgian and French commemorations.[32] In Flanders, Great Britain was put forward as a model to follow in opposition to Belgium's close connection with France. Moreover, it was in Ypres that France and Belgium had negotiated a secret military agreement which continued to cause agitation in Flanders where pacifism and pro-Flemish sentiments reinforced one another, compounded by anti-Belgian and anti-French feelings.

Very soon after the inauguration of the Menin Gate Memorial, the idea of a small daily ceremony was born. The proposal came from the municipal chief of police who suggested that a modest gesture be made every evening on behalf of the people of Ypres, honouring those who had given their lives defending the city. It was decided to sound the Last Post at sundown. The ritual took place from 1 July to 1 October 1928 and was resumed on 1 May 1929. Since then the ceremony has continued unbroken except during the German occupation in the Second World War. In the summer, the bugles sound at 9 p.m. and in the winter, one hour earlier. One minute before, traffic stops. The stillness is, at most, broken by a quacking duck on the moat. As the Last Post fades away under the Gate's arches, one cannot but be moved by the sight of the hundreds of panels of white Portland stone, with their 54,896 incised names of the unidentified missing who fell before 15 August 1917. The somewhat offensive pomposity of Blomfield's architecture notwithstanding, this site, with its permanent process of ritualizing and memorializing, is laden with a significance few other sites from the Great War, *lieux de mémoire*, can match. Even those who find the Menin Gate absolutely ugly and politically detestable, must admit that every evening this brief sonnerie justifies its existence: 'when the music of the bugles resounds, then all pomp and misplaced grandeur fade, then there is nothing but the Missing, somewhere deep in the clay of Ypres, who are embraced, comforted, cradled by the tones of that evensong'.[33]

Ypres was not alone in getting its zone of silence. A network of silent cities came into being throughout the Ypres Salient. There are more than 150 burial places, 169 to be exact, within an area of less than 140 square kilometres or 54 square miles. In other words, at least one cemetery per square kilometre or three at least per square mile. The dead occupy a great deal of space round about Ypres.[34] This is of course connected with the large number of British casualties (139,090 fell in Belgium), but, more influential still, was the ban on repatriation imposed by the British Red Cross in April 1915, since otherwise the wealthy would be the only ones who could afford to bring their dead home. It is a tribute to the otherwise so class-conscious Britain that its enlisted men and its officers were buried where they fell, regardless of rank or class. The French families, on the other hand, came in great numbers to dig up their dead.

Another reason why the dead occupy so much space is that the British chose to commemorate each fallen man with his own stone. This had not been a universal practice. In the War of 1870, the French and the Prussians still made use of common graves, and even in the First World War the

French had not quite made up their minds: there is a French cemetery near Ypres, Saint-Charles-de-Potyze, with both individual graves and two ossuaries, whereas in Kemmel in 1926, 5,294 unknown Frenchmen were interred in a common grave. Such collective burials must necessarily produce a sense of anonymity where the individual counts for little and associations with cannon-fodder arise. As early as the Boer War, the British had followed the example of the Americans who gave individual burial plots to the victims of the Civil War (1861–1865). In both cases, of course, typically Anglo-Saxon respect for each individual person played a part. The orderly arrangement of the British grave-markers, row on row, made a huge impression on the Continent, and certainly left its mark on Flanders' fields.

Following the French example, in 1917, the Belgian nation committed itself to provide burial grounds in perpetuity for its own fallen and for the Allied dead. The Belgian state remained the owner of the ground purchased for this purpose, giving the Allies the 'usufruct' thereof, a somewhat heartrending term in this context. One can be sure that this was not always what the farmers would have wanted. Upon their return, they found not only goods and chattels destroyed, but here and there a piece of land – fertile land, their most precious possession – transformed into an eternal field of the dead.

The British cemeteries seem scattered at random round the Ypres Salient, at times only a few hundred metres from each other, often far from the road, forlornly isolated in the middle of the fields. That this is so is a consequence of military topography and the bizarre course of the front-line. 'As much as possible, the graves are still where they always were, and thus they keep the war in their grasp'.[35] Most of the burial places came into being while the war was still on. They were laid out in haste, in the heat of battle, near a command post or a field hospital. Such were the Mending-hem, Bandage-hem and Dozing-hem Military Cemeteries, all three near Proven, all three witnesses to the Third Battle of Ypres. Their curious and ironic names were invented by soldiers who drew their inspiration from the numerous Casualty Clearing Stations in the area and the names of count-less Flemish villages which end in -hem or -gem. The largest British cemetery in Europe, Tyne Cot in Passchendaele, was originally a real Battle Cemetery. The dates on the markers are those of the terrible Third Battle of Passchendaele which lasted from 31 July to 10 November 1917. The word Tyne refers, of course, to a river in the north of England, Cot, reput-edly to the industrial housing on its banks, but to the locals it sounds like the West-Flemish word for chicken-coop, and with this homely and familiar word they have made the grandly conceived necropolis their own. The long semi-circular wall with the names of the 34,957 who were numbered among the missing after 15 August 1917 is a symbolic repre-sentation of the Salient. From here the towers of Ypres can be made out. Tyne Cot is the target of school trips and senior citizen excursions. Of late, Passchendaele has also become a culturally dense, symbolic focus for the renewed interest among the young in the tragedy of the Great War. Its influence further afield has been enhanced by concerts, radio programmes and publications.

Much of the fascination of the British cemeteries can be explained by their atmosphere. It is British, but not chauvinistic, and this appeals to many Flemings. In the twentieth century, generation after Flemish generation had to wrestle with the notions of peoplehood and fatherland, and they wanted nothing to do with the *mort pour la patrie* of French and Belgian military cemeteries. The British solders were simply 'killed in action' and were assigned no national function, nor were they encumbered with a posthumous hero's role. The unfortunate ones who were shot at dawn and who turn up sporadically in diaries, village war-lore and media contention, could always count on the tolerance of the Flemish; having their own 'tiny nation' syndrome, they could easily identify with the underdog.

The precise notation of the identity and burial location of each of the dead, the respect for the historic link between burial spot and military action, the extreme attention paid to the establishment and maintenance of the cemeteries so that they always looked like new – all this was the quintessence of the British cult of the dead. These elements of concreteness and accuracy sharpen one's awareness of history. The war becomes individualized; is brought near. Remembrance becomes a fresh contact with individual tragedies which would otherwise have been swallowed up by a grey past.

It is fortunate that the Belgian state did not assume responsibility for maintaining the British cemeteries. The Belgian cemeteries were soon in a sorry state and remained so until the 1950's. The British lawns nearby are kept trimmed to the millimetre by the great numbers of gardeners of the War Graves Commission. Until the Second World War they were all of them British veterans, and about 275 of them lived in Ypres. Using mainly English plants, year after year they transform the plots in Flanders' fields into English gardens – some corner of a foreign field that is for ever England – as Rupert Brooke had dreamed near Gallipoli. The War Graves Commission called in young architects who had been in the war to design the cemeteries. Their immediate superiors were the two stars of British architecture, Sir Edwin Lutyens and Sir Reginald Blomfield, whose respective works, Stone of Remembrance and Cross of Sacrifice, also help to set the tone. The ghost of Palladio now hovered over every *campo santo* of Flanders. In the mental landscape of Flanders, where the Middle Ages were cherished, this was a *Fremdkörper* indeed, a foreign import. But it was accepted. The British cemeteries are now so omnipresent that they have shaped our perceptions; for the Flemish, British funerary architecture has become the norm. It is a dignified classicism which cannot give offence except where it takes on imperial airs in the larger monuments. How different the macabre symbolism of the French memorials of which there are not many in the Salient; one must visit the phallic utopia of the Ossuaire de Douaumont near Verdun to see them at their most lugubrious.

The desolate expressionism of the German cemeteries along the edge of the Salient is almost breathtaking. The sculptor, Käthe Kollwitz, found the English cemeteries too friendly. Mourning the son she had lost on the battlefield, she sculpted a pair of Grieving Parents who seem to be sheer petrified woe. Originally the crosses of the German cemeteries were painted black, as the humiliating Treaty of Versailles had decreed. *Vae victis!* Nor could they have their plots in perpetuity; they were cleared at the end of the 1950's and concentrated into four large cemeteries. Sombre humility characterized the new burial grounds too. This attitude was perhaps typical of the Federal Republic and its timid attempts to be integrated into the West European setting, just as the German cemeteries with their tall lime trees and encircling pollard willows appear truly integrated into the Flemish landscape, moreso than the British. Indicative of a change of attitude among the Germans, was the recent demand that the Kollwitz figures be transferred to Berlin, as though they were the Elgin marbles. The sculptor's family and the German authorities finally abandoned the repatriation scheme, so that the strong links with the locality have been preserved.[36]

In stark contrast to the uniformity of the British memorials, the delirious eclecticism of the Belgians precipitated a veritable inflation in monuments. No thought had as yet been given to cemeteries when a tombstone was introduced at state expense in 1920, *une sepulture décente* for the fallen. Its style was very Belgian and slightly frivolous, with its art nouveau swirls that were somewhat outmoded and passé for the 'twenties'. The design was a bit too reminiscent of *la Belle Epoque*, that brief period when Belgium entertained the illusion that it was a great power with a cosmopolitan citizenry intent on overseas expansion.

There was yet another Belgian tombstone with a composition that was, if possible, even stranger. It was a Celtic cross designed by the artist Joe English of Bruges, carrying the motto of the Flemish Movement: 'All for Flanders, Flanders for Christ' in the form of its Dutch initials AVV-VVK. In August of 1916, a small group of Flemish intellectuals formed a committee to make these stones available to soldiers who wished to honour their slain comrades. The soldiers paid for the headstone out of their own pockets, often unbeknown to the family who were generally on the other side of the front, in Occupied Belgium. When, in 1925, the Belgian state at last laid out cemeteries, only fifty families chose to retain the Flemish tombstone. Meanwhile, the originators of the tombstone had begun to organize Yser Pilgrimages, radically Flemish in tone, and they now attempted to recover the other tombstones. At that very moment, a number of them were crushed, by order of the Belgian government, to make a road to a military cemetery. In Flanders this was, naturally, felt to be a slap in the face, particularly since the tombstones had been profaned by anti-Flemish elements while the war was still on. In the end, over two hundred tombstones were given back to the Committee for the Yser Pilgrimages. Once again, as the result of ill-will and misunderstandings, Flanders and Belgium were on opposing sides – a lamentable confrontation in the midst, as it were, of the First World War's tombs.

Whereas the British, with their national monuments, had succeeded in providing a solid base for their memorializing, the Belgians imitated the French, who left everything in the hands of the local authorities. Every mayor wanted a memorial in the town square and a field of honour in the village churchyard. *L'art tumulo-patriotique* threatened to become a national industry. Monuments shot up like mushrooms. They came in all shapes and sizes, for all segments of society, from the 1924 national monument for the 28 operators of fun-fair stands who had died for the fatherland to the 1926 national monument for the football-players who had made the supreme sacrifice, though by then the rage was beginning to subside. Between 1921 and 1924 three or four monuments were unveiled every week from April to November. Most had no artistic quality and may be categorized as *folies de l'industrie*.[37] It is said that King Albert, whose duty it was to unveil the greater part of them, termed them *les horreurs de la guerre*. The only truly Belgian national monument – his own equestrian statue in a brick rotunda near Nieuwpoort's sluices – is fortunately of higher quality. This is also true of the only really Flemish monument, the Yser Tower in Diksmuide. Both are the work of the same sculptor, Karel Aubroeck. There the similarity ends. It was the Flemish tombstone incident which provided the decisive impulse for the erection of the tower, fifty metres tall, actually an enormously enlarged version of the humble Flemish-Celtic cross, with the letters AVV-VVK again at the top. In the crypt under the tower, eight who fell in action were interred as a symbol. A Walloon was unintentionally included since his remains could not be separated from those of two heroic Flemish brothers.[38] Apart from the mystical implications of the Celtic cross, this Flemish monument is undoubtedly the most modernistic of those in and around the Salient. The entire complex is of brick, the Flemish building-material par excellence. The block-like tower and Aubroeck's robust statuary which has been compared to that of the German sculptor, Ernst Barlach, displays expressionism. Critics would later contend, however, that all that compressed power was a prologue to the militaristic aberrations of the Flemish Movement in the 1930's.

Apart from one inscription on the tower with a clear pacifist message ('no more war') in four languages on its flanks, the Yser Tower was from the very beginning a militant Flemish symbol. The inscription, 'Here their remains as seed in the sand, hope for the harvest, oh Flanders Land', a paraphrase of *sanguis martyrum, semen christianorum*, was a manifestly positive one. Flemish grievances were aired with annual regularity during the Pilgrimage, and the discrimination against Flanders in the State of

Belgium was exposed. During the Second World War, the Yser Pilgrimage was perverted by the collaborating sector of the Flemish Movement. Later, the Yser Tower was blown up, in circumstances that have never been explained. A professor at the University of Louvain (now Leuven) proposed a new tower, 350 metres tall (taller, of course, than the Eiffel Tower), in which motorbuses could drive to the top on a spiral ramp. This was rejected as an Americanism that would profane the Yser plain. The new tower was less pretentious. The Flemish Community, having gained a measure of independence, has now proclaimed the Yser Tower a national monument, though this was contested by part of the Flemish Left. Here again one could see how the Second World War can affect the perceptions of the First World War.

There is a network of trenches close by the Yser Tower called 'de Dodengang', 'Boyau de la Mort', the Trench of Death. It was one the most hazardous Belgian positions just in front of the German bastion of Diksmuide. These First World War trenches have recently become a bone of legal contention between Francophone Belgian ministers and the radical-Flemish Committee for the Yser Pilgrimages, the former deeming the latter unfit to oversee this Belgian patriotic monument. This resembles nothing so much as a fresh vaudeville act on the theme: people and patrie, and it has not yet been played to the end.

As a result of all the post-World War Two dissension about people and *patrie*, about resistance and collaboration, the Great War has been obscured in Belgian public debate. In West Flanders, nonetheless, the Great War is still intensely present, in landscape and memory. As for the landscape, it continues to suffer, never having been fully healed; it is barer, more treeless than before 1914. It was townscaping, not landscaping which consumed the energies of the reconstruction generation. Today, moreover, the serenity of Flanders' fields is threatened by unrestrained development. Huge, factory-like pig farms have positioned themselves at the very boundaries of the cemeteries.

As for the memory of the Great War, it has never completely disappeared. It still survives in local history and war chronicles and in private, self-proclaimed museums installed in back-rooms filled with stereopticons and their sepia images from the war's cabinet of horrors. In recent decades moreover, a young generation has come to the fore, wanting to rescue the war from oblivion, to stress its local importance, especially in the Ypres Salient where they have discovered a strong affinity with the British war experience. Yet there is no patriotism involved; the preoccupation with 'fatherland' and *patrie* has lost all meaning. Ypres is now associated with other martyred cities such as Mostar and Dubrovnik. This is a new, popular pacifism that nevertheless has its roots in the war experience of previous generations in the Ypres Salient: 'Whenever you come to West-Flanders . . . /It's the war that you'll find here/And the graves of thousands and thousands of soldiers/Always someone's father always someone's child.'[39]

Notes

The author and the editor are very grateful to Mrs. Ardis Dreisbach who has translated the original Dutch text. The subtitle was inspired by the famous book of Simon Schama, *Landscape and Memory*, London 1995.

1   T.F. Bumpus, *The Cathedrals and Churches of Belgium*, London, s.d., p. 116.
2   *Oorlogsdagboeken over Ieper (1914–1915)*, vol. II, Bruges, 1977, p. 119.
3   E. Balduck, *Krijgskerkhoven en oorlogsmonumenten in het Ieperse*, Antwerp, 1966, p. 9.
4   C. Gezelle, *De dood van Yper*, Amsterdam, 1916, p. 28.
5   *Up the Line to Death. The War Poets 1914–1918*, London, 1982, p. 125. quoted by C. & K. Brants, *Velden van weleer. Reisgids naar de Eerste Wereldoorlog*, Amsterdam–Antwerp, 1995, p. 80.
6   See the painting by Briton Rivière, in *King Albert's Book. A Tribute to the Belgian King from representative Men and Women throughout the World* (The Daily Telegraph), London, 1914, p. 56.
7   E. Lüthgen, *Belgische Baudenkmäler*, Leipzig, 1915, p. 47 and p. 88.
8   C. Gezelle, *De dood van Yper*, Amsterdam, 1916, p. 10.
9   *Dictionnaire encyclopédique de géographie historique du royaume de Belgique*, vol. II, Brussels, 1897, p. 633.
10 F. Deflo, *De literaire oorlog. De Vlaamse prozaliteratuur over de Eerste Wereldoorlog*, Aartrijke, 1991, p. 61.
11 R. Baccarne, *Poelkapelle en de Eerste Wereldoorlog* in *Iepers Kwartier*, 1995, nr. 3, p. 110.
12 P. & W. Chielens, *De troost van schoonheid. De literaire Salient (Ieper 1914–1918)*, Groot-Bijgaarden, 1996, p. 17.
13 M. Vinck, *Kruiden in Vlaanderen's Woestenij ten jare O.H. 1920*, in *Biekorf*, 1921, p. 1.
14 H. Brutsaert, L. Boereboom, R. Verwilghen, *Nieuw-Vlaanderen*, Antwerp, 1923 (about the agricultural and architectural reconstruction).
15 H. Bossier, *Verwoeste Gewesten* in *Iepers Kwartier*, 1969, nr. 4, p. 120.
16 R. Baccarne, *ibidem*, pp. 111–112.
17 H. Brutsaert, L. Boereboom, R. Verwilghen, *ibidem*, p. 50.
18 R. Gobyn, *De woningnood en het probleem van de voorlopige huisvesting in België na de eerste wereldoorlog*, in *Resurgam. De Belgische wederopbouw na 1914*, Brussels, 1985, pp. 169–187.
19 R. Gobyn, *ibidem*, p. 177.
20 Jan Maes, *De tuinwijkexperimenten in het kader van de Belgische wederopbouw na 1918*, in *Resurgam*, p. 194.
21 M. Heistercamp, *Wederopbouw van Ieper na de Eerste Wereldoorlog*, thesis University Leuven, 1979, p. 36.
22 P. Uyttenhove, *Internationale inspanningen voor een modern België*, in *Resurgam*, pp. 33–68.
23 M. Heistercamp, *ibidem*, p. 16.
24 *Oorlogsdagboeken over Ieper (1914–1915)*, vol. II, Bruges, 1977, p. 125.
25 V. de Deyne, *Ypres before and after the Great War*, Liège, 1927, p. 76.
26 M. Heistercamp, *ibidem*, p. 80.
27 M. Heistercamp, *ibidem*, p. 15.
28 H. Stynen, *Opvattingen over het herstel van de hal te Ieper*, in *Wonen TABK*, March 1983, pp. 32–43.

29 Private papers of Huib Hoste (P64) (map on reconstruction) in University Archives, Catholic University Leuven.
30 H. Brutsaert, L. Boereboom, R. Verwilghen, *ibidem*, p. 80.
31 P. & W. Chielens, *ibidem*, p. 10.
32 *De Standaard*, 25 July 1927, p. 1.
33 P. & W. Chielens, *ibidem*, p. 8.
34 Luc Schepens, *In pace. Soldatenkerkhoven in Vlaanderen*, Tielt, 1974, p. 9.
35 P. Chielens, *We're Here Because We're Here. Concert Party: Passchendaele*, Renningelst, 1994, p. 41.
36 *De Standaard*, 13 februari 1997.
37 J.-M. de Busscher, *Les folies de l'industrie*, Brussels, 1981.
38 Luc Schepens, *ibidem*, p. 79.
39 Song by Willem Vermandere, see P. Chielens, *We're Here Because We're Here. Concert Party: Passchendaele*, p. 10.

Chapter 28

Passchendaele and Material Culture – the Relics of Battle.

Peter Liddle and Matthew Richardson

There are of course relics surviving from battles and warfare from the earliest times to the present day – artefacts which were present, for example, at Marathon in 490 BC, at Crécy, Pavia, Blenheim, Austerlitz, Antietam and then in our own time, at Goose Green. No one with a sensual awareness of the past can deny the tingling of his nerve ends as he sees and perhaps is even allowed to touch these fragments of the past, so strong is their power and magic. This is perhaps well exemplified by an artefact held by the museum of the South Wales Borderers at Brecon – the lid of a British Army ammunition box recovered from the battlefield of Isandhlwana in January 1879 – seemingly innocuous, but in fact one of the very same boxes with severely screwed down lids denying ammunition to the British in the face of the Zulu onslaught, and leading ultimately to the deaths of over a thousand British soldiers on that day. The intention of this paper is to examine with particular reference to the Third Battle of Ypres the lasting but changing significance of such vestiges of war, and their intrinsic interest.

There are relics of the Third Battle of Ypres to be found in most regimental museums and military collections in the country (we show but two, the shattered helmet worn by tank commander Gerry Brooks, and the mud-encrusted watch worn by Harry Oldham, among the illustrations of this book). Why is it that such objects have been retained, both from the time of the battle and then in succeeding years. What was their significance and meaning to their original owners and then how has this been passed on to and changed by later custodians?

The public image of the First World War, and of Passchendaele in particular, is of warfare at its most grim. The battle is seen as an experience beyond redemption, one of thousands of unfortunates, dead, dying and destined to die, sinking in a muddy wilderness, drowning in a flooded nightmare of desolation. The worst event in a war made up of terrible events. Even in some military circles the battle is not acknowledged as if it were to

459

have had a justifiable purpose – Cambrai is seen by some authors almost as a desperate attempt to even up the balance sheet for 1917. Why is it then that so many men keep souvenirs from such an abomination if it were really such unexpurgated misery, a misery tainted by failure at the time, later considered pointless, as well as costly to an indictable degree, and worse still, a verdict endorsed to a large extent by succeeding generations?

Before we can answer that question properly we must first of all acknowledge, as Susan Pearce has argued, in *Interpreting Objects and Collections* [1] that an object has many meanings depending on who interacts with it. Indeed its meaning will change over time as it is passed on from its original owner to succeeding generations, who do not experience the events of the First World War themselves, but instead, as history.

To the man who acquired or kept the object in question, its purpose as he looks at it or holds it, senses its familiar shape, weight and texture, even smell, is to reawaken the associated memories and feelings which he, the individual, had at the time of the object's original significance to him when he was young and strong, in the prime of his life. We may gain some insight into this by looking at the contemporary attitudes of soldiers to souvenirs; M.L.Walkington wrote in 1916 that he was sending "two bosch bayonets home. Please guard them jealously as I got them in a place where I had quite a lot of fun and excitement" [2], while Charles Carrington, in a 1918 letter to his mother, describes a medal ribbon which he took from the corpse of a German unteroffizier during the Battle of the Somme as "my favourite souvenir" [3].

In later years, the man in question – the original wearer, keeper, looter of such an item, may ask himself, "How could I have been there, and done those things? I certainly could not do them now. I did that, in the days now long gone, of my youth. What a lad I must have been! I didn't please myself as I do today, and as others seem to. I behaved as I was told that I had to, and I did what everyone else did – I did my bit. What I was doing it for – my country – was more important than my own ease, comfort and safety, and I knew that". It reminds him of a special time of comradeship, the like of which he had never seen again, of special friends lost, and of achievements gained. He knows he will never forget it and "no one can say I wasn't there because I was and I've got this to prove it". His experiences can never be taken away from him – whether it were terrible or wonderful, it made him as a man, and whatever he might have done since, this was the yardstick by which he would measure the rest of his life – and the helmet or watch would be his proof to himself, if he were to begin to forget, that it was he who was there and who did those things.

But, we must also acknowledge that as years pass by, and the last of the men who fought at Ypres passes on, these items must necessarily pass into the hands of men and women who were NOT there, and the meaning of the objects must necessarily change. As Pearce argues, the meaning of the object changes with each new person who interacts with it. This interaction is a two way process, and the meaning of the object will depend largely on the prior knowledge and the set of values which the viewer brings to it. Each generation will view the artefact through a perspective conditioned by contemporary values. Even one who is in communion with those values of the past can only **begin** to visualize what it must have been like to be there. The widow who lost her husband at Passchendaele, or the mother her son, may be reduced to a state of emotional turmoil by it. Other generations may regard it variously as a disgusting symbol of the consequences of expansionist capitalism, man's inhumanity to man, the power of propaganda and indeed the frailty of the human spirit in the face of it, or indeed, one must recognize, with complete indifference.

Nevertheless, as the years go by, an object which was part of an individual's past now becomes part of our own individual past, part of all our pasts, as it comes to symbolize the past of the society to which we belong. There is a certain universality about this, because objects which have an association with a society's past have always had value and inspired reverence, be that society a near-stone age community of bushmen in the Kalahari desert, or one of the most technologically advanced western nations.

Behind such ideas lie the disciplines of sociology and philosophy. If we were to turn to a more museological approach, argued by those engaged

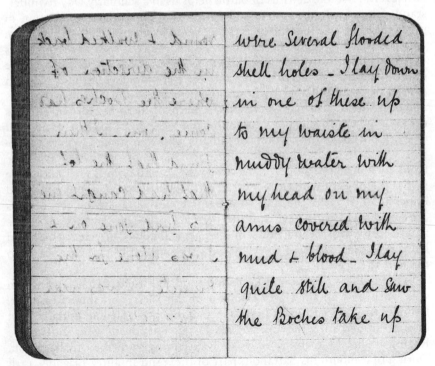

(xxxv) A page from Lieutenant Brooks' contemporary account of his experience on 22 August 1917. *(G.Brooks, Liddle Collection)*

in the curating, conservation and presentation of artefacts before the public, it would be that society's relationship with an object changes over its lifetime. To illustrate this briefly, when an object is new, it has value, but as it is used and becomes worn its value decreases until it has no value, it is effectively rubbish, and has no cultural status. Then, *if it survives*, its value over time begins to increase once more until again it has prestige. Indeed, it can be observed that even the lowliest cultural icons, domestic refuse (quite literally, rubbish) will gain status if sufficient time is allowed to elapse.

However, it can be further claimed that military objects, and some in particular, do not follow this pattern – their life cycles are cut short by an act of violence, some split second moment of human tragedy which not only concludes their useful life, but also imbues them with a potentially powerful emotional aura – we are all familiar with the bullet-holed cigarette case or wallet, which was carried in a soldier's breast pocket when he was wounded or killed.

We might also offer a historiographical approach to this subject. In respect of four particular artefacts, associated with Third Ypres, this will be done, but initially, one should understand that this approach works on two levels. First, the detritus of battle helps us in a scholarly way to understand more clearly the course and nature of a particular engagement, in much the same way that the objects recovered by an archaeologist help him to piece together the past. The clearest example of this in recent times occurred at the Custer Battlefield Memorial Park. A grass fire exposed the ground surface for the first time in over a hundred years, and through careful study of Indian arrowheads and artefacts, and US army cartridges and other items, historians were able to piece together the story of Custer's running fight with the Sioux, pinpoint the location of his last stand, and to work out rough proportions of Indians who were armed with the superior Winchester repeating rifle, all information not previously available from documentary sources[4]. However, the second point to be made here is that the object found or recovered on the battlefield is anonymous and impersonal, it lacks the link to a named individual which the objects presented here clearly have. It is this personal provenance which allows us to empathise with the individual human being involved in that conflict, and helps us to piece together an eye witness's viewpoint bringing us nearer to the human experience.

In the Liddle Collection at Leeds is a mud encrusted watch. This watch was worn by Captain Harry Oldham of the West Yorkshire Regiment. Oldham was an Old Boy of Leeds Grammar School. He had initially been commissioned into the Leeds Pals (15th Battalion West Yorkshire Regiment) but by October of 1917 was serving with the 9th Battalion. During that month his battalion, part of the 32nd Infantry Brigade, 11th (Northern) Division, was involved in fighting in the Ypres Salient, and on 5 October he wrote to his brother "out of the line again quite fit and happy. The old hun is really having a bad time and going through it"[5]. However it was during the battle of Poelcappelle four days later, as his battalion advanced astride the village, that he was buried by a shell burst, and dug out again by his men. His wrist watch, caked in mud, he retained as a souvenir of this experience. What must it have meant to him, and later to his family? A few brief moments of terror, coupled with the relief and exhilaration that he was still alive? Perhaps a reminder of the closest occasion that he ever came to death, but that he survived the experience? We may never know for certain, but for us, at the very least, as students of military history, it reminds us forcefully of the cloying ground conditions over which the infantry had to operate. The very mud of the Salient is there for us to see today, on Harry Oldham's watch.

The second object selected is the helmet of a tank commander. This helmet was worn by 2nd Lieutenant Gerry Brooks of "F" battalion, Tank Corps. While at school, Brooks' intention was to prepare for a career in law, much like his father. However, the outbreak of war interrupted his training to become a solicitor. He was initially unable to obtain a commission in the Royal West Kent Regiment because of his age. Instead he went to an officer cadet battalion at Cambridge. While there he volunteered to join what was to become the Tank Corps. All that he knew about it was that it was mechanical and involved machine-guns. After extensive training in the UK and France, his first experience of active service was to come at the Third Battle of Ypres. He went into action in command of an "F" battalion tank at zero hour on the morning of 22 August 1917, part of a four tank section, but quickly encountered swampy ground, which made turning difficult. The tanks advanced as best they could through shells bursting all around, showering them with mud and water, until they reached the British infantry, sheltering in shell holes. Brooks' contemporary account takes up the story: "The ground was now a mass of shell holes and I had the greatest difficulty in guiding the bus as the bullets were getting near to my [vision] flap ... I guided the bus in the direction of where I thought that the bullets were coming from – where there was a ruin. After a bit Arnold told me to turn as they were getting very uncomfortable behind. Soon after we had turned, the old bus stuck". Abandoning the tank, Brooks and his crew attempted to crawl back towards the British lines: "We crawled back for some way towards the infantry ... our guns got full of mud and became useless. We had to keep low as we could see the bullets hitting up the earth all around us. We got covered with mud and wet through as we had to practically swim through shell holes". Shortly afterwards, Brooks was hit in the forehead by a shell fragment, causing the damage to his helmet. For the rest of the day he feigned death, surviving a German bayonet charge in this way, until nightfall allowed him safely to return to the British lines. In this particular case we have supporting documentation which increases the power of the aura around the helmet, there are the notes quoted here from a small notebook written up while the young officer was recuperating in hospital and then there are Brooks' voiced memories responding to detailed questions on the incident many years later[6]. Together, helmet, notebook and voice do much to dissolve the years which distance us today from the hours of drama in the life of a young officer in August 1917.

As a third example, there is the mud and water-stained trench map used by Arthur Foreman, Lieutenant with the 1st/5th battalion Royal Warwickshire Regiment during the attack on Poelcappelle, 4 October 1917. In November 1971, 54 years later, Foreman recalled,

> our ultimate objective was Poelcappelle which we did not reach, we were supposed to have had tanks, but they were stuck in the mud and became a target for the enemy guns. You will note the farms marked where there were pillboxes. We i.e. what was left of us got to Winchester farm . . . the map you will note still has stains of Flanders mud on it . . . It was not nice, and I remember after reorganising we took over a trench held by the New Zealanders under the command of a Captain Parry[7]. I with what was left of my platoon was sent to arrange a take over – it was a trench in the middle of nowhere and the enemy had been registering the range of the trench, and while there Parry was buried, a shell at rear of his HQ landing bang on. We had 10 days more of this trench and the mud if I remember correctly was half way up our puttees, and when we came out to rest they cut puttees and boots off as they were caked with mud.[8]

In Foreman's case again, there was no hesitancy in putting into words the 1917 circumstance and the importance he still attached to an artefact which bound him to it as if the fifty four year gap were an insignificant passage of time.

The fourth item selected here for its association with Third Ypres tells a quite different story of personal experience of the battle. For each of the fighting men in the front line, we should not forget there were far more supporting them in rear areas, without whom those men in the front line could not be there, let alone in active operation. This is the story of one such man, D.G.McIntyre, and his tunic, worn at the time and subsequently kept over the years until his death. McIntyre was a Corporal with the 6th Battalion KOYLI in 1917, and a senior signaller in that unit. On Thursday 23 August, his battalion moved into the front line at Inverness Copse, but McIntyre was ordered to remain behind with battalion HQ. The next day, the battalion was attacked in force and suffered heavy casualties. McIntyre's diary records his reactions to the events:

> The battalion went into action. I was left behind i/c of recruit signallers at transport camp and was very thankful as the battn are going through a terrible time up Ypres way near Sanctuary Wood. Reports came down of men killed and wounded and I am wondering how Bob and Jimmy and the rest are faring. Today [Friday 24 August] I was detailed to go up with rations but was sent back at last moment. Truly I am very fortunate!

McIntyre's good fortune was not to last because he was soon to be gassed but he is a perfect example of a man who cherished a physical connection with the objects associated with an unanticipated and extraordinary life experience, that of soldiering at war. He even kept, among many other souvenirs, the eye shades protecting his gas-damaged eyes. His treasured souvenirs were cherished too by his sons who placed them with filial reverence in the archives being developed by Peter Liddle.

The last item for consideration concerns a Corporal in the Royal Engineers Cable Section, (later Royal Signals), L.H.Matthews. Matthews served on Westhoeke ridge during the Third Battle of Ypres, where his unit was in heavy fighting, and we are lucky enough to have his cabling equipment which he used at that time. For Matthews, the war was a searing experience, but it was one which drew him back to it again and again, for he was to remain a stalwart of his Old Comrades Association until his death, and kept numerous souvenirs of his experiences in France and Belgium, and later in the British Army of Occupation on the Rhine[10]. Interestingly, just as with McIntyre, there is an attractive family association here, for Matthews' daughter knew intimately the specific background of each of her father's many souvenirs. Her notes, verified from other sources, are invaluable in charting the specific importance of objects gathered at stages of a soldier's campaign service.

What can one make of these disparate items and the stories that lie behind them? Clearly, the First World War and Passchendaele were not events that these men wanted to obliterate from their conscience, they had experienced searing events which had marked them as men, yet they obviously drew strength from having tangible objects, reminders of those days, around them. Of course it must be recognized that some men kept nothing or jettisoned what they had and tried entirely to forget all association with the Great War – objects of the war rejected as of no interest, perhaps inspiring repulsion. But for those men who did keep their war souvenirs, though they may not reflect the totality of their experience, (perhaps self-protective shutters closing off some happenings), the objects symbolize a large part of the story. Today this should remind us that these relics of battle have a great deal to tell us about what life was like at the time. They speak softly and we should listen carefully, but they rarely lie and if those into whose care they pass were to be 'responsible', the personal associations linked to the object will not be lost. All that is required of us is knowledge and sensitivity to the value and fragility of these echoes from the past.

Notes

1   S. Pearce (ed.), "Interpreting Objects and Collections", London, Routledge, 1994.
2   M.L. Walkington papers, Liddle Collection, Library, University of Leeds (hereafter LC). Letter December 1916.
3   C.E. Carrington papers, LC, letter 141 (7 July 1918).

4   National Geographic, Vol 170, No. 6, December 1986 "Ghosts on the Little Bighorn", p787.
5   H. Oldham papers, LC, letter 4 October 1917.
6   G. Brooks papers, LC, mss notebook and tape recording number 424, March 1977.
7   12/2904 Captain E.C. Parry, 1st Auckland Infantry Regiment, killed in action 6 October 1917.
8   Arthur Foreman, letters to Peter H. Liddle 9 November 1971 and 18 November 1971.
9   D.G. McIntyre papers, LC, diary 23 August 1917.
10   L.H. Matthews papers, LC.

Chapter 29

Vestiges of War: Passchendaele Revisited

Paul Reed

The battlefields around the small Belgian town of Ypres (now known as Ieper) are among the most visited anywhere along the whole Western Front. As interest in the study of the war has grown, the number of visitors making the pilgrimage to the old Salient has grown with it. They come each year, on foot, by bike, in cars or coaches, to see the ground where great or even great great grandfathers fought and died. From books, videos or even family tradition, each visitor has a single word in mind. They are often confused as to its meaning, lost as to its location on a map, but they know it is close. It is a place which for them has become the microcosm of the Great War – it is Passchendaele.

The journey to Passchendaele, which lies only a few miles north east from Ypres, can be a tortuous one, and just as the men of the British Expeditionary Force slogged their way across the ridges which lay before them in 1917, there are many objectives to be reached, places to visit. This essay will look at some of them, and examine the way in which attitudes towards the battlefields have changed since the first tours began around Ypres in 1919.

Modern visitors begin at Ypres. Now it is a smart Belgian town with classy shops and expensively dressed inhabitants in fast, clean cars. Restaurants and bars surround the main square where once it was death to be seen in daylight, where, in mid 1917, the carcasses of horses killed bringing up ammunition and supplies for the offensive, rotted in the summer sunshine. The main square, or Grote Markt, is overlooked by the imposing Cloth Hall; in the fourteenth century, Ypres was the centre of the European cloth trade, and the Cloth Hall was where all the business took place. Destroyed completely during the war, it was rebuilt using the original plans – and was not properly finished until the 1960s. Today it houses the impressive Ypres Salient Museum; a vast hall with well-organized exhibits, photographs, models and maps. Illustrations of the Passchendaele battlefield adorn the walls and give rise to images which are often difficult to visualize among the verdant farmland out in the Salient itself. One particular feature of this museum is "the pieces of Ypres" – numerals from clock towers, wooden figures of Christ from local churches, sections of stained glass window – which British soldiers "souvenired" during the war. In later life either they, or their families, thought better of their plundering and in a gesture almost begging forgiveness returned their booty to the place of its origin. Apparently there are rooms of such material in the museum's reserve collection.

Beyond the Cloth Hall one finds St George's Memorial Church on the road to Poperinghe. Erected by the not inconsiderable British community in Ypres after the Great War, it was and remains a quiet place of meditation for those visiting the Ypres Salient. The walls are covered in brass plaques commemorating battalions, regiments, and divisions. Each chair is in memory of a man who " . . . fell at Passchendaele" or some other place in the Salient. As recently as the 1980's, the warden was an old soldier who had fought in the Passchendaele battle himself, but now one only meets other visitors seeking escape from fast cars, happy faces in the Groot Markt and the incessant boom of rock music in the cafés and bars.

In the past fifteen years, many features of the Ypres Salient have disappeared under the ever increasing development around the town. Life moves on, and progress has swallowed up the trench sites, particularly on the Third Ypres battlefield. Factories obscure the view towards Poelcappelle and Kitchener's Wood. New roads have obliterated old tracks and bunkers near St Jean. But one thing remains, immortal and indifferent to the changing world which grows and alters around them; the military cemeteries, those silent cities of the dead which circle Ypres like a crown of thorns.

On the Passchendaele battlefield these cemeteries take many forms. Large burial grounds with many thousands of dead are 'concentration' cemeteries, made after the war incorporating men who died in many parts of the battlefield. Smaller ones commemorate particular actions, divisions or battalions; 'comrade' cemeteries where the men buried there are united by date or unit. Due to their nature, these are often well off the beaten track; down footpaths, up cobbled roads or muddy trails. Finally there are cemeteries which began on the sites of Advanced Dressing Stations (ADS) or Casualty Clearing Stations (CCS). These can be further back from the battlefield, and are the last resting place of men who only too often succumbed to their wounds. In the approaches to Passchendaele one finds all these types of cemetery. Just outside Ypres, on the road to Boesinghe, is the frequently visited Essex Farm Cemetery. With nearly 1,200 dead from Britain, Canada and even Germany, this was a burial ground opened in 1915. Close by, on a side road that leads to the nearby Yser Canal, are the concrete bunkers that once formed part of the original Essex Farm, an Advanced Dressing Station where Canadian medic and poet, John McCrae, penned the immortal "In Flanders Fields" in 1915. Many of the graves here are of soldiers killed in the "quiet periods" between the major engagements around Ypres, but, during the Passchendaele battle, the

Dressing Station was in constant use. This cemetery is also on the tourist route, and most visitors come to see the grave of Pte V.J.Strudwick, a fifteen year old Rifle Brigade soldier. His grave is swamped with poppy crosses, and the visitors' book, common to all Commonwealth War Graves Commission cemeteries, makes mention of him frequently. Modern visitors are surprised to find such a young boy, perhaps the same age as their own children.

Further out to the east lies Buffs Road Cemetery. Named after a lane which ran from Wieltje, it was begun after the first day of Third Ypres – 31 July 1917 – and is a good example of a 'comrades' cemetery. In several rows, one finds the graves of men from the 11th, 12th and 13th (Southdowns) Battalions of the Royal Sussex Regiment who were killed in the attack on Kitchener's Wood and St. Julien. Their's was a successful operation on that day, but they still had their dead and here at Buffs Road there are forty-six of them. It is a good sample of a typical unit taking part in the battle. Of the forty-six, only ten are "originals", that is men who served with the units from their formation in 1914. With a few Lord Derby men, most of them are conscripts who joined as reinforcements after the costly Somme fighting . Their ages run from eighteen to thirty-nine, with the majority in their early twenties. Of the conscripts, less than half originate from Sussex, where the regiment recruited. Of the 'originals', most are of the rank of Lance Corporal or above, reflecting well a Passchendaele battalion commanded by the old hands, consisting mainly of young conscripts with no geographical connection to the county regiment in which they serve.

Further up the battlefield is a 'concentration' cemetery, New Irish Farm. With nearly 5,000 graves, some seventy-five percent of which are men whose identity is not known, it represents the amalgamation of dozens of smaller cemeteries which once existed on the Passchendaele battlefield. Most were small 'comrades' cemeteries, such as Fusilier Farm Cemetery at Boesinghe which contained the graves of seventeen men of the Royal Welsh Fusiliers killed in the attack on Poelcappelle. Although the Belgian Government was happy to give land in perpetuity for British cemeteries, the many small burial grounds such as Fusilier Farm were impractical to maintain and were concentrated into larger cemeteries like New Irish Farm – itself an original cemetery begun in August 1917. Here there is an infrequently visited grave, that of a man who fell in the Passchendaele fighting; Private W.W. Speight died with the Royal Welsh Fusiliers, aged sixty-two. He was the oldest soldier killed during Third Ypres, indeed, the oldest to die in the four years of fighting in the Salient.

Further behind the lines is a cemetery located close to a former Advanced Dressing Station; Canada Farm Cemetery, close to Elverdinghe. Canada Farm was the name given to the Flemish farm located nearby which housed the ADS, and the cemetery was opened in June 1917 as men died of their wounds. It remained in use through the Third Ypres battle, and, of the 907 graves here, nearly half are men from the Royal Field or Royal Horse

YPRES

INTENDING PASSENGERS FOR THE

Ypres Salient

SHOULD TRAVEL FROM

VICTORIA   (S. E. & C. R.)

The Belgian Government
TURBINE   STEAMERS

RUN IN THE SERVICES

DOVER—OSTEND

For fares and further particulars application should be made to the Superintendent of the Line (S. E. & C. R.) London Bridge Station, S.E.1 and at the Enquiry Offices, Victoria (S.E. & C.R.) or Charing Cross Stations.

Owing to the existing conditions affecting Continental Travel, intending passengers are advised to make their journey arrangements well in advance.

BY ORDER.

Artillery whose battery sites were also close by. It is often forgotten that the gunners suffered heavily during the bombardments for Passchendaele, and this cemetery certainly testifies to their losses. Casualties among senior officers are also evident here with three Lieutenant-Colonels buried in the cemetery; two are Guards officers, one of whom has his second in command and another Major buried next to him, killed the same day. In Plot 3, Row G, are nineteen graves from another aspect of the Third Battle of Ypres; these were men of the British West Indies Regiment, killed carrying shells and other ammunition across the Passchendaele battlefield. Recruited in 1914 as an infantry regiment, the War Office was reluctant to use them as front line troops and they undertook a labour rôle throughout their service on the Western Front. Few visitors to the main battle sites in the Salient realize that any black soldiers died at Passchendaele in the service of King and Empire.

Back on the battlefield, the approaches to Passchendaele village itself are guarded by one last cemetery; Tyne Cot. The largest British military cemetery in the world, with 11,976 graves, a veritable forest of graves. Tyne Cot is where all visitors come – the altar of the Ypres Salient. From King George V in the 1920's, to school parties today, it has been a centre piece of battlefield pilgrimage. Here, with the rows and rows of seemingly endless graves, people's prejudices about Third Ypres are either overturned or reinforced. Once, visitors to the cemetery had a different perspective. These were the relatives of the men buried here. The visitors' books recording their opinions have long since gone, but they left their mark on the headstones themselves in the form of the inscriptions which the next of kin could request be added, on payment of a fee. If you were to sample such inscriptions in any one plot at Tyne Cot Cemetery, you will note the post-war language of remembrance, clearly religious in its tone, with reference to King, Empire and Sacrifice. Families had to make some sense of their loss with inscriptions like "How sleep the brave" and "The noblest death a man could die, fighting for good". Others marked regret or sought peace with "Sadly missed", "Only son" and "After conflict rest". Comparing such epitaphs with the present-day comments left in the visitors' book, you will see such phrases as "At what price?", "Never again" and "Why?". They speak a different language, and characterize the popular approach not only to Third Ypres but the First World War as a whole. Today, these visitors see sacrifice as, "Such a waste"; the word *duty* is lost or fails to register. A second world war, loss of Empire and any number of "wars in peace" have made the modern world more reluctant to commit itself to conflict and the consequences of conflict.

In Tyne Cot Cemetery itself there are several unique features, quite apart

---

Opposite page
(xxxvi) An early indication [from 1920] of the need to make special provision for the surge of pilgrims to the Salient. *(From The Pilgrim's Guide to the Ypres Salient)*

from its size. Graves from every phase of the four years of fighting at Ypres can be found here. There are three German pillboxes in the confines of the boundary wall, and one just outside it, which formed the original site on trench maps known as Tyne Cot. One now doubles as the foundations of the Cross of Sacrifice, and from it one can see all the way back into Ypres on a clear day. Even Kemmel Hill is visible from here. At last the significance of these low ridges becomes apparent, but more often visitors are overwhelmed by the ranks of white headstones laid out before them – like a division on parade. But they are not all in regular lines. Behind the Cross of Sacrifice is a group of scattered graves marking the original burials; the pillbox was used as an aid post by the Canadians, and then there are the units holding the line at Passchendaele during the winter of 1917/18, and these graves are from their losses. The thousands of other burials were added after the war when smaller cemeteries were closed and isolated graves moved into Tyne Cot. Among them are three Passchendaele Victoria Cross winners; two Australians and a Canadian[1]. One of them, Captain C.S.Jeffries of the 34th Battalion AIF, is frequently visited, not least for the inscription on his grave, "On fame's eternal camping ground, their silent tents are spread."

The low wall behind is the Tyne Cot Memorial commemorating those who died at Passchendaele from mid-August 1917 to the conclusion of the battle. Men killed in the German Spring offensives of 1918 are also found here – in total, some 33,707 British, 1,179 New Zealanders and one Newfoundlander. Again there are three Victoria Cross winners, two of them from the Passchendaele battle; Lieutenant-Colonel P.E.Bent VC DSO of the 9th Leicesters and Corporal W.Clamp VC of the 6th Yorkshires[2]. A father and son are found under the King's Own Yorkshire Light Infantry panel. Lieutenant-Colonel H.Moorhouse DSO of the 1/4th Battalion was killed near the Ravebeek on 9 October 1917 and his son, Captain R.W.Moorhouse MC, a company commander in the same battalion, was killed in the same attack. The names reel on, the impression is, endlessly: these the men who, through popular myth, simply disappeared in the mud of Passchendaele. However, students of Third Ypres will know how the battlefield was strewn with corpses, and how either the shells buried the dead or made post-war identification of them impossible. The "missing" is often a misnomer which confuses modern visitors; a great many of those commemorated on Tyne Cot Memorial are buried in any number of cemeteries under an unknown soldier's headstone which simply reads "Known unto God".

But visitors do not come to the Ypres Salient just to see cemeteries. Here and there are the few remaining sites from the old battlefield. Most woods have trenches in, but at Sanctuary Wood they are preserved in a 'Trench Museum'. Lacking are the sandbags, duckboards and firesteps, but among the macabre arrangement of animal bones and stunted original trees, the aura of death is occasionally in the air. Not far away is 'Frontline Hooge'; the old mine craters and shell holes in the grounds of Hooge Château have been preserved and are open to the public. A section of trench line is currently under excavation which has unearthed items as diverse as army socks, mess tins and bayonets. At the bottom of one trench, the original duckboarding was found. Only a few hundred yards from 'Frontline Hooge' is the Hooge Crater Museum. Built inside the old Hooge chapel, it contains a staggering array of military uniforms and hardware. Many of the weapons and equipment are displayed in classic museum fashion; large cases full of rifles, grenades, bayonets, helmets, personal gear, gas masks. However, the centre-pieces of the collection are life-size dioramas in which well-made and realistic mannequins are convincingly dressed in the attire of the day; there are dugout scenes, trench settings and a moving case with a typical Passchendaele Tommy standing by the cross of a fallen comrade. In the background, classical music is played, the walls are lined with photographs of the old Salient, and a video screen runs a sequence of visions from the Passchendaele battle.

The most obvious reminders of Third Ypres are the German pillboxes; the bunkers constructed for various uses – artillery positions, observation posts, headquarters and machine-gun fortresses. These concrete structures are as numerous as the cemeteries, despite the efforts of post-war farmers to blow them up; such fruitless exercises were given up years ago. Along with the mud, they epitomize the Passchendaele battle as nothing else does. Indeed, despite the experience of the Hindenburg Line at Arras in the Spring of 1917, this was the first time in any battle of the war that they had been encountered in such numbers. British soldiers were killed or wounded attacking them, or turned them to their own use as headquarters or aid posts, and some were even awarded gallantry medals for capturing them. One post-war guide felt that,

> There can be no finer memorial to the indomitable spirit and magnificent fighting qualities of the British infantry soldier than these historic relics, and future generations may well marvel at the prowess and determination of those men who accomplished such feats of arms in effecting their capture.[3]

Pillboxes are particularly numerous around St Julien. On the road into the village is Van Heule Farm, a well-sited defence work looking back towards the British lines, which became a battalion headquarters when captured by units of the 39th Division on 31 July 1917. Later the same day, an unlucky shell came through a back door and over thirty officers and men were killed or wounded; in one battalion the whole headquarters section was all but wiped out. The well-known Alberta pillbox, originally built inside a ruined farm building, guards the approaches to the Steenbeek river north of St Julien. Nearby is a very impressive piece of concrete; a long massive shelter used as a headquarters by the Germans. Beyond St Julien, just east of the cross-roads where the moving Canadian "brooding soldier" memorial stands, is the location of Triangle Farm and Maison du Hibou. These pillboxes resisted several attacks by the infantry, and

Triangle Farm was only put out of action by the appearance of a British tank. It was one of the few occasions in the whole Third Ypres battle when the use of tanks could be seen to have a definite success; quite often they stuck in the mud and became virtual pillboxes themselves.

In Zonnebeke is perhaps the finest museum on the Passchendaele front. Located in the old Château – itself scene of fierce fighting – the 'Streekmuseum' at first gives the appearance of just being concerned with local history; the displays open with the prehistory of the Zonnebeke-Becelaere-Passchendaele area and abound with broken pots and tiles. However, this leads into a chronological history of the war in this part of the Salient. Each year or phase of the fighting is explained with the usual uniforms and hardware, but, rarely seen, here the illustrative material far outshadows the physical objects. There are colour reproductions of British and German trench maps. Private photographs from German sources of Zonnebeke and Passchendaele show the villages before the punishing Third Ypres bombardments. Superb panoramic oblique aerial photographs, taken by German pilots over the Zonnebeke area in 1917, add an impression of the battlefield not conveyed by any other means.

Just outside Zonnebeke is another battlefield site – Bremen Redoubt. This was a circular defence work constructed by the Germans in 1916, and captured during the October 1917 operations. Below the redoubt was a network of tunnels and dugouts, many later used by Australian troops as rest areas before moving up to the line nearer Passchendaele itself. After the war, the Belgian Government ruled that the entrances to such underground complexes should be filled in, as without the constant attention of working parties, they were beginning to become dangerous. Within a generation, they were forgotten by the locals. By the early 1980s, the sight of Bremen Redoubt was part of a large brickworks where the ground was continually being turned over. During one such excavation, earth rapidly gave way to the bulldozer and a wooden ladder was observed. Vertically, it led down a deep shaft. The workers followed it into a large complex of rooms and passageways. It was the last remains of the Bremen Redoubt.

Today, the dugout has been preserved and the entrances made secure by concrete. Electric light assists the visitor down the original access stairs, once connected to a front line trench. The whole dugout is supported with original timbers, which line the walls and floor. Bunk beds, which once had chicken-wire matting, indicate that the quarters were designed to sleep a unit of roughly platoon strength. There is a separate ante-room by the main stairs; possibly for officers or NCOs. The ladder which originally led the workmen into the shelter can still be seen and there is evidence that at some time it continued down to an even lower level. It is an impressive and unique location. Nowhere else on the whole Western Front is there a dugout in what is virtually its original condition; usually the passage of time rots the timber, or the roof caves in. On visiting it for the first time, one can only be mindful of Wilfred Owen's poem, "The Sentry", and the feeling that,

"What murk of air remained stank old and sour
With . . . the smell of men who'd lived there years"[4]

For here at Bremen Redoubt the *smell* of the First World War is certainly still in evidence.

Passchendaele is preordained as the ultimate destination for all visitors to the Salient. Like all villages in the area, it has a new Flemish title – Passendale. The hissing "s" sound of its pronunciation making the name even more sinister. But today's Passchendaele is better known for its local cheese production and yearly cheese festival than being the final objective in one of the most controversial battles of the First World War. On the western outskirts, the Canadian memorial at Crest Farm overlooks the valley through which men of the CEF made their final slog on the ruins of the village in November 1917. Further down are Waterfields and Marsh Bottoms; locations on wartime maps which only hint at the conditions which prevailed here. Like Ypres, Passchendaele has been completely rebuilt and the locals are used to visitors trying to make some sense of their mental pictures of shell holes and misery with what is now a pleasant

PRIVATE VISITS
— TO —
Battlefields & War-Graves
— IN —
FRANCE AND BELGIUM

First-class Travel & Hotels & Private Cars.   From 10 Gns. inclusive.

APPLY :

CAPTAIN R. S. P. POYNTZ,
(B.A. Oxon, B.E.F. 1914, and 1915—1918.)

12 REGENT STREET, LONDON, S.W.
Gerrard 8389.

(xxxvii) Need and opportunity, in several senses, meeting in this advertisement for specially tailored tours. *(From The Pilgrim's Guide to the Ypres Salient)*

Flemish village. Only a small memorial erected in the main square by the Western Front Association in the 1980s, pays testimony to what happened in 1917. Usually, visitors are disappointed with what they find here: the name has penetrated their consciousness to such an extent that they might have expected something more impressive; but Passchendaele is a picture of normality perhaps little different from where they themselves live. What they had hoped to find, might be difficult to articulate, but it is not Passendale.

Guidebooks are the means by which most visitors, past and present, have found their way round the Passchendaele battlefield. The first appeared as early as 1919 when the Michelin Tyre Company published "Ypres and the Battles of Ypres"[5]. It portrayed an image of a battlefield still very much in ruin, with directions round the battle sites like " . . . keep along the road, leaving on the left the ruins of the church, and . . . the remains of the Château"[6]. In 1920, "The Pilgrim's Guide to the Ypres Salient" was published on behalf of Toc H. As we have seen with the inscriptions on headstones in Tyne Cot Cemetery, the early years of battlefield visiting were characterised with religious association. Visitors in those days were known as "pilgrims", and an introduction to the book, written by Noel Mellish VC (himself a former army chaplain), told the reader that, " . . . yours is a pilgrimage in memory of those who passed this way. You will tread reverently, for it is Holy Ground."[7]

The pilgrimage aspect continued with "The Immortal Salient" in 1925, when even then there was talk of "chivalry, knighthood, heroism, self-sacrifice . . . a region consecrated forever to Britain by the valour of her sons."[8] "The Battle Book of Ypres"[9] in 1927 began at last to put some of the places into their historical setting via access to war diaries and unpublished sources, but from then there is a gap of over half a century before the *real* guides to the Salient began to appear. Today with access to archives and papers never available to the "pilgrims" of the 1920s, modern authors have begun to look at specific areas within the Ypres Salient in much greater detail. The best of these guides have been in the "Battleground Europe" series published by Pen & Sword. Nigel Cave's "Sanctuary Wood and Hooge"[10] covers many Third Ypres sites, and another, entitled "Passchendaele", is to follow in 1997.

Organized tours to the battlefields today are many and varied, and fifty seater coaches bearing the logo of any number of tour companies can often be seen outside Tyne Cot or parked in the square at Ypres. Such tours, like the printed guides, began as early as 1919, when unemployed ex-officers widely advertised their services to the thousands of relatives who were flooding in to the old battlefields in search of a loved one's grave. Advertisements for many of these early guides appear in the publications quoted above. One mentions the services of Captain R.S.P.Poyntz, "BEF 1914 & 1915–18", who arranged private visits to the battlefields and wargraves for ten guineas. Elsewhere the "Wipers Auto Service", run entirely by ex-servicemen, advertised private touring cars for hire. They catered for a demand which existed for at least twenty years after the war, and then died off by the time Europe stood on the threshold of another. Long gone are the ex-officers of the BEF, but an indication of today's interest in the battlefields is that these tours have returned to Ypres. A one and a half hour "Taxi Tour 14–18" run by a local taxi company, follows a thirty-five kilometre route covering a limited number of battlesites. Fifteen minutes are spent at Tyne Cot. Another company, "Salient Tours", is run by an Englishman who, twice a day, takes groups round in a specially converted minibus on " . . . an in-depth trip through the whole Salient". For some people, a day looking at cemeteries and memorials is more than enough; for others such visits awaken an interest in the First World War which is part of an ever-growing national fascination with the period.

On any tour, all roads eventually turn the pilgrim or the tourist, or the simply curious, back into Ypres and to the Menin Gate, that huge arch guarding the eastern walls of the town. On it are engraved the names of nearly 55,000 officers and men who were killed in the Ypres Salient from 1914 until midnight on 15 August 1917 and who have no known grave[11]. The missing from Australia and Canada who died at Third Ypres are also commemorated here. Siegfried Sassoon felt it a "sepulchre of crime"[12], but Field Marshal Plumer, who unveiled the memorial in July 1927, comforted the thousands of next of kin assembled for the ceremony with, "They are not missing – they are here". This was the aim of the Imperial War Graves Commission between the wars – to commemorate the legions of men who had often simply disappeared. The names on the Menin Gate represent the myriad of faces which made up the British forces in the Salient. There are senior officers, battalion commanders, winners of the Victoria Cross, and on the other extreme, men executed for desertion. Black soldiers from Africa and India are found. The name of every regiment of the British Army is represented on these walls. Some families have two, even three, sons commemorated here. One cannot but reflect that these men, had they lived, would have made some contribution, no matter how large or small, to the post-war world. How many lost endeavours? Lost hopes and promises?

Of them all, one name might be selected, today forgotten even in his native land. Talbot Mercier Papineau was a Major in the Princess Patricia's Canadian Light Infantry when he was killed near Passchendaele on 30 October 1917. From a French Canadian family, his grandfather had fought against the British. Although his profession was that of a solicitor, Talbot Papineau was actively involved in Canadian politics and was a protégé of the then Prime Minister. Volunteering in 1914, he was awarded the Military Cross at Ypres in 1915 and was subsequently transferred to the staff, a job he hated. In mid–1917, he finally managed to get a posting back to his beloved battalion, and was killed only a few weeks later. With his death Canada had lost a prospective leader. Given his French-Canadian connections, who can know what route the post-war history of Canada would have followed had he been spared?

Each night at eight o'clock, Papineau and the others named here are commemorated in a ceremony which dates back to those early pilgrims of the 1920s. The local Fire Brigade sounds the Last Post, with bugles specially tuned to the resonance of the archway. It has continued ever since, uninterrupted, save for the years of occupation in the Second World War. Once, thousands came to hear it, then for a long time only a mere handful. Today the numbers yearly increase, and even the most hardy of travellers cannot fail to be moved by the experience. Henry Williamson felt that, "Wipers exists in the memory only"[13] . Each night at Ypres that memory is revived.

Notes

1   The three VC winners buried in Tyne Cot Cemetery are: Captain C.S. Jeffries, 34th Battalion AIF, VC earned posthumously 12 October 1917; Sergeant L. McGee, 40th Battalion AIF, VC earned 4 October 1917, killed in action 13 October 1917; Private J.P. Robertson, 27th Battalion Canadian Infantry, posthumously earned 6 November 1917.

2   The two Third Ypres VC winners on the Tyne Cot Memorial are: Lieutenant-Colonel P.E. Bent, 9th Leicesters, posthumously earned 1 October 1917; Corporal W. Clamp, 6th Yorkshire Regiment, posthumously earned 9 October 1917.

3   Thurlow DSO, Colonel E.G.L. *The Pill-Boxes of Flanders*, (Ivor, Nicolson & Watson Ltd. 1933), p. 38.

4   Owen, Wilfred, "The Sentry", in Stallworthy, J. (ed.), *The Poems of Wilfred Owen*, (Chatto & Windus Ltd., 1990), p. 165.

5   Anon. *Ypres and the Battles of Ypres*, (Michelin Tyre Co., 1919).

6   ibid, p. 66.

7   Anon., *The Pilgrim's Guide to the Ypres Salient*, (Herbert Reach Ltd. for Talbot House c. 1920), p. vii.

8   Brice, B. & Pultney, Lt-Gen Sir W., *The Immortal Salient*, (John Murray, 1925), p. 54.

9   Brice, B., *The Battle Book of Ypres*, (John Murray, 1927).

10   Cave, N., *Battleground Europe; Hooge and Sanctuary Wood*, (Leo Cooper, 1993).

11   The Menin Gate was originally designed as the memorial to the missing for all the battles of Ypres, however, during its construction, it was realised that it would not offer sufficient wall-space for all the names. In consequence it was decided that all British and New Zealand missing after 15 August, an arbitrarily chosen date, would be commemorated on the walls of Tyne Cot cemetery, Passchendaele.

12   Sassoon, S., "On Passing the New Menin Gate", in Hart-Davies, R. (ed.), *Siegfried Sassoon: The War Poems*, (Faber & Faber, 1993), p. 153.

13   Williamson, H., *The Wet Flanders Plain*, (Faber & Faber, 1929), p. 58.

Chapter 30

Passchendaele: Verdicts, Past and Present

Brian Bond

In recent years the battle of the Somme, and particularly its first disastrous day – 1 July 1916 – has become the popular reference point for Britons of the 'horror' of the First World War, epitomizing notions of mud, blood and futility resulting from military incompetence. But it was not always so. Until the fiftieth anniversaries in the 1960's which stimulated a renewed surge of interest in the First World War, that doubtful distinction was bestowed on Flanders and especially Ypres. This was more appropriate since the main British effort was concentrated there from October 1914, culminating in the third Ypres offensive in 1917 which was fought in more hellish conditions, gained less ground and was harder to justify politically than the Somme. The final phase of this offensive produced the perfect name for critics of British generalship – Passchendaele (Passion dale) – an infernal battlescape in which thousands of British soldiers met their sacrificial deaths.

Paradoxically, despite its dreadful reputation, the campaign received comparatively few extensive studies by historians. Basil Liddell Hart, C.R.M.F. Cruttwell, Cyril Falls and others devoted only brief chapters in their general histories, and the relevant volume of the Official History did not appear until 1948. Hence the surprising but justified sub-title of Robin Prior and Trevor Wilson's book, *Passchendaele* – 'the untold story'.[1]

In this brief survey, only a few of the most influential or controversial authors will be discussed. Probably the most influential, due not only to his numerous publications but also his indispensable archive and assistance to other, younger historians, has been BH (later Sir Basil) Liddell Hart. From the 1920's on, he became increasingly critical of key aspects of the campaign, notably Haig's generalship, the choice of theatre and tactics. In reacting to post-war apologists he was especially severe on alleged justifications for launching the offensive in late summer when the best weather was over and persisting with it until November.

Thus, in *A History of The World War, 1914–1918*, he called Passchendaele 'a synonym for military failure – a name black-bordered in

479

the records of the British Army'.[2] The powers of endurance shown by the combatants and improved executive leadership in the later stages had been 'eclipsed in memory by the futility of the purpose and result'. In Liddell Hart's opinion, Haig believed optimistically that he could defeat the German armies in Flanders with minimal Allied assistance, and he disregarded the evidence produced by his meteorological advisers. Hence he doomed the offensive to failure before it had even begun through the long and intensive preparatory bombardment which destroyed the intricate drainage system. In concluding his ten-page account, Liddell Hart described the campaign as a 'pitiful tragedy' which had brought the British forces to the verge of exhaustion. In order to absorb the enemy's attention and draw in his reserves, Haig had chosen the spot most difficult for himself and least vital to his enemy.

The same year (1934), witnessed the appearance of C.R.M.F. Cruttwell's *A History Of The Great War* which has long remained in print and generally deserved its academic reputation as a scholarly work by an ex-combatant and Oxford don published by the University's Clarendon Press.[3] Cruttwell was less restrained than usual in the eight pages he devoted to the 1917 campaign in Flanders, partly due perhaps to confidential information received from Sir James Edmonds. All the combatants on either side, he wrote, regarded it as the culmination of horror. Strategically 'nothing whatever had been effected'; indeed the final British position was even more precarious than at the start. Cruttwell was not convinced that German morale was more deeply or permanently affected than the British. British casualties were higher and it was significant they had lost three times as many officers.

Cyril Falls, another former officer and later a professor at Oxford, by contrast, was more sympathetic to Haig's generalship and the British Army's performance in the campaign. His judicious history, *The First World War*, was not published until 1960, but originated in the inter-war period when Falls had been an official historian.[4] Calling his six page chapter 'The Mud and Blood of Third Ypres', Falls argued that the delay between the success at Messines and the opening of the offensive had been crucial. He wrote approvingly of Plumer's battles in September before the onset of the appalling autumn rains. Falls robustly challenged the notion that the offensive was 'mere blind bashing': on the contrary, he asserted, tactics were seldom more skilful. British artillery, with the co-operation of the Royal Flying Corps, had repeatedly frustrated enemy counter-attacks; while the infantry had also displayed tactical skills in tackling the formidable German defences-in-depth. Falls even defended Haig's persistence in the offensive after the weather had broken. At the start, Falls stated, the Germans often out-fought the British, whereas towards the end the latter could count on winning if they could get to close quarters. Despite the hellish conditions in the final phase, Falls concluded on a positive note which would sound discordant in the more radical 1960's. The battle 'called for nerve and endurance, which were not wanting'.

In contrast to these short accounts in general histories of the war, Leon Wolff's *In Flanders Fields* (1958), as one of the most striking volumes in a new wave of angry young authors 'rediscovering' the First World War, focused attention firmly on the events of 1917.[5] Wolff, who had served as an officer in the American Air Force in the Second World War, strove to provide a rounded account of the Flanders campaign from both sides and at all levels, but he was passionately convinced that the First World War was excessively wasteful and futile, and his critical view of British military and political leadership is evident. Whether access to official documents, then still closed to researchers, would have seriously modified his judgements, may be doubted.

There was, he concluded, no argument about the worthlessness of the few miles of muddy ground captured. Haig clung to his irrational hope of a German collapse and a British breakthrough until the offensive came to an ignominious end: only later did he and his supporters invoke the arguments for a calculated strategy of attrition and the need to shield the French Army from enemy attack. Wolff was rightly sceptical about the accuracy of comparative casualty figures, but he did allow that the Germans could afford their losses less than the Allies and that 'pragmatically the campaign hurt them more than the British'. After an incisive and generally fair review of the historiography, he concluded that no overall verdict was possible: 'human judgement is inadequate to categorize its ultimate meaning, if, indeed it has any meaning within the larger surge of life'. Ignoring the great political issues at stake, Wolff concluded that the war had 'meant nothing, solved nothing and proved nothing', and in doing so had killed eight and a half million men.

Liddell Hart kept the main controversies of the Third Ypres campaign high on the agenda with his combative article 'The Basic Truths of Passchendaele' in the *RUSI Journal* (November 1959).[6] Responding to a previous article and letters on the subject, Liddell Hart was chiefly concerned to demolish myths which were again flourishing due to uncritical acceptance of Edmonds' official history of the campaign, and of the post-1918 justifications by Haig's defenders. Liddell Hart assailed two myths in particular: first he convincingly showed that Haig had not been under overt pressure from French generals to begin or persist in the offensive. Second, he proved that Edmonds' method of calculating comparative casualty statistics was unreliable and, furthermore, that whatever the method adopted, British casualties clearly exceeded the enemy's, though his own figures were necessarily somewhat speculative. The numerous letters published in the two succeeding issues of the *Journal* revealed fundamental differences of approach between those of Michael Howard and Denis Richards who criticized specific failings in Haig and Edmonds, and the more numerous 'conservatives' such as John North and Brigadiers Jack and Bidwell who preferred to dwell on the Army's achievements in adverse conditions and the victory won under Haig's command in 1918.

481

The sixtieth anniversary of the campaign was notable for the publication of John Terraine's *The Road to Passchendaele: The Flanders Offensive of 1917*.[7] Reviewers reasonably took issue with the tendentious sub-title 'A Study in Inevitability' and the author's attempt to let history 'speak for itself' by relying heavily on an assemblage of quotations from a wide range of sources as distinct from a reasoned argument. In his brief concluding remarks, Terraine asserted that the offensive was justified in strategic terms: in contrast to the Somme, the Germans could not afford to retreat because of their logistical dependency on the Flanders rail network with its crucial junction at Roulers, only a few miles from Passchendaele. John Bourne endorses Terraine's reasoning in the present volume.[8] Similarly, Terraine argues that the tactical problems, though great, were not insurmountable. Critics, in his view, have dwelt too exclusively on British difficulties, on the false assumption that it was much easier for the German defenders. Paddy Griffith's contribution to this volume could be cited in support of Terraine's position.[9] However, the latter cannot be accused of taking an entirely uncritical stance. He allows, for example, that it was a serious command error to permit a delay of nearly eight weeks between the success at Messines and the launch of the main offensive on 31 July, exacerbated by Haig's decision to shift the main initial thrust from Plumer's Second to Gough's Fifth Army. Terraine reflects that this was Haig's most serious mistake because it affected both the timing and the method or style of operations: It should have always been Plumer's battle with Gough in support, not vice versa.

On the critical issue of John Charteris' role in encouraging Haig's optimistic faith that German morale was being so undermined by attrition that it could be completely broken, Terraine takes a compromise standpoint. Charteris and his chief were not so wide of the mark as other historians (such as Falls) alleged: in the final stages, the Germans *did* come close to cracking but the British were too exhausted themselves to clinch the matter. Werth, in the present volume, makes no effort to deny the seriousness of the condition to which the German Army had been reduced. This comes close to the consensus view that both sides fought themselves to a standstill and both had suffered a comparable slump in morale. In opposition to Terraine's positive interpretation of the effects of attrition on German morale in the autumn of 1917, it may be pointed out that they attacked vigorously and effectively after the initial setback at Cambrai on 20 November and, more generally, that the German spirits would be lifted by success on the Eastern Front. There, the imminent collapse of Russia would signify a momentous victory – and the transfer of up to fifty divisions to the west.

Terraine seems on safer ground in challenging the implications of the story (which originated with Edmonds in 1927 and was publicized by Liddell Hart) that Haig's Chief of Staff, Kiggell, on visiting the battlefield after the campaign ended in 1917, had burst into tears and exclaimed 'Good God, did we send men to fight in that?'[10] Whatever were to be the truth in the Kiggell affair, Terraine shows that Haig and G.H.Q. were well-informed about the dreadful conditions in October and November. Whether that knowledge should have caused Haig to halt the offensive earlier, remains as debatable as ever. His contemporary diary entries do not suggest that he agonised over the issue.

Finally, Terraine accepts that the campaign had a tragic quality and endorses Sir Philip Gibbs' opinion, albeit with the qualification that it was ephemeral: 'For the first time the British Army lost its spirit of optimism, and there was a sense of deadly depression among many officers and men with whom I came in touch'.[11]

Most recently, Prior and Wilson's *Passchendaele* (1996), referred to earlier, goes a fair way to substantiate their sub-title's claim to be telling 'the untold story'. In particular, they have made admirable use of official documents and other archival sources, especially on the British side, to enhance our understanding of the tactical development of the battle through its various phases. They are equally good on the command and logistical aspects, but perhaps neither as original nor persuasive as they claim in linking political and military aspects – a difficult objective anyway in precisely two-hundred pages of text.

As recognised authorities on the development of British tactics in the First World War, Prior and Wilson must be taken seriously in concluding that, given appropriate conditions, Haig's forces had good prospects of delivering a series of hammer blows to the enemy without suffering unacceptable casualties. But the essential conditions were good weather and strictly limited objectives. They convincingly rebut the notion that the tragic course and outcome of the campaign were in any sense 'inevitable'. Haig was unfortunate with the weather but, from the outset, he aimed at (and would not modify) grandiose territorial goals which were most unlikely to be achieved, given the obstacles to mobility imposed by the terrain and the depth of the German defensive system. In this over-ambitious strategy he was, for the most part, supported by his Army commanders and not seriously challenged by his prime minister and the War Cabinet. Consequently, their two main and related criticisms are that either Haig or Lloyd George could have halted the offensive at several points but opted to let it continue; and, operationally, there was no switch to a doctrine of limited 'bite and hold' offensives. Even Plumer is included in this indictment. Finally, as Prior and Wilson emphasise, the fighting did not end in any decisive way but merely petered out in conditions which have bequeathed a nightmarish image to the whole campaign. The British success in occupying the Passchendaele ridge ironically left them in an exposed and vulnerable position with greatly weakened reserves and the devastated battle area just behind their front line. The scene was set for the German breakthrough in March 1918.

It remains for me to review some of the main issues which have been raised in the historiography and by contributors to the present volume. There is, first, general agreement that the delay between 7 June and 31 July was to prove fatal to the prospects of a breakthrough to the Belgian coast. The delay was due in part to Haig's decision to give the leading role to Gough's Fifth Army on the left flank and later, in July, to General Anthoine's request for more time to prepare the French First Army on Gough's left. These lost weeks of fine weather naturally seemed more serious in retrospect in view of the unexpectedly wet August, but that is a separate issue.

Second, Haig and his supporters were later, after 1918, to stress the British obligation to launch, and continue, the offensive to shield the French armies which had suffered widespread mutinies in the Spring. This may have been one of Haig's concerns in planning the offensive, but his diaries and correspondence show that he was confident that his armies could secure a breakthrough and achieve decisive results even without French assistance. More to the point, there is no evidence that either Pétain or Foch urged him to continue the offensive to distract the enemy from attacking on their front. Quite the contrary, both expressed pessimism regarding Haig's ambitious plan. According to Sir Henry Wilson's diary, on 2 June 1917, Foch referred sarcastically to a "duck's march through the inundations to Ostend and Zeebrugge", and called Haig's plan 'futile, fantastic and dangerous'.[12]

Third, critics of the Passchendaele campaign, such as Liddell Hart, have always stressed Haig's obstinacy in launching the offensive despite the clear warning of his meteorological advisers that weather statistics, based on the records of eighty years, showed that he could not hope for more than a fortnight of fine weather. In his meticulous examination of this often-repeated charge, John Hussey shows that it is unjustified.[13] Haig was advised that the late summer weather in Flanders would be generally favourable to British plans. The effects of a normal rainfall would be offset by sun and wind. Hussey shows that August 1917 was exceptionally wet to the extent that the low-lying ground was unable to dry out. The popular notion of the campaign as being fought from first to last in heavy rain and mud has always avoided the awkward fact that Plumer's successful battles in September were fought in conditions of heat and dust. Less easy to counter, however, is the criticism that even with the normal rainfall in August, the long and intensive preparatory bombardment would destroy the intricate drainage system and so raise serious obstacles to a rapid advance, particularly in the low-lying sector where Gough was given ambitious objectives.

Fourth, as already noted, Prior and Wilson, in their recent study, are critical of Haig's style of command, particularly his failure to impress on his senior commanders that, after initial setbacks, limited advances on a 'bite and hold' basis were the only solution in view of the terrain and the depth of the German defences. Even John Terraine is critical of Haig's decision to allot the main attacking role to Gough and then, in late August, to switch the priority to Plumer. In this volume, Ian Beckett makes some interesting remarks on Haig's inconsistent exercise of his role as commander-in-chief, interfering in operational matters on some occasions while failing to assert his authority on others.[14] Beckett suggests that Haig added to Gough's command problems by failing to clarify precisely what was required of his Army. It is a serious charge that, after failing to achieve the ambitious objectives on the first day 'Haig appears to have counselled a more step-by-step approach, but this was never made clear to Gough and, equally Haig's wish that Gough seize the whole of the dominating Gheluvelt Plateau was another message that was not impressed sufficiently clearly . . .' Some contributors raise the wider issue of how much Haig learnt from these command and operational problems, but the answers lie beyond the scope of this volume.

A fifth issue of controversy which has concerned every student of the campaign from 1917 to the present is whether the offensive could and should have been called off at some point, perhaps in early August when it was already clear that a rapid advance towards the coast, thus permitting the intended amphibious landings, would not be possible; and certainly before the hellish phase in later October and November which has come to represent the whole operation in the popular imagination.

Prior and Wilson contend that either Lloyd George or Haig could have stopped the offensive at various points and censure both for not so doing. The Prime Minister certainly had the constitutional authority to intervene and, if necessary, dismiss the Commander-in-Chief. But in practice he had to be sure of the support of the War Cabinet and the other members of the Government and upon this he knew he could not rely. When, for example, the Prime Minister contemplated intervening in September, he was persuaded to desist by Milner lest the soldiers (ie., Haig and Robertson) 'defend their position by engaging the sympathies of the Opposition and the Press'.[15] In October, Lloyd George was advised that if he forced Robertson to resign then Cecil, Balfour, Carson and Curzon would also go and so bring down the Government. It should be added that, after his failed gamble in the Spring of 1917 in backing Nivelle against his own generals, Lloyd George simply lacked confidence in his own judgement in a direct confrontation with Haig; hence his furtive consultation with Generals French and Wilson during the Autumn of 1917. Haig's expectation of imminent victory through a German collapse remained remarkably buoyant throughout the campaign, even though the final weeks were devoted to capturing the Passchendaele ridge to deny the enemy its advantages as a defensive line from which they could overlook the Ypres salient. When the campaign ended Haig began to contemplate a renewed offensive in the Spring of 1918.

An important omission from many of the more bitter indictments of the campaign, including Leon Wolff's, is any sense of tactical development, or what is now termed 'the learning curve', on the British side. As we have noted, Cyril Falls was remarkably positive on this aspect, and even Prior and Wilson allow that there were signs of improvement at the tactical level though in their view the operational doctrine of 'bite and hold' was not consistently inculcated. In his forthright and combative contribution, Paddy Griffiths pushes further the notion of British tactical skills and increasing superiority on the battlefield.[16] While giving due stress to the marshy conditions which rendered tanks almost useless and seriously handicapped the artillery in advancing, Griffith argues that the enemy's ingenious defensive system – making the most of concrete pill boxes and, later, of dispersed machine-gun teams – was gradually worn down. In his opinion, the British 'fought and won Third Ypres by virtue of the dominance of their artillery and the endurance of their infantry'. By the time the advance became bogged down in November, the British Army had developed an effective system of offensive tactics against which the Germans had no answer. As he sombrely concludes, however, the events of March 1918 showed that British defensive tactics were less well developed.

The last controversy to be discussed is the crucial issue of casualty statistics. Since Haig had manifestly failed to achieve his strategic objectives in 1917, and since the German breakthrough in March 1918 suggested that their morale had not been broken earlier, the most convincing defence of 'Passchendaele' (other than its debatable success in shielding the French), came to be that attrition succeeded, in the long term, in depriving Germany of irreplaceable military manpower.

Unfortunately, to clinch this assertion, accurate comparative casualty statistics were needed and these have never been established to achieve consensus. This can be quickly demonstrated by reference to the different figures quoted in the publications discussed above and in this volume. Three factors account for these quite wide discrepancies and suggest that precise statistics may never be forthcoming. First the casualty records, especially on the German side, are incomplete. Second, the opposing sides did not compile casualty statistics on a common basis or with a view to settling historical arguments: British and German records in 1917 relate to different periods and different sectors of the front. Third, and most problematic of all, the Germans did not include in their casualty lists lightly wounded men who soon returned to active duty whereas the British did. In compiling the British official history of the Somme campaign, the chief historian, Sir James Edmonds, decided that 30 per cent should be added to German casualty statistics to offset this discrepancy. Critics, such as Liddell Hart, argued that this was an unconvincing attempt to conceal that British casualties in 1916 has been far in excess of those suffered by the enemy. Careful researches by Dr. M.J. Williams in the mid–1960's,[17] proved that Edmonds' methods were unreliable and in effect amounted to 'cooking the books', but the different criteria for lightly wounded casualties remained intractable. In his book on Passchendaele discussed above, John Terraine devotes an appended Note to casualties in the Third Battle of Ypres and concludes that it is reasonable to add 20 per cent to the German official figures, thus giving a total of 260,400 for the period up to 31 December which was roughly equal to British and French casualties during the Third Ypres campaign. In this volume, Ian Beckett gives a British total of 275,000 (including the operation at Messines) and suggests 220,000 for German casualties as against 400,000 claimed by the British official history.[18] It is possible that painstaking research on 1917 records, comparable to M.J. Williams' work on 1916, would produce more authoritative totals, or at least reduce the discrepancies between the extreme totals produced for either side. But, in the present state of our knowledge, and given the problems noted earlier, we can only conclude that in the gruesome compilation of casualty statistics it cannot be said that either side gained a clear advantage in the Third Ypres campaign.[19]

While no historian or commentator on either side has described Passchendaele as a 'famous victory', we may still conclude by posing little Peterkin's disturbing question after the battle of Blenheim; namely, 'what good came of it at last?' In the short term, the Germans had been pushed back and suffered heavy losses; their morale was badly shaken. Yet within a few months, with reinforcements from the eastern front and employing new infiltration tactics, Ludendorff's March 1918 offensive achieved a dramatic breakthrough and came close to his aim of winning the war before American intervention became effective. Thereafter, historians have the difficult task of weighing Germany's self-inflicted losses – through persisting in a failed offensive – and growing domestic war-weariness, with positive improvements in the Allied command system, operational direction and tactical superiority.

In trying to assess the ultimate significance of Passchendaele in this wider historical context, the historian is driven back towards Leon Wolff's scepticism regarding the individual's capacity to interpret the 'blank and imperturbable face of history'. Nevertheless one may sharply dissent from his conclusion that this was merely a dreadful episode in a meaningless war. It was a remarkable and decidedly worthwhile achievement for the Allies to win the war in the West in 1918 after the failures in that theatre and in Italy in 1917 and the crushing defeat of Russia. But the precise contribution of the Passchendaele campaign to the eventual victory must remain speculative. The very wide-ranging contents of this volume should serve to revive the long historical debate and will certainly raise new issues concerning a most controversial yet seldom studied campaign.

Notes

1   Robin Prior & Trevor Wilson *Passchendaele: the Untold Story* (London, 1996).
2   B.H. Liddell Hart *A History of the World War 1914–1918* (London, 1934) pp423–434.
3   C.R.M.F. Cruttwell *A History of the Great War 1914–1918* (Oxford, 1964) pp436–443.
4   Cyril Falls *The First World War* (London, 1960) pp280–286.
5   Leon Wolff *In Flanders Fields: the 1917 Campaign* (New York, pbk 1963) 388–413.
6   B.H. Liddell Hart 'The Basic Truths of Passchendaele' *R.U.S.I. Journal*

November 1959 pp433–439 and correspondence pp503–505. See also *R.U.S.I. Journals* February 1960 pp105–111 and May 1960 pp283–285.

7   John Terraine *The Road to Passchendaele: The Flanders Offensive of 1917* (London, 1977) pp336–347 and see A.J.P. Taylor's review 'Back on their pedestals' in *The Observer* 1 January 1978.

8   Bourne p.12.

9   Griffith. chapter 5.

10 Liddell Hart Centre for Military Archives LH Mss 11/1927/17 'Note on conversation with Edmonds', 7 October 1927.

11 Gibbs quoted by Terraine *The Road to Passchendaele* p341.

12 C.E. Callwell *Field-Marshal Sir Henry Wilson. His Life and Diaries.* (London, 1927) Volume I p359.

13 Hussey see chapter 10.

14 Beckett pp. 108, 109.

15 David French *The Strategy of the Lloyd George Coalition 1916–1918* (Oxford, 1995) pp130–132, 148–149, 158.

16 Griffith pp. 65 et seq.

17 M.J. Williams 'Thirty Per Cent: a Study in Casualty Statistics' *R.U.S.I. Journal* February 1964 pp51–55 and 'The Treatment of the German Losses on the Somme in the British Official History', *R.U.S.I. Journal* February 1966 pp69–74. See also Brian Bond 'The First World War' in C.L. Mowat (ed) *The New Cambridge Modern History* Vol XII Cambridge, 1968) pp197–199.

18 Beckett p. 112.

19 Brian Bond 'Passchendaele' in *The Listener* 4 January 1968 pp12–13.

Bibliography

This bibliography is not designed to be comprehensive, but seeks to embrace every aspect of battle examined within the book. The intention, throughout, has been to include books and articles which are readily available, but there are necessarily some exceptions.

GENERAL

Blake, R.: *The Unknown Prime Minister: the Life and Times of Andrew Bonar Law*, London, Eyre & Spottiswoode, 1955.

Blake, R. (ed): *The Private Papers of Douglas Haig*, London, Eyre & Spottiswoode, 1952

Bond, B. & Robbins, S. (eds): *Lord Moyne, Staff Officer: The Diaries of Lord Moyne 1914- 1918*, London, Leo Cooper, 1987.

Bonham-Carter, V.: *Soldier True: the Life and Times of Sir William Robertson, 1860–1933*, London, Muller, 1963.

Boraston, J. H. (ed): *Sir Douglas Haig's Despatches*, London, J. M. Dent, 1919.

Bourne, J.: *Britain and the Great War, 1914–1918*, London, Edward Arnold, 1989.

Cecil, H. & Liddle, P. H. (eds): *Facing Armageddon*, London, Leo Cooper/Pen & Sword, 1996.

Charteris, Brigadier-General J.: *At GHQ*, London, Cassell, 1931.

Charteris, Brigadier-General J.: *Field Marshal Earl Haig*, London, Cassell, 1929.

Cooper, Duff: *Haig* (2 vols), London, Faber & Faber, 1935.

Davidson, Major-General Sir J.: *Haig: Master of the Field*, London, Peter Nevill, 1953.

Dewar, G. A. B. & Boraston, Lt-Col J. H.: *Sir Douglas Haig's Command: December 19, 1915 to November 11, 1918* (2 vols), London, Constable, 1922.

Edmonds, Brigadier-General Sir James E.: *The Official History Of Military*

Operations, France and Belgium, 1917, Volume II, London, H.M.S.O., 1948.

Farrar-Hockley, A. H.: *Goughie: The Life of General Sir Hubert Gough*, London, Hart-Davis/MacGibbon, 1975.

French, D.: *The Strategy Of The Lloyd George Coalition 1916–1918*, Oxford, Clarendon Press, 1995.

Gollin, A. M.: *Proconsul in Politics: a Study of Lord Milner in Opposition and in Power*, New York, Macmillan, 1964.

Hancock, W. K. & Van der Poel, J. (eds): *Selection From The Smuts Papers*, 7 vols, Cambridge, Cambridge University Press, 1966–73.

Hankey, Lord: *The Supreme Command, 1914–1918*, 2 vols, London, Allen & Unwin, 1961.

Ingham, K.: *Jan Christian Smuts*, London, Weidenfeld & Nicholson, 1986.

Liddle, P. H. (ed): *Home Fires And Foreign Fields*, London, Brassey's, 1985.

Liddle, P. H.: *The Soldier's War 1914–1918*, London, Arms & Armour, 1988.

Lloyd George, D.: *War Memoirs*, London, Odhams Press, 1938 [2 vol edition].

McCarthy, C.: *The Third Ypres, Passchendaele, The Day-by-Day Account*, London, Arms and Armour, 1995.

Marshall-Cornwall, General Sir J.: *Haig as Military Commander*, London, Batsford, 1973.

Offer, A.: *The First World War: An Agrarian Interpretation*, Oxford, Clarendon Press, 1989.

Patterson, A. T.: *Jellicoe*, London, Macmillan, 1969.

Powell, G.: *Plumer: The Soldier's General*, London, Leo Cooper, 1990.

Prior, R. & Wilson, T.: *Passchendaele, the Untold Story*, London, Yale University Press, 1996.

Prior, R. & Wilson, T.: *Command on the Western Front: The Military Career of Sir Henry Rawlinson, 1914–18*, Oxford/Cambridge, Mass., Blackwell, 1992.

Pugh, M.: *Lloyd George*, London, Longman, 1988.

Riddell, Lord: *Lord Riddell's War Diary, 1914–1918*, London, Ivor Nicholson & Watson, 1933.

Robbins, K.: *The First World War*, Oxford & New York, OUP, 1993.

Robertson, General Sir W.: *Soldiers And Statesmen, 1914–1918*, London, Cassell, 1926.

Rose, K.: *Curzon*, London, Weidenfeld & Nicholson, 1969.

Roskill, S.: *Hankey: Man of Secrets*, London, Collins, 1970.

Sixsmith, E. K. G.: *Douglas Haig*, London, Weidenfeld & Nicholson, 1976.

Taylor, A. J. P.: *Beaverbrook*, London, Hamish-Hamilton, 1972.

Taylor, A. J. P.: *Lloyd George: A Diary by Frances Stevenson*, London, Hutchinson, 1971.

Terraine, J.: *Douglas Haig: The Educated Soldier*, London, Hutchinson, 1963.

Terraine, J.: *The Road To Passchendaele: The Flanders Offensive Of 1917*, London, Leo Cooper, 1977.

Terraine, J.: *White Heat: The New warfare 1914–18*, London, Sidgwick & Jackson, 1982.

Travers, T.: *The Killing Ground*, London, Allen and Unwin, 1987.

Travers, T.: *How The War Was Won*, London, Routledge, 1992.

Turner, J.: *British Politics and the Great War: Coalition and Conflict 1915–1918*, London & New Haven, Connecticut, Yale University Press, 1992.

Wilson, T.: *The Myriad Faces of War*, Cambridge, Polity Press, 1986.

Winter, J. M.: *The Great War and the British People*, London, MacMillan, 1985.

Woodward, D.: *Lloyd George And The Generals*, Newark, University of Delaware Press, 1983.

Woodward, D. (ed): *The Military Correspondence of Field-Marshal Sir William Robertson 1915–1918*, London, Army Records Office/Bodley Head, 1989.

GERMAN

[a selection of books in English and German; for further references see Chapters Four and Twenty]

Asprey, R. B.: *The German High Command At War*, New York, Morrow, 1991.

Groener, W.: *Lebenserinnerungen. Jugend Generalstab Weltkrieg.* Stuttgart, 1957.

Hindenburg, P. von: *Aus meinem Leben*, Leipzig, 1920.

Kielmansegg, Peter Graf: *Deutschland und der Erste Weltkrieg*, Stuttgart, 1980.

Kitchen, M.: *The Silent Dictatorship. The Politics of the German High Command under Hindenburg and Ludendorff, 1916–1918*, London, 1976.

Lossberg, F. von: *Meine Tätigkeit im Weltkriege 1914–1918*, Berlin, 1939.

Ludendorff, E.: *My War Memories, 1914–1918*, London, Hutchinson, 1919.

Lupfer, T. L.: *The Dynamics of Doctrine: The Changes in German Tactical Doctrine during the First World War*, Fort Leavenworth, 1981.

Michalka, W. (ed), *Der Erste Weltkrieg. Wirkung, Wahrnehmung, Analyse*, München 1994.

Müller, G. A. von: *Regierte der Kaiser? Kriegstagebücher, Aufzeichnungen und Briefe des Chefs des Marine-Kabinetts Admiral Georg Alexander von Müller 1914–1918. Herausgegeben von Walter Görlitz*, Berlin/Frankfurt, 1959.

Militärgeschichtliches Forschungsamt (Eds): *deutsche Militärgeschichte in sechs Bänden 1648- 1939*.Band V, VI. Begründet von Hans Meier-Welcker. München, 1983.

Kronprinz Rupprecht von Bayern: *Mein Kriegstagebuch*. 3 Bände. München, 1929.

Thaer, A. von: *Generalstabsdienst an der Front und in der O.H.L.*, Göttingen, 1958.

Der Weltkrieg 1914–1918. Herausgegeben vom Reichsarchiv, Reichskriegsministerium und Oberkommando des Heeres. 14 Bände, Berlin, 1925–1956.

TACTICS

Bailey, J. B. A.: *The First World War And The Birth of Modern Warfare*, Strategic And Combat Studies Institute, the Staff College, Camberley, *Occasional Paper No. 22*, 1996.

Bidwell, S. & Graham, D.: *Firepower: British Army Weapons and Theories of War 1904–1905*, London, Allen and Unwin, 1982.

Griffith, P.: *Battle Tactics Of The Western Front: The British Army's Art of Attack*, London and New Haven, Connecticut, Yale University Press, 1994.

Griffith, P. (ed): *British Fighting Methods in the Great War*, London, Frank Cass, 1996.

Wynne, G. C.: *The development of the German defensive battle in 1917 and its influence on British defence tactics*, Army Quarterly, 1937, Vol 34 (April, pp 15–32; July pp 248–266) and Vol 35 (October pp 14-)

THE MARITIME DIMENSION AND THE PLANNED AMPHIBIOUS ASSAULT

Bacon, Admiral Sir R.: *The Dover Patrol*, London, Hutchinson & Co, 1929.

Callwell, C. E.: *Military Operations and Maritime Preponderance: Their Relations and Interdependence* [ed. C. S. Gray], Annapolis, Maryland, 1996.

Corbett, J. S.: *Some Principles Of Maritime Strategy* [ed. E. Grove], Annapolis, Maryland, 1988.

Dobbie, Colonel W.: *The Operations of the First Division on the Belgian Coast in 1917*, Royal Engineers Journal, 38, No. 2, June 1924.

Halpern, P. G.: *A Naval History of World War I*, London, UCL Press, 1994.

Liddle, P. H.: *The Sailor's War 1914–1918*, Poole, Blandford Press, 1985.

Marder, A. J.: *From Dreadnought to Scapa Flow*, Vol 4, *Years of Crisis*, London, Oxford University Press, 1969.

Newbolt, H.: *Official History, Naval Operations*, Vol IV, London, Longmans, 1934.

Patterson, A. T.: *Tyrwhitt of the Harwich Force*, London, Military Book Society, 1973.

Wiest, A.: *Passchendaele And The Royal Navy*, London & New York, Greenwood Press, 1995.

FRENCH
[a selection of books in English and French; for further references see Chapter Seven]

Duffour Daille, Hellot, Tournes, Généraux: *Histoire de la Guerre mondiale*, Paris, Payot, 1934–36, 4 volumes.

Fridenson, P.: *The French Home Front*, Providence, RI & Oxford, Berg, 1992.

Gambiez, Général F. & Suire, Colonel N.: *Histoire de la Première Guerre mondiale*, Paris, Fayard, 1968, 2 volumes.

Miquel, P.: *La grande Guerre*, Paris, Fayard, 1983.

Pedroncini, G.: *Le Haute Commandement, la conduite de la guerre (mai 1917-novembre 1918)* Paris, 1971.

Philpott, W.: *Anglo-French Relations and Strategy on the Western Front*, London, MacMillan, 1996.

Renouvin, P.: *La Première Guerre mondiale*, Paris, P.U.F., 1987.

Sumner, I.: *The French Army 1914–18*, London, Osprey, 1995.

CARTOGRAPHY AND ARTILLERY SURVEY
Bragg, Dowson and Hemming: *Artillery Survey in the First World War*, London, Field Survey Association, 1971.

Chasseaud, P.: *Artillery's Astrologers - A History of British Field Survey on the Western Front 1914–18*, Lewes, Mapbooks, 1997.

Chasseaud, P.: *Topography of Armageddon, A British Trench Map Atlas of the Western Front 1914–18*, Lewes, Mapbooks, 1991.

Innes, J.: *Flash Spotters and Sound Rangers*, London, George Allen & Unwin, 1935.

Jack, E. M.: *Report on Survey on the Western Front*, London, War Office, 1920.

Winterbotham, H. St J. L.: *British Survey on the Western Front*, Geographical Journal, 1919.

WEATHER
Cotton, H.: *Memoirs of a Meteorologist, Meteorological Magazine*, vols 108, 109 in six parts, 1979'80. [Editorial note: Cotton papers and recollections are held in the Liddle Collection, Brotherton Library, University of Leeds].

Gold, E.: *Weather in War, Army Quarterly*, Vol. 47, October 1943.

Griffiths, P.: *The Effects of Weather Conditions on the Third Battle of Ypres, 1917, University of Birmingham School of Geography*, Working Paper No. 51, 1989.

THE AERIAL DIMENSION
Balfour, H.: *An Airman Marches*, London, Greenhill Books, 1985.

Barker, R.: *The Royal Flying Corps in France: from Bloody April 1917 to Final Victory*, London Constable 1995.

Boyle, A.: *Trenchard, Man of Vision*, London, Collins, 1962.

Bruce, J. M.: *Aeroplanes of the Royal Flying Corps*, London, Putnam, 1982.

Cole, C.: *McCudden VC*, London, William Kimber, 1967.

Douglas, Lord: *Years of Combat*, London, Collins, 1963.

Henshaw, T.: *The Sky their Battlefield*, London, Grub Street, 1995.

Imrie, A.: *Pictorial History of the German Army Air Service 1914–18*, London, Ian Allan, 1971.

Jefford, Wing Commander C. G.: *RAF Squadrons*, Shrewsbury, Airlife, 1988.

Jones, H. A.: *Official History: The War In The Air*, Vol. IV, O.U.P., 1934.

Kilduff, P.: Richthofen: *Beyond the Legend of the Red Baron*, New York, John Wiley, 1993.

Kilduff, P. (ed & trans): *Germany's Last Knight of the Air, The Memoirs of Major Carl Degelow*, London, William Kimber, 1979.

Lee, A. G.: *No Parachute*, London, Jarrolds, 1968.

Liddle, P. H.: *The Airmen's War 1914–1918*, Poole, Blandford, 1987.

McCudden, J. T. B.: *Five Years in the Royal Flying Corps*, London, Aeroplane and General Publishing Co Ltd, 1918.

MacMillan, N.: *Into The Blue*, London, Duckworth, 1929 [Revised edit, London, Jarrolds, 1969].

'McScotch', *Fighter Pilot*, London, Greenhill Books, 1985.

Mead, P.: *The Eye in the Air*, London, H.M.S.O., 1983.

MEDICINE AND THE WAR

Barrett, J. W.: *A Vision Of The Possible: What The R.A.M.C. Might Become*, London, H. K. Lewis, 1919.

Bayly, H. W.: *Triple Challenge: War, Whirligigs And Windmills: A Doctor's Memoirs*, London, Hutchinson, 1935.

Begg, R. C.: *Surgery on Trestles*, Norwich, Jarrold, 1967.

Bennett, J. D. C.: *Medical Advances Consequent To The Great War, 1914–1918*, Journal Of The Royal Society Of Medicine, 83, 1990, pp. 738–742.

Bosanquet, N.: *Health Systems in Khaki: The British and American Medical Experience*, in Cecil, H. & Liddle, P. H. (eds): *Facing Armageddon*, London, Leo Cooper/Pen & Sword, 1996.

Brown, T.: *Shell Shock in the Canadian Expeditionary Force 1914–1918: Canadian Psychiatry in the Great War*, in Roland, C. G. (ed): *Health, Disease and Medicine*, Toronto, The Hannah Institute, 1984.

Butler, A. G.: *The Australian Army Medical Services in the War of 1914–1918*, 3 vols, Melbourne, Australian War Memorial, 1940–1943.

Carberry, A. D.: *The New Zealand Army Medical Service in the Great War*, Auckland, Whitcombe & Tombs, 1924.

494

Colebrooke, L.: *Almroth Wright: Provocative Doctor And Thinker*, London Heinemann, 1954.

Cooter, R.: *Medicine and the goodness of war*, Canadian Bulletin of Medical History, 1990, 7, pp. 147–159.

Cooter, R.: *Surgery and Society in Peace and War: Orthopaedics and the Organization of Modern Medicine, 1880–1948*, London, MacMillan, 1993.

Cushing, H.: *From A Surgeon's Journal, 1915–1918*, London, Constable, 1936.

Dearden, H.: *Medicine And Duty: A War Diary*, London, Heinemann, 1940.

Gabriel, R. A. & Metz, K. S.: *A History of Military Medicine, Vol II: From the Renaissance Through Modern Times*, New York & London, Greenwood Press, 1992.

Gosse, P.: *Memoirs Of A Camp Follower: Adventures And Impressions Of A Doctor In The Great War*, London, Longmans, 1934.

Herringham, Sir W.: *A Physician In France*, London, Edward Arnold, 1919.

Hurst, Sir A.: *Medical Diseases Of War*, Baltimore, Williams & Welkins, 1944.

MacDonald, L.: *The Roses Of No Man's Land*, Harmondsworth, Penguin, 1993.

McLaughlin, R.: *The Royal Army Medical Corps*, London, Leo Cooper, 1972.

MacPhail, Sir A.: *Official History of the Canadian Forces in the Great War, 1914–1919: The Medical Services*, Ottawa, F. A. Acland, 1925.

MacPherson, W. G. (ed): *Official History Of The War - Medical Services - Diseases Of The War* (2 volumes), London, H.M.S.O., 1923.

MacPherson, W. G. (ed): *Official History Of The War - Medical Services - General History* (4 volumes), London, H.M.S.O., 1921–1923.

MacPherson, W. G. (ed): *Official History Of The War - Medical Services - Hygiene Of The War* (2 volumes), London, H.M.S.O., 1923.

MacPherson, W. G. (ed): *Official History Of The War - Medical Services - Surgery Of The War* (2 volumes), London, H.M.S.O., 1923.

Mitchell, T. J. & Smith, G. M.: *Official History Of The War - Medical Services - Casualties And Medical Statistics*, London, H.M.S.O., 1931.

Myers, C. S.: *Shell Shock In France, 1914–1918*, Cambridge, C.U.P., 1940.

Rorie, D.: *A Medico's Luck In The War*, Aberdeen, Milne & Hutchison, 1929.

Whitehead, I. R.: *Not a Doctor's Work? The Role of the British Regimental Medical Officer in the Field*, in Cecil, H. & Liddle, P. H. (eds): *Facing Armageddon*, London, Leo Cooper/Pen & Sword, 1996.

THE BRITISH DIVISIONS

Anon: *History of the 50th Infantry Brigade 1914–1919*, London, 1919.

Anon: *War History of the 1st/4th Battalion, the Loyal North Lancashire Regiment*, Preston, Toulmin, 1921.

Atkinson, C.: *The Seventh Division 1914–1918*, London, Murray, 1927.

Atteridge, A.: *History of the 17th (Northern) Division*, Glasgow, Maclehose, 1929.

Bewsher, F.: *The History of the 51st (Highland) Division 1914–1918*, Edinburgh, Blackwood, 1921.

Boraston, J. & Bax, C.: *The Eighth Division in War 1914–1918*, London, Medici Society, 1926.

Bradbridge, E.: *Record of the 59th (North Midlands) Division 1915–1918*, Chesterfield, Edmunds, 1928.

Coop, J.: *The Story of the 55th (West Lancashire) Division 1916–1919*, Liverpool, Daily Post, 1919.

Croft, W.: *Three Years With The Ninth Division*, London, Murray, 1919.

Dawson, H.: *The History of the 35th Division in the Great War*, London, Sifton Praed, 1927.

Denman, T.: *Ireland's Unknown Soldiers: The 16th (Irish) Division in the Great War*, Dublin, Irish Academic Press, 1992.

Ewing, J.: *History of the 9th (Scottish) Division 1914–1919*, London, Murray, 1921.

Falls, C.: *The History of the 36th (Ulster) Division*, London, M'Caw, Stevenson & Orr, 1922.

Headlam, C.: *History of the Guards Division in the Great War*, 2 vols, London, Murray, 1924.

Hussey, A. & Inman, D.: *The Fifth Division in the Great War*, London, Nisbet, 1921.

Hutchison, G.: *The 33rd Division in France and Flanders 1915–1919*, London, Waterloo, 1921.

Inglefield, V: *History of the 20th (Light) Division*, London, Nisbet, 1921.

Jerrold, D.: *The Royal Naval Division*, London, Hutchinson, 1923.

Kincaid-Smith, M.: *The 25th Division in France and Flanders*, London, Harrison, 1920.

Maude, A.: *The 47th (London) Division 1914–1919*, London, Stapleton, 1922.

Mitchinson, K. W.: *Gentlemen and Officers: The Impact and Experience of War on a Territorial Regiment 1914–1918*, London, Imperial War Museum, 1995.

Munby, J.: *A. History of the 38th Welsh Division*, London, Rees, 1920.

Nichols, G.: *The 18th Division in the Great War*, London, Blackwood, 1922.

Ross, R.: *The Fifty-first in France*, London, Hodder & Stoughton, 1918.

Sandilands, H.: *The 23rd Division 1914–1919*, London, Blackwood, 1925.

Shakespear, J.: *The Thirty Fourth Division 1915–1919*, London, Witherby, 1921.

Stanley, F.: *The History of the 89th Brigade 1914–1918*, Liverpool, Daily Post, 1919.

Stewart, J. & Buchan, J.: *The Fifteenth (Scottish) Division 1914–1919*, London, Blackwood, 1926.

Ward, C.: *The 56th Division (1st London Territirial Division)*, London, Murray, 1921.

Wyrall, E.: *History of the 19th Division 1914–1918*, London, Arnold, 1932.

Wyrall, E.: *The History of the 50th Division 1914–1919*, London, Lund Humphries, 1939.

THE AUSTRALIANS

Bean, C. E. W.: *The Australian Imperial Force in France* [first published 1933], vol IV, *The Official History of Australia in the War of 1914–1918*, 12 vols, Sydney, Angus & Robertson, 1943.

Bean, C. E. W.: *Anzac to Amiens* [first published 1946], Canberra, Australian War Memorial, 1983.

Beaumont, J. (ed): *Australia's War, 1914–18*, St Leonards, NSW, Allen & Unwin, 1995.

Belford, W. C.: *Legs Eleven: Being the Story of the 11th Battalion AIF in the Great War of 1914–1918*, Perth, Imperial Printing Co., 1940.

Chataway, T. P.: *History of the 15th Battalion, Australian Imperial Force: War of 1914–1918*, Brisbane, William Brooks, 1948.

Colliver, Captain E. J. & Richardson, Lieutenant B. H.: *The Forty Third: The Story and Official History of the 43rd Battalion AIF*, Adelaide, Rigby, 1920.

Dean, A. & Gutteridge, E. W.: *The Seventh Battalion AIF: A Résumé of the Activities of the Seventh Battalion in the Great war, 1914–1918*, Melbourne, Dean & Gutteridge, 1933.

Freeman, R. R.: *Hurcombe's Hungry Half Hundred: A Memorial History of the 50th AIF, 1916–1919*, Adelaide, Peacock Publications, 1991.

Gammage, B.: *The Broken Years: Australian Soldiers in the Great War*, Ringwood Vic & Harmondsworth, Penguin, 1990.

Horner, D.: *The Gunners: A History of Australian Artillery*, Sydney, Allen & Unwin, 1995.

Pederson, P.: *Monash as Military Commander*, Melbourne, Melbourne University Press, 1985.

Winter, D.: *Making the Legend: The War Writings of C. E. W. Bean*, St Lucia, Queensland University Press, 1992.

THE CANADIANS

Brown, I. M.: *Not Glamorous, But Effective: The Canadian Corps and the Set-piece Attack, 1917–1918, Journal of Military History*, 58/2, July 1994, pp. 424 & 425.

Dancocks, D. G.: *Legacy of Valour: The Canadians at Passchendaele*, Edmonton, Hurtig Publishers, 1986.

Corrigall, E. J.: *The History of the Twentieth Canadian Battalion (Central Ontario regiment) Canadian Expeditionary Force in the Great War*, Toronto, Stony & Cox, 1935.

Hyatt, M. J.: *General Sir Arthur Currie: A Military Biography*, Toronto, Toronto University Press, 1987.

Morton, D.: *When Your Number's Up: The Canadian Soldier in the First World War*, Toronto, Random House of Canada, 1993.

Morton, D. & Granatstein, J. L.: *Marching to Armageddon: Canadians and the Great War, 1914- 1919*, Toronto, Lester & Orpen Dennys, 1989.

Murray, W. W.: *The History of the 2nd Canadian Battalion (East Ontario Regiment) Canadian Expeditionary Force in the Great War, 1914–1919*, Ottawa, Mortimer/Historical Committee, 2nd Battalion, CEF, 1947.

Nicholson, G. W. L.: *Canadian Expeditionary Force: Official History of the Canadian Army in the First World War*, Ottawa, Queen's Printer, 1962.

Rawling, B.: *Surviving Trench Warfare: Technology and the Canadian Corps, 1914–1918*, Toronto, University of Toronto Press, 1987.

Stewart, W.: *Attack Doctrine in the Canadian Corps*, MA thesis, University of New Brunswick, 1982.

Swettenham, J.: *McNaughton: Volume I, 1887–1939*, Toronto, Ryerson Press, 1968.

Swettenham, J.: *To Seize The Victory: The Canadian Corps in World War I*, Toronto, Ryerson Press, 1965.

THE NEW ZEALANDERS

Austin, Lt-Col W. S.: *The Official History of the New Zealand Rifle Brigade*, Wellington, Watkins, 1924.

Baker, P.: *King and Country Call: New Zealanders, Conscription and the Great War*, Auckland, Auckland University Press, 1988.

Byrne, Lt. J. R.: *New Zealand Artillery in the Field 1914–1918*, Auckland, Whitcombe & Tombs, 1922.

Phillips, J., Boyack, N. & Malone, E. P. (eds): *The Great Adventure*, Allen & Unwin, Wellington, 1988.

Pugsley, C.: *On the Fringe of Hell: New Zealanders and Military Discipline in the First World War*, Auckland, Hodder & Stoughton, 1991.

Stewart, Colonel H.: *The New Zealand Division*, Christchurch, Whitcombe & Tombs, 1921.

THE SOUTH AFRICANS

Buchan, J.: *The History of the South African Forces in France*, Edinburgh, Nelson, 1920.

Digby, P. K. A.: *Pyramids and Poppies: The 1st South African Infantry Brigade in Libya, France and Flanders 1915–1919*, Rivonia, Ashanti, 1993.

Official History - Union of South Africa and the Great War 1914–1918, Pretoria, Government Printer, 1924.

UNIFORMS, EQUIPMENT, WEAPONS

Chappell, M.: *The British Soldier In The 20th Century: 1, Service Dress 1902–1940*, Dorchester, Wessex Military Publishing, 1987.

Chappell, M.: *The British Soldier In The 20th Century: 4, Light Machine Guns*, Dorchester, Wessex Military Publishing, 1988.

Chappell, M.: *British Infantry Equipments 1908–1980*, London, Osprey, 1980.

Chappell, M.: *British Battle Insignia (1): 1914–18*, London, Osprey, 1986.

Mitchell, F.: *Tank Warfare: the story of the tanks in the Great War*, London, Nelson & sons, 1933.

Pegler, M.: *The British Tank Crew's War 1916–1918*, Military Illustrated, No. 40, September 1991.

Scott, P. T.: *Mr Stokes's Educated Drainpipe, The Great War*, Vol. 2, No. 3, May 1990, pp 88–94.

Skennerton, I. D.: *The British Service Lee: Lee Metford & Lee Enfield Service Rifles & Carbines 1880–1980*, London, Arms & Armour Press, 1982.

Stern, A. G.: *Tanks 1914–1918: The Logbook of a Pioneer*, Hodder and Stoughton, 1919.

Westlake, R.: *British Territorial Units 1914–1918*, London, Osprey, 1991.

MORALE AND ARMY DISCIPLINE

Ashworth, T.: *Trench warfare 1914–1918: The Live And Let Live System*, London, MacMillan, 1980.

Babington, A.: *For The Sake Of Example: Capital Courts-Martial 1914–1920*, London, Leo Cooper, 1993 "Revised" Edition.

Baynes, J.: *Morale: A Study Of Men And Courage: The Second Scottish Rifles at the Battle of Neuve Chapelle*, 1915, London, Cassell, 1967 [London, Leo Cooper, 1987, revised edn.].

Childs, Major-General Sir W.: *Episodes And Reflections*, Cassell, 1930.

Cornwallis-West, G. F. M.: *Edwardian Hey-Days*, London, Putnam, 1930.

Dallas, G. & Gill, D.: *The Unknown Army [Mutinies in the British Army in World War I]*, London, Verso, 1985.

Field Punishment: *Some Correspondence And Notes, Stand To! The Journal Of The Western Front Association*, No. 13, Spring, 1985, pp. 40–44.

Fuller, J. G.: *Troop Morale and Popular Culture in the British and Dominion Armies 1914-1918*, Oxford, Clarendon Press, 1990.

James, L.: *Mutiny In The British And Commonwealth Forces, 1797–1956*, London, Buchan & Enright, 1987.

Macready, General Sir N.: *Annals of an Active Life*, London, Hutchinson, 1924 [2 vols].

Moran, Lord: *The Anatomy Of Courage*, London, Constable, 1945.

Putkowski, J. & Sykes, J.: *Shot at Dawn; executions in World War One by authority of the British Army Act*, Barnsley, Leo Cooper, 1992.

Richardson, Major-General F. M.: *Fighting Spirit: A Study Of Psychological Factors In War*, London, Leo Cooper, 1978.

Rubin, G. R.: *The Legal Education Of British Army Officers, 1860–1923*, The Journal of Legal History, Vol. 15, No. 3, June 1996, pp. 223–251.

Schell, A. von: *Battle Leadership: Some Experiences of a Junior Officer of the German Army with Observations on Battle Tactics and the Psychological Reactions of Troops in Campaign*, Marine Corps Association, Quantico, VA, 1988.

Shepherd, B.: *Shell Shock on the Somme* in RUSI Journal, Vol. 141, No. 3, June 1996, pp. 51–56.

PROPAGANDA

Carmichael, J.: *First World War Photographers*, London, Routledge, 1989.

Grieves, K.: *War Correspondents and Conducting Officers on the Western Front from 1915* in Cecil, H. & Liddle, P. H. (eds) *Facing Armageddon*, London, Leo Cooper, 1996.

Messinger, G. S.: *British Propaganda and the State in the First World War*, Manchester, Manchester University Press, 1992.

Reeves, N.: *Official British Film Propaganda in the First World War*, London, Croom Helm, 1986.

Sanders, M. L. and Taylor, P. M.: *British Propaganda during the First World War*, London, MacMillan, 1982.

Steed, A.: *British Propaganda and the First World War* in Stewart, I. & Carruthers, S. L. (eds): *War, Culture and Media: Representations of the Military in Twentieth Century Britain*, Trowbridge, Flicks, 1996.

MANPOWER ISSUES ON THE BRITISH HOME FRONT

Adams, R. J. Q. & Poirier, P. P.: *The Conscription Controversy in Great Britain*, London, Macmillan, 1987.

Braybon, G.: *Women Workers in the First World War*, Croom Helm, London, 1981.

Dewey, P. E.: *Military recruiting and the British labour force during the First World War*, Historical Journal, XXVII (1984), pp 199–223.

Dewey, P. E.: *British Agriculture in the First World War*, London, Routledge, 1989.

French, D.: *The Strategy of the Lloyd George Coalition 1916–18*, Oxford, Clarendon Press, 1995.

Grieves, K.: *The Politics of Manpower, 1914–18*, Manchester, Manchester University Press, 1988.

Official History of the Ministry of Munitions, 8 Vols., London, H.M.S.O., 1921–22.

Reid, A.: *Dilution, trade unionism, and the state in Britain during the First*

World War in Tolliday, S. and Zeitlin, J. (eds), *Shop floor bargaining and the state*, Cambridge, Cambridge University Press, 1985.

Statistics of the Military Effort of the British Empire, London, H.M.S.O., 1922.

Sweetman, J.: *The Smuts Report of 1917: Merely Political Window Dressing?*, Journal of Strategic Studies, 4/2, 1981.

Waites, B.: *A Class Society at War: England 1914–1918*, Leamington Spa, Berg, 1987.

Woodward, D. R. (ed): The Military Correspondence of Field-Marshal Sir William Robertson 1915–1918, London, Army Records Office/Bodley Head, 1989.

Wrigley, C. J.: *Lloyd George and the British Labour Movement*, Hassocks, Harvester Press, 1976.

Wrigley, C. J.: *The First World War and state intervention in industrial relations, 1914–1918*, in Wrigley, C. J.: *A History of British Industrial Relations*, vol. 2, Hassocks, Harvester Press, 1987.

ART AND THE WAR

Cork, R.: *A Bitter Truth: Avant Garde Art and the Great War*, New Haven, Connecticut, Yale University Press, 1994.

Eberle, M.: *The First World War and the Weimar Artists*, New Haven, Connecticut, University Press, 1985.

Harries, M. & S.: *The War Artists*, London, Michael Joseph and Tate Gallery, 1983.

Holmes, C. (ed): *The War Depicted by Distinguished British Artists*, London, The Studio, 1918.

Malvern, S.: *War as it is*, Art History, Vol. 9, No. 4, December 1986.

Mayes, W. P.: *The Origins of an Art Collection (First World War)*, unpublished manuscript, Imperial War Museum, London.

Nash, P.: *Outline: An Autobiography and Other Fragments*, London, Faber, 1949.

Orpen, W.: *An Onlooker in France*, London, Williams and Norgate, 1924.

Quigley, H.: *Passchendaele and the Somme*, London, Methuen, 1928.

Tippett, M.: *Art at the Service of War: Canada, Art and the Great War*, Toronto, University of Toronto Press, 1984.

Wyndham Lewis, P.: *Blasting and Bombardiering*, London, Eyre and Spottiswoode, 1937.

BRITISH AND GERMAN WAR VETERAN LITERATURE

The Memoirs

Binding, R.: *A Fatalist at War* (tr. F. D. Morrow), London, Allen & Unwin, 1929.

Blunden, E.: *Undertones of War*, London, R.. Cobden-Sanderson, 1928; Harmondsworth, Penguin edn. 1938.

Browne, Captain D. G.: *The Tank In Action*, London, Blackwood, 1920.

Burrage, A. M. (`Ex-Private X'): *War Is War*, London, Victor Gollancz, 1930.

Campbell, P. J.: *In The Cannon's Mouth*, London, Hamish Hamilton, 1979.

Carrington, C.: *Soldier from the Wars Returning*, London, Hutchinson, 1965.

Carstairs, C.: *A Generation Missing*, London, Heinemann, 1930.

Cecil, H.: *Edmund Blunden and First World War Writing, 1919–36, Focus on Robert Graves and his Contemporaries*, vol. 2, no. 1, Spring 1993, pp. 13–21.

Chapman, G.: *A Kind of Survivor*, London, Gollancz, 1975.

Chapman, G.: *A Passionate Prodigality*, London, Ivor, Nicholson & Watson, 1933.

Edmonds, C.: *A Subaltern's War*, London, Duckworth, 1929.

Ewart, W.: *Three Days*, in *When Armageddon Came, Studies In Peace And War*, London, Rich & Cowan, 1933, pp. 124–156.

Gladden, N.: *Ypres 1917: a Personal Account*, London, Wm. Kimber, 1967.

Harvey, A.D., *Oh What a Literary War!*, *London Magazine*, Dec-Jan 1993–4.

Jünger, E.: *Storm of Steel*, (tr. Basil Creighton, London, Chatto & Windus, 1929 (1st edn. 1920).

An "O.E.": *Iron Times With The Guards*, London, John Murray, 1918.

Richards, F.: *Old Soldiers Never Die*, London, Faber & Faber, 1933.

Steuart, R. H. J., S. J.: *March, Kind Comrade*, London, Sheed & Wards, 1931.

Saint-Mandé, W. (John Henry Parkyn Lamont): *War, Wine and Women*, London, Cassell, 1936 [see above, Harvey, A. D.: Oh What A Literary War!, which reveals this as a fabrication].

Wade, A.: *The War of the Guns*, London, Batsford, 1936, ch. 8.

The Poetry

Blunden, E.: *Undertones Of War*, London, R.. Cobden-Sanderson, 1928; Harmondsworth, Penguin edn. 1938.

Brereton, F. (ed): *An Anthology of War Poems*, London, Collins, 1930.

Dante: *The Inferno*, tr. Laurence Binyon, London, MacMillan, 1935 edition, Cantos 6, 23, 28, for Passchendaele-like torments.

Hibberd, D. & Onions, J. (eds): *Poetry of the Great War: an Anthology*, London, Macmillan, 1986.

Holt, T. & V., with Zeepvat, C.: *Violets from Oversea: Poets of the First World War*, London, Leo Cooper/Pen & Sword, 1996.

Hurd, M.: *The Ordeal of Ivor Gurney*, Oxford, O.U.P., 1984.

Jones, D.: *In Parenthesis*, London, Faber & Faber, 1937.

Parsons, I. (ed): *The Collected Works of Isaac Rosenberg*, London, Chatto & Windus, 1984.

Powell, A.: *A Deep Cry*, Aberporth, Paladour, 1993.

Read, H.: *Kneeshaw Goes To War* in *Naked Warriors*, London, Art & Letters, 1919.

Sassoon, S.: *Collected Poems, 1908–56*, London, Faber & Faber, 1961.

Schreibman, S. (ed): *Collected Poems of Thomas MacGreevy*, Dublin, Anna Livia Press, 1991.

Stephen, M. (ed): *Poems of the First World War: Never Such Innocence*, London, Everyman (J. M. Dent), 1993.

Stephen, M.: *The Price of Pity: Poetry, History and Myth in the Great War*, London, Leo Cooper/Pen & Sword, 1996.

The Novels

Blaker, R.: *Medal Without Bar*, London, Hodder & Stoughton, 1930.

Bracco, R. M.: *Merchants of Hope, British Middlebrow Writers and the First World War*, 1919–39, Oxford, Berg, 1993.

Briffault, R.: *Europa in Limbo*, London, Robert Hale, 1937, ch. 13.

Cecil, H.: *The Flower of Battle, How Britain Wrote The Great War*, S. Royalston, Vermont; London, Steerforth Press, 1996.

Cecil, H.: *The Post-War British War Novel of Experience* in Liddle, P. (ed), *Home Fires And Foreign Fields*, London, Brassey's, 1985.

Deeping, W.: *No Hero - This*, London, Cassell, 1936.

Ewart, W.: *Way of Revelation*, London, Putnam, 1921.

Grabenhorst, G.: *Zero Hour (Fahnenjunker Volkenborn)* [tr. from German by A. Featherstonehaugh], London, Brentano's, 1929, ch. 3 (1st pub. 1928).

Gurner, R.: *Pass Guard at Ypres*, London, Dent, 1929.

Hope, T. S.: *The Winding Road Unfolds*, London, Putnam, 1937.

Ingram, K.: *Out of Darkness*, London, Chatto and Windus, 1927.

Manning, F.: *The Middle Parts of Fortune*, London, Piazza Press, 1929.

Miller, P.: *The Natural Man*, Grant Richards, 1924, ch. 3.

Onions, J.: *English Fiction and Drama of the Great War, 1918–1939*, London, MacMillan, 1990.

Raymond, E.: *The Jesting Army*, London, Cassell, 1930, Part III, chs. 3 10.

Sassoon, S.: *Memoirs of an Infantry Officer*, London, Faber & Faber, 1930.

Schauwecker, F.: *The Fiery Way (Der feurige Weg)*, London, Dent, 1929 (1st pub. Berlin, 1926).

Williamson, A.: *Henry Williamson: Tarka and the Last Romantic*, Far Thrupp, Alan Sutton, 1995.

Williamson, H.: *Love and the Loveless: a Soldier's Tale*, London, MacDonald, 1958, chs 13- 18.

BELGIAN

[a selection of books in English, French and Flemish; for further references see Chapter Twenty-seven]

Borg, A.: *War Memorials from Antiquity to the Present*, London, 1991.

Brants, C. & K.: *Velden van weeler. Reisgids naar de Erste Wereldoorlog*, Amsterdam- Antwerp, 1995.

de Busscher, J.-M.: *Les folies de l'industrie*, Brussels, 1981.

Chielens, P. & W.: *De Troost van Schoonheid. De literaire Salient (Ieper 1914–1918)*, Groot- Bijgaarden, 1996.

Christens, R. & De Clerq, K.: *Frontleven 14/18. Het dagelijks leven van de Belgische soldaat aan de IJzer* (Reeks Retrospectief), Tielt-The Hague, 1987.

Deseyne, A. & A.: *Zonnebeke 1914–1918. Dood en heropstanding van een dorp*, Zonnebeke, 1976.

Devliegher, L.: *Oorlagsdagboeken uit de streek tussen IJzer en Leie*, Bruges, 1972.

Devliegher, L. & Schepens, L.: *Front 14/18*, Tielt-The Hague, 1968.

Durnez, G.: *Zeg mij waar de bloemen zijn. Beelden uit de Eerste Wereldoorlog in Vlaanderen*, Leuven, 1988.

Elfnovembergroep: *Van den groten Oorlog. Volksboek*, Kemmel, 1978.

Geldhof, J. (ed): *Oorlagsdagboeken over Ieper (1914–1915)*, Bruges, 1974–1977.

Lampaert, R.: *Modder voor het vaderland. De ongrijpbare stad. Ypres Salient 14/18* (Reeks Retrospectief), Tiels-The Hague, 1987.

Notebaert, A., Neumann, C. & Vanden Eynde, W.: *Inventaire des Archives de l'Office des Régions dévastées* (Archives Générales du Royaume), Brussels, 1986.

Schepens, L.: *14/18 Een oorlog in Vlaanderen* (Reeks Retrospectief), Tielt-The Hague, 1984.

Smets, M. (ed): *Resurgam. De Belgische wederopbouw na 1914*, Brussels, 1985.

Verleyen, H.: *In Flanders Fields, her verhaal van John McRae, zijn gedicht en de klaproos*, Veurne, 1995.

de Volder, J.: *Benoit XV et la Belgique durant la Grande Guerre*, Brussels-Rome, 1996.

de Vos, L.: *De Eerste Wereldoorlog*, Leuven, 1996.

de Vos, L.: *Veldslagen in de Lage Landen*, Leuven, 1995.

MATERIAL CULTURE

Hodder, I.: *Reading In Past*, Cambridge, Cambridge University Press, 1986.

Merriman, N.: *Beyond the glass case: the past, the heritage, and the public in Britain*, Leicester, Leicester University Press, 1991.

Miller, D.: *Artefacts as categories*, Cambridge, Cambridge University Press, 1985.

Miller, D.: *Material Culture and mass consumption*, Oxford, Blackwell, 1987.

Pearce, S. (ed): *Museums, Objects, Collections*, London, Routledge, 1994.

Pearce, S.: *Interpreting Objects and Collections*, London, Routledge, 1994.

Schlereth, T. (ed): *Material Culture Studies in America*, Nashville, Tenn., American Association for State and Local History, 1982.

PILGRIMAGE AND GUIDEBOOKS

Anon, *The Pilgrims Guide to the Ypres Salient*, Herbert Reach Ltd for Talbot House, c. 1920

Anon, *Handbook to Belgium and the Battlefields*, London, Ward Lock, c. 1930.

Anon, *The Western Front; Then and Now*, London, C. Arthur Pearson, 1938.

Bix, B.: *The Battle Book of Ypres*, London, John Murray, 1927.

Cave, N.: *Battleground Europe: Hooge and Sanctuary Wood*, London, Leo Cooper, 1993.

Chandler, D. (ed) *A Traveller's Guide to the Battlefields of Europe*, London, Hugh Evelyn, 1965.

Coombs, R. E. B.: *Before Endeavours Fade*, London, Battle of Britain Prints Int. Ltd., 1976.

De Deyne, V.: *Ypres Before And After the Great War*, Liège, Benard, 1927.

Giles, J.: *Flanders then and now*, London, Leo Cooper, 1970.

Holmes, R.: *Army Battlefield Guide* (Belgium and Northern France), London, H.M.S.O., 1995.

Jones, N. H.: *The War Walk (A Journey along the Western Front)*, London, Robt. Hale, 1983.

Michelin Guides, *Ypres and the Battles of Ypres - An Illustrated History and Guide*, 1919.

Pulteney, Lieut.Gen. Sir W.: *The Immortal Salient*, London, John Murray, 1925.

Scott, M.: *Cemeteries and Memorials of the Ypres Salient*, 1992.

Seton-Hutchinson, Lt.Col. G., *Pilgrimage*, London, Rich & Cowan, 1935.

Spagnoly, T.: *Salient Points*, London, Leo Cooper, 1995.

Taylor, H. A.: *Goodbye to the Battlefields*, London, Stanley Paul, 1928.

Thurlow, Col. E. G. L.: *The Pill Boxes of Flanders*, Ivor, Nicholson and Watson Ltd, 1933.

Williamson, H.: *The Wet Flanders Plain*, London, Faber & Faber, 1929.

Notes on Contributors

Dr Stephen Badsey [Royal Military Academy, Sandhurst].
Stephen Badsey is a leading specialist on the media in warfare. He was principal contributor to Roger Smither [ed], *The First World War Archive* and has written several books on warfare in the 19th and 20th centuries.

Professor Ian F W Beckett [University of Luton].
Ian Beckett is Head of the Department of History at Luton. He is the author of the biography, *Johnnie Gough VC*, of *The Amateur Military Tradition*, has written extensively on the British Army and co-edited, *A Nation at War, a social study of the British Army in the First World War*.

Colonel Allain Bernède
Dr Bernède is a Professor of History at the Direction de l'enseignement militaire supérieur de l'Armée de Terre in Paris and Director of a Department of Historical Research at Paul Valery University in Montpellier. He has published books on the French Army and contributed to research publications and conferences on this subject.

Professor Brian Bond [King's College, London].
Brian Bond is President of the British Commission for Military History. His numerous publications include [as editor], *The First World War and British Military History* and, most recently, *The Pursuit of Victory: Napoleon to Saddam Hussein* [1997].

Dr John M Bourne [The University of Birmingham].
John Bourne is the author of *Great Britain and the First World War*. He contributed to *Facing Armageddon: the First World War experienced*, and is one of the team working on a computer-based study of British Army divisions and their commanders in the First World War.

Jack M Bruce
A former Visiting Professor at the Smithsonian Institute, Washington DC, Jack Bruce, through his monumental work, *The Aeroplanes of the Royal Flying Corps* and from subsequent aeroplane monographs, is a recognized world expert on British aeroplanes of the First World War. He has been Chairman of the Historical Group Committee of the Royal Aeronautical Society, Deputy Director of the Royal Air Force Museum at Hendon and for many years, Vice President of Cross and Cockade International.

Dr Hugh P Cecil [The University of Leeds].
Hugh Cecil is an acknowledged authority on the literature of the First World War. He is the author of numerous articles and books including, *The Flower of Battle: How Britain wrote the First World War* [US edition 1996] and was the co-editor of *Facing Armageddon: the First World War experienced* [1996].

Peter Chasseaud [Honorary Archivist of the Field Survey Association].
Peter Chasseaud has for long been researching British cartography and field survey during the First World War. His published works include, *Trench Maps - A Collector's Guide* and *Topography of Armageddon - A British Trench Map Atlas of the Western Front 1914–18*. He is currently working on an operational history of field survey on the Western Front.

Mark Derez [Archivist of the Catholic University of Leuven, Belgium].
Mark Derez has published on the history of Universities and Higher Education and contributed to the volume, *Facing Armageddon: the First World War experienced*.

Ashley Ekins [The Australian War Memorial, Canberra].
Ashley Ekins, who is completing a study of discipline and punishment within the Australian army during the First World War, is an historian with the Official History Unit at the War Memorial working on Australia's involvement in the Vietnam War. He is co-author of a forthcoming volume in the series.

Paul Gough [The University of the West of England, Bristol].
Paul Gough has written numerous articles on aspects of art in the First World War and, as a painter, he has exhibited widely. He contributed to the volume, *Facing Armageddon: the First World War experienced*.

Dr Keith Grieves [Kingston University, Kingston-upon-Thames].
Keith Grieves is the author of *The Politics of Manpower 1914–18* and the biographer of Sir Eric Geddes, who organized the British Expeditionary Force railways on the Western Front. His recent publications have been on the management of the war economy, voluntary recruiting and rural social structure and on the writings of C E Montague.

Dr Paddy Griffith [independent writer and publisher].
Paddy Griffith has written a number of influential analytical books on military tactics in the 19th and 20th centuries, most notably, *Battle Tactics of the Western Front* and *British Fighting Methods in the Great War* [1996].

Dr Heinz Hagenlücke [Heinrich Heine University, Düsseldorf].
Dr Hagenlücke has published on aspects of German party political activity in the 19th and 20th centuries, *Die Deutsche Vaterlandspartei* [1996] but the First World War is one of his prime research interests.

John Hussey
John Hussey has had a life-long interest in British Naval and Military History. Since his retirement from the British Petroleum Group, he has had articles and book reviews published in numerous journals of military history including, *The British Army Review* and *War in History*.

Kevin Kelly
An acknowledged authority on the First World War in the air, Kevin Kelly has published articles in *Cross and Cockade* and *Over the Front*. He has given invaluable assistance to Peter Liddle in the production of several books, most notably, *The Airman's War 1914–18* [1987].

John Lee
John Lee is currently completing a biography of Sir Ian Hamilton while continuing to work as a member of a team studying the operational effectiveness of British divisions and their commanders in the First World War.

Dr Peter H Liddle [The Liddle Collection, The University of Leeds].
Peter Liddle is Founder and Keeper of the World War personal experience archive in the Library of the University of Leeds. His publications include, *The Battle of the Somme; The Worst Ordeal: Britons at Home and Abroad 1914–18* and, co-edited, *Facing Armageddon: the First World War experienced* [1996].

Dr Bill Nasson [The University of Capetown, Republic of South Africa].
Bill Nasson has written journal articles and a book on The South African War 1899–1902 and has also published work on aspects of South African service in the First World War.

Dr Dean Oliver [Carleton University, Ottawa, Canada].
Dr Oliver, formerly Assistant Director at York University's Centre for International and Security Studies in Canada, is a post-doctoral research fellow at the Norman Paterson School of International Affairs, Carleton University, Ottawa, and External Affairs and National Defence contributor for the Canadian Annual Review of Politics and Public Affairs.

Christopher Pugsley [The University of New England, Armidale, N.S.W., Australia].
Christopher Pugsley served as an officer in the New Zealand Army and has lectured on aspects of New Zealand's military history at Waikato and Massey Universities. He has published, *Gallipoli: The New Zealand story*; *On the Fringe of Hell: New Zealanders and Military Discipline in the First World War* and *Scars on the Heart* [1996], the subject of a permanent exhibition [for which he was the curator at the Auckland War Memorial Museum] on two centuries of New Zealand at War.

Paul Reed
Paul Reed now lives at Courcelette on the Somme in France after his work as a First World War freelance researcher in the Public Record Office at Kew. He has written journal articles for *Stand To: the Journal of the Western Front Association*. His exceptional knowledge of the British Western Front battlefields is expressed in his recent publication, *Walking the Somme* [1997].

Matthew Richardson [The Liddle Collection, The University of Leeds].
Matthew Richardson, is the Assistant Keeper of the Liddle Collection with special responsibility for the three-dimensional items. He has written articles for *Stand To: the Journal of the Western Front Association* and his interest in recollected testimony has led to the publication with Peter Liddle of an article in the *Journal of Contemporary History* [1996] on the validity of soldier oral testimony [1996].

Peter T Scott
Peter Scott has assisted the research of many through his knowledge of published work on the First World War. He was founding editor of *Stand To: the Journal of the Western Front Association* and published his own, highly regarded journal, *The Great War, 1914–18: an illustrated journal of First World War history* [1988–91]. *Home for Christmas: Cards, Messages and Legends of the Great War* and *"Dishonoured": the "Colonels' surrender" at St Quentin* are his books on the First World War.

Dr Phil Taylor [The University of Leeds].
Phil Taylor is Reader in Communications Studies at Leeds. His publications include, *British Propaganda in the First World War* [with M L Sanders] and *Munitions of the Mind: a history of propaganda from the ancient world to the present era* [1995].

Professor Geoffrey Till [Royal Naval College, Greenwich].
Geoffrey Till holds the Chair of History and International Affairs at the Royal Naval College. His published work includes, *Modern Sea Power*. He contributed a chapter on the Dardanelles / Gallipoli campaign to *Facing Armageddon: the First World War experienced*.

Professor John Turner [Royal Holloway, University of London].
John Turner is Professor of Modern History and Vice Principal of Royal Holloway. He has written and edited a number of works on British politics in the 20th Century including *Lloyd George's Secretariat*, and, most recently, *British Politics and the Great War: Coalition and Conflict 1915–18* [1992].

Emeritus Professor Frank Vandiver [Texas A&M University, College Station, Texas, USA].
Dr Vandiver, President Emeritus of his University, has many books to his name on the American Civil War and is the biographer of General Pershing, *Black Jack*. He is currently researching a biography of Field Marshal Sir Douglas Haig.

Dr Andrew A. Wiest [The University of Southern Mississippi, Hattiesburg, USA].
Dr Wiest was recently Visiting Senior Lecturer at the Royal Military Academy, Sandhurst. His book on *Passchendaele and the Royal Navy* was published in 1995.

German Werth [German Radio, Cologne].
German Werth works in the field of Literature and the Arts for the German Broadcasting Corporation. He has been responsible for TV documentaries on Germany in the First World War and his long-held interest in recording German testimony of experience on the Western Front led to his book, *Verdun, the Battle and the Myth*.

Dr Ian Whitehead [The University of Derby].
Ian Whitehead's 1914–18 research is in the sphere of medical care of wounded on the Western Front. He contributed a chapter on the British Medical Officer in the Field to *Facing Armageddon: the First World War experienced* and has played a major supportive rôle in the editing of this book on Passchendaele.

Index